International Foundation of Employee Benefit Plans
WorldatWork

WorldatWork

WorldatWork, formerly American Compensation Association, is a 45-year-old global not-for-profit professional association dedicated to knowledge leadership in disciplines associated with attracting, retaining, and motivating employees. More than 25,000 HR professionals, consultants, educators, and others are members of the association. WorldatWork emphasizes total rewards, specifically focusing on compensation and benefits, as well as other components of the work experience such as work/life balance, recognition, culture, professional development, and work environment issues. In addition to membership, WorldatWork offers highly acclaimed certification and education programs, online information resources, publications, conferences, research, and networking opportunities. Founded in 1955, the organization is governed by a board of directors elected by its membership (*www.worldatwork.org*).

Third Edition

STRATEGIC COMPENSATION

A Human Resource Management Approach

Joseph J. Martocchio

University of Illinois at Urbana-Champaign

UPPER SADDLE RIVER, NEW JERSEY 07458

Library of Congress Cataloging-in-Publication Data
Martocchio, Joseph J.
Strategic compensation: a human resource management approach / Joseph J.
Martocchio.—3rd ed.
p. cm.
Includes bibliographical references and index.
ISBN 0-13-182476-7
1. Compensation management. I. Title.
HF5549.5C67 M284 2003
658.3′22—dc21
2002038133

Acquisitions Editor: Michael Ablassmeir
Editor-in-Chief: Jeff Shelstad
Assistant Editor: Melanie Olsen
Editorial Assistant: Jill Wasiowich
Executive Marketing Manager: Shannon Moore
Marketing Assistant: Christine Genneken
Managing Editor (Production): John Roberts
Production Editor: Kelly Warsak
Production Assistant: Joe DeProspero
Permissions Coordinator: Suzanne Grappi
Associate Director, Manufacturing: Vincent Scelta
Production Manager: Arnold Vila
Manufacturing Buyer: Michelle Klein
Cover Design: Bruce Kenselaar
Associate Director, Multimedia Production: Karen Goldsmith
Composition: UG / GGS Information Services, Inc.
Full-Service Project Management: UG / GGS Information Services, Inc.
Printer/Binder: Courier-Westford
Cover Printer: Phoenix Color Corporation

Credits and acknowledgments borrowed from other sources and reproduced, with permission, in this textbook appear on appropriate page within text.

Pearson Education LTD
Pearson Education Singapore, Pte. Ltd
Pearson Education, Canada, Ltd
Pearson Education—Japan
Pearson Education Australia PTY, Limited
Pearson Education North Asia Ltd
Pearson Educación de Mexico, S.A. de C.V.
Pearson Education Malaysia, Pte. Ltd

10 9 8 7 6 5 4 3
ISBN 0-13-182476-7

To my parents, Rose and Joe Martocchio.
Their belief in the value of education
has enabled me to create many opportunities.

Brief Contents

Contents

PREFACE

Companies' success in the marketplace is as much a function of the way business practitioners manage employees as it is a function of companies' structures and financial resources. Compensating employees represents a critical human resource management practice: Without sound compensation systems, companies cannot attract and retain the best-qualified employees.

Compensation systems can promote companies' competitive advantage when they are properly aligned with strategic goals. Likewise, compensation practices can undermine competitive advantage when they are designed and implemented haphazardly. The title of this book—*Strategic Compensation: A Human Resource Management Approach*—reflects the importance of employees as key elements of strategic compensation programs.

The purpose of this book is to provide knowledge of the art of compensation practice and its role in promoting companies' competitive advantage. Students will be best prepared to assume the roles of competent compensation professionals if they possess a grounded understanding of compensation practices and the environments in which business professionals plan, implement, and evaluate compensation systems. Thus, we examine the context of compensation practice, the criteria used to compensate employees, compensation system design issues, employee benefits, and the contemporary challenges that compensation professionals will face well into this century.

ABOUT THIS BOOK

This book contains 14 chapters, lending itself well to courses offered as 10-week quarters or 15-week semesters. The chapters are organized in five parts:

- Part I: Setting the Stage for Strategic Compensation
- Part II: Bases for Pay
- Part III: Designing Compensation Systems
- Part IV: Employee Benefits
- Part V: Contemporary Strategic Compensation Challenges

Course instructors on a 10-week schedule might consider spending 2 weeks on each part. Given a 15-week schedule, course instructors might consider spending 1 week on each chapter.

Each chapter contains a chapter outline, learning objectives, key terms, and discussion questions. In addition, each chapter includes two features. The "Stretching the Dollar" features describe examples of how companies or employees experience greater-than-anticipated benefits from expenditures on compensation and on developing compensation systems. The "Flip Side of the Coin" features point out possible inconsistencies of particular compensation issues or discuss how well-intended practices fall short of benefiting companies or employees. Each chapter contains new features designed to promote student learning and student–instructor interactions. These features are described in *New to the Third Edition*.

This textbook is well suited to a variety of students, including undergraduate and master's degree students. In addition, the book was prepared for use by all business students, regardless of their majors. Both human resource management majors and other majors (accounting, finance, general management, international management, marketing, and organizational behavior) will benefit equally well from *Strategic Compensation*. After all, virtually every manager, regardless of functional area, will be involved in making compensation decisions. Practitioners beginning work in compensation or current professionals will find *Strategic Compensation* a useful reference.

NEW TO THE THIRD EDITION

The third edition includes some exciting new features.

Compensation in Action

The brief introductions in each chapter focus on compensation practice issues, often citing compensation consultants or referencing companies' experiences with compensation. Exciting articles follow at the end of each chapter that give a more detailed treatment of the issues. These articles come from the practitioner-oriented literature such as *Workspan* (the official journal of WorldatWork) and *HR Magazine* (the official magazine of the Society for Human Resource Management).

Compensation Online

This feature follows the discussion questions. Compensation Online engages students in timely compensation issues by having them surf the Internet or their college library's online resources. These exercises can serve as a basis for class discussion and other course requirements.

Each chapter contains two sets of Compensation Online exercises (three exercises per set). The first set is written for students assigned to explore compensation online with the goal of leading class discussion, writing short papers, or engaging in a debate with fellow students. The second set is written from the perspective of HR or compensation professionals who are about to learn more information about compensation issues that may be facing their companies.

Flip Side of the Coin

This in-text feature, with new or revised content, has been brought back from the first edition by popular demand.

What's New in Compensation?

Compensation, like most business practices, is subject to a variety of influences from within and outside the company. Certainly, practices change after the publication of a textbook. Although including state-of-the-art articles from leading sources such as the *New York Times* in textbooks is usually considered to be desirable pedagogy from course instructor and student perspectives, reprinted articles are simply not current as changes in the world occur. This feature draws on the student *New York Times* subscription offered as a supplement to *Strategic Compensation*. It allows course instructors and students to follow changes in compensation practices in near real-time, providing them with the resources to answer the question, "What's new in compensation?" Course instructors can take advantage of this feature to promote in-class discussions, group projects, individual papers, or other activities as deemed appropriate for students in the course.

Of course, all of the chapters have been thoroughly revised. First, summary statistics in every chapter represent the most current available information at the time this edition was prepared. More references to company examples are included. Second, state-of-the-art information sources for developing sound compensation systems are discussed. For instance, Chapter 8 describes the newest compensation survey programs offered by the U.S. Bureau of Labor Statistics. Third, the "Stretching the Dollar" features appear with mostly new content. Content carried over from the second edition transcends time and is key to compensation professionals. Last, but certainly not least, I incorporated the constructive feedback of course instructors and students who used the previous editions. As always, their insights were invaluable.

AVAILABLE TEACHING AND LEARNING AIDS

The teaching and learning accessories are designed to promote a positive experience for both instructors and students. Dr. David W. Oakes developed the teaching and learning aids for *Strategic Compensation*.

Instructor's Resource Manual with Test Item File

The instructor's resource manual contains learning objectives, chapter outlines, and discussion questions. In addition, the instructor's resource manual contains multiple-choice and short essay test questions. There are at least 25 multiple-choice questions and approximately 3 short essay questions for each chapter. The test item file contains the answers to the multiple-choice questions and suggested answers for the short essay questions. The test item file is also available in a Windows format. Prentice Hall's custom test generating software, TestGen-EQ, allows manipulation of questions and easy test preparation.

Custom Web Site with Study Guide

Students and instructors can find a variety of usefully information on the custom Web site. Students can find a study guide at *www.prenhall.com/martocchio*. Dr. David W. Oakes designed this study guide to help students prepare for quizzes and tests. It includes key learning points, sample multiple-choice questions, and short, thought-provoking essay questions. Instructors can find resources for their lectures.

PowerPoint Lecture Presentations

Strategic Compensation is accompanied by lecture visual presentations for each chapter based on Microsoft PowerPoint. These may be downloaded from the *Strategic Compensation* custom Web site with a password available from Prentice Hall or they can be accessed on the Instructor's Resource CD-ROM.

Instructor's Resource CD-ROM

The Instructor's Resource CD-ROM contains the electronic files for the Instructor's Manual with Test Item File, the PowerPoint lecture presentations, and the TestGen-EQ test generating software. The test program permits instructors to edit, add, or delete questions from the test bank; add existing graphics and create new graphics; analyze test results; and organize a database of student results. This new software allows for greater flexibility and ease of use. It provides many options for organizing and displaying tests, along with a search and sort feature.

ACKNOWLEDGMENTS

Many individuals made valuable contributions to the first and second editions. I am indebted to the reviewers who provided thoughtful remarks on chapter drafts during the development of this textbook:

Martha Andrews, Florida State University
Eric Austin, Alltel Co. (University of Central Arkansas)
Cam Caldwell, Washington State University
Shawn Carraher, Indiana University—Gary
Robert Figler, University of Akron
Daniel Hoyt, Arkansas State University
Deborah Knapp, Cleveland State University
Maria Kraimer, University of Illinois at Chicago
LaVelle Mills, West Texas A&M University
Lyle Schoenfeldt, Appalachian State University
Steve Thomas, Southwest Missouri State University

Hats off to Robert L. Kucik. As a student in my compensation course, Rob eagerly and very competently assisted me with this revision. Rob vigorously researched compensation topics, and he contributed substantially to the Compensation Online feature. Thanks, Rob. I would never have made the deadline without your fine work.

As in past editions, I thank Margaret Chaplan and Katie Dorsey. Margaret Chaplan, a labor librarian, provided invaluable assistance by sharing her wealth of knowledge. Katie Dorsey, a library clerk, also offered excellent reference assistance.

At Prentice Hall, I thank the following individuals for their guidance and expertise: Mike Ablassmeir, Kevin Glynn, Jeff Shelstad, Kelly Warsak, Jill Wasiowich, and Kelly Wendrychowicz. Many other professionals worked behind the scenes in the design, marketing, and production of this edition. I thank each and every one of those individuals for their contributions.

Joseph J. Martocchio

CHAPTER 1

STRATEGIC COMPENSATION

A Component of Human Resource Systems

Chapter Outline

- Exploring and Defining the Compensation Context
  - What Is Compensation?
  - Core Compensation
  - "Fringe" Compensation or Employee Benefits
- A Historical Perspective on Compensation: The Road Toward Strategic Compensation
- Strategic versus Tactical Decisions
  - Competitive Strategy Choices
  - Tactical Decisions That Support the Firm's Strategy
- Compensation Professionals' Goals
  - How HR Professionals Fit into the Corporate Hierarchy
  - How the Compensation Function Fits into HR Departments
  - The Compensation Department's Main Goals
- Stakeholders of the Compensation System
- Summary
- Key Terms
- Discussion Questions
- Exercises
- Endnotes

Learning Objectives

In this chapter, you will learn

1. Basic compensation concepts and the context of compensation practice
2. A historical perspective on compensation—from an administrative function to a strategic function

3. The difference between strategic and tactical compensation
4. Compensation professionals' goals within a human resource department
5. How compensation professionals relate to various stakeholders

For most of the 20th century, the predecessor to contemporary human resource management practices was initially referred to as manpower planning or personnel management. In the earlier part of that century, manpower planning often focused on the effective deployment of employees in factories to achieve the highest manufacturing output per employee per unit of time. For instance, management sought to increase the number of handmade garments per hour. Later, extensive government regulation involving payroll taxes, minimum wage laws, and antidiscrimination laws gave rise to the personnel management function. Legal compliance necessitated that personnel management take on the role of an administrative, support function. Since the 1970s, there has been widespread recognition that managing employees or human resources can contribute to company success. In recent years, researchers and HR practitioners have worked steadily to quantify the impact of managing human resources on business success. The "Compensation in Action" feature, listed at the end of the chapter, describes the evolving HR professional's role from compliance (policing) to consultation with a carpenter's eye toward quality HR system design.

EXPLORING AND DEFINING THE COMPENSATION CONTEXT

The compensation function does not operate in isolation. To the contrary, it is just one component of a company's human resource systems. In addition, compensation professionals interact with members of various constituencies, including union representatives and top executives. We will explore these ideas in more detail after we have introduced some fundamental compensation concepts.

What Is Compensation?

Compensation represents both the intrinsic and extrinsic rewards employees receive for performing their jobs. **Intrinsic compensation** reflects employees' psychological mind-sets that result from performing their jobs. **Extrinsic compensation** includes both monetary and nonmonetary rewards. Organizational development professionals promote intrinsic compensation through effective job design. Compensation professionals are responsible for extrinsic compensation. Although extrinsic compensation is our focus in this book, let's take a moment to briefly explore the intrinsic compensation concept.

Intrinsic Compensation

Intrinsic compensation represents employees' critical psychological states that result from performing their jobs. **Job characteristics theory** describes these critical psychological states. According to this job theory, employees experience enhanced psychological states (that is, intrinsic compensation) when their jobs rate high on five core job dimensions: skill variety, task identity, task significance, autonomy, and feedback [1]. Jobs that lack these core characteristics do not provide much intrinsic compensation.

Figure 1-1 illustrates the influence of core job characteristics on intrinsic compensation and subsequent benefits to employers.

- Skill variety is the degree to which the job requires the person to perform different tasks and involves different skills, abilities, and talents.
- Task identity is the degree to which a job enables a person to complete an entire job from start to finish.
- Task significance is the degree to which the job has an impact on the lives or work of other people.
- Autonomy is the amount of freedom, independence, and discretion the employee enjoys in determining how to perform the job.
- Feedback is the degree to which the job or employer provides the employee with clear and direct information about job outcomes and performance.

What are some examples of these critical psychological states, or intrinsic compensation? According to job characteristics theory, jobs that demand skill variety, task identity, and task significance enable employees to experience meaningfulness of work (for example, cancer researchers). Jobs that provide autonomy lead to experienced responsibility for outcomes of work (for example, farmers). Jobs that convey feedback enhance employees' knowledge of the actual results of their work activities, or how well they have performed (for example, automobile salespeople). Ultimately, employers hope to benefit from increased job performance, lower absenteeism, and higher employee satisfaction.

How do these characteristics translate into practice? Let's consider the problem of turnover of information technology employees. In general, company demand for these employees outpaces supply. Over time, base salaries and bonuses have risen dramatically to promote the recruitment and retention of the very best, but turnover has not slowed down. A recent market compensation survey by *people*[3], a consulting firm that specializes in human resource issues for information technology employee populations, suggests that enhanced intrinsic compensation may help reduce excessive

FIGURE 1-1 The Influence of Core Job Characteristics of Intrinsic Compensation and Subsequent Benefits to Employers

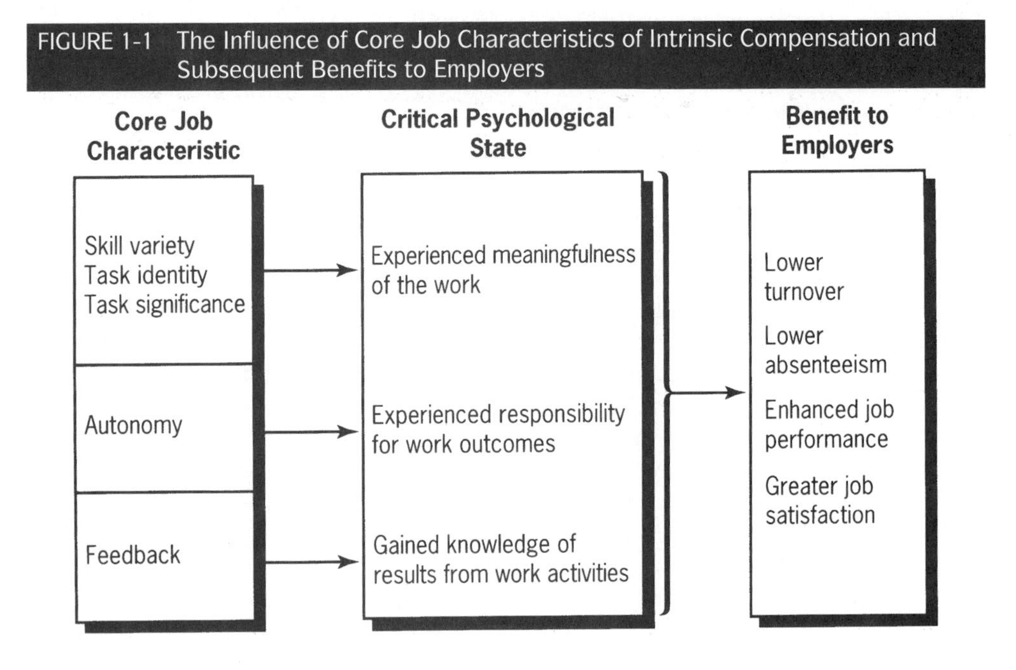

STRETCHING THE DOLLAR

RECOGNITION: PATS ON THE BACK MOTIVATE EMPLOYEES

Employee recognition programs continue to grow and earn respect as a strategic attraction and retention tool in today's lagging economy.

Quick Look

- 86 percent of companies in a recent survey reported having a rewards and recognition program.
- 91 percent of companies report employee morale as the main objective of their program.
- 65 percent of companies are doing more recognition than they were 3 years ago.

Amid all the stories and rumors about the lagging economy and struggling markets, companies have determined that it is more important to keep top performers than to cut costs completely. Layoffs continue to lead headlines, but companies responding to a recent survey say that employee recognition is a very important part of their current HR strategy.

The Role of Recognition survey by WorldatWork and the National Association for Employee Recognition (NAER) shows that 86 percent of companies have an employee recognition program. Of those with a program, respondents say senior management and line managers consider it to be important to their success in attracting and retaining key talent.

"Everyone likes credit or even a pat on the back for hard work and a job well done," said Anne C. Ruddy, Executive Director of WorldatWork. "It only makes sense that employees are going to feel more valued and respected if they are recognized for their performance."

The survey gauged opinions on employee recognition programs and their administration from 539 senior-level HR professionals.

Of the 14 percent of companies that do not have a recognition program, 62 percent are considering implementing one in the next 12 months. This shows the importance of these programs in the face of hard economic times. Human capital will continue to be the greatest asset companies can have in lean times, and recruiting and keeping those top workers will be essential. Making sure employees are motivated may require more than a competitive salary and other compensation and benefits programs. People always want to feel appreciated, and employee recognition programs play to that basic human need.

In fact, 91 percent of responding companies report that boosting employee morale is the main objective of their recognition programs.

How important is employee recognition? Well, some companies (3 percent) have gone as far as creating a formal recognition department solely responsible for administration of the program.

"I think it's important to note that companies see recognition as a strategic initiative," said Greg Boswell, NAER executive vice president. "More than 75 percent of those surveyed said they have a strategy behind their recognition programs."

Recognition continues to grow in use and popularity as well. Sixty-five percent of respondents said their companies are doing more recognition than they were 3 years ago. Experts expect this to continue, despite the struggling economy.

"For the best companies, recognition will continue to be a priority," Boswell said. "When economic times are tough, it is more important than ever to recognize people. If raises and other cash bonuses are hard to find, recognition is something companies can do to show employees that they are valued and appreciated."

THE TDK WAY

TDK Electronics Corp. is one company that feels recognition is one of their most important tools in building employee morale and attracting and retaining top talent. TDK sponsors a continuous reward and recognition committee of employees who represent all shifts and departments companywide. Jill Gray, director of general affairs for TDK, said the purpose of the program is to find fun and unique ways to recognize and thank employees who go the extra mile in accomplishing their work or exhibit outstanding team behavior.

"Employees like this program very much, and management is especially appreciative of the program because it creates an efficient avenue for thanking employees and increasing their motivation to do a good job," Gray said.

TDK's program provides awards to all supervisors and managers that they spontaneously can give to employees for doing something good. These awards, called "hats off" awards this year, afford employees a sticker or paper recognition. Any employee who has collected four of these recognitions is eligible to play "the game" at the next monthly employee meeting, according to Gray. The reward and recognition committee sets up some sort of game (roulette wheel, fishing, bowling, etc.) at the meeting, which allows those who have qualified a chance for a prize, which can be as simple as a beach towel sporting the TDK logo, sunglasses, lunch bag, movie passes or more. Gray said the target price for the awards is $5 to $7 per award.

Gray said the program has drawn rave reviews and the committee's creativity and excitement flows over into the employee base. She added that she doesn't see the slowing economy having any effect on TDK offering this recognition program.

"It is now part of our culture. TDK's reward and recognition program has never been very expensive in the first place," she said. "As the sponsor, I have always emphasized that the purpose of rewards and recognition is not to compensate employees for their extra effort on the job; it is a small token for a large amount of thanks and gratitude to our teammates."

TELL THE WORLD

Many companies view rewards and recognition as so important that they feel the need to tell everyone about them. Of the responding companies, 87 percent have a communication plan for employees and prospective employees. Seventy-two percent use company newsletters, 62 percent use Internet/intranet sites and 52 percent communicate them in employee orientations. Letting employees know there is a chance to get recognition for their work provides the motivational aspect of the program. Employees know there is something out there that they can be working toward achieving, other than a potential bonus or other recognition that may not be in the budget.

Perhaps even more important is telling people when and what employees have been awarded. Just knowing about a program is probably not as great a motivation as knowing the person sitting in the cubicle down the hall just got a $100 gift certificate and recognition plaque for suggesting a new cost-cutting measure. Companies feel that public recognition is important both to the person receiving the award and their coworkers.

WHAT'S NEXT?

Even with the economy slumping, employees being let go and money belts tightening at companies across the country, employee recognition appears to be a mainstay. With 86 percent of companies already having recognition programs and 62 percent of those without considering implementing one, it appears recognition is a strategic initiative that companies do not want to dismiss.

"With so much attention being placed on finding, hiring, training and keeping the best employees, I think recognition initiatives will continue to grow in the future," Boswell said. "Companies that align recognition programs with competitive compensation and benefits packages will increase employee satisfaction which, in turn, ultimately will help the company through these rocky economic times."

NOTES

Visit our Web site at *www.worldatwork.org* and go to Information Central. There you will find ResourcePRO, a powerful database that holds almost 7,000 full-text documents on total rewards topics.

For more information related to this article:

- Log in to ResourcePRO Search and select Simple Search
- Do Not Select a Rewards Category
- Type in this key word string on the search line: "employee recognition or rewards" OR "employee morale" OR "motivate or motivation."

Source: Jeremy Handel, WorldatWork, *Workspan*, December 2001, volume 44, number 12. © WorldatWork, 14040 N. Northsight Blvd., Scottsdale, AZ 85260 U.S.A.; 480/951-9191; Fax 480/483-8352; *www.worldatwork.org*; E-mail worldatwork@worldatwork.org

turnover [2]. Examples include new technologies, learning and training opportunities, and challenging technical environments.

Principles of intrinsic compensation also provide the basis for nonmonetary recognition awards. The "Stretching the Dollar" feature reports survey results that emphasize the strategic importance of nonmonetary recognition. This feature also describes TDK Electronic Corporation's nonmonetary recognition program.

Extrinsic Compensation

Extrinsic compensation includes both monetary and nonmonetary rewards. Compensation professionals establish monetary compensation programs to reward employees according to their job performance levels or for learning job-related knowledge or skills. As we will discuss shortly, monetary compensation represents **core compensation**. Nonmonetary rewards include protection programs (for example, medical insurance), paid time-off (for example, vacations), and services (for example, day care assistance). Most compensation professionals refer to nonmonetary rewards as **employee benefits** or **fringe compensation**.

Core Compensation

There are six types of monetary, or core, compensation. The elements of base pay adjustments are listed in Table 1-1.

Base Pay

Employees receive **base pay**, or money, for performing their jobs (Chapter 8). Base pay is recurring; that is, employees continue to receive base pay as long as they remain in their jobs. Companies disburse base pay to employees in either one of two forms—as **hourly pay** or **wage** or as **salary**. Employees earn hourly pay for each hour worked. They earn salaries for performing their jobs, regardless of the actual number of hours worked. Companies measure salary on an annual basis. The Fair Labor Standards Act (Chapter 3) established criteria for determining whether employees should be paid hourly or by salary.

Companies typically set base pay amounts for jobs according to the level of skill, effort, and responsibility required to perform the jobs and the severity of the working conditions. Compensation professionals refer to skill, effort, responsibility, and working conditions factors as **compensable factors** because they influence pay level (Chapters 3 and 7). Courts of law use these four compensable factors to determine whether jobs are equal per the Equal Pay Act of 1963. Compensation professionals use

TABLE 1-1 Elements of Core Compensation

Base Pay

- Hourly pay
- Annual salary

How Base Pay Is Adjusted over Time

- Cost-of-living adjustments
- Seniority pay
- Merit pay
- Incentive pay
- Pay-for-knowledge and skill-based pay

these compensable factors to help meet three pressing challenges, which we introduce later in this chapter: internal consistency (Chapter 7), market competitiveness (Chapter 8), and recognition of individual contributions (Chapter 9).

Over time, employers adjust employees' base pay to recognize increases in the cost of living, differences in employees' performance, or differences in employees' acquisition of job-related knowledge and skills. We discuss these core compensation elements next.

Cost-of-Living Adjustments (COLAs)

Cost-of-living adjustments (COLAs) represent periodic base pay increases that are based on changes in prices as indexed by the consumer price index (CPI). COLAs enable workers to maintain their purchasing power and standard of living by adjusting base pay for inflation. COLAs are most common among workers represented by unions. Union leaders fought hard for these improvements to maintain their members' loyalty and support. Many employers use the CPI to adjust base pay levels for newly hired employees.

Seniority Pay

Seniority pay systems reward employees with periodic additions to base pay according to employees' length of service in performing their jobs (Chapter 4). These pay plans assume that employees become more valuable to companies with time and that valued employees will leave if they do not have a clear idea that their wages will progress over time. This rationale comes from **human capital theory** [3], which states that employees' knowledge and skills generate productive capital known as **human capital**. Employees can develop such knowledge and skills from formal education and training, including on-the-job experience. Over time, employees presumably refine existing skills or acquire new ones that enable them to work more productively. Seniority pay rewards employees for acquiring and refining their skills as indexed by length (years) of employment.

Merit Pay

Merit pay programs assume that employees' compensation over time should be determined, at least in part, by differences in job performance. Employees earn permanent increases to base pay according to their performance. Merit pay rewards excellent effort or results, motivates future performance, and helps employers retain valued employees.

Incentive Pay

Incentive pay or **variable pay** rewards employees for partially or completely attaining a predetermined work objective. Incentive pay is defined as compensation (other than base wages or salaries) that fluctuates according to employees' attainment of some standard based on a preestablished formula, individual or group goals, or company earnings (Chapter 5).

Pay-for-Knowledge Plans and Skill-Based Pay

Pay-for-knowledge plans reward managerial, service, or professional workers for successfully learning specific curricula (Chapter 6). **Skill-based pay**, used mostly for employees who perform physical work, increases these workers' pay as they master new skills (Chapter 6). Both skill- and knowledge-based pay programs reward employees for the range, depth, and types of skills or knowledge they are capable of applying productively to their jobs. This feature distinguishes pay-for-knowledge plans from merit pay, which rewards employees' job performance. Said another way, pay-for-knowledge programs reward employees for their potential to make meaningful contributions on the job.

"Fringe" Compensation or Employee Benefits

Earlier, we noted that fringe compensation represents nonmonetary rewards. Fringe compensation or employee benefits include any variety of programs that provide paid time-off, employee services, and protection programs. The U.S. government requires most employers to provide particular sets of benefits to employees. We refer to these as **legally required benefits** (Chapter 10). In addition, companies offer addi-

TABLE 1-2 Employer Costs per Hour Worked for Employee Compensation and Costs As a Percent of Total Compensation: Civilian Workers, by Major Occupational Group, March 2002

Compensation component	*Civilian workers*		*White collar*		*Blue collar*		*Service*	
	Cost	*Percent*	*Cost*	*Percent*	*Cost*	*Percent*	*Cost*	*Percent*
Total compensation	$23.15	100.0	$28.02	100.0	$20.41	100.0	$13.09	100.0
Wages and salaries	16.76	72.4	20.57	73.4	14.14	69.3	9.60	73.3
Total benefits	6.39	27.6	7.45	26.6	6.27	30.7	3.49	26.7
Paid leave	1.59	6.9	2.07	7.4	1.20	5.9	.76	5.8
Vacation	.74	3.2	.94	3.4	.60	2.9	.34	2.6
Holiday	.54	2.3	.69	2.5	.43	2.1	.25	1.9
Sick	.23	1.0	.33	1.2	.12	0.6	.13	1.0
Other	.08	0.3	.11	0.4	.05	0.2	.04	0.3
Supplemental pay	.56	2.4	.59	2.1	.72	3.5	.25	1.9
Premium[a]	.22	1.0	.11	0.4	.50	2.4	.13	1.0
Shift differentials	.06	0.3	.05	0.2	.07	0.3	.05	0.4
Nonproduction bonuses	.28	1.2	.42	1.5	.15	0.7	.07	0.5
Insurance	1.61	7.0	1.84	6.6	1.66	8.1	.88	6.7
Life	.04	0.2	.06	0.2	.04	0.2	.02	0.2
Health	1.50	6.5	1.70	6.1	1.55	7.6	.84	6.4
Short-term disability	.04	0.2	.04	0.1	.05	0.2	.02	0.2
Long-term disability	.03	0.1	.04	0.1	.02	0.1	b	c
Retirement and savings	.80	3.5	.97	3.5	.72	3.5	.40	3.1
Defined benefit	.42	1.8	.46	1.6	.43	2.1	.30	2.3
Defined contribution	.38	1.6	.52	1.9	.29	1.4	.10	0.8
Legally required benefits	1.80	7.8	1.94	6.9	1.95	9.6	1.19	9.1
Social Security[d]	1.34	5.8	1.60	5.7	1.20	5.9	.79	6.0
OASDI	1.07	4.6	1.27	4.5	.97	4.8	.64	4.9
Medicare	.27	1.2	.33	1.2	.23	1.1	.16	1.2
Federal unemployment insurance	.03	0.1	.03	0.1	.03	0.1	.03	0.2
State unemployment insurance	.09	0.4	.08	0.3	.10	0.5	.08	0.6
Workers' compensation	.35	1.5	.23	0.8	.62	3.0	.29	2.2
Other benefits[e]	.03	0.1	.04	0.1	.03	0.1	b	c

[a]Includes premium pay for work in addition to the regular work schedule (such as overtime, weekends and holidays).

[b]Cost per hour worked is $0.01 or less.

[c]Less than 0.05 percent.

[d]The total employer's cost for Social Security is comprised of an OASDI portion and a Medicare portion. OASDI is the acronym for Old-Age, Survivors, and Disability Insurance.

[e]Includes severance pay and supplemental unemployment benefits.

Note: The sum of individual items may not equal totals due to rounding.

Source: U.S. Department of Labor (June 19, 2002). Employer costs for employee compensation, March 2002 (USDL: 02-346) [online]. Available: *www.bls.gov/ect/htm*, accessed July 8, 2002.

tional benefits on a discretionary basis. We refer to these as **discretionary benefits** (Chapter 11).

Legally Required Benefits

The U.S. government has established programs to protect individuals from catastrophic events such as disability and unemployment. Legally required benefits are **protection programs** that attempt to promote worker safety and health, maintain the influx of family income, and assist families in crisis. The key legally required benefits are mandated by the Social Security Act of 1935, various state workers' compensation laws, and the Family and Medical Leave Act of 1993. All provide protection programs to employees and their dependents (Chapter 10).

Discretionary Benefits

Discretionary benefits fall into three broad categories: protection programs, paid time-off, and services (Chapter 11). Protection programs provide family benefits, promote health, and guard against income loss caused by catastrophic factors such as unemployment, disability, or serious illness. Not surprisingly, **paid time-off** provides employees with pay for time when they are not working, such as vacation. **Services** provide enhancements such as tuition reimbursement and day care assistance to employees and their families.

Employers typically spend substantial amounts to pay employees and provide benefits. Table 1-2 lists the major legally required and discretionary benefits and the typical expenses incurred by employers to offer these benefits as of March 2002 [4]. This table also includes the cost of wages and salaries. The costs are expressed on an hourly basis per employee. For example, in March 2002, employers characteristically spent $6.39 per employee per hour worked.

A HISTORICAL PERSPECTIVE ON COMPENSATION: THE ROAD TOWARD STRATEGIC COMPENSATION

Agriculture and small family craft businesses were the bases for the U.S. economy before the 1900s. The turn of the 20th century marked the beginning of the Industrial Revolution in the United States. During the Industrial Revolution, the economy's transition from agrarian and craft businesses to large-scale manufacturing began. Increasingly, individuals were becoming employees of large factories instead of self-employed farmers or small-business owners. This shift from the agricultural sector to the industrial sector promoted the beginnings of the field of human resources management [5].

The factory system gave rise to divisions of labor based on differences in worker skill, effort, and responsibilities. The growth in the size of the workplace necessitated practices to guide such activities as hiring, training, setting wages, handling grievances, and terminating employment. At the time, practitioners referred to these activities as personnel administration, which is the predecessor of modern human resource management.

The early personnel (and compensation) function emphasized labor cost control and management control over labor. Many employers instituted so-called **scientific management practices** to control labor costs, as well as welfare practices to maintain control over labor. Scientific management practices gave rise to individual incentive pay systems. Welfare practices represent the forerunner of modern discretionary employee benefits practices.

Scientific management practices promoted labor cost control by replacing inefficient production methods with efficient production methods. Factory owners used time-and-motion studies and job analysis to meet that objective. **Time-and-motion studies** analyzed the time it took employees to complete their jobs. These studies literally focused on employees' movements and the identification of the most efficient steps to complete jobs in the least amount of time [6]. Job analysis is a systematic process for gathering, documenting, and analyzing information in order to describe jobs. At the time, employers used job analysis to classify the most efficient ways to perform jobs.

How did scientific management methods influence compensation practices? Scientific management methods gave rise to the use of piecework plans (Chapter 5). Under piecework plans, an employee's compensation depends on the number of units she or he produces over a given period. Specifically, these plans reward employees on the basis of their individual hourly production against an objective output standard, determined by the pace at which manufacturing equipment operates. For each hour, workers receive piecework incentives for every item produced over the designated production standard.

Welfare practices were generous endeavors undertaken by some employers, motivated in part to minimize employees' desire for union representation, to promote good management, and to enhance worker productivity. Welfare practices were "anything for the comfort and improvement, intellectual or social, of the employees, over and above wages paid, which is not a necessity of the industry nor required by law" [7]. Companies' welfare practices varied. For example, some employers offered facilities such as libraries and recreational areas; others offered financial assistance for education, home purchases, and home improvements. In addition, employer sponsorship of medical insurance coverage became common. The use of welfare practices created the need to administer them. Welfare secretaries served as an intermediary between the company and its employees, and they were essentially predecessors of human resource (HR) professionals [8].

The U.S. government instituted major legislation aimed at protecting individual rights to fair treatment in the workplace. Most often, fair treatment means making employment-related decisions according to job performance—for example, awarding higher merit pay increases to the better performers.

Federal laws led to the bureaucratization of compensation practice. Personnel and compensation administrators took the lead in developing and implementing employment practices that upheld the myriad federal employment laws. These professionals also maintained records, creating documentation in the event of legal challenges to employment practices. In short, compensation professionals were largely administrators who reacted to government regulation.

Personnel administration was transformed from a purely administrative function to a competitive resource in many companies during the 1980s. Since the early 1980s, compensation professionals have been designing and implementing compensation programs that contribute to companies' competitive advantage [9].

Competitive advantage describes a company's success. Specifically, **competitive advantage** refers to a company's ability to maintain market share and profitability over a sustained period of several years. Employers began to recognize that employees are key resources necessary for a company's success, particularly in changing business environments characterized by rapid technological change and intense business competition from foreign countries. Employers' recognition that employees represent an important resource led to the view of employees as human resources. In line with this view, companies design human resource management practices to promote competitive advantage.

As technology leads to the automation of more tasks, employers combine jobs and confer broader responsibilities on workers. For example, the technology of advanced automated manufacturing, such as that used in the automobile industry, began doing the jobs of people, including the laborer, the materials handler, the operator-assembler, and the maintenance person. Now, a single employee performs all of these tasks in a position called "manufacturing technician." The expanding range of tasks and responsibilities in this job demands higher levels of reading, writing, and computation skills than did the jobs that it replaced, which required strong eye-hand coordination. Most employees must possess higher levels of reading skills than before because they must be able to read the operating and troubleshooting manuals (when problems arise) of automated manufacturing equipment that is based on computer technology. Previously, manufacturing equipment had a relatively simple design, based on easily understood mechanical principles such as pulleys, and it was easy to operate.

Increased global competition has forced companies in the United States to become more productive. Now, more than ever, companies must provide their employees with leading-edge skills and encourage them to apply their skills proficiently to sustain competitive advantage. Evidence suggests that workers in other countries are more skilled and able to work more productively than U.S. employees [10].

Compensation practices contribute to competitive advantage by developing more productive and highly skilled workforces [11]. Well-designed merit pay programs reinforce excellent performance by awarding pay raises commensurate with performance attainments. The use of incentive pay practices is instrumental in changing the prevalent entitlement mentality U.S. workers have toward pay and in containing compensation costs by awarding one-time increases to base pay once work objectives have been attained. Pay-for-knowledge and skill-based pay programs are key to giving employees the necessary knowledge and skills to use new workplace technology effectively. Management can use discretionary benefit offerings to promote particular employee behaviors that have strategic value. For instance, when employees take advantage of tuition reimbursement programs, they are more likely to contribute to the strategic imperatives of product or service differentiation and cost-reduction objectives.

STRATEGIC VERSUS TACTICAL DECISIONS

Business professionals make two kinds of decisions—strategic decisions and tactical decisions. **Strategic decisions** guide the activities of companies in the market; **tactical decisions** support the fulfillment of strategic decisions. Business professionals apply these decisions to companies' functions, including manufacturing, engineering, research and development, management information systems, human resources, and marketing. For example, HR professionals make strategic compensation decisions and tactical compensation decisions. Figure 1-2 shows the relationship between strategic decisions and tactical decisions.

Strategic management entails a series of judgments, under uncertainty, that companies direct toward achieving specific goals [12]. Companies base strategy formulation on environmental scanning activities (as described later in this chapter). Discerning threats and opportunities is the main focus of environmental scanning. Strategic management is an inexact process because companies distinguish between threats and opportunities based on interpretation. A threat suggests a negative situation in which loss is likely and over which an individual has relatively little control. An opportunity implies a positive situation in which gain is likely and over which an individual has a fair amount of control [13].

For instance, Mercedes-Benz, a manufacturer of luxury automobiles, stepped outside its typical product offerings by introducing the C230, a well-equipped hatchback

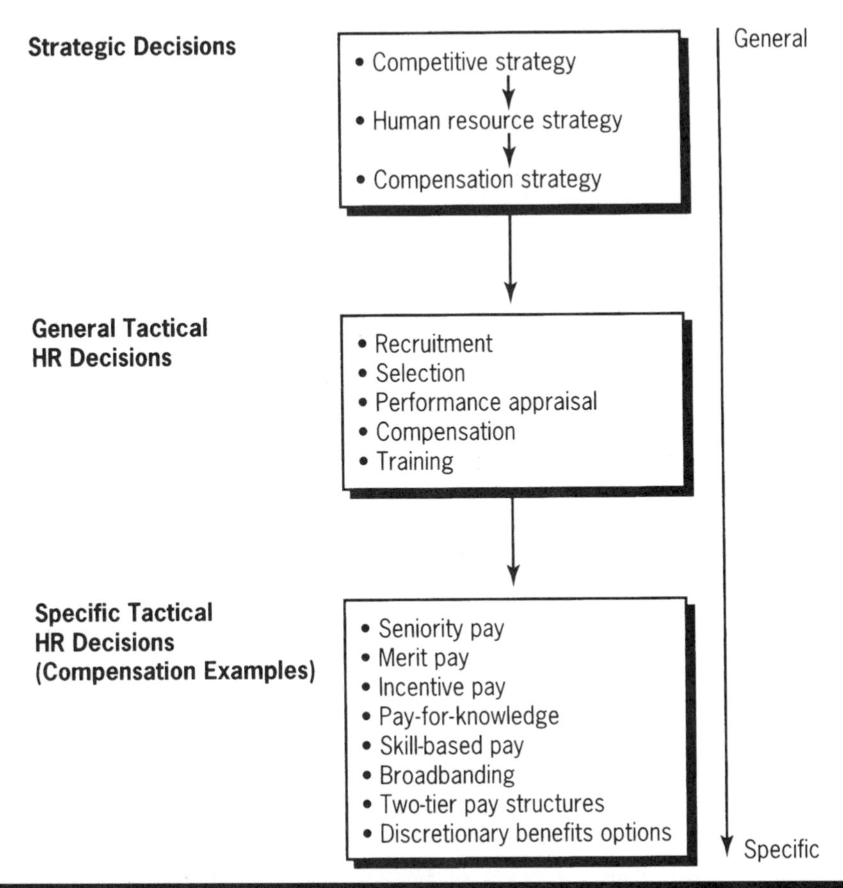

FIGURE 1-2 Relationship between Strategic and Tactical Decisions

model in the $25,000 to $30,000 price range. Most new well-equipped Mercedes vehicles retail well above the $40,000 level and are bought by affluent individuals who are into their 40s and beyond. The new Mercedes offering is geared toward extending its market base to car buyers in their 20s and 30s who typically cannot afford the Mercedes price tag. Given so many fine car alternatives, Mercedes hopes to build loyalty among a younger following of car buyers with the idea that loyal Mercedes owners will continue to buy Mercedes in the future. Table 1-3 illustrates additional threats and opportunities.

Tactical decisions support the fulfillment of strategic decisions, which we discuss shortly. Figure 1-2 shows this relationship between strategic decisions and tactical decisions. We look at Lilly corporation's Web site to illustrate these practices in the following paragraphs.

Strategic planning supports business objectives. Companies' executives communicate business objectives in competitive strategy statements. **Competitive strategy** refers to the planned use of company resources—technology, capital, and human—to promote and sustain competitive advantage. The time horizon for strategic decisions may span 2 or more years. Lilly's competitive strategy:

> Everything at Lilly begins with the unmet medical needs of people. We provide answers for these often complex, difficult problems in two ways: through the discovery and development of breakthrough medicines and through the

TABLE 1-3 Threats and Opportunities in Sample Industries

Sporting Goods

Growth in the $150 billion global sporting goods industry is slowing down following years of moderate growth. Much of the industry's slowdown can be attributed to the decline of children's participation in sports. Many children choose to watch television or videos, surf the Internet, and play video games.

Wireless Communications Services

Wireless services are on the rise as e-mail capabilities and Internet access are becoming increasingly mobile. Nowadays, this industry has provided services that deliver voice and data over cellular telephones, pagers, and handheld computers. There is a rapid trend toward personalizing these services to appeal to users of smaller devices. Growth in subscriptions to mobile phone service is accelerating quickly in large part due to these trends in service options and decreasing prices. Also, moving from analog networks to digital networks has contributed to rises in subscriptions because digital networks provide higher quality service, such as better sound quality and data services.

Apparel, Shoes, and Accessories

As signs of economic slowdown became apparent, sales increased for some retailers but not for others. Many consumers have quickly changed their focus from upscale retail stores such as Federated Department Stores, the May Department Store Company, and Dillard's to discount retail stores, including Wal-Mart, and Target. In response to these trends, many upscale stores have reduced the number of name brands, which are often associated with hefty designer fees. Instead, these stores are carrying high-quality private-label brands that come at a lower cost than name brands.

Many apparel, shoe, and accessory manufacturers have made efforts to sell goods to retail stores at lower costs. One of the main strategies has entailed opening production facilities in foreign countries where labor costs are lower and closing domestic production facilities. Weaker labor laws in Mexico and Southeast Asia permit employers to pay workers at substantially lower rates than in U.S. facilities.

Restaurant Industry

The restaurant industry distinguishes between two kinds of restaurants: full service and fast food. Full-service restaurants include family restaurants (such as Advantica's Denny's), dinner houses (Darden Restaurants' Red Lobster), and grill or buffet types of eateries (Metromedia's Ponderosa). The fast-food sector includes sandwich shops, Mexican food, and pizza, such as Burger King, KFC, McDonald's, Pizza Hut, and Taco Bell. The sluggish economy has resulted in slower sales in full-service restaurants. Some of the people who have cut back on their visits to full-service restaurants have opted for less expensive fast food. Both types of restaurants are facing a labor shortage, as the supply of workers age 16 to 24 has been declining. This age group represents the primary population of restaurant employees. Restaurants have attempted to maintain staffing by recruiting retirees, a growing segment of the population.

> health information we offer. To ensure that our customers get the maximum benefits from our products, we provide important information about our medicines and the diseases they treat.
>
> We are strengthening our ability to identify high-potential drug candidates by improving our research and development processes, investing in new research technologies, and expanding our research team. At the same time, we have entered into dozens of research alliances worldwide to gain access to new research capabilities and additional promising compounds [14].

Human resource executives collaborate with other company executives to develop human resource strategies. **Human resource strategies** specify the use of multiple HR practices. These statements are consistent with a company's competitive strategy.

> At Lilly, people are the source of all our abilities, all our successes. Our future depends on our global community of employees whose varied perspectives, experience and training fuel the creativity and the energy to pioneer pharmaceutical innovation.

Compensation and benefits executives work with the lead HR executive and the company's chief budget officer to prepare total compensation strategies. Total compensation strategies describe the use of compensation and benefits practices that support both human resource strategies and competitive strategies.

> The mission of Lilly's Work/Life Program is to provide the tools necessary for the company to pursue the highest level of effectiveness within the context of a changing work force. The company strives to create an environment that enables individuals to optimize their contribution over the course of their careers by reducing barriers to productivity that can be caused by conflicts between work and personal life.
>
> As part of this effort, Lilly provides its employees with numerous programs and options, which may vary according to job and location. These include flexible work options; on-site child care; parenting resources; maternity and dependent care leave; adoption assistance; nursing mother stations; health and dental benefits; health and wellness programs; and on-site conveniences, such as a credit union, a dry cleaner, a convenience store and ready-to-serve hot meals; and special events.

Competitive Strategy Choices

Lowest-Cost Strategy

The **cost leadership** or **lowest-cost strategy** focuses on gaining competitive advantage by being the lowest-cost producer of a product or service within the marketplace, while selling the product or service at a price advantage relative to the industry average. Lowest-cost strategies require aggressive construction of efficient-scale facilities and vigorous pursuit of cost minimization in such areas as operations, marketing, and human resources.

Southwest Airlines is an excellent illustration of an organization that pursues a lowest-cost strategy because its management successfully reduced operations costs. At least two noteworthy decisions have contributed to Southwest's goals. First, Southwest's training and aircraft maintenance costs are lower than similar competitors' costs because the airline uses only Boeing 737 aircraft. Southwest enjoys substantial cost savings because it does not need to buy different curricula for training flight attendants, mechanics, and pilots to learn about procedures specific to different aircraft makes (such as Boeing and McDonnell-Douglas) and models (such as Boeing 737 and Boeing 777). Second, Southwest passengers may sit anywhere they like as long as they get there first, and the airline uses ticketless travel. These choices greatly reduce administrative costs.

Differentiation Strategy

Companies adopt **differentiation strategies** to develop products or services that are unique from those of its competitors. Differentiation strategy can take many forms, including design or brand image, technology, features, customer service, and price.

Differentiation strategies lead to competitive advantage through building brand loyalty among devoted consumers. Brand-loyal consumers are less sensitive to price increases, which enables companies to invest in research and development initiatives to further differentiate themselves from competing companies.

The Iams Company, a cat and dog food manufacturer, successfully pursues a differentiation strategy based on brand image and price premiums. The company offers two separate dog food lines—Iams, a super-premium line that is nutritionally well balanced for dogs and uses high-quality ingredients, and Eukanuba, an ultra-premium line, that contains more chicken and vital nutrients than the Iams line, as well as OmegaCOAT Nutritional Science (fatty acids) that promotes shiny and healthy coats. Together, Iams and Eukanuba appeal to a substantial set of dog owners. The Iams Company distinguishes Eukanuba from Iams by claiming that Eukanuba is the "Vital Health System for Your Dog." The Eukanuba slogan is the company's basis for brand image.

Besides brand image, the Iams Company also differentiates its Eukanuba line by charging a price premium. This price premium has enabled the Iams Company to be an innovator in canine nutrition by investing heavily in product research and development. Eukanuba offers several formulas to meet the needs of small, medium, and large breeds of dogs according to life stage and activity level.

Tactical Decisions That Support the Firm's Strategy

Human resource tactics and practices in other functional areas support a company's competitive strategy. Functional area capabilities include manufacturing, engineering, research and development, management information systems, human resources, and marketing. Compensation and HR professionals can orchestrate human resource and other functional tactics to promote competitive strategy. In addition, HR practices support competitive advantage through energizing employees to perform the jobs for which they were hired.

Tactics in Other Functional Areas

Companies must determine which functional capabilities are most crucial to maintaining a competitive advantage. For example, rapid advances in medical science are moving toward less invasive surgical procedures that require special surgical instruments. One noteworthy example is arthroscopic surgery. Arthroscopes enable surgeons to perform knee and shoulder surgeries without invasive surgical openings. A competitive advantage in this industry depends largely on researching, developing, and manufacturing leading-edge surgical instruments for these new, less invasive surgical procedures.

Employee Roles Associated with Competitive Strategies

HR professionals must decide which employee roles are instrumental to the attainment of competitive strategies [15]. Knowledge of these required roles should enable HR professionals to implement HR tactics that encourage their enactment of these roles. Of course, compensation professionals are responsible for designing and implementing compensation tactics that elicit strategy-consistent employee roles.

For the lowest-cost strategy, the imperative is to reduce output costs per employee. The desired employee roles for attaining a lowest-cost strategy include repetitive and predictable behaviors, a relatively short-term focus, primarily autonomous or individual activity, high concern for quantity of output, and a primary concern for results [16].

The key employees' roles for differentiation strategies include highly creative behavior, a relatively long-term focus, cooperative and interdependent behavior, and a greater degree of risk taking [17]. Compared with lowest-cost strategies, successful attainment of differentiation strategies depends on employee creativity, openness to novel work approaches, and willingness to take risks. In addition, differentiation strategies require longer time frames to provide sufficient opportunity to yield the benefits of these behaviors.

COMPENSATION PROFESSIONALS' GOALS

Understanding compensation professionals' goals requires knowing the role of human resources within companies and specific HR practices, particularly how HR professionals fit into the corporate hierarchy and how the compensation function fits into HR departments.

How HR Professionals Fit Into the Corporate Hierarchy

Line function and staff function broadly describe all employee functions. **Line employees** are directly involved in producing companies' goods or delivering their services. Assembler, production worker, and salesperson are examples of line jobs. **Staff employees'** functions support the line functions. Human resource professionals and accountants are examples of staff employees. Human resource professionals are staff employees because they offer a wide variety of support services for line employees. In a nutshell, HR professionals promote the effective use of all employees in companies. Effective use means attaining work objectives that fit with the overall mission of the company. According to Jay Hannah, BancFirst Corp. executive vice president of financial services, "The HR department is the source and keeper of critical information, which is key in today's workplace. With the information they provide, we in turn can build and design strategies to hire and retain the best workforce possible. And this may sound cliché, but it's very true—the real competitive advantage is our company's human resources." [18]

Human resource professionals design and implement a variety of HR practices that advance this objective. Besides compensation, HR practices include:

- Recruitment
- Selection
- Performance appraisal
- Training
- Career development
- Labor-management relations
- Employment termination
- Managing human resources within the context of legislation

Most company structures include an HR department. Traditionally, HR departments were thought of as an administrative or support function for the company because the financial or market value of HR was not as readily apparent as sales, manufacturing, or marketing functions. Some practitioners and researchers are suspect about the future of internal HR functions. The "Flip Side of the Coin" feature describes how the HR function must change to remain a viable function for companies.

FLIP SIDE OF THE COIN

PUTTING HR ON THE SCORECARD

The challenge to GTE HR managers was tantalizing: Find a credible way to measure HR's contribution to the business.

Garrett Walker, GTE's director of HR planning, measurement, and analysis, was elated. He was in a meeting with seven other human resources specialists to tackle the challenge that the HR executive vice president had just handed them.

Their charter? To do work that had never been done before at GTE: to create and implement a tool that would measure HR's contribution to the business.

To accomplish this, they'd have to fold HR's vision and strategy into GTE's business objectives, integrate them in all the company's work units, and then measure their effectiveness.

It wasn't going to be easy.

The team, made up of members from each HR functional area, knew it was an immense task that would have far-reaching impact. First, they had to understand how to measure success in human terms. Then they had to find out if there was a tool that could be used to measure success.

The group identified their areas of concern and learned what they could from already available tools. They couldn't find an overall model that quantitatively measured the bottom-line impact of HR services, so they began to construct one of their own.

"Our senior HR leaders understood from the business strategy that we needed to deliver a lot of new skill sets to help our employees become more competitive in the current environment," says Walker. That drove HR strategies. "Once those were defined and we knew what our actions were going to be, we needed to know, quantitatively, if HR was delivering on the strategy. We needed a state-of-the-art way of measuring the effectiveness of HR."

They ultimately came up with the "HR Balanced Scorecard": a strategic measurement system that would use hard data to demonstrate HR's contribution to the bottom line. Based on the model created by David Norton and Robert Kaplan of Harvard Business School in "The Balanced Scorecard: Translating Strategy into Action" (Harvard Business School Press, 1996), it would measure and continually monitor activity over the entire enterprise, and gauge whether the activities were driving the company toward success.

The HR Balanced Scorecard would allow managers to react to the data, predicting problems and focusing their energy on solutions for those problems rather than symptoms. Another benefit of this system is that it underscored the culture change within GTE where functions were no longer working within silos to an environment where they were sharing information across the organization to improve productivity.

All of this was becoming increasingly important because the world in which GTE operates was changing dramatically. Since the Telecom Act, their industry had been deregulated, and there were increased pressures from investors as well as competitors. Accelerating technology had brought about vast changes in the services that telecommunications companies could offer, global expansion offered new opportunities, and customers had become very savvy, wanting more choices and expecting outstanding quality.

Finally, the workforce had also changed. All of these factors created an eagerness to excel—and to be able to use hard information to make sure the company was meeting its goals.

Let's take it from the top.

The team began its work in April 1998. First, it met with upper HR management to develop key questions that would become the framework of a measurement model. It began with identifying subject matter experts and asking them what they thought was important and how they suggested collecting data to measure it. They wanted to discover the ways and information already available, but also wanted to think in new creative modes.

"We've taken general business strategy and translated that to HR strategy. Then we created an instrument to use hard quantitative measures to translate that into basic actionable metrics," says Walker. "It's the first time ever within our company that a support unit, such as human resources, can actually use an instrument to see how you are contributing to business success."

(Continued)

(Continued)

The team had five targets to measure:

1. Managing talent
2. Developing world-class leadership
3. Customer service and support
4. Organizational integration
5. HR capability

Then, from August through November, came the process of interviewing dozens and dozens of individuals in HR to collect data. "it was a grueling process," says Walker. "Data collection is always a challenge in a company, especially one as large as GTE. But we wanted to challenge our colleagues to think through the measures that would be most valuable to them and then work backwards to see how to go about finding the information."

By January 1999, the HR Balanced Scorecard team had taken the next step. They linked the measurement system to performance criteria for the broad-based incentive pay program, which was followed quickly by a phased communication to explain the process throughout the HR organization.

Next, the group made the HR Balanced Scorecard and in-depth explanations (called the HR Briefing Book) available via the HR Web site, and allowed employees to view quarterly results.

How does the scorecard work?

After the major areas of focus are defined, divisions within the company answer questions and enter data into the scorecard based on key issues. After the information has been calculated and interpreted, it's posted on the company's intranet site so that all HR professionals can see how well the company is doing in its key target areas.

For example, take the area of leadership development, a high priority for GTE. The strategic questions would be, "Does the company have the talent needed to be successful in the future? Does it have leadership 'bench strength'?"

The scorecard would measure the acquisition of talent, the diversity of the workforce, targeted capabilities, and the ability to retain these individuals. Detailed measurements would be collected on two fronts: Is GTE doing well in its recruiting and are these individuals the correct ones? The raw data each unit feeds into the scorecard illustrate the effectiveness of HR's efforts in this critical strategic area.

Furthermore, through the scorecard measurements, management can see exactly what high-potential individuals are doing. They can quantify what key jobs high-potentials are filling and how they're doing. They track retention of these major contributors.

"If we had the next Jack Welch in our organization and they were an early career professional, we would need to identify them and engage them in order to maximize their value," says Walker. "We can compare how frequently we're moving them through developmental assignments as compared to the rest of the organization. [In this case,] it should be at a more frequent rate because for future senior leaders in the company, we have already created a development plan and we need to move them through jobs to gain experience. We don't want them to end up in a job for three years that they could have learned in six months."

Seeing is believing for GTE's HR accountability.

Through the information that the units provide for the scorecard, HR is able to watch the movement and development of these people on a quarterly basis. If greater executive education is desired, for example, that will become apparent quickly. This way, it drives accountability into human resources, and it also provides a way to communicate HR's contributions to the overall business.

"There was some resistance within the organization and we needed to go out and sell the project," says Walker. "It was important that we had established a good track record of credibility as we had been developing the product. However, we couldn't point to another company and say, 'That's what we're doing.' It was brand-new stuff—a concept and a theory."

But when they were finally able to produce the scorecard, people were surprised, and saw that it was very effective. Every quarter, the group publishes the results, not only to the 2,000-plus HR staff but to GTE's business leaders as well. The results are a fundamental way to see how the company is performing against its strategic objectives.

While it is not a full transformation, the team believes that GTE has made a quantum leap toward a quantitatively accountable culture.

"Although it seems cutting edge right now, we're at the very beginning of the journey here within HR. We're using it as a tool for cultural transformation and to drive accountability into human resources," says Walker. "As HR professionals, we are no longer a back room transaction-based necessary evil. We are a partner, experts helping the company maximize the value of people."

CHARTING A COURSE OF ACTION

GTE's goals led to a strategy with five major targets. Growth in these areas is critical to HR's mission to position the company as a worldwide player in telecommunications.

HR Strategic Thrust 1: Talent

- Grow the talent pool.
- Invest in our people.
- Provide growth opportunities.
- Leverage diversity.
- Build an environment that fosters creativity and innovation.

HR Strategic Thrust 2: Leadership

- Invest in leadership growth.
- Define leadership competencies.
- Structure rewards to foster leadership behavior.

HR Strategic Thrust 3:
Customer Service and Support

- Create an environment that supports employee engagement.
- Build service capability.

HR Strategic Thrust 4:
Organization Integration

- Leverage total GTE capabilities.
- Partner with our unions.
- Foster business unit teaming.
- Structure rewards to foster integration.

HR Strategic Thrust 5: HR Capability

- Invest in our own growth development.
- Organize to deliver excellent service.
- Enhance our technological capabilities.

WHAT DO YOU EXPECT FROM EMPLOYEES?

One of the most important questions GTE asked itself in its introspective look at HR was: What do we need from our people? Here are a few of HR's answers both in current needs as well as critical future needs.

Current

- Network management skills
- Customer support skills
- Voice product expertise

Enhanced

- Leadership capabilities
- Partnering with unions
- Learning and innovation focus

New

- Shared mindset toward achieving business results
- Partnering/alliance management capability
- Integration capability

Source: Charlene Marmer Solomon, 1998. Shaping our direction. GTE Human Resources; Workforce 94–98 79, no. 3 (March 2000): pp. 94–98, ISSN: 1092-8332, Number: 50835526, Copyright ACC Communications, Inc. "Shaping Our Direction," GTE Human Resources, 1998.

How the Compensation Function Fits into HR Departments

Human resource practices do not operate in isolation. Every HR practice is related to others in different ways. For example, Microsoft Corporation publicly acknowledges the relationships between compensation and other HR practices:

> We've said this for years, and it's still as true as it ever was: our employees are our greatest asset. And as such, we believe in making a long-term investment in you. That includes your financial well-being and your progress within our company. In this section you'll find three areas of discussion—covering career development, compensation and investment programs—designed to help you

better understand the concerted effort we make to ensure your experience at Microsoft is future-focused and enriching from day one. [19]

Let's consider additional relationships between compensation and each of the HR practices.

Compensation, Recruitment, and Selection

Job candidates choose to work for particular companies for a number of reasons, including career advancement opportunities, training, the company's reputation for being a "good" place to work, location, and compensation. Companies try to spark job candidates' interest by communicating the positive features of the core and fringe compensation programs. As we discuss in Chapter 8, companies use compensation to compete for the very best candidates. In addition, companies may offer such inducements as one-time signing bonuses to entice high-quality applicants. It is not uncommon for signing bonuses to amount to as much as 20 percent of starting annual salaries. Signing bonuses are useful when the supply of qualified candidates falls short of companies' needs for these candidates.

The next three sections address performance appraisal, training, and career development. Before discussing these issues, let's look at how Microsoft explicitly acknowledges the relationship between compensation and these HR practices:

> Once a year, you'll have the opportunity to take the long view on your performance and, with your manager, assess the value of your work and plan for your next move at Microsoft. This is done through a process called "reviews," and it provides a forum for you to evaluate your work and progress against measurable objectives you've previously identified and agreed upon with your manager. Your manager will also independently evaluate your work—again, in the context of those previously identified objectives and with regard to your role and team. You'll then meet with your manager to review your previous year's work and to set new goals to challenge you, expand your abilities, and grow your career in the coming year. It's also during this review process that merit bonuses and salary increases are determined, as they are generally reflective of your contribution in the context of your team and group at Microsoft.
>
> To complement this review, you will have a discussion with your manager halfway through the year to discuss your career objectives and planning. This is a time to review your personal goals in a formal setting, make changes as needed and carve your 3–5 year career path. At this time, strategic educational planning will also be implemented.
>
> Achieve your goals and measure your success. Depending on how you've moved toward accomplishing and surpassing the personal goals that you've set for yourself, we're ready to express our appreciation. We expect you to move forward on your career path and we're always ready to inspire your next step.
>
> Base pay. Our salaries are competitive within the industry, and specifics will be provided if we reach an offer stage with you.
>
> Bonus awards. Employees are eligible for a cash bonus award that may be determined during their formal review as described above. Bonus awards are based on the ability to meet specific personal performance goals that have been outlined and accessed periodically by both the employee and the employee's manager.

> Merit increases. Employees may be considered for merit increases during their formal review as described above. Merit increases are based on skill, experience, contribution and performance on your own personal goals.
>
> Stock option grants. Microsoft believes employees who become shareholders have an even bigger interest in working hard to help the company succeed. Microsoft's stock option program recognizes employee contribution and potential, and it provides a long-term incentive for future performance and contribution. Stock option grants may be awarded on a discretionary basis to employees at their time of hiring and/or annually. [20]

Compensation and Performance Appraisal

Accurate performance appraisals are key to effective merit pay programs. For merit pay programs to succeed, employees must know that their efforts toward meeting production quotas or quality standards will lead to pay raises. Job requirements must be realistic, and employees must be prepared to meet job goals with respect to their skills and abilities. Moreover, employees must perceive a strong relationship between attaining performance standards and receiving pay increases. Merit pay systems require specific performance appraisal approaches. Administering successful merit pay programs depends as much on sound performance appraisal practices as on the compensation professional's skill in designing and implementing such plans.

Compensation and Training

Successful pay-for-knowledge plans depend on a company's ability to develop and implement systematic training programs. When training is well designed, employees should be able to learn the skills needed to increase their pay, as well as the skills necessary to teach and coach other employees at lower skill levels. Companies implementing pay-for-knowledge plans typically increase the amount of classroom and on-the-job training. Pay-for-knowledge systems make training necessary rather than optional. Accordingly, companies that adopt pay-for-knowledge systems must ensure that all employees have equal access to the training needed to acquire higher-level skills.

Compensation and Career Development

Most employees expect to experience career development within their present companies. Employees' careers develop in two different ways. First, some employees change the focus of their work—for example, from supervisor of payroll clerks to supervisor of inventory clerks. This change represents a lateral move across the company's hierarchy. Second, others maintain their focus and assume greater responsibilities. This change illustrates advancement upward through the company's hierarchy. Advancing from payroll clerk to manager of payroll administration is an example of moving upward through a company's hierarchy. Employees' compensation changes to reflect career development.

Compensation and Labor-Management Relations

Collective bargaining agreements describe the terms of employment (for example, pay, work hours) reached between management and the union. Compensation is a key topic. Unions have fought hard for general pay increases and regular COLAs to promote their members' standard of living. In Chapter 3, we review the role of unions in compensation, and in Chapter 4, we indicate that unions have traditionally bargained for seniority pay systems in negotiations with management. More recently, unions have been willing to incorporate particular incentive pay systems. For example, unions appear to be receptive to behavioral encouragement plans because improving worker safety and minimizing absenteeism serve the best interests of both employees and employers.

Compensation and Employment Termination

Employment termination takes place when an employee's agreement to perform work is terminated. Employment terminations are either involuntary or voluntary. The HR department plays a central role in managing involuntary employment terminations. Companies initiate involuntary terminations for a variety of reasons, including poor job performance, insubordination, violation of work rules, reduced business activity due to sluggish economic conditions, and plant closings. Discharge represents involuntary termination for poor job performance, insubordination, or gross violation of work rules. Involuntary layoff describes termination under sluggish economic conditions or because of plant closings. In the case of involuntary layoffs, HR professionals typically provide outplacement counseling to help employees find work elsewhere. Companies may choose to award **severance pay**, which usually amounts to several months' pay following involuntary termination and, in some cases, continued coverage under the employer's medical insurance plan. Employees often rely on severance pay to meet financial obligations while they search for employment. In the past, companies commonly offered a year or more of severance pay. These days, severance benefits tend to be less generous. For example, Electronic Data Services (EDS), a global information technology company, prior to a large layoff recently reduced severance pay from 26 weeks to 4 weeks.

Employees initiate voluntary terminations, most often to work for other companies or to retire. In the case of retirement, companies sponsor pension programs. **Pension programs** provide income to individuals throughout their retirement. Sometimes, companies use **early retirement programs** to reduce workforce size and trim compensation expenditures. Early retirement programs contain incentives designed to encourage highly paid employees with substantial seniority to retire earlier than they had planned. These incentives expedite senior employees' retirement eligibility and increase their retirement income. In addition, many companies continue retirees' medical benefits. For example, Corning Incorporated announced that it would offer early retirement packages to approximately 600 employees as part of an overall plan to control costs because of the slowdown in capital spending by telecommunications companies.

Compensation and Legislation

Employment laws establish bounds of acceptable employment practices, as well as employee rights. Federal laws that apply to compensation practices are grouped according to four themes:

- Income continuity, safety, and work hours
- Pay discrimination
- Accommodation of disabilities and family needs
- Prevailing wage laws

Table 1-4 lists for each theme the major laws that influence compensation practice.

The federal government enacted income continuity, safety, and work hours laws (for example, the Fair Labor Standards Act of 1938) to stabilize individuals' incomes when they became unemployed because of poor business conditions or workplace injuries, as well as to set pay minimums and work-hour limits for children. The civil rights movement of the 1960s led to the passage of key legislation (for example, the

TABLE 1-4 Laws That Influence Compensation

Income Continuity, Safety, and Work Hours
Minimum wage laws—Fair Labor Standards Act of 1938
  Minimum wage
  Overtime provisions
    Portal-to-Portal Act of 1947
    Equal Pay Act of 1963
  Child labor provisions
Work Hours and Safety Standards Act of 1962
McNamara-O'Hara Service Contract Act of 1965

Pay Discrimination
Equal Pay Act of 1963
Civil Rights Act of 1964, Title VII
Bennett Amendment (1964)
Executive Order 11246 (1965)
Age Discrimination in Employment Act of 1967 (amended in 1978, 1986, 1990)
Executive Order 11141 (1964)
Civil Rights Act of 1991

Accommodating Disabilities and Family Needs
Pregnancy Discrimination Act of 1978
Americans with Disabilities Act of 1990
Family and Medical Leave Act of 1993

Prevailing Wage Laws
David-Bacon Act of 1931
Walsh-Healey Public Contracts Act of 1936

Equal Pay Act of 1963 and the Civil Rights Act of 1964) designed to protect designated classes of employees and to uphold their individual rights against discriminatory employment decisions, including matters of pay. Congress enacted legislation (for example, the Pregnancy Discrimination Act of 1978, the Americans with Disabilities Act of 1990, and the Family and Medical Leave Act of 1993) to accommodate employees with disabilities and pressing family needs. Prevailing wage laws (for example, the Davis-Bacon Act of 1931) set minimum wage rates for companies that provide paid services—such as building maintenance—to the U.S. government.

The Compensation Department's Main Goals

Compensation professionals promote effective compensation systems by meeting three important objectives: internal consistency, market competitiveness, and recognition of individual contributions.

Internal Consistency

Internally consistent compensation systems clearly define the relative value of each job among all jobs within a company. This ordered set of jobs represents the job structure or hierarchy. Companies rely on a simple, yet fundamental, principle for building internally consistent compensation systems: Employees in jobs that require greater qualifications, more responsibilities, and more complex job duties should be paid more than employees whose jobs require lesser qualifications, fewer responsibilities, and less complex job duties. Internally consistent job structures formally recognize differences in job characteristics, which enable compensation managers to set pay accordingly.

Compensation professionals use job analysis and job evaluation to achieve internal consistency. **Job analysis** is a systematic process for gathering, documenting, and analyzing information in order to describe jobs. Job analyses describe content or job duties, worker requirements, and sometimes the job context or working conditions.

Compensation professionals use **job evaluation** to systematically recognize differences in the relative worth among a set of jobs and to establish pay differentials accordingly. Whereas job analysis is almost purely descriptive, job evaluation partly reflects the values and priorities that management places on various positions. Based on job content differences (that is, job analysis results) and the firm's priorities, managers establish pay differentials for virtually all positions within the company.

Market Competitiveness

Market-competitive pay systems play a significant role in attracting and retaining the most qualified employees. Compensation professionals build market-competitive compensation systems based on the results of strategic analyses (Chapter 2) and compensation surveys.

A **strategic analysis** entails an examination of a company's external market context and internal factors. Examples of external market factors are the industry profile, information about competitors, and long-term growth prospects. Internal factors encompass the company's financial condition and functional capabilities—for example, marketing and human resources. Strategic analyses permit business professionals to see where they stand in the market based on external and internal factors.

Compensation surveys collect and then analyze competitors' compensation data. Traditionally, compensation surveys focused on competitors' wage and salary practices. Now, fringe compensation is also a target of surveys because benefits are a key element of market-competitive pay systems. Compensation surveys are important because they enable compensation professionals to obtain realistic views of competitors' pay practices. In the absence of compensation survey data, compensation professionals would have to use guesswork to build market-competitive compensation systems.

Recognizing Individual Contributions

Pay structures represent pay rate differences for jobs of unequal worth and the framework for recognizing differences in employee contributions. No two employees possess identical credentials or perform the same jobs equally well. Companies recognize these differences by paying individuals according to their credentials, knowledge, or job performance. When completed, pay structures should define the boundaries for recognizing employee contributions. Well-designed structures should promote the retention of valued employees.

Pay grades and pay ranges are structural features of pay structures. **Pay grades** group jobs for pay policy application. Human resource professionals typically group jobs into pay grades based on similar compensable factors and value. These criteria are not precise. In fact, no single formula determines what is sufficiently similar in terms of content and value to warrant grouping into a pay grade. Pay ranges build upon pay grades. **Pay ranges** include minimum, maximum, and midpoint pay rates. The minimum and maximum values denote the acceptable lower and upper bounds of pay for the jobs in particular pay grades. The midpoint pay value is the halfway mark between the minimum and maximum pay rates.

STAKEHOLDERS OF THE COMPENSATION SYSTEM

The HR department provides services to stakeholders within and outside the company. These include:

- Employees
- Line managers
- Executives
- Unions
- U.S. government

The success of HR departments depends on how well they serve various stakeholders. "Each constituency [stakeholder] has its own set of expectations regarding the personnel department's activities; each holds its own standards for effective performance; each applies its own standards for assessing the extent to which the department's activities meets its expectations; and each attempts to prescribe preferred goals for the subunit or presents constraints to its sphere of discretion. Multiple stakeholders often compete directly or indirectly for the attention and priority of the personnel department." [21] Our focus is on some of the ways compensation professionals serve these stakeholders.

Employees

As we discussed earlier, successful pay-for-knowledge programs depend on a company's ability to develop and implement systematic training programs. Compensation professionals must educate employees about their training options and how successful training will lead to increased pay and advancement opportunities within the company. These professionals should not assume that employees will necessarily recognize these opportunities unless they are clearly communicated. Written memos and informational meetings conducted by compensation professionals and HR representatives are effective communication media.

Discretionary benefits provide protection programs, paid time-off, and services. As compensation professionals plan and manage fringe compensation programs, they should keep these functions in mind. Probably no single company expects its fringe compensation program to meet all these objectives. Therefore, compensation professionals as representatives of company management, along with union representatives, must determine which objectives are the most important for their particular workforce.

Line Managers

Compensation professionals use their expert knowledge of the laws that influence pay and benefits practices to help line managers make sound compensation judgments. For example, the Equal Pay Act of 1963 (discussed in Chapter 3) prohibits sex discrimination in pay for employees performing equal work, so compensation professionals should advise line managers to pay the same hourly pay rate or annual salary for men and women hired to perform the same job.

Line managers turn to compensation professionals for advice about appropriate pay rates for jobs. Compensation professionals oversee the use of job evaluation to establish pay differentials among jobs within a company. In addition, they train line managers how to properly evaluate jobs.

Executives

Compensation professionals serve company executives by developing and managing sound compensation systems. Executives look to them to ensure that the design and implementation of pay and benefits practices comply with pertinent legislation.

Violation of these laws can lead to substantial monetary penalties to companies. Also, executives depend on compensation professionals' expertise to design pay and benefits systems that will attract and retain the best-qualified employees. As we discuss in Chapter 2, employees play a major role in a company's success.

Unions

As noted earlier, collective bargaining agreements describe the terms of employment reached between management and the union. Compensation professionals are responsible for administering the pay and benefits policies specified in collective bargaining agreements. Mainly, they ensure that employees receive COLAs and seniority pay increases on a timely basis.

U.S. Government

The U.S. government requires that companies comply with all employment legislation. Compensation professionals apply their expertise regarding pertinent legislation to design legally sound pay and benefits practices. In addition, since the passage of the Civil Rights Act of 1991, compensation professionals have applied their expertise to demonstrate that alleged discriminatory pay practices are a business necessity. As we discuss in Chapter 3, compensation professionals possess the burden of proof to demonstrate that alleged discriminatory pay practices are not discriminatory.

SUMMARY

This chapter introduced basic compensation concepts and the context of compensation practice. We distinguished between intrinsic and extrinsic compensation, noting that our focus is on extrinsic compensation. Next, we reviewed the evolution of compensation from an administrative function to a strategic function, as well as the strategic role of compensation in attaining competitive advantage. Then, we looked at how HR professionals fit in the corporate hierarchy and how compensation professionals fit into HR departments. Specifically, we learned that compensation professionals focus on internal and external pay differentials among jobs, as well as on creating pay structures that recognize employees for their particular contributions. Finally, we concluded with how compensation professionals relate to a company's various stakeholders.

Students of compensation should keep the following in mind: Compensation systems are changing. Change creates many exciting challenges for those who wish to work as compensation professionals. This book highlights those challenges.

Key Terms

- intrinsic compensation, 2
- extrinsic compensation, 2
- job characteristics theory, 2
- core compensation, 6
- employee benefits, 6
- fringe compensation, 6
- base pay, 6
- hourly pay, 6
- wage, 6
- salary, 6
- compensable factors, 6
- cost-of-living adjustments, 7
- seniority pay, 7
- human capital theory, 7
- human capital, 7
- merit pay, 7
- incentive pay, 7
- variable pay, 7
- pay-for-knowledge, 7
- skill-based pay, 7
- legally required benefits, 8
- discretionary benefits, 9
- protection programs, 9
- paid time-off, 9
- services, 9
- scientific management practices, 9
- time-and-motion studies, 10
- welfare practices, 10
- competitive advantage, 10
- strategic decisions, 11
- tactical decisions, 11
- strategic management, 11
- competitive strategy, 12
- human resource strategies, 13
- cost leadership, 14
- lowest-cost strategy, 14
- differentiation strategies, 14
- line employees, 16
- staff employees, 16

- severance pay, 22
- pension programs, 22
- early retirement programs, 22
- internally consistent compensation systems, 23
- job analysis, 24
- job evaluation, 24
- market-competitive pay systems, 24
- strategic analysis, 24
- compensation surveys, 24
- pay structures, 24
- pay grades, 24
- pay ranges, 24

Discussion Questions

1. Define compensation.
2. Presumably, five core job characteristics promote intrinsic compensation. Give examples of jobs that you believe rate highly on these core job characteristics. Explain your answer.
3. Identify two companies—one that you believe pursues a lowest-cost strategy and another that pursues a differentiation strategy. Relying on personal knowledge, company annual reports, or articles in newspapers and business periodicals, discuss these companies' competitive strategies.
4. Describe your reaction to the following statement: Compensation has no bearing on a company's performance.
5. Are the three main goals of compensation departments equally important, or do you believe that they differ in importance? Give your rationale.

Exercises

Compensation Online

For Students

Exercise 1: Find relevant journal articles
Use your school library's online catalog or Web sites to locate articles pertaining to compensation and competitive strategy. Find and read several of the articles to get a feel for topics that are currently important in these areas. If you were asked to write a short paper on the topic of most interest to you, what topic would you choose? Why?

Exercise 2: Use an Internet search engine
Each search engine allows its users to narrow their searches in order to better locate the sites they are looking for.

Go to the Yahoo! search engine at *www.yahoo.com*

Type the words *strategic compensation*, and click on the search button. How many sites were found? Click on a couple of the sites. How could you use the information on these sites to demonstrate knowledge and understanding to a job interviewer?

Exercise 3: Conduct an advanced search
Go back to the Yahoo! homepage and click on the advanced search link (located next to the search button). Type in *strategic compensation* again in the "exact phrase" box. Click on the search button. How did the results change from the regular search? Now, go back to the advanced search page and select "more options." Select English language, show pages only from the United States, and show pages updated in the last three months. How did the changes affect the search results?

Using a different search engine, go to the same Web site or find a related site. Compare and contrast the two search engines for ease of accessibility and amount of information available.

For Professionals

Exercise 1: Search for government documents
Your budget for securing compensation information is limited. A colleague points you to a free resource, the federal government. Search government sites for the Bureau of Labor Statistics and the Department of Labor for documents regarding human

resources. Also use Yahoo to search for "federal government" or "federal laws." Visit several of the sites listed. What are some of the key topics covered on these sites?

Exercise 2: Review a company Web page

Assume you are a compensation professional in some industry of interest to you. You have been assigned the task of finding out as much as you can about your competitors' strategies. Using Yahoo, find the homepages of a few of your competitors. These sites will have links about employment and investor information. Click these links. Using the information from these sites as well as information from Chapter 1, try to estimate each company's competitive strategy.

Use a different search engine, like Google.com, and search for the same companies. Compare and contrast the two search engines for ease of accessibility and the amount of information available.

Exercise 3: Review a compensation Web site

Your company is seeking to develop a new compensation system, and you are in charge of finding a compensation consulting firm. Use the Internet to identify firms. Research what resources and services each consulting firm offers.

Endnotes

1. Hackman, J. R., & Oldham, G. R. (1976). Motivation through the design of work: Test of a theory. *Organizational Behavior and Human Performance*, *16*, pp. 250–279.
2. people[3] [online]. Available: *www.people3.com*, accessed July 1, 2002.
3. Becker, G. (1976). *Human Capital*. New York: National Bureau of Economic Research.
4. U.S. Department of Labor (June 19, 2002). Employer cost for employee compensation March 2002 (USDL: 02–346) [online]. Available: *www.bls.gov/ect/home.htm*, accessed July 8, 2002.
5. Baron, J. N., Dobbin, F., & Jennings, P. D. (1986). War and peace: The evolution of modern personnel administration in U.S. industry. *American Journal of Sociology*, *92*, pp. 350–383.
6. Person, H. S. (1929). The new attitude toward management. In H. S. Person (Ed.), *Scientific Management in American Industry*. New York: Harper & Brothers.
7. U.S. Bureau of Labor Statistics. (1919). Welfare work for employees in industrial establishments in the United States. *Bulletin #250*, pp. 119–123.
8. Eilbirt, H. (1959). The development of personnel management in the United States. *Business History Review*, *33*, pp. 345–364.
9. Pfeffer, J. (1995). Producing sustainable competitive advantage through the effective management of people. *Academy of Management Executive*, *9*, pp. 55–69.
10. Carnevale, A. P., & Johnston, J. W. (1989). *Training in America: Strategies for the Nation*. Alexandria, VA: National Center on Education and the Economy and the American Society for Training and Development.
11. Pfeffer, J. (1995). Producing sustainable competitive advantage through the effective management of people. *Academy of Management Executive*, *9*, pp. 55–69.
12. Lengnick-Hall, C. A., & Lengnick-Hall, M. L. (1990). *Interactive Human Resource Management and Strategic Planning*. New York: Quorum Books.
13. Dutton, J. E., & Jackson, S. E. (1987). The categorization of strategic issues by decision makers and its links to organizational action. *Academy of Management Review*, *12*, pp. 76–90.
14. Lilly's competitive strategy statement (2002) [online]. Available: *www.lilly.com/about/overview/do.html*, accessed June 3, 2002.
15. Schuler, R. S., & Jackson, S. E. (1987). Linking competitive strategies with human resource management practices. *Academy of Management Executive*, *1*, pp. 207–219.
16. Ibid.
17. Ibid.
18. Quotation excerpted from "Straight talk: Executives sound off on why they think HR professionals lost strategic ground, and what they can do to earn a place 'at the table.'" *HR Magazine*, Journal 2002 [online] from Findarticles.com, accessed October 28, 2002.
19. Microsoft's statement on employee enrichment (2002) [online]. Available: *www.microsoft.com/mba/benefits/default.asp*, accessed June 10, 2002.
20. Microsoft's statement on employee enrichment (2002) [online]. Available: *www.microsoft.com/mba/benefits/default.asp*, accessed June 10, 2002.
21. Tsui, A. S. (1984). Personnel department effectiveness: A tripartite approach. *Industrial Relations*, *23*, p. 187.

COMPENSATION IN ACTION

THE COMPENSATION CARPENTER

The number one factor that will restrict a company's growth in the next decade is its inability to attract and retain employees. While many people perceive this statement as a given, the compensation profession has not responded. Human resources executives report that only about half of their companies' rewards strategies are linked to business or people strategies. This has powerful implications for compensation professionals, who need to rethink their roles in organizations. Management needs them to apply their expertise in a way that helps run business. This is hardly the case.

Most compensation processes are geared to control managers rather than facilitate their success. Examples of control are top-down salary and merit budgets, job evaluation schemes, salary grades, salary increase matrices and limitations governing short- and long-term variable plans. Intended to help managers run their businesses, these processes constrain managers, as shown when they regularly push the bounds of "acceptable" practice. If HR management and business management are true partners, leaders need to be provided with tools, not rules.

FROM COP TO CONSULTANT

As American industry grew out of World War II, it created myriad management command and control systems. The HR profession established an army of compensation police, who were brought into companies to oversee the fiscal responsibility of payroll. In the 1980s, there was a shift from the role of cop to that of compensation consultant. HR professionals acknowledged that their new role was not to police the compensation arena, but consult with managers in the appropriate application of the programs. Unfortunately, these consultants did not fundamentally alter the programs; they simply took off their police uniforms and attempted to assist managers in making those policies work.

Today, many organizations are managing compensation programs that have not kept pace with the changes in their businesses. These programs were developed when workforce demographics and factors influencing the business environment were dramatically different than they are today.

FROM CONSULTANT TO CARPENTER

In the New Economy, rules need to be replaced by tools that help managers run business. The consultant's new role is that of a master compensation carpenter, who designs and teaches. (See Figure 1.)

To implement the role of master carpenter, compensation professionals need to:

- Skillfully and creatively apply the fundamentals of their trade to build management tools that fit within the context of their businesses
- Teach managers how to use those management tools to unleash the potential within their workforce to drive the business forward in quantum leaps
- Let go, viewing their roles as process facilitators, not owners

FIGURE 1 The Evolving Role of the Compensation Professional

Business Era	*Fundamental Business Model*	*The Role of the Compensation Professional*
Post-War Industrial Revolution	Structural Hierarchy in Command-and-Control	Compensation Cop
Service Economy	Customer-Focused Solutions	Compensation Consultant
The New Economy	Knowledge and Speed	Compensation Carpenter

(Continued)

(Continued)

MASTERING A NEW ROLE

The transformation from compensation consultant to master compensation carpenter requires three things:

- **A solid foundation in a company's business environment, strategy and organizational structure, processes and culture should exist.** A Certified Compensation Professional (CCP) has the skill required to build a technically correct plan. One must marry that expertise with the competency to know how to design that plan according to the needs of a particular business. That deeper understanding only comes from thoroughly knowing the nuances of a company and industry, and being able to apply the sound technical knowledge.
- **A manager's toolbox should contain the tools required to run the business.** A set of tools should be created that is appropriate for the environment and allows managers to do the right thing in each unique situation. Historically, managers have been given only one tool to deal with a variety of situations across the bulk of populations—merit pay. This is akin to the master carpenter giving an apprentice a hammer and then trying to teach him to build something: Everything the apprentice looks at appears to be a nail. As a master carpenter, compensation professionals are expert builders.
- **Managers should be taught how to use each tool.** Any carpenter can build, but the master carpenter teaches. More importantly, the master carpenter teaches both the right use and application for each tool, knowing that, although he has many tools available to him, he only applies a tool appropriate for a specific time, place or situation.

IT'S NOT OVER

Compensation professionals need to radically redesign their programs in a way that gives their companies quantum leaps forward in performance. This is embedded in their ability to give managers both the tools they need to free the untapped potential within the work force and the knowledge to do so freely!

Furthermore, the master carpenter constantly improves. Rewards programs need to be reviewed, updated and rethought regularly. It is the master carpenter's role to assess how changes in businesses dictate changes in the tools and whether to sharpen, redesign, throw away or add tools to the toolbox. In short, compensation professionals must renew, recycle and reteach.

Source: Todd M. Manas, CCP, Arthur Andersen LLP, *Workspan*, September 2001, volume 44, number 9.

WHAT'S NEW IN COMPENSATION?

Laid-Off Workers Accept Jobs with Lower Pay

Employment termination is one of the HR practices discussed in Chapter 1. Layoffs represent one type of involuntary termination instigated by the employer. Oftentimes, employers institute layoffs to control costs when business activity slows down. This practice is also known as downsizing. During the recent economic recession, when most business activity slowed, announcements of company layoffs were common newspaper headlines.

Not surprisingly, most laid-off workers seek employment elsewhere after company downsizing. It is reasonable to assume that displaced workers will find jobs that pay at least as much as they were earning prior to being laid off. However, the slowing economy has substantially reduced the number of comparable available jobs, creating a situation in which the supply of qualified job applicants exceeds company demand for these individuals. In addition, more company layoffs are permanent now, which means that the jobs will not be filled in the future. As a result, many job seekers have accepted comparable jobs at lower pay. For example, the featured *New York Times* article indicates that those who managed to find full-time employment after having been laid off (from 1999 through 2001) earned a median weekly wage of $571, compared with $609 in the jobs they lost.

Log into your *New York Times* account. Search the database for articles on "layoffs," "downsizing," "job loss," and "economic conditions." Also, if you know the names of companies with recent downsizing activity, search for articles about these companies. Following your course instructor's specific directions, be prepared to describe the current situation and relate it to the article that follows. ■

The New York Times

Data Show Growing Trend toward Permanent Layoffs

Permanent layoffs surged from 1999 through 2001, the Bureau of Labor Statistics reported yesterday in releasing the results of a survey that is the government's most comprehensive assessment of how frequently workers are dismissed from their jobs.

The 9.9 million people who lost their jobs in that 3-year period represented an unusually high 7.8 percent of the nation's work force. The economy moved from boom in 1999 to recession in 2001, and half of the layoffs came in that last hard year, when the unemployment rate suddenly shot up.

Compounding the damage from the surge in layoffs, employers cut back on hiring. More than 800,000 job openings disappeared from May of last year to May of this year, a decline of nearly 19 percent, the bureau reported last month.

"You can have a high job displacement rate in a dynamic economy when there are lots of job openings for people to go to," said Lawrence Katz, a Harvard University labor economist. "But now there is a lot of displacement with a low level of job openings," and that is hardship.

Even in 1999 and 2000, which were years of strong growth and unemployment rates at 25-year lows, permanent layoffs were sufficiently frequent and widespread to suggest to many economists that the practice had become entrenched in the American workplace in the best as well as the worst of times.

"These numbers show a relatively high level of job displacement even when the unemployment rate was very low," said Ryan Helwig, the economist at the Bureau of Labor Statistics who wrote the latest job displacement report. It is based on a survey every 2 years of 60,000 households.

The new report confirmed trends that have been developing for more than a decade. Permanent layoffs, also known as downsizing, no longer dip as sharply in the expansion periods between recessions.

In addition, their constant presence has generated job insecurity, many economists say. That insecurity, in turn, has damped wage demands.

In fending off pressure to increase interest rates in the late 1990s, for example, Alan Greenspan, the chairman of the Federal Reserve, cited job insecurity as a reason the falling unemployment rate would not produce the inflationary wage pressures characteristic of tight labor markets in the 1970s and 1980s. His resistance to rate increases, in turn, helped to sustain the expansion. The low rates encouraged borrowing to finance spending.

Among the 9.9 million people who said in the latest survey, conducted in January, that they had lost a job in the previous 3 years, 64.4 percent were working again at the time of the survey, in most cases full time. An additional 22 percent were unemployed and seeking work, while 14 percent had dropped out of the labor force.

The 64.4 percent re-employment rate was significantly below the rate in the three previous surveys. It matched, in fact, the difficulty in landing another job during the early 1990s recession, when the unemployment rate rose above 7 percent. It is 5.9 percent now, up from 4.3 percent early last year.

Those who managed to land full-time jobs after having been laid off from 1999 through 2001 did so at a sacrifice. Their median weekly wage in their new job was $571, down from $609 in the lost jobs.

The Bureau of Labor Statistics instituted the job displacement survey in the early 1980s in response to political pressure as downsizing surged. The survey initially focused on workers who had been laid off after holding a job for at least 3 years. The bureau still gives a lot of attention to these "long tenured" workers. In the most recent 3 years, 4 million lost their jobs, or 40 percent of the total.

That is down from 45 percent in the mid-1990s and 50 percent in the early 1990s. This shift has occurred as downsizing has spread from blue-collar workers in manufacturing to white-collar workers in every industry, and well up into management ranks, becoming "much more egalitarian," as Mr. Katz put it.

Reflecting the spreading practice, the displacement rate of 7.8 percent in the latest three-year period was up from 6.1 percent from 1997 through 1999. These were the peak boom years. By comparison, during the peak years of the 1980s expansion—1987 through 1989—the displacement rate dipped to 5.5 percent.

The latest surveys, however, may understate the frequency of permanent layoffs in recent years, some economists say. When members of the 60,000 households report having lost a job, they are then asked if the loss was because the factory or company where they had worked had closed or moved, or whether their job was abolished, or whether there was insufficient work. If the answer is yes to any of these alternatives, the job loss becomes a permanent layoff.

But over the years, permanent layoffs have increasingly come in other guises. Employers often press workers into accepting early retirement packages that sweeten pensions in exchange for leaving their jobs. They have turned much more to the use of contract workers and temporary workers who come and go as companies need them, but are not considered laid off until the firm that sponsors them—a temporary help agency, for example—stops sending them out to new assignments.

"These could be problematic areas," Thomas Nardone, the chief of labor force statistics at the bureau, acknowledged. "If we tried to account for them, I don't know how that would affect the numbers."

SOURCE: Louis Uchitelle, Data show growing trend toward permanent layoffs (August 22, 2002) [online]. Available: *www.nytimes.com*, accessed October 28, 2002.

CHAPTER

2 STRATEGIC COMPENSATION IN ACTION

Strategic Analysis and Contextual Factors

Chapter Outline

- Strategic Analysis
  External Market Environment
  Internal Capabilities
- Factors That Influence Companies' Competitive Strategies and Compensation Practices
  National Culture
  Organizational Culture
  Organizational and Product Life Cycles
- Summary
- Key Terms
- Discussion Questions
- Exercises
- Endnotes

Learning Objectives

In this chapter, you will learn about

1. Strategic analysis factors
2. Industry classification: North American Industry Classification System (NAICS)
3. External market aspects of strategic analysis
4. Internal capabilities dimensions of strategic analysis
5. Factors that influence companies' competitive strategies and compensation practices

Compensation professionals should be knowledgeable about their company's competitive situation. Such knowledge enables them to guide the development and implementation of strategic compensation practices—that is, compensation practices for promoting competitive advantage. The "Compensation in Action" feature, listed at the end of the chapter, persuasively argues for the importance of investing in human resources to promote competitive advantages. A strategic analysis represents an important step toward attaining competitive advantage.

A **strategic analysis** entails an examination of a company's external market context and internal factors. Examples of external market factors include industry profile, information about competitors, and long-term growth prospects. Internal factors encompass financial condition and functional capabilities—for example, marketing and human resources. Strategic analyses permit business professionals to see where they stand in the market based on external and internal factors. Companies with strong potential to increase sales levels tend to have a better standing than companies with weak potential to maintain or increase sales. Companies with a strong standing should be able to devote more financial resources to fund compensation programs than weaker companies.

Compensation professionals also should be familiar with several factors that influence a company's choice of competitive strategies and compensation tactics. These include national culture, organizational culture, and organizational and product (or service) life cycle.

STRATEGIC ANALYSIS

We illustrate a strategic analysis for a hypothetical company named Fly-You-There. Fly-You-There operates in the scheduled passenger air transportation industry. The airline offers no-frills commercial flights along the West Coast, including several cities throughout California, Oregon, Washington, and Alaska. The company, located in San Francisco, is pursuing a lowest cost strategy. Its goal is to be the number one or two commercial airline in its markets by the year 2010. Key to Fly-You-There's success are operating efficiencies as measured through average cost per passenger, passenger safety, and on-time arrivals and departures.

The company was founded 20 years ago. Its workforce and enplanements grew slowly, but steadily, until the economic slowdown that began in the year 2000 and intensified after the September 11 terrorist attacks in 2001. During these 20 years, Fly-You-There has maintained a union-free workforce. The airline compensated its pilots, flight attendants, and ground crew about 5 percent higher than its competitors' average pay and benefits while maintaining profitability. Although many people have returned to commercial flights, enplanements are still below normal levels prior to the economic slowdown. As a result, Fly-You-There cannot afford to maintain its market lead in pay and compensation.

Barbara Viera has just joined Fly-You-There as the compensation director. Before joining Fly-You-There, Barbara served as a successful compensation manager for one of its main competitors. Based on her experience, Barbara's first task is to prepare an overview of the competitiveness of Fly-You-There's compensation program. Then, she must recommend compensation policies to Fly-You-There's CEO.

Strategic analyses begin with the identification of a company's industry classification because companies compete among each other for customers' business. For example, Verizon Wireless and Sprint PCS compete against each other for consumers who want wireless telephone service. The **North American Industry Classification System Manual** classifies industries based on the **North American Industry Classification System (NAICS)**. NAICS codes represent keys to pertinent information for strategic analyses. As we'll see shortly, the U.S. Federal government publishes different bulletins that contain information about industry and employment outlooks based on the NAICS. These bulletins permit compensation professionals and top managers to answer questions such as "Will consumer demand increase for regional air service on the West Coast over the next 5 years?" "Are there sufficient numbers of well-trained commercial airline pilots?" and "What do commercial airline pilots typically earn?"

The NAICS provides an excellent starting point because it enables companies to identify direct product or service market competitors. The NAICS is the classification system for industries used in all federal government economic statistics. Many private-sector companies also rely on the NAICS to conduct strategic analyses. The federal government publishes NAICS codes in the North American Industry Classification System Manual [1]. It created the NAICS in cooperation with the Canadian and Mexican governments to cover the entire field of economic activities common to all three countries—20 major sectors in all. Table 2-1 lists these 20 sectors. Fly-You-There falls in the Transportation and Warehousing sector.

The NAICS generally uses five-digit classification codes that are common to the United States, Canada, and Mexico. In many instances, you will find six-digit NAICS codes that represent U.S. industries. The sixth digit represents specialized industries that are unique to the United States. Figure 2-1 shows the elements of NAICS codes and a sample—71312. The first two digits represent the **sector**, which is the broadest classification of economic activities (based on the list presented in Table 2-1). The numbers 71 denote the arts, entertainment, and recreation sector. The first three digits stand for the **subsector**, classifying broad sectors into particular subsets of the arts, entertainment, and recreation sector. The numbers 713 represent the amusement, gambling, and recreation subsector. The first four digits represent the **industry group**. The numbers 7131 stand for amusement and theme parks. The five-digit code stands for the **industry**. The numbers 71312 represent video game arcades (nongambling).

TABLE 2-1 NAICS Sectors

Code	*NAICS Sectors*
11	Agriculture, Forestry, Fishing, and Hunting
21	Mining
22	Utilities
23	Construction
31–33	Manufacturing
42	Wholesale Trade
44–45	Retail Trade
48–49	Transportation and Warehousing
51	Information
52	Finance and Insurance
53	Real Estate and Rental and Leasing
54	Professional, Scientific, and Technical Services
55	Management of Companies and Enterprises
56	Administrative and Support and Waste Management and Remediation Services
61	Education Services
62	Health Care and Social Assistance
71	Arts, Entertainment, and Recreation
72	Accommodation and Food Services
81	Other Services (except Public Administration)
92	Public Administration

Source: http://www.census.gov/epcd/www/naicsect.htm

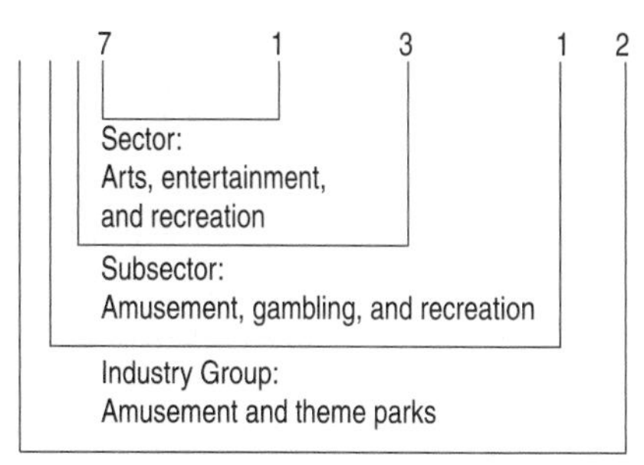

FIGURE 2-1 NAICS Code Elements

Fly-You-There's NAICS code is 48111. The digits 48 represent the sector Transportation and Warehousing. Companies in this sector engage in some of the following activities:

- Air transportation (passenger and cargo)
- Rail transportation
- Water transportation
- Truck transportation

The digits 481 stand for Air Transportation subsector, including two industry groups (four-digit classifications):

- Scheduled air transportation (4811), including commercial passenger airlines such as American Airlines, Delta Airlines, Northwest Airlines, and United Airlines
- Nonscheduled air transportation (4812), including commercially chartered airplanes and aerial sightseeing tours

Fly-You-There's industry group is scheduled air transportation (4811), and this NAICS industry group contains two NAICS industries (five-digit classifications):

- Scheduled passenger air transportation (48111)
- Scheduled freight air transportation (48112)

Fly-You-There's NAICS industry code is 48111—scheduled passenger air transportation. Companies in this industry primarily engage in providing air transportation of passengers and/or cargo over regular routes and on regular schedules. Companies in this industry operate flights even if they are partially loaded. Scheduled air passenger carriers, including commuter and helicopter carriers (except scenic and sightseeing), fall in this industry.

External Market Environment

Compensation professionals, top management, and consultants examine five elements of the external environment as they conduct strategic analyses.

- Industry profile
- Competition
- Foreign demand
- Industry's long-term prospects
- Labor market assessment

Several sources provide detailed information about external markets. Government sources are available at no cost. These sources include the U.S. Bureau of Labor Statistics (*www.bls.gov*), the U.S. Census Bureau's (*www.census.gov*) annual publication titled *Statistical Abstract of the United States*, and the U.S. Department of Commerce (*www.commerce.gov*). Private companies also provide excellent information about external markets, but they generally charge a fee. Some of these sources include *Business Week* (*www.businessweek.com*), Hoovers (*www.hoovers.com*), and the *Wall Street Journal* (*www.wsj.com*).

Industry Profile

Industry profiles describe such basic industry characteristics as sales volume, the impact of relevant government regulation on competitive strategies, and the impact of recent technological advancements on business activity. Compensation professionals use industry profile information to determine the kinds of compensation practices they should recommend to top management. For example, pay-for-knowledge programs may be appropriate if employees must learn to use new technology. In the case of sales stagnation, companies might choose to use incentive pay plans geared toward rewarding employees for contributing to increased sales activity.

The U.S. airline industry has experienced marked changes since the year 2000. Fewer airlines serve markets because of mergers and acquisitions. For example, United Airlines has acquired Continental Airlines, and American Airlines has acquired Trans World Airlines. Fewer competitors and consolidation of many air routes have made it easier for airlines to increase airfares somewhat because consumers face limited flight alternatives.

However, the widespread economic recession since the year 2000 and the uncertainties about passenger safety due to the September 11 attacks has weakened the airline industry. The general economic recession has led companies to reduce business travel in their quest to limit expenditures. Widespread layoffs and worries about job security cut into leisure travel. Not surprisingly, terrorists' downing of four commercial airline flights on September 11 raised fears about the safety of air travel, in large part because of gaps in airport security. Airlines reduced capacity by as much as 20 percent. That is, on average, one of every five flights was eliminated.

Competition

Companies take stock of competitors' business activities to help position themselves in the market. Companies can distinguish themselves from the competition in different ways (for example, top-notch customer service or state-of-the-art products), and they can achieve lowest-cost objectives in various ways (for example, reducing advertising expenditures versus minimizing staffing levels). Compensation professionals play a role by recommending pay systems (Chapters 4, 5, and 6) and setting pay levels (Chapter 8) that support differentiation or lowest-cost objectives.

Fly-You-There competes mainly with companies in the passenger airline business that serve markets along the West Coast and Alaska. Southwest Airlines and Alaska Air are among Fly-You-There's competitors. Fly-You-There must carefully establish a competitive strategy that distinguishes itself from these competitors. For example, Fly-You-There may introduce no-frills service in markets where only a few, high-priced competitors operate. In practice, compensation professionals would give careful consideration to the specific factors that make their competitors successful and to how compensation practices can be used to create competitive advantages for their own company.

Foreign Demand

Most companies are interested in foreign demand for their products or services because such demand is an indicator of additional sales revenue potential. Compensation professionals factor in this impact of foreign demand when making their pay policy recommendations. In general, compensation professionals may feel that higher base pay rates or incentive awards are warranted in the presence of higher foreign demand. In addition, the anticipated level of demand over time is important. Compensation professionals are unlikely to alter pay policy recommendations for short-term increases (or decreases, for that matter) in foreign demand.

Foreign demand does not apply to Fly-You-There, simply because the airline operates exclusively as a regional carrier within the United States. However, foreign demand is pertinent to U.S. airlines that serve cities outside the United States. For example, U.S. airlines face stiff competition from such airlines as KLM and Lufthansa that regularly add air service from large U.S. cities to destinations outside the United States.

Industry's Long-Term Prospects

Long-term prospects set the backdrop for strategic planning because these prospects are indicators of companies' futures. Companies establish strategic plans that fit with their industries' long-term prospects. For example, the cost of paper used in book printing has increased dramatically in recent years. Publishing companies will contain costs in other areas to limit substantial price increases because consumers will probably not purchase as many books if book prices increase commensurably with paper costs. In this type of situation, compensation professionals employed by publishing companies are apt to recommend pay policies that contribute to cost-containment objectives. At the same time, many publishers are providing access to publications through secured computer networks on the Internet, somewhat protecting them from increasing paper costs.

Long-term prospects for companies in the U.S. airline industry are unclear. Future success will turn on factors such as general national economic health, greater comfort with air transportation, and fuel costs. Of course, sluggish economic conditions, insecurities about flying safely, and higher fuel costs will curb the industry's success.

Labor Market Assessment

General Considerations

Labor market assessments represent key activities. Companies should carefully assess the labor market to determine the availability of qualified employees. In the future, many industries such as telecommunications will find staffing more challenging [2]. The U.S. Bureau of Labor Statistics (BLS) expects that the growth in the size of the U.S. labor force will slow down substantially through 2010. In addition, there will be fewer new workforce entrants (that is, individuals aged 16 to 24 years) but significantly more older workers (that is, individuals aged 45 and over) in the labor force.

These labor force trends have direct implications for compensation practice. In general, there will be more competition among companies for fewer qualified individuals. Higher demand for labor relative to labor supply should lead to higher wages. Companies will have to increase wages to entice the best individuals to choose employment in their companies rather than their competitors' companies. The greater prevalence of older employees also should increase typical wage levels. As we discuss in Chapter 4, older workers will probably have higher wages than younger workers. The prevalence of older workers relative to younger workers should translate into higher compensation costs to companies.

STRETCHING THE DOLLAR

BUILDING A FOUNDATION FOR EFFECTIVE PAY PROGRAMS

Strategy and culture should lay the groundwork for pay programs, while proper implementation and execution cement their success.

Quick Look

- Rewards programs are a critical tool to balancing identification and execution of the right business strategy.
- Grounding pay design in strategy and culture drives home the point that pay is a strategic tool.
- The major benefit of focusing on culture does not come primarily from determining what it is, but more importantly how the organization desires to change it.

T. J. Rogers may have said it best: Most companies do not fail for lack of talent or strategic vision; they fail for lack of execution.

Several studies in the 1990s illustrated that pay programs at higher performing companies better reinforced the business strategy and culture. These companies used their rewards programs as a tool to execute strategy.

Historically, identifying the strategy seemed to be the primary focus of senior management. The mindset appeared to be that, "If we just find the right strategy, all the pieces will fall into place." However, countless organizations with sound strategies proved this to be incorrect—a great strategy is important, but not enough to be successful.

Today's executives seem to agree that implementation and execution of the strategy demands more attention, and strategy identification needs to be balanced with execution. Executives also seem to agree that the rewards program is a critical tool to make this happen.

Culture is a main topic of discussion among executives, as well, becoming one of the forces that makes organizations successful. The power of culture becomes clear when considered against countless failed mergers or new CEOs who could not implement their vision and strategy because they ran against existing cultures.

The difficulty has been managing culture. True cultural change can only come about by changing employee behavior. And how are employee behaviors changed? While not the sole tool, rewards are certainly a critical part of the solution.

TAKING A STRATEGIC APPROACH TO COMPENSATION DESIGN

Given the power of rewards to support the business strategy and create the desired culture, the proper starting point in pay program design or the assessment of an existing pay program is to identify the strategy and culture. However, this often is overlooked in practice, or the importance and effort to do this is underestimated.

Often, organizations start a pay program design by examining why employees leave, then building a pay program around these issues. In effect, the employees drive the pay program, which then drives the business strategy and culture. This is the proverbial tail wagging the dog.

Another common approach often found in practice is gathering pay practice data from peers and competitors, then building an identical mousetrap. There are two significant issues here:

- It is unlikely that these peers have an identical strategy, culture, structure, etc.
- If these peers are identical, an organization is, at best, setting itself up to be equal to its peers or, in other words, average. This is not truly using pay to create competitive advantage.

STARTING WITH A FOUNDATION OF STRATEGY AND CULTURE

Starting with strategy and culture makes pay program design more difficult and takes considerable time. Why go through all the effort?

- As mentioned, several studies of high-performing companies show this method creates a more effective program.
- Grounding pay design in strategy and culture drives home the point that pay is a strategic tool.
- It enhances executive involvement and, therefore, buy-in to the design. Most executives do not want to "waste" their time on administrative tasks such as benchmarking pay levels. However, there is an intense interest in determining, communicating, and executing strategy and culture.

(Continued)

(Continued)

OBSTACLES TO A STRATEGIC APPROACH TO COMPENSATION DESIGN

Given these benefits, why do pay designs often not start with a diagnosis of the fundamentals of business strategy and culture? The reasons include:

- **Lack of direction.** The organization's strategy and culture is not clearly defined and articulated. The organization is reactive to the external environment or, though it has goals, it has not defined how it will attain these goals.
- **Desire to maintain secrecy.** The strategy and culture is defined, but only known by a few people who are not willing to share it out of fear that, if word gets out, the competitive advantage will be lost.
- **Conflict among executives.** Each executive has his or her unique idea of what the strategy and culture should be. Often, each person's view is at odds with others' and thereby creates an internal political minefield best left unexposed.
- **Pay is an administrative tool.** Pay is not viewed as a strategic tool, so why waste time evaluating strategy and culture?

This article provides a blueprint to help organizations evaluate their strategy and culture.

STRATEGY

Certainly, there is no end to books on strategy development. In an oversimplification of corporate strategy, the most common core business strategies are listed. . . . It is important to realize that these are only core strategies. Often, an organization will pursue two or three of these core strategies at any one time. Also, if the company is organized into business units, often the business units may pursue very distinct strategies.

EXAMPLES OF BUSINESS STRATEGY DRIVING PAY DESIGN

How does the business strategy affect the compensation program design? Take, for example, a company pursuing a retrenchment strategy. This organization typically would be in a "firefighting" mode. The focus would be on the short-term; long-term business issues would be far less important because if the company does not turn around in the short-term, there will be no long-term. It likely would see a heavy focus on retention programs, such as stay bonuses and short-term incentives to support a turnaround.

Compare that to an organization that is pursuing a product development strategy. This company would have a very long investment horizon and the short-term would be far less relevant. The critical issue is the payoff down the road from the current investments in research and development. The compensation mix in this case would be much more focused on long-term incentives. The long-term goal would be the development of new revenue sources and profit derived from new product sources. Also, the company would be recruiting the best and brightest in its research area and may be targeting above-market pay packages for these employees.

Finally, consider an organization pursuing a market penetration-cost strategy. In this situation, there would be incentives that heavily focus on cost control and margin.

BEYOND THE CORE STRATEGY

It is important that once the compensation program designer works with management to identify the core strategy, he/she does not stop. A thorough analysis and articulation should be made of specific tactics and initiatives to execute the strategy.

. . . Business strategy typically is broken into short-term tactics. These short-term initiatives or tactics often are referred to as the annual business plan. The real power of starting with strategy is not just identifying the core strategy, but in defining the specific short- and long-term initiatives to execute the strategy. Once the specific core strategy is determined, it is important to identify the specific initiatives of how the company is executing the strategy.

For example, determining that your organization is pursuing a "market penetration differentiation" strategy has limited value for the compensation designer. This alone tells little and provides a limited foundation for compensation design. However, it is the correct starting point.

In the case of a "market-penetration-differentiation strategy," the differentiating market factor may be based on product quality. Once this is determined, the compensation designer now has a firmer foundation to build a compensation program. If, for example, the company is a manufacturer and incentives are paid based on labor efficiencies, this may drive behavior counter to a product-differentiation strategy, but appropriate for a cost-based strategy.

COMPENSATION ALIGNMENT: AN ONGOING PROCESS

If an organization is within a stable economy, in a stable industry, and operating in a status-quo operation, a pay program can be designed and forgotten. It wouldn't need to change. But, for most organizations, the macroeconomy is constantly changing, as is the industry and company. In these organizations, having a strategically aligned compensation program is not a one-time effort.

Unfortunately, many organizations put a pay design in place and, other than periodic market-based pay level adjustments, forget about it. Unfortunately, this does not work. The business world is dynamic.

Business strategy will change over time given external business conditions, and the strategy process is an ongoing cycle of formulation, implementation, and evaluation. Therefore, compensation programs need to be continually tweaked and fine-tuned. Failure to undertake this ongoing alignment is a major source of misalignment resulting in effective pay programs.

CULTURE

As mentioned, good pay design should reinforce the organization's culture, as it is becoming an increasingly important tool for high-performing organizations. For example, any literature about General Electric or Southwest Airlines inevitably will mention culture as a competitive advantage.

The idea of using culture as a business tool is relatively young. It was not until the early 1980s that culture and its effect on promoting or inhibiting business success really became a common topic in the executive suite.

The tough question is, "What is culture?" Ask any executive to articulate his/her organization's culture and the answers likely will equal the number of people asked. Culture often is defined as an organization's values and behaviors.

While the basic definition helps clarify what culture is, it still provides little structure to define an individual organization's culture. A more meaningful analysis of an organization's culture can be made if culture is defined into various components. . . .

This table of culture attributes is not all-inclusive, nor does it fit every organization. It does, however, provide a good starting point to tailor a culture assessment tool for specific situations.

A major benefit of this tool is the ability to take an obscure topic, such as culture, and put it into more workable terms. The major benefit of focusing on culture does not come primarily from determining what it is, but more importantly how the organization desires to change it. In that respect, compensation can be better utilized in its role as a driver of employee behavior and a critical tool to drive lasting cultural change.

Once the culture is defined, how can it be used to design a pay program? Assume, for example, that a company wants to be highly risk-oriented in relation to its market. To support this, the pay program design also should have a higher risk rewards position in relation to the market. Or, assume the business is very short-term focused, as it might be in a turnaround or bankruptcy situation. The pay program should be more heavily focused on short-term incentives and less on long-term incentives than in market comparison.

The compensation design's outcome only will be effective by starting it with the foundation blocks of strategy and culture. It is imperative to use an assessment tool to evaluate these two areas and approach them objectively and systematically.

NOTES

For more information related to this article:

- Log in to ResourcePRO Search and select Simple Search
- Select the Rewards Category: Compensation
- Type in this key word string on the search line: "strategic or strategy and culture" OR "pay or salary and design" OR "assessment"

Source: Paul Gilles, CCP, CPA, SPHR, Aon Consulting, *workspan*, September 2001, volume 44, number 9.

Occupation-Specific Considerations

Companies should keep tabs on the occupational mix of their workforces and the relative importance of these occupations to maintaining competitive advantage. Compensation levels generally increase with the strategic importance of jobs to companies' strategic values and, as mentioned previously, the relative supply of labor.

For illustrative purposes, let's consider the labor market status of commercial airline pilots. Naturally, every airline needs pilots to operate aircraft to ensure the safety of passengers. An excellent starting point is the BLS *Occupational Outlook Handbook*. This handbook contains pertinent information for conducting effective strategic analyses:

- Qualifications and training
- Job outlook
- Typical earnings range

First, information about qualifications and training helps companies focus recruitment efforts on individuals with the necessary qualifications. Pilots who are paid to transport passengers or cargo must possess a commercial pilot's license with an instrument rating. The Federal Aviation Administration (FAA) issues this license and rating to a pilot based on sufficient flight experience in designated conditions, good health and vision, and written and flight tests to demonstrate acceptable knowledge and skills. In addition, candidates for positions with airlines must have an airline transport pilot's license. Earning this license entails at least 1,500 hours of flying experience, including night and instrument experience, and successful completion of additional written and flight tests. Further, applicants must possess advanced ratings that certify their competence to fly particular kinds of aircraft based on job requirements. For example, pilots assigned to fly Boeing 747 aircraft must have demonstrated competence to fly this type of plane before they may be compensated to transport passengers in Boeing 747s. Finally, some airlines may require applicants to pass tests of judgment under stress conditions.

Second, the BLS job outlook provides companies an indication of job prospects. Three scenarios describe possible job outlooks—retrenchment, status quo, and growth. Retrenchment means that fewer jobs will be available for a designated period. Status quo suggests that the present level of job opportunities will remain constant for a designated period. Under the growth scenario, job opportunities will be higher than present levels for a designated period. The BLS predicts that airline pilots will face status quo at least until 2010.

Third, the typical earnings range helps companies establish competitive pay levels. Companies would find it difficult to attract well-qualified candidates if they set pay levels and benefits too low. Also, paying and setting benefits well above the market may present a cost burden to companies. According to the BLS:

> Earnings of aircraft pilots and flight engineers vary greatly depending on whether they work as airline or commercial pilots. Earnings of airline pilots are among the highest in the Nation, and depend on factors such as the type, size, and maximum speed of the plane and the number of hours and miles flown. For example, pilots who fly jet aircraft usually earn higher salaries than do pilots who fly turboprops. Airline pilots and flight engineers may earn extra pay for night and international flights. In 2000, median annual earnings of airline pilots, copilots, and flight engineers were $110,940. The lowest 10 percent earned less than $36,110. Over 25 percent earned more than $145,000.

> Airline pilots usually are eligible for life and health insurance plans financed by the airlines. They also receive retirement benefits and, if they fail the FAA physical examination at some point in their careers, they get disability payments. In addition, pilots receive an expense allowance, or "per diem," for every hour they are away from home. Per diem can represent up to $500 each month in addition to their salary. Some airlines also provide allowances to pilots for purchasing and cleaning their uniforms. As an additional benefit, pilots and their immediate families usually are entitled to free or reduced fare transportation on their own and other airlines.
>
> More than one-half of all aircraft pilots are members of unions. Most of the pilots who fly for the major airlines are members of the Airline Pilots Association, International, but those employed by one major airline are members of the Allied Pilots Association. Some flight engineers are members of the Flight Engineers' International Association. [3]

In sum, labor market assessments are key elements of strategic analyses. Based on our analysis of Fly-You-There's situation, their compensation professionals should include a labor market assessment of pilots. Obviously, pilots are key to airline operations.

Internal Capabilities

Compensation professionals, top management, and consultants should examine three internal capabilities as part of strategic analyses:

- Functional capabilities
- Human resource capabilities
- Financial condition

Functional Capabilities

Companies must determine which functional capabilities are most crucial to maintaining competitive advantage. Functional capabilities include manufacturing, engineering, research and development, operations, management information systems, human resources, and marketing. Competition among airlines necessitates that Fly-You-There maintains strong functional capabilities such as marketing and operations to spread the word that the airline offers competitive fares and regular on-time arrivals and departures.

Research and development is not a critical function for all companies. For example, companies such as PepsiCo rely on marketing savvy to remain competitive. Many consumers of diet soft drinks complain that their taste is not as appealing as regular soft drinks containing sugar. PepsiCo's recent introduction of the Pepsi One diet soft drink represents the corporation's attempt to increase sales and market share by identifying with diet soft drink consumers who want a taste that more closely resembles sugared soft drinks.

Human Resources Capabilities

State-of-the-art research equipment, manufacturing systems, and efficient marketing distribution systems do not provide competitive advantage unless staffed with knowledgeable and productive employees. Pay-for-performance and pay-for-knowledge programs promote productive and knowledgeable employees. Merit pay programs reinforce prior excellent job performance with permanent base pay increases. Incentive pay programs reward employees for attaining predetermined performance standards. Employees generally know in advance that rewards increase with higher performance attainments, as well as how much they will earn for achieving particular performance goals. Companies design pay-for-knowledge programs to reward self-improvement, and these programs are essential when technology advances rapidly.

Financial Condition

A company's **financial condition** is a key consideration for top management officials and HR professionals. Financial condition has implications for a company's ability to compete. Sound financial conditions enable companies to meet operating and capital requirements; poor financial conditions prevent companies from adequately meeting operating and capital requirements.

Operating requirements encompass all HR programs. Top management limits funding increases for compensation programs when financial conditions are poor. As a result, employees' salaries stagnate, and job offers to potential employees will probably not be competitive. Salary stagnation leads to turnover, particularly among highly qualified employees, because they will have higher-paying job opportunities elsewhere.

Capital requirements include automated manufacturing technology and office and plant facilities. Companies that pursue differentiation strategies require state-of-the-art instruments and work facilities to conduct leading-edge research. Lowest-cost companies need efficient equipment that keeps cost per unit as low as possible.

FACTORS THAT INFLUENCE COMPANIES' COMPETITIVE STRATEGIES AND COMPENSATION PRACTICES

Several factors influence a company's choice of competitive strategies and compensation tactics. These include national culture, organizational culture, and organizational and product (or service) life cycle. Table 2-2 lists the particular dimensions of these influences on competitive strategy and compensation tactics.

National Culture

National culture refers to the set of shared norms and beliefs among individuals within national boundaries who are indigenous to that area. National culture increasingly has become an important consideration in strategic compensation and influences the effectiveness of various forms of pay as motivators of proficient employee behavior. The U.S. managers responsible for managing compensation programs abroad may find that cultural differences reduce the effectiveness of U.S. compensation practices. This problem is particularly troublesome, given the rise in U.S. companies' presence in foreign countries. Foreign offices or plants of multinational corporations tend to employ local nationals who may not understand U.S. culture. In the People's Republic of China, native Chinese who work for U.S.–Chinese joint venture companies are not accustomed to performance-based pay because the Communist influence in China led to need-based pay programs.

Compensation experts maintain that understanding the normative expectations of different national cultures should promote competitive advantage [4]. Thus, it is important to be familiar with differences in national culture and to understand how those differences may influence the effectiveness of alternative pay programs. Geert Hofstede, a renowned researcher of national cultures, categorizes national cultures among four dimensions—power distance, individualism-collectivism, uncertainty avoidance, and masculinity-femininity [5]. This categorization of variations in national culture facilitates a discussion of how they may affect compensation tactics.

TABLE 2-2 Influences on Competitive Strategy
National Culture
• Power distance • Individualism-collectivism • Uncertainty avoidance • Masculinity-femininity
Organizational Culture
• Traditional organizational hierarchy • Flatter organizational structures • Team orientation
Organizational and Product Life Cycle
• Growth • Maturity • Decline

Power distance is the extent to which people accept a hierarchical system or power structure in companies. Status differentials between employees and employers are typical in high power distance cultures. Cultures that highly value power distance are likely to have compensation strategies that reinforce status differentials among employees, perhaps using visible rewards that project power. For example, Venezuela, the Philippines, and Arab nations rate high on power distance, according to Hofstede. Where power distance is not a dominant value, compensation strategies probably should endorse egalitarian compensation tactics as well as participatory pay programs. Australia, Sweden, and the Netherlands rate lower on power distance.

Individualism-collectivism is the extent to which individuals value personal independence or group membership. Individualist cultures value personal goals, independence, and privacy. Collectivist cultures favor social cohesiveness and loyalty to such groups as coworkers and families. Individualist cultures adopt compensation strategies that reward individual performance, as well as acquisition of skill or knowledge. In collectivist societies, employers reward employees on the basis of group performance and individual seniority to recognize the importance of employees' affiliations with groups. Shortly, we contrast U.S. and Japanese cultures, which exemplify individualism and collectivism, respectively.

Uncertainty avoidance represents the method by which society deals with risk and instability for its members. Fear of random events, value of stability and routines, and risk aversion are hallmarks of high uncertainty avoidance. Italy and Greece are examples of countries that rate high on uncertainty avoidance. On the other hand, welcoming random events, valuing challenge, and seeking risk characterize low uncertainty avoidance. Where uncertainty avoidance is high, employers probably use bureaucratic pay policies, emphasize fixed pay as more important than variable pay, and bestow little discretion to supervisors in distributing pay. Where uncertainty avoidance is low, employers probably use incentive pay programs and grant supervisors extensive latitude in pay allocation. Singapore and Denmark rate low on uncertainty avoidance.

Masculinity-femininity refers to whether masculine or feminine values are dominant in society. "Masculinity" favors material possessions. "Femininity" encourages caring and nurturing behavior. The compensation strategies of masculine cultures are likely to contain pay policies that allow for inequities by gender, as well as paternalistic benefits for women in the form of paid maternity leave and day care. Mexico and Germany possess masculine national cultures. In contrast, the compensation strategies of feminine cultures may encourage job evaluation regardless of gender composition, as well as offer perquisites on bases other than gender. Finland and Norway possess feminine national cultures.

In sum, national culture is a complex phenomenon that is related to differences in compensation practices. Hofstede provides a useful framework for describing the dimensions of national culture. Next, we contrast the national cultures of the United States and Japan to illustrate the influence of national culture on compensation practices. The individualism-collectivism dimension characterizes the differences between U.S. and Japanese culture.

U.S. Culture

The U.S. culture is a good example of individualism and emphasizes instrumentality. Employees strive for high levels of performance when they believe that better performance leads to better pay. Money derives importance from what it can buy, the sense of security it creates, its perception as a sign of achievement, and its definition of personal relationships. As we discuss throughout this book, with few exceptions most compensation practices in U.S. companies reward individual performance (that is, merit pay and incentive pay) or individuals' acquisition of job-relevant knowledge or skills (that is, pay-for-knowledge and skill-based pay).

Japanese Culture

Japan's national culture is collectivist. Influenced by the Zen, Confucian, and Samurai traditions, the predominant values of Japanese culture are social cooperation and responsibility, and acceptance of reality, and perseverance [6]. People hold dear their membership in groups. Duty to group needs prevails over each individual's needs and personal feelings. Failure to meet group needs results in personal shame because society disapproves of individuals who do not hold group interests in high esteem.

These principles apply to all aspects of Japanese life, including employment. Traditionally, employers have highly valued employees' affiliations, and they have taken personal interest in employees' personal lives as well as their work lives. The value placed on group membership leads employers to care about the well-being of their employees' families because families are important groups in Japan. Employers generally award base pay to meet families' needs and also according to seniority to honor affiliation as employees.

Compared with North Americans, the Japanese are more likely to produce at high levels because of the values that they embrace rather than because of what is in it for them [7]. This contrast holds implications for compensation tactics in these two countries. Traditionally, compensation professionals designed U.S. compensation systems to reward individual performance. Also, the time orientation tends to be short-term—typically 1 year or less [8]. In Japan, compensation professionals design pay systems to reward employees' loyalty and to meet the personal needs of the individual because Japanese employers value employees' affiliation with their companies. Japanese compensation systems focus on the long term, changing as employees' needs change throughout their work lives.

Organizational Culture

Organizational culture is an organization's system of shared values and beliefs that produce norms of behavior [9]. These values are apparent in companies' organizational and work structures. Also, organizational culture influences HR systems designs, including compensation.

Traditional Hierarchy

The traditional design of U.S. companies emphasizes efficiency, decision making by managers, and dissemination of information from the top of the company to lower levels. Figure 2-2 illustrates a traditional organizational hierarchy. The company's executive vice president is the intermediary for the company's chief executive officer and the vice presidents of the functional areas. Within the functional areas, the decision making flows downward from the vice presidents to managers of specialties within the functions.

For example, a company's top executives recognize the need to motivate employees to learn new skills associated with changing workplace technology. As discussed in Chapter 1, systematic training programs and pay-for-knowledge programs go hand in hand. Thus, the executive vice president communicates the strategic imperative for developing a pay-for-knowledge program to the vice presidents of training and compensation. In turn, these vice presidents charge their directors and managers with the

FIGURE 2-2 Traditional Organizational Structure

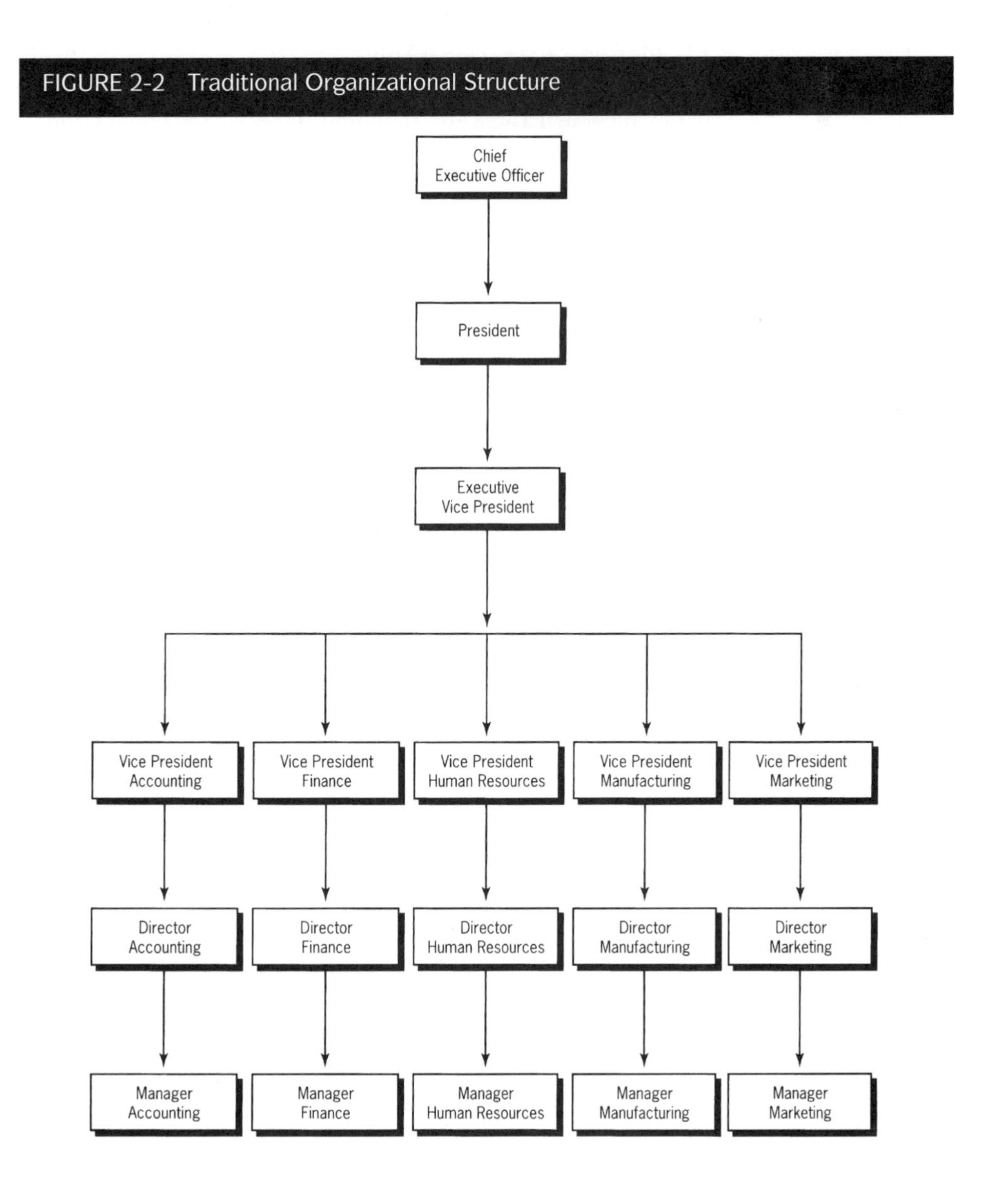

responsibility of developing such programs. The managers identify the major design considerations of pay-for-knowledge programs (Chapter 9). Table 2-3 lists these main considerations.

Seniority pay (Chapter 4) and such pay-for-performance programs as merit pay (Chapter 4) fit best with traditional hierarchical structures. Seniority pay programs create hierarchies based on length of time in a job. Under seniority systems, employees performing the same jobs may receive markedly different pay. Likewise, merit pay programs create hierarchies: The use of narrower pay grades (that is, pay grades that contain relatively few jobs) tends to promote hierarchy. As we discussed in Chapter 1, pay grades group jobs for pay policy application, and pay ranges indicate acceptable minimum, midpoint, and maximum pay rates for each pay grade. In addition, we discussed that compensation professionals group jobs into pay grades based on such compensable factors as skill, effort, responsibility, and working conditions. In general, minimum, midpoint, and maximum pay rates increase as the level of compensable factors (for example, greater skill) increases.

Flattening the Organization

Although traditional hierarchical organizational structures still are prevalent, many companies' structures are flattening, or becoming less bureaucratic [10]. Many companies have recognized the need to move to an adaptive, high-involvement organizational structure. In the adaptive organizational structure, employees are in a constant state of learning and performance improvement [11]. Employees are free to move wherever they are needed in the company. Employees, managers, vendors, customers, and suppliers work together to improve service quality and to create new products and services. Line employees are trained in multiple jobs, communicate directly with suppliers and customers, and interact frequently with engineers, quality experts, and employees from other functions.

Broadbanding (Chapter 9) represents the increasing organizational trend toward flatter, less hierarchical corporate structures that emphasize teamwork over individual contributions alone [12]. Broadbanding uses only a few large salary ranges, spanning levels within the organization previously covered by several pay grades. Thus, HR professionals place jobs that were separated by one or more pay grades in old pay structures into the same band under broadbanding systems, minimizing hierarchical differences among jobs. Figure 2-3 illustrates the broadbanding concept.

TABLE 2-3 Designing Pay-for-Knowledge Programs

Establishing Skill Blocks

- Skill type
- Number of skills
- Grouping of skills

Transition Matters

- Skills assessment
- Aligning pay with the knowledge structure
- Access to training

Training and Certification

- In-house or outsourcing training
- Certification and recertification

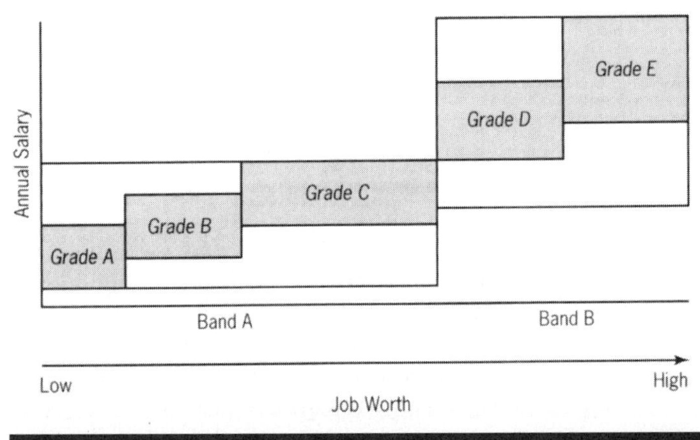

FIGURE 2-3 Broadbanding Structure and Its Relationship to Traditional Pay Grades and Ranges

Team Orientation

Employers in the United States are increasingly using teams to get work done. Two main changes in the business environment have led to this development [13]. First, in the 1980s, the rise in the number of Japanese companies conducting business in the United States was dramatic. The team approach to work is a common feature of Japanese companies. Second, team-based job design promotes innovation in the workplace [14]. Whirlpool Corporation uses teams to manufacture appliances, and Saturn uses teams to manufacture automobiles.

Companies need to change individualistic compensation practices so that groups are rewarded for their collaborative behavior [15]. Accordingly, team-based pay plans should emphasize cooperation between and within teams, compensate employees for additional responsibilities they often must assume in their roles as members of a team, and encourage team members to attain predetermined objectives for the team [16].

Team-based organizational structures encourage team members to learn new skills and assume broader responsibility than is expected of them under traditional pay structures that are geared toward individuals. Employees who work in teams must initiate plans for achieving their team's production goals. Usually, a pay plan for teams emphasizes cooperation, rewarding its members for the additional responsibilities they must take on and for the skills and knowledge they must acquire. Chapter 5 addresses the design of team incentive pay plans. Chapter 6 shows how skill-based pay plans and knowledge-based pay can address these additional responsibilities.

Organizational and Product Life Cycles

Many business professionals set competitive strategies on the basis of organizational and product life cycles. **Organizational and product life cycles** describe the evolution of companies and products in terms of human life cycle stages. Much as people are born, grow, mature, decline, and die, so do companies, products, and services. Business priorities, including human resources, vary with life cycle stages [17]. In particular, life cycle stages influence the choice of competitive strategies and such specific HR strategies as compensation.

Growth Phase

Differentiation strategies are most appropriate for companies in the growth phase. In competitive markets, newcomers must distinguish themselves from the established competitors in ways that appeal to prospective consumers and clients. Failure to do so will create competitive disadvantages. After all, why purchase a product or service from a new, unknown company when you can get exactly the same thing from a well-known company?

Companies that provide services on the Internet are growth companies. The Internet is a single network that connects millions of computers around the world. The number of computers connected to the Internet has grown exponentially. Likewise, the amount of information on the Internet has grown exponentially. There does not appear to be a foreseeable slowdown in the expansion of the Internet. Lycos and Google are examples of growth companies that provide services on the Internet. These companies offer "search engines" that enable individuals to systematically locate, identify, and edit material on the Internet on the basis of key words and concepts. Research and development is a key focus because these companies continually develop new software to increase their search capabilities.

Growth companies experience cash demands to finance capital expansion projects (for example, new buildings, manufacturing equipment, or enhanced telecommunications services). These companies also strive to employ the best-qualified employees for key positions. Often, getting the most talented executives and professional employees requires exorbitant expenditures on compensation, discounting labor cost containment strategies [18]. As a result, growth companies tend to emphasize market-competitive pay systems over internally consistent pay systems.

Not all core compensation tactics are appropriate for growth companies. Long-term incentive programs with annual or longer goals for professionals and executives are suitable. Rewarding engineers' innovations in product design requires a long-term orientation: It takes an extended amount of time to move through the series of steps required to bring the innovation to the marketplace—patent approval, manufacturing, and market distribution. The incentives that executives receive are based on long-term horizons because their success is matched against the endurance of their companies over time (Chapter 13). Lucrative long-term incentive awards may be able to maintain key employees' commitment to growth objectives over time.

Core compensation tactics for staff (for example, compensation specialist) and lower-level line employees (for example, first-line supervisors) typically consist of base pay, periodically increased with modest merit awards. Base pay levels usually are consistent with external market pay rates. Although these employees are not directly responsible for company growth, they do contribute by offering consistency in the product manufacturing or service delivery processes. In some cases, growth companies may set base pay levels somewhat below external market rates to maximize cash flow for R&D activities or marketing campaigns. As we discuss in Chapter 9, setting base pay too low may make it difficult for companies to recruit and retain well-qualified employees.

Growth companies tend to keep discretionary benefits offerings to a minimum. As we discuss in Chapter 11, discretionary benefits represent a significant fiscal cost to companies. In March 2002, U.S. companies spent an average $9,547 per year per employee to provide discretionary benefits [19]. Such discretionary benefits accounted for approximately one-third of employers' total payroll costs (that is, the sum of core compensation and all fringe compensation costs). For too many years, companies have awarded benefits to employees regardless of employee's performance or the cost impact of these benefits on company performance. Growth companies cannot afford expenditures that do not contribute directly to growth objectives.

FLIP SIDE OF THE COIN

COMPENSATION STRATEGY: A GUIDE FOR SENIOR MANAGERS

Most senior managers wish, at least at times, that they could ignore compensation. No other organizational system is so weighted with values and emotions, so visible to employees or so much the subject of internal dissent. Nearly everyone has opinions—usually strong opinions—about rewards. Any change in compensation usually attracts loud complaints from employees who feel disadvantaged by the change.

The topic of rewards is rife with myths that are widely accepted but contradicted by extensive research (see "Myths about Rewards That Never Die #1 and #2"). In view of these difficulties, can busy senior managers safely take the easy way out and leave compensation decisions to their compensation specialists? Or should they devote significant personal attention to compensation? Senior managers should be heavily involved in setting the strategic direction for compensation, and there are some fundamental choices senior managers need to make during this process.

Compensation systems demanded less senior management attention only a few years ago. At that time, senior managers generally left the design of employee compensation systems to technical specialists. This was possible partly because professionally managed compensation systems looked very much alike from one company to another. For most firms, the goal of compensation design was simply to avoid a competitive disadvantage by keeping labor costs in line with those of competitors, and the goal of compensation administration was to keep employee noise down.

The picture has changed greatly during the past decade, as companies throughout the economy have begun to rethink their compensation systems in the search for competitive advantage. Base pay, incentives, benefits and pay for corporate performance all have changed dramatically. Studies of Fortune 1000 firms (Lawler, Mohrman and Ledford, 1998; see Figure 1) from 1986 to 1997 show large increases in the percentage of Fortune 1000 firms using a variety of compensation innovations. For example, there has been a 50 percent increase in companies using pay for skills, knowledge and competencies; a 50 percent increase in companies using work group or team incentives; and a 100 percent increase in firms using flexible benefit systems. The strategic demands of new competitive forces, new organizational forms, and increase in knowledge work and recognition of the importance of compensation to organizational effectiveness have largely driven these changes. Top managers can no longer afford to leave compensation solely in the hands of compensation professionals.

There are some basic principles of compensation strategy senior managers need to understand. The alignment of compensation with business needs, the goals of the compensation system, reward system levers and basic choices managers

FIGURE 1 Use of Selected Reward Practices by Fortune 1000 Firms, 1987–1996

	1987	*1990*	*1993*	*1996*
Knowledge/Skill-based Pay	40	51	60	62
All-Salaried Pay System	71	64	73	70
Flexible, Cafeteria-Style Benefits	34	54	68	68
Work Group or Team Incentives	NA	59	70	87
Gainsharing (unit performance incentives)	26	39	42	45
Profit Sharing	65	63	66	69
Employee Stock Ownership Plan	61	64	71	68

Note: Numbers are the percentage of Fortune 1000 firms using the practice with any employees.

Source: Lawler, Mohrman & Ledford, 1998.

(Continued)

(Continued)

need to make are among these principles. A foundation of knowledge will help senior managers use compensation as an important tool for managing the business.

MYTHS ABOUT REWARDS THAT NEVER DIE #1: "MONEY DOESN'T MOTIVATE, IT'S ONLY A HYGIENE FACTOR"

Bad ideas about compensation never die, they just recirculate.

The idea that money doesn't motivate employees has been around for decades. It received its most famous formulation in the work of Frederick Herzberg (1968). He claimed that intrinsic sources of motivation arising from the design of work are much more important than extrinsic sources, such as pay, in determining the level of employee motivation. In Herzberg's view, extrinsic sources are "hygiene" factors that can have a negative effect but not a positive effect on motivation, while intrinsic sources are true motivators. However, while Herzberg is remembered for his emphasis on the importance of intrinsic motivation, contemporary motivations scholars almost universally reject his claim that extrinsic rewards do not motivate.

A more recent view is expressed by Alfie Kohn (1993), a polemicist whose highly biased and incomplete review of the reward literature might have remained obscure had it not been excerpted in the *Harvard Business Review*. Kohn argues that extrinsic rewards cannot work for several reasons. He argues that extrinsic rewards such as pay need to be provided continually to be effective, whereas intrinsic rewards such as work design are available to employees without continuous management action.

However, we are unimpressed with the discovery that you can't pay employees for performance just once—you have to *keep* paying them. Kohn rehashes Herzberg's discredited arguments about motivators and hygiene factors. Further, Kohn relies heavily on studies by Deci and his colleagues, who argue based on lab experiments that extrinsic rewards undermine intrinsic motivation. However, contemporary scholars have rejected Deci's work. For example, a review of 96 studies (Eisenberg and Cameron, 1996) found that extrinsic rewards are more likely to *increase* rather than decrease intrinsic motivation and creativity. The argument that money doesn't motivate simply collapses under the weight of the research evidence. For example, a recent analysis of 39 studies of financial incentives published in a leading academic journal (Jenkins, Mitra, Gupta and Shaw, 1998) found a relatively strong correlation of .34 between the use of financial incentives and job performance. The vast majority of motivation researchers agree that money motivates.

What explains the enduring appeal of this myth? Managerial self-interest is possibly a primary explanation. What manager would be unhappy to learn that there is no penalty for simply avoiding all the headaches, design dilemmas and compensation costs involved in trying to link pay and performance? Managers want to believe, even when their experience denies the myth.

MYTHS ABOUT REWARDS THAT NEVER DIE #2: "A HAPPY WORKER IS A PRODUCTIVE WORKER"

One of the most enduring myths about reward systems is "a happy worker is a productive worker." That is, if we just make employees happier (or more modestly, if we just increase their job satisfaction), productivity will follow as day follows night.

This myth dates back at least to the dawn of the industrial revolution. It has great appeal for a number of reasons (Ledford, 1999). It lets managers ignore pay system issues altogether. Why bother with costly, complicated pay systems if a friendly management style, or an employee-centered culture, or generous benefits can make workers both happier and more productive? In fact, management may hope that employees will work for less money if they are happier (while being more productive).

Employees also adopt this myth and use it to turn the tables on management, arguing that any improvement in pay or working conditions will reward management with higher productivity, ultimately making the added rewards "free." This is like asking Santa Claus for presents. Seemingly, no one has to pay for them.

Unfortunately, the popular belief that happiness leads to productivity is not supported by the evidence. Literally hundreds of studies have examined the relationship between employee attitudes such as job satisfaction and productivity.

(Of course, satisfaction is not the same thing as happiness, but the two obviously are closely related.)

In every decade since the 1950s, a major review of this ever-growing literature has reached the same conclusions: that is, the relationship between satisfaction and productivity is detectable, but too small to be of practical significance. Where the relationship exists, it may well be because more productive people tend to be rewarded for their higher performance, and thus happiness may be the indirect *result* rather than the *cause* of productivity. Making people happier makes them stay in the organizational longer—that is, it reduces turnover—but it does not necessarily make them more productive.

We ask skeptical readers to reflect on their own experiences. Think about the times in your life when you were most and least productive. Were you uniformly happy when you were most productive and miserable when you were least productive? Our personal experience does not support the idea that a happy worker is necessarily a productive worker, and we think the same is true for most readers.

Thus, managers cannot take the easy way out. They cannot substitute the things that make employees happy for rewards that are linked to performance. Indeed, an effective reward system may increase unhappiness by paying top performers more than poor performers. Poor performers may resent the outcome, but be motivated to increase their performance as a result.

REFERENCES

Eisenberg & Cameron. (1996). Detrimental effects of rewards: Reality or myth? *American Psychologist, 51*, pp. 1153–1166.

Herzberg, F. (January–February 1968). One more time: How do you motivate employees? *Harvard Business Review*.

Jenkins, G. D. Jr., A. Mitra, N. Gupta, & J. D. Shaw. (1998). Are financial incentives related to performance? A meta-analytic review of empirical research. *Journal of Applied Psychology, 83*, pp. 777–787.

Kohn, A. (1993). *Punished by Rewards*. Boston: Houghton-Mifflin.

Lawler, E. E. III, S. A. Mohrman, & G. E. Ledford Jr. (1998). *Strategies for High Performance Organizations*. San Francisco: Jossey-Bass.

Ledford, G. E. Jr. (1999). Happiness and productivity revisited. *Journal of Organizational Behavior, 20*, pp. 25–30.

Source: Gerald E. Ledrod, Jr., Ph.D., and Elizabeth J. Hawk, CCP, *ACA Journal*, first quarter 2000, volume 9, number 1, pp. 28–38.

Maturity

Lowest-cost strategies are most appropriate for mature companies. Products and services have fully evolved within the constraints of technology. Mature companies strive to maintain or gain market share. Efficient operations are paramount to striking a balance between cost containment and offering the best possible quality products or services.

Southwest Airlines is an exemplar of a mature company that successfully pursues a lowest-cost strategy. Several features of Southwest's operations account for its success as a low-cost yet safe and reliable airline. Southwest does not offer as many nonstop flight arrangements as its competitors. For example, flying from New Orleans to Indianapolis may require three separate flights—New Orleans to Houston, Houston to St. Louis, and St. Louis to Indianapolis. By offering shorter flights, Southwest can more easily fill its planes, increasing cost efficiency. Southwest also saves money by using an open seating policy on its flights. This open seating policy frees up reservationists' time for booking additional reservations. Finally, Southwest Airlines manages costs by not offering full meal services on its flights.

Mature companies usually have large, well-developed internal labor markets. Internal labor markets are pools of skills and abilities from among a company's current workforce. As companies mature, employees presumably become more skilled and able to make greater contributions to the attainment of companies' goals. Management can capitalize on internal labor markets through the implementation of career development programs. Current excellent performers may receive promotions, leaving mainly entry-level job openings available to external candidates.

As we discuss in Chapter 6, pay-for-knowledge and skill-based pay programs are suitable for companies that pursue lowest-cost strategies. Both programs are instrumental in developing internal labor markets. In the short run, pay-for-knowledge and skill-based pay programs may undermine the imperatives of lowest-cost strategies because of the associated training costs. However, productivity enhancements and increased flexibility should far outweigh the short-run costs.

Other core compensation programs may be appropriate for lowest-cost strategies as well. Logically, base pay rates should be set below the market average to contain costs. However, compensation professionals must recommend pay rates that strike a balance between efficiency mandates and the need to retain valued employees. Often, setting base pay to meet market averages strikes this balance when this tactic is augmented with incentive pay. Lowest-cost strategies demand reduced output costs per employee. As we discussed in Chapter 1, incentive pay fluctuates according to employees' attainment of some standard based on a preestablished formula, individual or group goals, or company earnings [20]. Merit pay systems are most appropriate only when the following two conditions are met: (1) Pay increases are commensurate with employee productivity, and (2) employees maintain productivity long after receiving permanent increments to base pay.

Decline

Companies in decline experience diminishing markets and, subsequently, poor business performance. Several factors, including limited financial resources and changes in consumer preferences, can result in decline. Business leaders can respond to decline in either of two ways. They can allow decline to continue until the business is no longer profitable, or they can make substantial changes that reverse decline. A company's response to decline determines whether lowest-cost or differentiation strategies are most appropriate.

Differentiation strategies become the focus when companies choose to redirect activities toward distinguishing themselves from the competition by modifying existing products or services in some creative way or by developing new products or services. American Express Corporation differentiated itself in response to the declining market for its charge cards. Changes in preferences have led consumers to choose credit cards over charge cards. These changes created problems for American Express, which is well known for charge cards. Charge card agreements require cardholders to pay balances in full, typically on a monthly basis. Credit cards are based on revolving debt. Credit card holders have the option to pay balances in full, typically on a monthly basis, without paying interest charges. Alternatively, credit card holders may pay only a small percentage (usually 5 percent or less) of their debt every month but pay interest on remaining balances to the credit card companies. Credit card purchases are consistent with the trend in U.S. consumer purchasing patterns toward spending now and paying much later. The American Express Company lost considerable market share and revenue because of this trend in consumer purchasing patterns. In response to these changing consumer preferences, the American Express Company began offering a variety of credit cards to suit various consumer preferences for repayment options (for example, repayment over extended periods, repayment in full some months later) and rewards programs (for example, airline frequent flyer miles, discounts on shopping).

Lowest-cost strategies are most appropriate when companies allow decline to continue to business closure. The era of small, family-owned furniture stores is coming to an end as large discount furniture stores take hold. This trend is the result of two factors. First, small, family-owned furniture stores generally charge substantial price premiums (anywhere from 200 percent to 300 percent more than the manufacturers' suggested prices). Large discount stores usually price furniture well below manufacturers' suggested rates—anywhere from 30 percent to 80 percent below. Second, showroom space is quite limited in family-owned stores relative to the large discount stores. As a result, the family-owned businesses display far less furniture, giving the consumer fewer options from which to choose. These factors make it virtually impossible for family-owned furniture stores to compete. Many of these small businesses choose to go out of business. Upon making this decision, these businesses adopt lowest-cost strategies in which they offer deep discounts to sell remaining inventories as quickly as possible. Although profit margins are lower under these circumstances, business owners are more likely to minimize losses by eliminating sooner overhead expenses such as rent, utilities, insurance, and compensation.

SUMMARY

This chapter reviewed strategic compensation in action. We discussed the importance of strategic analysis in identifying competitive forces facing companies. Strategic analyses enable compensation professionals to better understand the internal and external contexts of their companies, giving them a better sense of how much they can afford to compensate employees. We then discussed factors that influence competitive strategies and compensation practices—national culture, organizational culture, and organizational and product life cycle. As competition increases, compensation professionals must move into action by skillfully choosing compensation practices to promote the attainment of competitive advantage.

Key Terms

- strategic analysis, 34
- North American Industry Classification System Manual, 34
- North American Industry Classification System (NAICS), 34
- sector, 35
- subsector, 35
- industry group, 35
- industry, 35
- industry profiles, 37
- labor market assessments, 38
- financial condition, 44
- operating requirements, 44
- capital requirements, 44
- national culture, 44
- power distance, 45
- individualism-collectivism, 45
- uncertainty avoidance, 45
- masculinity-femininity, 45
- organizational and product life cycles, 49

Discussion Questions

1. Discuss what strategic compensation means to you.
2. Describe the purpose of the NAICS.
3. Earlier, we referred to a few of Fly-You-There's competitors. Go to the Web sites of three competitors and summarize similarities and differences between two competitors' business objectives.
4. Describe why a company's long-term prospects are an important consideration to compensation professionals.
5. National culture is a more important influence on compensation systems than organizational culture. Discuss whether you agree or disagree with this statement.
6. Identify three products or services with which you are familiar. Discuss whether these are in growth, maturity, or decline stages.

Exercises

Compensation Online

For Students

Exercise 1: Find relevant journal articles

Use your school library's online catalog to locate articles pertaining to competitive strategies, organizational cultures, and organizational life cycles. Find and read several current articles in these areas. As a student who will be looking for employment in the near future, what sort of culture will you look for in prospective employers?

Exercise 2: Review a research site

An assignment requires you to analyze a certain industry that you are not familiar with. Using the Yahoo search engine, type in "NAICS" and click on the search button. Find the NAICS homepage. Read over their homepage to understand what information is available in the NAICS manual.

Using a different search engine, go to the same Web site or find a related site. Compare and contrast the two search engines for ease of accessibility and amount of information available.

Exercise 3: Research a government document

Go to the NAICS Web site, click on the *New Code System* link, which is located on the left side of the homepage. Review the information on this page. Write a brief description of how this information will affect you in your career.

For Professionals

Exercise 1: Research trade magazines and newsletters

You have just begun working for a company in an industry that is entirely new to you. Use a search engine to find examples of trade magazines and newsletters of any industry you are interested in. Read about different aspects of the industry environment, and try to think how you might use this information if you were working in this industry.

Exercise 2: Examine industry profiles

Your company is set to overhaul policies and operations, including pay. You must get your department started on some basic industry analysis. Search for "industry profile" and use the resulting sites to learn characteristics of different industries. How will things like nature of business, number of competitors, and industry regulation affect you in your HR career?

Exercise 3: Analyze an organization's Web page

You have been asked to sit in on a meeting with representatives of the World Trade Organization. Naturally, you want to be as prepared as you can. Using the Yahoo search engine, type in "World Trade Organization" and click on the search button. Under the Web sites listing, click on the World Trade Organization (WTO) link. Read over the page and click on a couple of the links to see what information is available.

Using a different search engine, go to the same Web site or find a related site. Compare and contrast the two search engines for ease of accessibility and amount of information available.

What does the WTO do? What interactions might you have with the WTO when you begin your career? Think about working in a few different industries and how much the WTO would be involved with each.

Endnotes

1. U.S. Office of Management and Budget. (1998). *North American industry classification system manual.* [online]. Available: http://www.nits.gov/naics, accessed March 29, 2000.
2. Braddock, D. (1999). Occupational employment projections to 2008. *Monthly Labor Review*, *122*, pp. 51–77.
3. U.S. Bureau of Labor Statistics. (2000). *Occupational*

Outlook Handbook (2000–2001 edition). Washington, DC: Author, pp. 564–565.

4. Gòmez-Mejía, L. R., & Welbourne, T. (1991). Compensation strategies in a global context. *Human Resource Planning, 14*, pp. 29–41.
5. Hofstede, G. (1980). *Culture's Consequences*. Newbury Park, CA: Sage.
6. Terpstra, V., & David, K. (1991). *The Cultural Environment of International Business* (3rd ed.). Cincinnati, OH: South-Western Publishing.
7. Muczyk, J. P., & Hastings, R. E. (1985). In defense of enlightened hardball management. *Business Horizons*, July–August, pp. 23–29.
8. Heneman, R. L. (1992). *Merit pay: Linking Pay Increases to Performance Ratings*. Reading, MA: Addison-Wesley.
9. Smircich, L. (1983). Concepts of culture and organizational analysis. *Administrative Science Quarterly, 28*, pp. 339–358.
10. Marcus, S. (1991). Delayering: More than meets the eye. *Perspectives, 3*, pp. 22–26.
11. Rosow, J., & Zager, R. (1988). *Training: The Competitive Edge*. San Francisco: Jossey-Bass.
12. Risher, H. H., & Butler, R. J. (1993–94). Salary banding: An alternative salary-management concept. *ACA Journal, 2*, pp. 48–57.
13. Jackson, S. E. (1992). Team composition in organizational settings: Issues in managing an increasingly diverse workforce. In S. Worchel, W. Wood, & J.A. Simpson (Eds.), *Group Process and Productivity* (pp. 138–173). Newbury Park, CA: Sage.
14. Kanter, R. M. (1988). When a thousand flowers bloom: Structural, collective, and social conditions for innovation in organizations. In B. M. Staw & L. L. Cummings (Eds.), *Research in Organizational Behavior* (vol. 10, pp. 169–211). Greenwich, CT: JAI Press.
15. Worchel, S., Wood, W., & Simpson, J. A. (Eds.). (1992). *Group Process and Productivity*. Newbury Park, CA: Sages.
16. Kanin-Lovers, J., & Cameron, M. (1993). Team-based reward systems. *Journal of Compensation and Benefits*, January–February, pp. 55–60.
17. Schuler, R. S. (1989). Strategic human resource management and industrial relations. *Human Relations, 42*, pp. 157–184.
18. Galbraith, J. R. (1983). Strategy and organizational planning. *Human Resource Management, 22*, pp. 63–77.
19. U.S. Bureau of Labor Statistics. (2002). Employer Cost Index, March 2002. Washington, DC: U.S. Government Printing Office.
20. Peck, C. (1993). Variable pay: Nontraditional programs for motivation and reward. New York: Conference Board.

COMPENSATION IN ACTION

BUILD A CASE FOR HR'S BOTTOM-LINE IMPACT

WHAT WORKS

The next time you're looking for a training video about human resources, workplace culture, and the bottom line, drive to your nearest video-rental store and pick up a copy of *Jerry Maguire*. That's right, skip the usual stuff about paradigms and fish markets, and get the 1996 release starring Tom Cruise, Renee Zellweger, and Cuba Gooding Jr.

In the movie, Cruise plays Maguire, a high-flying sports agent who starts feeling that his work is too self-serving. Am I "just another shark in a suit?" he asks.

Things reach a crisis point while he's out of town on business. He stays up all night, thinking, agonizing, sucking down coffee and writing a multi-page mission statement titled: "The Things We Think and Do Not Say: The Future of Our Business."

It's an on-paper liberation, and Maguire makes copies for his 110 colleagues. They politely take it, read it and gulp hard. The "statement" takes shots at their business and calls for people to be more caring, more humane. All of his coworkers (except Zellweger, who goes on to team up with him) begin to ostracize him. Eventually he gets his walking papers, and is left with just one client, a wide receiver named Rod Tidwell (Gooding).

Tidwell has no shortage of self-confidence and couldn't care less about emotion-laden mission statements. What he wants from Maguire is a better contract and a fatter paycheck. In fact, his guiding mantra is just four words: "Show me the money!" He says it on the phone. He says it in the shower. He says it while dancing. He practically grabs Maguire by the collar and says, "It's all about the bottom line, stupid." Show me the money!

In all of my years working with organizations, I've never seen CEOs, CFOs, or accountants dancing on their desks shouting, "Show me the money!" But I've had the sense that they're saying it inside, and some have grabbed me by the figurative collar and said, "That stuff about improving the workplace culture is all well and good, but how will it help our bottom line?" I've often felt like Maguire, full of mission, pitted against the Rod Tidwells of the world.

For change agents who have a Maguire-like missionary zeal, its tempting to pull away and let the money-minded people live in their own world. But nothing is more self-defeating. In most cases, change agents do have to show the money. It's a necessary step in winning over fence-sitters and skeptics.

Fortunately, there are plenty of studies showing that investments to improve human resources end up increasing the overall worth of an organization. You're probably familiar with *Fortune* magazine's annual list of the "Best Companies to Work For." A group of numbercrunchers took the 1999 list, sorted out the 55 companies whose stocks had been publicly traded for at least five years, and compared the results to those of the Russell 3000. (The comprehensive Russell 3000 Index of U.S. stocks includes companies that are comparable to those on the "best" list.) Over the same five-year period, Fortune's 55 best companies had an average annual appreciation of 25 percent—well ahead of the 19 percent gain by the Russell index.

In a similar study, consulting firm Hewitt Associates teamed up with the University of Wisconsin and Vanderbilt University to analyze the average stock returns from the "best companies to work for." Their findings made it clear that people-friendly practices benefit the bottom line. During a measurement period of seven years, the data showed that companies on a 1993 "best" list outpaced a broad market index by 87 percentage points. The top 1998 Fortune companies bested their index counterparts by 56 percentage points, over four years.

Watson Wyatt surveyed 405 publicly traded companies of all types, posing 72 wide-ranging questions on everything from training to workplace culture to communications. In order to come up with a so-called Human Capital Index (HCI) score for each company, a statistical formula was applied. Then the subject companies were sorted into three HCI-rating categories: low, medium, and high. The companies in the high-HCI group delivered a 103 percent total return to shareholders over a five-year period, compared to 53 percent for low-HCI and 88 percent for medium-HCI companies.

So when someone asks you to show them the money, graciously accept their invitation and share one of the above studies. And if they respond with more skepticism, mention the Malcolm Baldrige National Quality Award, which was launched in 1988 and is regarded by many business leaders as the top award for organizational performance. Its criteria cover seven areas: human resources, leadership, strategic planning, customer and market focus, information and analysis, process management, and business results. Baldrige winners have consistently outperformed the S&P 500—by a margin of 4.4 to 1, according to an April 2001 analysis.

Also, you might want to rent *Jerry Maguire*. Check out Rod Tidwell's jig to "Show Me the Money." I guarantee that when you're equipped with several solid studies showing the bottom-line impact of culture change in the workplace, you'll be dancing, too.

Source: Tom Terez, *Workforce* 22–24 81, no. 3 (March 2002): p. 22–24 ISSN: 1092-8332, Number: 110436465, Copyright ACC Communications, Inc., March 2002.

WHAT'S NEW IN COMPENSATION?

Industry Conditions and Trends Are Key to Developing Strategic Compensation

Compensation systems developed without regard to industry conditions could negatively affect competitive advantage. For example, compensating sales professionals according to job seniority simply does not fit the imperative of increasing the customer base and sales volume. Under a seniority system, motivation to achieve higher sales is not supported because employees can expect regular pay increases based on length of service. As another example, setting pay levels too low for strategically important jobs will keep a company from attracting and retaining the very best people.

The featured *New York Times* article describes major activities and trends in the vaccine industry. Many pharmaceutical companies and vaccine development companies are striving to find vaccines for such catastrophic health conditions as AIDS, cocaine addiction, and Alzheimer's disease. Recent scientific breakthroughs in the fields of immunology and biotechnology have raised the possibility that vaccines may limit the incidence of these catastrophic health conditions. In addition, government legislation has created a fund from which vaccine makers may draw in the event of lawsuits against them (for example, when an individual's death is associated with a well-tested vaccine). Further, rapid increases in the cost of health care will be slowed because successful vaccines will reduce the cost of treatment. Health insurance companies and employers that purchase health insurance on behalf of employees will be better able to control the costs of health insurance coverage.

Log into your *New York Times* account. Search the database for articles on "industry trends," or specify the name of an industry that interests you. When reading these articles, identify possible threats and opportunities to the industry. You might also speculate how industry conditions and trends could influence compensation practices. Following your course instructor's specific directions, be prepared to describe the current situation, and relate it to the article contained in this text. ■

The New York Times

Big Steps for Vaccine Industry; Fresh Approaches and Technology Ignite New Interest

Una S. Ryan, president and chief executive of Avant Immunotherapeutics, used to tread carefully when describing the cholesterol fighter her company was developing. Facing criticism from numerous skeptics, she started calling it an "inhibitor," not a vaccine.

That seemed a good idea at the time, since she was repeatedly hearing that the vaccine business was a money-losing proposition, that the risks outweighed any possible rewards. But suddenly all that has changed.

Avant's vaccine has produced some encouraging—if still preliminary—test results in people in the last year. And now, Dr. Ryan no longer hides the fact that her company's cholesterol fighter is a vaccine. The skeptics, she said, "are finally coming about."

Until fairly recently, almost no one was interested in vaccines. Rocked by the threat of liability lawsuits in the 1970s and early 1980s, vaccine marketers jumped ship, and the number of large companies in the business shrank from roughly a dozen to just four.

But over the last decade, vaccine development has bounced back, with many new products aimed at adults. Analysts point to the roughly 100 vaccines now in development in the United States alone.

Developing a safe and effective AIDS vaccine remains a holy grail for some companies, like Merck. But vaccine research is now also tackling a previously unimaginable variety of conditions, like osteoporosis, cocaine addiction, ulcers, multiple sclerosis, and even Alzheimer's. Some efforts are focusing on friendlier delivery technologies, like administering vaccines through needleless skin patches, while others are trying to develop more combination products, perhaps to pack a dozen or so vaccines together.

In Gaithersburg, Maryland, MedImmune is developing two vaccines that might be given to women for preventing urinary tract infections and also infections from the human papilloma virus, a major cause of cervical cancer.

To be sure, most of these vaccines are all highly experimental, with no guarantee that they will succeed or pass muster with the Food and Drug Administration. But that has not slowed this resurgence.

Four companies still dominate the market—Merck, GlaxoSmithKline, American Home Products, and Aventis Pasteur (part of the French drug giant Aventis). And they now account for 80 percent of sales. Because of the huge costs associated with developing and manufacturing vaccines, these companies, which controlled just half the market in 1988, will continue to grow stronger, predicts Pamela Bassett, president of BioTrend, a market research and consulting firm in Manhattan. Still, when it comes to developing vaccines, large companies are battling perhaps four dozen smaller ones, as well as a new group of medium-size ones like Baxter, Chiron, and Corixa.

At $5 billion a year, total worldwide sales of vaccines are still minuscule compared with the roughly $300 billion in total drug sales. But vaccines are picking up momentum. While sales had been growing recently by about 7 percent annually, Ms. Bassett, for one, expects sales to grow 12 percent annually for the next decade, eventually reaching $15 billion. As reasons, she cites the introduction of far more vaccines for preventing diseases, as well as the rollout of "therapeutic" vaccines, which bolster the body's defenses. While vaccines are now almost always used to prevent disease, not treat it, Ms. Bassett estimates that roughly half the vaccines in development are aimed at therapeutic use.

That represents a sea change for the industry. Ms. Bassett predicts that most future growth will come from products never available before, like vaccines against herpes, colon and stomach cancer, and malignant melanoma, the deadliest form of skin cancer.

Such mammoth projections help explain why some vaccine makers seem to be jockeying to lead the industry, a scene almost unthinkable a few years ago. Aventis Pasteur, for example, says it now has the broadest range of vaccines worldwide and produces more vaccine doses—more than a billion annually—than any other company. But in mid-May, Robert Essner, the new president and chief executive of American Home Products, told analysts and investors that his company was "on track to be the world's No. 1 vaccine producer" by 2003.

How did a virtual orphan within the drug industry stage such a comeback?

Analysts point to the federal legislation that established a liability fund for vaccine makers in 1986, as well as the attention that Bill and Melinda Gates got when they set up a $100 million fund in 1998 for ensuring that new vaccines get to developing countries. But analysts also point to the strides that immunology and biotechnology have made in the last 20 years. At Merck, for example, vaccines now under development use science "that was not available a decade or two ago," said Dr. Adel Mahmoud, head of vaccine efforts.

Lately, the business has gotten yet another lift: the almost unprecedented success of Prevnar, which fights pneumococcal disease, the major cause of meningitis, blood poisoning, and pneumonia in young children. While most childhood vaccines now cost $6 to $20 a dose, Prevnar, the first vaccine of its kind, costs a hefty $232 for a four-dose round.

Despite its price tag, Prevnar, introduced in February 2000, racked up sales of $461 million last year. According to Kevin L. Reilly, president of the vaccine division at Wyeth-Ayerst Pharmaceuticals, which is part of American Home Products, Prevnar is meeting little, if any, resistance from the managed care industry. Wyeth-Ayerst hopes the FDA will approve Prevnar soon for fighting ear infections in children, which prompt some 27 million doctor visits a year in the United States.

"Prevnar is a classic example of how the vaccine business is changing," said Kris Jenner, manager of the T. Rowe Price Health Sciences Fund. "It's much more expensive than the typical vaccine, but it carries tremendous potential benefit."

American Home Products expects Prevnar sales to exceed $1 billion eventually. But it also has high hopes for FluMist, the nasal-spray flu vaccine it is developing that is now under review by the FDA.

Health experts say FluMist may finally make it practical to vaccinate not just adults but also children.

Mr. Jenner, the fund manager, says American Home Products is an emerging leader in vaccines. And he expects its future earnings growth to get a "meaningful" lift from new vaccines like Prevnar and FluMist.

Still, companies like American Home Products have their work cut out for them, especially as they take on unusually complex diseases that may have a multitude of causes, like Alzheimer's. "We've already tackled the easy diseases, so we're getting progressively further and further into more difficult diseases, where vaccines are extremely difficult to develop," Mr. Reilly said.

Vaccine development times already mirror the difficulty. In the early 1960s, the first DTP vaccine, for fighting diphtheria, tetanus, and pertussis in children, took just a year to develop, said John Lambert, who heads the vaccine business at the Chiron Corporation. But now, he said, development times of 15 or 17 years are not uncommon, while combination products can take 6 more years to ensure that the vaccines are both safe and work without interfering with one another.

Still, Chiron now has about 20 major vaccines in development, while smaller companies are also turning up the heat, either by snapping up other small developers or by trying to carve out a profitable niche. Avant, for example, based in Needham, Massachusetts, is developing vaccines for travelers, a market some analysts say might reach $2 billion by 2005. One vaccine is aimed at traveler's diarrhea. Here, Dr. Ryan said, the goal is to develop a product that would confer immunity in a matter of days, not weeks.

Lately, the race to develop cancer vaccines has become especially crowded. While the vaccines have not yet come on the market in the United States, when they do, analysts expect them to cost $10,000 to $20,000 for one round. And despite their experimental nature, analysts expect them to produce profits almost as high as what newer drugs command.

According to their developers, cancer vaccines are not intended to replace surgery or radiation; rather, they are geared toward stimulating the body's immune system to mop up any residual cancer cells left after such therapies. Still, Peter L. Ginsberg, a biotechnology analyst at U.S. Bancorp Piper Jaffray, says there are more than a dozen publicly traded biotech companies focusing on cancer vaccines, and probably at least as many private companies. For prostate cancer alone, he says, the number of vaccines in human tests jumped from 5 in 1997 to 16 now.

Lately, as cancer vaccines have gone into more advanced testing, investors have taken note. When Progenics Pharmaceuticals of Tarrytown, New York, announced in May 2000 that an affiliate of the National Cancer Institute had stopped testing the company's vaccine for preventing a relapse of melanoma, investors reacted with venom. In just one day, its stock plummeted from $33 to $10. But this May, Progenics's stock, then trading around $14, started climbing, even after Bristol-Myers Squibb, the world's largest cancer drug company, said it, too, was parting ways with the company.

Analysts say investors probably decided to bet on the overall promise of the vaccine, especially since Progenics had just announced plans to test it on 1,300 European patients, the largest test ever on melanoma patients with any new form of therapy.

The race to develop vaccines has left a few older, and presumably less profitable, vaccines in the lurch. In January, Wyeth-Ayerst Pharmaceuticals withdrew its vaccine for fighting tetanus and diphtheria in children—in part because two other companies were also making the vaccine, and also because it needed to free manufacturing space for vaccines like Prevnar. But now Aventis Pasteur is the only company making the vaccine, and earlier this year that caused troublesome shortages in some areas.

Wayne Pisano, senior vice president for marketing at Aventis Pasteur, said his company was still committed to children's vaccines. In fact, he said, such vaccines could use some tinkering as well. While the average child in the United States now receives almost two dozen shots by age 5, some routine doctor visits require administering up to four shots at a time. Aventis wants to raise the number of vaccines that can be packed into a single shot.

To Mr. Pisano, the effort is part of his company's "renewed commitment to vaccines." But to Mr. Jenner, of T. Rowe Price, such efforts add up to just good sense.

"I think very highly of companies that are pursuing vaccine strategies," he said. "As we look to technology to both improve the quality of life and also decrease the cost of health care, vaccines fit that desire perfectly."

SOURCE: Sana Siwobp, Big steps for vaccine industry: Fresh approaches and technology ignite new interest (dated July 25, 2001) [online]. Available: *www.nytimes.com*, accessed September 30, 2002.

CHAPTER

3 CONTEXTUAL INFLUENCES ON COMPENSATION PRACTICE

Chapter Outline

Learning Objectives

In this chapter, you will learn about

1. Compensation and the social good
2. Various laws that influence private sector companies' and labor unions' compensation practices
3. Contextual influences on the federal government's compensation practices
4. Labor unions' influence on companies' compensation practices
5. Market factors' impact on companies' compensation practices

As competition increased in the textile industry, the original concern of the mill owners for their employees gave way to stricter controls that had nothing to do with the well-being of the workers. Employers reduced wages, lengthened hours, and intensified work. For a workday ranging from 11½ to 13 hours, making up an average week of 75 hours, the women operatives were generally earning less than $1.50 a week (exclusive of board) by the late 1840s, and they were being compelled to tend four looms whereas in the 1830s they had only taken care of two. . . . [The manager] ordered them [the female textile workers] to come before breakfast. "I regard my work-people just as I regard my machinery. So long as they can do my work for what I choose to pay them, I keep them, getting out of them all I can." [1]

Anne Brown, the claims department manager of a small insurance company, said to Bill Smith, the human resource manager, "I'm sick and tired of having clerks who just don't work out. The quality of their work is not very good nor are they reliable—they are frequently absent or late. They are limiting my ability to maintain timely and accurate claims processing." Bill replied, "You get no argument from me. It's been nearly impossible to recruit top quality clerks ever since ABC Automobile Parts Company established a manufacturing facility across town. After all, ABC's clerks earn nearly 40 percent more than our clerks."

The previous quotations illustrate three major contextual influences on companies' compensation practices. The first quotation captures the inherent conflict between employers and employees—employers' profit maximization objectives and employees' desire for equitable and fair treatment. This conflict gave rise to the first two contextual influences that we will review in this chapter—federal protective legislation and labor unions. The "Compensation in Action" feature at the end of this chapter describes how attorneys' and judges' interpretations of protective laws influence HR practice. This particular feature describes changes in the interpretation of the Family and Medical Leave Act of 1993 and the Americans with Disabilities Act of 1990.

The second quotation represents a third contextual influence, market forces. In particular, this quotation illustrates a potential consequence of interindustry compensation differentials—the inability to recruit top quality employees. We will address these differentials later in the chapter.

COMPENSATION AND THE SOCIAL GOOD

The social good refers to a booming economy, low levels of unemployment, progressive wages and benefits, and safe and healthful working conditions. Compensation promotes the social good by enabling citizens to actively participate as consumers in the economy. However, conflicting goals among employees, employers, and the government can threaten the social good. Figure 3-1 illustrates the relationships among employees', employers', and the government's goals [2]. The overlapping areas represent the mutual goals between any two or all three groups. The nonoverlapping areas represent unique goals that can undermine the social good.

Employees, employers, and the government do share some common goals. Each group wants a booming economy. Employers' profits and the demand for their products and services tend to be high within booming economies. Employees prosper because unemployment is low and consumers tend to have confidence in the future, which leads to higher spending. Higher income tax revenues enable the government to fund programs—for example, national defense—and government employees' compensation packages.

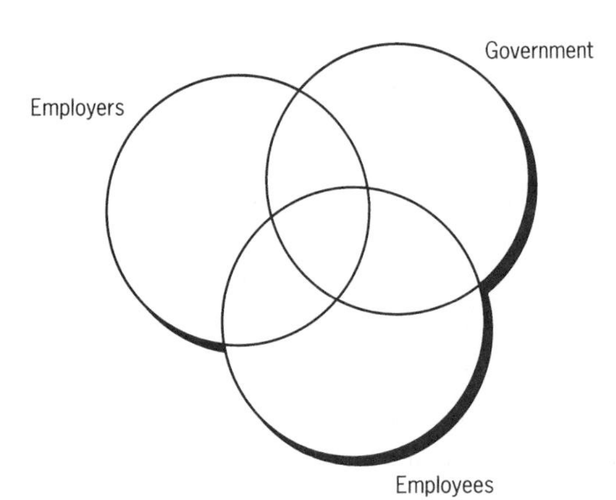

FIGURE 3-1 Employers', Employees', and Government's Goals

Employees' Goals

Employees' fundamental goals are to attain high wages, comprehensive benefits, safe and healthful work conditions, and job security. Prior to the 1930s, employees did not possess the right to negotiate with their employers over terms and conditions of employment. As a result, many workers were subjected to poor working conditions, low pay, and excessive work hours [3], as illustrated by the first opening quotation. Unemployment was an employee's main alternative to enduring these conditions. Nowadays, employment legislation and labor unions protect workers' rights and status. Employer abuses are much less prevalent than before the passage of legislation and the rise of labor unions. Nevertheless, employers still maintain the fundamental profit maximization objective, which necessitates legal and labor union impacts.

Employers' Goals

The employers depicted in Figure 3-1 are private sector companies. Private sector employers strive to increase profits, market share, and returns on investment. These employers expect workers to be as productive as possible and to produce the highest quality of products and services. The majority of U.S. civilian employees work under this objective. In 2001, 84 percent of all U.S. civilian employees worked for private sector businesses, and the remaining 16 percent worked for the government (municipal, state, or federal) [4].

Government's Goals

The government's ultimate goal is to promote the social good without extensive involvement in private sector employers' operations. It must operate as both an employer and consumer to achieve the social good. In 2001, the government employed 16 percent—about 20 million employees—of all U.S. civilian employees to ensure national security and legal compliance [5].

In addition, the government is both a buyer and consumer of the products and services that private sector companies produce. In fiscal year 2001, the federal government's expenditures totaled $1.77 trillion [6]. The government uses energy to run its buildings, and it engages in contracts with private sector companies for a multitude of goods and services, such as building construction and multimillion-dollar defense systems. Nearly 85 percent of the government's expenditures were for nondefense purposes. The federal government awarded contracts to private sector companies totaling $246 billion.

EMPLOYMENT LAWS THAT INFLUENCE COMPENSATION TACTICS

Employment laws establish bounds of acceptable employment practices as well as employee rights. The **federal constitution** forms the basis for employment laws. The following four amendments of the Constitution are most applicable:

> Article I, Section 8. "The Congress shall have Power . . . to regulate Commerce with foreign Nations, and among the several States, and with the Indian Tribes. . . ."
>
> First Amendment. "Congress shall make no law respecting an establishment of religion, or prohibiting the free exercise thereof; or abridging the freedom of speech, or of the press; or the right of the people peaceably to assemble, and to petition the Government for a redress of grievances."
>
> Fifth Amendment. "No person shall . . . be deprived of life, liberty, or property, without due process of law. . . ."
>
> Fourteenth Amendment, Section 1. ". . . No state shall make or enforce any law which shall abridge the privileges or immunities of citizens of the United States, nor shall any State deprive any person of life, liberty, or property without due process of law; nor deny any person within its jurisdiction the equal protection of the laws."

Government in the United States is organized at three levels roughly defined by geographic scope:

- Federal
- State
- Local

A single **federal government** oversees the entire United States and its territories. The vast majority of laws that influence compensation were established at the federal level. Next, individual **state governments** enact and enforce laws that pertain exclusively to their respective regions, for example, Illinois and Michigan. Finally, **local governments** enact and enforce laws that are most pertinent to smaller geographic regions, for example, Champaign County in Illinois and the city of Los Angeles. Many of the federal laws have counterparts in state and local legislation. State and local legislation may be concurrent with federal law or may exist in the absence of similar federal legislation. Federal law prevails wherever state or local laws are inconsistent with federal legislation.

The federal government has three branches:

- Legislative branch
- Executive branch
- Judicial branch

Congress creates and passes laws within the **legislative branch**. The **executive branch** enforces the laws of various quasi-legislative and judicial agencies.The president of the United States possesses the authority to establish **executive orders** that influence the operation of the federal government and companies that are engaged in business relationships with the federal government. The **judicial branch** is responsible for interpreting the laws. The U.S. Supreme Court, which consists of nine life-appointed justices, is the forum for these interpretations.

Federal laws that apply to compensation practices are grouped according to key themes:

- Income continuity, safety, and work hours
- Pay discrimination
- Accommodating disabilities and family needs
- Prevailing wage laws

Income Continuity, Safety, and Work Hours

Three factors led to the passage of income continuity, safety, and work hours legislation. First was the **Great Depression**, the move from family businesses to large factories, and divisions of labor within factories. During the Great Depression, which took place in the 1930s, scores of businesses failed, and many workers became chronically unemployed. Government enacted key legislation designed to stabilize the income of an individual who became unemployed because of poor business conditions or workplace injuries. The **Social Security Act of 1935 (Title IX)** provided temporary income to workers who became unemployed through no fault of their own. **Workers' compensation** programs granted income to workers who were unable to work because of injuries sustained on the job. Supporting workers during these misfortunes promoted the well-being of the economy: These income provisions enabled the unemployed to participate in the economy as consumers of essential goods and services. We will defer a more detailed discussion of the Social Security Act of 1935 and workers' compensation laws until Chapter 10 because these laws represent legally required employee benefits.

Second, the main U.S. economic activity prior to the 20th century was agriculture and small family businesses that were organized along craft lines. Workers began to move from their farms and small family businesses to capitalists' factories for employment. The character of work changed dramatically with the move of workers to factories. An individual's status changed from owner to employee. This status change meant that individuals lost control over their earnings and working conditions.

Third, the factory system also created divisions of labor characterized by differences in skills and responsibilities. Some workers received training while others did not, which contributed greatly to differences in skills and responsibilities. Workers with higher skills and responsibilities did not necessarily earn higher wages than workers with fewer skills and responsibilities. Paying some workers more than others only increased costs, which factory owners avoided whenever possible.

In sum, factory workers received very low wages, and the working conditions were often unsafe. Factory workers received low wages and worked in unsafe conditions because factory owners sought to maximize profits. Offering workers high wages and providing safe working conditions would have cut into factory owners' profits. These conditions led to the passage of the **Fair Labor Standards Act of 1938 (FLSA)**. The FLSA addresses major abuses that intensified during the Great Depression and the transition from agricultural to industrial enterprises. These include substandard pay, excessive work hours, and the employment of children in oppressive working conditions.

Fair Labor Standards Act of 1938

The FLSA addresses three broad issues:

- Minimum wage
- Overtime pay
- Child labor provisions

The U.S. Department of Labor enforces the FLSA.

Minimum Wage

The purpose of the minimum wage provision is to ensure a minimally acceptable standard of living for workers. The original minimum wage was 25¢ per hour. Since the act's passage in 1938, the federal government has raised the minimum wage several times. The most recent minimum wage increase, to $5.15 per hour, was signed into law in August of 1996. The change from 25¢ per hour to $5.15 per hour represents a 1,960 percent minimum wage increase! Unfortunately, most minimum wage earners struggle to sustain a minimally acceptable standard of living because the costs of goods and services have increased at a much greater rate (see the "Stretching the Dollar" feature in Chapter 8).

Specific FLSA exemptions permit employers to pay some workers less than the minimum wage. Students employed in retail or service businesses, on farms, or in institutions of higher education may be paid less than the minimum wage with the consent of the Department of Labor. With explicit permission from the Department of Labor, employers can pay less than the minimum wage for trainee positions or to prevent a reduction in the employment of mentally or physically disabled individuals. Table 3-1 lists the six factors that define trainees.

Overtime Provisions

The FLSA requires employers to pay workers at a rate equal to time and one-half for all hours worked in excess of 40 hours within a 7-day period. For example, a worker's regular hourly rate is $10 for working 40 hours or less within a 7-day period. The FLSA requires the employer to pay this employee $15 per hour for each additional hour worked beyond the regular 40 hours within this 7-day period.

There are some general exceptions to this rule: Negotiated overtime pay rates contained within collective bargaining agreements prevail over the one and one-half time rule. In health care facilities, a base work period is 80 hours during 14 consecutive days rather than 40 hours during 7 consecutive days. Workers in health facilities receive overtime base pay for each hour worked over 80 within a 14-day period.

The overtime provisions and basic exceptions are based on employees' working set hours during fixed work periods. However, many employees work irregular hours that fluctuate from week to week (Chapter 14). A Supreme Court ruling (***Walling v. A. H. Belo Corp.***) [7] requires employers to guarantee fixed weekly pay when the following conditions prevail:

- The employer typically cannot determine the number of hours employees will work each week, and
- The workweek period fluctuates both above and below 40 hours per week.

TABLE 3-1 Six Defining Factors of a Trainee for the FLSA

- The training, even though it includes actual operation of the employers' facilities, is similar to that which would be provided in a vocational school.
- The training is for the benefit of the trainee.
- The trainee does not displace regular employees but works under closer supervision.
- The employer providing the training gains no immediate advantage from the trainees' activities; on occasion, the employer's operation may in fact be hindered.
- The trainee is not guaranteed a job at the completion of the training.
- The employer and the trainee understand that the employer is not obligated to pay wages during the training period.

Source: J. E. Kalet, *Primer on wage and hour laws* (Washington, DC: Bureau of National Affairs, 1987).

Overtime work becomes necessary when employees cannot meet higher than normal workloads during the standard workweek. Oftentimes, overtime pay is typically more cost effective than hiring additional permanent employees: Companies pay a fixed amount to provide employees' fringe benefits. In other words, benefits costs generally do not increase with the number of hours worked. Overtime practices increase wage costs. However, hiring additional permanent workers leads to higher total wage and fixed fringe benefits costs. Awarding existing employees overtime pay also is less expensive than hiring temporary workers. Temporary workers may be less productive in the short run because they are not familiar with specific company work procedures.

The overtime provision does not apply to all jobs. Generally, administrative, professional, and executive employees are **exempt** from the FLSA overtime and minimum wage provisions. Table 3-2 describes criteria that exempt executive, administrative, and professional jobs from this act. Most other jobs are **nonexempt**. Nonexempt jobs are subject to the FLSA overtime pay provision.

Classifying jobs as either exempt or nonexempt is not always clear-cut. In ***Aaron v. City of Wichita, Kansas*** [8], the city contended that its fire chiefs were exempt as executives under the FLSA because they spent more than 80 percent of their work hours managing the fire department. The fire chiefs maintained that they should not be exempt from the FLSA because they did not possess the authority to hire, fire, authorize shift trades, give pay raises, or make policy decisions. The court offered several criteria to determine whether these fire chiefs were exempt employees, including:

- Relative importance of management as opposed to other duties
- Frequency with which they exercised discretionary powers
- Relative freedom from supervision
- Relationship between their salaries and wages paid to other employees for similar nonexempt work

TABLE 3-2 FLSA Exemption Criteria for Executive, Administrative, and Professional Employees

Executive Employees

- Primary duties include managing the organization
- Regularly supervise the work of two or more full-time employees
- Authority to hire, promote, and discharge employees
- Regularly use discretion as part of typical work duties
- Devote at least 80 percent of work time to fulfilling the previous activities

Administrative Employees

- Perform nonmanual work directly related to management operations
- Regularly use discretion beyond clerical duties
- Perform specialized or technical work, or perform special assignments with only general supervision
- Devote at least 80 percent of work time to fulfilling the previous activities

Professional Employees

- Primary work requires advanced knowledge in a field of science or learning, including work that requires regular use of discretion and independent judgment, or
- Primary work requires inventiveness, imagination, or talent in a recognized field or artistic endeavor

Source: 29 Code of Federal Regulations, Sec. 541.3. 29; Sec. 541.1.

Based on these criteria, the court determined that the City of Wichita improperly exempted fire chiefs from the FLSA overtime pay provisions.

The federal government broadened the scope of the FLSA twice since 1938 through the passage of two acts:

- Portal-to-Portal Act of 1947
- Equal Pay Act of 1963

The **Portal-to-Portal Act of 1947** defines the term "hours worked" that appears in the FLSA. Table 3-3 lists the compensable activities that precede and follow the primary work activities. For example, time spent by state correctional officers caring for police dogs at home is compensable under the FLSA (***Andres v. DuBois***) [9]. The care of dogs, including feeding, grooming, and walking, is indispensable to maintaining dogs as a critical law enforcement tool, it is part of officers' principal activities, and it benefits the corrections department. However, this court ruled that time spent by state correction canine handlers transporting dogs between home and correctional facilities is not compensable under FLSA.

The **Equal Pay Act of 1963** prohibits sex discrimination in pay for employees performing equal work. We will discuss the Equal Pay Act of 1963 later in this chapter.

Child Labor Provisions

The FLSA child labor provisions protect children from being overworked, working in potentially hazardous settings, and having their education jeopardized due to excessive work hours. The restrictions vary by age:

- Children under age 14 usually cannot be employed.
- Children ages 14 and 15 may work in safe occupations outside school hours if their work does not exceed 3 hours on a school day (18 hours per week while school is in session). When school is not in session, as in the summer, children cannot work more than 40 hours per week.
- Children ages 16 and 17 do not have hourly restrictions; however, they cannot work in hazardous jobs—for example, the use of heavy industrial equipment or exposure to harmful substances.

Work Hours and Safety Standards Act of 1962

Coverage extends to all laborers and mechanics who are employed by contractors who meet the following criterion: Federal loans or grants fund part or all the contracts. The act requires that contractors pay employees one and one-half times their regular hourly rate for each hour worked in excess of 40 hours per week.

TABLE 3-3 Compensable Activities That Precede and Follow Primary Work Activities

- The time spent on the activity was for the employee's benefit.
- The employer controlled the amount of time spent.
- The time involved is categorized as "suffered and permitted," meaning that the employer knew the employee was working on incidental tasks either before or after the scheduled tour of duty.
- The time spent was requested by the employer.
- The time spent is an integral part of the employee's principal duties.
- The employer has a union contract with employees providing such compensation, or, as a matter of custom or practice, the employer has compensated the activities in the past.

McNamara-O'Hara Service Contract Act of 1965

The **McNamara-O'Hara Service Contract Act of 1965** applies to all contractors who employ service workers. The term *contractor* refers to companies doing business with the United States. For this act, service employees work in recognized trades or crafts other than skilled mechanical or manual jobs. Plumbers and electricians are recognized trades workers. The act contains two main provisions. First, all contractors must pay at least the minimum wage as specified in the FLSA. Second, contractors holding contracts with the federal government that exceed $2,500 in value must pay the local prevailing wages. In addition, contractors must offer fringe compensation equal to the local prevailing benefits.

Pay Discrimination

The civil rights movement of the 1960s led to the passage of key legislation designed to protect designated classes of employees and to uphold their rights individually against discriminatory employment decisions. Some of these laws such as the **Civil Rights Act of 1964** apply to all employment-related decisions (recruitment, selection, performance appraisal, compensation, and termination). Other laws such as the Equal Pay Act of 1963 apply specifically to compensation practices. These laws limit employers' authority over employment decisions.

Equal Pay Act of 1963

Congress enacted the Equal Pay Act of 1963 to remedy a serious problem of employment discrimination in private industry: "Many segments of American industry [have] been based on an ancient but outmoded belief that a man, because of his role in society, should be paid more than a woman even though his duties are the same" [10]. The Equal Pay Act of 1963 is based on a simple principle. Men and women should receive equal pay for performing equal work.

The Equal Employment Opportunity Commission (EEOC) enforces the Equal Pay Act of 1963. The EEOC possesses the authority to investigate and reconcile charges of illegal discrimination. The act applies to all employers and labor organizations. In particular,

> "No employer . . . shall discriminate within any establishment in which such employees are employed, between employees on the basis of sex by paying wages to employees in such establishment at a rate less than the rate at which he pays wages to employees of the opposite sex . . . for equal work on jobs the performance of which requires equal skill, effort, and responsibility, and which are performed under similar working conditions. . . ." (29 USC 206, Section 6, paragraph (d))

The Equal Pay Act of 1963 pertains explicitly to jobs of equal worth. Companies assign pay rates to jobs according to the skill, effort, responsibility, and working conditions required. Skill, effort, responsibility, and working conditions represent **compensable factors**. The U.S. Department of Labor's definitions of these compensable factors are listed in Table 3-4.

How do we judge whether jobs are equal? The case ***EEOC v. Madison Community Unit School District No. 12*** [11] sheds light on this important issue. The

TABLE 3-4 U.S. Department of Labor Definitions of Compensable Factors

Factor	***Definition***
Skill	Experience, training, education, and ability as measured by the performance requirements of a job
Effort	The amount of mental or physical effort expended in the performance of a job
Responsibility	The degree of accountability required in the performance of a job
Working conditions	The physical surroundings and hazards of a job, including dimensions such as inside versus outside work, heat, cold, and poor ventilation

Source: U.S. Department of Labor, *Equal pay for equal work under the Fair Labor Standards Act* (Washington, D.C.: U.S. Government Printing Office, December 31, 1971).

school district paid female athletic coaches of girls' sports teams less than it paid male athletic coaches of boys' teams. The judge concluded:

> The jobs that are compared must be in some sense the same to count as "equal work" under the Equal Pay Act of 1963; and here we come to the main difficulty in applying the Act; whether two jobs are the same depends on how fine a system of job classification the courts will accept. If coaching an athletic team in the Madison, Illinois, school system is considered a single job rather than a [collection] of jobs, the school district violated the Equal Pay Act prima facie by paying female holders of this job less than male holders. . . . If on the other hand coaching the girls' tennis team is considered a different job from coaching the boys' tennis team, and if coaching the girls' volleyball or basketball team is considered a different job (or jobs) from coaching the boys' soccer team, there is no prima facie violation. So the question is how narrow a definition of *job* the courts should be using in deciding whether the Equal Pay Act is applicable. We can get some guidance from the language of the Act. The act requires that the jobs compared have "similar working conditions," not the same working conditions. This implies that some comparison of different jobs is possible . . . since the working conditions need not be "equal," the jobs need not be completely identical. . . . Above the lowest rank of employee, every employee has a somewhat different job from every other one, even if the two employees being compared are in the same department. So, if "equal work" and "equal skill, effort, and responsibility" were taken literally, the Act would have a minute domain. . . .

The courts have thus had to steer a narrow course. The cases do not require an absolute identity between the jobs, but do require substantial identity.

Pay differentials for equal work are not always illegal. Pay differentials between men and women who are performing equal work are acceptable where:

> . . . such payment is made pursuant to (i) a seniority system; (ii) merit system, (iii) a system which measures earnings by quantity or quality of production; or (iv) a differential based on any other factor other than sex: Provided, that an employer who is paying a wage rate differential . . . shall not . . . reduce the wage rate of any employee. (29 USC 206, Section 6, paragraph (d))

As an aside, comparable worth is an ongoing debate in American society that differs from the issues addressed in the Equal Pay Act of 1963. The debate centers on the pervasive pay differentials between men and women who perform comparable, but not equal, work [12]. In a nutshell, jobs held predominantly by women are paid at substantially lower rates than jobs held predominantly by men that require comparable skill, effort, responsibility, and working conditions. Researchers have compared female-dominated jobs to male-dominated jobs, for example:

- Nurses to tree trimmers
- Clerical workers to parking lot attendants
- Clerk typists to delivery van drivers

These comparisons show that the jobs require comparable skill, effort, responsibility, and working conditions. However, the female-dominated jobs received substantially lower compensation, on average, than male-dominated jobs. **Comparable worth** advocates maintain that employers should pay employees holding predominantly female jobs the same as employees holding predominantly male jobs if these jobs require comparable skills, effort, responsibility, and working conditions.

Civil Rights Act of 1964

The Civil Rights Act of 1964 is a comprehensive piece of legislation. **Title VII** of the Civil Rights Act is the most pertinent to compensation. Legislators designed Title VII to promote equal employment opportunities for underrepresented minorities. According to Title VII:

> It shall be an unlawful employment practice for an employer—(1) to fail or refuse to hire or to discharge any individual, or otherwise to discriminate against any individual with respect to his compensation, terms, conditions, or privileges of employment, because of such individual's race, color, religion, sex, or national origin; or (2) to limit, segregate, or classify his employees or applicants for employment in any way which would deprive or tend to deprive any individual of employment opportunities or otherwise adversely affect his status as an employee, because of such individual's race, color, religion, sex, or national origin. (42 USC 2000e-2, Section 703)

The courts have distinguished between two types of discrimination covered by Title VII—disparate treatment and disparate impact. **Disparate treatment** represents intentional discrimination, occurring whenever employers intentionally treat some workers less favorably than others because of their race, color, sex, national origin, or religion. Applying different standards to determine pay increases for blacks and whites may result in disparate treatment. For example, awarding pay increases to blacks according to seniority and to whites based on performance may lead to disparate treatment, particularly if blacks have significantly less seniority than whites.

Disparate impact represents unintentional discrimination. It occurs whenever an employer applies an employment practice to all employees, but the practice leads to unequal treatment of protected employee groups. Awarding pay increases to male and female production workers according to seniority could lead to disparate impact if females had less seniority, on average, than men.

Title VII applies to companies with 15 or more employees, employment agencies, and labor unions. Title VII excludes employees of the U.S. government. The EEOC enforces the Civil Rights Act.

Bennett Amendment

This provision is an amendment to Title VII. The **Bennett Amendment** allows employees to charge employers with Title VII violations regarding pay only when the employer has violated the Equal Pay Act of 1963. The Bennett Amendment is necessary because lawmakers could not agree on the answers to the following questions:

- Does Title VII incorporate both the Equal Pay Act of 1963's equal pay standard and the four defenses for unequal work [(i) a seniority system; (ii) merit system, (iii) a system which measures earnings by quantity or quality of production; or (iv) a differential based on any other factor other than sex]?
- Does Title VII include only the four exceptions to the Equal Pay Act of 1963 standard?

Some lawmakers believed that Title VII incorporates the equal pay standard (that is, answering yes to the first question and no to the second question). However, other lawmakers believed that Title VII did not incorporate the equal pay standard (that is, answering no to the first question and yes to the second question). If Title VII did not incorporate the equal pay standard, then employees could raise charges of illegal discrimination (on the basis of race, religion, color, sex, or national origin) for unequal jobs.

Executive Order 11246

This executive order extends Title VII standards to contractors holding government contracts worth more than $10,000 per year. In addition, **Executive Order 11246** imposes additional requirements on contractors with government contracts worth more than $50,000 per year and 50 or more employees. These contractors must develop written plans each year—**affirmative action** plans. Contractors specify in affirmative action plans goals and practices that they will use to avoid or reduce Title VII discrimination over time.

Age Discrimination in Employment Act of 1967 (as Amended in 1978, 1986, 1990)

Congress passed the **Age Discrimination in Employment Act of 1967** (**ADEA**) to protect workers age 40 and older from illegal discrimination. This act provides protection to a large segment of the U.S. population known as the **baby boom generation** or "baby boomers." The baby boom generation was born roughly between 1946 and 1964, representing a swell in the American population. Some members of the baby boom generation reached age 40 in 1986. By the year 2004, all members of the baby boom era will be at least age 40, accounting for approximately 150 million people [13].

A large segment of the population will probably continue to work beyond age 65, the "traditional" retirement age, because many fear that Social Security retirement income (Chapter 10) will not provide adequate support. The U.S. Census Bureau predicts that individuals aged 65 and over will increase from about 25 million in 2001 (12.4 percent of the population) to about 77 million (20.3 percent of the population) by 2050. [14] Thus, the ADEA should be extremely relevant for some time to come.

The ADEA established guidelines prohibiting age-related discrimination in employment. Its purpose is "to promote the employment of older persons based on their ability rather than age, to prohibit arbitrary age discrimination in employment, and to help employers and workers find ways of meeting problems arising from the impact of age on employment." The ADEA specifies that it is unlawful for an employer:

> (1) to fail or refuse to hire or to discharge any individual or otherwise discriminate against any individual with respect to his compensation, terms, conditions, or privileges of employment, because of such individual's age; (2) to limit, segregate or classify his employees in any way which would deprive or tend to deprive any individual of employment opportunities or otherwise adversely affect his status as an employee, because of such individual's age; or (3) to reduce the wage rate of any employee in order to comply with this act. (29 USC 623, Section 4)

The ADEA applies to employee benefits practices as well:

> . . . any employer must provide that any employee aged 65 or older, and any employee's spouse aged 65 or older, shall be entitled to coverage under any group health plan offered to such employees under the same conditions as any employee, and the spouse of such employee, under age 65. (29 USC 623, Section 4, paragraph (g)(1))

The ADEA also sets limits on the development and implementation of employers' "early retirement" practices, which many companies use to reduce workforce sizes. Most early retirement programs are offered to employees who are at least 55 years of age. These early retirement programs are permissible when companies offer them to employees on a voluntary basis. Forcing early retirement upon older workers represents age discrimination (***EEOC v. Chrysler***) [15].

The **Older Workers Benefit Protection Act (OWBPA)**—the 1990 amendment to the ADEA—placed additional restrictions on employers' benefits practices. Under particular circumstances, employers can require older employees to pay more for health care insurance coverage than younger employees. This practice is permissible when older workers collectively do not make proportionately larger contributions than the younger workers [16]. Moreover, employers can legally reduce older workers' life insurance coverage only if the costs for providing insurance to them is significantly greater than the cost for younger workers. Further, the OWBPA enacts the **equal benefit or equal cost principle**: Employers must offer benefits to older workers that are equal to or more than the benefits given to younger workers with one exception. The OWBPA does not require employers to provide equal or more benefits to older workers when the costs to do so are greater than for younger workers.

The ADEA covers private employers with 20 or more employees, labor unions with 25 or more members, and employment agencies. The EEOC enforces this act.

Executive Order 11141

This executive order extends ADEA coverage to federal contractors.

Civil Rights Act of 1991

Congress enacted the **Civil Rights Act of 1991** to overturn several Supreme Court rulings. Perhaps most noteworthy is the reversal of ***Atonio v. Wards Cove Packing Co.*** [17]. The Supreme Court ruled that plaintiffs (employees) must indicate which employment practice created disparate impact and demonstrate how the employment practice created disparate impact. Since the passage of the Civil Rights Act of 1991, employers must show that the challenged employment practice is a business necessity. Thus, the Civil Rights Act of 1991 shifted the burden of proof from employees to employers.

FLIP SIDE OF THE COIN

UPDATE: WOMEN STILL HITTING AN IMPENETRABLE GLASS CEILING DESPITE AFFIRMATIVE ACTION AND THE GLASS CEILING COMMISSION

BACKGROUND

The purpose of affirmative action is to promote the employment of individuals who are protected under the Civil Rights Act of 1964. Many companies began using affirmative action plans nearly 40 years ago. Although great strides have been made in promoting the employment of women and underrepresented minorities, affirmative action has not benefited everyone. In 1991, the **Glass Ceiling Act** was included under **Title II** of the Civil Rights Act of 1991. The term ***glass ceiling*** describes the artificial barriers that prevent qualified women and minority men from reaching their full career potentials in the private sector. Ultimately, the main focus was on the status of women. The Glass Ceiling Act established the Glass Ceiling Commission, a 21-member bipartisan body appointed by President George Bush (U.S. president between 1989 and 1993) and Congressional leaders and chaired by the secretary of labor. The committee conducted a study of opportunities for, and artificial barriers to, the advancement of minority men and all women into management and decision-making positions in U.S. businesses. The Glass Ceiling Commission completed its deliberations in 1995 with a finding that three artificial barriers continue to limit the advancement of minorities and women: societal barriers that may be outside the direct control of business, internal structural barriers within the direct control of business, and governmental barriers.

UPDATE

A recent study by the U.S. General Accounting Office (GAO) reviewed the status of women in management in positions in ten selected industries.* The GAO compiled data from the Current Population Survey (CPS) to determine how women in management were faring in 2000 compared with 1995 and to further understand the continuing impact of the glass ceiling on women's advancement to the top.

Despite a sense of continued progress toward gender equality in the workplace, in ten industries employing 71 percent of U.S. women workers and 73 percent of U.S. women managers, the data show that women managers continue to lag behind their male counterparts in both advancement and pay.

Perhaps even more startling, the data show that in seven of the ten industries the wage gap between male and female managers actually widened between 1995 and 2000. In other words, the majority of women managers actually did better, relative to men, in 1995 than they did in 2000. Occurring as it did during a time of economic prosperity, this increased wage gap is particularly troubling.

The GAO study also shows that women continue to be underrepresented in management. In only five of the ten industries reviewed do women hold a share of management jobs proportionate to their share of the industry workforce. Thus, women's record presence in the workforce is not matched by their presence in the more influential and economically advantageous positions.

*U.S. Government Accounting Office. (2001). Women in management: Analysis of selected data from the Current Population Survey (GAO-02-156). Washington, DC: Author.

Source: Federal Glass Ceiling Commission, *Good for business: Making full use of the nation's human capital* (Washington, DC: U.S. Government Printing Office, March, 1995).

Two additional sections of the Civil Rights Act of 1991 apply to compensation practice. The first feature pertains to seniority systems. As we discuss in Chapter 4, public sector employers make employment decisions based on employees' seniority. For example, public sector employers award more vacation days to employees with higher seniority than to employees with lower seniority. The Civil Rights Act of 1991 overturns the Supreme Court's decision in ***Lorance v. AT&T Technologies*** [18], which allowed employees to challenge the use of seniority systems only within 180 days from the system's implementation date. Now, employees may file suits claiming discrimination either when the system is implemented or whenever the system negatively affects them.

A second development addresses the geographic scope of federal job discrimination. Prior to the Civil Rights Act of 1991, the U.S. Supreme Court (***Boureslan v. Aramco***) [19] ruled that federal job discrimination laws do not apply to U.S. citizens working for U.S. companies in foreign countries. Since the act's passage, U.S. citizens working overseas may file suit against U.S. businesses for discriminatory employment practices.

The Civil Rights Act of 1991 provides coverage to the same groups protected under the Civil Rights Act of 1964. The 1991 act also extends coverage to Senate employees and political appointees of the federal government's executive branch. The EEOC enforces the Civil Rights Act of 1991. Since the passage of the 1991 act, the EEOC helps employers avoid discriminatory employment practices through the Technical Assistance Training Institute.

Accommodating Disabilities and Family Needs

Congress enacted the Pregnancy Discrimination Act of 1978, the Americans with Disabilities Act of 1990, and the Family and Medical Leave Act of 1993 to accommodate employees with disabilities and pressing family needs. These laws protect a significant number of employees: In 2000, approximately 68 percent of employed women were responsible for children under the age of 18 [20]. The preamble to the Americans with Disabilities Act states that it covers 43 million Americans. Many employees will benefit from the Family and Medical Leave Act if they need substantial time away from work to care for newborns or elderly family members. Two trends explain this need. First, many elderly and seriously ill parents of the employed baby boom generation depend on their children. Second, both husbands and wives work full-time jobs now more than ever before, necessitating extended leave to care for newborns or for children who become ill.

Pregnancy Discrimination Act of 1978

The **Pregnancy Discrimination Act of 1978** (**PDA**) is an amendment to Title VII of the Civil Rights Act of 1964. The PDA prohibits disparate impact discrimination against pregnant women for all employment practices. Employers must not treat pregnancy less favorably than other medical conditions covered under employee benefits plans. In addition, employers must treat pregnancy and childbirth the same way they treat other causes of disability. Further, the PDA protects the rights of women who take leave for pregnancy-related reasons. The protected rights include:

- Credit for previous service
- Accrued retirement benefits
- Accumulated seniority

Americans with Disabilities Act of 1990

The **Americans with Disabilities Act of 1990** (**ADA**) prohibits discrimination against individuals with mental or physical disabilities within and outside employment settings, including public services and transportation, public accommodations, and employment. It applies to all employers with 15 or more employees, and the EEOC is the enforcement agency. In employment contexts, the ADA:

> . . . prohibits covered employers from discriminating against a "qualified individual with a disability" in regard to job applications, hiring, advancement, discharge, compensation, training or other terms, conditions, or privileges of employment. Employers are required to make "reasonable accommodations" to the known physical or mental limitations of an otherwise qualified individual with a disability unless to do so would impose an "undue hardship." [21]

Title I of the ADA requires that employers provide "reasonable accommodation" to disabled employees. Reasonable accommodation may include such efforts as making existing facilities readily accessible, job restructuring, and modifying work schedules. Every "qualified individual with a disability" is entitled to reasonable accommodation. A qualified individual with a disability, however, must be able to perform the "essential functions" of the job in question. Essential functions are those job duties that are critical to the job.

Let's apply these principles to an example. Producing printed memoranda is a key activity of a clerical worker's job. Most employees manually keyboard the information by using a word processing program to generate written text. In this case, the essential function is producing memoranda using word processing software. However, manual input represents only one method to enter information. Information input based on a voice recognition input device is an alternative method for entering information. If a clerk develops crippling arthritis, the ADA may require that the employer make reasonable accommodation by providing him with a voice-recognition input device.

Family and Medical Leave Act of 1993

The **Family and Medical Leave Act of 1993 (FMLA)** aimed to provide employees with job protection in cases of family or medical emergency. The basic thrust of the act is guaranteed leave, and a key element of that guarantee is the right of the employee to return either to the position he or she left when the leave began or to an equivalent position with the same benefits, pay, and other terms and conditions of employment. We will discuss this act in greater detail in Chapter 10 because compensation professionals treat such leave as a legally required benefit.

Prevailing Wage Laws

Davis-Bacon Act of 1931

The **Davis-Bacon Act of 1931** establishes employment standards for construction contractors holding federal government contracts valued at more than $2,000. Covered contracts include highway building, dredging, demolition, and cleaning, as well as painting and decorating public buildings. This act applies to laborers and mechanics who are employed on-site. Contractors must pay wages at least equal to the prevailing wage in the local area. The U.S. Secretary of Labor determines prevailing wage rates based on compensation surveys of different areas. In this context, "local" area refers to the general location where work is performed. Cities and counties represent local areas. The "prevailing wage" is the typical hourly wage paid to more than 50 percent of all laborers and mechanics employed in the local area. The

STRETCHING THE DOLLAR

AVOIDING ADA LAWSUITS WHILE "DOING THE RIGHT THING"

Intervene early and intervene often. The wisdom of this principle was borne out once again by the recent Supreme Court Opinion, *Chevron U.S.A. Inc., Petitioner v. Mario Echazabal*. Chevron did intervene early and often. This case contrasts nicely to an earlier Supreme Court case, *Toyota Motor Manufacturing, Kentucky, Inc. v. Williams*. While both cases involved litigation and court appeals, the Chevron case benefited from clearly documented, direct communication with the worker, while the Toyota case involved a period in which communication broke down as disability concerns (in the employee) increased. In contrast to both cases, it is easy to see that the best cases are those that are resolved apart from litigation, as in a representative instance of a large corporation's dealings with an employee suffering from carpal tunnel syndrome.

No matter the legal defense a corporation may be able to garner, nothing substitutes for vigilance in establishing clear-cut health guidelines for job requirements and carefully managing employees in the event they encounter disabling conditions. Companies that prevent litigation always win, more so than companies that go to court and are exonerated. And, of course, the business losses only increase when the final court decision sides against the employer, a situation that is common but not within the scope of this article. In all disability claims, strategic intervention should be implemented for many reasons—the welfare of the employee, the productivity of the company and the desire to avoid litigation.

CHEVRON V. ECHAZABAL

The legal contention of this recent ruling (June 10, 2002) springs from a "regulation of the Equal Employment Opportunity Commission [that] authorizes refusal to hire an individual because his performance on the job would endanger his own health, owing to a disability." Chevron refused to hire Echazabal on this ground, claiming that because of Echazabal's liver condition, "the job would endanger his own health." Echazabal, however, preferred to take the risk and took Chevron to court on the grounds that the Americans with Disabilities Act of 1990 does not permit such a regulation, in as much as it discriminates against those with a "disability."

Chevron ultimately presented the case to the Supreme Court, which concluded that the ADA does permit such a regulation. Although the final Opinion does not state the matter in these words, Chevron had been put into an impossible situation: asked at once to protect the health of its employees under OSHA regulations and, at the same time, challenged under the ADA for refusing employment to a high-risk candidate.

One element of the case that probably motivated Echazabal and made his case tenable was the fact that he already had worked in the Chevron plant for about 20 years (through an independent contractor). From his point of view, he simply wanted to continue being at risk, but with the increased security and benefits that would come through direct employment under Chevron.

From Chevron's point of view, they were following standard operating procedures by subjecting him to a medical examination before hire. He was examined twice, diagnosed with hepatitis C, and was refused the job on the grounds that the chemical levels could seriously damage his liver and eventually kill him (chemical levels that met OSHA safety levels for healthy individuals). The second time Echazabal was diagnosed, Chevron requested that the independent contractor either remove Echazabal from the Chevron site or find him a position that protected him from contact with the chemicals.

It was that level of vigilance that allowed Chevron to convincingly claim it was working in Echazabal's best medical interests. Far from applying medical diagnoses as an afterthought, Chevron applied them proactively and acted upon them responsibly. The Supreme Court's interest was not, of course, in determining the validity of the medical diagnoses, but in examining the compatibility of the Equal Employment

(Continued)

(Continued)

Opportunity Commission (EEOC) regulation with the ADA. However, if Chevron had examined Echazabal reactively instead of proactively, the tenor of their argument would have contrasted negatively with their implied argument that the EEOC regulation is ethically consistent with the ADA.

TOYOTA V. WILLIAMS: INEFFICIENT INTERVENTION

This Supreme Court case, like *Chevron v. Echazabal*, was decided in favor of the employer, although the interactions between Toyota and Williams were not as clear as those between Chevron and Echazabal. While this ruling has established a narrower definition of "disability" in terms of the ADA, it came only after a series of previous settlements and appeals.

This decision (Jan. 8, 2002) limited the breadth of the term "disability" when applied to the ADA. The Supreme Court opinion assured employers that the ADA is applicable only to cases in which one's daily life and work life are severely impaired by a disability, not to cases in which specific job functions extend beyond a worker's physical or psychological capacity. The ruling determined that, while an individual may be limited in certain abilities, such a limitation does not constitute being disabled in the individual's daily life.

In the case of Emma Williams, it was unanimously acknowledged that she experienced physical conditions that prevented her from performing certain types of work. The in-house medical staff diagnosed her with bilateral carpal tunnel syndrome and bilateral tendonitis, and prescribed modified work conditions. Between 1990 and 1993, she was given modified duties, found them insufficient, filed two legal actions and obtained a settlement for both. She then was given a job that primarily consisted of paint inspection and, for about two years, seemed to find the job amenable.

In 1996, this inspection job was broadened to include rubbing oil onto each car's paint surface to highlight possible flaws. Williams found the tasks impossible. At this point, the Supreme Court judgment suggests that the employer-employee relationship broke down, followed by confusion about which party was primarily responsible for a loss of communication. Toyota perceived that Williams was ignoring her employer by missing work; Williams thought that Toyota was ignoring her by not modifying her work. She stopped working in December 1996, was terminated by letter in January 1997, and began a series of legal actions.

The relationship breakdown between employer and employee is suggested by the court record that "the parties disagree about what happened next," and it touches a common theme in case management: When documentation is most needed for future determinations, it is most difficult to obtain. At the time this breakdown occurred between Toyota and Williams, there may have been an opportunity for mediation that may have precluded the next seven years of litigation. We cannot know that, but we can pinpoint that phase as a critical one that may have determined the course of the future. By the time the Supreme Court reviewed the case, the communication breakdown was history and what counted was the appropriateness of the suit to the protection offered by the ADA.

The Court ruled that someone may be disabled from performing a specific job, but not disabled according to the ADA. This legal distinction reminds us how easily the meaning of important terms may shift in our usage. The Social Security Disability Fund has its own definition of disability. Group disability insurance plan language may have another. If someone designates him- or herself as disabled, the overriding question must be "In relation to what?" The inherent vagaries of these definitions make it even more important for employers to communicate with precision.

DAVE: SUCCESSFUL CASE MANAGEMENT

Inevitably, disability claims will arise. The employer's response, however, can complicate or help resolve the situation.

Good case management intervention resolved the following disability case instead of allowing its potential for delays and litigation to take root. In this example, the employer had contracted a third-party case management company who assigned the case to a nurse case manager

(Nurse CM). Dave, like Emma Williams, also suffered from carpal tunnel syndrome and was plagued with severe physical pain and ambivalence toward his workplace.

The sequence of events is as follows:

- June 6, 2000: Dave informed the Nurse CM that he had pain extending from his back to his shoulders, as well as tingling in his fingers on both hands.
- June 7: He had an exam scheduled and planned on being back at work June 11, contingent on the results of the exam. In addition to his physical problems, he doubted the goodwill of the company and the company doubted Dave's commitment to his work.
- June 8: During this week, the Nurse CM contacted Dave's HR department, his attending physician, and Dave again.
- June 11: Dave was not back at work.
- June 14: Another exam confirmed carpal tunnel syndrome. In this case, the employee was ambivalent toward the workplace, but responsive to phone calls from the Nurse CM.
- June 15: Dave, clearly troubled, responded and worked closely with the Nurse CM to avoid unnecessary delays.
- June 19: Under the Nurse CM's influence, Dave moved up his next medical exam (originally June 25).
- June 7 through Aug. 31: Physician recommended disability duration.
- June 21: The Nurse CM intervened because there was insufficient medical documentation from Dave's treating physician to support and authorize a disability absence for this extended period of time to make the recommendation to his employer. Therefore, she approved a recovery period through July 5, and requested more clinical information.
- June 29: Surgery provides needed information, and the disability leave was extended through Aug. 9 to accommodate recovery from the surgical procedure and return to work.

Although this could have been a troublesome case, active case management produced a positive outcome for the employer and employee. The employee felt "heard," while the Nurse CM remained objective, consistently applied the benefit, and requested corroborative evidence to justify the physician's recommended disability period. Case management intervention reduced the absence duration by 22 days.

This case shows that successful case management should involve the following three ingredients:

- Frequent communication
- Good documentation
- An inclusive approach that blends together medical expertise with objectivity, employer policy and employee education.

Vigilance cannot be sacrificed to anyone's convenience because each party (including the employee and the physician) has eccentricities, because disabilities, such as carpal tunnel syndrome, can have highly varied effects on individuals, and because the loss in morale that logically accompanies a disability can further obstruct communication. Early and frequent intervention will reduce the likelihood of unnecessary loss, whether that loss registers in the loss of an individual's dignity, the company's bottom line or litigation costs.

Source: Presley Reed, M.D., *workspan*, August 2002, volume 45, number 8. © 2002 WorldatWork, 14040 N. Northsight Blvd., Scottsdale, AZ 85260 U.S.A.; 480/951-9191; Fax 480/483-8352; *www.worldatwork.org*; E-mail worldatwork@worldatwork.org

act also requires that contractors offer fringe benefits that are equal in scope and value to fringe compensation that prevails in the local area.

Walsh-Healey Public Contracts Act of 1936

This act covers contractors and manufacturers who sell supplies, materials, and equipment to the federal government. Its coverage is more extensive than in the Davis-Bacon Act. The **Walsh-Healey Public Contracts Act of 1936** applies to both construction and nonconstruction activities. Also, this act covers all of the contractors' employees except office, supervisory, custodial, and maintenance workers who do any work in preparation for the performance of the contract. The minimum contract amount that qualifies for coverage is $10,000 rather than the $2,000 amount under the Davis-Bacon Act of 1931.

The Walsh-Healey Act of 1936 mandates that contractors with federal contracts meet guidelines regarding wages and hours, child labor, convict labor, and hazardous working conditions. Contractors must observe the minimum wage and overtime provisions of the FLSA. In addition, this act prohibits the employment of individuals younger than 16, as well as convicted criminals. Further, this act prohibits contractors from exposing workers to any conditions that violate the **Occupational Safety and Health Act of 1970**. This act was passed to assure safe and healthful working conditions for working men and women by authorizing enforcement of the standards under the act.

CONTEXTUAL INFLUENCES ON THE FEDERAL GOVERNMENT AS AN EMPLOYER

As we discussed previously, federal government employees do not receive protection under Title VII, ADEA, and the Equal Pay Act of 1963. Shortly after the passage of these acts during the 1960s, the president of the United States and Congress enacted executive orders and laws to prohibit job discrimination and promote equal opportunity in the federal government. These executive orders and laws apply to employees who work within:

- Military service (civilian employees only)
- Executive agencies
- Postal service
- Library of Congress
- Judicial and legislative branches

Table 3-5 contains a summary of these key executive orders and laws. We already discussed the FMLA because it applies to private sector employers as well.

TABLE 3-5 Executive Orders and Laws Enacted to Protect Federal Government Employees

- **Executive Order 11478** prohibits employment discrimination on the basis of race, color, religion, sex, national origin, handicap, and age (401 *FEP Manual* 4061).
- **Executive Order 11935** prohibits employment of nonresidents in U.S. civil service jobs (401 *FEP Manual* 4121).
- The **Rehabilitation Act** mandates that federal government agencies take affirmative action in providing jobs for individuals with disabilities (401 *FEP Manual* 325).
- The **Vietnam Era Veterans Readjustment Assistance Act** applies the principles of the Rehabilitation Act to veterans with disabilities and veterans of the Vietnam War (401 *FEP Manual* 379).
- The **Government Employee Rights Act of 1991** protects U.S. Senate employees from employment discrimination on the basis of race, color, religion, sex, national origin, age, and disability (401 *FEP Manual* 851).
- The **Family and Medical Leave Act of 1993** grants civil service employees, U.S. Senate employees, and U.S. House of Representative employees a maximum of 12-weeks unpaid leave in any 12-month period to care for a newborn or a seriously ill family member (401 *FEP Manual* 891).

LABOR UNIONS AS CONTEXTUAL INFLUENCES

Since the passage of the **National Labor Relations Act of 1935 (NLRA)**, the federal government requires employers to enter into good-faith negotiations with workers over the terms of employment. Workers join unions to influence employment-related decisions, especially when they are dissatisfied with job security, wages, benefits, and supervisory practices.

Since the 1950s, the percentage of U.S. civilian workers in both the public and private sectors represented by unions declined steadily to a 14.8 percent representation rate in 2001 [22]. The unionization rate of government workers was 42 percent, compared with 9.8 percent among private sector employees in 2001. As we will discuss shortly, union representation will probably continue to decline in the future. This decline may be attributed to the reduced influence of unions. Later in this section, we will present reasons for this conclusion. Nevertheless, 14.8 percent of the U.S. civilian workforce stands for a large number of workers—approximately 20 million.

National Labor Relations Act of 1935

The purpose of this act was to remove barriers to free commerce and to restore equality of bargaining power between employees and employers. Employers denied workers the rights to bargain collectively with them on such issues as wages, work hours, and working conditions. Consequently, employees experienced poor working conditions, substandard wage rates, and excessive work hours. Section 1 of the NLRA declares the policy of the United States to protect commerce:

> . . . by encouraging the practice and procedure of collective bargaining and by protecting the exercise by workers of full freedom of association, self-organization, and designation of representatives of their own choosing for the purpose of negotiating the terms and conditions of employment. . . .

Sections 8(a)(5), 8(d), and 9(a) are key provisions of this act. Section 8(a)(5) provides that it is an unfair labor practice for an employer ". . . to refuse to bargain collectively with the representatives of his employees subject to the provisions of Section 9(a)."

Section 8(d) defines the phrase "to bargain collectively" as the "performance of the mutual obligation of the employer and the representative of the employees to meet at reasonable times and confer in good faith with respect to wages, hours, and other terms and conditions of employment. . . ."

Section 9(a) declares:

> Representatives designated or selected for the purposes of collective bargaining by the majority of employees in a unit appropriate for such purposes, shall be the exclusive representatives of all the employees in such unit for the purposes of collective bargaining in respect to rates of pay, wages, hours of employment, or other conditions of employment. . . .

The National Labor Relations Board (NLRB) oversees the enforcement of the NLRA. The president of the United States appoints members to the NLRB for 5-year terms.

Compensation Issues in Collective Bargaining

Union and management negotiations usually center on pay raises and fringe benefits [23]. Unions fought hard for general pay increases and regular cost-of-living adjustments (COLAs) [24]. COLAs represent automatic pay increases that are based on changes in prices, as indexed by the consumer price index (CPI). COLAs enable workers to maintain their standards of living by adjusting wages for inflation. Union leaders fought hard for these improvements to maintain the memberships' loyalty and support.

Unions generally secured high wages for their members through the early 1980s. In fact, it was not uncommon for union members to earn as much as 30 percent more than their nonunion counterparts. Unions also improved members' fringe compensation. Most noteworthy was the establishment of sound retirement income programs [25].

Unions' gains also influenced nonunion companies' compensation practices. Many nonunion companies offered similar compensation to their employees. This phenomenon is known as a **spillover effect**. Why? Management of nonunion firms generally offered higher wages and benefits to reduce the chance that employees would seek union representation [26].

Unions' influence has declined since the 1980s for three key reasons. First, union companies demonstrated consistently lower profits than nonunion companies [27]. As a result, management has been more reluctant to agree on large pay increases, which represent costs that lead to lower profits. Second, drastic employment cuts have taken place in various industries, including the highly unionized automobile and steel industries [28]. Technological advances and foreign competition have contributed to these declines. Automated work processes in both the automobile and steel industries made many workers' skills obsolete. Foreign competition dramatically reduced market share held by domestic automobile manufacturers and steel plants. Third, foreign automobile manufacturers produced higher-quality vehicles than U.S. automobile manufacturers. Although more expensive, U.S. consumers were willing to pay higher prices in exchange for better quality.

As a result of the changing business landscape, unions tempered their stance in negotiations with management. Many unions focused more heavily on promoting job security than securing large pay increases. This is known as **concessionary bargaining**. Available data indicates that annual negotiated pay raises declined steadily since 1980. During the 1980s, concessions were most prevalent in small companies, in high-wage companies, and in companies with a small percentage of employees covered by unions [29].

MARKET INFLUENCES

In competitive labor markets, companies attempt to attract and retain the best individuals for employment partly by offering lucrative wage and benefits packages. Unfortunately, some companies were unable to compete on the basis of wage and benefits as illustrated in the second opening quotation. Indeed, there are differences in wages across industries. These differences are known as **interindustry wage or compensation differentials**. Table 3-6 displays the average weekly earnings in various industries for selected years between 1980 and 2002. Construction and mining establishments paid the highest wages throughout this period; retail trade and service companies paid the lowest wages.

Interindustry wage differentials can be attributed to a number of factors, including the industry's product market, the degree of capital intensity, and the profitability of the industry [30]. Companies that operate in product markets where there is relatively little competition from other companies tend to pay higher wages because these companies exhibit substantial profits. This phenomenon can be attributed to such factors as

TABLE 3-6 Average Weekly Earnings by Industry Group, 1980 to April 2002

Industry	*1980*	*1985*	*1990*	*1995*	*1998*	*2002*
Mining	$397	$520	$603	$684	$744	$756
Construction	$368	$464	$526	$587	$643	$720
Manufacturing	$289	$386	$442	$515	$563	$620
Transportation, public utilities	$351	$450	$496	$557	$606	$659
Wholesale trade	$267	$351	$411	$476	$538	$616
Finance, insurance, real estate	$210	$289	$357	$442	$512	$586
Services	$191	$257	$319	$369	$420	$488
Retail trade	$147	$175	$194	$221	$255	$287

Source: U.S. Department of Commerce, *Statistical abstracts of the United States*. 121st ed. (Washington, D.C.: U.S. Government Printing Office, 2001) and U.S. Bureau of Labor Statistics.

higher barriers to entry into the product market and an insignificant influence of foreign competition. Government regulation and extremely expensive equipment represent entry barriers. The U.S. defense industry and the public utilities industry have high entry barriers and no threats from foreign competitors.

Capital intensity—the extent to which companies' operations are based on the use of large-scale equipment—also explains pay differentials between industries. The amount of average pay varies with the degree of capital intensity. On average, capital-intensive industries (for example, manufacturing) pay more than industries that are less capital intensive (service industries). Service industries are not capital intensive, and most have the reputation of paying low wages. The operation of service industries depends almost exclusively on employees with relatively common skills rather than on employees with specialized skills to operate physical equipment such as casting machines or robotics. Retail sales and the myriad "1-900" phone lines are just two examples of service businesses.

Finally, companies in profitable industries tend to pay higher compensation, on average, than companies in less profitable industries. Presumably, employees in profitable industries receive higher pay because their skills and abilities contribute to companies' success.

SUMMARY

This chapter provided a discussion of the various contextual influences on compensation practice. These include laws, labor unions, and market forces. These contextual influences pose significant challenges for compensation professionals. Aspiring compensation professionals must be familiar with the current contextual influences and anticipate impending ones. For example, most companies must adjust in order to accommodate workers with disabilities.

Key Terms

- federal constitution, 66
- federal government, 66
- state governments, 66
- local governments, 66
- legislative branch, 66
- executive branch, 66
- executive orders, 66
- judicial branch, 66
- Great Depression, 67
- Social Security Act of 1935 (Title IX), 67
- workers' compensation, 67
- Fair Labor Standards Act of 1938 (FLSA), 67
- *Walling v. A. H. Bello Corp.*, 68
- exempt, 69
- nonexempt, 69
- *Aaron v. City of Wichita, Kansas*, 69

- Portal-to-Portal Act of 1947, 70
- *Andres v. DuBois*, 70
- Equal Pay Act of 1963, 70
- McNamara-O'Hara Service Contract Act of 1965, 71
- Civil Rights Act of 1964, 71
- compensable factors, 71
- *EEOC v. Madison Community Unit School District No. 12*, 71
- comparable worth, 73
- Title VII, 73
- disparate treatment, 73
- disparate impact, 73
- Bennett Amendment, 74
- Executive Order 11246, 74
- Affirmative Action, 74
- Age Discrimination in Employment Act of 1967 (ADEA), 74
- baby boom generation, 74
- *EEOC v. Chrysler*, 75
- Older Workers Benefit Protection Act (OWBPA), 75
- equal benefit or equal cost principle, 75
- Civil Rights Act of 1991, 75
- *Atonio v. Wards Cove Packing Co.*, 75
- Glass Ceiling Act, 76
- Title II, 76
- glass ceiling, 76
- *Lorance v. AT&T Technologies*, 76
- *Boureslan v. Aramco*, 77
- Pregnancy Discrimination Act of 1978 (PDA), 77
- Americans with Disabilities Act of 1990 (ADA), 77
- Title I, 78
- Family and Medical Leave Act of 1993 (FMLA), 78
- Davis-Bacon Act of 1931, 78
- Walsh-Healy Public Contracts Act of 1936, 81
- Occupational Safety and Health Act of 1970, 82
- Executive Order 11478, 82
- Executive Order 11935, 82
- The Rehabilitation Act, 82
- The Vietnam Era Veterans Readjustment Assistance Act, 82
- The Government Employee Rights Act of 1991, 82
- National Labor Relations Act of 1935 (NLRA), 83
- spillover effect, 84
- concessionary bargaining, 84
- interindustry wage or compensation differentials, 84

Discussion Questions

1. Identify the contextual influence that you believe will pose the greatest challenge to companies' competitiveness, and identify the contextual influence that will pose the least challenge to companies' competitiveness. Explain your rationale.
2. Should the government raise the minimum wage? Explain your answer.
3. Do unions make it difficult for companies to attain competitive advantage? Explain your answer.
4. Select one of the contextual influences presented in this chapter. Identify a company that has dealt with this influence, and conduct some research on the company's experience. Be prepared to present a summary of the company's experience in class.
5. Some people argue that there is too much government intervention, while others say there is not enough. Based on the presentation of laws in this chapter, do you think there is too little or too much government intervention? Explain your answer.

Exercises

Compensation Online

For Students

Exercise 1: Find relevant journal articles

One of your classes will hold a debate next week. You have been given the topic of affirmative action. Your opponent will argue that affirmative action is reverse discrimination and infringes upon the right of the company to select the best person for each job. You will have to convince the rest of the class otherwise. Search your library's online catalog for affirmative action and read up to prepare for the debate.

Exercise 2: Review a government document

Imagine that you must write a short history on workplace legislation. Using Yahoo, search for Title VII. Find the text and read over Sec. 2000e1–4. What is this section about? Using a different search engine, go to the same Web site or find a related site. Compare and contrast the two search engines for ease of accessibility and amount of information available.

Exercise 3: Review an organization's Web site
Your class will be performing a mock negotiation next week, and you will play the role of union representation. To best prepare for the project, use Yahoo and search for AFL-CIO. Go to the AFL-CIO official site. Read through the information on the site. Write a brief abstract on the topics covered in this chapter from the perspective of organized labor.

Next, return to the top of the home page and click on the Working Women link (top left-hand corner). Review the page and click on the links at the bottom of the page. From the way the information is presented on these links, how would you summarize the union's stance on the issue of equal pay for women?

For Professionals

Exercise 1: Research a compliance with federal law
You are a human resources consultant, and one of your clients, concerned about legal issues, has asked you to review their policies for compliance. Using the search engine of your choice, search for FMLA. Visit a few of the sites and determine what compliance is and what common mistakes are made in this area.

Exercise 2: Research compliance services
Your own company has not had any legal problems but would like to review current policies and practices. You have been asked to find a consultation firm to aid in the process. From the Yahoo homepage, click the Business & Economy link, then the Business to Business link, and then Consulting and Human Resources. From here, find a few firms that fit the needs of the project and compare their services.

Exercise 3: Review professional references
As an HR consultant, an issue has arisen for which you do not have an immediate answer. Using at least two search engines, search for "human resources law." Review some of the sites and determine which sites would be most helpful as quick references and simple-to-use guides in day-to-day practice.

Endnotes

1. Dulles, F. R. & Dubofsky, M. (1984). *Labor in America: A History* (4th ed.). Arlington Heights, IL: Harlon Davidson Inc., p. 72.
2. Dunlop, J. T. (1993). *Industrial Relations Systems* (Rev. ed.). Boston: Harvard Business School Press.
3. Dulles, F. R. & Dubofsky, M. (1984). *Labor in America: A History* (4th ed.). Arlington Heights, IL: Harlon Davidson Inc., p. 72.
4. U.S. Bureau of Labor Statistics. (2002). Employment situation: June 2002 (USDL 02-376) [online]. Available: *http//stats.bls.gov/newsrels.htm*, accessed July 10, 2002.
5. Ibid.
6. U.S. Census Bureau. (2000). Consolidated federal funds report, fiscal year 2001 [online]. Available: *http//www.census.gov/govs/www/cffr.html*, accessed July 10, 2002.
7. *Walling v. A.H. Belo Corp.*, 316 U.S. 624 1942, 2 WH Cases 39 (1942).
8. *Aaron v. City of Wichita, Kansas*, 54 F. 3d 652 (10th Cir. 1995), 2 WH Cases 2d 1159 (1995).
9. *Andres v. DuBois*, 888 F. Supp. 213 (D.C. Mass 1995), 2 WH Cases 2d 1297 (1995).
10. S. Rep. No. 176, 88th Congress, 1st Session, 1 (1963).
11. *EEOC v. Madison Community Unit School District No. 12*, 818 F. 2d 577 (7th Cir. 1987).
12. Anker, R. (1998). Gender and jobs: Sex segregation of occupations in the world. Washington, DC: International Labor Organization.
13. U.S. Bureau of Census. (January 2000). Projections of the total resident population by 5-year age groups, and sex with special age categories: Middle series, 2001 to 2005 (table NP-T3-B) [online]. Available: *http//www.census.gov*, accessed July 10, 2002.
14. U. S. Department of Commerce. (2001). Statistical abstracts of the United States (121st ed), U. S. Department of Census (May 2001). Profile of general demographic statistics, table DP-1 [online]. Available: *http://www.census.gov*, accessed July 10, 2002.
15. *EEOC v. Chrysler Corp.*, 652 F. Supp. 1523 (D.C. Ohio 1987), 45 FEP Cases 513.
16. Myers, D. W. (1989). *Compensation Management.* Chicago: Commerce Clearing House.
17. *Atonio v. Wards Cove Packing Co.*, 490 U.S. 642, 49 FEP Cases 1519 (1989).
18. *Lorance v. AT&T Technologies*, 49 FEP Cases 1656 (1989).

19. *Boureslan v. Aramco*, 499 U.S. 244, 55 FEP Cases 449 (1991).
20. U.S. Department of Commerce. (2001). Statistical abstracts of the United States (121st ed.).
21. Bureau of National Affairs. (1990). Americans with Disabilities Act of 1990: Text and analysis. *Labor Relations Reporter, 134* (3). Washington, DC: Author.
22. U.S. Bureau of Labor Statistics. (2002). Union members in 2001 (USDOL-02-28) [online]. Available: *http//stats.bls.gov/newsrels.htm*.
23. Kochan, T. R., Katz, H. C., & McKersie, R. B. (1994). *The Transformation of American Industrial Relations.* Ithaca, NY: ILR Press.
24. Ferguson, R. H. (1976). *Cost-of-Living Adjustments in Union Management Agreements*. New York: Cornell University Press.
25. Allen, S., & Clark, R. (1988). Unions, pension wealth, and age-compensation profiles. *Industrial and Labor Relations Review, 42*, pp. 342–359.
26. Solnick, L. (1985). The effect of the blue collar unions on white collar wages and benefits. *Industrial and Labor Relations Review, 38*, pp. 23–35.
27. Blanchflower, D. G., & Freeman, R. B. (1992). Unionism in the United States and other advanced OFCD countries. *Industrial Relations, 31*, pp. 56–79.
28. Kochan, T. R., Katz, H. C., & McKersie, R. B. (1994). *The Transformation of American Industrial Relations*. Ithaca, NY: ILR Press.
29. Bell, L. (1995). Union concessions in the 1980s: The importance of firm specific factors. *Industrial and Labor Relations Review, 48*, pp. 258–275.
30. Krueger, A. B., & Summers, L. H. (1987). Reflections on inter-industry wage structure. In K. Lang & J. S. Leonard (Eds.), *Unemployment and the Structure of the Labor Market* (pp. 14–17). New York: Basil Blackwell.

COMPENSATION IN ACTION

THE NEW YEAR BRINGS KEY DECISIONS FOR HR

As the new year begins, it's an auspicious time to review recent changes in employment law, and to look at new workplace legislation. Last year brought significant changes in the Family and Medical Leave Act, and continued trends in the sexual harassment arena. In 2002, HR professionals should be aware of additional decisions on the FMLA, as well as crucial rulings that may affect the way employers can use mandatory arbitration. In addition, the Supreme Court will hear a case that could reshape the Americans with Disabilities Act. Maria Danaher, an employment attorney with the firm of Dickie, McCarney & Chilcote, reviews the key issues from 2001, and looks to the year ahead.

LOOKING AT LAST YEAR, WHAT WERE THE SIGNIFICANT DECISIONS?

One would be the Washington, D.C., circuit decision ruling that nonunion employees are entitled to have a coworker present at an investigatory meeting. In this case, there were two guys who were trying to improve work conditions at a nonunion shop. One was called into a meeting; he asked to have the other with him and the employer said no. The court ruled against the employer. That doesn't mean that employers must inform employees that they have the right to have a coworker present at an investigatory meeting. But if the individual asks, you can't say no—if there's a reasonable expectation that the outcome of the meeting will include discipline. That's important for nonunion employers to note.

WHAT WAS THE HOT LEGAL ISSUE FOR 2001?

The hot issue of 2001 was the FMLA. There were a number of circuit courts that decided issues regarding the FMLA. There was one major ruling: An employer's mistake in granting FMLA leave to an ineligible employee doesn't make that person eligible. In that case, an employer gave an employee FMLA leave, then found the employee had not worked for the requisite number of hours to be eligible for FMLA leave. But the employee demanded it anyway, because the employer had agreed to it. The court said no. So the courts have been using a commonsense approach in not expanding the language of the FMLA.

WHAT WERE OTHER BIG CASES THAT HELPED INTERPRET THE FMLA?

The Seventh Circuit ruled that the right to be reinstated to employment after FMLA leave is not absolute. The court allowed a nursing-home employer to terminate an employee on her return from maternity leave because she had mismanaged her position. That's a big issue for employers: "I've sent someone out on FMLA leave. When they come back, I can't terminate them because the law requires me to keep their job open." But in the Seventh Circuit case, there had been documentation of performance problems before the employee left. While she was out, the employer put somebody in her position who did a better job. When she came back, she was told about the complaints and offered an opportunity to resign, and she said they'd have to fire her. So they did. And when she sued them, the court ruled for the employer because there were discrepancies in the employee's performance. It's another tap on the shoulder to employers to understand how critical documentation is in these performance issues. The employer prevailed because it had documented her performance problems before she went on leave.

HAVE THERE BEEN ANY OTHER BIG ISSUES THAT HAVE BEEN WORKED OUT IN THE COURTS IN THE PAST YEAR?

We're continuing on the path started by the 1999 Faragher and Ellerth sexual harassment decision: What kind of a response to an employee's sexual harassment complaint really insulates an employer from legal liability? That's come up in a number of circuits. The decisions are pretty consistently rational. There was a recent case in the Seventh Circuit where the court basically said: If you have managers with hiring authority and you don't train them in the basic features of anti-discrimination law, then, in the

(Continued)

(Continued)

court's words, you are making an extraordinary mistake. So employers are understanding they need to put their managers through some kind of awareness training for how to investigate, respond, and follow up on these claims.

IN 2002, IT LOOKS LIKE THE FMLA WILL REMAIN AN ISSUE

The Supreme Court will actually be looking at some FMLA cases in this term. One is *Ragsdale v. Wolverine Worldwide*. This concerns a DOL regulation stating that FMLA leave doesn't start until an employer informs the employee he or she is on FMLA leave. So people were going on leave, then returning and demanding their 12 weeks of FMLA leave. They were getting chunks of medical leave they weren't entitled to. In *Ragsdale*, the Eighth Circuit Court ruled that the regulation was invalid because it creates a right the statute didn't confer. The statute only requires an employer to provide 12 weeks of unpaid leave, and under the DOL regulations, an employer can be forced to provide many more than 12 weeks. So this is the big one. It's the case everyone's looking at.

WHAT IS THE EXPECTED OUTCOME?

The Supreme Court is hesitant to allow a statute to be expanded—in a nonlegislative manner—by the DOL. So it's likely this Eighth Circuit Court decision will be upheld, but there's no way to tell for sure.

MANDATORY ARBITRATION IS ANOTHER ISSUE THAT WILL TURN UP THIS YEAR, CORRECT?

Yes, *EEOC v. Waffle House* will come in front of the Supreme Court. The question: Can the EEOC pursue a case on behalf of an individual who's already agreed to arbitrate any employment claims? This is a big one for employers. "If I go through the trouble of getting my employees to sign an arbitration agreement, can the EEOC pick it up and take it to court anyway?" It really nullifies half of the benefits of having the arbitration agreement, because you still suffer the disruption and expense of the litigation you were trying to avoid. So that will be a big decision.

AND FINALLY, LET'S TALK ABOUT THE MAJOR ADA CASE THAT WILL BE RESOLVED THIS YEAR

It's huge: *Toyota Motor v. Williams*, about an ADA claim from a woman with carpal tunnel. It will be interesting to see whether the Supreme Court looks at this case narrowly or broadly. The narrow question is: Is carpal tunnel a disability? The broad question is: When is somebody truly disabled? The Sixth Circuit Court ruled in *Williams* that a woman's carpal tunnel was sufficiently disabling to cover her under the ADA. The employer argued that to be covered by the ADA, you have to be substantially limited in a major life function and working is a major life function. So even if I can eat, sleep, read, write, walk, if I can't work—I'm not just unable to do one job function, but I'm unable to work—then I can be considered disabled. Toyota said the employee wasn't unable to work. The only thing she couldn't do was one particular job, where she had to hold brushes at shoulder level. But the court bypassed that rationale; it said that performing manual tasks is a major life activity. Even though it was only one aspect of her job, the fact that she can't do manual tasks keeps her from performing a major life function.

SO THAT'S A MAJOR DEVELOPMENT FOR EMPLOYERS

That's scary. Because that means people who aren't necessarily disabled in a broad sense would be disabled for purposes of the ADA, if they had carpal tunnel syndrome. So the question is: What will the Supreme Court do with this? Will it deal narrowly with the Sixth Circuit's rationale that performing manual tasks is a major life activity? Or will it rule on what it takes to include a person as disabled under the ADA? This is the one employers should keep their eyes on.

Source: Gillian Flynn, *Workforce* (January 2002): pp. 68–69 ISSN: 1092-8332, Number: 97951355, Copyright: ACC Communications, Inc., January 2002.

WHAT'S NEW IN COMPENSATION?

Labor and Management Renegotiate Collective Bargaining Agreements in Effect

The National Labor Relations Act of 1935 gives workers the right to bargain collectively with management over many terms of employment, including wages and hours. Reaching mutually acceptable terms leads to a collective bargaining agreement that documents the results of the bargaining process. Both workers and management are obligated to fulfill the terms of the agreement throughout the duration, usually between 3 and 7 years. However, management may open negotiations during the life of a current agreement when the financial solvency of the company is in jeopardy.

A very clear example of companies in financial strife is the airline industry. As discussed in Chapter 2, the airline industry is in financial straits in large part because of the widespread economic recession since the year 2000 and the uncertainties about passenger safety since the September 11 attacks. The *New York Times* article featured here refers to US Airways's negotiations with the various labor unions representing different employee groups. This article indicates that management attempted to cut nearly $1 billion in labor costs in order to receive $1 billion in loans. The nearly $2 billion dollars (half financed through labor cost reductions such as pay and benefits and the other half financed with loans) should help the airline restructure to operate more efficiently in the face of significantly less air travel.

Log into your *New York Times* account. Search the database for articles on "US Airways," "airlines," or the names of other airlines. When reading these articles, look for information about the current state of the industry or specific airlines. Also, identify issues about labor costs and compensation issues. Are airlines still cutting costs? Following your course instructor's specific directions, be prepared to describe the current situation, and relate it to the article. ■

The New York Times

US Airways and Unions Still Negotiating over Cuts

Labor officials said yesterday that US Airways and several of its largest unions were not ready to settle on concessions from employees even though they have to agree quickly on cuts to bolster the company's application for a federal loan guarantee. The airline is also continuing to talk with it competitors on a partnership that would be critical to its recovery.

US Airways has been working this month to persuade its unions to agree to cuts that would save $950 million a year in labor costs because the government expects to see that the carrier can successfully restructure if it receives a guarantee. US Airways applied last week for a $900 million guarantee for $1 billion in loans. But federal officials will probably reject the application if the carrier cannot prove that it will cut costs. The filing came as a surprise because David N. Siegel, the chief executive, had said he wanted to reach an agreement on concessions before making the application.

At least one union is reluctant to start final negotiations until it sees whether the airline obtains concessions from the pilots, which is the group with the largest costs.

"The holdup is that management and the pilots are attempting to reach agreement first," said a posting on the Web site of the Association of Flight Attendants. "Everyone knows that the pilots' deal is the one with the most money in it for the company. If management can't reach a deal with the pilots, everything falls apart in terms of getting the loan guarantee from the government."

On June 12, the flight attendants offered management a concession package of $61 million a year, about two-thirds of what executives had said they wanted. The union has not changed that number since, said Jeff Zack, a union spokesman.

"We haven't given the company another proposal, and we won't until we see what happens with the pilots," he said. "In order to finish these talks, we need the pilots to finish theirs."

The Web site posting said that the flight attendants did not plan to give up a larger percentage of their wages and benefits than the pilots did.

Last week, the pilots offered $400 million in concessions, also two-thirds of what management is seeking.

"There's no sense of how close we are," said Roy Freundlich, a spokesman for the Air Line Pilots Association. "There are a lot of open issues at this point."

Representatives of the machinists' union met with management on Tuesday, and financial advisers were reviewing the numbers yesterday, said Joe Tiberi, a spokesman for the union, the International Association of Machinists and Aerospace Workers. The carrier initially asked the union for $261 million in cuts, and labor leaders and management have exchanged counterproposals.

"Our meetings and discussions with the company do not depend on what the pilots do," Mr. Tiberi said.

The varying stands taken by the unions highlight the difficulties that often prevent management and labor from working together in the airline industry. But US Airways said it needed the federal loan guarantee to survive. It lost $269 million last quarter and $2 billion last year.

"We're making progress," David Castelveter, a US Airways spokesman, said of the talks. "We're all focused on a common goal and trying to meet that goal."

As part of its recovery plan, the airline is also looking for a domestic and international code-share partner, which would allow it to expand routes with another carrier and share revenue, Mr. Freundlich said that although the pilots' contract with US Airways forbids any kind of code-sharing because of job concerns, the union has agreed to allow the carrier to seek a partner. Once the airline finds a partner, then the pilots will review the agreement to determine whether they need to demand job or wage protection, he said.

One person close to the discussion said yesterday that US Airways was closer to an agreement with United Airlines than with any other carrier. US Airways said it "cannot confirm or deny any public speculation." At a luncheon in New York yesterday, Gordon M. Bethune, the chief executive of Continental Airlines, scoffed at the idea that US Airways might strike a deal soon with United.

"I think they're going well," Mr. Bethune said of his own airline's talks with US Airways. "They would be a wonderful partner, especially here in New York."

United is trying to untangle its own labor problems because it has said it would like to file for a loan guarantee. The airline reached a tentative agreement on concessions with its pilots last week, and the leaders of their union approved concessions last night that included pay cuts of 10 percent.

Leaders of the flight attendants' union are meeting this week to review a proposal that United gave them on Monday. But the machinists' union, the largest labor group at the airline, said it was not in serious talks with management.

SOURCE*:* Edward Wong, US Airways and unions still negotiating over cuts (June 20, 2002) [online]. Available: *www.nytimes.com*, accessed October 5, 2002.

CHAPTER 4 TRADITIONAL BASES FOR PAY

Seniority and Merit

Chapter Outline

Learning Objectives

In this chapter, you will learn about

1. The U.S. business traditional practice of setting employees' base pay on their seniority or longevity with the company
2. The fit of seniority pay practices with the two competitive strategies—lowest cost and differentiation
3. The U.S. business traditional practice of setting employees' base pay on their merit
4. The role of performance appraisal in the merit pay process
5. Ways to strengthen the pay-for-performance link
6. Some possible limitations of merit pay programs
7. How merit pay programs fit with the two competitive strategies—lowest cost and differentiation

For decades, companies have awarded raises to base pay according to employees' seniority or job performance. Many companies such as IBM tended to pay employees according to performance, but the system became one of entitlements. That is, employees expected pay raises regardless of performance. Changes in the global marketplace forced IBM to reconsider its approach to employee compensation. After careful planning, IBM revamped its compensation program to reflect the realities of fierce global competition and changing technology. The "Compensation in Action" feature at the end of this chapter describes the process IBM used to develop, implement, and evaluate a true performance-based compensation system.

SENIORITY AND LONGEVITY PAY

Seniority pay and **longevity pay** systems reward employees with periodic additions to base pay according to employees' length of service in performing their jobs. These pay plans assume that employees become more valuable to companies with time and that valued employees will leave if they do not have a clear idea that their salaries will progress over time [1]. This rationale comes from **human capital theory** [2], which states that employees' knowledge and skills generate productive capital known as **human capital**. Employees can develop such knowledge and skills from formal education and training, including on-the-job experience. Over time, employees presumably refine existing skills or acquire new ones that enable them to work more productively. Thus, seniority pay rewards employees for acquiring and refining their skills as indexed by seniority.

Historical Overview

A quick look back into U.S. labor relations history can shed light on the adoption of seniority pay in many companies. President Franklin D. Roosevelt advocated policies designed to improve workers' economic status in response to the severely depressed economic conditions that had started in 1929. Congress instituted the National Labor Relations Act (NLRA) in 1935 to protect worker rights, predicated on a fundamental, but limited, conflict of interest between workers and employers. President Franklin D. Roosevelt and other leaders felt that companies needed to be regulated to establish an appropriate balance of power between the parties. The NLRA established a collective bargaining system nationwide to accommodate employers' and employees' partially conflicting and partially shared goals.

Collective bargaining led to **job control unionism** [3], in which collective bargaining units negotiate formal contracts with employees and provide quasi-judicial grievance procedures to adjudicate disputes between union members and employers. Union shops establish workers' rights and obligations and participate in describing and delineating jobs. In unionized workplaces, terms of collective bargaining agreements may determine the specific type of seniority system used, and seniority tends to be the deciding factor in nearly all job scheduling, transfer, layoff, compensation, and promotion decisions. Moreover, seniority may become a principal criterion for selecting one employee over another for transfer or promotion. Table 4-1 on page 96 illustrates the rules for a seniority pay program contained in the collective bargaining agreement between The Chauffeurs, Teamsters and Helpers, Local 26 (affiliated with International Brotherhood of Teamsters, AFL-CIO). It shows the actual rates for job classification and seniority level, effective August 4, 2003.

Employees shall be paid a rate equal to eighty percent (80.0%) of the full base rate of the job classification and shall advance to the full base rate as follows:

Number of months worked	*% of full base rate*
9	85
18	90
27	95
36	100

Political pressures probably drive the prevalence of public sector seniority pay. Seniority-based pay systems essentially provide automatic pay increases. Performance assessments tend to be subjective rather than objective (for example, production data including dollar volume of sales and units produced, and human resource data including accidents and absenteeism) because accurate job performance measurements are very difficult to obtain. In contrast, employees' seniority is easily indexed—time on the job is a relatively straightforward and concrete concept. Implementing such a system that specifies the amount of pay raise an employee will receive according to his or her seniority is automatic. Politically, "automatic" pay adjustments protect public sector employees from the quirks of election-year politics [4]. In addition, the federal, state, and local governments can avoid direct responsibility for pay raises, so employees can receive fair pay without political objections.

Who Participates?

Today, most unionized private sector and public sector organizations continue to base salary on seniority or length of employee service. The total number of unionized employees in both sectors is quite large [5]. In 2001, unions covered approximately 9.8 million workers in the private sector, and government (federal, state, and municipal) employed approximately 8 million workers with union representation. Members of union bargaining units whose contracts include seniority provisions, usually rank-and-

TABLE 4-1 Rantoul Hourly Classification Rates Effective 08-04-2003

Classification Title	*Start*	*9 Months*	*18 Months*	*27 Months*	*36 Months*
Assembler	$ 9.56	$10.16	$10.76	$11.35	$11.95
Injection Molding Press Oper.	$ 9.56	$10.16	$10.76	$11.35	$11.95
Central Stores Attendant	$ 9.56	$10.16	$10.76	$11.35	$11.95
Utility Attendant	$ 9.56	$10.16	$10.76	$11.35	$11.95
Fork Lift Driver	$ 9.88	$10.50	$11.12	$11.73	$12.35
Shipping/Receiving Driver	$ 9.88	$10.50	$11.12	$11.73	$12.35
Quality Control Auditor	$ 9.88	$10.50	$11.12	$11.73	$12.35
Emp Involvement Coordinator	$11.36	$12.07	$12.78	$13.49	$14.20
Facilitator	$11.36	$12.07	$12.78	$13.49	$14.20
Building Maintenance	$11.36	$12.07	$12.78	$13.49	$14.20
Mold Setter	$11.68	$12.41	$13.14	$13.87	$14.60
Set-up Worker (Paint Line)	$12.00	$12.75	$13.50	$14.25	$15.00
Maintenance Electrician	$13.40	$14.24	$15.08	$15.91	$16.75
Maintenance General	$13.40	$14.24	$15.08	$15.91	$16.75
Tool & Die Maker	$13.84	$14.71	$15.57	$16.44	$17.30
Maintenance Tech.	$15.08	$16.02	$16.97	$17.91	$18.85
Inj. Mold Repair Tech.	$16.68	$17.72	$18.77	$19.81	$20.85
Leader @ $.50 over Class Led					

Source: Agreement between Textron Automotive Company Rantoul Products and the Chauffeurs, Teamsters and Helpers, Local 26. Affiliated with International Brotherhood of Teamsters, AFL-CIO.

file as well as clerical workers, receive automatic raises based on the number of years they have been with the company. In the public sector—municipal, state, and federal government organizations—most administrative, professional, and even managerial employees receive such automatic pay raises.

Effectiveness of Seniority Pay Systems

Virtually no systematic research has demonstrated these pay plans' effectiveness, nor is there any documentation regarding their prevalence. Seniority or longevity pay plans are likely to disappear from for-profit companies in increasingly competitive markets. External influences such as increased global competition, rapid technological advancement, and skill deficits of new and current members of the workforce necessitate a strategic orientation toward compensation. These influences will probably force companies to establish compensation tactics that reward their employees for learning job-relevant knowledge and skills and for making tangible contributions toward companies' quests for competitive advantage. Seniority pay meets neither goal.

Until recently, public sector organizations have faced less pressure to change these systems because they exist to serve the public rather than make profits. For example, the Internal Revenue Service is responsible for collecting taxes from U.S. citizens. Paying taxes to the federal government is an obligation of virtually all U.S. citizens. The amount of taxes each citizen pays is based on established tax codes. The Internal Revenue Service is not in the business of finding new customers to pay taxes. It does not compete against any other businesses for taxpayers.

Nowadays, however, the federal government has raised questions about the effectiveness of its seniority pay system for white-collar workers, the General Schedule, which we discuss shortly. Questions about the effectiveness of its seniority pay system are based on how the world of work has dramatically changed since the system's inception in 1949. The "Flip Side of the Coin" feature describes how the

FLIP SIDE OF THE COIN

A SYSTEM WHOSE TIME HAS COME—AND GONE

The fundamental nature of the federal compensation system was established at the end of the 1940s, a time when over 70 percent of federal white-collar jobs consisted of clerical work. Government work today is highly skilled and specialized "knowledge work." Yet in the age of the computer, the federal government still uses—with few modifications—pay and job evaluation systems that were designed for the age of the file clerk. The divergence between the federal pay system and the broader world of work where the war for talent must be fought has led observers to call for reform of the federal system. To support achievement of the government's strategic goals, a new, more flexible system may be called for, one that better supports the strategic management of human capital and allows agencies to tailor their pay practices to recruit, manage, and retain the talent to accomplish their mission.

The formidable challenges of World War II were overcome by breaking them into their component problems and solving those problems through centralized planning and the application of uniform methods. At the end of the 1940s, the federal government's civilian workforce was ripe for application of this scientific management approach, as embodied in the Classification Act of 1949. Over 70 percent of federal white-collar jobs consisted of clerical work—work such as posting census figures in ledgers or retrieving taxpayer records from vast file rooms. It made sense to manage this work by breaking it into clearly describable positions. It made sense to sort these positions based on clear-cut, enduring differences in the difficulty, responsibility, and skill requirements of the work employees carried out. It made sense to use such differences as the foundation for all aspects of human resources management, such as setting pay, thus making position the principal driver of most federal personnel administration systems.

That focus on position rather than performance made sense for this army of clerks in the late 1940s. Indeed, it made little sense for pay to reflect variations in employee performance—most of the work was so cut and dried that employees had scant opportunity to distinguish themselves from their peers. As for using comparisons with pay outside the government, that was not even on the map yet. Specific pay rates and pay raises for federal employees were established by Congress though legislation, not through any sort of administrative, market-based procedure.

The Classification Act of 1949 used work level descriptions that date to 1912 to extend a centralized job evaluation system to all white-collar positions, thereby establishing internal equity—a fairness and consistency criterion aimed at ensuring that each job is compensated according to its relative place in a single hierarchy of positions—as the centerpiece of federal compensation. The act also merged several separate "schedules" of pay rates into one "General Schedule." Finally—and fatefully—it defined the federal government's pay and job evaluation structure in statute, where it has remained essentially unchanged for over 50 years.

During this 50-year period, much has changed, including:

- **The nature of work.** When the General Schedule was created, the federal government was largely a "government of clerks." But most government work no longer revolves around the execution of established, stable processes or the application of physical effort. Instead, as illustrated in the chart on page 98, federal white-collar work has become highly skilled and increasingly specialized "knowledge work" that is properly classified at higher grade levels.

  Some of the work-related features of the General Schedule are not just dated, they are counterintuitive. If two employees perform similar jobs but one employee has a much greater workload, can that employee's salary be higher? Not under the General Schedule—if the level of difficulty of two jobs is the same, they are in the same salary range. If one employee performs a wider variety of tasks than other employees, can that result in higher pay? Not if the tasks are at the same level. If the busier employees complain that this is inequitable, what can the agency do? Take work away from the busier employees. Years ago, spreading clerical tasks

(Continued)

(Continued)

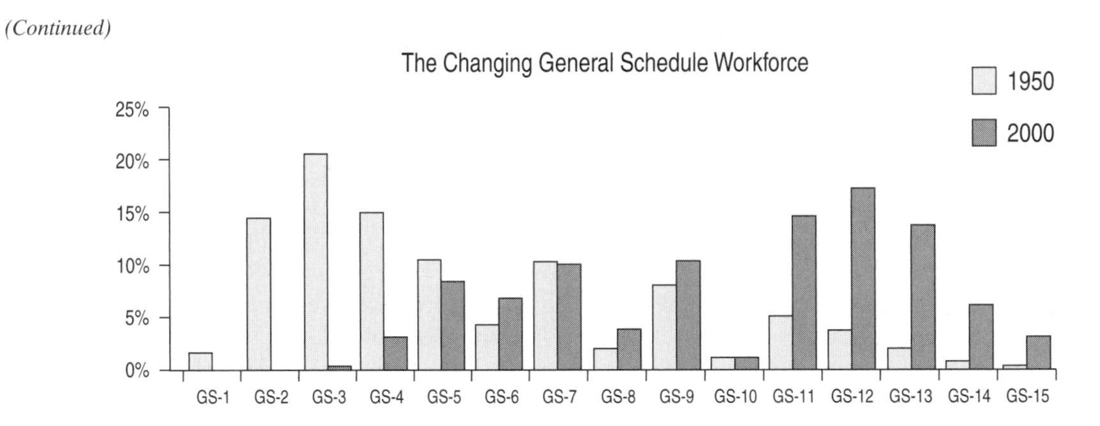

across similar, stable positions made sense; in today's multi-tasking workplace, the system appears illogical.

- **The role of compensation in organizations.** In most organizations, particularly those in the private sector, compensation management has become considerably more than simply calculating and paying the bill for employee efforts. The concept of compensation and rewards has broadened. Organizations have come to view their compensation and reward systems as much more than schemes managed out of the comptroller's office and designed to contain salary and related benefits costs.[1] Today, organizations manage their rewards systems out of their human resources offices.[2] They design them to use pay, awards, benefits, learning and development, challenging and satisfying work, work-life balance, and a supportive work environment strategically to attract, manage, develop, and retain high-quality, diverse workforces that meet their specific human capital needs.

  The purpose and tactics of compensation have also broadened. Organizations no longer view their annual compensation budgets simplistically as the bill for "another year's worth of labor inputs." Instead, they use flexible, targeted compensation tools to acquire and retain critical talent. Compensation's role in recruiting gets considerable attention from both employers and potential employees. Organizations no longer use compensation principally to encourage and reward unquestioning loyalty from undifferentiated "human resources"; instead, they use compensation to communicate and reward desired values, behaviors, and outcomes. Federal agencies are similarly poised to use compensation as a strategic tool, rather than a merely administrative tool. This shift is already visible in a wide variety of demonstration projects and alternative personnel systems that align agency pay practices and bonus and award programs with agency strategic goals.
- **Employee expectations.** The employees of the 1940s and 1950s shared the experiences of economic depression and war. They sought stability and security. The federal compensation system, with its career ladders (where employees start their careers in positions at low grades with the prospect of advancement over time to higher-grade positions), time-based pay increases, and benefits keyed to length of service, reflects a conception of employment predicated on a 30-year career with the same employer. That model is designed to reward loyalty by providing stable and secure employment, reflecting and meeting those needs. But increasingly employees neither expect nor seek that form of security from their employer. Instead, they expect immediate rewards and recognition for their individual

[1]For every dollar increase in basic pay, or "benefits-bearing compensation," agencies routinely budget an additional 20 to 30 cents as an estimate of related benefits cost obligations that dollar will generate. In a related development within the federal government, President Bush's FY 2003 budget for the first time displays agencies' future cost accruals for employee benefits as the agency level, thereby reinforcing this administration's policy that agencies must be strategic in their use of all human resources-related funding. The president's proposed Managerial Flexibility Act includes statutory changes that would effect this accounting change permanently.

[2]*Private Sector Compensation Practices*, Booz • Allen & Hamilton—Report to the U.S. Office of Personnel Management, Washington DC, February 2000.

accomplishments and consider continued employability the key to security.

- **Stakeholder expectations.** Employees and their representatives, as well as agencies and other stakeholders, have expectations about how human resources management systems are developed and implemented today. With a consistent migration away from tightly legislated systems to administrative authorities that lend themselves to decentralization and delegation, stakeholders expect to influence how those administrative authorities will be designed and used. Agencies want the latitude to adapt system features to support their strategic needs. At the same time, elected employee representatives expect to have a voice in systems affecting their members. Engaging unions in fundamental workplace change is a sound human capital practice and recognizes that labor and management have a shared stake in building a more effective government that delivers results to the American people.

Although the federal white-collar pay system has been refined in response to these changes, these refinements have not changed its fundamental character, which remains focused on internal equity (to reflect relative place in a hierarchy of positions) and leaves little meaningful room for external equity (to accommodate changes in labor market rates for different occupations) or individual equity (to reward excellent performance). Consequently, the outdated beliefs and expectations underlying our pay and classification systems have diverged from those of the broader world of work where the war for talent must be fought today. This divergence has led observers and architects of government human resources management systems to contemplate possible modernization of the federal compensation system.[3] During the 1980s and early 1990s, these observers advocated reform of various aspects of the federal compensation system, such as the classification system[4] and the pay-setting process,[5] as well as benefits.[6] The calls for reform continue.

[3]The possibility of a need for systemic change was acknowledged and anticipated in the Civil Service Reform Act of 1978, which authorized the establishment of "demonstration projects" by the Office of Personnel Management under 5 U.S.C. §4703 to test progressive human resources practices for possible governmentwide adoption.

[4]See *Modernizing Federal Classification: An Opportunity for Excellence*, National Academy of Public Administration, Washington, DC, 1991.

[5]See Robert W. Hartman, *Pay and Pensions for Federal Workers*, The Brookings Institution, Washington, DC, 1983.

[6]Ibid.

Source: U.S. Office of Personnel Management. (2002). A White Paper. A Fresh Start for Federal Pay: The Case for Modernization. Washington, DC: Author.

federal government's seniority pay system may limit the government's mission to strategically serve the public.

Design of Seniority Pay and Longevity Pay Plans

Although seniority pay and longevity pay are similar, there are some important distinctions between them. The object of seniority pay is to reward job tenure or employees' time as members of a company explicitly through permanent increases to base salary. Employees begin their employment at the starting pay rate established for the particular jobs. At specified time intervals—as short as 3 months and as long as 3 years—employees receive designated pay increases. These pay increases are permanent additions to current pay levels. Over time, employees will reach the maximum pay rate for their jobs. Companies expect that most employees will earn promotions into higher paying jobs that have seniority pay schedules. Figure 4-1 illustrates a seniority pay policy for a junior clerk job and an advanced clerk job. Pay rates are associated with seniority. Presumably, when employees reach the top pay rate for the junior clerk position, they are qualified to assume the duties of the advanced clerk position.

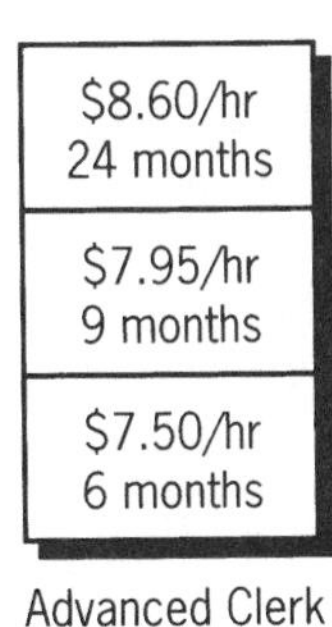

FIGURE 4-1 A Sample Seniority Policy for Junior and Advanced Clerk Jobs

Longevity pay rewards employees who have reached pay grade maximums and who are not likely to move into higher grades. State and local governments often use longevity pay as an incentive to reduce employee turnover and to reward employees for continuous years of service. Longevity pay may take the form of a percentage of base pay, a flat dollar amount, or a special step increase based on the number of years the employee has spent with the organization [6].

Federal employees are subject to longevity pay via the **General Schedule (GS)**, which is shown in Table 4-2. The General Schedule classifies federal government jobs into 15 classifications (GS-1 through GS-15) based on such factors as skill, education, and experience levels. In addition, jobs that require high levels of specialized education (for example, a physicist), influence public policy significantly (for example, law judges), or require executive decision making are classified in separate categories: Senior Level (SL), Scientific & Professional (SP) positions, and the Senior Executive Service (SES). The government typically increases all pay amounts annually to adjust for inflation.

Employees are eligible for 10 within-grade step pay increases. At present, it takes employees 18 years to progress from Step 1 to Step 10. The waiting periods within steps are as follows:

- Steps 1–3: 1 year
- Steps 4–6: 2 years
- Steps 7–9: 3 years

The aging of the baby boom generation may make companies' use of seniority or longevity infeasible. Most individuals in the baby boom generation, born roughly between 1946 and 1964, are currently in the workforce, and only a small segment of them are presently approaching retirement age. Companies that use seniority plans are likely to find the costs burdensome.

Advantages of Seniority Pay

Seniority pay offers a number of advantages to both employees and employers. Employees are likely to perceive they are treated fairly because they earn pay increases according to seniority, which is an objective standard. Seniority stands

TABLE 4-2 Salary Table 2002-GS, 2002 General Schedule Incorporating a 3.60% General Increase Effective January 2002, Annual Rates by Grade and Step

	1	*2*	*3*	*4*	*5*	*6*	*7*	*8*	*9*	*10*	*Within-Grade Increase Amounts*
GS-1	$14,757	$15,249	$15,740	$16,228	$16,720	$17,009	$17,492	$17,981	$18,001	$18,456	VARIES
2	$16,592	$16,985	$17,535	$18,001	$18,201	$18,736	$19,271	$19,806	$20,341	$20,876	VARIES
3	$18,103	$18,706	$19,309	$19,912	$20,515	$21,118	$21,721	$22,324	$22,927	$23,530	$603
4	$20,322	$20,999	$21,676	$22,353	$23,030	$23,707	$24,384	$25,061	$25,738	$26,415	$677
5	$22,737	$23,495	$24,253	$25,011	$25,769	$26,527	$27,285	$28,043	$28,801	$29,559	$758
6	$25,344	$26,189	$27,034	$27,879	$28,724	$29,569	$30,414	$31,259	$32,104	$32,949	$845
7	$28,164	$29,103	$30,042	$30,981	$31,920	$32,859	$33,798	$34,737	$35,676	$36,615	$939
8	$31,191	$32,231	$33,271	$34,311	$35,351	$36,391	$37,431	$38,471	$39,511	$40,551	$1,040
9	$34,451	$35,599	$36,747	$37,895	$39,043	$40,191	$41,339	$42,487	$43,635	$44,783	$1,148
10	$37,939	$39,204	$40,469	$41,734	$42,999	$44,264	$45,529	$46,794	$48,059	$49,324	$1,265
11	$41,684	$43,073	$44,462	$45,851	$47,240	$48,629	$50,018	$51,407	$52,796	$54,185	$1,389
12	$49,959	$51,624	$53,289	$54,954	$56,619	$58,284	$59,949	$61,614	$63,279	$64,944	$1,665
13	$59,409	$61,389	$63,369	$65,349	$67,329	$69,309	$71,289	$73,269	$75,249	$77,229	$1,980
14	$70,205	$72,545	$74,885	$77,225	$79,565	$81,905	$84,245	$86,585	$88,925	$91,265	$2,340
15	$82,580	$85,333	$88,086	$90,839	$93,592	$96,345	$99,098	$101,851	$104,604	$107,357	$2,753

Source: U.S. Office of Personnel Management [online]. Available: *http://www.opm.gov*, accessed August 2, 2002.

in contrast to subjective standards based on supervisory judgment. The inherent objectivity of seniority pay systems should lead to greater cooperation among coworkers.

Seniority pay offers two key advantages to employers. First, seniority pay facilitates the administration of pay programs. Pay increase amounts are set in advance, and employers award raises according to a pay schedule, much like the federal government's General Schedule. A second advantage is that employers are less likely to offend some employees by showing favoritism to others because seniority is an objective basis for making awards. The absence of favoritism should enable supervisors and managers to effectively motivate employees to perform their jobs.

Fitting Seniority Pay with Competitive Strategies

Seniority pay does not fit well with the imperatives of competitive strategies because employees can count on receiving the same pay raises for average and exemplary performance, and this fact represents the greatest disadvantage of seniority pay systems. Employees who make significant contributions in the workplace receive the same pay increases as coworkers who make modest contributions. In addition, employees receive pay raises without regard to whether companies are meeting their differentiation or cost goals. Employees clearly do not have any incentives to actively improve their skills or to take risks on the job because they receive pay raises regardless of any initiative they show.

So, in light of increased external pressures on companies to promote productivity and product quality, will seniority or longevity pay be gradually phased out? With the exception of companies that are shielded from competitive pressures—for example, public utilities—it is likely that companies that intend to remain competitive will set aside seniority pay practices. Although seniority pay plans reflect employees' increased worth, they measure such contributions indirectly rather than based on tangible contributions or the successful acquisition of job-related knowledge or skills. Now more than ever, companies need to be accountable to shareholders, which will require direct measurement of employee job performance.

To further illustrate the incompatibility of seniority pay structures with the attainment of competitive strategy, Toyota, a manufacturer of automobiles, abandoned its seniority-based wage system for a performance-based pay system. Traditional Japanese companies defined seniority as employee age. Despite Toyota's worldwide reputation as a manufacturer of high-quality automobiles, company management continually adopts employment practices that encourage even better quality products. Performance-based pay fits with Toyota's mission.

MERIT PAY

Merit pay programs assume that employees' compensation over time should be determined, at least in part, by differences in job performance [7]. Employees earn permanent merit increases based on their performance. The increases reward excellent effort or results, motivate future performance, and help employers retain valued employees. Merit increases are usually expressed as a percentage of hourly wages for nonexempt employees and as a percentage of annual salaries for exempt employees. In 2001, nonexempt workers earned average merit increases of 4.3 percent (nonunion) or 4.4 percent (union), and exempt employees earned 4.5 percent [8].

Who Participates?

Merit pay is one of the most commonly used compensation methods in the United States. Various small-scale surveys of no more than a few thousand companies [9], conducted by compensation consulting firms and professional associations, demonstrate that merit pay plans are firmly entrenched within U.S. business. Its popularity may result from the fact that merit pay fits well with U.S. cultural ideals that reward individual achievement [10]. Merit pay programs occur most often in the private "for-profit" sector of the economy rather than in public sector organizations such as local and state governments [11].

Exploring the Elements of Merit Pay

Managers rely on objective as well as subjective performance indicators to determine whether an employee will receive a merit increase and the amount of increase warranted. As a rule, supervisors give merit increases to employees based on subjective appraisal of employees' performance [12]. Supervisors periodically review individual employee performance to evaluate how well each worker is accomplishing assigned duties relative to established standards and goals. Thus, as we discuss later in this chapter, accurate performance appraisals are key to effective merit pay programs.

For merit pay programs to succeed, employees must know that their efforts in meeting production quotas or quality standards will lead to pay raises. Job requirements must be realistic, and employees must have the skills and abilities to meet job goals. Moreover, employees must perceive a strong relationship between attaining performance standards and receiving pay increases.

Further, companies that use merit programs must ensure that the funds needed to fulfill these promises to compensate employees are available. For now, we assume that adequate funding for merit pay programs is in place. In Chapter 9 we address the ramifications of insufficient budgets for funding merit pay programs.

Finally, companies should make adjustments to base pay according to changes in the cost of living or inflation before awarding merit pay raises. Merit pay raises should always reward employee performance rather than represent adjustments for inflation. Inflation represents rises in the cost of consumer goods and services (for example, food and health care) that boost the overall cost of living. Over time, inflation erodes the purchasing power of the dollar. No doubt, you've heard, "It's harder to stretch a dollar these days." Employees are concerned about how well merit increases raise purchasing power. Compensation professionals attempt to minimize negative inflationary effects by making permanent increases to base pay known as cost-of-living adjustments. For now, let's assume that inflation is not an issue. (As an aside, this principle also applies to seniority pay. Pay increases should reflect additional seniority after making specific adjustments for inflation.)

Although fairly common, merit pay systems are not appropriate for all companies. Compensation professionals should consider two factors—commitment from top management and the design of jobs—before endorsing the use of merit pay systems. Top management must be willing to reward employees' job performances with meaningful pay differentials that match employee performance differentials. Ideally, companies should grant sufficiently large pay increases to reward employees for exemplary job performance and to encourage similar expectations about future good work.

The amount of a merit pay increase should reflect prior job performance levels and motivate employees toward striving for exemplary performance. The pay raise amount should be meaningful to employees. The concept of **"just-meaningful pay**

TABLE 4-3 Performance Engineer

Description
This deep-skill position will be a member of Bank One's Performance Engineering team within Enterprise Computing. As part of this high-performance group, this individual will be responsible for the day-to-day support of Bank One's mainframe SMF, RMF, Mainview, MICS & MXG data and reporting facilities. This position will work closely with several Infrastructure and Operations organizations such as Mainframe Engineering, Level III Technical Support, MF Operations, Enterprise Systems Management, Production Assurance and Enterprise Command Center to define and deliver quality systems performance reports and metrics. This high-energy, results-oriented job requires a balance of strong technical skills and business processes, a sense of urgency resolving problem issues, creativity, work schedule flexibility, adaptability to changing business conditions and a commitment to customer satisfaction. Responsibilities include: Develop strategy and plans for mainframe systems performance reporting using MICS, MXG, SAS and Mainview. Develop strategy and plans for internal charge-back system/reporting. Deliver and support Web interface for performance reporting "drill-down" capability. Develop standard and exception reports. Research and apply proactive software maintenance. Provide input to engineering on infrastructure architecture related issues. Use performance reports/metrics to identify improvement opportunities. Use historical data to determine production readiness of proposed changes, assessing impacts and risks. Develop wellness check scripts, processes and procedures for level II support personnel. Contribute to Root Cause Investigation. Document changes to infrastructure configuration. Support and contribute to Bank One projects and initiatives. Update system configuration and resource definitions when required. Develop and communicate IT standards.
Skills
General knowledge of systems software, communications software, database software and applications software processed on the corporate computing equipment. General knowledge of all computing hardware installed. Demonstrated interviewing techniques to obtain application information for tactical and strategic planning. Ability to assess business planning requirements and develop tactical and strategic plans to meet those requirements. In depth understanding of what makes an application perform well or poorly. Ability to quickly learn systems software, database software and hardware capabilities, adapt to rapidly changing situations and apply knowledge to the environment. Familiarity with Personal Computer techniques and ability to apply them to defined projects. Demonstrated complex problem solving capabilities. Demonstrated statistical analysis capabilities. Demonstrated effective written and oral communication skills. Ability to understand and develop technical direction. One year of project management experience including the ability to manage complex projects with limited supervision and demonstrated skill in project planning and control techniques. Implement and tune mainframe computer systems to meet all computer performance business requirements with minimal costs. Recommend configuration changes to exploit available technology options for achieving Information Systems' mission. MVS Internal Performance. Systems Programmer experience in at least two of the following areas: OS/390, CICS, DB2, IMS, VTAM/NCP. DESIRED SKILLS/EXPERIENCE: OS/390 Systems Performance Tuning, ZOS (the new MVS), Tape Management, IODF gens, Storage Management, Capacity Planning, Sysplex, Goal Mode, and DASD Management & Optimization. Performance Tuning for DB2, IMS and CICS. EDUCATION: Four-year college degree or equivalent work experience. Over 8+ years data processing work experience. Over 5 years SAS experience a plus.
Work Days
Mon, Tue, Wed, Thu, Fri
Work Shift
1st Shift

Source: www.bankone.com, accessed November 16, 2002.

increase" refers to the minimum pay increase that employees will see as making a meaningful change in compensation [13]. The basic premise of this concept is that a trivial pay increase for average or better employees is not likely to reinforce their performance or to motivate enhanced future performance. We take up the specifics of the just-meaningful pay increase concept in Chapter 9.

In addition to top management's commitment to merit pay programs, HR professionals must design jobs explicitly enough that employees' performance can be measured accurately. Merit programs are most appropriate when employees have control over their performances and when conditions outside employees' control do not substantially affect their performance. Conditions beyond employees' control that are likely to limit job performance vary by the type of job. For sales professionals, recessionary economic spells generally lead consumers to limit spending on new purchases because they anticipate the possibility of layoffs. Certainly, sales professionals do not create recessionary periods, nor can they allay consumers' fears about the future. For production workers, regular equipment breakdowns will lead to lower output.

Further, there must be explicit performance standards that specify the procedures or outcomes against which employees' job performance can be clearly evaluated. At Pratt & Whitney, HR professionals and employees worked together to rewrite job descriptions. The purpose was to define and put into writing the major duties of a job and to specify written performance standards for each duty to ensure that the job requirements provided a useful measurement standard for evaluation. The main performance standards included such factors as quality, quantity, and timeliness of work.

Table 4-3 displays a job description for a manager for performance engineering at Bank One Corporation. The duties describe the activities the jobholder performs, prior experience, and necessary skills to perform this job at an acceptable level. For instance, a successful candidate must demonstrate evidence of statistical analysis capabilities.

PERFORMANCE APPRAISAL

Effective performance appraisals drive effective merit pay programs. Merit pay systems require specific performance appraisal approaches, as noted previously. Administering successful merit pay programs depends as much on supervisors' appraisal approaches as on the professionals' skills in designing and implementing such plans.

Types of Performance Appraisal Plans

Performance appraisal methods fall into four broad categories:

- Trait systems
- Comparison systems
- Behavioral systems
- Goal-oriented systems

The four kinds of performance appraisal methods are next described in order.

Trait Systems

Trait systems ask raters to evaluate each employee's traits or characteristics, such as quality of work, quantity of work, appearance, dependability, cooperation, initiative, judgment, leadership responsibility, decision-making ability, or creativity. Appraisals

TABLE 4-4 A Trait-Oriented Performance Appraisal Rating Form

Employee's Name:			***Employee's Position:***	
Supervisor's Name:			***Review Period:***	
Instructions: For each trait below, circle the phrase that best represents the employee.				
1. Diligence				
a. outstanding	b. above average	c. average	d. below average	e. poor
2. Cooperation with others				
a. outstanding	b. above average	c. average	d. below average	e. poor
3. Communication skills				
a. outstanding	b. above average	c. average	d. below average	e. poor
4. Leadership				
a. outstanding	b. above average	c. average	d. below average	e. poor
5. Decisiveness				
a. outstanding	b. above average	c. average	d. below average	e. poor

are typically scored using descriptors ranging from unsatisfactory to outstanding. Table 4-4 contains an illustration of a trait method of performance appraisal.

Trait systems are easy to construct, use, and apply to a wide range of jobs. They are also easy to quantify for merit pay purposes. Increasingly, trait systems are becoming common in companies that focus on the quality of interactions with customers. For example, Leon Leonwood Bean, founder of L. L. Bean, made customer service the foundation of his business from its beginning in 1912. Bean referred to the necessity of positive customer service as one of the business's golden rules: Sell good merchandise at a reasonable profit, treat your customers like human beings, and they will always come back for more [14].

The trait approach does have limitations. First, trait systems are highly subjective [15], as they are based on the assumption that every supervisor's perception of a given trait is the same. For example, the trait "quality of work" may be defined by one supervisor as "the extent to which an employee's performance is free of errors." To another supervisor, quality of work might mean "the extent to which an employee's performance is thorough." Human resource professionals and supervisors can avoid this problem by working together in advance to clearly specify the definition of traits.

Another drawback is that systems rate individuals on subjective personality factors rather than objective job performance data. Essentially, trait assessment focuses attention on employees rather than on job performances. Employees may simply become defensive rather than trying to understand the role that the particular trait plays in shaping their job performance and then taking corrective actions.

Comparison Systems

Comparison systems evaluate a given employee's performance against the performance of other employees. Employees are ranked from the best performer to the poorest performer. In simplest form, supervisors rank each employee and establish a performance hierarchy such that the employee with the best performance receives the highest ranking. Employees may be ranked on overall performance or on various traits.

An alternative approach, called a **forced distribution** performance appraisal, assigns employees to groups that represent the entire range of performance. For exam-

TABLE 4-5 A Forced Distribution Performance Appraisal Rating Form

Instructions: You are required to rate the performance for the previous 3 months of the 15 workers employed as animal keepers to conform with the following performance distribution:

- *15 percent* of the animal keepers will be rated as having exhibited poor performance.
- *20 percent* of the animal keepers will be rated as having exhibited below average performance.
- *35 percent* of the animal keepers will be rated as having exhibited average performance.
- *20 percent* of the animal keepers will be rated as having exhibited above average performance.
- *10 percent* of the animal keepers will be rated as having exhibited superior performance.

Use the following guidelines for rating performance. On the basis of the five duties listed in the job description for animal keeper, the employee's performance is characterized as:

- Poor if the incumbent performs only two of the duties well.
- Below average if the incumbent performs only two of the duties well.
- Average if the incumbent performs only three of the duties well.
- Above average if the incumbent performs only four of the duties well.
- Superior if the incumbent performs all five of the duties well.

ple, three categories that might be used are best performers, moderate performers, and poor performers. A forced distribution approach, in which the rater must place a specific number of employees into each of the performance groups, can be used with this method. Table 4-5 displays a forced distribution rating form for an animal keeper job with five performance categories.

Many companies use forced distribution approaches to minimize the tendency for supervisors to rate most employees as excellent performers. This tendency usually arises out of supervisors' self-promotion motives. Supervisors often provide positive performance ratings to most of their employees because they do not want to alienate them. After all, their performance as supervisors depend largely on how well their employees perform their jobs.

Forced distribution approaches have drawbacks. The forced distribution approach can distort ratings because employee performance may not fall into these predetermined distributions. Let's assume that a supervisor must use the following forced distribution to rate her employees' performance:

- 15 percent well below average
- 25 percent below average
- 40 percent average
- 15 percent above average
- 5 percent well above average

This distribution is problematic to the extent that the actual distribution of employee performance is substantially different from this forced distribution. If 35 percent of the employees' performance were either above average or well above average, then the supervisor would be required to underrate the performance of 15 percent of the employees. Based on this forced distribution, the supervisor can rate only 20 percent of the employees as having demonstrated above average or well above average job performance. Ultimately, management-employee relationships suffer because workers feel that ratings are dictated by unreal models rather than by individual performance.

TABLE 4-6 A Paired Comparison Performance Appraisal Rating Form

Instructions: Please indicate by placing an X which employee of each pair has performed most effectively during the past year.

X	Bob Brown	X	Mary Green
___	Mary Green	___	Jim Smith
X	Bob Brown	___	Mary Green
___	Jim Smith	X	Allen Jones
___	Bob Brown	___	Jim Smith
X	Allen Jones	X	Allen Jones

A third comparative technique for ranking employees establishes **paired comparisons**. Supervisors compare each employee to every other employee, identifying the better performer in each pair. Table 4-6 displays a paired comparison form. Following the comparison, the employees are ranked according to the number of times they were identified as being the better performer. In this example, Allen Jones is the best performer because he was identified most often as the better performer, followed by Bob Brown (identified twice as the better performer) and Mary Green (identified once as the better performer).

Comparative methods are best suited for small groups of employees who perform the same or similar jobs. They are cumbersome for large groups of employees or for employees who perform different jobs. For example, it would be difficult to judge whether a production worker's performance is better than a secretary's performance because the jobs are substantively different. The assessment of a production worker's performance is based on the number of units she produces during each work shift; a secretary's performance is based on the accuracy with which she types memos and letters.

As do trait systems, comparison approaches have limitations. They tend to encourage subjective judgments, which increase the chance for rater errors and biases. In addition, small differences in performance between employees may become exaggerated by using such a method if supervisors feel compelled to distinguish among levels of employee performance.

Behavioral Systems

Behavioral systems rate employees on the extent to which they display successful job performance behaviors. In contrast to trait and comparison methods, behavioral methods rate objective job behaviors. When correctly developed and applied, behavioral models provide results that are relatively free of rater errors and biases. The three main types of behavioral systems are the critical incident technique (CIT), behaviorally anchored rating scales (BARS), and behavioral observation scales (BOS).

The **critical incident technique (CIT)** [16] requires job incumbents and their supervisors to identify performance incidents—on-the-job behaviors and behavioral outcomes—that distinguish successful performances from unsuccessful ones. The supervisor then observes the employees and records their performance on these critical job aspects. Usually, supervisors rate employees on how often they display the behaviors described in each critical incident. Table 4-7 illustrates a CIT form for an animal keeper job. Two statements represent examples of ineffective job performance (numbers 2 and 3), and two statements represent examples of effective job performance (numbers 1 and 4).

TABLE 4-7 A Critical Incidents Performance Appraisal Rating Form

Instructions: For each description of work behavior below, circle the number that best describes how frequently the employee engages in that behavior.

1. The incumbent removes manure and unconsumed food from the animal enclosures.

1	2	3	4	5
Never	Almost never	Sometimes	Fairly often	Very often

2. The incumbent haphazardly measures the feed items when placing them in the animal enclosures.

1	2	3	4	5
Never	Almost never	Sometimes	Fairly often	Very often

3. The incumbent leaves refuse dropped by visitors on and around the public walkways.

1	2	3	4	5
Never	Almost never	Sometimes	Fairly often	Very often

4. The incumbent skillfully identifies instances of abnormal behavior among the animals, which represent signs of illness.

1	2	3	4	5
Never	Almost never	Sometimes	Fairly often	Very often

The CIT tends to be useful because this procedure requires extensive documentation that identifies successful and unsuccessful job performance behaviors by both the employee and the supervisor. But the CIT's strength is also its weakness: Implementation of the CIT demands continuous and close observation of the employee. Supervisors may find the record keeping to be overly burdensome.

Behaviorally anchored rating scales (BARS) [17] are based on the critical incident technique, and these scales are developed in the same fashion with one exception. For the CIT, a critical incident would be written as "the incumbent completed the task in a timely fashion." For the BARS format, this incident would be written as "the incumbent is expected to complete the task in a timely fashion." The designers of BARS write the incidents as expectations to emphasize the fact that the employee does not have to demonstrate the exact behavior that is used as an anchor in order to be rated at that level. Because a complete array of behaviors that characterize a particular job would take many pages of description, it is not feasible to place examples of all job behaviors on the scale. Therefore, experts list only those behaviors that they believe are most representative of the job the employee must perform. A typical job might have 8 to 10 dimensions under BARS, each with a separate rating scale. Table 4-8 contains an illustration of a BARS for one dimension of an animal keeper job—cleaning animal enclosures and removing refuse from the public walkways. The scale reflects the range of performance on the job dimension from ineffective performance (1) to effective performance (7).

As with all performance appraisal techniques, BARS has its advantages and disadvantages [18]. Among the various performance appraisal techniques, BARS is the most defensible in court because it is based on actual observable job behaviors. In addition, BARS encourages all raters to make evaluations in the same way. Perhaps the main disadvantage of BARS is the difficulty of developing and maintaining the volume of data necessary to make it effective. The BARS method requires companies to maintain distinct appraisal documents for each job. As jobs change over time, the documentation must be updated for each job.

Another kind of behavior system, a **behavioral observation scale (BOS)** [19], displays illustrations of positive incidents (or behaviors) of job performance for various job dimensions. The evaluator rates the employee on each behavior according to the

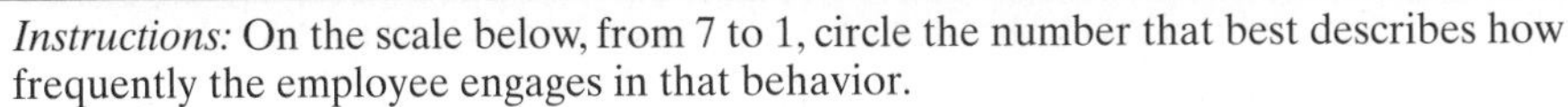
TABLE 4-8 A Behaviorally Anchored Rating Scale

Instructions: On the scale below, from 7 to 1, circle the number that best describes how frequently the employee engages in that behavior.

7 The incumbent could be expected to thoroughly clean the animal enclosures and remove refuse from the public walkways as often as needed.

6

5 The incumbent could be expected to thoroughly clean the animal enclosures and remove refuse from the public walkways twice daily.

4

3 The incumbent could be expected to clean the animal enclosures and remove refuse from the public walkways in a haphazard fashion twice daily.

2

1 The incumbent could be expected to rarely clean the animal enclosures or remove refuse from the public walkways.

extent to which the employee performs in a manner consistent with each behavioral description. Scores from each job dimension are averaged to provide an overall rating of performance. BOS is developed in the same way as a BARS instrument, except that it incorporates only positive performance behaviors. The BOS method tends to be difficult and time-consuming to develop and maintain. Moreover, to assure accurate appraisal, raters must be able to observe employees closely and regularly. Observing employees on a regular basis may not be feasible where supervisors are responsible for several employees.

Goal-Oriented Systems

Management by objectives (MBO) [20] is possibly the most effective performance appraisal technique because supervisors and employees determine objectives for employees to meet during the rating period and employees appraise how well they have achieved their objectives. Management by objectives is used mainly for managerial and professional employees and typically evaluates employees' progress toward strategic planning objectives.

Together, employees and supervisors determine particular objectives tied to corporate strategies. Employees are expected to attain these objectives during the rating period. At the end of the rating period, the employee writes a report explaining his or her progress toward accomplishing the objectives, and the employee's supervisor appraises the employee's performance based on accomplishment of the objectives.

Management by objectives can promote effective communication between employees and their supervisors. On the downside, management by objectives is time-consuming and requires a constant flow of information between employees and employers. Moreover, its focus is only on the attainment of particular goals, often to the exclusion of other important outcomes. This drawback is known as a "results at any cost" mentality [21]. Historically, the role of automobile sales professionals was literally limited to making sales. Once these professionals and customers agreed on the price of a car, the sales professionals' work with customers was completed. Nowadays, automobile salespeople remain in contact with clients for as long as several months following the completion of the sale. The purpose is to ensure customer satisfaction and build loyalty to the product and dealership by addressing questions about the vehicle's features and reminding clients about scheduled service checks.

Oftentimes, goal-oriented systems are a component of broader development programs that help employees achieve career goals. Honeywell blends goal-oriented systems with performance discussions between managers and employees:

> To guide your development and career path at Honeywell, you will have annual performance discussions with your supervisor. These discussions review a number of topics including:
>
> Your strengths and accomplishments during the year
> Significant milestones you have achieved
> Ratings on each corporate competency area
> Personal goals for the next 12 months
> Developmental suggestions for future growth
> Ideas for your next assignment or placement
>
> From these discussions, you will begin to map your Learning Plan for the year. In addition to the annual reviews, supervisors will engage in mid-year reviews. These reviews are opportunities to check the learning and development of the individual to ensure that all team members are on the road to success. [22]

Exploring the Performance Appraisal Process

Performance appraisals represent a company's way of telling employees what is expected of them in their jobs and how well they are meeting those expectations. Typically, performance appraisals require supervisors to monitor employees' performance, complete performance appraisal forms about the employees, and hold discussions with employees about their performance. Companies that use merit pay plans must assess employee job performance, which serves as a basis for awarding merit pay raises. Awarding merit pay increases on factors other than job performance, but for four exceptions (a seniority system, merit system, quality or quantity of production, and any factor besides sex), could lead some employees to level charges of illegal pay discrimination against the employer based on the Equal Pay Act of 1963.

One such violation of the Equal Pay Act involved two female employees of Cascade Wood Components Company, which remanufactures lumber products [23]. The job in question was the sawyer job; a sawyer is responsible for cutting the best grade wood segments that will be manufactured into the highest grade lumber. Cascade awarded pay increases to male sawyers before awarding pay increases to more experienced female sawyers. The court found Cascade in violation of the Equal Pay Act because the higher pay raises awarded to the male sawyers could not be accounted for by commensurate differences in job performance, seniority, a merit system that measures earnings by quantity or quality of production, or any factor other than sex.

Chapter 3 emphasized how U.S. civil rights laws protect employees from illegal discrimination based on age, race, color, religion, sex, national origin, or qualified disability. Because negative performance appraisals can affect an individual's employment status and related decisions such as pay levels and increases, promotions, and discharges, appraisals must be based on job-related factors and not on any discriminatory factors.

Legislation and court decisions have subjected performance appraisals to close scrutiny. In ***Brito v. Zia Company***, the court found that the Zia Company violated Title VII when a disproportionate number of protected class individuals were laid off on the basis of low performance appraisal scores. Zia's action was a violation of Title VII because the use of the performance appraisal system in determining layoffs was indeed an employment test. In addition, the court ruled that the Zia Company had not demonstrated that its performance appraisal instrument was valid. In other words, the appraisal did not assess any job-related criteria based on quality or quantity of work [24].

Four Activities to Promote Nondiscriminatory Performance Appraisal Practices

Since the *Brito v. Zia Company* decision, court opinions and compensation experts suggest the following four points to ensure nondiscriminatory performance appraisal practices and to protect firms using merit pay systems if legal issues arise [25]. Nondiscriminatory performance appraisal systems are key to effective merit pay systems because they accurately measure job performance.

1. Conduct job analyses to ascertain characteristics necessary for successful job performance.

Companies must first establish definitions of the jobs and then discover what employee behaviors are necessary to perform the jobs. Job analysis is essential for the development of content-valid performance appraisal systems. Content validity displays connections between the measurable factors upon which the employee is being appraised and the job itself. For example, customer service associates' performance might be judged on the basis of courtesy and knowledge of the company's products or services, and these measures would be content-valid dimensions. Both measures are representative of and relative to the job. On the other hand, knowledge of the company's financial accounting practices would not be a content-valid criterion of customer service associates' performance.

Human resource and compensation experts must review performance appraisal tools regularly to ensure that the tools adequately reflect the key behaviors necessary for effective job performance. Jobholders, supervisors, and clients can often give the most relevant input to determine whether a performance appraisal system contains dimensions that relate to a particular job.

2. Incorporate these characteristics into a rating instrument.

Although the professional literature recommends rating instruments that are tied to specific job behaviors (for example, behaviorally anchored rating scales), the courts routinely accept less sophisticated approaches such as simple graphic rating scales and trait ranges. Regardless of the method, HR departments should provide all supervisors and raters with written definitive standards.

The examples given earlier about the animal keeper job indicate that effective performance appraisal instruments are based on explicitly written job duties conveyed in the job description.

3. Train supervisors to use the rating instrument properly.

Raters need to know how to apply performance appraisal standards when they make judgments. The uniform application of standards is extremely important. In addition, evaluators should be aware of common rater errors, which are discussed later in this chapter.

4. Several cases demonstrate that formal appeal mechanisms and review of ratings by upper-level personnel help make performance appraisal processes more accurate and effective.

Allowing employees to voice their concerns over ratings they believe to be inaccurate or unjust opens a dialogue between employees and their supervisors that may shed light on the performance appraisal outcomes. Employees may be able to point out instances of their performances that may have been overlooked in the appraisal process or explain particular extreme instances as the result of extraordinary circumstances. For example, an ill parent in need of regular attention is the reason for an employee's absence rather than an employee's deliberate breach of work responsibilities because the employee chose to relax at the beach.

Sources of Performance Appraisal Information

Information for performance appraisal can be ascertained from five sources:

- Employee (that is, the individual whose job performance is being appraised)
- Employee's supervisor
- Employee's coworkers
- Employee's supervisees
- Employee's customers or clients

More than one source can provide performance appraisal information. Although supervisory input is the most common source of performance appraisal information, companies are increasingly calling on as many sources of information as possible to gain a more complete picture of employee job performance. Performance appraisal systems that rely on many appropriate sources of information are known as **360-degree performance appraisals**.

Companies are increasingly relying on the 360-degree performance appraisal methods to reduce the costs of recruiting and hiring new employees. This method helps companies develop a more complete understanding of current employee performance by formulating a judgment on input from multiple sources. Oftentimes, companies feel more confident about promoting employees from within when multiple sources of information support positive performance judgments.

Three criteria should be used to judge the appropriateness of the information source [26]. First, the evaluators should be aware of the objectives of the employee's job. Second, the evaluators should have occasion to frequently observe the employee on the job. Third, the evaluators should be capable of determining whether the employee's performance is satisfactory.

The use of 360-degree performance appraisals is on the rise in U.S. businesses. Three main factors account for this trend. First, as companies downsize, the organizational structures are becoming less hierarchical. As a result, managers and supervisors are increasingly responsible for more workers. With responsibility for more employees, it has become difficult for managers and supervisors to provide sufficient attention to each employee throughout the appraisal period.

Second, the use of 360-degree performance appraisal methods is consistent with the increased prevalence of work teams in companies. At Whirlpool Corporation, members of semiautonomous work teams communicate their work goals to the entire team. At the end of the designated appraisal period, team members judge others' performances based on the prior statement of work goals.

Third, companies are placing greater emphasis on customer satisfaction as competition for a limited set of customers increases. Nowadays, companies turn to customers as a source of performance appraisal information. For example, it is common for restaurants, furniture stores, moving companies, and automobile manufacturers to ask customers to complete short surveys designed to measure how well they were satisfied with various aspects of their interactions. Volkswagen of America uses the services of a professional survey company to call VW car owners to rate their experiences with VW dealer service departments. Table 4-9 illustrates a major moving company's customer satisfaction survey, which it mails to customers following a move.

TABLE 4-9 Sample Customer Satisfaction Survey

Before and During Your Move:	***Yes***	***No***
1. Did our moving consultant help with packing and moving day suggestions?	☐	☐
2. Were we on time?	☐	☐
3. Was our packing service satisfactory?	☐	☐
4. Were our moving personnel courteous?	☐	☐
5. Did your possessions arrive in good condition?	☐	☐
6. Would you recommend us to your friends?	☐	☐

Why did you choose us?

☐ Reputation	☐ Contacted by salesperson
☐ Have used before	☐ Recommended by friends
☐ Selected by employer	☐ Recommended by employer
☐ Contacted by telemarketer	☐ Other:_______________

How can we better serve you?

____

____

____

Errors in the Performance Appraisal Process

Almost all raters make rating errors. **Rating errors** reflect differences between human judgment processes versus objective, accurate assessments uncolored by bias, prejudice, or other subjective, extraneous influences [27]. Rating errors occur because raters must always make subjective judgments. Human resource departments can help raters minimize errors by carefully choosing rating systems and raters to recognize and avoid common errors. Major types of rater errors include [28]:

- Bias errors
- Contrast errors
- Errors of central tendency
- Errors of leniency or strictness

Bias Errors

Bias errors happen when the rater evaluates the employee based on a personal negative or positive opinion of the employee rather than on the employee's actual performance. Four ways supervisors may bias evaluation results are first impression effects, positive and negative halo effects, similar-to-me effects, and illegal discriminatory biases.

A manager biased by a **first-impression effect** might make an initial favorable or unfavorable judgment about an employee and then ignore or distort the employee's actual performance based on this impression. For instance, a manager expects that a newly hired graduate of a prestigious Ivy League university will be an exemplary performer. After 1 year on the job, this employee fails to meet many of the work objectives; nevertheless, the manager rates the job performance more highly because of the initial impression.

A **positive halo effect** or **negative halo effect** occurs when a rater generalizes an employee's good or bad behavior on one aspect of the job to all aspects of the job. A secretary with offensive interpersonal skills is a proficient user of various computer software programs and an outstanding typist. The secretary's supervisor receives frequent complaints from other employees and customers. At performance appraisal time, the supervisor gives this employee an overall negative performance rating.

A **similar-to-me effect** refers to the tendency on the part of raters to judge favorably employees whom they perceive as similar to themselves. Supervisors biased by this effect rate more favorably employees who have attitudes, values, backgrounds, or interests similar to theirs. For example, employees whose children attend the same elementary school as their manager's children receive higher performance appraisal ratings than employees who do not have children. "Similar-to-me" errors or biases easily can lead to charges of **illegal discriminatory bias**, wherein a supervisor rates members of his or her race, gender, nationality, or religion more favorably than members of other classes.

Contrast Errors

Supervisors make **contrast errors** when they compare an employee to other employees rather than to specific, explicit performance standards. Such comparisons qualify as errors because other employees are required to perform only at minimum acceptable standards. Employees performing at minimally acceptable levels should receive satisfactory ratings, even if every other employee doing the job is performing at outstanding or above-average levels.

Errors of Central Tendency

When supervisors rate all employees as average or close to average, they commit **errors of central tendency**. Such errors are most often committed when raters are forced to justify only extreme behavior—high or low ratings—with written explanations. Therefore, HR professionals should require justification for ratings at every level of the scale and not just at the extremes.

Errors of Leniency or Strictness

Raters sometimes place every employee at the high or low end of the scale, regardless of actual performance. With a **leniency error**, managers tend to appraise employees' performance more highly than they really rate compared with objective criteria. Over time, if supervisors commit positive errors, their employees will expect higher-than-deserved pay rates.

On the other hand, **strictness errors** occur when a supervisor rates an employee's performance lower than it would be if compared against objective criteria. If supervisors make this error over time, employees may receive smaller pay raises than deserved, lower their effort, and perform poorly. In effect, this error erodes employees' beliefs that effort varies positively with performance and that performance influences the amount of pay raises.

STRENGTHENING THE PAY-FOR-PERFORMANCE LINK

Ultimately, companies who don't consider these possible limitations weaken the relationship between pay and performance. HR managers can employ a number of approaches to strengthen the link between pay and job performance.

Link Performance Appraisals to Business Goals

The standards by which employee performance is judged should be linked to a company's competitive strategy or strategies. For example, each member of a product development team that is charged with the responsibility of marketing a new product might be given merit increases if certain sales goals are reached.

Analyze Jobs

Job analysis (Chapter 7) is vital to companies that wish to establish **internally consistent compensation systems**. Job descriptions (Chapter 7)—a product of job analyses—can be used by supervisors to create objective performance measures, as discussed earlier. Job descriptions note the duties, requirements, and relative importance of a job within the company. Supervisors appraising performances can match employees' performances to these criteria. This approach may help reduce supervisors' arbitrary decisions about merit increases by clarifying the standards against which employees' performances are judged.

Communicate

For merit pay programs to succeed, employees must clearly understand what they need to do to receive merit increases and what the rewards for their performances will be. Open communication helps employees develop reasonable expectations and encourages them to trust the system and those who operate it. Figure 4-2 illustrates worksheets both supervisors and employers may use to establish performance expectations.

FIGURE 4-2 Supervisor's and Employee's Performance Planning Worksheets

Supervisor's Performance Planning Worksheet

To be filled out by supervisor

Name of Employee: **Date:**

Employee Title: **Department:**

1. List what you consider to be the primary job duties or assignments at this time (list in order of priority):

2. Describe contributions, achievements, or improvements made by the employee during the past appraisal period:

3. Describe any specific change, improvements, or goals desired for the employee's performance in the next appraisal period:

4. Describe the coaching, training, or development activities you would support in pursuit of improved performance, employee growth, learning, and/or career development:

Employee ______ Date ______ Supervisor ______ Date ______

FIGURE 4-2 (*cont.*)

Employee's Performance Planning Worksheet

To be filled out by employee

Name of Employee: **Date:**

Employee Title: **Department:**

1. List what you consider to be your primary job duties or assignments at this time (list in order of priority):

2. Describe contributions or achievements that indicate your success at improving your performance or exceeding job requirements during the past appraisal period:

3. Describe any specific changes or improvements you want to make in your performance in the next appraisal period. Describe obstacles to getting your job done and suggest possible solutions:

4. Describe the coaching, training, or development activities that would help you pursue improved performance, job growth, learning, and/or career development:

____________________ ______

Employee Signature Date

______ (*Initial*) I have been given the opportunity to fill this out and choose not to do so.

Establish Effective Appraisals

During performance appraisal meetings with employees, supervisors should discuss goals for future performance and employee career plans. When performance deficiencies are evident, the supervisor and employee should work together to identify possible causes and develop an action plan to remedy these deficiencies. The performance standards listed within job descriptions should serve as the guides for establishing performance targets. For example, a company's job description for a secretary specifies that the job incumbent must be able to use one word processing software package proficiently. The supervisor should clearly explain what software usage proficiency means. Proficiency may refer to the ability to operate certain features of the software well, including the mail merge utility, the table generator, and the various outlining utilities, or proficiency may refer to the ability to operate all features of the software well.

Empower Employees

Because formal performance appraisals are conducted periodically—maybe only once per year—supervisors must empower their employees to make performance self-appraisals between formal sessions [29]. Moreover, supervisors need to take on a coach's role to empower their workers [30]. As coaches, supervisors must ensure that employees have access to the resources necessary to perform their jobs. Supervisors-as-coaches should also help employees interpret and respond to work problems as they develop. Empowering employees in this fashion should lead to more self-corrective actions rather than reactive courses of action to supervisory feedback and only to the criticisms addressed in performance appraisal meetings.

Differentiate Among Performers

Merit increases should consist of meaningful increments. If employees do not see significant distinctions between top performers and poor performers, top performers may become frustrated and reduce their levels of performance. When companies' merit increases don't clearly reflect differences in actual job performances, they may need to provide alternative rewards. For example, fringe compensation—additional vacation days or higher discounts on the company's product or service—can complement merit pay increases.

POSSIBLE LIMITATIONS OF MERIT PAY PROGRAMS

Despite the popularity of merit pay systems, these programs are not without potential limitations, which may lessen their credibility with employees. If employees do not believe in a merit pay program, the pay system will not bring about the expected motivational impacts. Supervisors, HR managers, and compensation professionals must address the following eight potential problems with merit pay programs.

Failure to Differentiate Among Performers

Employees may receive merit increases even if their performance does not warrant them, because supervisors want to avoid creating animosity among employees. Therefore, poor performers may receive the same pay increase as exemplary performers, and poor performers may come to view merit pay increases as entitlements. Consequently, superior performers may question the value of striving for excellent performance.

Poor Performance Measures

Accurate and comprehensive performance measures that capture the entire scope of an employee's job are essential to successful merit pay programs. In most companies, employees' job performances tend to be assessed subjectively, based on their supervisors' judgments. As discussed, merit pay programs rely on supervisors' subjective assessments of employees' prior job performances. Unfortunately, developing performance measures for every single job is not only difficult but also expensive.

Supervisors' Biased Ratings of Employee Job Performance

As we discussed earlier, supervisors are subject to a number of errors when they make subjective assessments of employees' job performances. These errors often undermine the credibility of the performance evaluation process. Performance evaluation processes that lack credibility do little to create the perception among employees that pay reflects performance.

STRETCHING THE DOLLAR

MERIT BONUSES COST LESS MONEY

Merit increases have traditionally been permanent increases to employees' base pay. Thus, companies carry merit pay increase expenses as long as employees remain employed. This design feature essentially rewards employees over time for some prior performance accomplishments, even though employer benefits have typically expired long ago. Past exemplary performers can slack off and still enjoy high compensation based on past performance. On the other hand, newcomers who are capable performers must perform well for several years in order to reach the same pay level as longer-service employees.

Although merit increases aren't supposed to be given as an entitlement to employees, many employees see it as a regular increase nonetheless. According to an American Compensation Association study [31], approximately one out of every three companies are shifting toward variable pay programs that do not add permanent increases to base pay. Incentive pay represents the majority of available variable pay programs to companies.

Many companies use alternative kinds of merit pay awards known as **merit bonuses**. The merit bonus differs from the traditional merit pay increase in an important way. The merit bonus is not added to base pay as a permanent increment. Employees must earn the bonus each year. Companies that use merit bonuses find it less costly than companies that rely solely on permanent merit pay increases. In addition, employees who choose to slack off will be at a disadvantage because merit bonuses are not added as permanent increments to base pay.

Table 4-10 illustrates the cost burden to companies that is associated with awarding permanent merit pay increases versus merit bonuses.

TABLE 4-10 The Costs of Permanent Merit Increases versus Merit Bonus Awards: A Comparison

At the end of 2002, Angela Johnson earned an annual salary of $20,000.

		Cost of Increase (Total Current Salary—2002 Annual Salary)		*Total Salary Under:*	
Year	*Increase Amount*	*Permanent Merit Increase*	*Merit Bonus*	*Permanent Merit Increase (% Increase × Previous Annual Salary)*	*Merit Bonus (% Increase × 2002 Annual Salary)*
2003	3%	$ 600	$ 600	$20,660	$20,600
2004	5%	$ 1,630	$ 1,000	$21,630	$21,000
2005	4%	$ 2,496	$ 800	$22,496	$20,800
2006	7%	$ 4,070	$ 1,400	$24,070	$21,400
2007	6%	$ 5,514	$ 1,200	$25,514	$21,200
2008	5%	$ 6,790	$ 1,000	$26,790	$21,000
2009	3%	$ 7,594	$ 600	$27,594	$20,600
2010	6%	$ 9,250	$ 1,200	$29,250	$21,200
2011	8%	$11,590	$ 1,600	$31,590	$21,600
2012	7%	$13,801	$ 1,400	$33,801	$21,400
Total increase amount		$63,335	$10,800		

Lack of Open Communication Between Management and Employees

If managers cannot communicate effectively with employees, employees will not trust performance appraisal processes. Trust is difficult to build when decisions are kept secret and employees have no influence on pay decisions. Thus, merit pay decision systems can cause conflict between management and employees. If mistrust characterizes the relationship, then performance appraisals will mean little to employees and could even lead to accusations of bias. In an environment of secrecy, employees lack the information necessary to determine if pay actually is linked to job performance.

Undesirable Social Structures

We acknowledged that relative pay grades can reflect status differentials within a company: Employees with lucrative salaries are usually granted higher status than lower-paid employees. Permanent merit increases may rigidify the relative pay status of employees over time [32]. Table 4-11 shows the permanence of the relative pay difference between two distinct jobs that each receive a 5 percent merit increase each year. Even though both employees performed well and received "equal" merit increases in percentage terms, the actual salary differentials prevail each year. Thus, where pay level is an indicator of status, permanent merit increases may reinforce an undesirable social structure. Lower-paid employees may resent never being able to catch up.

Factors Other Than Merit

Merit increases may be based on factors other than merit, which will clearly reduce the emphasis on job performance. For example, supervisors may subconsciously use their employees' ages or seniority as bases for awarding merit increases. Studies show that the extent to which supervisors like the employees for whom they are responsible determines the size of pay raises in a merit pay program [33]. In addition, company politics assumes that the value of an employee's contributions depends on the agenda, or goals, of the supervisor [34] rather than on the objective impact of an employee's contributions to a rationally determined work goal. For instance, an accounting manager wishes to employ different accounting methods

TABLE 4-11 The Impact of Equal Pay Raise Percentage Amounts for Distinct Salaries

At the end of 2000, Anne Brown earned $50,000 per year as a systems analyst, and John Williams earned $35,000 per year as an administrative assistant. Each received a 5 percent pay increase every year until the year 2005.

	Anne Brown	*John Williams*
2001	$52,500	$36,750
2002	$55,125	$38,587
2003	$57,881	$40,516
2004	$60,775	$42,542
2005	$63,814	$44,669

than top management's accounting methods. She believes that she can gain top management support by demonstrating that the accounting staff agrees with her position. The accounting manager may give generally positive performance evaluations, regardless of demonstrated performance, to those who endorse her accounting methods.

Undesirable Competition

Because merit pay programs focus fundamentally on individual employees, these programs do little to integrate workforce members [35]. With limited budgets for merit increases, employees must compete for a larger share of this limited amount. Competition among employees is counterproductive if teamwork is essential for successfully completing projects. Thus, merit increases are best suited for jobs where the employee works independently, such as clerical positions, and many professional positions from job families such as accounting.

Little Motivational Value

Notwithstanding their intended purpose, merit pay programs may not positively influence employee motivation. Employers and employees may differ in what they see as "large enough" merit increases to really motivate positive worker behavior. For example, increases diminish after deducting income taxes and contributions to Social Security, and differences in employees' monthly paychecks may be negligible.

LINKING MERIT PAY WITH COMPETITIVE STRATEGY

As you will recall, in Chapter 2 we reviewed a framework for establishing a basis for selecting particular compensation tactics to match a company's competitive strategy. How do merit systems fit with the two fundamental competitive strategies—lowest cost and differentiation? Ultimately, merit pay systems, when properly applied, can contribute to meeting the goals of lowest-cost and differentiation strategies. However, the rationale for the appropriateness of merit pay systems differs according to the imperatives of the lowest-cost and differentiation competitive strategies.

Lowest-Cost Competitive Strategy

Lowest-cost strategies require firms to reduce output costs per employee. Merit pay systems are most appropriate only when the following two conditions are met: (1) Pay increases are commensurate with employee productivity, and (2) employees maintain productivity levels over time. Unfortunately, factors outside companies' control may lead to lower employee productivity from time to time. Personal illness and a shortage of raw materials for production are examples of factors that undermine employee productivity. Companies that typically experience such slowdowns are likely to find that merit pay systems run counter to cost-containment goals.

Differentiation Competitive Strategy

A differentiation strategy requires creative, open-minded, risk-taking employees. Compared to lowest-cost strategies, companies that pursue differentiation strategies must take a longer-term focus to attain their preestablished objectives. Merit pay has the potential to promote creativity and risk taking by linking pay with innovative job accomplishments. However, objectives that are tied to creativity and risk taking must be established on a regular basis for merit pay to be effective under differentiation strategies. Granting merit pay raises for past performance would be tantamount to rewarding employees long after the impact of their past performance has subsided.

SUMMARY

This chapter provided a discussion of the seniority pay and merit pay concepts. Companies should move away from rewarding employees solely on the basis of seniority and toward rewarding employees for measurable accomplishments. To be successful, merit pay programs must be founded on well-designed performance appraisal systems that accurately measure performance. In addition, rewards commensurate with past performance should be rewarded. Perhaps the greatest challenge for companies is to ensure that employees are given the opportunity to perform at exemplary levels.

Key Terms

- seniority pay, 94
- longevity pay, 94
- human capital theory, 94
- human capital, 94
- job control unionism, 95
- General Schedule (GS), 100
- merit pay programs, 102
- just-meaningful pay increase, 103
- trait systems, 105
- comparison systems, 106
- forced distribution, 106
- paired comparisons, 108
- behavioral systems, 108
- critical incident technique (CIT), 108
- behaviorally anchored rating scales (BARS), 109
- behavioral observation scale (BOS), 109
- management by objectives (MBO), 110
- *Brito v. Zia Company*, 111
- 360-degree performance appraisals, 113
- rating errors, 114
- bias errors, 114
- first-impression effect, 114
- positive halo effect, 114
- negative halo effect, 114
- similar-to-me effect, 115
- illegal discriminatory bias, 115
- contrast errors, 115
- errors of central tendency, 115
- leniency error, 115
- strictness errors, 115
- internally consistent compensation systems, 116
- merit bonuses, 119

Discussion Questions

1. Human capital theory has been advanced as a rationale underlying seniority pay. Identify two individuals you know who have performed the same job for at least 2 years. Ask them to describe the changes in knowledge and skills they experienced from the time they assumed their jobs to the present. Discuss your findings with the class.
2. Subjective performance evaluations are subject to several rater errors, which makes objective measures seem a better alternative. Discuss when subjective performance evaluations might be better (or more feasible) than objective ratings.
3. Consider a summer job that you have held. Write a detailed job description for that job. Then, develop a behaviorally anchored rating scale (BARS) that can be used to evaluate an individual who performs that job in the future.
4. This chapter indicates that merit pay plans appear to be the most common form of compensation in the United States. Although widely used, these systems are not suitable for all kinds of jobs. Based on your knowledge of merit pay systems, identify at least three jobs for which merit pay is

inappropriate. Be sure to provide your rationale given the information in this chapter.

5. Select three distinct jobs of your choice—for instance, a clerical job, a technical job, and a professional job. For each job, identify what you believe is the most appropriate performance appraisal method. Based on your choices, sketch a performance appraisal instrument. Discuss the rationale for your choice of performance appraisal methods.

Exercises

Compensation Online

For Students

Exercise 1: Search for relevant journal articles
Search article databases for seniority and merit pay. Using the information you find through your search and the information in Chapter 4, write a short explanation of the pros and cons of each system, which you would advocate, and why.

Exercise 2: Search for government salary schedules
Using Yahoo, go to the federal government's General Schedule by clicking on the *advance search* link, typing in "general schedule," selecting the *exact phrase match*, and clicking on the *search* button. Scroll down to the *General Schedule Classification System* link and click on it. Read over the page and then click on the *Classification Standards* (located at the bottom of the page under Related Topics). Review the page and click on a couple of the links. Write a brief description about the contents of this site, describing what information it contains and how valuable you think this site might be for you as a student.

Exercise 3: Research employment discrimination laws
Using the search engine of your choice, search for Equal Pay Act of 1963. Find articles or government Web sites, and gather information on how this law has been interpreted over the years and what sorts of cases have been most common. Write a short timeline of how the Equal Pay Act and related cases have changed over the life of the act.

For Professionals

Exercise 1: Research an organizational Web site
Using Yahoo, click on the *advanced search* button. Type the "Institute of Management and Administration" in the window, click on the exact phrase match and the Web sites options, and then click on the *search* link. Read over its homepage (*www.ioma.com*). Review the page and then click on some of the topics. Do you think this site might be of value to you as a professional? Describe the features of the IOMA organization that you would find most helpful.

Exercise 2: Search for a union's Web sites
Sometimes, certain Web resources are not what you need. For instance, you would like specifically to find only current events and recent issues pertaining to the United Auto Workers. Using Yahoo, click on the *advanced search* button and type in "United Auto Workers." Select the exact phrase match and Web sites options, and click on the *search* button. Click on each of the *Categories, Web Pages,* and *News and Stories* buttons and review the information available on each one. What did you find when you clicked on each button? When would you use one button rather than the other? Find a site that pertains to the UAW and collective bargaining. Describe the relevant information for a human resource professional.

Exercise 3: Research different performance management practices

The VP of human resources has expressed dissatisfaction with your company's current performance management system. Search for performance appraisal and/or performance management. Find consulting firms that specialize in these areas. Compare and contrast the services offered by each firm. How would you determine the reputability of each firm?

Endnotes

1. Cayer, N. J. (1975). *Public Personnel Administration in the United States*. New York: St. Martin Press.
2. Becker, G. (1975). *Human Capital*. New York: St. Martin Press.
3. Kochan, T. R., Katz, H. C., & McKersie, R. B. (1994). *The Transformation of American Industrial Relations*. Ithaca, NY: ILR Press.
4. Cayer, N. J. (1975). *Public Personnel Administration in the United States*. New York: St. Martin Press.
5. U.S. Bureau of Labor Statistics. (2002). Union members in 2001 (USDOL-02-28) [online]. Available: *http://stats.bls.gov/newsrels.htm*, accessed July 13, 2002.
6. Kernel, R. C., & Moorage, K. S. (1990). Longevity pay in the States: Echo from the past or sound of the future? *Public Personnel Management, 19*, pp. 191–200.
7. Peck, C. (1984). Pay and performance: The interaction of compensation and performance appraisal (*Research Bulletin No. 155*). New York: The Conference Board.
8. WorldatWork (2002). 2001–02 Total salary increase budget survey [online]. Available: *worldatwork.org*, accessed June 17, 2002.
9. Ibid.
10. Gómez-Mejía, L. R., & Welbourne, T. (1991). Compensation strategies in a global context. *Human Resource Planning, 14*, pp. 29–41.
11. Heneman, R. L. (1992). *Merit Pay: Linking Pay Increases to Performance*. Reading, MA: Addison-Wesley.
12. Latham, G. P., & Wexley, K. N. (1982). *Increasing Productivity through Performance Appraisal*. Reading, MA: Addison-Wesley.
13. Krefting, L. A., & Mahoney, T. A. (1977). Determining the size of a meaningful pay increase. *Industrial Relations, 16*, pp. 83–93.
14. Bean, Leon Leonwood. Today's commitment to customer values: L. L. Bean's golden rule. [online]. Available: *http://www.llbean.com*, accessed: July 11, 2002.
15. Bernadin, H. J. & Beatty, R. W. (1984). *Performance Appraisal: Assessing Human Behavior at Work*. Boston: Kent.
16. Fivars, G. (1975). The critical incident technique: A bibliography. *JSAS Catalog of Selected Documents in Psychology, 5*, p. 210.
17. Smith, P., & Kendall, L. M. (1963). Retranslation of expectation: An approach to the construction of unambiguous anchors for rating scales. *Journal of Applied Psychology, 47*, pp. 149–155.
18. Latham, G. P., & Wexley, K. N. (1982). *Increasing Productivity through Performance Appraisal*. Reading, MA: Addison-Wesley.
19. Latham, G. P., & Wexley, K. N. (1977). Behavioral observation scales for performance appraisal purposes. *Personnel Psychology, 30*, pp. 255–268.
20. Bernardin, H. J., & Beatty, R. W. (1984). *Performance Appraisal: Assessing Human Behavior at Work*. Boston: Kent.
21. Bernardin, H. J., & Beatty, R. W. (1984). *Performance Appraisal: Assessing Human Behavior at Work*. Boston: Kent.
22. Excerpt from Honeywell's Web site: How will my career develop? [online]. Available: *http://www.honeywell.com*, accessed July 11, 2002.
23. *Coe v. Cascade Wood Components*, 48 FEP Cases 664 (W.D. OR. 1988).
24. *Brito v. Zia Company*, 478 F2d 1200, CA 10 (1973).
25. Barrett, G. V., & Kernan, M. C. (1987). Performance appraisal and terminations: A review of court decisions since *Brito v. Zia Company* with implication for personnel practices. *Personnel Psychology, 40*, pp. 489–503.
26. Latham, G. P., & Wexley, K. N. (1982). *Increasing Productivity through Performance Appraisal*, Reading, MA: Addison-Wesley.
27. Blum, M. L., & Naylor, J. C. (1968). *Industrial Psychology: Its Theoretical and Social Foundations*. New York: Harper & Row.
28. Bernardin, H. J., & Beatty, R. W. (1984). *Performance Appraisal: Assessing Human Behavior at Work*. Boston: Kent.
29. Gómez-Mejía, L. R., Balkin, D. R., & Cardy, R. L. (1995). *Managing Human Resources*. Upper Saddle River, NJ: Prentice Hall.
30. Evered, R. D., & Selman, J. C. (1989). Coaching and the art of management. *Organizational Dynamics, 18*, pp. 16–33.

31. Lawler, E. E. III, & Cohen, S. G. (1992). Designing a pay system for teams. *American Compensation Association Journal, 1,* pp. 6–19.
32. Haire, M., Ghiselli, E. E., & Gordon, M. E. (1967). A psychological study of pay. *Journal of Applied Psychology Monograph, 51* (Whole No. 636).
33. Cardy, R. L., & Dobbins, G. H. (1986). Affect and appraisal: Liking as an integral dimension in evaluating performance. *Journal of Applied Psychology, 71*, 672–678.
34. Murphy, K. R., & Cleveland, J. N. (1991). *Performance Appraisal: An Organizational Perspective*. Boston: Allyn & Bacon.
35. Lawler, E. E. III, & Cohen, S. G. (1992). Designing a pay system for teams. *American Compensation Association Journal, 1*, pp. 6–19.

COMPENSATION IN ACTION

STREAMLINING A COMPETITIVE PAY PACKAGE IN AN UNCERTAIN MARKET

In revamping its pay mix, IBM took all variables into account, right down to the letter.

Quick Look

- Companies need to be aware of how market implications affect their compensation package.
- Employee pay is linked directly to performance in IBM's global variable pay program.
- In assessing its pay package, IBM focused on employee values, perceptions, and motivators.
- It's important to continually communicate the value of the pay package to executives and employees.

Volatility, uncertainty, and turbulence are words that paint a stormy picture of today's economic environment. For compensation professionals, that means spending money wisely, using real-time knowledge of market trends and pay levels, and rethinking employees' pay mix. Companies also need to be fast and flexible, with contingency plans in hand, when facing market uncertainty.

"The market can take the shape of the letter V, U, or L, when rebounding," Doreen T. Griffen, director of executive compensation at International Business Machines (IBM), told attendees at the Conference Board's Compensation Conference in Coronado, California.

"In a V, growth picks up as quickly as it slides," Griffen said. "When the market slows down for a while then picks up, it's in the shape of a U. In an economic slowdown where output continues at low levels, it takes on an L shape." (See Figure 1.)

"If there is a major downturn in your business, you need to know the implications on compensation," she continued. "It's also important to look at it as an opportunity to drive the business to get results."

FIGURE 1 Labor Market Volatility

V Market sharply declines, then rapidly regains momentum, like a V.

U Market declines slowly, then slowly rallies, like a U.

L Market declines sharply with output continuing at new low levels, like an L.

OUT WITH THE OLD

IBM's old rewards system consisted of socialized pay, Griffen said. "This is the belief that everyone should share in equity, without regard to performance," she said.

At IBM, an internal equity system superceded marketplace demands in a rule-driven bureaucracy dominated by entitlements, such as merit raises, serial promotions, paternalistic benefits, and managed communications.

"Employees believed that IBM took care of them for life," Griffen explained.

IN WITH THE NEW

To combat a volatile market, IBM now is taking a different approach to rewards by using pay differentiation in a market-driven company. Entitlements have been replaced with pay for individual contribution. Employees also are responsible for their own personal career development and choose their benefits with shared costs.

"Rather than handing out serial promotions left and right, it's up to individuals to develop their own career path," Griffen said.

Managed communications also are a thing of the past. Straight talk between managers and employees is strongly encouraged. "Managers are telling it like it is," Griffen said.

INVESTING IN PEOPLE

In IBM's global variable pay program, employee pay is linked directly to performance, Griffen said. IBM spends more than $30 billion per year in compensation and benefits expenses for more than 300,000 employees, including nearly $2 billion in variable pay for all employees, and nearly 50 million shares valued at $5 billion (face value price of $100 per share).

IBM's new pay-for-performance approach consists of:

- Allocating pools of bonus dollar, cash increases, and stock options
- Differentiating businesses based on high-level guidelines and principles
- Providing IT tools to expedite decision making and measuring program results

In addition, managers have ultimate discretion to spend dollars as they see fit, within their budgets. This approach resulted in:

- Fifteen percent average cash increases to top executives; 25 percent did not receive cash increases.
- Executives with the highest leadership or management potential received the largest option grants.
- Top employee increases were four times the bottom-level increases. For example, if the bottom-level increase was 4 percent, top increases were 16 percent. Fifteen percent of employees did not receive increases.
- Managers directed funds to greatest attrition areas (e.g., Silicon Valley).
- Options were directed to employees based on performance skill. "Not all employees received stock options," Griffen said. "Those who did, though, received sizable grants."

IBM's goal is to pay the best performers like the best in the marketplace. "We give employees the opportunity to get to the top of the market," Griffen said.

Employees should be paid appropriately compared to the range of pay in the local marketplace, based on the level of their contributions. Employees participate in the success and risk of the business through variable performance-based pay.

Total rewards at IBM follows three principles:

- Rewards are seen as a total package.
- The package supports a high-performance culture.
- The package needs to be competitive in terms of opportunity and cost to the company.

"How do we determine if we're delivering a competitive pay package?" Griffen asked. "There is a need for competitive intelligence, not only through surveys, but also by tracking industry trends and data and doing 'deep dives' on key competitors."

Griffen explained that people who do "deep dives" are assigned to know all the details of competitors' pay practices.

Other ways of obtaining information are via a network of company experts, a quest for real-time pay level data on positions, or creating customized surveys to ensure the company captures the right market for talent.

WHATEVER FLOATS THEIR BOAT

In assessing its pay package, IBM assessed employee motivators. "What do employees value in their compensation package?" Griffen asked. It's critical to understand employees' values and perceptions and what motivates them. "Taking it a step further, how do motivators vary by skill and location? How can compensation be tailored to employees' needs?" she added.

IBM took a market-based total compensation approach to determine market total cash and total compensation levels and filled the gap with equity value. (See Figure 2.)

MIX IT UP

To determine the appropriate mix of pay needed, IBM asked the following questions in designing its new compensation package:

- Should cash be targeted at the market in the 50th percentile and total compensation targeted at the 75th percentile for executives?
- Given market uncertainty, should cash pay be targeted higher at the expense of equity?
- What is the right mix of equity? Of stock options vs. full-value stock awards or performance units?

Market volatility is a consideration in the final package. IBM uses value-based award guidelines based on a planning price. If the planning

FIGURE 2 Market-Based Total Compensation Approach

— Total Comp

$ Equity Value

— Total Cash

(Continued)

(Continued)

price is far off the actual grant price, should the shares be adjusted? The alternatives are:

- Do nothing and the market will correct itself.
- Move to share-based guidelines or percentage of shares outstanding.
- Set the planning price based on a fixed six-month or longer average price.

FAST AND FLEXIBLE

IBM ensures that it can direct funds to the hottest emerging skills. The company is prepared to consider replacement options at a lower strike price. Approval processes were streamlined to empower managers to act quickly. Business had retention budgets in place for off cycles.

"It's important to have contingency plans in place, if you don't already," Griffen emphasized. Companies should be prepared with a list of actions that can be taken to cut expenses and understand the cost and employee relations impact of each item. For example, companies can cut international assignments by 50 percent or freeze off-cycle employee cash increases.

ABOVE ALL: COMMUNICATE!

"Companies need `to communicate programs to employees and executives so they understand the value of their compensation package," Griffen said. High-technology vehicles, such as Lotus Notes, the intranet and the extranet, are excellent remote communications. "But, person-to-person communication still counts," Griffen said.

"You can't please all the people all of the time," Griffen continued. "Rewards are a zero-sum game—a fixed pot. Companies are dealing with an exercise in distributive justice."

LOOKING AHEAD

What is the future of compensation? Griffen said companies should consider the following in designing their pay packages:

- Role of compensation
- Tailor compensation to individual needs
- Flexibility in compensation design to address business needs and experiment with emerging big opportunities
- Real-time market pay levels, headhunter data and trends with tools, such as Towers Perrin's Comp Online, a Web-based tool.

"In light of economic uncertainty, it's an excellent time to create shareholder value and competitive advantage," Griffen concluded.

Source: Barbara Parus, WorldatWork, *Workspan*, August 2001, volume 44, number 8. © 2002 WorldatWork, 14040 N. Northsight Blvd., Scottsdale A2 85260 USA: 480/951-9191; *www.worldatwork. org*; E-mail worldatwork @ worldatwork.org

WHAT'S NEW IN COMPENSATION?

Challenges to Performance Evaluation for Potential Employment Discrimination

By now, you've received the message that performance evaluation is an essential feature of successful pay-for-performance compensation systems. We know that poorly designed performance evaluation systems can undermine the effectiveness of pay-for-performance systems by failing to clearly distinguish between low- and high-performing employees. Sometimes, performance evaluation plans may lead to biased results that disfavor protected class employees such as blacks or Hispanics (compared with white males), women (compared with men), or older workers (compared with younger workers). The featured *New York Times* article refers to serious reservations some workers have expressed about the fairness of forced rankings or distributions in performance evaluation systems and some companies' endorsement of these methods. In fact, some companies' practices are being challenged in courts of law based on claims of alleged age, sex, and race discrimination.

Log into your *New York Times* account. Search the database for articles on "age discrimination," "sex discrimination," or "employment discrimination." When reviewing these articles, identify the HR practice or practices under scrutiny (for example, pay, benefits, hiring, termination, performance evaluation). Also, how have these practices led to claims of discrimination or proof of actual discrimination? Following your course instructor's specific directions, be prepared to describe the current situation and relate it to the article. ■

The New York Times

Companies Turn to Grades, and Employees Go to Court

An increasingly popular technique for evaluating employees is prompting lawsuits charging discrimination at three big companies.

At issue is the ranking of managers, professionals, and sometimes lower-level employees from best to worst, or grading them on a bell curve, and then using that ranking to help determine pay and sometimes whether to fire someone.

In their suits, all filed over the last year or so, employees at Microsoft, Ford Motor, and Conoco say the rating systems are unfair because they favor some groups of employees over others: white males over blacks and women, younger managers over older ones, and foreign citizens over Americans.

A growing number of companies are turning to grading systems, also known as forced rankings or distributions, as a way of making sure managers evaluate employees honestly and make clearer distinctions among them. At companies that do not compare employees with one another this way, nearly every employee can come away feeling above average, like the children of Lake Wobegon. But under the grading system, managers are forced to identify some people as low performers.

At General Electric, for example, supervisors identify the top 20 percent and bottom 10 percent of their managerial and professional employees every year. The bottom 10 percent are not likely to stay.

As John F. Welch Jr., General Electric's chief executive, wrote last month to shareholders, "A company that bets its future on its people must remove that lower 10 percent, and keep removing it every year—always raising the bar of performance and increasing the quality of its leadership."

Ranking or grading employees is also common at technology companies like Cisco Systems and Hewlett-Packard. But recently the concept has been catching on more broadly, according to management consultants. One reason is that as the economy slows, companies often lay off employees. Cisco, for example, announced earlier this month that it would let go as many as 5,000 workers—and would use grading as one way to identify people to lay off.

"Companies are playing their version of 'Survivor,' " said David Thomas, a professor at the Harvard Business School.

Another reason is that some companies are eager to copy Mr. Welch, long viewed as one of the most successful managers in America.

Defenders of these systems say anyone who gets a low grade is likely to view the process as unfair. " 'A' students love grades; 'F' students hate grades," said John Sullivan, a human resources professor at San Francisco State University.

But the techniques, which some employees label with terms like "rank and yank," have come under sharp criticism. While they appear to offer an objective way to judge employees, they can be vulnerable to bias, Mr. Thomas said. Managers may stereotype employees when evaluating them on vague criteria like career potential—deciding that older workers, for example, may have a harder time keeping up with new technology.

In some cases managers can view these systems "as a tool to be used to weed out the ones you don't want," said Thomas S. McLeod, a lawyer in Canton, Michigan, who represents employees suing Ford in another case.

Critics of the system also argue that companies should not apply a bell curve, in which a small number of employees get the highest and lowest rankings and a much larger number are grouped in the middle. The bell curve model assumes a normal distribution among a very large group of random individuals, not small groups.

What is more, across a company, people who belong to a particularly talented unit will suffer if a certain number of them must be given poorer grades than they would get in another unit.

"You end up with dysfunctional results," said Edward E. Lawler III, a business professor at the University of Southern California.

Some lawsuits contend that Microsoft's grading systems are discriminatory. One, filed last October, seeks class-action status on behalf of blacks and women. The suit states that the rating system "permits managers, who are predominantly white males, to rate employees based upon their own biases rather than based upon merit."

According to the lawsuit, employees are rated on a five-point scale, with only a certain percentage permitted to receive each score. Employees doing the same job in the same unit are also given a "stack ranking," from most to least valuable. Managers decide those rankings largely using what are called "lifeboat discussions," where they choose which employees they would want with them if stuck in a lifeboat. Managers had no other clear criteria, according to Christine Webber, a lawyer at Cohen, Milstein, Hausfeld & Toll who is representing the employees.

Grading is highly subjective at Microsoft, according to Peter M. Browne, a former executive who is also suing the company, charging discrimination. Mr. Browne, who is black, said managers were forced to use a curve in evaluating even small groups. He said he had to rate a group of five on a curve, for example, in deciding which ones would not receive stock options.

"You weren't told anything—just meet the curve," Mr. Browne said.

He says managers ended up favoring people with whom they socialized. "People gravitate to people who are like them, and the system just forces that," he said.

Microsoft defends its system as fair and helpful. "We want to give the highest compensation to the very top performers," said Deborah Willingham, senior vice president for human resources, adding that the system included checks and balances to ensure fair treatment. Employees can appeal their ratings, for example, and are largely responsible for developing the criteria by which they are evaluated.

Ms. Willingham also said the company did not ask its managers to give a fixed percentage of their employees any given score. "We don't force that curve to look any certain way," she said.

Microsoft has no formal "stack rank" policy, she said. And when managers do have lifeboat discussions, they are a tool to consider which employees they would want to keep if they were starting again.

While the company would not comment on the lawsuits, Microsoft "expressly prohibits discrimination," Ms. Willingham said.

Similar criticisms emerged in a lawsuit brought last month against Ford. It argues that the company's new grading system discriminates against older workers. The company, which adopted what it calls its performance management process a year ago, gives its 18,000 managers A, B, or C grades. Last year, the company awarded 10 percent an A, 80 percent a B, and 10 percent a C.

Ford also faces a second lawsuit asserting that it unfairly discriminated against older white males in its grading. It would not comment on the litigation but defended its use of grades. "We believe the system is fair and nondiscriminatory," a company spokeswoman said. "We are in a very competitive industry, and we need all of our employees to be the best they can be."

At Conoco, employees contend that the company discriminated against United States citizens and older workers when it laid off a dozen geophysicists and other scientists in 1999 based on a ranking from one to four, according to a lawsuit filed last year. The majority of those let go were Americans, according to the suit, as opposed to British, Norwegian, and Canadian professionals.

"The rating system was selectively enforced, and there were instances of manipulation," said John Zavitsanos, the lawyer representing the workers. Even though some were given higher ratings on earlier rankings, they were eventually given the lowest possible rating of four.

Conoco, based in Houston, has extensive operations in the North Sea, and many of the senior managers at the division in question are British, according to Mr. Zavitsanos.

While Conoco said it could not comment on the litigation, it said its evaluations were based on several factors, including performance, skills, and expertise. The company said ratings often changed as more information was collected and people were evaluated in larger groups. Conoco company also denied that decisions were based on anything other than individual capabilities.

Companies "do need something in making pay decisions, downsizing decisions," said Jim Kochanski, a consultant with Nextera Enterprises. The problem is that companies may not take enough care in deciding how people should be ranked. "They can get it very wrong," he said.

SOURCE: Reed Abelson, Companies turn to grades, and employees go to court (March 19, 2001) [online]. Available: *www.nytimes.com,* accessed October 9, 2002.

CHAPTER

5 INCENTIVE PAY

Chapter Outline

Learning Objectives

In this chapter, you will learn about

1. How incentive pay and traditional pay systems differ
2. Plans that reward individual behavior
3. A variety of plans that reward group behavior
4. The most broadly used corporatewide incentive programs—profit sharing and employee stock option plans
5. Considerations for designing incentive pay plans
6. How individual, group, and gain sharing incentive plans contribute to differentiation and lowest-cost competitive strategies

As we discuss momentarily, incentive pay places some portion of employee compensation at risk. When employees, groups of employees, or entire companies fail to meet preestablished performance standards (for example, annual sales), they forfeit some or all of their compensation. Expert incentive pay consultants argue that a critical element of successful incentive pay plans is the provision of regular, honest communication to employees. The "Compensation in Action" feature at the end of this chapter describes the necessity of communication to help employees maintain realistic expectations about variable pay from the vantage of successful compensation consultants, including Schuster-Zingheim and Associates, Synygy, and Towers Perrin.

EXPLORING INCENTIVE PAY

Incentive pay or **variable pay** rewards employees for partially or completely attaining a predetermined work objective. Incentive or variable pay is defined as compensation, other than base wages or salaries, that fluctuates according to employees' attainment of some standard, such as a preestablished formula, individual or group goals, or company earnings [1].

Effective incentive pay systems are based on three assumptions [2]:

- Individual employees and work teams differ in how much they contribute to the company, not only in what they do but also in how well they do it.
- The company's overall performance depends to a large degree on the performance of individuals and groups within the company.
- To attract, retain, and motivate high performers and to be fair to all employees, a company needs to reward employees on the basis of their relative performance.

Much like seniority and merit pay approaches, incentive pay augments employees' base pay, but incentive pay appears as one-time payments. Usually, employees receive a combination of recurring base pay and incentive pay, with base pay representing the greater portion of core compensation. Nowadays, more employees are eligible for incentive pay than ever before as companies seek to control costs and motivate personnel to continually strive for exemplary performance. Companies increasingly recognize the importance of applying incentive pay programs to various kinds of employees as well, including production workers, technical employees, and service workers.

Some companies use incentive pay extensively. Lincoln Electric Company, a manufacturer of welding machines and motors, is renowned for its use of incentive pay plans. At Lincoln Electric, production employees receive recurring base pay as well as incentive pay. The company determines incentive pay awards according to five performance criteria: quality, output, dependability, cooperation, and ideas.

Companies generally institute incentive pay programs to control payroll costs or to motivate employee productivity. Companies can control costs by replacing annual merit or seniority increases or fixed salaries with incentive plans that award pay raises only when the company enjoys an offsetting rise in productivity, profits, or some other measure of business success. Well-developed incentive programs base pay on performance, so employees control their own compensation levels. Companies can choose incentives to further business objectives. For example, the management of H. Lee Moffitt Cancer Center and Research Institute at the University of South Florida continually strives to improve patient care as well as control costs. Moffitt's incentives are usually tied to net income or operating surplus, quality of care measures, patient satisfaction scores, and operating efficiencies.

CONTRASTING INCENTIVE PAY WITH TRADITIONAL PAY

In traditional pay plans, employees receive compensation based on a fixed hourly pay rate or annual salary. Annual raises are linked to such factors as seniority and past performance. Some companies use incentive pay programs that replace all or a portion of base pay in order to control payroll expenditures and to link pay to performance. Companies use incentive pay programs in varying degrees for different kinds of positions. Some compensation programs consist of both traditional base pay and incentive pay; other programs, usually for sales jobs, offer only incentive pay, in which case all pay is at risk [3].

Traditional core compensation generally includes an annual salary or hourly wage that is increased periodically on a seniority or merit basis. Companies usually base pay rates on the importance they place on each job within their corporate structure and on the "going rate" that each job commands in similar companies. For example, Lincoln Electric determines the importance of the jobs within its job structure based on job evaluation techniques. The five criteria on which Lincoln evaluates jobs are skill, responsibility, mental aptitude, physical application, and working conditions. Then, Lincoln Electric surveys the pay rates of competitors, and it uses these data to set base pay rates.

As we discussed in Chapter 4, employees under traditional pay structures earn raises according to their length of service in the organization and to supervisors' subjective appraisals of employees' job performance. Again, both merit pay raises and seniority pay raises are permanent increases to base pay. Annual merit pay increase amounts usually total no more than a small percentage of base pay—nowadays, 2 to 10 percent is not uncommon—but the dollar impact represents a significant cost to employers over time. Table 5-1 shows the contrast in rate of compensation increase between a traditional merit compensation plan and an incentive plan.

Companies use incentive pay to reward individual employees, teams of employees, or whole companies based on their performance. Incentive pay plans are not limited solely to production or nonsupervisory workers. Many incentive plans apply to categories of employees such as sales professionals, managers, and executives. Typically, management relies on business objectives to determine incentive pay levels. At Taco

TABLE 5-1 Permanent Annual Merit Increases Versus Incentive Awards: A Comparison

(At the end of 2003, John Smith earned an annual salary of $35,000.)

		Cost of Increase (Total Current Salary—2003 Annual Salary)		***Total Salary Under:***	
Year	***Increase Amount***	***Permanent Merit Increase***	***Incentive Award***	***Permanent Merit Increase (% Increase × Previous Annual Salary)***	***Incentive Award (% Increase × 2003 Annual Salary)***
2004	3%	$1,050	$1,050	$36,050	$36,050
2005	5%	$2,853	$1,750	$37,853	$36,750
2006	4%	$4,367	$1,400	$39,367	$36,400
2007	7%	$7,122	$2,450	$42,122	$37,450
2008	6%	$9,649	$2,100	$44,649	$37,100
2009	5%	$11,881	$1,750	$46,881	$36,750
2010	3%	$13,287	$1,050	$48,287	$36,050
2011	6%	$16,185	$2,100	$51,185	$37,100
2012	8%	$20,279	$2,800	$55,279	$37,800
2013	7%	$24,148	$2,450	$59,148	$37,450

Bell, restaurant managers receive biannual bonuses based on the attainment of three objectives [4]:

- Target profit levels
- Quality of customer service based on an independent assessment by a market research company
- Store sales

Management then communicates these planned incentive levels and performance goals to restaurant managers. Although merit pay performance standards aim to be measurable and objective, incentive levels tend to be based on even more objective criteria, such as quantity of items an employee produces per production period or market indicators of a company's performance (for example, an increase in market share for the fiscal year). Moreover, supervisors communicate in advance the incentive award amounts that correspond to objective performance levels. On the other hand, supervisors generally do not communicate the merit award amounts until after they offer subjective assessments of employees' performances.

Incentive pay plans can be broadly classified into three categories:

- **Individual incentive plans.** These plans reward employees whose work is performed independently. Some companies have piecework plans, typically for their production employees. Under piecework plans, an employee's compensation depends on the number of units she or he produces over a given period.
- Group incentive plans. These plans promote supportive, collaborative behavior among employees. Group incentives work well in manufacturing and service delivery environments that rely on interdependent teams. In gain sharing programs, group improvements in productivity, cost savings, or product quality are shared by employees within the group.
- Companywide plans. These plans tie employee compensation to a company's performance over a short time frame, usually from a 3-month period to a 5-year period.

TABLE 5-2 Typical Performance Measures for Individual, Group, and Companywide Incentive Plans

Individual Incentive Plans
Quantity of work output
Quality of work output
Monthly sales
Work safety record
Work attendance
Group Incentive Plans
Customer satisfaction
Labor cost savings (base pay, overtime pay, benefits)
Materials cost savings
Reduction in accidents
Services cost savings (e.g., utilities)
Companywide Incentive Plans
Company profits
Cost containment
Market share
Sales revenue

Table 5-2 lists common performance measures used in individual, group, and companywide incentive plans.

INDIVIDUAL INCENTIVE PLANS

Individual incentive pay plans are most appropriate under three conditions. First, employees' performances can be measured objectively. Examples of objective performance measures include:

- Number of units produced—an automobile parts production worker's completion of a turn signal lighting assembly
- Sales amount—a Mary Kay Cosmetics sales professional's monthly sales revenue
- Reduction in error rate—a word processor's reduction in typing errors

Second, individual incentive plans are appropriate when employees have sufficient control over work outcomes. Factors such as frequent equipment breakdowns and delays in receipt of raw materials limit employees' ability to control their performance levels. Employees are not likely to be diligent when they encounter interference: Chances are good that employees who previously experienced interference will expect to encounter interference in the future. Employees' resistance threatens profits because companies will find it difficult to motivate people to work hard when problem factors are not present.

Third, individual incentive plans are appropriate when they do not create a level of unhealthy competition among workers that ultimately leads to poor quality. For example, a company may create unhealthy competition when it limits the number of incentive awards to only 10 percent of the employees who have demonstrated the highest levels of performance. If the company judges performance according to volume, then employees may sacrifice quality as they compete against each other to outmatch quantity. In addition, under an incentive plan that rewards quantity of output, those employees who meet or exceed the highest standard established by their employer may be subject to intimidation by workers whose work falls below the standard [5]. Unions may use these intimidation tactics to prevent plan standards from being raised.

Defining Individual Incentives

Individual incentive plans reward employees for meeting work-related performance standards such as quality, productivity, customer satisfaction, safety, or attendance. Any one of these standards or a combination may be used. Ultimately, a company should employ the standards that represent work that an employee actually performs. For instance, take the case of telemarketers. Customer satisfaction and sales volume measures indicate telemarketers' performance. Tardiness would not be as relevant unless absenteeism was a general management problem.

Managers should also choose factors that are within the individual employee's control when they create individual performance standards. Further, employees must know about standards and potential awards before the performance period starts. When designed and implemented well, individual incentive plans reward employees based on results for which they are directly responsible. The end result should be that excellent performers receive higher incentive awards than poor performers.

Types of Individual Incentive Plans

There are four common types of individual incentive plans:

- Piecework plans
- Management incentive plans
- Behavioral encouragement plans
- Referral plans

Piecework Plans

Generally, companies use one of two **piecework plans** [6]. The first, typically found in manufacturing settings, rewards employees based on their individual hourly production against an objective output standard and is determined by the pace at which manufacturing equipment operates. For each hour, workers receive piecework incentives for every item produced over the designated production standard. Workers also receive a guaranteed hourly pay rate regardless of whether they meet the designated production standard. Table 5-3 illustrates the calculation of a piecework incentive.

Companies use piecework plans when the time to produce a unit is relatively short, usually less than 15 minutes, and the cycle repeats continuously. Piecework plans are usually found in manufacturing industries such as textiles and apparel.

Quality is also an important consideration. Companies do not reward employees for producing defective products. In the apparel industry, manufacturers attempt to minimize defect rates because they cannot sell defective clothing for the same price as nondefective clothing. Selling defective clothing at a lower price reduces company profits.

The second type of piecework incentive plan establishes individual performance standards that include both objective and subjective criteria. Units produced

TABLE 5-3 Calculation of a Piecework Award for a Garment Worker

Piecework standard: 15 stitched garments per hour

Hourly base pay rate awarded to employees when the standard is not met: $4.50 per hour. That is, workers receive $4.50 per hour worked regardless of whether they meet the piecework standard of 15 stitched garments per hour.

Piecework incentive award: $0.75 per garment stitched per hour above the piecework standard

	Guaranteed Hourly Base Pay	*Piecework Award (No. of Garments Stitched Above the Piecework Standard × Piecework Incentive Award)*	*Total Hourly Earnings*
First hour	$4.50	10 garments × $0.75/garment = $7.50	$12.00
Second hour	$4.50	Fewer than 15 stitched garments, thus piecework award equals $0	$4.50

represent an objective standard. Overall work quality is a subjective criterion that is based on supervisors' interpretations and judgments. For example, supervisors may judge customer service representatives' performances to be higher when sales professionals emphasize the benefits of purchasing extended product warranties than when sales professionals merely mention the availability and price of extended product warranties.

Management Incentive Plans

Management incentive plans award bonuses to managers when they meet or exceed objectives based on sales, profit, production, or other measures for their division, department, or unit. Management incentive plans differ from piecework plans in that piecework plans base rewards on the attainment of one specific objective and management incentive plans often require multiple complex objectives. For example, management incentive plans reward managers for increasing market share or reducing their budgets without compromising the quality and quantity of output. The best-known management incentive plan is management by objectives (MBO) [7]. In Chapter 4, MBO was presented as an outcome-oriented performance appraisal technique for merit pay systems. When MBO is used as part of merit pay systems, superiors make subjective assessments of managers' performances, and they use these assessments to determine permanent merit pay increases. When used as part of incentive programs, superiors communicate the amount of incentive pay managers will receive based on the attainment of specific goals.

Behavioral Encouragement Plans

Under **behavioral encouragement plans**, employees receive payments for specific behavioral accomplishments, such as good attendance or safety records. For example, companies usually award monetary bonuses to employees who have exemplary attendance records for a specified period. When behavioral encouragement plans are applied to safety records, workers earn awards for lower personal injury or accident rates associated with the improper use of heavy equipment or hazardous chemicals. Table 5-4 contains an illustration of a sample behavioral encouragement plan that rewards employees for excellent attendance. Employees can earn $250 for perfect attendance during a 3-month period. With perfect attendance for an entire year, employees can earn $1,000.

TABLE 5-4 A Sample Behavioral Encouragement Plan That Rewards Employee Attendance

At the end of each 3-month period, employees with exemplary attendance records will receive monetary incentive awards according to the following schedule. Note that the number of days absent does not refer to such company-approved absences as vacation, personal illness, jury duty, bereavement leave, military duty, scheduled holidays, and educational leave.

Number of Days Absent	*Monetary Incentive Award*
0 days (perfect attendance)	$250
1 day	$200
2 days	$100
3 days	$ 50
4 days	$ 25

Referral Plans

A recent WorldatWork survey shows that nearly 60 percent of companies rely on referral bonuses to enhance recruitment of highly qualified employees [8]. Employees may receive monetary bonuses under referral plans for referring new customers or recruiting successful job applicants. In the case of recruitment, employees can earn bonuses for making successful referrals for job openings. For example, there has been a tremendous shortage of nurses for the past several years. Because of the shortage, hospitals offer sign-on bonuses of up to $15,000 to recruit nurses and referral bonuses of up to $5,000. A successful referral usually means that companies award bonuses only if hired referrals remain employed with the company in good standing beyond a designated period, often at least 30 days. **Referral plans** rely on the idea that current employees' familiarity with company culture should enable them to identify viable candidates for job openings more efficiently than employment agencies could, because agents are probably less familiar with client companies' cultures. Employees are likely to make only those referrals they truly believe are worthwhile because their personal reputations are at stake.

Advantages of Individual Incentive Pay Programs

There are three key advantages of individual incentive pay plans. First, individual incentive plans can promote the relationship between pay and performance. As discussed in Chapter 1, employees in the United States are motivated primarily by earning money. Employees strive for excellence when they expect to earn incentive awards commensurate with their job performance.

Second, individual incentive plans promote an equitable distribution of compensation within companies. That is, the amount employees earn depends upon their job performance. The better they perform, the more they earn. Ultimately, equitable pay enables companies to retain the best performers. Paying better performers more money sends a signal that the company appropriately values positive job performances.

A third advantage of individual incentive plans is their compatibility with individualistic cultures such as the United States. Because U.S. employees are socialized to make individual contributions and be recognized for them, the national culture of the United States probably enhances the motivational value of individual incentive programs.

Disadvantages of Individual Incentive Pay Programs

Although individual incentive plans can prove effective in certain settings, these programs also have serious limitations. Supervisors, human resource managers, and compensation professionals should know about three potential problems with individual incentive plans.

Individual incentive plans possess the potential to promote inflexibility [9]. Because supervisors determine employee performance levels, workers under individual incentive plans become dependent on supervisors for setting work goals. If employees become highly proficient performers, they are not likely to increase their performance beyond their reward compensation. For example, let's assume that management defines the maximum incentive award as $500 per month, which is awarded to employees whose productivity rates 15 percent above the performance standard. Employees who produce more than 15 percent above the production standard will not receive additional incentive pay beyond the $500. With this design, employees would not be motivated to improve their performance.

With merit pay systems, supervisors must develop and maintain comprehensive performance measures to properly grant incentive awards. Individual incentive programs pose measurement problems when management implements improved work methods or equipment. When such changes occur, it will take some time for employees to become proficient performers. Thus, it will be difficult for companies to determine equitable incentive awards, which may lead to employees' resistance to the new methods.

A third limitation of individual incentive plans is that they may encourage undesirable workplace behavior when these plans reward only one or a subset of dimensions that constitute employees' total job performances. Let's assume that an incentive plan rewards employees for quantity of output. If employees' jobs address various dimensions such as quantity of output, quality, and customer satisfaction, employees may focus on the one dimension—in this case, quantity of output—that leads to incentive pay, and thereby neglect the other dimensions.

GROUP INCENTIVES

Increasingly, U.S. employers are using teams to get work done. Two main changes in the business environment have led to an increased use of teams in the workplace [10]. First, in the 1980s, many Japanese companies began conducting business in the United States, particularly in the automobile industry. A common feature of Japanese companies was the use of teams, which contributed to superior product quality. General Motors's Saturn division is an excellent example of quality improvement based on teamwork. Second, team-based job design promotes innovation in the workplace [11]. At Rubbermaid, a manufacturer of such plastic household products as snap-together furniture and storage boxes, product innovation has become the rule since the implementation of project teams. Team members represent various cross-functional areas, including research and development (R&D), marketing, finance, and manufacturing. Rubbermaid attributes the rush on innovation to the cross-fertilization of ideas that has resulted from the work of these diverse teams.

Companies that use work teams need to change individualistic compensation practices so that groups are rewarded for their behavior together [12]. Accordingly, team-based pay plans should emphasize cooperation between and within teams, compensate employees for additional responsibilities they often must assume in their roles as members of a team, and encourage team members to attain predetermined objectives for the team [13]. Merit, seniority, or individual incentives do not encourage team behaviors

STRETCHING THE DOLLAR

INCENTIVE PROGRAMS BOOST EMPLOYEE MORALE AND PRODUCTIVITY

Reward and recognition programs help motivate employees in changing times while enabling companies to do more with less.

Quick Look

- Restoring worker productivity levels in changing times is a vital issue for companies.
- Studies show that incentive programs work in achieving company performance.
- Incentive programs build a culture of high morale, performance, and recognition.
- Many companies use software to successfully manage enterprisewide incentive programs

To say that September 11 had a negative impact on the American workforce—from both an attitudinal and productivity standpoint—would be an understatement. Motivating employees and restoring previous levels of productivity is a hot business topic.

In most industries, human capital costs represent an overwhelming percentage of overall corporate spending. Compensation and benefits professionals are particularly sensitive to this, since they see firsthand that maximizing employee productivity determines a company's overall successes.

According to *Contented Cows Give Better Milk*, by Robert J. Kriegel, Ph.D., companies that manage and recognize their people outperform companies that don't by 30 percent to 40 percent. And nothing drives revenue and profitability more than motivated and happy employees. An energetic workforce distinguishes the world's thriving companies from those that are either barely passing or outright failing. When corporations fail to motivate employees, there are consequences. Employees who don't feel appreciated and properly acknowledged become a liability to their companies rather than an asset—productivity dives and both voluntary and involuntary attrition soars.

NO LONGER JUST A WELL-KEPT SECRET

When benefits and compensation professionals discuss motivating employees, the conversation typically turns to 401(k) plans, health care plans, stock options, and other more traditional compensation vehicles. Rarely does one hear incentive and recognition programs mentioned in the context of that conversation, despite the fact that roughly 78 percent of companies have at least one type of performance-related program, according to a Hewitt Associates 2000 study.

Incentive programs commonly are associated with sales initiatives, so few benefits and compensation professionals have fully embraced them as tried-and-true methods for raising overall employee productivity. But the fact is, corporate America has learned that incentive programs—when leveraged properly—can be used to inspire employees enterprisewide, from employees in sales to customer service, and every department in between. A recent WorldatWork study found that 85 percent to 95 percent of all incentive programs reach or exceed their goals, and that the return on investment (ROI) on non-sales employee programs (200 percent) is actually greater than the ROI on sales incentives (134 percent).

DOING MORE WITH LESS

A recent Gallup survey found that in the U.S. working population, 26 percent of employees are engaged (loyal and productive), 55 percent are not engaged (just putting in time), and 19 percent are disengaged (unhappy and spreading their discontent).

Tough times, such as layoffs, can cripple workplaces and create uncertainty about long-term viability. Those employees remaining after the layoffs often are as devastated as those headed to the unemployment office. This presents a serious dilemma for corporations—the vast majority of which are already being tasked to "do more with less" and, therefore, rely on these remaining employees to perform at even greater levels.

Employees have an emotional need to feel appreciated. And that emotional need has been pushed to the extreme as the events of

(Continued)

(Continued)

September 11 have exacerbated the already evident impact of a full-blown recession. U.S. corporations are working with smaller and, often times, less motivated staffs. Yet, they are asked to increase overall productivity and revenue in order to survive. But how can you motivate disgruntled employees when restricted cash flow prohibits pulling out all the stops and offering the benefits and compensation characteristics of the last few years, such as profit sharing, cash bonuses, and stock options?

Do it by appealing to employees' need to feel appreciated. Do it by giving them increased visibility within the organization. Do it by recognizing their accomplishments with non-cash incentives that carry tremendous "trophy value." Hence, the growing popularity of incentive programs, which enable corporations to get the most possible value out of existing employees, without breaking the bank.

Incentive and recognition programs are one of the most effective ways for companies to create a great place to work and to build a culture of high morale, performance, recognition, and improvement. By shining the spotlight on employees who perform, a company not only encourages them to do it repeatedly, they also encourage other employees to emulate that same behavior themselves. Too often, kudos are given in private, one-on-one meetings, due to fear that openly praising star employees will lead to a perception of favoritism or exclusivity.

Moreover, it's not just management-down, peer-to-peer incentives build loyalty and goodwill within the ranks.

However, to create a winning team, versus just a handful of winners, a company must create a "performance-based culture." That is, the everyday environment in the workplace must be one in which employees are fully cognizant of who is performing and what, specifically, they need to do to join the ranks of the company's elite members. When you applaud performance in a very open manner, you can tear down perceived "ceilings" to growth by illustrating that the company consistently awards employees whose performance is best aligned with overall company objectives. Nebulous standards of recognition are potentially damaging, because employees quickly lose sight of business goals that aren't frequently mentioned and rewarded.

STREAMLINING INTERNAL COMMUNICATIONS

A number of factors—including layoffs, mergers and acquisitions, and higher frequency of management changes—have made it increasingly difficult for today's executive to take new objectives and priorities established in the board room and effectively communicate them to the entire company (a.k.a. the proverbial "from the boardroom to the lunchroom"). It's always been tough for executives at large corporations to make each employee aware of new company goals in a timely fashion.

So if this is the Information Age, why is internal communication executed inefficiently at so many of the world's largest corporations?

The answer is actually quite simple. Too often, employees aren't aware of how their individual actions relate to the broader company goals. As creatures of habit, U.S. employees quickly grow accustomed to relying on their job descriptions as the marching order for their daily activities. However, the new economy is defined by ever-changing business goals, so a new protocol is required to communicate these new objectives.

Clearly, the overall mission is to foster a better link between each worker's daily regiment and the overall business goals—revenue numbers, customer satisfaction, etc.—that determine the company's ultimate success.

Incentive programs meet the market demand for a more effective way to streamline internal communication of company objectives. The best way to get every company employee "on the same page" is through a common Web-based experience that tracks his or her performance against predetermined objectives. Many of the world's leading corporations now are using "virtual scoreboards" that clearly track employee performance and rewards achievement with incentives.

Linking the actions of employees to a company's performance is one of the most fundamental building blocks of a performance-driven business.

BRINGING BETTER ROI TO INCENTIVE PROGRAMS

A Hewitt Associates study revealed that more than 78 percent of companies currently have at least one type of performance-related program in place. That number is up from 47 percent just 10 years ago, proving a surging adoption of performance programs. Yet, while incentive programs have been identified as one of the de facto methods of employee motivation and retention, few corporations have been able to determine the exact return of investment (ROI) figures on their own internal incentive programs.

In an economy where programs without proven ROI are readily dismissed, it's surprising that so many companies are running expensive recognition programs without taking a more accurate measure of their effectiveness.

Most companies have a number of disparate incentive programs that span across numerous departments. The most popular approach to date has been to allow each department head to implement a unique incentive program with goals and rewards specific to the employees in that sector. A sales department head, for example, will reward quotas met and exceeded, while a customer service department head will reward based on customer retention figures.

However, when there are many separate incentive programs within an organization, there is poor accountability to ROI and overall success. Running incentive programs manually can be a cost-intensive nightmare—sorting through thousands of spreadsheets at the end of each fiscal quarter to determine whether objectives were met. Most companies don't even realize how much they're spending on incentives programs—let alone how much value they're extracting from them.

Running a multitude of disparate incentive programs also undermines the overall performance-based culture mentioned earlier. Recognition programs should counteract divisiveness, not encourage it. In many organizations, certain departments are far more in the spotlight than others, despite the fact that their individual contributions are every bit as important to the overall goals of the organization. The customer service employee who retains a major account for a specific duration should receive comparable recognition as the sales employee who lands the next big account.

The idea of running a program throughout an entire organization could very well sound like a logistical nightmare for the person who has to administer it. Therefore, it probably comes as no surprise that many companies are using software to successfully manage enterprisewide incentive programs. Having a singular program, customized to specific company goals, helps to maximize the return on the incentive investment. It also gives a snapshot of not only individual and departmental performance, but the progress of the company as a whole—something that effectively demonstrates ROI. This "virtual scoreboard" approach shows CEOs which team members are meeting or exceeding goals at any given time, so they can calculate immediate returns on human investment. It also enables executives to link recognition program costs to measurable activity costs and periodically observe if the program has helped overall human capital management costs.

Source: Brendan P. Keegan, Bravanta, *Workspan*, March 2002, volume 45, number 3. © 2002 WorldatWork, 14040 N. Northsight Blvd., Scottsdale, AZ 85260 USA: 480/951-9191; Fax 480/483-8352; *www.worldatwork.org*; E-mail worldatwork@worldatwork.org

and may potentially limit team effectiveness. Experts suggest that traditional pay programs will undermine the ability of teams to function effectively [14]. Both merit- and seniority-based pay emphasize hierarchy among employees, which is incompatible with the very concept of a team.

Team-based organization structures encourage team members to learn new skills and assume broader responsibility than is expected of them under traditional pay structures that are geared toward individuals. Rather than following specific orders from a supervisor, employees who work in teams must initiate plans for achieving their team's production. Usually, a pay plan for teams emphasizes cooperation and rewards its members for the additional responsibilities they must take on, as well as the skills and knowledge they must acquire. Chapter 6 shows how skill- and knowledge-based pay plans can address these additional responsibilities.

Defining Group Incentives

Group incentive programs reward employees for their collective performance, rather than for each employee's individual performance. Group incentive programs are most effective when all group members have some impact on achieving the goal, even though individual contributions might not be equal. Boeing utilizes a team-based approach to manufacture its model 777 jumbo jet. More than 200 cross-functional teams contribute to the construction of each jet, and the contribution of each individual is clearly not equal. Installing the interior trim features such as upholstery is not nearly as essential to the airworthiness of each jet as are the jobs of ensuring the aerodynamic integrity of each aircraft.

Ultimately, well-designed group incentive plans reinforce teamwork, cultivate loyalty to the company, and increase productivity. For instance, at General Motors's Saturn division, each team is responsible for managing itself. As a result, each team manages its own budget and determines whom to hire. The renowned quality of Saturn automobiles has been attributed to the effective utilization of teams.

Types of Group Incentive Plans

Companies use two major types of group incentive plans:

- Team-based or small-group incentive plans. A small group of employees shares a financial reward when a specific objective is met.
- Gain sharing plans. A group of employees, generally a department or work unit, is rewarded for productivity gains.

Team-Based or Small-Group Incentive Plans

Team-based incentives are similar to individual incentives with one exception. Each group member receives a financial reward for the attainment of a group goal. The timely completion of a market survey report depends on the collaborative efforts of several individual employees. For example, some group members design the survey; another set collects the survey data; and a third set analyzes the data and writes the report. It is the timely completion of the market survey report, not the completion of any one of the jobs that are required to produce it, that determines whether group members will receive incentive pay.

There are many kinds of team incentive programs. Companies define these programs according to the performance criteria. Teams or groups may receive incentive pay based on criteria such as customer satisfaction, safety records, quality, and production records. Although these criteria apply to other categories of incentive programs as well (individual, companywide, and group plans), companies allocate awards to each worker based on the group's attainment of predetermined performance standards.

Human resource managers must devise methods for allocating incentives to team members. Although the team-based reward is generated by the performance of the team, the incentive payments typically are distributed to members of the team individually. Human resource experts allocate rewards in one of three ways:

- Equal incentive payments to all team members
- Differential incentive payments to team members based on their contribution to the team's performance
- Differential payments determined by a ratio of each team member's base pay to the total base pay of the group

The first method, the equal incentives payment approach, reinforces cooperation among team members except when team members perceive differences in members' contributions or performance. The second method, the differential incentive payments approach, distributes rewards based to some extent on individual performance. Obviously, differential approaches can hinder cooperative behavior. Some employees may focus on their own performance rather than the group's performance because they wish to maximize their income. As a compromise, companies may base part of the incentive on individual performance, with the remainder based on the team's performance. The third disbursement method, differential payments by ratio of base pay, rewards each group member in proportion to her or his base pay. This approach assumes that employees with higher base pay contribute more to the company, and so should be rewarded in accord with that worth.

Gain Sharing Plans

Gain sharing describes group incentive systems that provide participating employees with an incentive payment based on improved company performance for increased productivity, increased customer satisfaction, lower costs, or better safety records [15]. Gain sharing was developed so that all employees could benefit financially from productivity improvements resulting from the suggestion system. Besides serving as a compensation tool, most gain sharing reflects a management philosophy that emphasizes employee involvement. The use of gain sharing is most appropriate where workplace technology does not constrain productivity improvements. For example, assembly line workers' abilities to improve productivity may be limited. Increasing the speed of the conveyor belts may compromise workers' safety.

Most gain sharing programs have three components [16]:

- Leadership philosophy
- Employee involvement systems
- Bonus

The first component, leadership philosophy, refers to a cooperative organizational climate that promotes high levels of trust, open communication, and participation. The second component, employee involvement systems, drives organizational productivity improvements. Employee involvement systems use broadly based suggestion systems. Anyone can make suggestions to a committee made up of both hourly and management employees who oversee the suggestion implementation. This involvement system also may include other innovative employee involvement practices, such as problem-solving task forces.

The bonus is the third component of a gain sharing plan. A company awards gain sharing bonuses when its actual productivity exceeds its targeted productivity level. Usually, the gain sharing bonuses are based on a formula that measures productivity that employees perceive as fair and the employer believes will result in improvements in company performance. Employees typically receive gain sharing bonuses on a monthly basis. Most bonuses range between 5 and 10 percent of an employee's base annual pay. A noteworthy exception to this norm is AmeriSteel. On average, AmeriSteel's gain sharing plan pays out between 35 and 45 percent of base pay.

Although many accounts of gain sharing use can be found in the practitioner and scholarly literature, no one has completed a comprehensive, soundly designed investigation of the effectiveness of gain sharing programs [17]. Meanwhile, gain sharing programs' success has been attributed to company cultures that support cooperation among employees [18]. Some gain sharing attempts have failed. Organizational, external environment, and financial information factors, such as poor communications within and across departments, highly competitive product markets, and variable corporate profits, over time can inhibit effective gain sharing programs [19]. Poor communications will stifle the creativity needed to improve the efficiency of work processes when employees focus exclusively on their own work. Highly competitive product markets often require companies to make frequent changes to their production methods, as in the automobile industry, where such changes occur each year with the introduction of new models. When companies make frequent or sudden changes, employees must have time to learn the new processes well before they can offer productive suggestions. Companies that experience variable profits from year to year most likely do not use gain sharing because management sets aside as much excess cash as possible in reserve for periods when profits are down and excess cash is scarce.

The Scanlon, Rucker, and Improshare gain sharing plans are the most common forms used in companies, and they were also the first types of gain sharing plans developed and used by employers. In the early days of gain sharing, these plans were adopted wholesale. Today, employers generally modify one of these traditional plans to meet their needs or adopt hybrid plans.

The Scanlon Plan

Joseph Scanlon first developed the gain sharing concept in 1935 as an employee involvement system without a pay element. The hallmark of the **Scanlon Plan** is its emphasis on employee involvement. Scanlon believed that employees will exercise self-direction and self-control if they are committed to company objectives and that employees will accept and seek out responsibility if given the opportunity [20]. Current Scanlon plans include monetary rewards to employees for productivity improvements. Scanlon plans assume that companies will be able to offer higher pay to workers, generate increased profits for stockholders, and lower prices for consumers.

Scanlon plan is a generic term referring to any gain sharing plan that has characteristics common to the original gain sharing plan devised by Scanlon. Scanlon plans have the following three components [21]:

- An emphasis on teamwork to reduce costs, assisted by management-supplied information on production concerns
- Suggestion systems that route cost-saving ideas from the workforce through a labor-management committee that evaluates and acts on accepted suggestions
- A monetary reward based on productivity improvements to encourage employee involvement

Scanlon plan employee involvement systems include a formal suggestion program structured at two levels. Production-level committees, usually including a department foreman or supervisor and at least one elected worker, communicate the suggestion program and its reward features to workers. Production committee members encourage and assist workers in making suggestions and formally record suggestions for consideration. Production committees may also reject suggestions that are not feasible, but they must provide a written explanation of the reasons for the rejection to the worker who made the suggestion. Providing the written rationale under this circumstance is key to helping employees understand why the suggestions are not feasible and, thus, workers are not discouraged from making suggestions in the future. After employees' suggestions have been fully implemented, they typically receive bonuses on a monthly basis.

The production committee forwards appropriate suggestions to a companywide screening committee, which also includes worker representatives. This committee reviews suggestions referred by the production committees, serves as a communica-

TABLE 5-5 Illustration of a Scanlon Plan

For the past 3 years, the labor costs of XYZ Manufacturing Company have averaged $44,000,000 per year. During the same 3-year period, the sales value of XYZ's production (SVOP) averaged $83,000,000 per year. (As an aside, of the $83,000,000, $65,000,000 represents sales revenue, and $18,000,000 represents the value of goods held in inventory.) The Scanlon ratio for XYZ Manufacturing Company is:

$$\frac{\$44{,}000{,}000}{\$83{,}000{,}000} = 0.53$$

The ratio of 0.53 is the base line. Any benefits resulting from an improvement, such as an improvement in production methods that results in a reduction in labor costs, are shared with workers. In other words, when improvements lead to a Scanlon ratio that is lower than the standard of 0.53, employees will receive gain sharing bonuses.

The operating information for XYZ Manufacturing Company for March 2003 was as follows:

Total labor costs	$3,100,000
SVOP	$7,200,000

The Scanlon ratio, based on March 2003 information was

$$\frac{\$3{,}100{,}000}{\$7{,}200{,}000} = 0.43$$

The Scanlon ratio for March 2003 was less than the standard of 0.53, which was based on historical data. In order for there to be a payout, labor costs for March 2003 must be less than $3,816,000 (i.e., 0.53 × $7,200,000); $3,816,000 represents allowable labor costs for March 2003 based on the Scanlon standard established for XYZ Manufacturing.

In summary, the allowable labor costs for March 2003 were $3,816,000. The actual labor costs were $3,100,000. Thus, the savings $716,000 ($3,816,000 – $3,100,000) is available for distribution as a bonus.

---

tions link between management and employees, and reviews the company's performance each month.

Actual gain sharing formulas are designed to suit the individual needs of the company [22]. Usually, formulas are based on the ratio between labor costs and **sales value of production (SVOP)** [23]. The SVOP is the sum of sales revenue plus the value of goods in inventory.

Smaller Scanlon ratios indicate that labor costs are lower relative to SVOP. Companies definitely strive for lower ratios, as Table 5-5 illustrates. In addition, Table 5-5 shows the calculation for a bonus distribution under a Scanlon plan.

The Rucker Plan

Similar to Scanlon's plan, the **Rucker Plan** was developed by Allan W. Rucker in 1933. Both Scanlon and Rucker plans emphasize employee involvement and provide monetary incentives to encourage employee participation. The main difference lies in the formula used to measure productivity. Rucker plans use a **value-added formula** to measure productivity. Value added is the difference between the value of the sales price of a product and the value of materials purchased to make the product. The following example illustrates the concept of value added based on the sequence of events that eventually lead to selling bread to consumers. These events include growing the wheat, milling the wheat, adding the wheat to other ingredients to make bread, and selling the bread to consumers.

First, a farmer grows the wheat and sells it to a miller; the added value is the difference in the income the farmer receives for the wheat and the costs incurred for seed, fertilizer, fuel, and other supplies. The miller, in turn, buys the wheat from the farmer, mills it, and then sells it to a bakery. The difference in the cost of buying the wheat and the price it is sold for to the baker is the amount of "value" the miller "adds" in the milling processes. The same process is repeated by the baker, as the flour which was milled by the miller is mixed with other ingredients, baked, and sold as bread either to the consumer or to a retailer who in turn sells it to the consumer. The baker "adds value" by blending in the other ingredients to the flour and baking the bread. If the bread is sold to the consumer through a retailer, then the retailer also "adds value" by buying the bread from the bakery, transporting it to a store convenient for the consumer, displaying the bread, and selling it. The total of all the added values from each step along the way equals the total contribution to the overall economy from the chain of events [24].

The following ratio is used to determine whether bonuses will be awarded under a Rucker plan:

$$\text{Rucker ratio} = \frac{(\text{Value added}) - (\text{Costs of materials, supplies, and services rendered})}{\text{Total employment costs of plan participants (wages, salaries, payroll taxes, and fringe compensation)}}$$

In contrast to the Scanlon ratio, companies prefer a larger Rucker ratio. A larger Rucker ratio indicates that the value added is greater than total employment costs. Table 5-6 illustrates the calculation for bonus distribution under the Rucker plan.

Invented by Mitchell Fein in 1973, **Improshare**—Improved Productivity through Sharing—measures productivity physically rather than in terms of dollar savings as

TABLE 5-6 Illustration of a Rucker Plan

Last year, ABC Manufacturing Company generated net sales of $7,500,000. The company paid $3,200,000 for materials, $250,000 for sundry supplies, and $225,000 for such services as liability insurance, basic maintenance, and utilities. On the basis of these data, value added was $3,825,000 (i.e., net sales – costs of materials, supplies, and services rendered). For this example: $7,500,000 – ($3,200,000 + $250,000 + $225,000).

For the same year, total employment costs were $2,400,000, which includes hourly wages for nonexempt workers, annual salaries for exempt employees, payroll taxes, and all benefit costs. Based on the Rucker formula, the ratio of value added to total employment costs was 1.59. This ratio means that if there are to be bonuses, each dollar attributed to employment costs must be accompanied by creating at least $1.59 of value added.

The operating information for ABC Manufacturing Company for the month July 2003 was as follows:

Value added	$670,000
Total employment costs	$625,000

The Rucker ratio, based on July 2000 information, was:

$$\frac{\$670{,}000}{\$625{,}000} = 1.07$$

The Rucker ratio for July 2003 is less than the standard of 1.59, which was based on historical data. In order for there to be a payout, value added for July 2003 must be more than the standard, which would be $1,065,300 (1.59 × $670,000). However, based on the Rucker ratio obtained for July 2003 (1.07), value added was only $716,900. Therefore employees of ABC Manufacturing will not receive any gain sharing bonuses for July 2003 performance.

TABLE 5-7 Scanlon, Rucker, and Improshare Plans: A Comparison of Key Features

Feature	*Scanlon*	*Rucker*	*Improshare*
Program goal	Productivity improvement	Productivity improvement	Productivity improvement
Basis for savings	Labor costs	Labor costs plus raw materials costs plus services costs (e.g., utilities)	Completing work at or sooner than production standard
Employee involvement	Required	Required	NA
Type of employee involvement	Screening and production committees	Screening and production committees	NA
Bonus payout frequency	Monthly	Monthly	Weekly

used in the Scanlon and Rucker plans. These programs aim to produce more products with fewer labor hours. Under Improshare, the emphasis is on providing employees with an incentive to finish products.

The Improshare bonus is based on a **labor hour ratio formula**. A standard is determined by analyzing historical accounting data to find the number of labor hours needed to complete a product. Productivity is then measured as a ratio of standard labor hours and actual labor hours. Unlike the Rucker and Scanlon plans, employee participation is not a feature, and workers receive bonuses on a weekly basis.

Improshare plans feature a **buy-back provision**. Under this provision, a maximum productivity improvement payout level is placed on productivity gains. Any bonus money that is generated because of improvements above the maximum is placed in a reserve. If productivity improves to the point where the maximum is repeatedly exceeded, the firm buys back the amount of the productivity improvement over the maximum with a one-time payment to employees. This payment usually is equal to the amount in the reserve. The company then is permitted to adjust the standards so that a new ceiling can be set at a higher level of productivity. In unionized settings, management's discretion may be challenged by unions when union leadership believes that management is simply trying to exploit workers by making it more difficult for them to receive bonuses.

In summary, the Scanlon, Rucker, and Improshare plans are among the best-known kinds of gain sharing programs that are used by companies. Although the principle underlying these different plans is the same—a group incentive system that provides all or most employees a bonus payment based on improved company performance—they each rest on slightly different assumptions. Table 5-7 details a comparison of these three plans.

Advantages of Group Incentives

The use of group incentive plans has two advantages for companies. First, companies can more easily develop performance measures for group incentive plans than for individual incentive plans. There are obviously fewer groups in a company than individuals. Thus, companies generally use fewer resources such as staff time to develop performance measures. In addition, judging the quality of the final product makes the most sense because companies must deliver high-quality products to maintain competitiveness. During the late 1970s and early 1980s, U.S. automobile manufacturers (especially

Chrysler Corporation) lost substantial market share to foreign automobile manufacturers (for example, Honda and Toyota) because foreign automakers marketed automobiles of substantially higher quality than U.S. automakers. The trend did not change until U.S. automakers manufactured high-quality vehicles, which they began to market in the late 1980s.

Greater group cohesion is the second advantage associated with group incentive plans [25]. Cohesive groups usually work more effectively toward achieving common goals than do individual group members focusing on the specific tasks for which they are responsible. Undoubtedly, working collaboratively is in group members' best interests in order to maximize their incentive awards.

Disadvantages of Group Incentives

The main disadvantage of group incentive compensation is employee turnover. Companies' implementation of group incentive programs may lead to turnover because of the **free-rider effect**. Some employees may make fewer contributions to the group goals because they possess lower ability, skills, or experience than other group members. In some groups, members may deliberately choose to put forth less effort particularly when each group member receives the same incentive compensation regardless of individual contributions to the group goals. In any case, the free-rider effect initially leads to feelings of inequity among those who make the greatest contributions to the attainment of the group goal. Over time, members who make the greatest contributions are likely to leave.

Group members may feel uncomfortable with the fact that other members' performance influence their compensation level. Exemplary performers are more likely to feel this way when other group members are not contributing equally to the attainment of group goals. The lower performance of a few group members may lead to lower earnings for all members of the group. Discomfort with group incentive plans is likely to be heightened where incentive compensation represents the lion's share of core compensation.

COMPANYWIDE INCENTIVES

The use of companywide incentive plans can be traced to the nineteenth century. Companies instituted profit sharing programs to ease workers' dissatisfaction with low pay and to change their beliefs that company management paid workers substandard wages while earning substantial profits. Quite simply, management believed that workers would be less likely to challenge managerial practices if they received a share of company profits.

Defining Companywide Incentives

Companywide incentive plans reward employees when the company exceeds minimum acceptable performance standards, such as profits or the overall value of the company based on its stock price. As competitive pressures on companies increased, management sought methods to improve employee productivity. Nowadays, companies use companywide incentive programs to motivate employees to work harder for increased profits or increased company value to owners. Advocates of companywide incentive plans believe that well-designed programs make workers' and owners' goals more compatible as workers strive toward increasing company profits or value.

Types of Companywide Incentive Plans

Companies use two major types of companywide incentive plans:

- Profit sharing plans. Employees earn a financial reward when their company's profit objective is met.
- Employee stock option plans. Companies grant employees the right to purchase shares of company stock.

Profit Sharing Plans

Profit sharing plans pay a portion of company profits to employees, separate from base pay, cost-of-living adjustments, or permanent merit pay increases. Two basic kinds of profit sharing plans are used widely today. First, **current profit sharing** plans award cash to employees, typically on a quarterly or annual basis. Second, **deferred profit sharing** plans place cash awards in trust accounts for employees. These trusts are set aside on employees' behalf as a source of retirement income. Apart from the time horizon, these plans differ with regard to taxation. Current profit sharing plans provide cash to employees as part of their regular core compensation; thus, these payments are subject to IRS taxation when they are earned. Deferred profit sharing plans are not taxed until the employee begins to make withdrawals during retirement. Premature withdrawal of funds that were secured under a deferred compensation plan is subject to stiff tax penalties (up to 20 percent). The IRS established this penalty to discourage employees from making premature withdrawals. Some companies offer deferred compensation as one kind of retirement program. We discuss deferred profit sharing plans in Chapter 11. The focus here will be on current profit sharing plans because employees receive cash compensation as a reward for on-the-job performance.

Calculating Profit Sharing Awards

Human resource professionals determine the pool of profit sharing money with any of three possible formulas. A fixed first-dollar-of-profits formula uses a specific percentage of either pretax or posttax annual profits, contingent upon the successful attainment of a company goal. For instance, a company might establish that the profit sharing fund will equal 7 percent of corporate profits; however, payment is contingent on a specified reduction in scrap rates.

Second, companies may use a graduated first-dollar-of-profits formula instead of a fixed percentage. For example, a company may choose to share 3 percent of the first $8 million of profits and 6 percent of the profits in excess of that level. Graduated formulas motivate employees to strive for extraordinary profit targets by sharing even more of the incremental gain.

Third, profitability threshold formulas fund profit sharing pools only if profits exceed a predetermined minimum level but fall below some established maximum level. Companies establish minimums to guarantee a return to shareholders before they distribute profits to employees. They establish maximums because they attribute any profits beyond this level to factors other than employee productivity or creativity, such as technological innovation.

After management selects a funding formula for the profit sharing pool, they must consider how to distribute pool money among employees. Usually, companies make distributions in one of three ways—equal payments to all employees, proportional payments to employees based on annual salary, and proportional payments to employees based on their contribution to profits. Equal payments to all employees reflect a belief that all employees should share equally in the company's gain in order to promote cooperation among employees. However, employee contributions to profits probably vary. Accordingly, most employers divide the profit sharing pool among employees based on a differential basis.

Companies may disburse profits based on proportional payments to employees based on their annual salaries. As we detail in Chapters 7 and 8, salary levels vary based on both internal and external factors; in general, the higher the salary, the more work the company assigns to a job. Presumably, higher-paying jobs indicate more potential to influence a company's competitive position. For any given job, pay will differ according to performance or seniority. Chapter 4 notes that higher performance levels and seniority result in greater worth.

Still another approach is to disburse profits as proportional payments to employees based on their contribution to profits. Some companies measure employee contributions to profit based on job performance. However, this approach is not very feasible because it is difficult to isolate each employee's contributions to profits. For example, how does a secretary's performance (based on answering telephones, greeting visitors, and typing memos) directly contribute to company performance?

Companies can treat profit sharing distributions either as compensation awarded in addition to an employee's base pay or as "pay at risk." In the former case, base pay is set at externally competitive levels, which makes any profit sharing tantamount to a bonus. In the latter case, base pay is set below the average for competing employers, which creates a sense of risk. Employees' earnings for a given period may thus be relatively meager or relatively sizable, compared with what they could earn elsewhere.

Advantages of Profit Sharing Plans

The use of a profit sharing plan has two main advantages, one for employees and the other for companies. When properly designed, profit sharing plans enable employees to share in companies' fortunes. As employees benefit from profit sharing plans, they will be more likely to work productively to promote profits. Obviously, the upshot of enhanced employee productivity is greater profits for companies that use profit sharing plans.

Companies that use profit sharing programs gain greater financial flexibility. As we discussed, monetary payouts to employees vary with profit levels. During economic downturns, payout levels are significantly lower than during economic boom periods. This feature of profit sharing plans enables companies to use limited cash reserves where needed, such as for research and development activities.

Disadvantages of Profit Sharing Plans

There are two main disadvantages associated with profit sharing plans. The first one directly affects employees, and the second one affects companies. Profit sharing plans may undermine the economic security of employees, particularly if profit sharing represents a sizable portion of direct compensation. Because company profits vary from year to year, so do employees' earnings. Thus, employees will find it difficult to predict their earnings, which will affect their saving and buying behavior. If there is significant variability in earnings, a company's excellent performers are likely to leave for employment with competitors. Certainly, the turnover of excellent performers represents a significant disadvantage to companies.

Employers also find profit sharing programs to be problematic under certain conditions. Profit sharing plans may fail to motivate employees because they do not see a direct link between their efforts and corporate profits. Hourly employees in particular may have trouble seeing this connection, because their efforts appear to be several steps removed from the company's performance. For instance, an assembly line worker who installs interior trim—carpeting and seats—to automobiles may not find any connection between his or her efforts and the level of company profits because interior trim represents just one of many steps in the production of automobiles.

Employee Stock Option Plans

Under **employee stock option plans**, companies grant employees the right to purchase shares of company stock. **Company stock** represents total equity of a company. **Company stock shares** represent equity segments of equal value. Equity interest increases positively with the number of stock shares. **Stock options** describe an employee's right to purchase company stock. Employees do not actually own stock until they exercise the stock option rights. This is done by purchasing stock at a designated price after a company-chosen time period lapses, usually no more than 5 years. Employee stock options provide an incentive to work productively, with the expectation that collective employee productivity will increase the value of company stock over time. Employees earn monetary compensation when they sell the stock at a higher price than they originally paid for it.

Employee stock option plans represent just one type of general stock compensation plan. Two other basic kinds of stock plans are widely used today. First, **employee stock ownership plans (ESOPs)** place company stock in trust accounts for employees. The purpose of ESOPs is similar to deferred profit sharing because these trusts are set aside on employees' behalf as a source of retirement income, and these awards provide favorable treatment to employees. Discussion of ESOPs is deferred to Chapter 11. Second, **stock compensation plans** represent an important type of deferred compensation for executives. **Deferred compensation** is supposed to create a sense of ownership, aligning the interests of the executive with those of the owners or shareholders of the company over the long term. There are several kinds of stock compensation plans for executives. Discussion of these types of plans is set aside for Chapter 13.

DESIGNING INCENTIVE PAY PROGRAMS

When designing an incentive pay plan, HR professionals and line managers should consider five key factors:

- Whether the plan should be based on group or individual employee performance
- The level of risk employees will be willing to accept in their overall compensation package
- Whether incentive pay should replace or complement traditional pay
- The criteria by which performance should be judged
- The time horizon for goals—long term, short term, or a combination of both

Group Versus Individual Incentives

Companies considering various design alternatives should choose a design that fits the structure of the company. Group incentive programs are most suitable where the nature of the work is interdependent and the contributions of individual employees are difficult to measure. In such situations, companies require cooperative behavior among their employees. Companies may be able to encourage team behavior by linking compensation to the achievement of department or division goals and eliminating from the pay determination process factors that are outside the group's control, such as the late delivery of raw materials by an independent vendor.

On the other hand, individual incentive plans reward employees for meeting or surpassing predetermined individual goals, such as production or sales quotas. As with group incentive programs, the attainment of individual goals should be well within the control of the employees. Moreover, goals for individual incentive programs should be based on independent work rather than interdependent work. For example, it would be appropriate to base an employee's incentive on typing accuracy because the work can be performed independently and there are few external constraints on an employee's ability to complete such work. At the group level, it would be reasonable to provide incentives to the individual members of a sales team. In the case of computer hardware and networks, the sale and implementation of these products involve a team of marketing professionals and technical experts who depend on the others' expertise to identify the appropriate configuration of hardware and networking equipment—meeting the client's needs—and to successfully install the equipment in the client's company.

Level of Risk

Careful consideration should be given to the level of risk employees are willing to accept. As mentioned previously, incentive pay may complement base salary or may be used in place of all or a portion of base salary. Clearly, the level of risk increases as incentive pay represents a greater proportion of total core compensation. The level of risk tends to be greater among higher-level employees than among those who are at the lower levels of a company's job structure. Intuitively, it is reasonable to infer that the attainment of a first-line supervisor's goal of maintaining a packing department's level of productivity above a predetermined level is less risky than the achievement of a sales manager's goal of increasing market share by 10 percent in a market where the competition is already quite stiff. Apart from an employee's rank, the level of risk chosen should depend on the extent to which employees control the attainment of the desired goal. The adoption of incentive pay programs makes the most sense when participants have a reasonable degree of control over the attainment of the plan's goals. Logically, incentive programs are bound to fail when the goals are simply out of reach because they are too difficult or because extraneous factors are hampering employees' efforts to meet goals.

Complementing or Replacing Base Pay

When complementing base pay, a company awards incentive pay in addition to an employee's base pay and fringe compensation. Alternatively, companies may reduce base pay by placing the reduced portion at risk in an incentive plan. For instance, if a company grants its employees 10 percent raises each year, the company could, instead, grant its employees a 4 percent cost-of-living increase and use the remaining 6 percent as incentive by awarding none of it to below average performers, only half of it to employees whose performance is average, and the entire 6 percent to employees whose performance is above average. In this scenario, the 6 percent that was expected by the employees to become part of their base pay is no longer a guarantee because that potential salary has been placed at risk. By introducing risk into the pay program, employees have the potential to earn more than the 6 percent because poor performers will receive less, leaving more to be distributed to exemplary performers.

Companies in cyclical industries such as retail sales could benefit by including an incentive component in the core compensation programs they offer to employees. During slow business periods, the use of regular merit pay programs that add permanent increments to base pay can create budget problems. If incentive pay were used instead of permanent merit raises, then the level of expenditure on compensation would vary with levels of business activity. In effect, the use of incentive pay can lower payroll costs during lean periods and enhance the level of rewards when business activity picks up.

Performance Criteria

Obviously—from the discussion of performance appraisal in Chapter 4—the measures used to appraise employee performance should be quantifiable and accessible. For incentive pay programs, common measures of employee performance are company profits, sales revenue, and number of units produced by a business unit. Preferably, the measures chosen should relate to the company's competitive strategy. For instance, if a company is attempting to enhance quality, its incentive plan would probably reward employees on the basis of customer satisfaction with quality.

In reality, more than one performance measure may be relevant. In such instances, a company is likely to employ all of the measures as a basis for awarding incentives. The weighting scheme would reflect the relative importance of each performance criterion to the company's competitive strategy—for example, company performance (10 percent), unit performance (40 percent), and individual performance (50 percent), incorporating all of the organizational levels. Clearly, an employee would receive an incentive even if company or departmental performance was poor. In effect, the relative weights are indicative of the degree of risk to an employee that is inherent in these plans. Compared with the previous example, the following plan would be quite risky—50 percent company performance, 35 percent departmental performance, and 15 percent individual performance. Employees' earnings would depend mainly on company and departmental performance over which they possess less control than they do over their own performance.

Time Horizon: Short Term Versus Long Term

A key feature of incentive pay plans is the time orientation. There are no definitive standards to distinguish between short term and long term. A general rule of thumb is that short-term goals generally can be achieved in 5 years or less and that long-term goals may require even longer.

In general, incentives for lower-level employees tend to be based on short-term goals that are within the control of such employees. For example, production workers' performances are judged on periods as short as 1 hour. On the other hand, incentive programs for professionals and executives have a long-term orientation. For instance, rewarding an engineer's innovation in product design requires a long-term orientation because it takes an extended amount of time to move through the series of steps required to bring the innovation to the marketplace—patent approval, manufacturing, and market distribution. The incentives that executives receive are based on a long-term horizon because their success is matched against the endurance of a company over time.

FLIP SIDE OF THE COIN

ON THE FOLLY OF REWARDING A, WHILE HOPING FOR B

In the classic article titled "On the Folly of Rewarding A, While Hoping for B," Steven Kerr criticized organizational reward systems for some behaviors while ignoring other desirable work behaviors [26]. Although the article was published more than two decades ago, follies of this kind are quite pervasive in organizations today—case in point: research universities. Historically, research universities awarded faculty members various kinds of awards based on the quality and quantity of their scholarly publication records. These rewards include pay raises, promotions to the ranks of associate professor and full professor, and tenure. Unfortunately, university administrators did not place nearly as much emphasis on teaching effectiveness, which meant that faculty received rewards as long as they continued to publish scholarly articles, regardless of their performance as course instructors. Given this reality, many faculty members (but certainly not all) devoted much of their energy to research at the expense of teaching quality.

Currently, university administrators claim to place greater emphasis on the importance of teaching effectiveness. This "emphasis" came about in response to outcries from taxpayers whose dollars fund a significant portion of public university budgets, as well as the parents of children attending both private and public universities because of the rampant increases in tuition costs. Also contributing to this "emphasis" are widely publicized criticisms of faculty in newspaper articles and in books such as *Profscam* [27]. Certainly, emphasizing teaching effectiveness has merit. Unfortunately, the reward systems in research universities have not changed very much. In business school departments, faculty pay raises continue to be based almost exclusively on publication record rather than teaching effectiveness [28]. University administrators have not broken out of the old ways of thinking about reward and recognition practices. This lack of change may be due to the fact that university administrators, faculty, and students have not reached consensus on the meaning of teaching effectiveness or on valid methods for measuring teaching effectiveness.

LINKING INCENTIVE PAY WITH COMPETITIVE STRATEGY

As you will recall, in Chapter 2 we reviewed a framework for establishing a basis for selecting particular compensation tactics to match a company's competitive strategy. How do incentive pay systems fit with the two fundamental competitive strategies—lowest cost and differentiation? Ultimately, incentive pay systems, when properly applied, can contribute to meeting companies' goals of lowest-cost and differentiation strategies. However, the rationale for the appropriateness of incentive pay systems differs according to the imperatives of these strategies.

Lowest-Cost Competitive Strategy

Lowest-cost strategies demand reduced output costs per employee. In general, incentive pay appears to be suited to meeting this productivity focus, as we have shown in this chapter, by companies that are pursuing a lowest-cost strategy. The suitability of specific incentive pay programs merits comment.

Individual incentive programs such as piecework systems connect core compensation costs to employee productivity. From a company's perspective, a well-designed piecework system aligns its expenditure on compensation with the level of employee output. Piecework plans are especially effective when they motivate employees to keep up with the demand for companies' products. When employees' output matches market demand, then the company will cover its expenditure on incentive compensation and generate a profit.

Behavioral encouragement plans provide effective incentives for companies pursuing a lowest-cost strategy if these companies suffer excessive absenteeism or poor safety records. Absenteeism poses direct fiscal costs to employers and disrupts workflow that can lead to compromises in production or service delivery. Poor safety records cost employers stiff monetary penalties that arise from violations of the Occupational Safety and Health Act. In addition, employers are liable for on-the-job accidents and carry workers' compensation insurance (Chapter 10). The cost of workers' compensation insurance increases dramatically for companies with poor safety records.

Among the group incentives, gain sharing programs are appropriate for companies that pursue a lowest-cost strategy. Simply put, employee involvement facilitates productivity enhancements. Such improvements result from more efficient ways to conduct work and enhanced employee motivation that comes from greater participation in workplace matters.

Current profit sharing plans are probably the least likely form of incentive to support lowest-cost strategies. As mentioned earlier in this chapter, profit sharing can be an ineffective incentive when employees do not perceive links between their work contributions and company profits. When profit share awards do not motivate employees, then their productivity is unlikely to be influenced, and this money will be "wasted" from the company's standpoint.

Differentiation Competitive Strategy

Differentiation strategies mandate creativity, novel ways of approaching work, and risk taking. Compared with lowest-cost strategies, companies that pursue differentiation strategies hold a longer-term focus with regard to the attainment of preestablished objectives. Among the incentives that we reviewed earlier, team-based incentives and gain sharing are clearly the most appropriate for companies pursuing differentiation strategies. By their very nature, team-based incentives and gain sharing programs promote interaction among coworkers and some degree of autonomy to devise the "best" way to achieve the objectives set by management.

Piecework plans and current profit sharing plans provide inappropriate incentives if a company wishes to promote differentiation. Piecework plans focus on increasing employees' productivity on their existing jobs rather than encouraging employees to offer creative ideas that may lead to product or service differentiation. As before, profit sharing plans may be ineffective where employees see no link between job performance and profits.

SUMMARY

This chapter provided a discussion of the incentive pay concept—how incentive pay differs from traditional bases for pay such as seniority pay and merit pay; varieties of individual, group, and companywide incentives; issues about designing incentive pay programs; and its fit with competitive strategy. Companies should seriously consider adopting incentive pay programs when the conditions for using incentive pay programs are appropriate. Perhaps one of the greatest challenges for companies is to ensure that employees perceive a connection between job performance and the rewards they receive. Another challenge is for companies to balance the level of risk employees will bear, particularly given the fact that U.S. employees are accustomed to receiving base pay and regular permanent increases according to seniority or merit pay systems.

Key Terms

- incentive pay, 133
- variable pay, 133
- individual incentive plans, 135
- piecework plans, 137
- management incentive plans, 138
- behavioral encouragement plans, 138
- referral plans, 139
- group incentive programs, 144
- team-based incentives, 144
- gain sharing, 145
- Scanlon Plan, 146
- sales value of production (SVOP), 147
- Rucker Plan, 147
- value-added formula, 147
- Improshare, 148
- labor hour ratio formula, 149
- buy-back provision, 149
- free-rider effect, 150
- profit sharing plans, 151
- current profit sharing, 151
- deferred profit sharing, 151
- employee stock option plans, 153
- company stock, 153
- company stock shares, 153
- stock options, 153
- employee stock ownership plans (ESOPs), 153
- stock compensation plans, 153
- deferred compensation, 153

Discussion Questions

1. Indicate whether you agree or disagree with the following statement: "Individual incentive plans are less preferable than group incentives and companywide incentives." Explain your answer.
2. Currently, there is a tendency among business professionals to endorse the use of incentive pay plans. Identify two jobs for which individual incentive pay is appropriate and two jobs for which individual incentive pay is inappropriate. Be sure to include your justification.
3. Critics of profit sharing plans maintain that these plans do not motivate employees to perform at higher levels. Under what conditions are profit sharing plans not likely to motivate employees?
4. Unlike individual incentive programs, group and companywide incentive programs reward individuals based on group (for example, cost savings in a department) and companywide (for example, profits) performance standards, respectively. Under group and companywide incentive programs, it is possible for poor performers to benefit without making substantial contributions to group or company goals. What can companies do to ensure that poor performers do not benefit?
5. Opponents of incentive pay programs argue that these programs manipulate employees more than seniority and merit pay programs. Discuss your views of this statement.

Exercises

Compensation Online

For Students

Exercise 1: Find relevant journal articles

Use your school's online catalog to search for articles on incentive pay. Compare what you learned about merit pay in Chapter 4 with what you find out about incentive pay. What are the main differences between these two systems, and what type of behavior is each likely to reward?

Exercise 2: Search for stock prices

One of your classes deals at length with stock as compensation. You have been assigned the project of finding and tracking 10 stock prices over the course of the semester. Use three search engines: Yahoo, Lycos, and one of your choice. Using one search engine at a time, type in "stock prices," and click on the *search* button. Look up the New York Stock Exchange symbol for AT&T, and then search for the information available on AT&T. Click on the various buttons available and review the information each button presents. What is the NYSE symbol for AT&T? How did each search engine differ in the way they presented the information? Did you prefer one search engine over another? As a human resource professional, how could this type of search benefit you?

Exercise 3: Research the Scanlon Plan

One of your professors announces that there will be significant extra credit to the top five short essays on the Scanlon Plan. Essays will be judged solely on demonstrated understanding of how the Scanlon Plan came about and how it works. Using Yahoo, type "Scanlon Plan" into the search window, and click on the *search* link. Click on a site that concerns the history of the plan. Did you learn anything about the Scanlon Plan that you did not already know? Do you think this site might be of use to you in other classes or in your profession?

Using a different search engine, go to the same Web site or find a related site. Compare and contrast the two search engines for ease of accessibility and amount of information available.

For Professionals

Exercise 1: Research performance management issues

You have been asked to return to your alma mater and speak to current students about performance management issues. To make the most of this experience for yourself and the students, conduct an advanced search for "performance management" and particularly focus on news and articles. Read up on the current trends and thinking on the subject of performance management.

Exercise 2: Research employee stock ownership plans

Your company is about to extend its ESOP to a broader group of employees. You have been asked to work with colleagues from the finance department to develop a proper system. To bring yourself up to speed and start off on the right foot with your coworkers, you want to update your understanding of ESOP. Search for "employee stock ownership plans" and look at everything from consulting services to news articles.

Exercise 3: Research a company's Web site

Using the search engine of your choice, research both the Motorola and Sprint Web pages for information concerning the available compensation and benefits they offer. Which site did you find most informative? When you become a human resource professional, would you suggest your company promote its compensation and benefits packages like Motorola's or Sprint's? Why?

Endnotes

1. Peck, C. (1993). Variable pay: Nontraditional programs for motivation and reward. New York: The Conference Board.
2. Gòmez-Mejìa, L. R. & Balkin, D. R. (1992). *Compensation, Organizational Strategy and Firm Performance*. Cincinnati, OH: South-Western.
3. Schuster, J. R., & Zingheim, P. K. (1992). *The New Pay: Linking Employee and Organizational Performance*. New York: Lexington Books.
4. Caudron, S. (1993). Master the compensation maze. *Personnel Journal, 72* (June), pp. 64a–64o.
5. Dulles, F. R., & Dubofsky, M. (1984). *Labor in America: A History* (4th ed.). Arlington Heights, IL: Harlan Davidson.
6. Peck, C. (1993). Variable pay: Nontraditional programs for motivation and reward. New York: The Conference Board.
7. Drucker, P. (1954). *The Practice of Management*. New York: Harper.
8. WorldatWork. (2002). Referral bonus online survey 2002 [online]. Available: *//www.worldatwork.org*, accessed June 17, 2002.
9. Gòmez-Mejìa, L. R., Balkin, D. R., & Cardy, R. L. (1995). *Managing Human Resources*. Upper Saddle River, NJ: Prentice Hall.
10. Jackson, S. E. (1992). Team composition in organizational settings: Issues in managing an increasingly diverse work force. In S. Worchel, W. Wood, & J. A.

Simpson (Eds.), *Group Process and Productivity* (pp. 138–173). Newbury Park, CA: Sage.

11. Kanter, R. M. (1988). When a thousand flowers bloom: Structural, collective, and social conditions for innovation in organizations. In B. M. Staw & L. L. Cummings (Eds.), *Research in Organizational Behavior* (vol. 10, pp. 169–211). Greenwich, CT: JAI.
12. Worchel, S., Wood, W., & Simpson, J. A. (Eds.). (1992). *Group Process and Productivity*. Newbury Park, CA: Sage.
13. Kanin-Lovers, J., & Cameron, M. (1993). Team-based reward systems. *Journal of Compensation and Benefits*, January–February, pp. 55–60.
14. Schuster, J. R., & Zingheim, P. K. (1993). Building pay environments to facilitate high-performance teams. *ACA Journal, 2*, pp. 40–51.
15. Belcher, J. G., Jr. (1994). Gain sharing and variable pay: The state of the art. *Compensation & Benefits Review*, May–June, pp. 50–60.
16. Doyle, R. J. (1983). *Gain Sharing and Productivity*. New York: American Management Association.
17. Peck, C. (1993). Variable pay: Nontraditional programs for motivation and reward. New York: The Conference Board.
18. Milkovich, G. T., & Newman, J. M. (1993). *Compensation* (4th ed.). Homewood, IL: Irwin.
19. Ross, T. (1990). Why gain sharing sometimes fails. In B. Graham-Moore & T. Ross (Eds.), *Gain Sharing: Plans for Improving Performance* (pp. 100–115). Washington, DC: Bureau of National Affairs.
20. Lesiur, F. G. (Ed.). (1958). The Scanlon Plan: *A Frontier in Labor-Management Cooperation.* Cambridge, MA: MIT Press.
21. Bullock, R. J. & Lawlor, E. E. III. (1984). Gain sharing: A few questions and fewer answers. *Human Resource Management, 23*, pp. 18–20.
22. Smith, B. T. (1986). The Scanlon Plan revisited: A way to a competitive tomorrow. *Production Engineering, 33*, pp. 28–31.
23. Geare, A. J. (1976). Productivity from Scanlon type plans. *Academy of Management Review, 1*, pp. 99–108.
24. Myers, D. W. (1989). *Compensation Management.* Chicago: Commerce Clearing House.
25. Lawler, E. E., III, & Cohen, S. G. (1992). Designing a pay system for teams. *American Compensation Association Journal, 1*, pp. 6–19.
26. Kerr, S. (1975). On the folly of rewarding A, while hoping for B. *Academy of Management Journal, 18*, pp. 769–783.
27. Syles, C. J. (1988). *Profscam: Professors and the Demise of Higher Education*. Washington, DC: Regnery Gateway.
28. Gòmez-Mejía, L. R., & Balkin, D. B. (1992). The determinants of faculty pay: An agency theory perspective. *Academy of Management Journal, 35*, pp. 921–955.

COMPENSATION IN ACTION

WHAT GOES UP MAY COME DOWN

Undoubtedly there were a lot of disappointed workers at mid-year bonus time this summer. Companies that are tightening their belts for the first time in years are finding their variable pay plans put to the test.

"HR professionals are in for some noise from employees about variable pay this year," says Jay Schuster of Los Angeles–based compensation consultants Schuster-Zingheim and Associates.

During the recent boom times, variable pay awards and stock options with value have been treated like entitlements, Schuster believes. "At too many organizations, HR has not done a good job of helping leadership communicate the realities of variable pay—that value goes up and down over time and, if goals are missed, cash incentives do not pay off."

COMMUNICATE COME RAIN OR SHINE

The best-managed variable pay plans are clearly and continuously communicated to staff. "Every study of workforce attitudes suggests that honest and frequent communication of the facts creates improved employee understanding of the realities of how people can help a company thrive," says Schuster's partner, Patricia Zingheim. "And with better understanding comes better support, acceptance of what the company is doing and subsequently improved morale."

"Frequency is the key, whether the news is good or bad," according to Mark Stiffler, president and CEO of Synygy, a Conshohocken, Pennsylvania–based provider of enterprise incentive management software and services. Many companies fear having to disclose bad news to employees, but if it comes as part of a regular and frequent distribution, it may be easier for employees to understand and accept. A good rule of thumb, says Stiffler, "is to communicate incentive plan results two to three times as often as you pay them out." Employees "shouldn't just be issued a check and a statement."

So if bonuses are awarded quarterly, individual results and news about the incentive program should be disseminated monthly. If bonuses are paid annually, the company should communicate to all staff every four to six months. This also gives the organization a key opportunity to reinforce to employees the rules and the purpose of the variable pay plan.

Synygy recommends tailoring the information to individuals in confidential reports tracking their performance and bonus expectations. If the amount is tied to company performance as well, that component also should be disclosed. "Companies should aim for frequency, accuracy, and timeliness, as well as understandability" in these reports, Stiffler advises.

Diane Gherson, global practice leader for performance and rewards at Towers Perrin in Irvine, California, agrees that it's crucial to make employees understand how they are tracking against the company's goals throughout the year. "The better-managed plans do this. At least on a monthly basis, employees should know what their bonus would look like if they were paid out that day. If the numbers are disappointing, leadership should communicate what actions it is taking—and what actions employees should take—to get on track. When bonus time rolls around, they know the story; there are no surprises."

Even when the news is bad, don't be afraid to pass it along in exactly the same manner. "Don't make a special case out of it, like calling an all-hands meeting to explain," Gherson urges. "If you do, then your variable pay plan will be perceived as a benefit or entitlement that can be taken away."

Also, fight people's natural inclination to let diminished variable pay affect their morale, she adds. "It should not be a morale issue. Most leading companies aren't talking morale; they are talking engagement. Engaged employees are given enough information so they can make decisions and adjust their behavior."

Cranking up communications about variable pay is a major chance for HR to help the business—and become a business partner at the same time. When pay expectations are in danger of being dashed, "HR needs to communicate what is

(Continued)

(Continued)

going on, why this is happening and what the company is going to do—if anything—about going forward," Schuster advises.

According to Stiffler, before-and-after surveys show that the frequency and manner that plan information is communicated can have a very significant impact. When the communications efforts are changed for the better, "We've seen jumps from 40 percent to 90 percent of employees who say they understand the plan fully."

Make sure the plan's objectivity is demonstrated clearly and that all the rules are exposed. Hide none of the details. Make sure the formulas are very clear. "If people understand their plan, and company strategy is reflected there, they will change their behavior. Calls about the plan drop. HR spends less time fielding questions."

Plan communication also should cover expectation-setting. "Let them use 'what if' calculators to see the effect of improved performance on their bonus," Stiffler recommends. And remind them that, while variable pay will depend on the company's performance to some degree, an employee's performance counts even when the company does less well. "Employees don't have to be victims of the economy. Even when companies announce an across-the-board base pay cut, they can still earn great money with variable pay."

But what if a company hasn't been quite so consistent about its communications, letting the plan's success—up to now—speak for itself? "If your plan paid out a lot of money in the past, then expectation have been set," says Stiffler. "If you pay out a lot less this year, people are going to get upset and there will be turnover, as well as demands to 'make it up' to disgruntled workers in some way."

But it sets a damaging precedent if a company decides to override the plan parameters and supplement a disappointing payout. "It will send the message that the company will take care of you no matter what, and yours is no longer a pay-for-performance plan," he warns.

A Towers Perrin study of 750 variable pay plans last year showed that one-eighth made the mistake of paying out supplements, Gherson notes. "Each of those companies fell into the lowest category in terms of the effectiveness of their plans."

DON'T ABANDON VARIABLE PAY

In fact, having a plan that doesn't consistently provide employees with an annual windfall is an effective lesson about performance pay and gain sharing. "The current economic climate gives all HR professionals the chance to really add value to the business," believes Schuster. "Missing performance goals provides the business case for communicating the measures and goals needed to make the company a success. It is not a time to panic and return to a 'base pay only' mentality."

"You can't change the plan every time goals are missed," notes Schuster. "The [economy's] move from 2000 to 2001 was a unique change and must be communicated as such."

And you can't just scrap the variable pay plan because some vocal employees express their disenchantment. "The alternative is going to be more base pay or an automatic 'bonus' award granted retrospectively at the end of the year—both of which are probably unaffordable unless results improve," Zingheim explains.

"You need to educate your employees on the whys and what-fors of variable pay. The message must stress that variable pay is the company's agile reward—it can communicate new goals and directions as the company needs them addressed, while base pay does a good job of reflecting the skills and capabilities a person uses to perform a specific role." Variable pay is the best way to reward performance—whether by companywide, business unit, division, department, team or even individual. It is how the company creates a financial partnership with employees, Zingheim believes.

Stiffler believes that the companies catching the most flak about disappointing bonuses are those that had poor plan designs that paid out unrealistically. "You want your plan to be financially controllable in both up and down times."

"While an organization may have missed the mark relative to setting goals, or even choosing goals, in 2000 and 2001, that's part of the normal state of things under unusual economic circumstances, and it will do better now going forward,"

Zingheim notes. "The message is, 'We are learning, but we don't want to throw out the baby with the bath water.' "

DO IT RIGHT THE NEXT TIME

Instead, when a company's performance falters, it may be the perfect time to revisit the variable pay plan for a tune-up—not to ensure a bigger or more consistent payout, but to align it with a changing business strategy that takes into account the shifting economy. "Think of it as driving a car that's not properly tuned," Gherson says. "Variable pay plans have lots of moving parts, so they need to be checked and tuned regularly.

Changing the plan's metrics, performance expectations, and goals should not become commonplace or "people will lose confidence in the company's ability to achieve even short-term business plans," Zingheim warns. "But if the name of the game for the company has changed, the reward system should be aligned with these new directions."

And the strong message to employees should be about what has changed in the business, what leadership is doing about it and what everyone else can do to get the company engine running properly again. "It can't be, 'Well, we missed these goals so we picked some new ones we think we can now meet,' " she stresses. "It's necessary to build a case for why the new goals are better, why they are achievable, and how people can really influence goal performance as a result of doing things within their reach to make the company get to where it needs to be.

Consider outsourcing the plan design and communication program, Stiffler advises. "Everyone thinks they know how to do this, thinking 'How complex can this possibly be?' But it is challenging to create a variable pay plan that works correctly, especially in an up-and-down environment." When you change the design, it can take months to implement and revise payroll accounting systems, he says.

If the plan is changed, should the organization try to retroactively calculate and pay the previous period's bonuses? If staff turnover might be a problem, it's worth a shot. "Synygy has had clients do that, but your payroll staff will go into a tailspin without some professional help," says Stiffler.

According to Towers Perrin data, "We know that the most common plan out there is an organizationwide plan that has a 70 percent chance of failure," Gherson notes. "These are the plans that don't have 'line of sight'—that is, employees can't see clearly how their performance can make a difference."

Instead, do everything you can to get employees to believe in the company's success strategy, and demonstrate their important role. "Let them know that even in a tough economy, your company and its staff are winners," she says. "Remind them that there are lots of organizations doing well out there now because their people are very focused and intend to overcome every obstacle."

Source: Martha Frase Blunt. *HR, 46,* pp. 85–90.

WHAT'S NEW IN COMPENSATION?

Employee Empowerment Is Key to Suggestion System Success

Incentive pay programs are becoming more common in the workplace because employees continually strive to achieve higher levels of performance based on management communication of performance goals. These programs are also becoming more popular among managers because they help companies control costs by offering a one-time reward for the attainment of particular goals rather than a recurring increase, as in the case of merit pay programs. In this chapter, we discussed a variety of incentive pay plans. Most gain sharing plans in particular are premised on regular input by employees regarding more efficient ways of accomplishing work, thus helping companies to reduce costs. With gain sharing plans, companies share some of the gain (such as additional money) triggered by employee suggestions.

From the perspective of employees, formal input promotes a sense of empowerment because their initiatives may have made a real difference in the workplace. However, management may not always view employee participation so positively because some employees could feel disempowered when their suggestions are not adopted. The featured *New York Times* article discusses this and other management concerns that may arise from the use of formal employee input programs.

Log into your *New York Times* account. Search the database for articles on "incentive pay" and "employee participation." When reviewing these articles, pay attention to the types of incentive pay plans being discussed. Be prepared to discuss the types of incentive pay plans and the particular issues raised about them in the articles. Also, identify issues that come up about employee participation. Some of the articles will relate to incentive pay issues; others will emphasize different HR issues such as the choice to take training. Following your course instructor's specific directions, be prepared to describe the current situation and relate it to the article. ■

The New York Times

Management; Suggestions Rise from the Floors of U.S. Factories

MILFORD, CONN.—At 2:15 on a Friday afternoon, as the production lines churn out pens, razors, and cigarette lighters, 15 employees of the Bic Corporation abruptly leave their posts and file into a conference room. Machinists pull up chairs next to their managers at the table.

Charlie Tichy, an hourly employee with a tattoo left over from his service days, takes a seat at the head of the table. "Everyone ready?" he asks, although he has their attention. Mr. Tichy, who holds the title of employee-involvement administrator, begins reading aloud from the slips he has pulled during the last week from the plant's suggestion boxes. The ideas range from buying a $2 "gutter scoop" for cleaning underneath a pen-point machine to redesigning the factory's packaging area, with a hand-drawn diagram showing how.

Mr. Tichy does not read the names on the sheets of paper, but there are clues to the authors' identities. One slip offers a remedy for a machine that tends to spray oil on the floor. "That's a good idea," pipes up Mike Hanscom, a mechanic in the ballpoint manufacturing department, drawing laughter from friends who knew he suggested it.

Whenever the group voices its support for a proposal, its slip is passed down the table to the appropriate supervisor, who has 10 days to put the change in place. This is no management gimmick to stroke workers' egos, either. Bic, which is owned by Societe Bic S.A. of France, takes what it calls its employee-involvement program very seriously, viewing it as a way to spur morale and productivity and ultimately bolster corporate profits.

Suggestion boxes have a long history in the American workplace, of course, with the first documented program credited to Eastman Kodak in 1898. But increasingly, they are becoming more ambitious. In the early 1990s, corporations began instituting something they generally called workplace-involvement programs, aimed at picking workers' brains for ways to improve efficiency.

These programs are grounded in the premise that workers know more about their immediate surroundings than anybody else, and are smart enough to spot defects in products and procedures and to figure out solutions to them. Their proposals can save money, which is why many chief executives ask employees to send proposals directly to their e-mail in-boxes.

At Bic last year, 577 employees out of 684 hourly manufacturing employees wrote 2,999 suggestions, and every one was mulled over at a meeting like this one. Some 2,368 were carried out. One favorite was delightfully simple: A worker noticed that the trash was being collected twice each week, although the Dumpster was only half full. Cutting trash pickups saved $500 a week.

The employees were not necessarily looking to cash in; the most coveted award, Suggestion of the Month, nets the winner only a modest after-tax bonus of $100 and a reserved parking space. Yet these meetings have transformed the corporate culture from quiescent to teamwork-oriented, says Philip S. Preston, an employee-involvement specialist, who works with Mr. Tichy.

"When I came to Bic 20 years ago, the thinking was, 'I just have to press these buttons; I have engineers to do the thinking for me,' " Mr. Preston said. "Now, people think when they come to work."

Some companies are using these initiatives to mimic the enthusiasm common at start-ups. This year, Voyant Technologies Inc. of Westminster, Colorado, which makes voice-conferencing systems for telecommunications companies, began encouraging employees, from receptionists to management, to submit ideas for new products through its Bright Ideas program. Voyant plans to put up seed money for the best ideas and give the submitting employees leeway to help develop them.

The program itself was the bright idea of Brad Volin, director of product development, who headed a start-up of his own before joining Voyant. While his company, a vehicle-registration Web site called CarRegister, did not survive, Mr. Volin says he would like to reproduce the creative energy that permeated it.

The rewards come in the form of recognition, even for the ideas that are not good enough. For those, there is a consolation prize: the Elisha Gray award, named after the inventor who submitted a patent for the telephone just hours after Alexander Graham Bell. "We wanted to encourage risk with all the employees and really create a culture where we reward failure," Mr. Volin said. Employees need not fret that they lack the skills to write a polished proposal, he said. All they have to do is fill out a simple form on the company's internal Web site.

The employee-suggestion movement has plenty of room for growth. Automakers were the first American companies to promote the programs in a big way, partly because their Japanese rivals were reaping benefits from the practice, business specialists say. Yet today, only about 7 percent of companies have formal suggestion programs, said Andrew Wood, whose company, Ideas Management Ltd. in Gig Harbor, Washington, sets up such programs.

Chief executives have reason to be skeptical. These programs can backfire if they are not handled intelligently. If managers ask for ideas but fail to act on them, for example, they could sow resentment among workers. "People feel bad if they step forward and they're not responded to," said John Kao, a former professor at Harvard Business School who leads a consulting business in San Francisco called the Idea Factory. And no matter what managers do, some workers will view their efforts as window dressing.

But employee empowerment is very much on the minds of most corporate managers these days. Some 89 percent of the chief executives surveyed in 1999 by Robert Half International, a staffing service, said that companies had stepped up efforts to encourage creativity in their employees. "There is a renewed respect in the last 5 to 10 years of reality-based ideas coming from those in the thick of activity, on the front lines," said Lynn Taylor, the firm's vice president for research.

"They have seen the benefits of opening the channels, of encouraging smart risk-taking," she said. "Better to make a mistake and to have thought outside the box than to be afraid."

At the Dana Corporation, an automotive-parts manufacturer in Toledo, Ohio, employee suggestions are part of the company infrastructure. Management not only encourages suggestions, it provides a quota: two ideas from each employee a month. Changes that would cost less than $500 do not need the approval of a plant manager; employees can put them into action themselves.

Dana estimates it has saved millions of dollars because of the program, which like Voyant's initiative is titled Bright Ideas. One idea came from Kevin Young, a maintenance supervisor at the company's engine controls warehouse in Carlisle, Pennsylvania. He proposed installing automated light dimmers in the 405,000-square-foot plant. In the first two weeks, the dimmers reduced electricity bills by more than $6,000. "In down times, having an idea program will make the difference," said Gary Corrigan, a Dana spokesman. "It creates a competitive advantage."

At Procter & Gamble, an employee with an idea may first bounce it off a computer. The company's suggestion box is interactive, and it hangs on the company's internal Web site. When an employee submits an idea, the site hunts for key words in its database of suggestions.

"It comes back saying, 'By the way, here are some other ideas that may be close to what you have,' " said Ed Von Bargen, a chemist in the research and development department who administers the site.

One creative employee idea evolved into MoreThanACard.com, a commercial Web site that sells gift packages of Procter & Gamble products, he said.

"When Procter & Gamble put up its My Idea Web site two and a half years ago, we were originally going to have this just for the R&D folks," Mr. Von Bargen said. But John E. Pepper, then the chief executive, suggested a companywide site, he added. While the old suggestion system got about 100 ideas a year, he said, the new Web site receives 5 to 20 hits a day, and has built up a database of 10,000 ideas.

Mr. Von Bargen winces at the word suggestion.

"We tried to shy away from its being a suggestion box and more a place where you can share your ideas," he said. "Too many times a suggestion box is kind of like a black hole: They go in and you never know what's going to happen."

Mr. Tichy, who was the lead employee in the ball-grinding department when he volunteered in 1992 to help with Bic's fledgling suggestion program, remembers being skeptical that management cared what the workers had on their minds. Or that employees would bother filling out the forms if they were not receiving a cut of the savings. But now he sees even the gruffest line workers show pride and engage in a little primping when the camera comes around to take their picture for the employee-suggestion bulletin board.

"The guys are worse than the women," he said. "Some of these guys I've worked with for 25 years. I never know how vain they are until they get Employee of the Month."

SOURCE: Julie Flaherty, Management: Suggestions rise from the floors of U.S. factories (April 18, 2001) [online]. Available: *www.nytimes.com,* accessed October 12, 2002.

CHAPTER 6 PERSON-FOCUSED PAY

Chapter Outline

Learning Objectives

In this chapter, you will learn about

1. Differing opinions on the meaning of competency-based pay
2. Traditional person-focused pay plans-pay-for-knowledge pay and skill-based pay programs
3. Reasons that companies adopt pay-for-knowledge pay and skill-based pay programs
4. Pay-for-knowledge pay and skill-based pay variations

5. Contrasts between person-focused pay systems and incentive pay or merit pay concepts
6. Advantages and disadvantages of using pay-for-knowledge pay plans and skill-based pay plans
7. How pay-for-knowledge pay plans and skill-based pay plans fit with differentiation and lowest-cost competitive strategies

In Chapters 4 and 5, we discussed compensation systems that reward employees for performance. Since the 1980s, strong competitive pressures and technological changes often have swiftly left employees with obsolete knowledge and skills. In the health care industry, for example, patient financial specialists have faced many challenges. Patient financial specialists, typically employed in hospitals, clinics, and doctors' offices, ensure that insurance providers pay claims on behalf of insured patients. The increasing variety of different types of "insurance" (for example, indemnity plans, HMOs, and PPOs, all of which we discuss in Chapter 11) rendered many patient financial services employees outdated in their knowledge and skills. Also, the ongoing developments in diagnostic testing and treatments have added volumes to what these specialists must know. The "Compensation in Action" feature at the end of this chapter further illustrates the practical challenges companies face when considering the use of person-focused pay.

DEFINING COMPETENCY-BASED PAY, PAY-FOR-KNOWLEDGE, AND SKILL-BASED PAY

Person-focused pay plans generally reward employees for acquiring job-related competencies, knowledge, or skills rather than for demonstrating successful job performance. The "Stretching the Dollar" feature in this chapter titled "What Is a 'Competency'?" reviews the present confusion about the meaning of a "competency" among HR management professionals. **Competency-based pay** often refers to two basic types of person-focused pay programs: pay-for-knowledge and skill-based pay. Sometimes these competency-based pay programs incorporate a combination of both types of person-focused pay systems, which reward employees for successfully acquiring new job-related knowledge or skills. Other times, companies combine competency-based pay programs with traditional merit pay programs by awarding pay raises to employees according to how well they demonstrate competencies.

Pay-for-knowledge plans reward managerial, service, or professional workers for successfully learning specific curricula. The Federal Express Corporation pay-for-knowledge program rewards its customer service employees who learn how to calculate delivery rates and how to document packages for shipment from the United States to various foreign countries [2]. **Skill-based pay**, a term used mostly for employees who do physical work, increases these workers' pay as they master new skills. For example, both unions and contractors who employ carpenters use skill-based pay plans. As carpenters master more advanced woodworking skills such as cabinet-making, they earn additional pay.

Both skill- and knowledge-based pay programs reward employees for the range, depth, and types of skills or knowledge they are capable of applying productively to their jobs. This feature distinguishes pay-for-knowledge plans from merit pay, which rewards employees' job performance. Said another way, pay-for-knowledge programs reward employees for their potential to make meaningful contributions on the job.

WHAT IS A "COMPETENCY"?

Nowadays, many HR professionals and other functional managers (for example, marketing) comment on the importance of paying employees based on competencies. Unfortunately, there seem to be as many definitions of competencies as there are professionals' calls for competency-based pay. Typically, many HR professionals refer to competencies as uniquely combined characteristics of the person, including personality, attitudes, knowledge, skills, and behaviors that enable an employee to fulfill job requirements well. Others simply use the terms "knowledge" and "skills" as synonyms for competencies. Competency-based pay programs apply to technical, managerial, service, or professionals employees (HR manager, marketing director) for whom it is difficult to define job performance according to observable or concrete behaviors. For instance, an animal keeper can be observed removing debris from enclosed animal habitats. On the other hand, a compensation director may be responsible for overseeing the ongoing development and implementation of an effective compensation system.

There is uncertainty about the meaning of competencies. In fact, two of my colleagues who are experts in compensation recently stated that "a lack of consensus means that competencies can be a number of things; consequently they stand in danger of becoming nothing."[1] I wholeheartedly agree with their view of competencies.

Setting these concerns aside for the moment, **core competencies** are often derived from the overall strategic statements of companies. For example, General Electric (GE) emphasizes three strategic goals for corporate growth: Globalization, Product Services, and Six Sigma (quality improvement). GE's top management relies on four core competencies to drive business success, which they call the four "E's": high *E*nergy, the ability to *E*nergize others, *E*dge (the ability to make tough calls), and *E*xecute (the ability to turn vision into results).

Core competencies are very general as you can see from the previous example. Companies often offer training to help employees develop particular competency sets (e.g., technical skills, knowledge of the business) or to become more self-aware of competencies they already possess (e.g., leadership). GE offers a comprehensive training program to entry-level HR professionals. Table 6-1 describes the purpose of GE's training program and particular statements regarding competency sets they expect participants to acquire as successful business professionals.

TABLE 6-1 A Description of GE's Human Resources Leadership Program

The Human Resources Leadership Program (HRLP) is GE's premiere entry-level training program for high potential individuals seeking an accelerated career in human resources. HRLP is the cornerstone in the development of future HR leaders at GE. The program consists of three 8- to 12-month rotational assignments at a GE Business combined with training. HRLP candidates attend four developmental seminars, are provided a self-study program in basic financial skills, and are exposed to GE leaders through both formal and informal mentoring and networking opportunities.

The human resource leadership program provides formal training in advanced human resources:

- Techniques and business concepts, as well as hands-on field experience.
- Three challenging and in-depth 8-month rotations assignments.
- Broad-based skills developed via hands-on experiences in two HR assignments plus a third in a cross-functional assignment outside of HR such as finance, quality, or business development.
- Assignments are held at major GE locations, satellite plants, and field offices. Wherever the program leads, GE's supportive environment and free flow of information encourages people to take risks and stretch their capabilities.
- Formal classroom training in advanced HR techniques and business concepts.
- Extensive contact with peers and senior level business leaders from around the world.
- Program seminars provide exposure to key GE business initiatives and the opportunity to interact with senior-level business leaders from around the world.
- The Human Resource Leadership Program graduates emerge prepared to plan and implement the strategic initiatives that enable GE to build and maintain its diverse, global teams.
- The people involved in the program become a support network throughout a GE career.

Source: www.GE.com, accessed July 8, 2002.

In this chapter, we use the term "pay-for-knowledge" to refer to both pay-for-knowledge and skill-based pay programs. Although we noted differences between the two earlier, the basic principles underlying these programs are similar.

Human resource professionals can design pay-for-knowledge plans to reward employees for acquiring new horizontal skills, vertical skills, or a greater depth of knowledge or skills. Employees can earn rewards for developing skills in one or more of these dimensions based on the kind of skills the company wants to foster. **Horizontal skills** (or **horizontal knowledge**) refer to similar skills or knowledge. For example, clerical employees of a retail store might be trained to perform several kinds of record-keeping tasks. They may maintain employee attendance records, schedule salespeople's work shifts, and monitor the use of office supplies (for example, paper clips and toner cartridges for laser printers) for reordering. Although focused on different aspects of a store's operations, all three of these tasks are based on employees' fundamental knowledge of record keeping.

Vertical skills (or **vertical knowledge**) are those skills traditionally considered supervisory, such as scheduling, coordinating, training, and leading others. These types of supervisory skills are often emphasized in pay-for-knowledge pay plans designed for self-managed work teams, because team members often need to learn how to manage one another [3]. Such work teams—referred to as self-regulating work groups, autonomous work groups, or semiautonomous work groups—typically bring employees together from various functional areas to plan, design, and complete one product or service. At DaimlerChrysler Corporation, teams of skilled employees from a variety of functions—marketing, finance, engineering, and purchasing—redesign and manufacture DaimlerChrysler vehicle models. One of the most recent innovations resulting from this team approach is the redesigned Jeep Grand Cherokee, a popular sport utility vehicle. Its popularity can be attributed to the ingenuity of the work teams. These teams capitalized on the unique talents—both knowledge and skills—of different employees who together produced a reasonably priced sport utility vehicle with features (for example, four-wheel drive, leather seats) that met market demand.

Depth of skills (or **depth of knowledge**) refers to the level of specialization or expertise an employee brings to a particular job. Some pay-for-knowledge pay plans reward employees for increasing their depth of skills or knowledge. Human resource professionals may choose to specialize in managing a particular aspect of the HR function, such as compensation, benefits administration, training evaluation, or new employee orientation. To be considered a compensation specialist, HR professionals must develop depth of knowledge by taking courses offered by WorldatWork on job evaluation, salary survey analysis, principles of pay-for-knowledge pay system design, merit pay system design, and incentive pay system design, among others. The more compensation topics HR professionals master, the greater their depth of knowledge about compensation.

USAGE OF PAY-FOR-KNOWLEDGE PAY PROGRAMS

A wide variety of employers have established pay-for-knowledge pay programs [4]; however, no systematic survey research documents the actual number. Companies of various sizes use pay-for-knowledge pay programs. More than half of the companies known to be using this kind of pay system employ between 150 and 2,000 employees. The absence of detailed evaluative data makes it impossible to conclude whether size is related to the success of these programs.

These programs are most commonly found in continuous process settings, such as manufacturing companies that use assembly lines where one employee's job depends on the work of at least one other employee. At Bell Sports, manufacturer of motorcycle safety helmets, the assembly process includes applying enamel to the helmets and attaching visors to the helmets. Clearly, both tasks require different sets of skills.

FLIP SIDE OF THE COIN

DESPITE SIGNIFICANT EXPENSE, COMPANIES STRIVE FOR EXCELLENCE WITH SIX-SIGMA TECHNIQUES

Companies work diligently to maintain and improve profit levels. Achieving higher profits is especially difficult during sluggish economic times. Some companies boost profits by limiting operating expenses such as advertising and human resource programs. Other companies actually spend more money to achieve higher profits. Investments in Six Sigma Methodology can help companies boost profits.

Motorola invented the Six Sigma Methodology to enable business improvement in the late 1980s. The impact this methodology has on improving business performance is dramatic and well documented. Companies around the world have implemented Six Sigma and Black Belt programs to:

- Improve customer satisfaction
- Maximize process efficiencies
- Increase competitive advantage and market share
- Save millions of dollars in operating expenses

Whether your organization is public or private, local or global, mastering the Motorola University Six Sigma Methodology will deliver improved business results for your organization.

Six Sigma is a structured, data-driven methodology for eliminating defects, waste, or quality control problems of all kinds in manufacturing, service delivery, management and other business activities. Six Sigma methodology is based on the combination of statistical quality control techniques, data analysis methods, and the systematic training of all employees at every level in the organization involved in the activity or process targeted by Six Sigma.

The term Six Sigma defines an optimum measurement of quality: 3.4 defects per million events. The Greek letter Σ (sigma) is a mathematical term that represents a measure of variation, the spread around the mean or average of any process or procedure in manufacturing, engineering, services, or transactions. We discuss measures of variation and the mean in Chapter 8.

Source: www.mu.motorola.com, accessed July 15, 2002.

Applying enamel requires the ability to use automated sprayers. Specifically, this skill demands that workers possess strong literacy skills so that they can interpret read-outs from the sprayers that suggest possible problems. Attaching visors to the helmets requires proficient motor skills that involve eye-hand coordination. When employees learn how to perform different jobs, they can cover for absent coworkers. In the event of absenteeism or turnover, Bell Sports benefits from having cross-trained employees because it is more capable of meeting its production schedules.

Pay-for-knowledge pay programs that emphasize vertical skills work well at manufacturing companies that organize work flow around high-performance work teams in which employees are expected to learn both functional and managerial tasks, such as work scheduling, budgeting, and quality control. This means that groups of employees work together to assemble entire products such as cellular telephones (Motorola) and furniture (Steelcase, a manufacturer of office furniture), and each team member learns how to perform the jobs of other team members.

Increasingly, companies recognize the importance of using person-focused pay. Pay-for-knowledge pay programs have been adopted most widely in service and manufacturing industries. More recently, companies have been striving to adopt pay-for-knowledge pay programs for professional employees. Pay-for-knowledge pay programs also represent a prevalent basis for pay among clerical and skilled trade employees, such as carpenters and electricians.

REASONS TO ADOPT PAY-FOR-KNOWLEDGE PAY PROGRAMS

Pay-for-knowledge pay programs represent important innovations in the compensation field. Pay-for-knowledge pay systems imply that employees must move away from viewing pay as an entitlement. Instead, these systems treat compensation as a reward earned for acquiring and implementing job-relevant knowledge and skills. Advocates of pay-for-knowledge pay programs offer two key reasons that firms seeking competitive advantage should adopt this form of compensation: technological innovation and increased global competition [5].

Technological Innovation

In an age of technological innovation in which robots, telecommunications, artificial intelligence, software, and lasers perform routine tasks, some skills soon become obsolete [6]. Then jobs require new and different worker skills. The skills needed by automobile mechanics, for instance, have changed dramatically. Previously, competent automobile mechanics were adept at manually assembling and disassembling carburetors. Since then, electronic fuel injection systems, which are regulated by onboard computers, have replaced carburetors, necessitating that auto mechanics possess different kinds of skills. Specifically, auto mechanics must now be able to use computerized diagnostic systems to assess the functioning of fuel injectors.

As technology leads to the automation of more tasks, employers combine jobs and confer broader responsibilities on workers. For example, the technology of advanced automated manufacturing, such as in the automobile industry, has required some employees to begin doing the jobs of other employees, including the laborer, the materials handler, the operator-assembler, and the maintenance person. Nowadays, a single employee performs all of these tasks in a position called "manufacturing technician." The expanding range of tasks and responsibilities in this job demands higher levels of reading, writing, and computation skills than its predecessor, which required strong eye-hand coordination. Most employees must possess better reading skills than before because they must be able to read the operating manuals and, when problems arise, the troubleshooting manuals of automated manufacturing equipment based on computer technology. Previously, the design of manufacturing equipment was relatively simple and easy to operate, based on simple mechanical principles such as pulleys.

These technological changes have fostered increased autonomy and team-oriented workplaces, which also demand different job-related skills than employees needed previously [7]. The manufacturing technician's job is generally more autonomous than its predecessor. Thus, technicians must be able to manage themselves and their time.

Employers now rely on working teams' technical and interpersonal skills to drive efficiency and improve quality. Today's consumers often expect customized products and applications, and employees must have sufficient technical skill to tailor products and services to customers' needs, as well as the interpersonal skills necessary to determine client needs and handle customer service [8]. Long-distance telephone service providers such as AT&T and Sprint seek competitive advantage by serving clients' present needs as well as by anticipating possible changes in customers' long-distance service needs. Lower costs of cellular phone service, with the inclusion of domestic long-distance service, create an even stronger imperative for land-line service providers to be as responsive as possible to market needs and preferences. As a result, these companies offer programs to provide clients the most favorable long-distance telephone rates based on their particular calling patterns. To be successful, these companies must have customer service associates who maintain current knowledge of these programs as well as the skills needed to match service plans to clients' long-distance service requirements.

Increased Global Competition

Increased global competition has forced companies in the United States to become more productive. Now more than ever, to sustain competitive advantage, companies must provide their employees with leading-edge skills and encourage employees to apply their skills proficiently. Evidence clearly shows that the foreign workers are better skilled and able to work more productively than U.S. employees in at least two ways.

First, employers in both the European Common Market and some Pacific Rim economies emphasize learning. In both cases, employers use classes and instruction as proactive tools for responding to strategic change. In Ireland, the private sector offers graduate employment programs to employees in particular skill areas such as science, marketing, and technology [9]. An example of a marketing skill is the application of inferential statistics to a market analysis. Marketing professionals use inferential statistics to draw conclusions about whether the level of satisfaction with Brand A athletic shoes among a small sample of Brand A athletic shoe owners represents the level of satisfaction among every person who has purchased Brand A athletic shoes.

Second, both Western European and some Pacific Rim cultures provide better academic preparation and continuing workplace instruction for the non-college-bound portions of their workforces. Although the United States is well regarded for the quality of education its colleges and universities provide to skilled professionals such as engineers, the Europeans are much better at educating the "vocational" segment of their workforces. Western European workplaces emphasize applied rather than theoretical instruction for vocational employees. The European apprenticeship structure mixes academic and applied learning both in "high schools" and in continuing education for employees.

To establish and maintain competitive advantage, companies should carefully consider pay-for-knowledge pay systems. As discussed earlier, many companies already compensate employees on this basis because they have discovered the advantages of such plans. Of course, as companies consider adopting these pay systems, they must tailor compensation programs to the particular kinds of skills they wish to foster. Human resource professionals can guide employee development through a variety of pay-for-knowledge pay systems.

Companies strive to market the highest quality of products and services in the face of increased global competition and the availability of new technology. As previously indicated in the "Flip Side of the Coin" feature, many companies have adopted six-sigma techniques to do so. The adoption of six-sigma techniques signals many companies' plans to strive for excellence.

VARIETIES OF PAY-FOR-KNOWLEDGE PAY PROGRAMS

A **stair-step model** actually resembles a flight of stairs, much like the arrangement illustrated in Figure 6-1 for an assembly technician. The steps represent jobs from a particular job family that differ in terms of complexity. Jobs that require more skills are more complex than jobs with fewer skills. For example, an Assembly Technician 1 job requires employees to possess two skills—line restocking and pallet breakdown. An Assembly Technician 3 job requires employees to possess six skills—line restocking, pallet breakdown, burr removal, line jockey, major assembly, and soldering. In terms of the stairs, higher steps represent jobs that require more skills than lower steps. Compensation specialists develop separate stair-step models for individual job families; for example, clerks or accountants. Thus, a company may have more than one stair-step model, each corresponding to a particular job family such as accounting, finance, or clerical. No stair-step model should include both clerical workers and skilled trade workers such as carpenters, electricians, and plumbers.

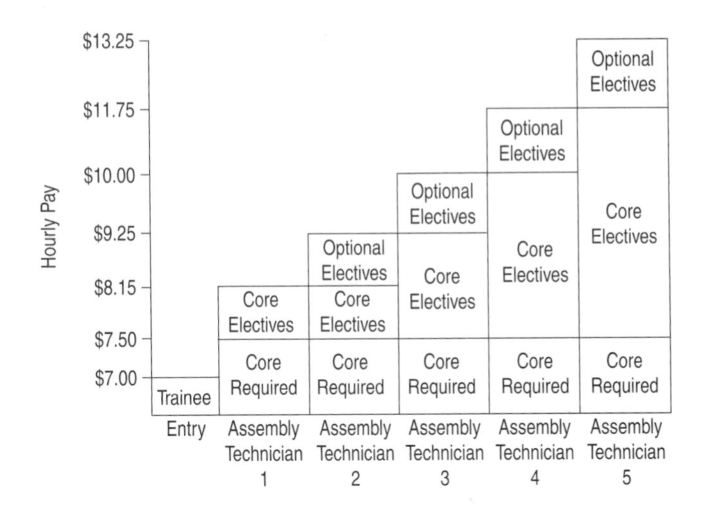

Core Required

Employees must complete all three workshops.

1. Orientation Workshop: The goal of this workshop is to familiarize employees with ABC's pay schedule, offerings of employee benefits, work hours, holiday and vacation policies, and grievance procedures.
2. Safety Workshop: The goal of this workshop is to educate employees about the procedures for ensuring the health and safety of themselves and coworkers while using and being around the machinery.
3. Quality Workshop: The goal of this workshop is to acquaint employees with ABC's procedures for maintaining quality standards for parts assembly.

Core Electives

Employees must complete all core elective courses for the designated job before they assume the commensurate duties and responsibilities.

Assembly Technician 1:
a. Line restocking
b. Pallet breakdown

Assembly Technician 2:
a. Core electives for Assembly Technician 1
b. Burr removal
c. Line jockey

Assembly Technician 3:
a. Core electives for Assembly Technician 2
b. Major assembly
c. Soldering

Assembly Technician 4:
a. Core electives for Assembly Technician 3
b. Acid bath
c. Final inspection

Assembly Technician 5:
a. Core electives for Assembly Technician 4
b. Equipment calibration
c. Training

FIGURE 6-1 A Stair-Step Model at ABC Company

Optional Electives

Employees may choose to complete up to two optional electives at each step.

Administrative procedures
Public relations
Group facilitation
Grievance resolution
Training
Marketing fundamentals (basic)
Marketing fundamentals (intermediate)
Finance fundamentals (basic)
Finance fundamentals (intermediate)
Accounting fundamentals (basic)
Accounting fundamentals (intermediate)
Human resource management fundamentals (basic)
Human resource management fundamentals (intermediate)

FIGURE 6-1 *(cont.)*

How do employees earn increases in hourly pay based on a stair-step model? Using the model in Figure 6-1, Howard Jones wants to become an assembly technician. ABC Manufacturing Company hires Howard as an assembly technician trainee at $7.00 per hour. Howard starts by completing three core workshops designed for Assembly Technician 1—a company orientation, a safety workshop, and a quality workshop. After successfully completing all three courses, based on earning greater than the minimum scores on tests for each subject, he receives a $0.50 per hour pay increase, making his total hourly pay $7.50. In addition, Howard completes the core electives designated for his Assembly Technician 1 job—he learns how to restock lines and break down pallets. Upon successfully completing both courses, he receives a $0.65 per hour pay raise, making his total hourly pay $8.15, earning him the Assembly Technician 1 title. Howard may continue to learn more skills for an assembly technician by completing the curriculum for the Assembly 2 level. Afterwards, if he chooses, Howard can complete the curricula to move to level 3.

Training courses may be offered in-house by the company, at a local vocational school, or at a local community college or four-year university. Companies usually offer specialized courses in-house for skills that pertain to highly specialized work or to work that bears on a company's competitive advantage. Federal Express sponsors customer service training internally because the skills and knowledge required to be an effective Federal Express customer service employee distinguish its service from other express mail companies, including United Parcel Service (UPS). For more common skills or skills that do not have an effect on competitive advantage, companies typically arrange to have their employees take training courses offered by external agents such as community colleges. Most companies require clerical employees to be able to effectively use word processing programs. Thus, companies commonly sponsor their employees' training in word processing at local community colleges.

The **skill blocks model** also applies to jobs from within the same job family. Just as in the stair-step model, employees progress to increasingly complex jobs. However, in a skill blocks program, skills do not necessarily build on each other. Thus, an employee may progress two or more steps, earning the pay that corresponds with each step. Although similar, the stair-step model and the skill blocks model differ in an important way. The stair-step model addresses the development of knowledge or skills depth. In particular, Howard Jones could develop his skills depth as an assembly technician by taking the five separate curricula. With the successful completion of each curriculum, Howard will enhance the depth of his skills as an assembly technician. As we will see shortly, the skill blocks model emphasizes both horizontal and vertical skills.

As shown in Figure 6-2, Pro Company hired Bobby Smith as a Clerk 1 because her employment tests demonstrated her proficiency in the skills and knowledge that she needs for this level job. These required skills correspond to Clerk 1 core requirements—filing, typing, and possessing a working knowledge of one word processing program. Moreover, Bobby knows transcription and shorthand, which are Level 1 core electives. During employee orientation for new clerical hires, an HR representative explained the pay-for-knowledge pay program available to this employee group. In particular, Bobby knows that she can advance to any level in the clerical pay structure by successfully completing the corresponding curriculum. To make her goal of becoming a Clerk 4, Bobby simply needs to complete the Level 4 curriculum. She need not take the curricula for the Clerk 2 and Clerk 3 jobs. Taking the Clerk 2, 3, or 4 curricula will enhance Bobby's horizontal skills. The Clerk 3 curriculum provides the knowledge required to successfully manage different types of ledgers. Taking the Clerk 5 curriculum will increase Bobby's vertical skills, including project scheduling and assigning personnel to projects.

A **job-point accrual model** encourages employees to develop skills and learn to perform jobs from different job families. A company would benefit if its employees were proficient in a small subset of jobs. Employees are generally not free to learn as many jobs as they would like. Companies limit the number of jobs employees are allowed to learn in order to avoid having them become "jacks of all trades." Job-point accrual methods create organizational flexibility and promote company goals by assigning a relatively greater number of points to skills that address key company concerns—such as customer relations. The more points employees accrue, the higher their core compensation level will be.

For example, let's assume that ZIP-MAIL is a new company that competes in express mail delivery service against established firms in the business—Federal Express and UPS. ZIP-MAIL couriers must meet their delivery promise of 7:30 A.M., which is at least a half-hour earlier than some of the competitors. They must also convey a professional image and establish rapport with corporate clients to encourage individuals and representatives from client companies to choose ZIP-MAIL over other competitors. In other words, customer relations skills are essential to ZIP-MAIL's success. ZIP-MAIL stands to benefit from a pay-for-knowledge pay program, particularly one that follows the job-point accrual model. Under this system, employees who successfully complete customer relations training courses would earn more points than they'd earn by taking other kinds of training offered by ZIP-MAIL, creating an incentive for employees to learn customer relations skills over other kinds of skills.

Although the job-point accrual model and the cross-departmental model are similar, the intended purposes of these programs differ. The job-point accrual model encourages employees to learn skills and acquire knowledge that bear directly on companies' attainment of competitive advantage, as in the case of ZIP-MAIL. **Cross-departmental models** promote staffing flexibility by training employees in one department with critical skills they would need to perform effectively in other departments. If the shipping department experienced a temporary staffing shortage, a production department supervisor who has been trained in distribution methods can be "lent" to the shipping department. The cross-departmental model can help production environments manage sporadic, short-term staffing shortages. Such cross-training can also help companies meet seasonal fluctuations in demand for their products or services.

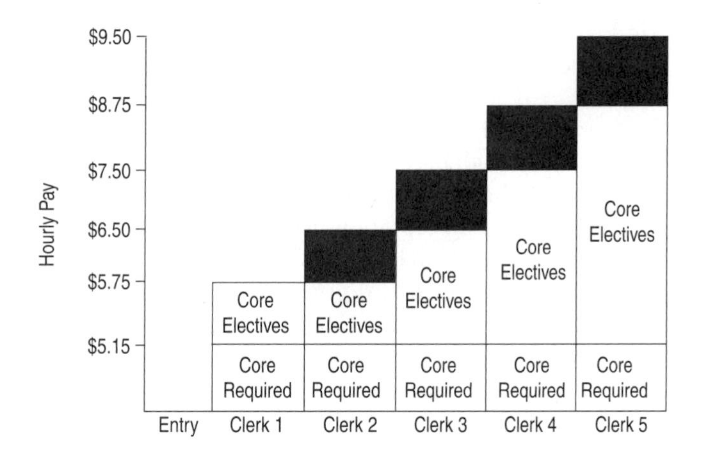

Core Required

All employees must be proficient in all of the following skills or take the necessary courses that are offered by Pro Company in order to become proficient.

Principles of filing

Typing skill, 40 words per minute minimum speed

Working knowledge of one word processing program such as *Word* or *Wordperfect*

Core Electives

Employees must complete all core elective courses for the designated job before they assume the commensurate duties and responsibilities.

Clerk 1:
a. Transcription
b. Shorthand

Clerk 2:
a. Maintaining office supplies inventory
b. Ordering office supplies from local vendor

Clerk 3:
a. Accounts receivable ledgers
b. Accounts payable ledgers
c. Working knowledge of one spreadsheet program, for example, *Lotus 1-2-3* or *Excel*

Clerk 4:
a. Payroll records
b. Maintaining records of sick pay usage, vacation usage, and performance bonus awards based on company policy

Clerk 5:
a. Project scheduling
b. Assigning personnel to projects

Optional Electives

Employees may choose to complete up to two optional electives at each step.

Public relations (basic, intermediate, advanced)

Supervisory skills

Resolving minor employee conflicts

Effective written communication skills (basic, intermediate, advanced)

Effective oral communication skills (basic, intermediate, advanced)

FIGURE 6-2 A Skill Blocks Model at Pro Company

The holiday shopping rush represents an excellent context in which a company can benefit from cross-departmental training systems. Retail business activity varies widely, with enhanced volume during the holiday shopping season during the fall months. For several months following this period, business activity tends to subside dramatically. Let's consider a company that manufactures and distributes custom-made shoes. For weeks prior to the holidays, employees in the production department are working rapidly to complete all the telephone gift orders that must be shipped before Chanukah and Christmas day. Within a few days of the holidays, the company is likely to receive fewer orders because purchasers of custom-made shoes recognize that they need to place orders well in advance of the date they expect to receive their shoes. As orders drop off, many workers in both sales and production will be less busy than workers in the distribution department. Under the cross-departmental pay-for-knowledge pay system, sales and production department workers will be rewarded for learning how to properly package shoes and how to complete express mail invoices so that they can assist the shipping department during its peak activity periods.

CONTRASTING PERSON-FOCUSED PAY WITH JOB-BASED PAY

Companies institute job-based pay plans or person-focused pay plans based on very different fundamental principles and goals. Table 6-2 lists the key differences between these two pay programs. **Job-based pay** compensates employees for jobs they currently perform. Human resource professionals establish a minimum and maximum acceptable amount of pay for each job. In the case of merit pay, managers evaluate employees based on how well they fulfilled their designated roles as specified by their job descriptions and periodic objectives. Managers then award a permanent merit addition to base pay, based on employee performance.

With incentive pay, managers award one-time additions to base pay. Pay raise amounts are based on the attainment of work goals, which managers communicate to employees in advance. Consider the executives of Acme Manufacturing Company, who are dissatisfied with their level of defective disk drives for computers, which is significantly higher than that of their competitor, Do-Rite Manufacturing Company. Acme's monthly defect rate is 6,500 disk drives per employee, and Do-Rite's monthly defect rate is significantly less, at 3,000 disk drives per employee. Acme executives decided to

TABLE 6-2 Person-Focused and Job-Based Pay: A Comparison

Feature	*Skill-Based*	*Job-Based*
Pay level determination	Market basis for skill valuation	Market basis for job valuation
Base pay	Awarded on how much an employee knows or on skill level	Awarded on the value of compensable factors
Base pay increases	Awarded on an employee's gain in knowledge or skills	Awarded on attaining a job-defined goal or seniority
Job promotion	Awarded on an employee's skills base and proficiency on past work	Awarded on exceeding job performance standards
Key advantage to employees	Job variety and enrichment	Perform work and receive pay for a defined job
Key advantage to employers	Work scheduling flexibility	Easy pay system administration

TABLE 6-3 Acme's Incentive Plan for Reductions in Monthly Defect Rates

Acme's goal is to achieve a monthly defect rate of 3,000 disk drives per employee to match Do-Rite's (the competition's) per employee defect rate. Employees whose monthly defect rates falls below 3,000 disk drives will receive an incentive award that is commensurate with the following schedule.

Reduction in Error Rate	*Monthly Incentive Award*
91–100%	$500
81–90%	$450
71–80%	$400
61–70%	$350
51–60%	$300
41–50%	$250
31–40%	$200
21–30%	$150
11–20%	$100
1–10%	$50

implement an incentive system to encourage employees to make fewer defective disk drives, with the ultimate goal of having a lower defect rate than Do-Rite. At the end of every month, Acme employees receive a monetary award based on their defect rate for that month. Table 6-3 displays the incentive plan for Acme. As you can see, employees earn a larger incentive award as the defect rate decreases.

Person-focused pay compensates employees for developing the flexibility and skills to perform a number of jobs effectively. Moreover, these programs reward employees on their potential to make positive contributions to the workplace based on their successful acquisition of work-related skills or knowledge. Job-based pay plans reward employees for the work they have done as specified in their job descriptions or periodic goals—that is, how well they have fulfilled their potential to make positive contributions in the workplace.

Finally, job-based pay programs apply to an organizationwide context because employees earn base pay rates for the jobs they perform. (We address how management establishes these pay rates in Chapter 8.) Pay-for-knowledge pay plans apply in more limited contexts because not all jobs can be assessed based on skill or knowledge. Table 6-4 describes the duties that toll booth operators perform. This position would

TABLE 6-4 Job Description for a Toll Collector

Collects toll charged for use of bridges, highways, or tunnels by motor vehicles, or fare for vehicle and passengers on ferryboats: Collects money and gives customer change. Accepts toll and fare tickets previously purchased. At end of shift balances cash and records money and tickets received. May sell round-trip booklets. May be designated according to place of employment as Toll-Bridge Attendant (government service), or type of fare as Vehicle-Fare Collector (motor trans.; water trans.). May admit passengers through turnstile and be designated Turnstile Collector (water trans.).

Source: Reprinted from *Dictionary of occupational titles*, Vol. 1, 4th ed. (Washington, DC: U.S. Government Printing Office, 1991).

clearly not be appropriate in a pay-for-knowledge pay system, because the job is narrowly defined, and the skills are very basic. Toll booth operators probably master the required skills and knowledge soon after assuming their responsibilities.

ADVANTAGES OF PAY-FOR-KNOWLEDGE PAY PROGRAMS

Although no large-scale studies have clearly demonstrated these benefits, case studies suggest that employees and companies enjoy advantages from pay-for-knowledge pay programs. Well-designed pay-for-knowledge pay systems, which are discussed in Chapter 9, can provide employees and employers with distinct advantages over traditional pay systems.

Advantages to Employees

Employees usually like pay-for-knowledge pay systems for the following two reasons. First, they can provide employees with both job enrichment and job security. Job enrichment refers to a job design approach that creates more intrinsically motivating and interesting work environments. Companies can enrich jobs by combining narrowly designed tasks so that an employee is responsible for producing an entire product or service [10].

According to job characteristics theory, employees are more motivated to perform jobs that contain a high degree of core characteristics, such as [11]:

1. Skill variety. The degree to which the job requires the person to do different tasks and involves the use of different skills, abilities, and talents.
2. Task identity. The degree to which a job enables a person to complete an entire job from start to finish.
3. Autonomy. The amount of freedom, independence, and discretion the employee enjoys in determining how to do the job.
4. Feedback. The degree to which the job or employer provides the employee with clear and direct information about job outcomes and performance.

At Volvo's Uddevalla manufacturing facility in Sweden, teams of 7 to 10 hourly workers produce entire vehicles rather than focusing solely on certain aspects such as installing a drivetrain assembly or attaching upholstery to a car's interior [12]. Contributing to all aspects of manufacturing automobiles expands the horizontal dimensions (skill variety) of workers' jobs. In some cases, an employer empowers teams to manage themselves and the work they do. These managing duties, including controlling schedules, dividing up tasks, learning multiple jobs, and training one another, represent the vertical dimensions (autonomy) of work. Pay-for-knowledge pay programs can help companies design such intrinsically motivating jobs, especially with regard to skill variety and autonomy. Both pay-for-knowledge pay programs and job enrichment programs expand both horizontal and vertical work dimensions.

So far, evidence does suggest that pay-for-knowledge pay plans lead to increased employee commitment, enhanced work motivation, and improved employee satisfaction [13]. These results are probably due to the fact that well-designed pay-for-knowledge pay plans promote skill variety and autonomy. Some experts attribute these positive outcomes of pay-for-knowledge pay programs to the fact that employees can increase their skills and be paid for it [14].

The second advantage for employees is that, because pay-for-knowledge pay programs create more flexible workers, these programs can actually represent better job security for employees. Rather than being laid off during periods of low product demand, employees can perform a variety of jobs that draw upon the skills they have attained through pay-for-knowledge pay programs. During periods of slow sales, many companies conduct inventories of their products. Customer service employees who have learned inventory accounting techniques are less likely to be laid off during periods of low sales than customer service employees who have not learned inventory techniques. Further, employees who update their skills will be more attractive applicants to other employers as well. Very definitely, clerical employees who become proficient in the use of Windows-based computer software will have more employment opportunities available to them than clerical employees who have resisted learning these programs. Likewise, HR professionals who become familiar with the constraints placed on compensation practice by recent laws (Civil Rights Act of 1991 and the Americans with Disabilities Act) will probably have more employment opportunities available to them than HR professionals who choose not to become familiar with these pertinent laws.

Advantages to Employers

Employers like pay-for-knowledge pay systems because, when properly designed and implemented, these programs can lead to enhanced job performance, reduced staffing, and greater flexibility. First, pay-for-knowledge pay programs can influence both the quantity and the quality of an employee's work. Employees who participate in a pay-for-knowledge pay program often exhibit higher productivity levels because employees who know more about an entire process may also be able to identify production shortcuts that result in increased productivity. For example, electrical wiring in an automobile runs along the vehicle's interior beneath the seats and carpeting. Members of auto assembly teams familiar with all aspects of the automobile manufacturing process could potentially identify and fix problems with the wiring before the seats and carpeting are installed. If such problems were identified after the seats and carpeting were installed, completion of the vehicle would be delayed, and fewer automobiles could be counted as finished.

Product or service quality should also gain from these programs. As employees learn more about the entire production process, the quality of both the product and its delivery often improve. Schott Transformers, a supplier of magnetic components and power systems to the computer and telecommunications industries, instituted a pay-for-knowledge pay program and experienced a significant increase in the quality of their service as measured by customer satisfaction surveys [15]. Such customer satisfaction increases usually follow a company's implementation of self-directed work teams in which employees develop both horizontal and vertical skills. If employees feel responsible for entire products, they take more care to ensure that customers are satisfied.

Second, companies that use pay-for-knowledge pay systems can usually rely on leaner staffing because multiskilled employees are better able to cover for unexpected absenteeism, family or medical leave, and training sessions that take individual employees away from their work. The successful operation of a restaurant depends on coordinated efforts from buspersons, waitstaff, chefs, and other food preparers. When one or two buspeople are absent, the restaurant will not be able to serve its reservations customers on time. If employees are cross-trained in a number of jobs, fewer employees will have to be on hand to provide backup for absent buspeople.

Third, pay-for-knowledge pay systems provide companies with greater flexibility in meeting staffing demands at any particular time. Quite simply, because participants in pay-for-knowledge pay plans have acquired a variety of skills, they can perform a wider range of tasks. This kind of staffing flexibility helps companies when unexpected changes in demand occur. After a tornado devastated a densely populated area in Illinois, the municipal water supply was not fit for drinking because areawide power outages disabled the pumps that purify the water. As a result, residents living in the affected areas rushed to grocery stores to purchase bottled water. Because this sudden demand exceeded the normal inventories of bottled water in grocery stores, wholesale distributors such as SuperValu had to respond quickly by moving bottled water inventories from their warehouses to the retail grocery stores. This spike in demand for bottled water overwhelmed the usual distribution and shipping staff.

DISADVANTAGES OF PAY-FOR-KNOWLEDGE PAY PROGRAMS

Although pay-for-knowledge pay programs present many advantages, they have the following two limitations. First, employers feel that the main drawback of pay-for-knowledge pay systems is that hourly labor costs, training costs, and overhead costs can all increase. Hourly labor costs often increase because greater skills should translate into higher pay levels for the majority of workers. Because training is an integral component of pay-for-knowledge pay systems, training costs are generally higher than at companies with job-based pay programs. These costs can be especially high during initial start-up periods, as HR professionals attempt to standardize employee backgrounds. This process begins with assessing the skills levels of employees. Federal Express tests its employees twice per year [16]. The company pays for 4 hours of study time and 2 hours of actual test time, which are bound to be quite expensive.

Second, pay-for-knowledge pay systems may not mesh well with existing incentive pay systems [17]. When both pay-for-knowledge and incentive pay systems are in operation, employees may not want to learn new skills when the pay increase associated with learning a new skill is less than an incentive award employees could earn based on skills they already possess. Oftentimes, employees place greater emphasis on maximizing rewards in the short term rather than preparing themselves to maximize the level of rewards over time, which can be facilitated through pay-for-knowledge pay programs.

An assembly line worker chooses to focus on his work because he receives monetary incentives for meeting weekly production goals set by management rather than taking skills training in inventory control for which he will earn additional pay upon successful completion of his training. In the short term, this worker is earning a relatively large sum of money; in the long term, however, he may be jeopardizing his earnings potential and job security. In the future, the company may experience reduced demand for its product, which would eliminate the incentive program. During such times, the company may also place production workers in other jobs, such as in the warehouse, until the demand for the product returns to normal. Without the skills required to work in the warehouse, this employee may be targeted for a layoff or a reduced work schedule, clearly leading to lower personal earnings.

LINKING PAY-FOR-KNOWLEDGE PAY WITH COMPETITIVE STRATEGY

As you will recall, in Chapter 2 we reviewed a framework for establishing a basis for selecting particular compensation tactics to match a company's competitive strategy. How do pay-for-knowledge pay systems fit with the two fundamental competitive strategies—lowest cost and differentiation? Ultimately, pay-for-knowledge pay systems, when properly applied, can contribute to meeting the goals of lowest-cost and differentiation strategies. However, the rationale for the appropriateness of pay-for-knowledge pay systems differs according to the imperatives of the lowest-cost and differentiation competitive strategies.

Lowest-Cost Competitive Strategy

Lowest-cost strategies require firms to reduce output costs per employee. Pay-for-knowledge pay systems are appropriate when the training employees receive enables them to work more productively on the job with fewer errors. Pay-for-knowledge pay plans may seem to contradict the lowest-cost imperative because of several factors in the short term. The cost of providing training, downtime while employees are participating in training, and inefficiencies that may result back on the job while employees work on mastering new skills can easily increase costs in the short term. Recall that Federal Express tests its employees twice per year [18]. Because the company pays for study time and actual test time, the lowest-cost strategy is expensive.

However, a longer-term perspective may well lead to the conclusion that pay-for-knowledge pay programs support the lowest-cost imperative. Over time, productivity enhancements and increased flexibility should far outweigh the short-run costs if a company ultimately provides exemplary service to its customers. For example, Federal Express is renowned for its worldwide express delivery service because of its remarkable track record in consistently meeting delivery promises in a timely fashion for a reasonable price. Much of Federal Express's success can be attributed to its knowledgeable customer service employees. These individuals play a key role in determining how to best manage the delivery of packages across time zones and through international customs checkpoints.

Differentiation Competitive Strategy

A differentiation strategy requires creative, open-minded, risk-taking employees. Compared with lowest-cost strategies, companies that pursue differentiation strategies must take a longer-term focus to attain their preestablished objectives. Pay-for-knowledge compensation is appropriate when employees are organized into teams that possess some degree of autonomy over how work will be performed. Employers that pursue differentiation strategies often rely on employees' technical and interpersonal skills in working teams to drive efficiency, quality improvements, and new applications for existing products and services. As discussed earlier, at DaimlerChrysler, teams of skilled employees from a variety of functions—marketing, finance, engineering, and purchasing—redesign and manufacture DaimlerChrysler vehicle models. One of the recent innovations resulting from this team approach is the redesigned Jeep Grand Cherokee, whose popularity can be attributed to the ingenuity of the work teams. Such "cutting-edge" companies often focus on new technology that employees must learn—a goal consistent with pay-for-knowledge pay programs.

New technology also allows customization of products, which requires employees with sufficient technical skills and imagination to tailor products and services to customers' needs, as well as the interpersonal skills necessary to provide good customer service. Clearly, Northern Telecom is an exemplar of a telecommunications company that continually provides differentiated service to its customers—both technically and interpersonally—because of its investment in pay-for-knowledge pay compensation programs.

SUMMARY

This chapter discussed pay-for-knowledge, reasons companies should adopt pay-for-knowledge pay programs, varieties of pay-for-knowledge pay programs, how pay-for-knowledge pay relates to merit pay and incentive pay programs, advantages as well as disadvantages of pay-for-knowledge pay programs, and the fit of these programs with competitive strategy. Companies should seriously consider adopting pay-for-knowledge pay programs in order to keep up with technological innovation and to compete internationally. Perhaps the greatest challenge for companies is to ensure that employees are given the opportunity to apply newly learned skills in productive ways.

Key Terms

- person-focused pay plans, 168
- competency-based pay, 168
- pay-for-knowledge, 168
- skill-based pay, 168
- horizontal skills, 170
- horizontal knowledge, 170
- vertical skills, 170
- vertical knowledge, 170
- depth of skills, 170
- depth of knowledge, 170
- stair-step model, 173
- skills blocks model, 175
- job-point accrual model, 176
- cross-departmental models, 176
- job-based pay, 178

Discussion Questions

1. "Pay-for-knowledge pay plans are least preferable compared with individual incentive pay programs" (Chapter 5). Indicate whether you agree or disagree with this statement. Detail your arguments to support your position.
2. Pay-for-knowledge pay is becoming more prevalent in companies. However, pay-for-knowledge pay programs are not always an appropriate basis for compensation. Discuss the conditions under which incentive pay (Chapter 5) is more appropriate than pay-for-knowledge pay programs. Be sure to include your justification.
3. Name at least three jobs that have been influenced by such technological advances as robotics, word processing software, fax machines, and electronic mail. Describe the jobs prior to the technological advances and explain how these jobs have changed or will change because of the technological advances. For each job, list the new skills that you feel are relevant for pay-for-knowledge pay programs.
4. Discuss your reaction to the following statement: "Companies should not provide training to employees because it is the responsibility of individuals to possess the necessary knowledge and skills prior to becoming employed."
5. As discussed in the chapter, pay-for-knowledge pay programs are not suitable for all kinds of jobs. Based on your understanding of pay-for-knowledge pay concepts, identify at least three jobs for which this basis for pay is inappropriate. Be sure to provide your rationale, given the information in this chapter.

Exercises

Compensation Online

For Students

Exercise 1: Find relevant journal articles
Search your school's online catalog for pay-for-knowledge plans. Select two or three of these topics and describe how each works to reward the employee and/or benefit the employer.

Exercise 2: Research a relevant topic on pay systems
Your professor wants you to find examples of the topics covered in Chapter 6 in practice. Using the advanced search link in Yahoo, use the "an exact phrase match" option for Web sites pertaining to "person-focused pay" and/or "performance appraisal." Select and review at least two of the sites. Compare and contrast the information on the two sites. What circumstances do you think affected the decision to use these different pay systems?

Exercise 3: Research the use of training
Visit company Web sites and look for the kind of training or career development they offer. Are there any companies with noteworthy or innovative training programs? Write a review of the one or two that you find most interesting.

For Professionals

Exercise 1: Review union Web sites

You work in human resources for a small manufacturer. There is talk of an organizing campaign, and you want to be prepared for any questions that might come up. One of the main issues is that workers find the training and development program at the company to be lacking. This is the issue you wish to be best prepared for. Search different unions' Web sites for articles or stances on training and development. What sorts of things do unions value, and what do they view as significant drawbacks?

Exercise 2: Research training and development services

Some firms provide in-house training programs; some companies choose to outsource them. From Yahoo, click Business and Economy > Business to Business > Consulting > Human Resources. Look for firms that provide training services. Write a short memo to the Director of Human Resourses on the benefits and drawbacks to using these services as opposed to developing the training programs from within the company.

Exercise 3: Research relevant news

As a practicing professional, it is important to keep up with issues. Conduct an advanced search on Yahoo for "pay for performance." Concentrate on the news section. Read through some articles and identify any major trends or stories that may have implications for HR professionals.

Endnotes

1. Milkovich, G. T., & Newman, J. M. (1999). *Compensation* (6th ed.). Boston: Irwin McGraw-Hill, p. 152.
2. Filipowski, D. (1992). How Federal Express makes your package its most important. *Personnel Journal, 71*, pp. 40–46.
3. Bureau of National Affairs (2002). Skill-based pay. *BNA's Library on Compensation & Benefits CD* [CD-ROM]. Washington, DC: Author.
4. Jenkins, G. D., Jr., Ledford, G. E., Jr., Gupta, N., & Doty, D. H. (1992). *Skill-based Pay: Practices, Payoffs, Pitfalls, and Prescriptions*. Scottsdale, AZ: American Compensation Association.
5. Schuster, J. R., & Zingheim, P. K. (1992). *The New Pay: Linking Employee and Organizational Performance*. New York: Lexington Books.
6. American Society for Training and Development. (1989). *Training America: Learning to Work for the 21st Century*. Alexandria, VA: Author.
7. Doeringer, P. B. (1991). *Turbulence in the American Workplace*. New York: Oxford University Press.
8. Manz, C. C., & Sims H. P., Jr. (1993). *Business without Bosses: How Self-Managing Work Teams Are Building High Performance Companies*. New York: John Wiley & Sons.
9. Carnevale, A. P., & Johnston, J. W. (1989). *Training in America: Strategies for the Nation*. Alexandria, VA: National Center on Education and the Economy and the American Society for Training and Development.
10. Lawler, E. E. (1986). *High Involvement Management*. San Francisco: Jossey-Bass.
11. Nadler, D. A., Hackman, J. R., & Lawler, E. E. (1979). *Managing Organizational Behavior*. Boston: Little, Brown.
12. Carrell, M. R., Elbert, N. F., & Hatfield, R. D. (1995). *Human Resource Management: Global Strategies for Managing a Diverse Workforce* (5th ed.). Upper Saddle River, NJ: Prentice Hall.
13. Gupta, N., Schweizer, T. P., & Jenkins, G. D., Jr. (1987). Pay-for-knowledge compensation plans: Hypotheses and survey results. *Monthly Labor Review, 110*, pp. 40–43.
14. Caudron, S. (1993). Master the compensation maze. *Personnel Journal, 72*, pp. 64a–64o.
15. Schilder, J. (1992). Work teams boost productivity. *Personnel Journal, 72*, pp. 64–71.
16. Filipowski, D. (1992). How Federal Express makes your package its most important. *Personnel Journal, 71*, pp. 40–46.
17. Jenkins, G. D., Jr., & Gupta, N. (1985). The payoffs of paying for knowledge. *National Productivity Review, 4*, pp. 121–130.
18. Filipowski, D. (1992). How Federal Express makes your package its most important. *Personnel Journal, 71*, pp. 40–46.

COMPENSATION IN ACTION

REASSESSING THE VALUE OF SKILL-BASED PAY

GETTING THE RUNAWAY TRAIN BACK ON TRACK

The demise of skill-based pay is premature, especially if employers learn how to pay only for those skills that clearly add value to the business.

As the idea of skill-based pay chugs along and struggles for credibility and practicality, one must consider whether it is worth saving at all. Has the time come for this compensation philosophy to be retired to the ancient-history files under the title "Reward Innovations Gone Afoul"?

The argument that paying for people skills and capabilities, rather than inanimate jobs, is powerful and compelling. People do the work of business, and can learn, grow and perform; jobs don't and can't. It makes sense to organize work around the capabilities of hires, rather than shoehorning people into jobs and expecting them to perform as the jobs are structured. Rewarding key skills and capabilities is one essential element to building a powerful workforce brand.[1] But employers should pay only for those skills that clearly add value to the business.

The total rewards model includes individual development as a rewards component. Skill and competency growth also provide a dimension of how to best align employees' efforts with goal performance. Paying for skill and competency is essential to designing base pay that rewards individual, ongoing value[2] and, to create a win-win situation for employers and employees, rewards solutions should be built around the skills and competencies that employers need and that employees obtain and apply.

For skill-based pay to prove its worth as a business tool, the importance of skills needs to be validated. Though some academic research favors paying for skills, no studies provide evidence that skill-based pay improves workforce performance. But other benefits are at least partially substantiated by self-reporting at the senior human resource levels. For example, research reports that companies deploy skill pay solutions to develop a more flexible, learning-oriented workforce that is helpful during times of organizational change and adaptable to customer needs.

The logic of skill-based pay repeatedly overpowers that of job-based pay from a conceptual perspective.[3] Skill-based pay makes good sense in nearly every way but has struggled from the first installation to the last, causing some employers to hesitate pursuing it for their organizations.

EARLY TROUBLES

Complexity is one of the first culprits to have thrown skill-based pay off track, and it still remains a primary issue. Organizations and change agents find that changing from job-based to skill-based pay programs is difficult to implement and even harder to communicate. For example, designers struggle to define "best practice." Broadly accepted, valid and reliable guidelines about what does and does not work have never been developed, so opinion and anecdote are taken at face value without enough of the hard, validating data needed to act on issues of this importance. Consider the following differences—that could make or break skill-based pay implementation—that often are overlooked:

- How to derive skill definitions
- How skills are acquired and demonstrated
- When skills should be paid
- How new skills are learned
- When new skills replace obsolete skills

Also, designers and researchers often are at odds with regard to skill-based pay expectations and success measurement. Considerable lore exists about skill-based pay, but no study proves that organizations are better with it than without it. That's just not enough for today's practical business leaders who need a solid foundation to build reasonable practices.

Pay changes are "hot," in that they get everyone's attention. Because pay change nearly always increases employee "noise" level and, thereby, organizational concern, it needs strong and persistent champions who understand the issues and challenges.[4] Because pay changes are tough to make stick, leaders have the right to expect measurable gain from the effort. Skill-based pay often does not generate bottom-line measurements, making those who are held accountable flinch. Why? Frequently when skill-based pay is sold on the front end, leaders are promised results and meaningful benefits that skill-based pay cannot deliver in the short term.

DERAILMENTS STALL DELIVERY

In the beginning, employers rushed to judgment with regard to skill-based pay. Change agents moved to champion skill-based pay, typically, with unrealistic expectations. Too often, skill-based pay was the latest fad—the latest and greatest—for advisers and consultants to advocate. In most instances, the early technology was not ready for prime time and, because employers had not properly prepared themselves or their workforces for dramatic pay changes, failures were inevitable.

In some cases, employers became interested in paying not only for measurable and observable skills related to the job but also for more vaguely defined competencies relevant to companies. These companies consumed significant resources and time fashioning competency models that they believed were unique. In the end, the design of skill/competency pay was burdensome and bureaucratic and, ironically, employers tended to use a combination of the same eight competencies:

Customer focus
Communication
Team orientation
Technical expertise
Results orientation
Leadership
Adaptability
Innovation[5]

Even the highly customized competency models came to these same competencies, and focusing on these eight, rather than attempting to reinvent the wheel, could have saved considerable time. What would have been the benefit of saving time?

The lost benefit was to focus on a major source of failure for skill-based pay plans: ill-defined skills and competencies. Employers spent so much time developing elaborate competency models that they had no time to work on the real deliverable: a pay solution everyone could understand and follow.

New pay innovations receive quick press, and skill-based pay was no exception. Many advisers and change agents received considerable attention from work-in-progress skill-based pay installations. Academics jumped into the fray quickly, trying to publish "findings" on skill-based pay in an attempt to uncover its workings or failings. The business and human resources press were not on the heels of this "new big thing" in pay, and often looked to publish information proving that the program didn't work.

The skill-based pay exploration process bowed out early because of a resistance to change. When employers gathered employee input and attitudes, the general response favored keeping a pay system that was understood, rather than a new and, in many instances, greatly misunderstood pay approach. Skill-based pay never got the fair break on the battlefield of good versus unacceptable pay practices.

THE LITTLE ENGINE THAT MIGHT

Is there value in imparting some new momentum to skill-based pay? Recent experience has solidified the hold on job-based pay. Skill-based pay is hard to relate to competitive practice because nearly all of the most popular surveys report on what jobs are worth in the market, not the worth of skills and capabilities. Because market pay has grown in popularity, it is difficult to move forward confidently with a pay solution that has had more publicized failures than successes.

While some highly successful skill-based pay installations do exist, they mostly are in manufacturing[6] and, to complicate matters, manufacturing is in a slump, thereby putting pressure on even the most workable and value-added skill-based pay solutions. Employers, of course, are hesitant to experiment when pay solutions based on market value are working so well. With concerns about labor costs, employers are not inclined to move to a pay foundation perceived as too

(Continued)

(Continued)

complex. Because skill-based pay started on the wrong foot, it likely will be necessary to overprove its value.

KICK-START IT OR TAKE IT TO THE GRAVEYARD

Skill-based pay works too well in some very specific work environments to completely do away with it. Rather, the issue is whether the number of new skill-based pay implementations will grow in the short or longer term. It is unlikely that skill-based pay will become the fad that broadbanding was in the 1990s.[7] Broadbanding, or "fat ranges," was easier to implement, had only minimal impact on the way people were paid before and after implementation, and did not result in nearly the revolutionary change that skill-based pay creates. Banding simply was a system of wide salary ranges intended to reduce the number of levels and layers necessary throughout a job structure.

To kick-start the skill-based pay solution, employers need to insist that the completed program be simple to explain and must match the communication concept of the "elevator speech." (If a trainer gets on an elevator on the ground floor of a 20-story building with someone else, that other individual should have a solid general understanding of how the program applies to him or her by the time they reach the top floor.)

A skill-based pay program should include:

- Skills and competencies—directly important to job performance—that can be defined in measurable and objective terms.
- Skills that employees apply on the job to gain desirable job performance objectives. Employers should pay for performance, not training.
- New and different skills that replace obsolete skills or skills that no longer are important to job performance. If additional skills are needed, the obsolete skill should be removed from the program.
- On-the-job skill training, not "in the classroom." Those who possess the skills should teach them. Also, include on-the-job assessment, which can be supplemented by paper-and-pencil exams administered on the job, as well.

These solutions should be implemented with the understanding that it will take several years for skill-based pay to bear fruit for the company and its employees. It is just a different way for companies and employees to think about pay.

Initially, skill-based pay seems to increase the cost of the employees included in the program. Transition charges often are considerable, and the overall labor cost relationship also can be a significant challenge. Kick-starting skill-based pay likely means building a new body of knowledge on what does—and doesn't—work. It also requires defining the reasons companies should consider it (e.g., what to expect in return for the time and resources required for installation). Also, more realistic timelines need to be developed for skill-based pay implementation from project startup to the realization of benefits.[8]

CRANKING THE ENGINE

Employers can consider skill-based pay as part of any total rewards solution. The technical issues should be easier to address than the social challenges of workforce involvement, acceptance, and commitment. An organization can perform preapproval processes on skill-based pay with the following steps:

- **Justify the application.** Determine the expected advantages derived from a skill-based pay program early. The most probable expectations are to encourage a more flexible workforce that seeks learning and uses needed skills and capabilities, along with a solution that pays more as people learn more and apply newfound skills to the job. Consider: Are these reasons enough to make implementing a skill-based pay program worth the effort?
- **Determine readiness.** Determine whether the company is ready, or can prepare, for skill-based pay. Consider different scenarios about how pay and rewards issues will be managed in an environment where people are paid for the skills they have, can obtain, and will apply, rather than for the jobs they already have or may not accurately fit.
- **Prepare for change.** How has the organization addressed major change regarding HR policy and programs in the past? Moreover, has it been tasked to address changes relative to people issues?
- **Define tolerances.** Decide whether the organization is willing to do what it takes to design, implement, communicate, and manage a skill-

based pay solution on a continual basis. What is the company's tolerance for workforce change that creates noise and resistance? Will leadership, aided by change supporters, have the patience to wait for its acceptance? Is any pain during the change process worth the effort?

- **Establish the plan and timelines.** Once the decision to proceed has been made (if it has been made), foster commitment to a plan for implementing skill-based pay, including specific timelines. Communicate the plan to those involved, describing the reasons for the decision and how the process will unfold. Do not plan on wishful thinking, but on your best estimate of the magnitude and challenge.
- **Follow the plan.** Act on what has been developed and work to make it successful. If adjustments need to be made along the way for unexpected occurrences, do them. Tell employees what's happening and why, and get the process moving steadily and as close to on time and on target as possible.

Preparation is essential when it has been determined that skill-based pay makes sense for an organization. Success does not need to be defined in terms of implementing a skill-based pay solution. It may result in not implementing skill-based pay, and it may result in moving to a solution that differs from the current plan, but does not include a total skill-based pay answer.

WHERE SKILL-BASED PAY CAN ADD MOST VALUE

Although the exception clearly proves the rule for skill-based pay, there are some guidelines to consider when selecting when and where skill-based pay is a viable business solution for pay management. Here are some possible skill-based pay applications:

- A company whose leadership has a realistic understanding of skill-based pay's challenges and opportunities, particularly from the perspective of how much time and energy it will take to make skill-based pay operational.
- An environment in which a skill progression exists and skills higher in this progression are more valuable to the business and to the employee than other skills.
- Situations where skills are concrete and can be defined so everyone knows when someone has the skill and when they do not. Where little controversy exists about who has and applies the skill to do the job.
- Circumstances where the opportunities for growth and rotation are not encumbered by arbitrary work rules and seniority systems that are "anti-skill."
- Organizations where employee involvement, strong communications, and mutual trust exist.
- Where experimental human resources systems can be explored.
- Where, if the solution doesn't work, the human resources situation is such that more experimentation is possible in the future.

Skill-based pay certainly is not dead and probably will not die, but we clearly are seeing fewer new applications. Businesses somehow do not seem to see a fit with the problems they are facing concerning pay at this time. Perhaps skill-based pay is just a "good time" answer that cannot stand the test of economic challenge. It's more likely that a solution for base pay that survives the need to create a high-performance business will focus on the actual people who have the most important skills and capabilities. The jury is still out on whether this will be some type of skill-based pay.

If skill-based pay can emphasize a value-added business formula by responding to both the skills the company needs for success and the market value of these skills, then some form of skill-based pay probably will have lasting value to the enterprise. It will need, however, to be more streamlined and easier to understand and communicate. And companies must have very clear and realistic expectations as to what skill-based pay can deliver.

ENDNOTES

1. Zingheim, P. K., and Schuster, J. R. (2001). Creating a powerful customized workplace reward brand. *Compensation & Benefits Review, 33*, pp. 30–33.
2. Zingheim, P. K., and Schuster, J. R. (2000). *Pay People Right? Breakthrough Reward Strategies to Create Great Companies*. San Francisco: Jossey-Bass.
3. Lawler, E. E. III (1990). *Strategic Pay: Aligning Organizational Strategies and Pay Systems*. San Francisco: Jossey-Bass.

(Continued)

(Continued)

4. Ledford, G. E., Jr. (1995). Designing nimble pay systems. *Compensation & Benefits Review, 27*, pp. 46–54.
5. Zingheim, P. K., Ledford, G. E., Jr., and Schuster, J. R. (1996). Competencies and competency models: Does one size fit all? *ACA Journal*, Spring, pp. 56–65.
6. Schuster, J. R., and Zingheim, P. K. (1996). *The New Pay: Linking Employee and Organizational Performance*. San Francisco: Jossey-Bass.
7. Abosch, K. S. (1998). The promise of broadbanding. *ACA Journal, 7*, pp. 28–36.
8. Lawler, E. E., III (2000). *Rewarding excellence: Pay Strategies for the New Economy*. San Francisco: Jossey-Bass.

WHAT'S NEW IN COMPENSATION?

Considerations for Developing Relevant Training Opportunities

Effective person-focused pay programs depend, in large part, on well-designed training programs. There is a lot at stake: Person-focused pay systems include costly training programs, and these systems award pay raises to employees who successfully complete training. Also, these programs require that employers bear the price of base pay and benefits while employees attend training during regular work hours. Finally, companies must wait patiently before realizing a return on investment for training. Several months may pass before employees apply newly learned knowledge and skills to their jobs. After all, practice makes perfect, and training programs cannot anticipate all the circumstances employees face when performing their jobs.

Training employees is not a guarantee of a positive return. The featured *New York Times* article raises questions about the effectiveness of training programs designed to promote teamwork. For example, some argue that it is difficult to teach employees to work effectively in teams outside the work environment where the politics of the workplace and stresses of job demands are not pressing issues.

Log onto your *New York Times* account. Search the database for articles on "employee training" and "job skills" to find articles about training. When reading these articles, identify the kinds of skills and knowledge needed for training. Following your course instructor's specific directions, be prepared to describe the current situation, and relate it to the article contained in this text. ■

The New York Times

Management; Training Programs Often Miss the Point on the Job

Nanette Solow remembers the day she stood in a row with 10 coworkers, tucked an orange under her chin and transferred it to the space beneath a colleague's chin. The goal was to move the orange down the entire line in less than five minutes. But there was a deeper purpose: to build teamwork, enhance communication and promote problem solving. And, oh yes: to have a hoot in the process.

"My team got so good we did it in 4 minutes and 30 seconds," said Ms. Solow, a travel-industry marketing executive in Manhattan. "It was childlike and fun and fairly inoffensive."

It worked, too—for about a day. But after the fun ended, employees returned to their desks, submerged themselves in daily chores and forgot about the great fruit exchange.

Why? Because they knew management played by a different set of rules than those the seminar organizers had preached, Ms. Solow said.

"People were still not getting raises, and they felt underappreciated," she said. "It didn't matter how fast we transferred oranges. It was demoralizing."

Ms. Solow's sentiments are being echoed by a lot of employees these days, especially in a climate in which more and more corporations—at least 70 percent, according to some estimates—are relying on external training programs to build leadership skills and companywide bonding.

According to the American Society for Training and Development in Alexandria, Va., companies spend about $55 billion a year on formal training of all kinds. Often, they use elaborate and eccentric methods to put their points across, like paintball wars, fighter-pilot simulations and a course at the BMW Performance Center in Spartanburg, S.C., that features driving a car while blindfolded.

Trouble is, many of these programs have no practical value.

"With corporate training, it's often: 'Let's spend the money and hope for the best,' " said Cary Cherniss, a psychology professor at Rutgers University and cochairman of the Consortium for Research on Emotional Intelligence in Organizations, a coalition of researchers and practitioners from business schools, government, consulting firms and corporations. Unfortunately, he added, "It takes a lot of time and effort to unlearn old ways of thinking and acting and develop new neural circuits; it's unlikely these programs have a lasting impact."

Promoters say training seminars can do some good by fostering teamwork. "So many companies are looking at ways to bring in new energy, they want to know how to take it to the next level," said Anthony Bourke, vice president of Afterburner Seminars, a half-day program in which management teams experience training and combat techniques used by fighter pilots. Both Mr. Bourke and the company's founder, James Murphy, author of the newly released *Business Is Combat* (HarperCollins), are Air National Guard pilots with a combined 30 years of sales-training experience.

"Here they're at an off-site meeting, and we set a tone that's different from anything they've ever done before," Mr. Bourke said.

But that may be precisely the problem. While many programs bolster self-esteem and promote good cheer—it can be fun, after all, to pelt the boss with paint—most take place away from the office and all the frustrations and power struggles that go with it. As a result, critics say, they tend to create an artificial, almost vacation-like atmosphere that has little relevance in the real corporate world.

Like all new recruits at Deloitte Consulting in Manhattan, for example, Lou DiLorenzo had to take a weeklong training program. While he had a good time, he says, he didn't really learn much. "What I found is that you went to these classes to learn how to do research, say, but there was no link to the office. It was just like being at college and taking a class," he recalled. He is now on a task force to overhaul the firm's training program.

Hard times can quickly expose the limitations of training programs. In 1998, the Vandor Corporation, a diversified manufacturer in Richmond, IN, with 100 employees, sent employees and managers to an intense paintball war with leadership training program with Leading Concepts, a company in Louisville, KY. Everyone raved about the experience, but when the company found itself in a sales-and-profit squeeze a few months later, it laid off several people.

"As employees witnessed team members being axed to their left and right, they ultimately lost trust and rapport with management, and they undermined their entire investment with us," said Dean Hohl, the president of Leading Concepts. (A Vandor spokesman, Bruce Richardson, disagreed. "It's true that lack of trust is a natural reaction to a downsizing," he said. But, he added, the paintball war probably helped employees cope with that ordeal.)

Providers of management-training seminars acknowledge that some programs lack substance, though they generally argue that theirs fit into the useful category.

"When programs work, they pay for themselves, most within the first five years or so," said Daniel Goleman, cochairman of the Consortium for Research on Emotional Intelligence in Organizations and author of *Working with Emotional Intelligence* (Bantam, 1998). But, he added, "When programs fail, they waste time and money."

Roger Lewin and Birute Regine, cofounders of Harvest Associates, a business consulting firm in Cambridge, Mass., believe most training programs do not work because they perpetuate an us-vs.-them mentality. Managers, they argue, are not really interested in establishing genuine team structures, nor are they interested in overhauling their power base. And since training programs are imposed from the outside in, many employees resent them.

"Organizations are dynamic, interconnected human systems, not machines," said Ms. Regine, who with Mr. Lewin is the author of *The Soul at Work* (Simon & Schuster, 2000). "If you want an organization that's adaptable, robust and flexible, the nexus of change is relationships. People need a sense of community. When people feel they're part of something they're more willing to change."

So what is the answer? Ms. Regine urges managers to skip the love-fests at lakeside resorts and sit down with employees for serious heart-to-heart talks about what makes them tick—what they care about, what their goals are and what their fears are. Then they should try to motivate them the old-fashioned way—with raises, promotions and other positive reinforcement.

"How are people interacting? Are managers providing opportunities for people to connect on all levels?" she asked. "It's incredible the impact that has on people. You need to gauge what is essentially human—people's desire to participate, contribute and be part of something greater than themselves."

SOURCE: Abby Ellin, Management; training programs often miss the point on the job (March 29, 2000) [online]. Available: *www.nytimes.com*, accessed September 5, 2002.

CHAPTER 7 BUILDING INTERNALLY CONSISTENT COMPENSATION SYSTEMS

Chapter Outline

- Internal Consistency
- Job Analysis
  - Steps in the Job Analysis Process
  - Legal Considerations for Job Analysis
  - Job Analysis Techniques
  - U.S. Department of Labor's Occupational Information Network (O*NET)
- Job Evaluation
  - Compensable Factors
  - The Job Evaluation Process
- Job Evaluation Techniques
  - The Point Method
  - Alternative Job-Content Evaluation Approaches
  - Alternatives to Job Evaluation
- Internally Consistent Compensation Systems and Competitive Strategy
- Summary
- Key Terms
- Discussion Questions
- Exercises
- Endnotes

Learning Objectives

In this chapter, you will learn about

1. The importance of building internally consistent compensation systems
2. The process of job analysis
3. Job descriptions
4. O*NET

5. The process of job evaluation
6. A variety of job evaluation techniques
7. Alternatives to job evaluation
8. Internally consistent compensation systems and competitive strategy

Job descriptions serve as a cornerstone in the development of internally consistent compensation systems as well as performance standards in performance evaluation systems. Nevertheless, HR professionals have debated over the usefulness of job descriptions. Opponents often say that job descriptions simply are not realistic depictions of what many employees actually do each day. The "Compensation in Action" feature at the end of this chapter describes some of the reasons why HR professionals feel this way, and it offers suggestions for developing more realistic job descriptions.

INTERNAL CONSISTENCY

Internally consistent compensation systems clearly define the relative value of each job among all jobs within a company. This ordered set of jobs represents the job structure or hierarchy. Companies rely on a simple yet fundamental principle for building internally consistent compensation systems: Jobs that require higher qualifications, more responsibilities, and more complex job duties should be paid more than jobs that require lower qualifications, fewer responsibilities, and less complex job duties. Internally consistent job structures formally recognize differences in job characteristics that enable compensation managers to set pay accordingly. Figure 7-1 illustrates an internally consistent job structure for employee benefits professionals. As Figure 7-1 indicates, a benefits manager should earn substantially more than a benefits counselor I: Benefits managers have far greater responsibility for ensuring effective benefits practices than the entry-level counselor. The difference in average pay rates between benefits counselor II and benefits counselor I jobs should be far less than the difference in average pay rates between benefits manager and benefits counselor I jobs. Why? The differences in responsibility between benefits counselor II and benefits counselor I are far less than the differences between benefits manager and benefits counselor I.

Compensation experts and HR professionals create internally consistent job structures through two processes—job analysis followed by job evaluation. **Job analysis** is almost purely a descriptive procedure; job evaluation reflects value judgments. Effective job analysis identifies and defines job content. **Job content** describes job duties and tasks as well as pertinent factors such as the skill and effort (compensable factors) needed to perform the job adequately.

Human resource specialists lead the job analysis process. As we will discuss shortly, they solicit the involvement of employees and supervisors, who offer their perspectives on the nature of the jobs being analyzed. Based on this information, HR specialists write job descriptions that describe the job duties and minimum qualifications required of individuals to perform their jobs effectively.

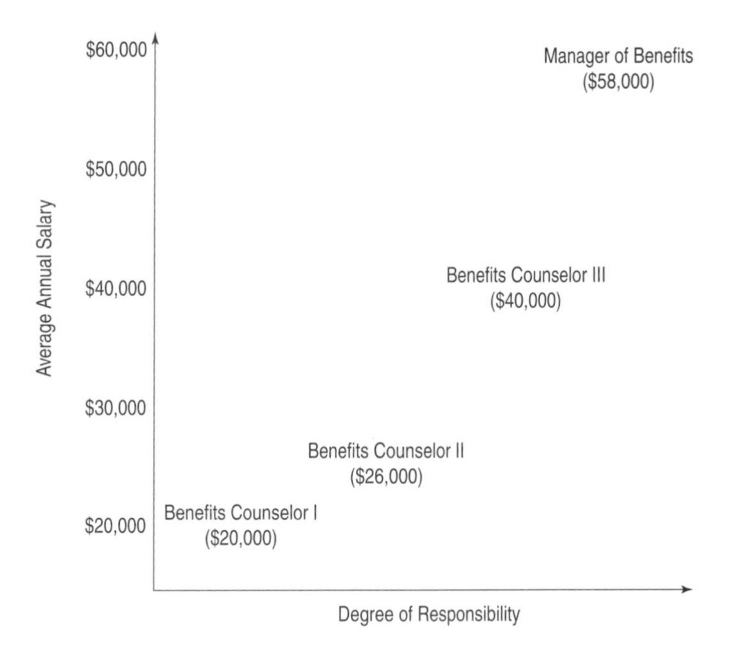

Benefits Counselor I

Provides basic counseling services to employees and assistance to higher-level personnel in more-complex benefits activities. Works under general supervision of higher-level counselors or other personnel.

Benefits Counselor II

Provides skilled counseling services to employees concerning specialized benefits programs or complex areas of other programs. Also completes special projects or carries out assigned phases of the benefits counseling service operations. Works under general supervision from Benefits Counselor III or other personnel.

Benefits Counselor III

Coordinates the daily activities of an employee benefits counseling service and supervises its staff. Works under direction from higher-level personnel.

Manager of Benefits

Responsible for managing the entire benefits function from evaluating benefits programs to ensuring that Benefits Counselors are adequately trained. Reports to the Director of Compensation and Benefits.

FIGURE 7-1 Internally Consistent Compensation Structure

Job evaluation is key for casting internally consistent compensation systems as strategic tools. Compensation professionals use job evaluation to establish pay differentials among employees within a company. The descriptive job analysis results directly aid compensation professionals in their pay-setting decisions by highlighting the key similarities and differences between jobs.

COMPANIES CAN BENEFIT WHEN THEY DISCLOSE PAY PROCESSES TO EMPLOYEES

Employers can raise employees' satisfaction with their pay without actually raising their salaries, according to a recent study sponsored by WorldatWork, an organization in Scottsdale, Ariz., for compensation and benefits professionals. The study found a correlation between employees' understanding of their companies' pay structure and their overall satisfaction with their pay.

The key to better attitudes about pay, the survey found, is better communication. Writing in the survey report—*The Knowledge of Pay Study: E-mails from the Front Line*—participant Susan Zelinski-Davis, CCP, manager of employee performance and rewards at Nationwide Insurance, said companies "don't need to throw money at the problem to increase pay satisfaction, [they] need to communicate the process better."

Indeed, employers don't seem to be communicating the process well at all. Although 76 percent of the survey's respondents said they understand the basic concept of the pay grade, band or level they are in, only 48 percent understand the rationale behind their being placed in that grade, band or level of pay. Furthermore, only 41 percent said they know how base pay increases are determined, and only 36 percent know how their pay range is determined, according to the study.

Even when companies disclose pay structure information, the study found, there is still a gap in understanding the key considerations that go into getting a promotion or a larger merit increase.

"Employees want you to translate the pay structure to what their opportunities are for pay increases and promotions," says a co-author of the study, Peter V. LeBlanc. He served as president of the LeBlanc Group, which conducted the study, and is now senior vice president of Sibson Consulting Group/The Segal Co. in Cary, N.C. "Employees have no clue as to what they might earn if they were to be promoted. That's an even greater mystery to them than what their next base pay increase would be. They don't know what they can aspire to if they meet certain key considerations."

Another misconception among employees, the study found, is the belief that managers have alot of discretion in distributing pay increases. "The ultimate irony is you hear disgruntled employees insinuate that there is favoritism involved [in merit increases]," LeBlanc says. "But managers' hands are handcuffed all too often because of the fairly narrow ranges and systems that are in place.

While many organizations use salary surveys and other market data to determine pay ranges, only 36 percent of respondents know how their organization's pay rates compare with market rates, the study found. "So many good efforts are made by compensation experts to link [pay rates] to the outside market, but it's hard to translate those efforts in a way that people believe its accuracy," LeBlanc explains. Employees question the selection of companies in salary surveys, the selection of regions, and, most often, the content of the job profiles compared.

Far from being just an exercise in good will, explaining pay processes can generate the benefits that flow from improved employee loyalty, because employees who are more satisfied with pay are more loyal, the report states. The survey found that organizations that disclosed this information had employees who were more satisfied with their overall compensation level, more likely to stay with the company, more committed to the organization and more trusting of management.

LeBlanc cites two reasons why companies may still hold pay structure information close to the vest. First, he says, the pay structure "might make sense to a compensation expert or a management team, but they aren't convinced it would make sense to the rank-and-file. The question becomes, 'Is it explainable?' " Second, he says, managers believe that if they explain the structure to employees, they become bound to the process and to the key considerations.

Still, the benefits of disclosing this information seem to outweigh the risks, according to the study. "In the era of low pay increases and zero or low bonuses, organizations that aren't revealing as much as they should can gain a lot in sharing knowledge of pay," LeBlanc concludes.

Source: Adrienne Fox, *HR Magazine* (2002), volume 47, number 7, p. 25.

JOB ANALYSIS

Competent compensation professionals are familiar with job analysis concepts, the process of conducting job analysis, and fundamental job analysis techniques. Job analysis is a systematic process for gathering, documenting, and analyzing information in order to describe jobs. Job analyses describe content or job duties, worker requirements, and, sometimes, the job context or working conditions.

Job content refers to the actual activities that employees must perform in the job. Job content descriptions may be broad, general statements of job activities or detailed descriptions of duties and tasks performed in the job. Greeting clients is common to receptionist jobs. The job activity of greeting clients represents a broad statement. Describing the particular activities associated with greeting clients—for example, saying "hello," asking the clients' names, using the telephone to notify the employees of their clients' arrivals, and offering beverages—represents a detailed statement.

Worker requirements represent the minimum qualifications and skills that people must have to perform a particular job. Such requirements usually include education, experience, licenses, permits, and specific abilities such as typing, drafting, or editing. For example, the minimum educational qualification for a lead research scientist in a jet propulsion laboratory is a Ph.D. in physics.

Working conditions are the social context or physical environment where work will be performed. For instance, social context is a key factor for jobs in the hospitality industry. Hospitality industry managers emphasize the importance of employees' interactions with guests. Hotel registration desk clerks should convey an air of enthusiasm toward guests and be willing to accommodate each guest's specific requests for a nonsmoking room or an early check-in time.

Physical environments vary along several dimensions, based on the level of noise and possible exposure to hazardous factors, including hazardous chemicals. Work equipment also defines the character of the physical environment. Nuclear power plant employees work in rather hazardous physical environments because of possible exposure to dangerous radiation levels. Accountants perform their jobs in relatively safe working environments because office buildings must meet local building safety standards.

Steps in the Job Analysis Process

The job analysis process has five main activities:

- Determine a job analysis program.
- Select and train analysts.
- Direct job analyst orientation.
- Conduct the study: Data collection methods and sources of data.
- Summarize the results: Writing job descriptions.

Determine a Job Analysis Program

A company must decide between using an established system or developing its own system tailored to specific requirements. Both established and custom job analysis programs vary in the method of gathering data. The most typical methods for collecting job analysis information are questionnaires, interviews, observation, and participation. Oftentimes, administrative costs represent a major consideration in selecting a job analysis method.

Select and Train Analysts

Generally speaking, job analysts must be able to collect job-related information through various methods, relate to a wide variety of employees, analyze the information, and write clearly and succinctly. Ideally, a task force of representatives from throughout the company conducts the analysis, and HR staff members coordinate it. Although some companies rely on HR professionals to coordinate and conduct job analysis, many use teams to represent varying perspectives on work, because virtually all employees interact with coworkers and supervisors.

Before the task force embarks on a job analysis, members need to be taught about the basic assumptions of the model and the procedures they must follow. The training should include discussions of the study's objectives, how the information will be used, methodology overviews, and discussions and demonstrations of the information-gathering techniques. Analysts also should be trained to minimize the chance that they will conduct ineffective job analyses. For example, analysts should involve as many job incumbents as possible within the constraints of staff time to have representative samples of job incumbents' perceptions.

Finally, job analysts must be familiar with the structure of pertinent job data. Job analysis data are configured in levels, hierarchically from specific bits of information to progressively broader categories that include the prior specific pieces. Table 7-1 defines representative analysis levels and lists examples of each one. The most specific information is a job element, and the broadest element is an occupation.

TABLE 7-1 Units of Analysis in the Job Analysis Process

1. An *element* is the smallest step into which it is practical to subdivide any work activity without analyzing separate motions, movements, and mental processes involved. Inserting a diskette into floppy disk drive is an example of a job element.
2. A *task* is one or more elements and is one of the distinct activities that constitute logical and necessary steps in the performance of work by the worker. A task is created whenever human effort, physical or mental, is exerted to accomplish a specific purpose. Keyboarding text into memo format represents a job task.
3. A *position* is a collection of tasks constituting the total work assignment of a single worker. There are as many positions as there are workers. John Smith's position in the company is clerk typist. His tasks, which include keyboarding text into memo format, running a spell check on the text, and printing the text on company letterhead, combine to represent John Smith's position.
4. A *job* is a group of positions within a company that are identical with respect to their major or significant tasks and sufficiently alike to justify their being covered by a single analysis. There may be one or many persons employed in the same job. For example, Bob Arnold, John Smith, and Jason Colbert are clerk typists. With minor variations, they essentially perform the same tasks.
5. A *job family* is a group of two or more jobs that call for either similar worker characteristics or similar work tasks. File clerk, clerk typist, and administrative clerk represent a clerical job family because each job mainly requires employees to perform clerical tasks.
6. An *occupation* is a group of jobs, found at more than one establishment, in which a common set of tasks are performed or are related in terms of similar objectives, methodologies, materials, products, worker actions, or worker characteristics. File clerk, clerk typist, administrative clerk, staff secretary, and administrative secretary represent an office support occupation. Compensation analyst, training and development specialist, recruiter, and benefits counselor represent jobs from the human resources management occupation.

Source: U.S. Department of Labor. (1991). *The revised handbook for analyzing jobs*. Washington, DC: U.S. Government Printing Office, 1991.

TABLE 7-2 Major Occupational Groups of the Standard Occupational Classification

- Management occupations
- Business and financial operations occupations
- Computer and mathematical occupations
- Architecture and engineering occupations
- Life, physical, and social science occupations
- Community and social services occupations
- Legal occupations
- Education, training, and library occupations
- Arts, design, entertainment, sports, and media occupations
- Healthcare practitioners and technical occupations
- Healthcare support occupations
- Protective service occupations
- Food preparation and serving related occupations
- Building and grounds cleaning and maintenance occupations
- Personal care and service occupations
- Sales and related occupations
- Office and administrative support occupations
- Farming, fishing, and forestry occupations
- Construction and extraction occupations
- Installation, maintenance, and repair occupations
- Production occupations
- Transportation and material moving occupations
- Military specific occupations

Source: U.S. Bureau of Labor Statistics. (1999). *Revising the standard occupational classification system* [Report 929]. Washington, DC: U.S. Government Printing Office.

The U.S. Office of Management and Budget published *The Standard Occupational Classification System* (SOC) that identifies 23 **major occupational groups**. The SOC system replaces the government's longstanding *The Dictionary of Occupational Titles* (published in 1938 and subsequently revised in 1949, 1964, 1977, and 1991). Table 7-2 lists the 23 major occupational groups.

These concepts are relevant for making compensation decisions. Ultimately, the units of analysis may influence compensation professionals' judgments about whether work is dissimilar or similar. Human resource manager, purchasing manager, and payroll clerk are dissimilar jobs because employees in these jobs perform different duties. However, HR manager and purchasing manager are similar at the occupational level because they fall under the management occupation. In addition, HR manager and payroll clerk are quite different at the occupational level because HR manager is classified as a management occupation, and payroll clerk falls under the office and administrative support occupation.

Direct Job Analyst Orientation

Before analysts start specific job analysis techniques, they must analyze the context in which employees perform their work to better understand influencing factors. In addition, analysts should obtain and review such internal information as organizational charts, listings of job titles, classifications of each position to be analyzed, job incumbent names and pay rates, and any instructional booklets or handbooks for operating equipment. Job analysts may also find pertinent job information in such external sources as *The Standard Occupational Classification System*, trade associations, professional societies, and trade unions.

Conduct the Study: Data Collection Methods and Sources of Data

Once analysts have gathered and made sense of these preliminary data, they can begin gathering and recording information for each job in the company. Analysts should carefully choose the method of data collection and the sources of data. The most common methods are questionnaires and observation. Questionnaires direct job incumbents' and supervisors' descriptions of the incumbents' work through a series of questions and statements, for example:

- Describe the task you perform most frequently.
- How often do you perform this task?
- List any licenses, permits, or certifications required to perform duties assigned to your position.
- List any equipment, machines, or tools you normally operate as part of your position's duties.
- Does your job require any contacts with other department personnel, other departments, outside companies, or agencies? If yes, please describe.
- Does your job require supervisory responsibilities? If yes, for which jobs and for how many employees?

Observation requires job analysts to record perceptions they form while watching employees perform their jobs.

The most common sources of job analysis data are job incumbents, supervisors, and the job analysts. Job incumbents should provide the most extensive and detailed information about how they perform job duties. Experienced job incumbents will probably offer the most details and insights. Supervisors also should provide extensive and detailed information, but with a different focus. Specifically, supervisors are most familiar with the interrelationships among jobs within their departments. They are probably in the best position to describe how employees performing different jobs interact. Job analysts also should involve as many job incumbents and supervisors as possible because employees with the same job titles may have different experiences.

For example, parts assembler John Smith reports that a higher level of manual dexterity is required than parts assembler Barbara Bleen reports. Parts assembler supervisor Jan Johnson indicates that assemblers interact several times a day to help each other solve unexpected problems, and supervisor Bill Black reports no interaction among parts assemblers. Including as many job incumbents and supervisors as possible will provide a truer assessment of the parts assembler job duties.

Of course, job analysts represent a source of information. In the case of observation, job analysts write descriptions. When using questionnaires, job analysts often ask follow-up questions to clarify job incumbents' and supervisors' answers. In either case, job analysts' HR expertise should guide the selection of pertinent follow-up questions.

Ultimately, companies strive to conduct job analyses that lead to reliable and valid job evaluation results. A **reliable job analysis** yields consistent results under similar conditions. For example, let's assume that two job analysts independently observe John Smith perform his job as a retail store manager. The method is reliable if the two analysts reach similar conclusions about the duties that constitute the retail store manager job. Although important, reliable job analysis methods are not enough. Job analyses also must be valid.

A **valid job analysis** method accurately assesses each job's duties. Unfortunately, neither researchers nor practitioners can demonstrate whether job analysis results are definitively accurate. At present, the "best" approach to producing valid job descriptions requires that results among multiple sources of job data (job incumbents, analysts, supervisors, customers) and multiple methods (interview, questionnaire, observation) converge [1].

Reliable and valid job analysis methods are essential to building internally consistent compensation systems. The factors that describe a particular job should indeed reflect the actual work. Failure to accurately match compensable factors with the work employees perform may result in either inadequate or excessive pay rates. Both cases are detrimental to the company. Inadequate pay may lead to dysfunctional turnover—the departure of high-quality employees. Excessive pay represents a cost burden to the company that can ultimately undermine its competitive position. Moreover, basing pay on factors that do not relate to job duties leaves a company vulnerable to allegations of illegal discrimination.

What can compensation professionals do to increase the likelihood that they will use reliable and valid job analysis methods? Whenever time and budgetary constraints permit, job analysts should use more than one data collection method, and they should collect data from more than one source. Including multiple data collection methods and sources minimizes the inherent biases associated with any particular one. For example, a job incumbent may view her work as having greater impact on the effectiveness of the company than the incumbent's supervisor. Observation techniques do not readily indicate why an employee performs a task in a specific way, but the interview method provides analysts with an opportunity to make probing inquiries.

Summarize the Results: Writing Job Descriptions

Job descriptions summarize a job's purpose and list its tasks, duties, and responsibilities as well as the skills, knowledge, and abilities necessary to perform the job at a minimum level. Effective job descriptions generally explain:

- What the employee must do to perform the job
- How the employee performs the job
- Why the employee performs the job in terms of its contribution to the functioning of the company
- Supervisory responsibilities, if any
- Contacts (and purpose of these contacts) with other employees inside or outside the company
- The skills, knowledge, and abilities the employee should have or must have to perform the job duties
- The physical and social conditions under which the employee must perform the job

Job descriptions usually contain four sections:

- Job title
- Job summary
- Job duties
- Worker specifications

Table 7-3 contains a job description for a training and development specialist.

Job titles indicate the name of each job within a company's job structure. In Table 7-3, the job title is training and development specialist. The **job summary** statement

TABLE 7-3 Job Description: Training and Development Specialist

Job Summary

Training and development specialists perform training and development activities for supervisors, managers, and staff to improve efficiency, effectiveness, and productivity. They work under general supervision from higher-level training and development professionals.

Job Duties

A training and development specialist typically:

1. Recommends, plans, and implements training seminars and workshops for administrators and supervisors, and evaluates program effectiveness.
2. Evaluates training needs of employees and departments by conducting personal interviews, questionnaires, and statistical studies.
3. Researches, writes, and develops instructional materials for career, staff, and supervisor workshops and seminars.
4. Counsels supervisors and employees on policies and rules.
5. Performs related duties as assigned.

Worker Specifications

1. Any one or any combination of the following types of preparation:
   (a) credit for college training leading to a major or concentration in education or other fields closely related to training and development (such as human resource management or vocational education).

   —or—

   (b) two years of work experience as a professional staff member in a human resource management department.
2. Two years of professional work experience in the training and development area in addition to the training and experience required in item 1 above.

concisely summarizes the job with two to four descriptive statements. This section usually indicates whether the job incumbent receives supervision and by whom. The training and development specialist works under general supervision from higher-level training and development professionals or other designated administrators.

The **job duties** section describes the major work activities and, if pertinent, supervisory responsibilities. For instance, the training and development specialist evaluates training needs of employees and departments by conducting personal interviews, questionnaires, and statistical studies.

The **worker specification** section lists the education, skills, abilities, knowledge, and other qualifications individuals must possess to perform the job adequately. **Education** refers to formal training. Minimum educational levels can be a high school diploma or a general equivalency diploma (GED) through such advanced levels as master's or doctoral degrees.

The **Equal Employment Opportunity Commission** (EEOC) guidelines distinguish among the terms *knowledge, skill,* and *ability*. **Skill** refers to an observable competence to perform a learned psychomotor act. Typing 50 words per minute with fewer than five errors is an example of a psychomotor act because it requires knowledge of the keyboard layout and manual dexterity. According to the EEOC, **ability** refers to a present competence to perform an observable behavior or a behavior that results in an observable product. For example, possessing the competence to successfully mediate a dispute between labor and management reflects an ability. **Knowledge** refers to a body of information applied directly to the performance of a function. Companies measure knowledge with tests, or they infer that employees have knowledge based on formal education completed. For instance, compensation professionals should know about the Fair Labor Standards Act's overtime pay requirements.

Legal Considerations for Job Analysis

The government does not require companies to conduct job analysis. However, conducting job analyses increases the chance that employment decisions are based solely on pertinent job requirements. Under the Equal Pay Act (Chapter 3), companies must justify pay differences between men and women who perform equal work. Different job titles do not suffice as justification. Instead, companies must demonstrate substantive differences in job functions. Job analysis helps HR professionals discern whether substantive differences between job functions exist.

Job analysis is also useful for determining whether a job is exempt or nonexempt under the Fair Labor Standards Act (FLSA). As we discussed in Chapter 3, failure to pay nonexempt employees an overtime hourly pay rate violates the FLSA. Table 7-4 lists the FLSA criteria that distinguish between exempt and nonexempt jobs. Job analysis can provide job descriptions to be judged on these criteria.

Companies may perform job analysis to see if they comply with the Americans with Disabilities Act (ADA), also discussed in Chapter 3. As long as disabled applicants can perform the essential functions of a job with reasonable accommodation, companies must not discriminate against these applicants by paying them less than other employees performing the same job. Human resource professionals use job analysis to systematically define essential job functions. Companies may consult the EEOC's interpretive guidelines to determine whether a job function is essential. Table 7-5 lists these guidelines.

TABLE 7-4 FLSA Exemption Criteria for Executive, Administrative, and Professional Employees

Executive Employees

- Primary duties include managing the organization
- Regularly supervise the work of two or more full-time employees
- Authority to hire, promote, and discharge employees
- Regularly use discretion as part of typical work duties
- Devote at least 80 percent of work time to fulfilling the previous activities

Administrative Employees

- Perform nonmanual work directly related to management operations
- Regularly use discretion beyond clerical duties
- Perform specialized or technical work, or perform special assignments with only general supervision
- Devote at least 80 percent of work time to fulfilling the previous activities

Professional Employees

- Primary work requires advanced knowledge in a field of science or learning, including work that requires regular use of discretion and independent judgment, or
- Primary work requires inventiveness, imagination, or talent in a recognized field or artistic endeavor

Source: 19 Code of Federal Regulations, Sec. 541.3.29; Sec. 541.1.

TABLE 7-5 EEOC Interpretive Guidelines for Essential Job Functions under the Americans with Disabilities Act

- The reason the position exists is to perform the function.
- The function is essential or possibly essential. If other employees are available to perform the function, the function probably is not essential.
- A high degree of expertise or skill is required to perform the function.
- The function is probably essential; and
- Whether a particular job function is essential is a determination that must be made on a case-by-case basis and should be addressed during job analysis. Any job functions that are not essential are determined to be marginal. Marginal job functions could be traded to another position or not done at all.

Source: From the text of the Americans with Disabilities Act, Federal Register 35734 (July 26, 1991).

Job Analysis Techniques

Human resource professionals can either choose from a variety of established job analysis techniques or custom design them. Most companies generally choose to use established job analysis techniques because the costs of custom-made job analysis techniques often outweigh the benefits. Besides, many of the established job analysis techniques apply to a wide variety of jobs, and both researchers and practitioners have already tested and refined them.

Choosing one established plan over another depends on two considerations—applicability and cost. Some job analysis techniques apply only to particular job families, such as managerial jobs, but others can be applied more broadly. Also, some methods are proprietary, yet others are available to the public at no charge. Private consultants or consulting firms charge substantial fees to companies that use their methods, but the U.S. Department of Labor does not charge fees to use its job analysis method. Next we review the U.S. Department of Labor's **Occupational Information Network** (O*NET).

U.S. Department of Labor's Occupational Information Network (O*NET)

The U.S. Department of Labor's Employment and Training Administration spearheaded the development of O*NET during the 1990s to replace its previous methods of analyzing and describing jobs (*Revised Handbook for Analyzing Jobs* [2] and *The Dictionary of Occupational Titles* [3]). O*NET is a database, and it was created for two reasons. First, it is designed to describe jobs in the relatively new service sector of the economy (for example, wireless telecommunications). Second, O*NET more accurately describes jobs that evolved as the result of technological advances (for example, software and hardware engineers).

O*NET is comprehensive because it incorporates information about both jobs and workers. The O*NET **Content Model** lists six categories of job and worker information. Job information contains the components that relate to the actual work activities of a job—information that HR professionals should include in the summary and duties sections of job descriptions. Worker information represents characteristics of employees that contribute to successful job performance. Figure 7-2 shows the six categories of the O*NET content model.

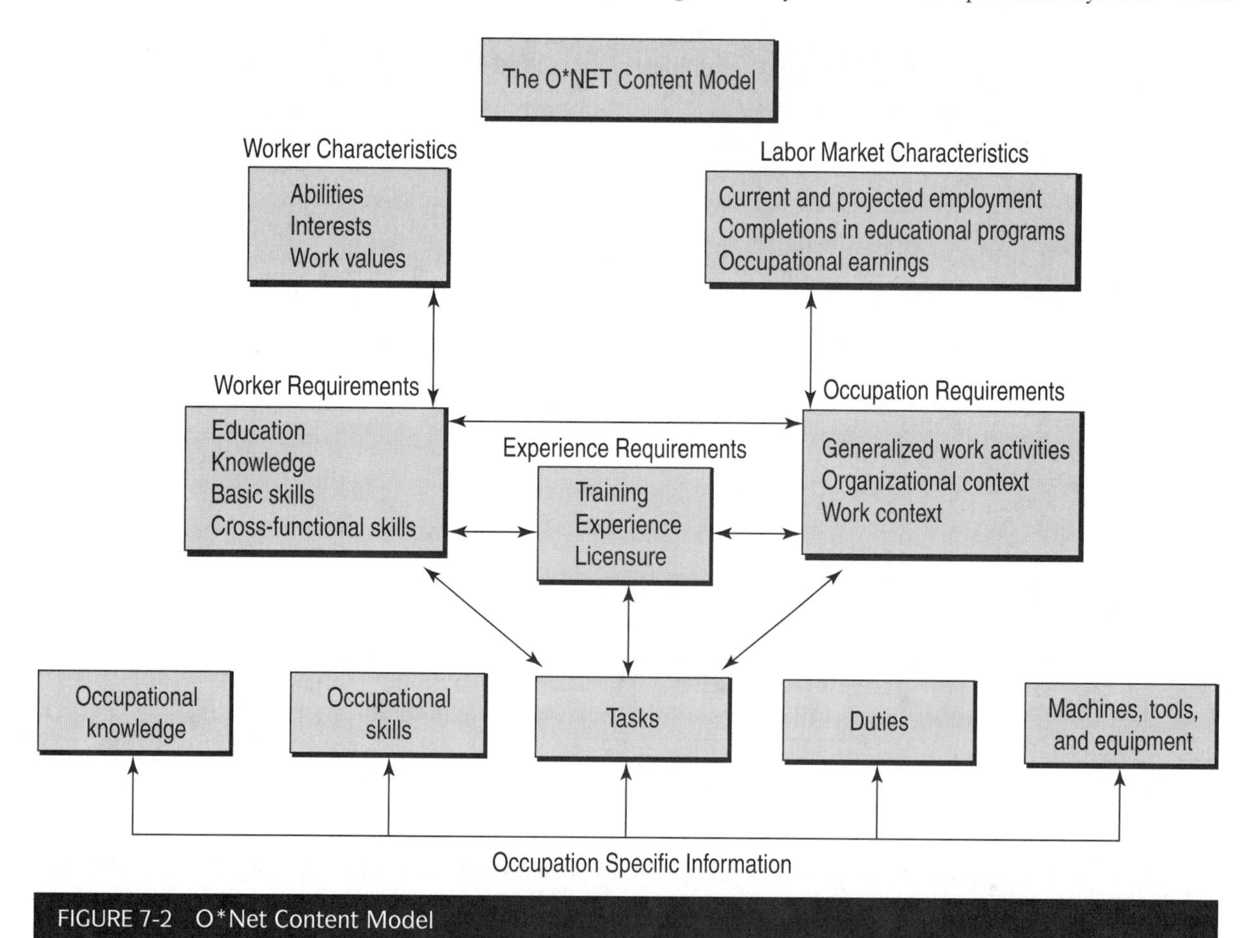

FIGURE 7-2 O*Net Content Model

Source: U.S. Department of Labor Employment and Training Administation. (2002). *O*NET*. Washington DC: Government Printing Office [online]. Available: *www.doleta.gov*.

Experience Requirements

Experience requirements include:

- Experience and training
- Licensing

Experience and training information describes specific preparation required for entry into a job plus past work experience contributing to qualifications for an occupation. **Licensing** information describes licenses, certificates, or registrations that are used to identify levels of skill or performance relevant to occupations. Table 7-6 lists the specific experience requirements.

Occupation Requirements

Occupation requirements include:

- Generalized work activities
- Organizational context
- Work context

Generalized work activities information describes general types of job behaviors occurring on multiple jobs. **Organizational context** information indicates the

TABLE 7-6 O*NET Content Model—Experience Requirements

Experience Requirements
• Experience and training 1. Related work experience 2. On-site or in-plant training 3. On-the-job training 4. Apprenticeship • Licensing ◦ License, certificate, or registration required ◦ Education, training, examination or other requirements for license, certificate, or registration 1. Post-secondary degree 2. Graduate degree 3. On-the-job training 4. Examination 5. Character references ◦ Additional education and training ◦ Organization and agency requirements 1. Legal requirement 2. Employer requirement 3. Union, guild, or professional association requirement

Source: U.S. Department of Labor Employment and Training Administration. (2002). *O*NET*. Washington, DC: Government Printing Office [online]. Available: *www.doleta.gov*.

characteristics of the organization that influence how people do their work. **Work context** information describes physical and social factors that influence the nature of work. Table 7-7 lists examples of particular occupational requirements.

Occupation-Specific Requirements

Occupation-specific requirements information describes the characteristics of a particular occupation. These particular requirements are occupational skills, knowledge, tasks, duties, machines, tools, and equipment.

Occupation Characteristics

Occupation characteristics information describes labor market information, occupational outlook, and wages. These data are available from the following sources: U.S. Bureau of Labor Statistics, National Occupational Information Coordinating Committee, U.S. Department of Education, and Office of Personnel Management. We discussed issues of labor market information and occupational outlook in Chapter 2 and address wage information in Chapter 8.

Worker Characteristics

Worker characteristics information includes:

- Abilities
- Interests
- Work styles

Abilities are enduring attributes of the individual that influence performance. **Interests** describe preferences for work environments and outcomes. **Work styles** are personal characteristics that describe important interpersonal and work style

TABLE 7-7 O*NET Content Model—Sample Occupation Requirements

- Generalized work activities
  - Information input
    - Looking for and receiving job-related information
    - Identifying/evaluating job-relevant information
  - Mental processes
    - Information/data processing
    - Reasoning/decision making
  - Work output
    - Performing physical and manual work activities
    - Performing complex/technical activities
  - Interacting with others
    - Communicating/interacting
    - Coordinating/developing/managing/advising others
- Organizational context
  - Structural characteristics
    - Organizational structure
      - Decision-making system
        - Decentralization and employee empowerment
        - Individual versus team structure
      - Job characteristics
        - Skill variety
        - Task significance
        - Task identity
        - Autonomy
        - Feedback
    - Human resources systems and practices
      - Recruitment and selection
        - Recruitment operations
        - Reward system
          - Basis of compensation
            - Which of the following is part of your compensation package?
            1. Profit sharing
            2. Gain sharing
            3. Knowledge/skill-based pay
            4. Pay based on your individual performance
            5. Pay based on the performance of your team
            6. Pay based on customer satisfaction
            7. Pay based on job tenure/seniority
            8. Pay based on job attributes
            9. None of the above
          - Benefits
            - Which of the following is part of your benefits?
            1. Stock ownership in the organization
            2. Retirement plan
            3. Major medical insurance
            4. Life insurance
            5. Disability insurance
            6. Flexible working hours
            7. Daycare

TABLE 7-7 *(cont.)*

- Benefits *(cont.)*
  8. Paid leave
  9. None of the above
- Social processes
  - Goals
    - Individual goal characteristics
    - Goal feedback
  - Roles
    - Role conflict
    - Role negotiability
    - Role overload
  - Culture
    - Organizational value
      - How important are each of the following?
        1. Taking chances; going out on a limb
        2. Fairness; justice
        3. Precision; paying attention to even the smallest details
  - Supervisor role
- Work context
  - Interpersonal relationships
    - Communication
    - Role relationships
      - Job interactions
    - Responsibility for others
    - Conflictual contact
  - Physical work conditions
    - Work setting
    - Environmental conditions
    - Job hazards
    - Body positioning
    - Work attire
  - Structural job characteristics
    - Criticality of position
    - Routine versus challenging work
    - Level of competition
    - Pace and scheduling

Source: U.S. Department of Labor Employment and Training Administration. (2002). *O*NET*. Washington, DC: Government Printing Office [online]. Available: *www.doleta.gov*.

requirements in jobs and occupations. Table 7-8 lists the particular abilities, interests, and work styles.

Worker Requirements

Worker requirements include:

- Basic skills
- Cross-functional skills
- Knowledge
- Education

TABLE 7-8 O*Net Content Model—Worker Characteristics

- Abilities
  - Cognitive abilities
    - Verbal abilities
      1. Oral comprehension
      2. Written comprehension
      3. Oral expression
      4. Written expression
    - Idea generation and reasoning abilities
      1. Fluency of ideas
      2. Originality
      3. Problem sensitivity
      4. Deductive reasoning
      5. Inductive reasoning
      6. Information ordering
      7. Category flexibility
    - Quantitative abilities
      1. Mathematical reasoning
      2. Number facility
    - Memory
      1. Memorization
    - Perceptual abilities
      1. Speed of closure
      2. Flexibility of closure
      3. Perceptual speed
    - Spatial abilities
      1. Spatial orientation
      2. Visualization
    - Attentiveness
      1. Selective attention
      2. Time sharing
  - Psychomotor abilities
    - Fine manipulative abilities
      1. Arm-hand steadiness
      2. Manual dexterity
      3. Finger dexterity
    - Control movement abilities
      1. Control precision
      2. Multilimb coordination
      3. Response orientation
      4. Rate control
    - Reaction time and speed abilities
      1. Reaction time
      2. Wrist-finger dexterity
      3. Speed of limb movement
  - Physical abilities
    - Physical strength abilities
      1. Static strength
      2. Explosive strength
      3. Dynamic strength
      4. Trunk strength

TABLE 7-8 (*cont.*)

- ■ Endurance
  1. Stamina
- ■ Flexibility, balance, and coordination
  1. Extent flexibility
  2. Dynamic flexibility
  3. Gross body coordination
  4. Gross body equilibrium
- ◦ Sensory abilities
  - ■ Visual abilities
    1. Near vision
    2. Far vision
    3. Visual color discrimination
    4. Night vision
    5. Peripheral vision
    6. Depth perception
    7. Glare sensitivity
  - ■ Auditory and speech abilities
    1. Hearing sensitivity
    2. Auditory attention
    3. Sound localization
    4. Speech recognition
    5. Speech clarity
- • Interests
  - ◦ Holland occupational classification
    1. Realistic
    2. Investigative
    3. Artistic
    4. Social
    5. Enterprising
    6. Conventional
  - ◦ Occupational values
    - ■ Achievement
      1. Ability utilization
      2. Achievement
    - ■ Comfort
      1. Activity
      2. Independence
      3. Variety
      4. Compensation
      5. Security
      6. Working conditions
    - ■ Status
      1. Advancement
      2. Recognition
      3. Authority
      4. Social values
    - ■ Altruism
      1. Coworkers
      2. Social service
      3. Moral values

TABLE 7-8 (*cont.*)

- ■ Safety
  1. Company policies and practices
  2. Supervision, human relations
  3. Supervision, technical
- ■ Autonomy
  1. Creativity
  2. Responsibility
  3. Autonomy

- Work Styles
  - ◦ Achievement orientation
    1. Achievement/effort
    2. Persistence
    3. Initiative
  - ◦ Social influence
    1. Energy
    2. Leadership orientation
  - ◦ Interpersonal orientation
    1. Cooperation
    2. Concern for others
    3. Social orientation
  - ◦ Adjustment
    1. Self-control
    2. Stress tolerance
    3. Adaptability/flexibility
  - ◦ Conscientiousness
    1. Dependability
    2. Attention to detail
    3. Integrity
  - ◦ Independence
  - ◦ Practical intelligence
    1. Innovation
    2. Analytical thinking

Source: U.S. Department of Labor Employment and Training Administration. (2002). *O*NET*. Washington, DC: Government Printing Office [online]. Available: *www.doleta.gov*.

Basic skills information describes developed capacities that facilitate learning or the more rapid acquisition of knowledge. **Cross-functional skills** information indicates developed capacities that facilitate performance of activities that occur across jobs. Knowledge information describes organized sets of principles and facts applying in general domains. Education information details prior educational experience required to perform in a job. Table 7-9 lists the particular basic skills, cross-functional skills, knowledge, and educational requirements.

Using O*NET

Human resource professionals use O*NET by consulting the **O*NET User's Guide** as well as the most current **O*NET database** [4]. Academic (college or university) and public libraries designated as government depositories keep these items. Alternatively, companies can purchase these publications for nominal fees from the

TABLE 7-9 O*NET Content Model—Worker Requirements

- Basic skills
  - Content
    1. Reading comprehension
    2. Active listening
    3. Writing
    4. Speaking
    5. Mathematics
    6. Science
  - Process
    1. Critical thinking
    2. Active learning
    3. Learning strategies
    4. Monitoring
- Cross-functional skills
  - Social skills
    1. Social perceptiveness
    2. Coordination
    3. Persuasion
    4. Negotiation
    5. Instructing
    6. Service orientation
  - Complex problem-solving skills
    1. Problem identification
    2. Information gathering
    3. Information organization
    4. Synthesis/reorganization
    5. Idea generation
    6. Idea evaluation
    7. Implementation planning
    8. Solution appraisal
  - Technical skills
    1. Operations analysis
    2. Technology design
    3. Equipment selection
    4. Installation
    5. Programming
    6. Testing
    7. Operation monitoring
    8. Operation and control
    9. Product inspection
    10. Equipment maintenance
    11. Troubleshooting
    12. Repairing
  - Systems skills
    1. Visioning
    2. Systems perception
    3. Identification of downstream consequences
    4. Identification of key causes
    5. Judgment and decision making
    6. Systems evaluation

TABLE 7-9 (*cont.*)

- Resource management skills
  1. Time management
  2. Management of financial resources
  3. Management of material resources
  4. Management of personal resources
- Knowledge—organized sets of principles and facts applying in general domains
  - Business and management
    1. Administration and management
    2. Clerical
    3. Economics and accounting
    4. Sales and marketing
    5. Customer and personal service
    6. Personnel and human resources
  - Manufacturing and production
    1. Production and processing
    2. Food production
  - Engineering and technology
    1. Computers and electronics
    2. Engineering and technology
    3. Design
    4. Building and construction
    5. Mechanical
  - Mathematics and science
    1. Mathematics
    2. Physics
    3. Chemistry
    4. Biology
    5. Psychology
    6. Sociology and anthropology
    7. Geography
  - Health services
    1. Medicine and dentistry
    2. Therapy and counseling
  - Education and training
    1. Education and training
  - Arts and humanities
    1. English language
    2. Foreign language
    3. Fine arts
    4. History and archeology
    5. Philosophy and theology
  - Law and public safety
    1. Public safety and security
    2. Law, government, and jurisprudence
  - Communications
    1. Telecommunications
    2. Communications and media
  - Transportation
    1. Transportation

TABLE 7-9 *(cont.)*

- Education
  - Level of education
    1. Less than a high school diploma
    2. High school diploma (or high school equivalency)
    3. Post-secondary certificate
    4. Some college courses
    5. Associate's degree (or other 2-year degree)
    6. Bachelor's degree
    7. Post-baccalaureate certificate
    8. Master's degree
    9. Post-master's certificate
    10. First professional degree
    11. Doctoral degree
    12. Post-doctoral certificate
  - Instructional program required
  - Level of education in specific subject
    1. Technical vocational
    2. Business vocational
    3. English/language arts
    4. Oral communication
    5. Languages
    6. Basic math
    7. Advanced math
    8. Physical science
    9. Computer science
    10. Biological science
    11. Applied science
    12. Social science
    13. Arts
    14. Humanities
    15. Physical education

Source: U.S. Department of Labor Employment and Training Administration. (2002). *O*NET*. Washington, DC: Government Printing Office [online]. Available: *www.doleta.gov*.

U.S. Government Printing Office or they may find the latest O*NET information on the U.S. Department of Labor Employment and Training Administration's Web site (*www.doleta.gov*). In addition, the American Psychological Association published an extensive treatment of O*NET, *An Occupational Information System for the 21st Century: The Development of O*NET* [5].

JOB EVALUATION

Compensation professionals use **job evaluation** to systematically recognize differences in the relative worth among a set of jobs and establish pay differentials accordingly. Whereas job analysis is almost purely descriptive, job evaluation partly reflects the values and priorities that management places on various positions. Based on job content and the firm's priorities, managers establish pay differentials for virtually all positions within the company.

Compensable Factors

Compensation professionals generally base job evaluations on **compensable factors**, which are the salient job characteristics by which companies establish relative pay rates. Most companies consider skill, effort, responsibility, and working conditions, which were derived from the Equal Pay Act. These four dimensions help managers determine whether dissimilar jobs are "equal."

Skill, effort, responsibility, and working conditions are **universal compensable factors** because virtually every job contains these four factors. So, how can meaningful distinctions regarding the value of jobs be made with such broad factors? Many companies break these general factors into more specific factors. For example, responsibility required could be further classified as responsibility for financial matters and responsibility for personnel matters.

Compensation professionals should choose compensable factors based on two considerations. First, factors must be job-related. The factors that describe a particular job should indeed reflect the actual work that is performed: Failure to accurately match compensable factors with the actual work may result in either inadequate or excessive pay rates. Both cases are detrimental to the company because inadequate pay may lead to dysfunctional turnover.

Second, compensation professionals should select compensable factors that further a company's strategies. For example, companies that value product differentiation probably consider innovativeness to be an important compensable factor for research scientist and marketing manager jobs. Companies that distinguish themselves through high-quality customer relations are likely to place great value on such compensable factors as product knowledge and interpersonal skills. Lowest-cost strategies may emphasize different kinds of compensable factors, such as efficiency and timeliness.

The Job Evaluation Process

The job evaluation process entails six steps:

- Determining single versus multiple job evaluation techniques
- Choosing the job evaluation committee
- Training employees to conduct job evaluations
- Documenting the job evaluation plan
- Communicating with employees
- Setting up the appeals process

Determining Single Versus Multiple Job Evaluation Techniques

Compensation professionals must determine whether a single job evaluation technique is sufficiently broad to assess a diverse set of jobs. In particular, the decision is prompted by such questions as "Can we use the same compensable factors to evaluate a forklift operator's job and the plant manager's job?" If the answer is yes, then a single job evaluation technique is appropriate. If not, then more than one job evaluation approach should be employed. It is not reasonable to expect that a single job evaluation technique, based on one set of compensable factors, can adequately assess diverse sets of jobs—operative, clerical, administrative, managerial, professional, technical, and executive. Clearly, a carpenter's job is distinct from a certified public accountant's position because manual dexterity is an important compensable factor that describes carpentry work and is not nearly as central to accounting positions.

Choosing the Job Evaluation Committee

Human resource professionals help put together a committee of rank-and-file employees, supervisors, managers, and, if relevant, union representatives to design, oversee, and evaluate job evaluation results. The functions, duties, responsibilities, and authority of job evaluation committees vary considerably from company to company. In general, committees simply review job descriptions and analyses and then evaluate jobs. Larger companies with a multitude of jobs often establish separate committees to evaluate particular job classifications such as nonexempt, exempt, managerial, and executive jobs. The immense number of jobs in large companies would otherwise preclude committee members from performing their regular duties.

Job evaluation is an important determinant of a job's worth within many companies. All employees, regardless of their functions, wish to be compensated and valued for their efforts. All employees strive for a reasonable pay-effort bargain—a compensation level consistent with their contributions. Managers strive to balance employee motivation with cost control because they have limited resources for operating their departments. Union representatives strive to ensure that members enjoy a good standard of living. Therefore, unions try to prevent the undervaluation of jobs.

Job evaluation committees help ensure commitment from employees throughout companies. They also provide a checks-and-balances system. Job evaluation procedures are not scientifically accurate because these evaluation decisions are based on ordinary human judgment. Therefore, a consensus of several employees helps to minimize the biases of individual job evaluators.

Training Employees to Conduct Job Evaluations

Individuals should understand the process objectives. Besides knowing company objectives, evaluators also should practice using the chosen job evaluation criteria before applying them to actual jobs. Similar to job analysis procedures, evaluators should base their decisions on sound job- and business-related rationales to ensure legal compliance.

Documenting the Job Evaluation Plan

Documenting the job evaluation plan is useful for legal and training purposes. From an employer's perspective, a well-documented evaluation plan clearly specifies job- and business-related criteria against which jobs are evaluated. Well-documented plans can allow employees to understand clearly how their jobs were evaluated and the outcome of the process. In addition, well-documented plans provide guidelines for clarifying ambiguities in the event of employee appeals or legal challenges.

Communicating with Employees

Job evaluation results matter personally to all employees. Companies must formally communicate with employees throughout the job analysis and evaluation processes to ensure employees' understanding and acceptance of the job evaluation process and results. Information sessions and memoranda are useful media. Not only should employers share basic information but also employees should be given the opportunity to respond to what they believe are either unsatisfactory procedures or inaccurate outcomes of the job evaluation process.

Setting Up the Appeals Process

Companies should set up appeals procedures that permit reviews on a case-by-case basis to provide a check on the process through reexamination. Such appeals reduce charges of illegal discrimination that would be more likely to occur if employees were not given a voice. Usually, compensation professionals review employees' appeals. Increasingly, companies process appeals through committees made up of compensation professionals and a representative sample of employees and supervisors. Grievants are more likely to judge appeals decisions as fair if committees are involved: Committee decisions should reflect the varied perspectives of participants rather than the judgment of one individual.

JOB EVALUATION TECHNIQUES

Compensation professionals categorize job evaluation methods as either market-based evaluation or job-content evaluation techniques. **Market-based evaluation** plans use market data to determine differences in job worth. Many companies choose market-based evaluation methods because they wish to assign job pay rates that are neither too low nor too high relative to the market. Setting pay rates too low will make it difficult to recruit talented candidates, and setting pay rates too high will result in an excessive cost burden for the employer. Compensation professionals rely on compensation surveys to determine prevailing pay rates of jobs in the relevant labor market. We address that issue in Chapter 8.

Job-content evaluation plans emphasize the company's internal value system by establishing a hierarchy of internal job worth based on each job's role in company strategy. Compensation professionals review preliminary structures for consistency with market pay rates on a representative sample of jobs known as benchmark jobs.

Ultimately, compensation professionals must balance external market considerations with internal consistency objectives. In practice, compensation professionals judge the adequacy of pay differentials by comparing both market rates and pay differences among jobs within their companies. They consult with the top HR official and chief financial officer when discrepancies arise, particularly if company pay rates are generally lower than the market rates. Upon careful consideration of the company's financial resources and the strategic value of the jobs in question, these executives decide whether to adjust internal pay rates for jobs with below-market pay rates.

Neither market-based nor job-content evaluation approaches alone enable compensation professionals to balance internal and external considerations. Therefore, most companies rely on both approaches. The point method is the most popular job-content method because it gives compensation professionals better control over balancing internal and market considerations. Chapter 8 fully addresses how compensation professionals combine point method results with market approaches. However, a brief overview follows our discussion of the point method in this chapter.

The Point Method

The **point method** is a job-content valuation technique that uses quantitative methodology. Quantitative methods assign numerical values to compensable factors that describe jobs, and these values are summed as an indicator of the overall value for the job. The relative worth of jobs is established by the magnitude of the overall numerical value for the jobs.

The point method evaluates jobs by comparing compensable factors. Each factor is defined and assigned a range of points based on the factor's relative value to the company. Compensable factors are weighted to represent the relative importance of each factor to the job. Job evaluation committees follow seven steps to complete the point method.

Step 1: Select Benchmark Jobs

Point method job evaluations use benchmark jobs to develop factors and their definitions to select jobs to represent the entire range of jobs in the company. **Benchmark jobs,** found outside the company, provide reference points against which jobs within the company are judged. Table 7-10 lists the characteristics of benchmark jobs [6].

Step 2: Choose Compensable Factors Based on Benchmark Jobs

Managers must define compensable factors that adequately represent the scope of jobs slated for evaluation. Each benchmark job should be described by these factors that help distinguish it from the value of all other jobs. Besides the "universal" factors—skill, effort, responsibility, and working conditions—additional factors may be developed to the extent that they are job- and business-related.

Compensable factor categories may be broken down further into specific related factors or subfactors. For example, skill may include job knowledge, education, mental ability, physical ability, accuracy, and dexterity. Effort may include factors relating to both physical and mental exertion. Responsibility may include considerations related to fiscal, material, or personnel responsibilities. Working conditions may be unpleasant because of extreme temperatures or possible exposure to hazardous chemicals.

How many compensable factors should companies use? It depends. Compensation professionals should select as many compensable factors as are needed to adequately describe the range of benchmark jobs.

Step 3: Define Factor Degrees

Although compensable factors describe the range of benchmark jobs, individual jobs vary in scope and content. Therefore, evaluators must divide each factor into a sufficient number of degrees to identify the level of a factor present in each job. Table 7-11 illustrates a factor definition for writing ability and its degree statements. Degree definitions should set forth and limit the meaning of each degree so that evaluators can uniformly interpret job descriptions. It is generally helpful to include a few actual work examples as anchors.

The number of degrees will vary based on the comprehensiveness of the plan. For example, if the plan covers only a limited segment of jobs such as clerical employees, fewer degrees will be required than if the plan covered every group of employees. Take education as an example. Only two degrees may be necessary to describe the educational requirements for clerical jobs—high school diploma or equivalent and an associate's degree. More than two degrees would be required to adequately describe the educational requirements for administrative, production, managerial, and professional

TABLE 7-10 Characteristics of Benchmark Jobs

1. The contents are well-known, relatively stable over time, and agreed upon by the employees involved.
2. The jobs are common across a number of different employers.
3. The jobs represent the entire range of jobs that are being evaluated within a company.
4. The jobs are generally accepted in the labor market for the purposes of setting pay levels.

Source: Milkovich, G. T., and Newman, J. M. (1996). *Compensation* (5th ed.) Homewood, IL: Irwin.

TABLE 7-11 Writing Ability: Factor Definition and Degree Statements

Definition	Capacity to communicate with others in written form.
First Degree	Print simple phrases and sentences, using normal work order and present and past tenses.
Sample Anchor	Prints shipping labels for packages, indicating the destination and the contents of the packages.
Second Degree	Write compound and complex sentences, using proper end punctuation and adjectives and adverbs.
Sample Anchor	Fills requisitions, work orders, or requests for materials, tools, or other stock items.
Third Degree	Write reports and essays with proper format, punctuation, spelling, and grammar, using all parts of speech.
Sample Anchor	Types letters, reports, or straight-copy materials from rough draft or corrected copy.
Fourth Degree	Prepare business letters, expositions, summaries, and reports, using prescribed format and conforming to all rules of punctuation, grammar, diction, and style.
Sample Anchor	Composes letters in reply to correspondence concerning such items as request for merchandise, damage claims, credit information, delinquent accounts, or to request information.
Fifth Degree	Write manuals or speeches.
Sample Anchor	Writes service manuals and related technical publications concerned with installation, operation, and maintenance of electronic, electrical, mechanical, and other equipment.

jobs—high school diploma or equivalent, associate's degree, bachelor's degree, master's degree, and doctorate. Most analyses anchor minimum and maximum degrees, with specific jobs representing these points.

Step 4: Determine the Weight of Each Factor

Weighting compensable factors represents the importance of the factor to the overall value of the job. The weights of compensable factors usually are expressed as percentages. Weighting often is done by management or by a job evaluation committee's decision. All of the factors are ranked according to their relative importance, and final weights are assigned after discussion and consensus. For example, let's assume the relative importance of skill, effort, responsibility, and working conditions to ABC Manufacturing Corporation:

- Skill is the most highly valued compensable factor, weighted at 60 percent.
- Responsibility is the next most important factor, weighted at 25 percent.
- Effort is weighted at 10 percent.
- The working conditions factor is least important, weighted at 5 percent.

Step 5: Determine Point Values for Each Compensable Factor

Compensation professionals set point values for each compensable factor in three stages. First, they must establish the maximum possible point values for the complete set of compensable factors. This total number is arbitrary, but it represents the possible maximum value jobs can possess. As a rule of thumb, the total point value for a set of compensable factors should be determined by a simple formula—the number of compensable factors times 250. ABC Manufacturing sets 1,000 (4 compensable factors × 250) as the possible maximum number of points.

Second, the maximum possible point value for each compensable factor is based on total weight as described in Step 4. Again, for ABC Manufacturing, skill equals 60 percent, responsibility equals 25 percent, effort equals 10 percent, and working conditions equals 5 percent:

- The maximum possible total points for skills equal 600 points (60% × 1,000 points).
- The maximum possible total points for responsibility equal 250 points (25% × 1,000 points).
- The maximum possible total points for effort equal 100 points (10% × 1,000 points).
- The maximum possible total points for working conditions equal 50 points (5% × 1,000 points).

Third, compensation professionals distribute these points across degree statements within each compensable factor. The point progression by degrees from the lowest to the highest point value advances arithmetically—that is, a scale of even incremental values. This characteristic is essential for conducting regression analysis—a statistical analysis method that we address in Chapter 8 in the discussion of integrating internal job structures (based on job evaluation points) with external pay rates for benchmark jobs.

How do compensation professionals assign point values to each degree? Let's illustrate this procedure by example, using the skill compensable factor. Let's also assume that the skill factor has five degree statements. Degree 1 represents the most basic skill level, and degree 5 represents the most advanced skill level. The increment from one degree to the next highest is 120 points (600 point maximum/5 degree statements).

- Degree 1 = 120 points (120 points × 1)
- Degree 2 = 240 points (120 points × 2)
- Degree 3 = 360 points (120 points × 3)
- Degree 4 = 480 points (120 points × 4)
- Degree 5 = 600 points (120 points × 5)

Step 6: Verify Factor Degrees and Point Values

Committee members should independently calculate the point values for a random sample of jobs. Table 7-12 shows a sample job evaluation worksheet. After calculating the point values for this sample, committee members should review the point totals for each job. Committee members give careful consideration to whether the hierarchy of jobs makes sense in the context of the company's strategic plan, as well as to the inherent content of the jobs. For instance, sales jobs should rank relatively high on the job hierarchy within a sales-oriented company such as the pharmaceuticals industry. Research scientist jobs ought to rank relatively high for a company that pursues a differentiation strategy. Messenger jobs should not rank more highly than claims analyst jobs in an insurance company. In short, where peculiarities are apparent, committee members reconsider compensable factor definitions, weights, and actual ratings of the benchmark jobs.

Step 7: Evaluate All Jobs

Committee members evaluate all jobs in the company once the evaluation system has been tested and refined. Each job then is evaluated by determining which degree definition best fits the job and by assigning the corresponding point factors. All points are totaled for each job, and all jobs are ranked according to their point values.

TABLE 7-12 Sample Job Evaluation Worksheet

Job Title: ____________
Evaluation Date: ____________
Name of Evaluator: ____________

Compensable Factor			***Degree***			***Total***
	1	***2***	***3***	***4***	***5***	
Skill						
Mental skill	60	120	180	240	(300)	300
Manual skill	60	(120)	180	240	300	120
Effort						
Mental effort	10	20	30	40	(50)	50
Physical effort	10	20	(30)	40	50	30
Responsibility						
Supervisory	25	50	(75)	100	125	75
Department budgeting	(25)	50	75	100	125	25
Working conditions						
Hazards	10	20	30	(40)	50	40
Total job value						640

Balancing Internal and Market Considerations Using the Point Method

How do compensation professionals balance internal and market considerations with point method results? They convert point values into the market value of jobs through regression analysis, a statistical technique. As we discuss in Chapter 8, regression analysis enables compensation professionals to set base pay rates in line with market rates for benchmark or representative jobs. Companies identify market pay rates through compensation surveys. Of course, a company's value structure for jobs based on the point method will probably differ somewhat from the market pay rates for similar jobs. Regression analysis indicates base pay rates that minimize the differences between the company's point method results and the market pay rates.

Alternative Job-Content Evaluation Approaches

Most other job-content approaches use qualitative methods. Qualitative methods evaluate entire jobs and typically compare jobs to each other or some general criteria. Usually, these criteria are vague—for example, importance of jobs to departmental effectiveness. The prevalent kinds of qualitative job evaluation techniques include:

- Simple ranking plans
- Paired comparisons
- Alternation ranking
- Classification plans

Simple Ranking Plans

Simple ranking plans order all jobs from lowest to highest according to a single criterion, such as job complexity or the centrality of the job to the company's competitive strategy. This approach considers each job in its entirety, usually in small companies that have relatively few employees. In large companies that classify many jobs, members of job evaluation committees independently rank jobs on a departmental basis. Different rankings will likely result. When this occurs, job evaluation committees discuss the differences in rankings and choose one set of rankings by consensus.

Paired Comparison and Alternation Ranking

Two common variations of the ranking plan are paired comparison and alternation ranking. The **paired comparison** technique is useful if there are many jobs to rate, usually more than 20. Job evaluation committees generate every possible pair of jobs. For each pair, committee members assign a point to the job with the highest value, and the lowest-value job does not receive a point. After evaluating each pair, the evaluator sums the points for each job. Jobs with higher points are more valuable than jobs with fewer points. The job with the most points is ranked the highest; the job with the fewest points is ranked the lowest.

The **alternation ranking** method orders jobs by extremes. Yet again, committee members judge the relative value of jobs according to a single criterion, such as job complexity or the centrality of the job to the company's competitive strategy. This ranking process begins by determining which job is the most valuable, followed by determining which job is the least valuable. Committee members then judge the next most valuable job and the next least valuable job. This process continues until all jobs have been evaluated.

Despite the simplicity of ranking plans, they exhibit three limitations. First, ranking results rely on purely subjective data; the process lacks objective standards, guidelines, and principles that would aid in resolving differences of opinion among committee members. Companies usually do not fully define their ranking criteria. For example, the criterion job complexity can be defined as level of education or as number of distinct tasks that the workers must perform daily.

Second, ranking methods use neither job analyses nor job descriptions, which makes this method difficult to defend legally. Committee members rely on their own impressions of the jobs.

Third, ranking approaches do not incorporate objective scales that indicate how different in value one job is from another. For instance, let's assume that a committee decides on the following ranking for training and development professionals (listed from most valuable to least valuable):

- Director of training and development
- Manager of training and development
- Senior training and development specialist
- Training and development specialist
- Training and development assistant

Rankings do not offer standards for compensation professionals to facilitate answering such questions as "Is the director of training and development job worth four times as much as the training and development assistant job?" Compensation professionals' inability to answer such questions makes it difficult to establish pay levels according to job content differences.

Classification Plans

Companies use **classification plans** to place jobs into categories based on compensable factors. Public sector organizations, such as civil service systems, use classification systems most prevalently. The federal government's classification system is a well-known example. As we discussed in Chapter 4, the General Schedule classifies federal government jobs into 15 classifications (GS-1 through GS-15) based on such factors as skill,

TABLE 7-13 Federal Government Factor Evaluation System

1. Knowledge required by the position
   a. Nature or kind of knowledge and skills needed
   b. How the skills and knowledge are used in doing the work
2. Supervisory controls
   a. How the work is assigned
   b. The employee's responsibility for carrying out the work
   c. How the work is reviewed
3. Guidelines
   a. The nature of guidelines for performing the work
   b. The judgment needed to apply the guidelines or develop new guides
4. Complexity
   a. The nature of the assignment
   b. The difficulty in identifying what needs to be done
   c. The difficulty and originality involved in performing the work
5. Scope and effect
   a. The purpose of the work
   b. The impact of the work product or service
6. Personal contacts
7. Purpose of contacts
8. Physical demands
9. Work environment

Source: U.S. Civil Service Commission. (1977). *Instructions for the factor evaluation system.* Washington, DC: U.S. Government Printing Office.

education, and experience levels. In addition, jobs that require high levels of specialized education (for example, a physicist), significantly influence public policy (for example, law judges), or require executive decision making are classified in separate categories: Senior Level (SL) positions, Scientific & Professional (SP) positions, and the Senior Executive Service (SES).

The federal government uses its factor evaluation system (FES) job evaluation methodology to classify most government jobs in the General Schedule. Jobs are evaluated based on nine general compensable factors. Four of the compensable factors have subfactors. Table 7-13 lists these factors and subfactors.

The GS classification system enables the federal government to set pay rates for thousands of unique jobs based on 18 classes. Pay administration is relatively simple because pay rates depend on GS level and the employees' relevant work seniority, as we discussed in Chapter 4. The most noteworthy disadvantage is the absence of regular procedures for rewarding exceptional performance, which, ultimately, discourages employees from working as productively as possible.

Alternatives to Job Evaluation

Compensation professionals assign pay rates to jobs in numerous ways other than through the job evaluation process as previously defined. These alternate methods include reliance on market pay rates, pay incentives, individual rates, and collective bargaining. Many companies determine the value of jobs by paying the average rate in the external labor market. The procedures for assessing market rates are addressed fully in Chapter 8.

Besides the market pay rate, pay incentives may also be the basis for establishing the core compensation for jobs. As we discussed extensively in Chapter 5, incentives

FLIP SIDE OF THE COIN

JOB EVALUATION HINDERS COMPETITIVE ADVANTAGE

Earlier, we indicated that job evaluation has strategic value. However, not everybody holds that view. Opponents of job evaluation argue that the development of internally consistent compensation structures may be detrimental to the attainment of competitive advantage.

The primary focus in traditional point-factor plans (that is, point plans) is internal equity across all jobs in the organization. It is difficult to determine what is internal equity beyond functional areas with consistent agreement among employees and managers. The "line of sight" for internal equity among employees, who need to believe the program is credible, is within functional areas (for example, within marketing, within manufacturing, within human resources, within engineering) rather than between them. Trying to create internal equity across functions is subject to individual interpretation and potential disagreement and therefore reduces the likelihood of program acceptance.

Often organizations complain that employees are too focused on internal equity and cannot be refocused. As long as the organization keeps a job evaluation system that attempts to create internal equity across the entire organization, however, the organization is communicating to employees to focus on internal equity. In this case, the job evaluation system and the focus of pay need to change so that they are able to refocus on what is important to the organization—results and organizational success.

Source: Schuster, J. R., & Zingheim, P. K. (1992). *The New Pay: Linking Employee and Organizational Performance*. New York: Lexington Books, pp. 121–122.

tie part or all of an employee's core compensation to the attainment of a predetermined performance objective. Next, both core and fringe compensation may be determined through negotiations between an individual and an employer. Typically, the employer uses the market rate as a basis for negotiations, agreeing to higher pay if the supply of talented individuals is scarce and the individual in question has an established track record of performance. Finally, when unions are present, pay rates are established through the collective bargaining process, which we already considered in Chapter 3.

INTERNALLY CONSISTENT COMPENSATION SYSTEMS AND COMPETITIVE STRATEGY

To this point, we have examined the principles of internally consistent compensation systems and the rationale for building them. Moreover, we reviewed the key processes—job analysis and job evaluation—that lead to internally consistent compensation systems. Although we made the case for building internally consistent pay systems, these systems do have some limitations.

Internally consistent pay systems may reduce a company's flexibility to respond to changes in competitors' pay practices because job analysis leads to structured job descriptions and job structures. In addition, job evaluation establishes the relative worth of jobs within the company. Responding to the competition may require employees to engage in duties that extend beyond what's written in their job descriptions whenever competitive pressures demand. In the process, the definitions of jobs become more fluid, which makes equity assessments more difficult.

Another potential limitation of internally consistent compensation structures is the resultant bureaucracy. Companies that establish job hierarchies tend to create narrowly defined jobs that lead to greater numbers of jobs and staffing levels [7]. Such structures promote heavy compensation burdens. Employees' core compensation depends on the jobs they perform, how well they perform their jobs, or the skills they possess. However, employee benefits (Chapters 10 and 11) represent fixed costs that typically do not vary with employees' job duties, their performances, or their skills.

SUMMARY

This chapter discussed internally consistent pay systems and described two important tools HR and compensation professionals use to build them—job analysis and job evaluation. Job analysis represents a descriptive process that enables HR professionals to systematically describe job duties, worker specifications, and job context. Compensation professionals use job evaluation to assess the relative worth of jobs within companies. Job analysis and job evaluation are an art because they require the HR and compensation professionals' sound judgments. We discussed the strategic role that job analysis and job evaluation play in companies' quests for competitive advantage. However, we also pointed out some of the shortcomings of these approaches. Compensation professionals must carefully weigh the possible benefits and consequences of these methods in attaining competitive advantage.

Key Terms

- internally consistent compensation systems, 194
- job analysis, 194
- job content, 194
- worker requirements, 197
- working conditions, 197
- major occupational groups, 199
- reliable job analysis, 200
- valid job analysis, 201
- job descriptions, 201
- job titles, 201
- job summary, 201
- job duties, 202
- worker specification, 202
- education, 202
- Equal Employment Opportunity Commission, 202
- skill, 202
- ability, 202
- knowledge, 202
- Occupational Information Network, 204
- content model, 204
- experience and training, 205
- licensing, 205
- occupation requirements, 205
- generalized work activities, 205
- organizational context, 205
- work context, 206
- occupation specific requirements, 206
- occupation characteristics, 206
- worker characteristics, 206
- abilities, 206
- interests, 206
- work styles, 206
- basic skills, 211
- cross-functional skills, 211
- O*NET User's Guide, 211
- O*NET database, 211
- job evaluation, 214
- compensable factors, 215
- universal compensable factors, 215
- market-based evaluation, 217
- job-content evaluation, 217
- point method, 217
- benchmark jobs, 218
- simple ranking plans, 221
- paired comparison, 222
- alternation ranking, 222
- classification plans, 222

Discussion Questions

1. Discuss the differences between job analysis and job evaluation. How do these practices help establish internally consistent job structures?
2. Conduct a job analysis of a person you know, and write a complete job description (no longer than one page) according to the principles described in this chapter. In class, be prepared to discuss the method you used for conducting the job analysis and some of the challenges you encountered.
3. This chapter provides rationale for conducting job analysis, and it indicates some of the limitations. Take a stand for or against the use of job analysis, and provide convincing arguments for your position.

4. Respond to the statement "Building an internally consistent job structure is burdensome to companies. Instead, it is best to simply define and evaluate the worth of jobs by surveying the market."
5. Do you consider job evaluation to be an art or a science? Please explain.

Exercises

Compensation Online

For Students

Exercise 1: Find relevant journal articles

Your professor has asked you to write an essay explaining why internal consistency is important from the company standpoint. Use your school library's online catalog to locate articles pertaining to job evaluation and job analysis. Find and read several current articles in these areas.

Exercise 2: Research online job search sites

As a student, you are no doubt currently looking for a job, or will be soon. This exercise will be useful in that regard but also will help you understand one of the topics covered in this chapter. Part of Chapter 7 focuses on job descriptions. One way to determine how businesses view the responsibilities it assigns to its employees is to examine how they choose to describe a position when they recruit to fill it. Go onto a job search site such as Monster at *www.monster.com* or Job Trak at *www2.jobtrak.com*. Review the descriptions companies provide for the openings they have, and answer the following questions: How thorough are the descriptions? How would you change the descriptions if you had to write them? Do you get a sense of how much the companies value the positions by reading the descriptions? Are the companies clear about the minimal qualifications they want the applicants to have?

Exercise 3: Calculate geographic pay differences

As a job seeker, the following exercise will help you understand what to expect and what you can ask for when it comes time to determine your salary. One of the major variables to consider is the cost of living differences between cities, which are, in part, based on their geographic location. Using these two different Web sites, calculate geographic differences in pay for the same two cities.

www.homefair.com:80/homefair/cmr/salcalc.html

www.datamasters.com

You can also use a search engine and search for "salary calculator." Are the numbers the same for each Web site? Why or why not? Take into consideration the validity of each Web site.

For Professionals

Exercise 1: Keep informed on current events related to human resources

As a human resources professional, it is important to keep abreast of current issues and developments. One site that will allow you to do this is the Web site for the Society for Industrial and Organizational Psychology. Click on their Web address at *www.siop.org/*

Click on SIOP Search and type in "job analysis." How many resources were available? Choose one, and write a brief abstract on the article.

Exercise 2: Research job evaluation methods

Conduct an advanced search for "job evaluation." Look for Web pages that allow you to look at and even fill out sample questionnaires or analysis forms. Put yourself in the place of an HR professional in a specific company. How would you adapt the questionnaire based on the material contained in this chapter?

Exercise 3: Write a job description

Conduct an advanced search for "job descriptions." Visit some of the resulting Web sites and view sample job descriptions. Identify the kind of information that is important, and then think of your current job or one you would like to hold as your career develops. Write a job description for yourself based on the samples you viewed on the Internet.

Endnotes

1. Harvey, R. J. (1991). Job analysis. In M. D. Dunnette & L. M. Hough (Eds.), *Handbook of Industrial and Organizational Psychology* (vol. 2). Palo Alto, CA: Consulting Psychologists Press.
2. U.S. Department of Labor. (1991). *The Revised Handbook for Analyzing Jobs*. Washington, DC: Government Printing Office.
3. U.S. Department of Labor. (1991). *The Dictionary of Occupational Titles*. Washington, DC: Government Printing Office.
4. U.S. Department of Labor, Employment and Training Administration. (2002). O*NET. Washington, DC: Government Printing Office [online]. Available: *http://www.doleta.gov*, accessed July 1, 2002.
5. Peterson, N. G., Mumford, M. D., Borman, W. C., Jeanneret, P. R., & Fleishman, E. A. (1999). *An Occupational Information System for the 21st Century: The Development of O*NET*. Washington, DC: American Psychological Association.
6. Milkovich, G. T., & Newman, J. M. (1996). *Compensation* (5th ed.). Homewood, IL: Richard D. Irwin.
7. Lawler, E. E., III. (1986). What's wrong with point-factor job evaluation? *Compensation and Benefits Review, 18*, pp. 20–28.

COMPENSATION IN ACTION

REFOCUSING JOB DESCRIPTIONS

Some employers are changing or replacing formal job descriptions in an attempt to focus on competencies that don't change, rather than skills that do.

"And other duties as assigned." Those can be five sweet words to harried HR departments too busy to keep job descriptions up to date. But the familiar catchall also can be a trap, lulling HR and supervisors into neglecting job descriptions. And neglect might seem easier than wrestling descriptions into shape in these days when volatile markets, new technologies and staff shortages can put HR on a nonstop merry-go-round of description changes.

To address these issues, some employers are refocusing job descriptions to make them more realistic and easier to update.

Some companies still use job descriptions that call for narrow matches between specific skills and required tasks. But others have shifted from basing descriptions on skills to basing them on the role the position plays. Some employers also use performance goals to augment role descriptions—creating descriptions that those employers say are as flexible as each project's new demands but still can withstand legal challenges.

BLUEPRINTS FOR PERFORMANCE

Traditional job descriptions range from outlines that merely cover generalities to finely turned blueprints that detail specific duties and how employees will perform them, the exact percentage of time employees will spend on each task, and what equipment they will use. Many descriptions also contain educational requirements, mandatory skills, and years of experience that dictate pay levels and promotion possibilities.

Altering descriptions can draw employees' skepticism. "Employees can feel that 'This is a management tactic to get me to do more work without paying me for it,' or that their job will be difficult to define," says Rick Powers, SPHR, vice president of HR with Nextview Technologies in Cary, N.C. "Some employees will never be satisfied without that three-page description."

Descriptions do have plenty of uses. "Job descriptions are needed for hiring and performance reviews, to determine an employee's ability to do a job and to define working conditions for regulatory requirements like the [Americans with Disabilities Act]," says Maria Fisher-Proulx, principal of Future Directives LLC, an HR consulting firm in Cheshire, Conn.

Job descriptions also can give clear career guidance to employees, according to Jean Rall, chief operating officer of New York–based IHS Help Desk, a division of Leveraged Technology that assists industries in using computers as business tools.

Rall says that job descriptions may not be necessary in a very small company where job functions are shared among a team. "At one time, that description fit our company," says Rall.

At first, IHS Help Desk found that giving employees verbal job descriptions when they were hired worked well enough. "There was a feeling that each of our clients would require something different, so why bother writing job descriptions?" Rall says.

"Then we started hearing employees say during exit interviews, 'I got hired to do this and I do it well, but you haven't provided me with any vision about what I'm doing next,' " Rall continues. "Employees didn't see a professional identity or career path and we couldn't manage employee expectations." Rall attributes an increased turnover to these and other problems and says the new job descriptions are helping IHS Help Desk hang onto more employees.

Rall believes that job descriptions provide clear expectations and responsibilities and give employees a vision of the opportunities available. "We don't set these structures up to restrain people. Job descriptions help develop careers," Rall says. "Supervisors need to know the differences between entry level and intermediate, and what the employee needs to do to move up; and employees can be prepared for other options that come along."

Employers that have used job descriptions for years agree that descriptions help with employee expectations and management planning but add that employers need options too. One option is moving away from skill-based descriptions and toward "job roles," focused on broader abilities, that are easier to alter as technologies and customer needs change.

MOVING FROM SKILLS TO ROLES

Job descriptions won't do much to help develop employees' careers if the descriptions no longer reflect their true duties, notes Jeff Standridge, organizational development leader for Acxiom Corp. in Little Rock, Ark. When Standridge arrived, the technology company was using a form of job description called skill blocks. Skill blocks delineated various levels through which employees could move for advancement and listed the skills employees were required to have at each level.

Under the skill block method, employees who wanted to advance from one level of a job to a higher level found that they had to document skills that were irrelevant to what they actually did, or were obsolete in their rapidly changing environment. A common complaint from employees was, "My job has evolved faster than my skill blocks," says Standridge. Information technology changes so fast that maintaining skill block descriptions was difficult.

The company moved to replace skill blocks with job roles and competency models. "Roles and competency models don't become outdated so quickly," says Standridge. "They describe what you do functionally. They don't describe who you are or where you sit within the org chart.

"Most companies cluster a group of related skills together and call it a competency," he adds. A communications competency, for example, would probably include common skills like writing, speaking, and making presentations.

"To change those [communications competencies] to behavior statements, upon which our job roles and competency models are based, you might say the person actively listens, builds trust, and adapts his style and tactics to fit the audience," Standridge says. "These behaviors won't change, even as the means of executing them evolve with technology."

To define job roles, the company examined the successful behaviors of its good performers. Standridge says, "When we asked a panel, 'What makes this employee a successful software developer?' the first answer would be, 'Well, he knows Java and C++, etc.' " Recognizing that these languages could become obsolete, he probed to discover what really made the developer successful in that position.

"When we asked, 'If Java becomes obsolete in 5 years, will this person no longer be successful?' The panel responded, 'Oh, no, he'll update his skills and be great in the new language,' " says Standridge. The employee's strength was not just in his specific skills but in his ability to learn. "What we did was move beyond skills to behaviorally anchored competencies like self-directed learning," Standridge says.

The company now uses very brief descriptions, along with a few statements that describe overall responsibilities, to nail down the essence of a role.

Specific expectations set by individual managers define the skills, such as knowledge of certain computer languages, that employees need in each position. Standridge emphasizes that those skills are not permanent parts of the job role.

GIVING PERFORMANCE MORE WEIGHT

Powers is another user of job roles, which he says have greater longevity and flexibility than descriptions. That flexibility also can reduce the tendency for employees to use the old "It's not in my job description" rationale to avoid work that seems to fall outside a formal description.

Powers adds that where an employer is not using traditional, skills-based job descriptions, a strong, frequently updated performance management system is critical in defining the specifics of an employee's work.

At Nextview, says Powers, "Seven brief sentences fit every manager in the company," and they typically are pithy and generic: "Supervises

(Continued)

(Continued)

at least two employees. . . . Implements policies, procedures, controls, and services. . . . Responsible for adherence to department budget guidelines."

What differentiates one type of manager from another are the specific functions required by each person's performance plan. "Each manager will need different skills to meet their specific goals," Powers says, noting that employees are measured against their performance in meeting goals, rather than whether or how they execute particular tasks.

Powers likens performance plans to "living" job descriptions. "The key is to have an accurate statement of what employees do so they can be fairly and equitably compensated, versus a job description that is perhaps revised once a year—and will be slow to reflect the changes that inevitably occur in jobs," he says.

In organizations reluctant to go as far as Nextview and Acxiom, the performance review process still can help management and HR keep existing job descriptions focused, Fisher-Proulx adds. Supervisors should review job duties and the description's accuracy during performance reviews to ensure that performance goals and descriptions mesh, she says.

CAUTIONS ABOUT CHANGE

Powers has a caution for companies considering changes to their job description structure: If your workplace is unionized, remember to consult with labor lawyers and the union before making any moves.

Many bargaining units have contracts specifying that employees have a tenure track and learn jobs through apprenticeship, Powers says. In such cases, the union and management need clearly defined terms and descriptions.

Unions typically direct their job-description efforts toward setting defined boundaries for positions, usually wanting to define the work that employees can perform within specific job classification, adds Dale Deitchler, a partner with the law firm Rider, Bennett, Egan, and Arundel in Minneapolis. Doing without job descriptions in a union environment, or not updating them, can give the union ammunition for contract violation grievances if, for example, supervisors appear to be doing work that belongs to bargaining unit members, he says.

Employers also must be careful about changes if jobs require certifications or other restrictions. For example, many medical jobs require licenses, and some financial jobs require certain training and certifications. Descriptions, roles, or other variations need to include these restrictions.

CONSIDER LEGAL IMPLICATIONS

Deitchler also advises employers who are interested in what he calls "free form or generic job descriptions" to weigh the benefits they offer against some potential legal risks.

"Newer, quicker-growing start-up companies in rapidly changing industries simply may not be able to accurately describe job expectations—or expectations that are meaningful for more than a few days," says Deitchler. "Almost by necessity, job descriptions within those types of organizations need to be worded loosely."

But any employer considering alterations to job descriptions, and especially an employer doing without any written descriptions, also should remember that descriptions have legal uses, Deitchler says.

"A job description can be a tool to discourage a disgruntled employee from later legally challenging an employer's actions," says Deitchler. "If an employee has an objective standard against which to measure his or her performance, and knows that the standard has not been achieved, he or she may be less likely to file suit."

Deitchler suggests job descriptions can be a strong defense against many kinds of claims, including those involving discrimination, negligence, retaliation, and the Americans with Disabilities Act.

Employers can use job descriptions to identify and establish the essential functions of the job, functions that become key in determining if a disabled employee can do the job.

In defending against discrimination claims, Deitchler says, an employer trying to show that an employee violated performance or behavior standards might need a written description to identify those standards.

And Equal Pay Act cases may be hard to defend if there are no descriptions that identify specific skill, effort, and responsibility levels.

Deitchler also describes cases in which employers defended themselves against employees' negligence claims by citing job descriptions. "A hospital defended itself in a case where psychologists [at the hospital] were assaulted by contending that the psychologists knew of the risk and danger of an assault because their written job description identified that risk," he says.

DUTIES TRUMP DESCRIPTIONS

While some form of written description can be a help if the employer faces a challenge, John Fraser, deputy administrator for the Department of Labor's Wage and Hour Division in Washington, D.C., emphasizes that investigators always will zero in on the work actually performed.

"We don't frown on the expression 'Other duties as assigned' nor do we require job descriptions," Fraser says. "With respect to the laws that we administer, job descriptions *per se* aren't relevant, and 'Other duties as assigned' is not a refuge. It's what people do, not what's on paper that matters."

Powers says experience has taught him that his system of job roles and living performance plans can stand up to legal challenges. The Wage and Hour Division investigated a Nextview employee's complaint about misclassification, and, Powers says, the job roles model prevailed.

The employee claimed he should have been classified as nonexempt and paid overtime, Powers says. The investigator asked for job descriptions, but Powers explained that he didn't have any. "I told her that I used role statements and then fleshed those out with specifics for each performance plan."

After the investigator asked for the department's performance plans, Powers was gratified when she told him that he had made life easier for her. "The investigator said that instead of looking at job descriptions—which didn't show what people do—I have her performance plans that showed exactly what people did." He successfully defended Nextview against the complaint.

Source: Carla Joinson, *HR Magazine* (2001), volume 46, number 1.

WHAT'S NEW IN COMPENSATION?

What Happens When Job Structures Change

Job descriptions are key building blocks in job structures. These descriptions convey information about various aspects of the job and necessary worker characteristics including job duties, reporting responsibilities, education, and experience requirements. As discussed in this chapter, job structures provide a basis for setting ranges of acceptable pay for jobs. Specific compensable factors help differentiate the relative worth of jobs, which ultimately translates into different pay amounts.

Many forces have an impact on job structures, including economic conditions and technology. When economic conditions are sluggish, companies often modify job structures by laying off workers, eliminating jobs, and combining job duties and responsibilities. These modifications often create larger workloads for employees who remain. As technology changes, so does the nature of work. Automobile technicians now use computers to diagnose engine malfunctions. In past decades, the operation of engines was based exclusively on mechanical components. Nowadays, complex electronic systems govern engine and drivetrain operation. For example, electronic stability control systems enable cars to safely maintain operations when encountering adverse road conditions. When these systems break down, automobile technicians interpret complex information to diagnose the source of malfunction.

The featured *New York Times* article describes changes in Time Inc., publisher of *Time* magazine, that have led to modifications of editor-at-large jobs. These jobs are based on very general job descriptions: "Find out where in the company you can do the best work you can." After a careful analysis of the contributions of editors-at-large, Time, Inc. decided to limit the scope of these jobs and to reduce pay befitting the limited job scope.

Log into your *New York Times* account. Search the database for articles on "downsizing," "technology," or "career management" to find articles that are likely to describe changes in company job structures. When reading these articles, think about whether there should be changes to pay as well as whether you agree or disagree with the company's actions. Following your course instructor's specific directions, be prepared to describe the current situation, and relate it to the article contained in this text. ■

The New York Times

MediaTalk; Time Inc. Reconsiders Some Coveted Positions

For several years, one of the most coveted jobs at Time Inc. has been editor-at-large. The job description is loose: "Find out where in the company you can do the best work you can," said one former editor-at-large.

The pay varies widely but can reach $300,000 a year, Time executives said. That is considered a pretty big salary, and one that produces relatively few editorial pages for the company, they added.

The payoff has always presumably been that the editors-at-large are considered a kind of brain trust for Time Inc., a squadron of senior advisors and chin-strokers available for provocative writing—and occasionally for troubleshooting.

The program has long been the project of Norman Pearlstine, the editor-in-chief of Time Inc. since 1994.

Now, as part of a reexamination of the bottom line, most of the editors-at-large have been encouraged by Mr. Pearlstine the last two weeks to renegotiate their deals with Time Inc. so that they are paid less.

Of the approximate dozen editors-at-large, it is expected that at least four will be eased out. Those who stay have been asked to concentrate on one magazine—for all intents and purposes becoming staff editors, not editors-at-large with all the wide-ranging freedom that job entailed.

Daniel Okrent is currently negotiating his arrangement as editor-at-large and may leave the company entirely, according to Time executives. Claire McHugh, the first editor of the American edition of *Maxim* magazine, is expected to stay and focus on *In Style* magazine, but plans for her women's magazine have been shelved. Roger Rosenblatt, who has written for *Sports Illustrated, Time* and *Life*, will now work on a contract basis for *Time*, rather than as a contributor to several magazines.

Danyel Smith, the former editor of *Vibe*, and Gregory Curtis, who writes for *Time* from Austin, Tex., are negotiating their status. Steve Lovelady, an editor-at-large, is expected to discuss his position with Mr. Pearlstine this week. (Last week, Steve Lopez, who wrote for *Time, People, Entertainment Weekly* and *Life*, resigned to join *The Los Angeles Times*, although executives said his departure was more closely linked to his dissatisfaction with the structure of the editor-at-large position and his desire to write a newspaper column.)

Donald L. Barlett and James B. Steele are expected to stay as editors-at-large.

Mr. Pearlstine had no comment. Peter Costiglio, a spokesman for Time Inc., confirmed that Mr. Pearlstine was having discussions with the editors-at-large. He said there had never been a fixed number of how many editors-at-large ought to be on staff.

"The number of editors-at-large has always been a number that is flexible and fungible," he said.

SOURCE: Alex Kuczynski, Media talk; Time Inc. reconsiders some coveted positions (April 2, 2001) [online]. Available: *www.nytimes.com,* accessed September 10, 2002.

CHAPTER

8 BUILDING MARKET-COMPETITIVE COMPENSATION SYSTEMS

Chapter Outline

Learning Objectives

In this chapter, you will learn about

1. Market-competitive compensation systems
2. Compensation surveys
3. Statistical analysis of compensation surveys
4. Integrating the internal job structure with external market pay rates
5. Compensation policies and strategic mandates

Companies rely on compensation surveys as a benchmark for setting pay and benefits to recruit highly qualified applicants and to retain valued employees. The number of salary surveys has risen with the popularity of the Internet. The "Compensation in Action" feature at the end of this chapter describes this phenomenon and offers suggestions for evaluating the quality of compensation survey information.

MARKET-COMPETITIVE PAY SYSTEMS: THE BASIC BUILDING BLOCKS

Market-competitive pay systems represent companies' compensation policies that fit the imperatives of competitive advantage. Market-competitive pay systems play a significant role in attracting and retaining the most qualified employees. Well-designed pay systems should promote companies' attainment of competitive strategies. Paying more than necessary can undermine lowest-cost strategies: Excessive pay levels represent an undue burden. Also, excessive pay restricts companies' abilities to invest in other important strategic activities—for example, research and development, training—because money is a limited resource. Companies that pursue differentiation strategies must strike a balance between offering sufficiently high salaries to attract and retain talented candidates and providing sufficient resources to enable them to be productively creative.

Compensation professionals create market-competitive pay systems based on four activities:

- Conducting strategic analyses
- Assessing competitors' pay practices with compensation surveys
- Integrating the internal job structure with external market pay rates
- Determining compensation policies

First, a **strategic analysis** entails an examination of a company's external market context and internal factors. Examples of external market factors include industry profile, information about competitors, and long-term growth prospects. Internal factors encompass financial condition and functional capabilities—for example, marketing and human resources. Refer to Chapter 2 for a detailed description of the components of strategic analysis.

Second, **compensation surveys** involve the collection and subsequent analysis of competitors' compensation data. Compensation surveys traditionally focused on competitors' wage and salary practices. More recently, fringe compensation has also become a target of surveys because benefits are a key element of market-competitive pay systems. Compensation surveys are important because they enable compensation professionals to obtain realistic views of competitors' pay practices. In the absence of compensation survey data, compensation professionals would have to use guesswork to try to build market-competitive compensation systems, and making too many wrong guesses could lead to noncompetitive compensation systems that undermine competitive advantage.

Third, compensation professionals integrate the internal job structure (Chapter 7) with the external market pay rates identified through compensation surveys. This integration results in pay rates that reflect both the company's and the external market's valuations of jobs. Most often, compensation professionals rely on regression analysis, a statistical method, to achieve this integration.

Finally, compensation professionals recommend pay policies that fit with their companies' standing and competitive strategies. As we discuss later in this chapter, compensation professionals must strike a balance between managing costs and attracting and retaining the best-qualified employees. Ultimately, top management makes compensation policy decisions after careful consideration of compensation professionals' interpretation of the data.

COMPENSATION SURVEYS

The second step compensation professionals undertake to assure external competitiveness is to consult or develop compensation surveys. Compensation surveys contain data about competing companies' compensation practices.

Preliminary Considerations

There are two important preliminary considerations compensation professionals take under advisement before investing time and money into compensation surveys:

- What companies hope to gain from compensation surveys
- Custom development versus use of an existing compensation survey

What Companies Hope to Gain from Compensation Surveys

Clarifying what companies hope to gain from compensation surveys is critical to developing effective compensation systems. Usually, compensation professionals want to learn about competitors' compensation practices and something about employees' preferences for alternative forms of compensation due to economic changes.

Information to be learned about competitors' compensation offerings includes base pay levels, incentive award structures, and both the mix and levels of discretionary benefits. Mix can be described as the percentage of employer compensation costs applied to compensation and benefits. For example, health insurance coverage accounts for 40 percent of total dollars spent on employee benefits. Levels refer to amounts actually or potentially paid to employees or beneficiaries. For instance, the average annual pay for day care workers is $13,000, and life insurance benefits are subject to a maximum payout of $250,000.

Compensation professionals wish to make sound decisions about pay levels based on what the competition pays its employees. Sound pay decisions promote companies' efforts to sustain competitive advantage, and poor pay decisions compromise competitive advantage. Compensation surveys enable compensation professionals to make sound judgments about how much to pay employees. Offering too little will limit a company's ability to recruit and retain high-quality employees. Paying well above the competition represents opportunity costs. Financial resources are limited. Therefore, companies cannot afford to spend money on everything they wish. Excessive pay represents an opportunity cost because it is money companies could have spent on other important matters.

Compensation professionals must also take into account employees' preferences for alternative forms of compensation amid changes in the economic climate. For instance:

> While stock options were the hot currency of the New Economy scarcely 12 months ago, employees today now regard cash—and freedom—as king, according to a new nationwide survey of working Americans. In the third annual BridgeGate Report, conducted in February 2001 by Market Facts TeleNation, Inc., of Atlanta for technology search firm *BridgeGate LLC*, employee retention is more likely to be influenced by salary increases than by improved benefits, flexible work schedules or stock options. A total of 682 part-time and full-time employees were asked which factors would be most likely to convince them to continue working for their current employer. The majority of respondents—slightly more than 50 percent—indicated that "a raise" would most influence them to remain with their present company, up from the 46 percent who cited a salary hike in last year's report. By contrast, just 40 percent of those surveyed placed non-monetary concerns ahead of increased pay. This year's survey marks the first time in the three-year history of the BridgeGate Report that significantly more respondents said they would remain at a job for higher compensation, over the combined total of respondents most interested in non-monetary offerings—benefits, flexibility, stock options and training. In perhaps the most significant finding of the report, fully 1 in 7 of those polled could not identify

any specific action employers could take to ensure retention, up from 1 in 16 two years ago. Stock options have taken a dive as a retention tool, thanks largely to a tumbling NASDAQ and diminished valuations of pre-IPO startups; just 7 percent of respondents placed stock options first, compared with 12 percent last year. The survey also recorded a small decrease in the number of workers who placed improved benefits at the top of their list. The latest BridgeGate Report did note a slight increase in the value of more flexible work schedules—14 percent in 2001, up from 12 percent in the year 2000 report. "Increasingly, people are again saying, 'show me the money,' I'll figure out the rest of my life on my own," said Dudley Brown, managing director, BridgeGate LLC.[1]

Custom Development Versus Use of an Existing Compensation Survey

Managers must decide whether to develop their own survey instruments and administer them or rely on the results of surveys conducted by others. In theory, customized surveys are preferable because the survey taker can tailor the questions the survey asks and select respondent companies to provide the most useful and informative data. Custom survey development should enable employers to monitor the quality of the survey developers' methodologies.

In practice, companies choose not to develop and implement their own surveys for three reasons. First, most companies lack employees qualified to undertake this task. Developing and implementing valid surveys requires specialized knowledge and expertise in sound questionnaire design, sampling methods, and statistical methods.

Second, rival companies are understandably reluctant to surrender information about their compensation packages to competitors because compensation systems are instrumental to competitive advantage issues. If companies are willing to cooperate, the information may be incomplete or inaccurate. For example, rival companies may choose to report the salaries for their lowest-paid accountants instead of the typical salary levels. Such information may lead the surveying company to set accountants' salaries much lower than if they had accurate, complete information about typical salary levels. Setting accountants' salaries too low may hinder recruitment efforts. Thus, custom development is potentially risky.

Third, custom survey development can be costly. Although cost figures are not readily available, it is reasonable to conclude that most companies use published survey data to minimize costs such as staff salaries and benefits (for those involved in developing a compensation survey as well as analyzing and interpreting the data), telephone and mail charges (depending upon the data collection method), and computers for data analyses.

Using Published Compensation Survey Data

Companies usually rely on existing compensation surveys rather than creating their own. Using published compensation survey data starts with two important considerations:

- Survey focus: core or fringe compensation
- Sources of published survey data

Survey Focus: Core or Fringe Compensation

Human resource professionals should decide whether to obtain survey information about base pay, employee benefits, or both. Historically, companies competed for employees mainly on the basis of base pay. Many companies offered similar, substantial benefits packages to employees without regard to the costs. Companies typically did not use benefits offerings to compete for the best employees.

Times have changed. Benefits costs are now extremely high, which has led to greater variability in benefits offerings among companies. As of March 2002, U.S. companies spent an average $9,547.20 per year per employee to provide discretionary benefits—for example, vacations and medical insurance coverage [2]. Such discretionary benefits accounted for approximately one-third of employers' total payroll costs. That is a huge cost to employers but one that cannot be avoided; benefits have become a basis for attracting and retaining the best employees. Consequently, employers are likely to use compensation surveys to obtain information about competitors' base pay and benefits practices so that they can compete effectively for the best candidates.

Sources of Published Compensation Surveys

Companies can obtain published survey data from various sources—professional associations, industry associations, consulting firms, and the federal government. Professional and industry associations survey members' salaries, compile the information in summary form, and disseminate the results to members. The survey data tend to be accurate because participants—as well as association members—benefit from the survey results. In addition, membership fees often entitle members to survey information at no additional cost.

For example, the Society for Industrial and Organizational Psychology's (SIOP) primary membership includes college and university faculty members and practitioners who specialize in such human resource management-related fields as selection, training, performance appraisal, and career development. SIOP periodically provides members' salary information based on gender, age, employment status (part-time versus full-time), years since earning degree, and geographic region according to metropolitan area (for example, Boston, San Francisco/San Jose, and Washington, DC). Employers use the survey results to judge whether they are paying employees too much or too little relative to the market and to determine how much to pay new hires. Employees use the survey results to judge the adequacy of job offers and to ask their deans for pay raises when their salaries fall below the market rates.

Professional associations that specialize in the field of compensation often conduct surveys that focus on broader types of employees and employers. WorldatWork (described on the inside of the front cover of this book) collects comprehensive data on an annual basis. The end-of-chapter appendix shows WorldatWork's 2002/2003 Total Salary Increase Budget Survey. As you will see, some of the survey topics include salary structures, promotions, and attraction and retention incentive practices.

Consulting firms are another source of compensation survey information. Some firms specialize on particular occupations (for example, engineers) or industries (for example, financial services); other firms do not. Examples of consulting firms that provide compensation services include Mercer Human Resource Consulting (*www.mercerhr.com*), Towers Perrin (*www.towers.com/towers*), and Watson Wyatt Worldwide (*www.watsonwyatt.com*). Clients may have two choices. First, consulting firms may provide survey data from recently completed surveys. Second, these firms may literally conduct surveys from scratch exclusively for a client's use. In most cases, the first option is less expensive to companies than the second option. However, the quality of the second option may be superior because the survey was custom-designed to answer a client's specific compensation questions.

The federal government is an invaluable source of compensation survey information. The U.S. Bureau of Labor Statistics (BLS) provides free salary surveys to the public. Highly qualified survey takers and statisticians are responsible for producing these surveys. Many factors contributed to the implementation of BLS pay and benefits surveys. The government began collecting compensation data in the 1890s to assess the effects of tariff legislation on wages and prices. Ever since, the government's survey programs have been rooted in competitive concerns.

Nowadays, the BLS conducts various surveys that provide the following types of information (the survey names are listed in parentheses):

- Wages (National Compensation Survey)
- Compensation cost trends (Employment Cost Index; Employer Costs for Employee Compensation)
- Benefits (National Compensation Survey)

The following summary of these programs was excerpted from the public domain BLS Web site (*www.bls.gov*). Survey data are available to the public on the Web site. There are no fees associated with accessing information from this Web site.

Wages

The **National Compensation Survey (NCS)** makes it easy to find information on occupational wages paid in or near your area. The data available (see Table 8–1) include:

- Average hourly wages for up to 480 occupations in more than 85 metropolitan and nonmetropolitan localities
- Weekly and annual earnings and hours for full-time workers
- Earnings by work level that permit wage comparisons across occupational groups
- Data presented at three levels: localities, broad regions, and the nation
- Workers as a total (all workers) and broken out by private industry and state and local government
- Wage data by industry, occupational group, full-time and part-time status, union and nonunion status, establishment size, time and incentive status, and job level

Compensation Cost Trends

The Employment Cost Index (ECI) is a quarterly measure of changes in labor costs. It is one of the principal economic indicators used by the Federal Reserve Bank. Some of its main features are that it:

- Shows changes in wages and salaries and benefit costs, as well as changes in total compensation
- Presents data as a total for all workers and separately for private industry and for state and local government workers
- Reports compensation changes by industry, occupational group, union and nonunion status, region, and metropolitan/nonmetropolitan status
- Provides seasonally adjusted and unadjusted data
- Presents historical data on changes in labor costs
- Uses fixed weights to control for shifts among occupations and industries

Why was the Employment Cost Index developed?

- The ECI was developed in the mid-1970s in response to the rapid acceleration of both wages and prices at that time.
- Monetary and fiscal policymakers needed a more accurate measure of the actual changes in employers' labor costs.
- The ECI was first published for the third quarter, September through December, of 1975.
- It was initially very limited, covering only wage and salary changes in private industry.

TABLE 8-1 Mean Hourly Earnings and Weekly Hours by Selected Characteristics, Private Industry and State and Local Government, United States, National Compensation Survey, 2000

Worker and Establishment Characteristics and Geographic Areas	Total		Private Industry		State and Local Government	
	Mean Hourly Earnings	Mean Weekly Hours	Mean Hourly Earnings	Mean Weekly Hours	Mean Hourly Earnings	Mean Weekly Hours
Total	$15.80	35.8	$15.08	35.7	$20.00	36.7
Worker characteristics:						
White-collar occupations	19.35	36.0	18.62	36.0	22.54	36.5
Professional specialty and technical	25.57	35.8	24.99	35.7	26.75	35.9
Executive, administrative, and managerial	28.37	40.0	28.64	40.3	27.03	38.6
Sales	13.40	33.0	13.41	33.0	13.01	32.7
Administrative support	12.55	36.4	12.50	36.4	12.81	36.5
Blue-collar occupations	13.41	38.2	13.30	38.2	15.45	37.6
Precision production, craft, and repair	17.01	39.6	16.97	39.6	17.64	39.8
Machine operators, assemblers, and inspectors	11.88	39.2	11.87	39.2	15.29	38.2
Transportation and material moving	13.31	37.3	13.19	37.7	14.30	34.1
Handlers, equipment cleaners, helpers, and laborers	10.15	35.8	10.01	35.7	12.75	38.5
Service occupations	9.59	31.8	8.28	30.7	14.97	36.8
Full time	16.66	39.6	15.97	39.8	20.41	38.8
Part time	9.06	20.5	8.69	20.6	13.46	19.4
Union	19.02	37.0	17.20	37.1	21.75	36.8
Nonunion	15.12	35.6	14.78	35.5	18.41	36.5
Time	15.57	35.7	14.76	35.6	20.00	36.7
Incentive	20.19	38.2	20.19	38.2	—	—
Establishment characteristics:						
Goods producing	—	—	16.37	39.5	—	—
Service producing	—	—	14.55	34.4	—	—
1 to 99 workers	13.71	34.7	13.67	34.7	16.14	35.8
100 to 499 workers	15.31	36.3	14.95	36.4	18.55	35.7
500 to 999 workers	17.58	36.9	16.74	37.1	20.32	36.0
1,000 to 2,499 workers	17.35	36.9	16.55	37.2	19.69	36.0
2,500 workers or more	21.44	37.3	22.10	37.0	20.90	37.6
Geographic areas:						
Metropolitan	16.08	35.7	15.37	35.6	20.76	36.6
Nonmetropolitan	13.22	37.0	11.89	37.1	16.68	36.8
New England	17.45	35.4	16.82	35.4	22.75	35.6
Middle Atlantic	18.25	34.7	17.40	34.6	23.02	35.3
East North Central	15.75	35.8	15.03	35.8	20.91	35.9
West North Central	14.99	35.3	14.22	35.0	19.19	37.2
South Atlantic	14.90	36.5	14.38	36.2	17.52	38.1
East South Central	12.64	37.0	12.08	37.0	16.93	36.7
West South Central	14.57	36.8	14.08	36.6	16.95	38.3
Mountain	14.67	35.6	13.81	35.3	19.51	36.9
Pacific	17.15	35.6	16.11	35.5	22.84	35.7

Source: U.S. Bureau of Labor Statistics. (2000). *National compensation survey* (Summary 01–04). Washington, DC: Author.

- Benefits and total compensation series were added in 1981.
- The ECI is being integrated into the NCS ECI Constant Dollar Time Series.
- It adjusts data for the current price level.
- It uses the Consumer Price Index for adjustment.

The Employer Costs for Employee Compensation (ECEC) product is an annual survey that shows employers' average hourly cost for total compensation and its components. As its key features it:

- Shows compensation costs as a total and broken out by (1) wages and salaries; (2) total benefit costs; (3) separate benefit costs for broad benefit categories such as paid leave, supplemental pay, insurance, retirement and savings, legally required benefits, and other benefits; or (4) separate benefit costs for detailed benefits such as paid holidays, health insurance, defined benefit pension, and workers' compensation
- Provides cost data in dollar amounts and as percentages of compensation
- Breaks out data on civilian workers into estimates for white-collar, blue-collar, and service groups or state and local government workers into estimates for white-collar workers, service occupations, and service industries
- Reports compensation costs by major occupation, industry, region, union and nonunion status, establishment size, and full- or part-time status
- Uses current weights to reflect today's labor force composition

Benefits

The National Compensation Survey (NCS) covers the incidence and detailed provisions of selected employee benefit plans in small private establishments, medium and large private establishments, and state and local governments. The data are presented as the percent of employees who have access to or participate in certain benefits or as average benefit provisions (for example, the average number of paid holidays provided to employees each year).

Estimates are published by:

- Broad occupational groups
- Full- and part-time status of employees
- Union and nonunion status
- Broad geographic regions and industry sectors

The NCS provides incidence and extensive provisions data for two major benefit areas:

- Health insurance
- Retirement (both defined benefit and defined contribution components)

In previous years, data were collected in three surveys:

- Medium and large private establishments (in odd years)
- Small private establishments (in even years)
- State and local governments (in even years)

With the exception of broad incidence data, which were produced by major region, all of the NCS benefits data were national. They were presented for three broad occupational groupings: professional, technical, and related; clerical and sales; and blue-collar and service employees. Broad incidence data were also available by goods- and service-producing, union affiliation, and full- and part-time status.

For the next several years, all private industry establishments, regardless of size, will be studied each year. Eventually, data on both private industry establishments and state and local government workers will be produced every year. Incidence and key provisions for all benefits plans, as well as detailed plan provisions for health care and retirement plans, will be studied each year; the plan is to make these data available by additional occupational and industry detail categories.

Benefits data will be added by such establishment and employee characteristics as:

- Establishment size
- Industry group
- Profit versus nonprofit status
- Time versus incentive status

The same detailed benefits data that are produced for the nation are also to be produced for the ten largest metropolitan areas and for nine census divisions. The NCS also conducts special studies in new benefit trends:

- Stock options
- Child care resource and referral services

Compensation Surveys: Strategic Considerations

Two essential strategic considerations are:

- Defining the relevant labor market
- Choosing benchmark jobs

Defining the Relevant Labor Market

Relevant labor markets represent the fields of potentially qualified candidates for particular jobs. Companies collect compensation survey data from the appropriate relevant labor markets. Relevant labor markets are defined on the basis of occupational classification, geography, and product or service market competitors.

Occupational classification refers to a group of two or more jobs that are based on similar work characteristics (such as blue- versus white-collar work), duties (such as work mainly with people or with machines), and responsibilities (such as supervision of other employees). The U.S. Bureau of Labor Statistics publishes the *Standard Occupational Classification Manual* that helps business professionals and government economists make proper occupational matches for collecting compensation data. In fact, the NCS survey program is based on nine major occupational groupings described in the manual with detailed information about specific occupations:

- Professional, technical, and related occupations
- Executive, administrative, and managerial occupations
- Sales occupations
- Administrative support occupations, including clerical
- Precision production, craft, and repair occupations
- Machine operators, assemblers, and inspectors
- Transportation and material-moving occupations
- Handlers, equipment cleaners, helpers, and laborers
- Service occupations, except private household

This manual was not available in printed form prior to the publication of this book; however, the entire manual is available to the public on the BLS Web site (*www.bls.gov/ncs/ocs/ocsm/commain.htm*).

Companies that plan to hire accountants and auditors should consider data about accountants and auditors only, rather than individuals from such other job families as engineers. After all, the worker characteristics and work tasks are clearly different:

Accountants and auditors prepare, analyze, and verify financial reports and taxes, as well as monitor information systems that furnish this information to managers in business, industrial, and government organizations. Engineers apply the theories and principles of science and mathematics to the economical solution of practical technical problems. For example, civil engineers design, plan, and supervise the construction of buildings, highways, and rapid transit systems.

Companies search over a wider geographical area for candidates for jobs that require specialized skills or skills that are low in supply relative to the demand. For instance, hospitals are likely to search nationwide for neurosurgeons because their specialized skills are scarce. Companies are likely to limit searches for clerical employees to more confined local areas because clerical employees' skills are relatively common, and their supply tends to be higher relative to companies' demand for them. An insurance company based in Hartford, Connecticut, restricts its search for clerical employees to the Hartford area.

Companies use product or service market competitors to define the relevant labor market when industry-specific knowledge is a key worker qualification and competition for market share is keen. For example, such long-distance telephone companies as Sprint and AT&T probably prefer to lure marketing managers away from industry competitors rather than from such unrelated industries as snack foods or medical and surgical supplies. Knowledge about customer preferences in snack foods has little to do with customers' preferences for long-distance telephone service.

Occupational classification, geographic scope, and product or service market competitors are not necessarily independent dimensions. For example, a company uses product or service market competitors as the basis for defining the relevant labor market for product managers. However, this dimension overlaps with geographic scope because competitor companies are located throughout the country (for example, Boston, San Francisco, Dallas, and Miami).

With many professional, technical, and management positions, all three factors—job family, geographic scope, and companies that compete on the basis of product or service—can be applicable. For more information about relevant labor markets for various occupations, employers can consult professional and industrial associations and consulting firms.

Choosing Benchmark Jobs

As we discussed in Chapter 7, benchmark jobs are key to conducting effective job evaluations. They also play an important role in compensation surveys. Human resource professionals determine the pay levels for jobs based on typical market pay rates for similar jobs. In other words, HR professionals rely on benchmark jobs as reference points for setting pay levels. As we discussed in Chapter 7, benchmark jobs have four characteristics [3]:

- The contents are well-known, relatively stable over time, and agreed upon by the employees involved.
- The jobs are common across a number of different employers.
- The jobs represent the entire range of jobs that are being evaluated within a company.
- The jobs are generally accepted in the labor market for the purposes of setting pay levels.

Why are benchmark jobs necessary? Ideally, HR professionals would match each job within their companies to jobs contained in compensation surveys. However, in reality, one-to-one matches are not feasible for two reasons. First, large companies may have hundreds of unique jobs, making one-to-one matches tedious, time-consuming, and expensive because of the salary and benefits paid to staff members responsible for making these matches. Second, it is highly unlikely that HR professionals will find perfect or close matches between each of a company's jobs and jobs contained in the compensation surveys: Companies adapt job duties and scope to fit their particular situations. In other words, jobs with identical titles may differ somewhat in the degrees of compensable factors. Perfect matches are the exception rather than the rule. For example, Company A's secretary I job may require only a high school education or GED equivalent. Company B's secretary I job may require an associate's degree in office administration.

TABLE 8-2 Comparing Companies' Jobs with Benchmark Jobs

Instructions to Job Incumbents: Compare elements of your job with elements of the survey benchmark job.

Instructions to Supervisors: Compare elements of your employee's job with elements of the survey benchmark job.

		Adjust Pay
Skill (Check the statement that most applies.)		
My (employee's) job requires substantially more skill than the benchmark job.	☐	+4%
My (employee's) job requires somewhat more skill than the benchmark job.	☐	+2%
My (employee's) job and benchmark job require equal skill.	☐	0%
My (employee's) job requires somewhat less skill than the benchmark job.	☐	–2%
My (employee's) job requires substantially less skill than the benchmark job.	☐	–4%
Effort (Check the statement that most applies.)		
My (employee's) job requires substantially more effort than the benchmark job.	☐	+2%
My (employee's) job requires somewhat more effort than the benchmark job.	☐	+1%
My (employee's) job and benchmark job require equal effort.	☐	0%
My (employee's) job requires somewhat less effort than the benchmark job.	☐	–1%
My (employee's) job requires substantially less effort than the benchmark job.	☐	–2%
Responsibility (Check the statement that most applies.)		
My (employee's) job requires substantially more responsibility than the benchmark job.	☐	+4%
My (employee's) job requires somewhat more responsibility than the benchmark job.	☐	+2%
My (employee's) job and benchmark job require equal responsibility.	☐	0%
My (employee's) job requires somewhat less responsibility than the benchmark job.	☐	–2%
My (employee's) job requires substantially less responsibility than the benchmark job.	☐	–4%

Pay adjustment calculation: Sum the percentages for the three checked items. Possible range is from +10% to –10%.

☐ Pay adjustment (For example, a total of 0% means no adjustment is required; +3% indicates that the job's pay rate be increased by 3%, and –3% indicates that the job's pay rate be decreased by 3%.)

Companies can make corrections for differences between their jobs and external benchmark jobs. These corrections are based on subjective judgment rather than on objective criteria. Job incumbents and compensation professionals should independently compare compensable factors for a company's jobs with the compensable factors for the external benchmark jobs. Table 8–2 illustrates a rating scale for this purpose. Both job incumbents and supervisors should complete this questionnaire separately to minimize rater biases (see Chapter 4, performance appraisal section). Differences in ratings can be reconciled through discussion.

Compensation Survey Data

Compensation professionals should be aware of three compensation survey data characteristics. First, compensation surveys contain immense amounts of information. A perusal of every datum point would be mind-boggling even to the most mathematically inclined individuals. In addition, there is bound to be wide variation in pay rates across companies, making it difficult to build market-competitive pay systems. Thus, compensation professionals should use statistics to efficiently describe large sets of data. Second, compensation survey data are outdated because there is a lag between when the data were collected and when employers implement the compensation plan based on the survey data. Third, compensation professionals must use statistical analyses to integrate their internal job structures (based on job evaluation points; see Chapter 7) with the external market based on the survey data. We discuss this matter in detail later in this chapter.

Table 8–3 contains sample salary information collected from a salary survey of 35 accounting jobs according to seniority. Accountant I incumbents possess less than 2 years of accounting work experience. Accountant II incumbents have 2 to less than 4 years of accounting work experience. Accountant III incumbents possess 4 to 6 years of work experience as accountants. Seven companies (A–G) from Atlanta participated in the survey, and most have more than one incumbent at each level. Company B has three accountant I incumbents, three accountant II incumbents, and two accountant III incumbents.

As a starting point, let's begin with basic tabulation of the survey data. Basic tabulation helps organize data, promotes decision makers' familiarization with the data, and reveals possible extreme observations—outliers. Table 8–4 displays a frequency table, and Figure 8–1 displays a histogram. Both indicate the number of job incumbents whose salaries fall within the specified intervals. For example, 11 accountants' annual salaries range between $30,000 and $35,000. Only one job incumbent falls in the $45,001 and above interval, which suggests the possibility of an outlier. We'll discuss the importance of outliers shortly.

Using the Appropriate Statistics to Summarize Survey Data

Two properties describe numerical data sets:

- Central tendency
- Variation

Central tendency represents the fact that a set of data clusters or centers around a central point. Central tendency is a number that represents the typical numerical value in the data set. What is the typical annual salary for accountants in our data set? Two types of central tendency measures are pertinent to compensation-arithmetic mean (often called mean or average) and median.

We calculate the **mean** annual salary for accountants by adding all the annual salaries in our data set and then dividing the total by the number of annual salaries in

TABLE 8-3 Raw Compensation Survey Data for Accountants in Atlanta, Georgia

Company	*Job Title*	*2001 Annual Salary*
A	Accountant I	$33,000
A	Accountant I	34,500
A	Accountant II	36,000
A	Accountant III	43,500
B	Accountant I	33,000
B	Accountant I	33,000
B	Accountant I	36,000
B	Accountant II	37,500
B	Accountant II	36,000
B	Accountant II	37,500
B	Accountant III	45,000
B	Accountant III	43,500
C	Accountant I	34,500
C	Accountant II	37,500
C	Accountant III	43,500
D	Accountant I	36,000
D	Accountant I	36,000
D	Accountant III	55,000
E	Accountant I	33,000
E	Accountant I	33,000
E	Accountant I	34,500
E	Accountant II	36,000
E	Accountant II	36,000
E	Accountant II	37,500
E	Accountant III	45,000
F	Accountant I	34,500
F	Accountant II	37,500
F	Accountant III	45,000
F	Accountant III	45,000
F	Accountant III	43,500
G	Accountant I	34,500
G	Accountant I	33,000
G	Accountant II	37,500
G	Accountant II	37,500
G	Accountant III	43,500

TABLE 8-4 Frequency Table for Accountants

Salary Interval	*Number of Salaries from Survey*
$30,000–$35,000	11
$35,001–$40,000	14
$40,000–$45,000	9
$45,000+	1

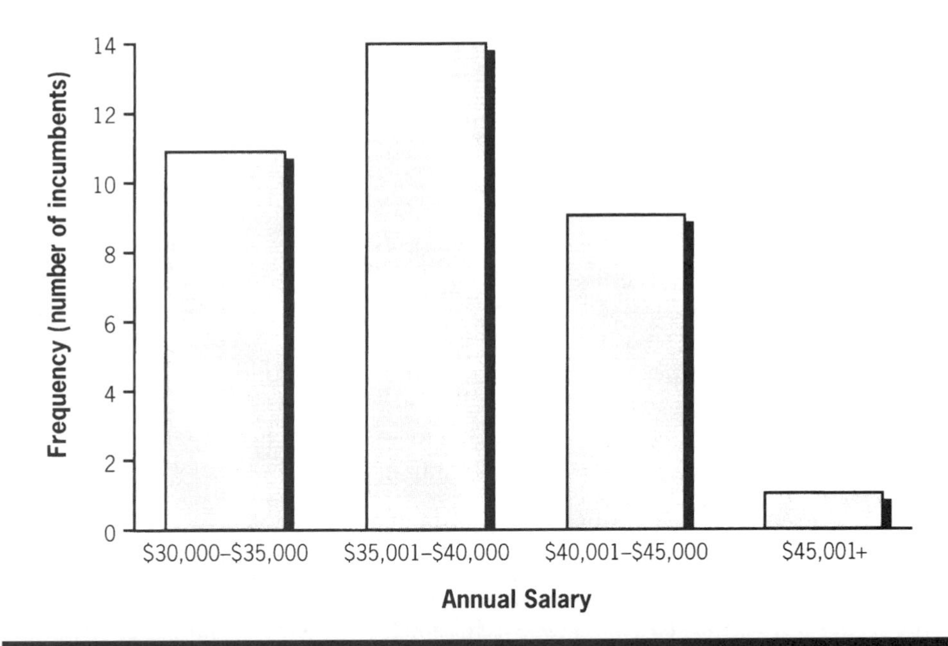

FIGURE 8-1 Histogram of Survey Data for Accountants

the data set. The sum of the salaries in our example is $1,337,500 based on 35 salaries. Thus, the mean equals $38,214.29 (that is, $1,337,500 divided by 35). In this example, the mean informs compensation professionals about the "typical" salary or going market rate for the group of accountants I, II, and III. Compensation professionals often use the mean as a reference point to judge whether employees' compensation is below or above the market.

We use every data point to calculate the mean. Consequently, one or more outliers can lead to a distorted representation of the typical value. The mean understates the "true" typical value when there is one or more extremely small value, and it overstates the "true" typical value when there is one or more extremely large value. The mean's shortcoming has implications for compensation professionals.

Understated mean salaries may cause employers to set starting salaries too low to attract the best qualified job candidates. Overstated mean salaries probably promote recruitment efforts because employers may set starting salaries higher than necessary, a condition that creates a cost burden to companies.

The **median** is the middle value in an ordered sequence of numerical data. If there is an odd number of data points, the median literally is the middle observation. Our data set contains an odd number of observations. The median is $36,000. Table 8–5 illustrates the calculation of the median.

If there is an even number of data points, the median is the mean of the values corresponding to the two middle numbers. Let's assume that we have four salaries, ordered from the smallest value to the highest value: $25,000, $28,000, $29,500, and $33,000. The median is $28,750. The median does not create distorted representations like the mean because its calculation is independent of the magnitude of each value.

Variation is the second property used to describe data sets. **Variation** represents the amount of spread or dispersion in a set of data. Compensation professionals find three measures of dispersion to be useful—standard deviation, quartile, and percentile.

STRETCHING THE DOLLAR

STAGNANT MINIMUM WAGE AND INFLATION MAKE IT HARDER FOR THE POOR TO MAKE ENDS MEET

The increase in cost of living relative to the increase in minimum wage is devastating when we consider the federal government's annual poverty threshold. The poverty guidelines, issued each year by the U.S. Department of Health and Human Services, represent the minimum annual earnings used by the federal government to determine financial eligibility for certain programs. An individual who earns the minimum wage has an annual income totaling $10,712 ($5.15 per hour × 40 hours per week × 52 weeks). The annual poverty threshold in 2002 for a household of two individuals was $8,860, according to the *Federal Register* (67, 631–6933). In 2002, assuming a single parent earns the minimum wage to care for a dependent child, this person's minimum wage income exceeded the poverty threshold by less than $2,000. The picture for individuals with additional dependents is not much better. Let's consider an individual who supports a spouse and two dependent children. This individual's minimum wage income barely exceeded the 2002 poverty threshold—$15,020—by $4,000.

Even though the poverty levels exceed minimum wage earnings, the picture is actually bleaker when we consider the difference between nominal dollars and real dollars. **Nominal dollars** refer to the face value of money. The nominal value of a $10 bill is 10 dollars; the nominal value of a quarter is 25 cents. **Real dollars**, on the other hand, represent the purchasing power of money. Over time, increases in the costs of goods and services, or inflation, diminish the value of nominal dollars. Let's consider the nominal and real values of the minimum wage over time.

Let's look at an example of the nominal and real differences between the minimum wage of $3.80 in 1990 and the minimum wage of $5.15 in July 2002. The nominal increase in minimum wage was $1.35 or 36 percent. At first glance, it appears that purchasing power increased by 36 percent over this 12-year period. This conclusion would be correct if the prices of goods and services did not increase between 1990 and July 2002. However, the cost of living increased dramatically during this period. In July 2002, a dollar, on average, purchased only 62 percent as much as it could in 1990. Said another way, the purchasing power of the dollar (or the value of the real dollar) eroded by nearly 40 percent between 1990 and July 2002. The level of erosion (40 percent) exceeded the level of nominal increase (36 percent). Thus, purchasing power of the minimum wage fell between 1990 and July 2002.

Standard deviation refers to the mean distance of each salary figure from the mean—how larger observations fluctuate above the mean and how smaller observations fluctuate below the mean. Table 8–6 demonstrates the calculation of the standard deviation for our data set.

The standard deviation equals $5,074.86. Compensation professionals find standard deviation to be useful for two reasons. First, as we noted previously, compensation professionals often use the mean as a reference point to judge whether employees' compensations are below or above the market. The standard deviation indicates whether an individual salary's departure below or above the mean is "typical" for the market. For example, Irwin Katz's annual salary is $27,500. His salary falls substantially below the typical average salary: The difference between the mean salary and Katz's salary is $10,714.29 ($38,214.29 – $27,500). This difference is much greater than the typical departure from the mean because the standard deviation is just $5,074.86.

TABLE 8-5 Calculation of the Median for Accountant Survey Data

The salary data are arranged in ascending order. The median is $(n + 1)/2$, where n equals the number of salaries. The median is item 18 ([35 + 1]/2). Thus, the median value is $36,000.

1. $33,000
2. $33,000
3. $33,000
4. $33,000
5. $33,000
6. $33,000
7. $34,500
8. $34,500
9. $34,500
10. $34,500
11. $34,500
12. $36,000
13. $36,000
14. $36,000
15. $36,000
16. $36,000
17. $36,000
18. $36,000 ⟵ median
19. $37,500
20. $37,500
21. $37,500
22. $37,500
23. $37,500
24. $37,500
25. $37,500
26. $43,500
27. $43,500
28. $43,500
29. $43,500
30. $43,500
31. $45,000
32. $45,000
33. $45,000
34. $45,000
35. $55,000

Second, the standard deviation indicates the range for the majority of salaries. The majority of salaries falls between $33,139.43 ($38,214.29 – $5,074.86) and $43,289.15 ($38,214.29 + $5,074.86). Remember, $38,214.29 is the mean, and $5,074.86 is the standard deviation. Compensation professionals can use this range to judge whether their company's salary ranges are similar to the market's salary ranges. A company's salary ranges are not typical of the market if most fall below or above the market range. A company will probably find it difficult to retain good employees when most salaries fall below the typical market range.

TABLE 8-6 Calculation of the Standard Deviation (S.D.) for Accountant Survey Data

$$\text{S.D.} = \sqrt{\frac{\sum_{i=1}^{n} X_i^2 - nM^2}{n-1}}$$

where:

$\sum_{i=1}^{n} X_i^2$ = the sum of the squares of the individual salary obervations.

nM^2 = the sample size (n; that is, 35 salaries) multiplied by the square of the mean for the 35 salaries.

$$\text{S.D.} = \frac{(\$33{,}000^2 + \$33{,}000^2 + \ldots + \$55{,}000^2) - 35(\$38{,}214.92)^2}{35 - 1}$$

$$\text{S.D.} = \sqrt{\frac{51{,}987{,}260{,}000 - 51{,}111{,}618{,}000}{34}}$$

S.D. = \$5,074.86

Both quartiles and percentiles describe dispersion by indicating the percentage of figures that fall below certain points. Table 8–7 illustrates the use of quartiles and percentiles for our survey data. **Quartiles** allow compensation professionals to describe the distribution of data—in this case, annual base pay amount—based on four groupings. The first quartile is \$34,500. In other words, 25 percent of the salary figures are less than or equal to \$34,500. The second quartile is \$36,000. Fifty percent of the salary figures are less than or equal to \$36,000. The third quartile is \$43,500. Seventy-five percent of the salary figures are less than or equal to \$43,500. The fourth quartile is \$55,000. One hundred percent of the salary figures are less than or equal to \$55,000. There are one hundred **percentiles** ranging from the first percentile to the

FLIP SIDE OF THE COIN

STATISTICS CAN TELL DIFFERENT STORIES

As we discussed, the mean and median are measures of central tendency. Oftentimes, the mean and median are different for a given set of data points. When the distribution of data is skewed to the left (that is, there is a higher frequency of larger values than smaller values), the mean will be less than the median. On the other hand, when the distribution of data is skewed to the right (that is, there is a lower frequency of larger values than smaller values), the mean will be greater than the median.

Let's look at an example. The mean hourly wage rate for production workers in Company A is \$8.72. The union in Company A is demanding that management grant pay raises to production workers because the mean hourly pay rate for production workers in Company B is higher—\$9.02. The mean value for Company B is based on the following survey of its production workers:

Hourly Wage Rate of Production Workers

\$8.15, \$8.39, \$8.51, \$8.55, \$8.60, \$10.25, \$10.72

Company A's management is unwilling to raise production workers' pay: Company A's production workers earn a higher mean hourly wage (\$8.72) than the median hourly wage rate of Company B's production workers (\$8.55).

TABLE 8-7 Percentile and Quartile Rank for Accountant Survey Data

Salary	
$33,000	
$33,000	
$33,000	← 10th percentile
$33,000	
$33,000	
$33,000	
$34,500	
$34,500	
$34,500	← 1st quartile
$34,500	
$34,500	
$36,000	
$36,000	
$36,000	
$36,000	
$36,000	
$36,000	
$36,000	← 2nd quartile
$37,500	(also 50th percentile)
$37,500	
$37,500	
$37,500	
$37,500	
$37,500	
$37,500	
$43,500	
$43,500	
$43,500	← 3rd quartile
$43,500	
$43,500	
$45,000	
$45,000	← 90th percentile
$45,000	
$45,000	
$55,000	← 4th quartile

one hundredth percentile. For our data, the tenth percentile equals $33,000, and the ninetieth percentile equals $45,000.

Quartiles and percentiles complement standard deviations by indicating the percentage of observations that fall below particular figures. Compensation professionals' reviews of percentiles and quartiles can enhance their insights into the dispersion of salary data. For example, compensation professionals want to know the percentage of accountants earning a particular salary level or less. If $33,000 represents the tenth percentile for accountants' annual salaries, then only 10 percent earn $33,000 or less. Compensation professionals are less likely to recommend similar pay for new accountant hires. Although paying at this level represents a cost savings, companies are likely

TABLE 8-8 The Consumer Price Index: Basic Facts and Interpretation Issues

Basic Facts

The CPI indexes monthly price changes of goods and services that people buy for day-to-day living. The index is based on a representative sample of goods and services, because obtaining information about all goods and services would not be feasible. The BLS gathers price information from thousands of retail and service establishments—for example, gasoline stations, grocery stores, and department stores. Thousands of landlords provide information about rental costs, and thousands of home owners give cost information pertaining to home ownership.

The CPI represents the average of the price changes for the representative sample of goods and services within each of the following areas:

- Urban United States
- 4 regions
- 4 class sizes based on the number of residents
- 27 local metropolitan statistical areas

The BLS publishes CPI for two population groups: a CPI for All Urban Consumers (CPI-U) and the CPI for Urban Wage Earners and Clerical Workers (CPI-W). The CPI-U represents the spending habits of 80 percent of the population of the United States. The CPI-U covers wage earners; clerical, professional, managerial, and technical workers; short-term and self-employed workers; unemployed persons; retirees; and others not in the labor force. The CPI-W represents the spending habits of 32 percent of the population, and it applies to consumers who earn more than one-half of their income from clerical or wage occupations. The distinction between the CPI-U and CPI-W is important because the CPI-U is most representative of all consumers, whereas unions and management use the CPI-W during negotiations to establish effective cost-of-living adjustments; most unionized jobs are clerical or wage jobs rather than salaried professional, managerial, or executive jobs.

Interpreting the CPI: Percentage Changes vs. Point Changes

The span 1982 to 1984 is the base period for the CPI-U and CPI-W, which is 100. Compensation professionals use the base period to determine the changes in prices over time. How much did consumer prices increase in Atlanta between the base period and December 31, 2001?

The *CPI Detailed Report* indicates that the 2001 CPI-U for Atlanta was 176.2. We know that the base period CPI is 100. Consumer prices in Atlanta increased 76.2 percent between 2001 and the base period. We determine price change with the formula:

$$\frac{(\text{Current CPI} - \text{Previous CPI})}{\text{Previous CPI}} \times 100\%$$

For this example:

$$\frac{(176.2 - 100)}{100} \times 100\% = 76.2\%$$

Compensation professionals are most concerned with annual CPI changes because they are updating recently collected survey data. The same formula yields price changes between periods other than the base period. How much did prices increase in Atlanta between 1999 and 2001? The *CPI Detailed Report* (January 2002) indicates that the 1999 annual CPI-U for Atlanta was 161.2, and we know that the 2001 annual average is 176.2.

$$\frac{(176.2 - 161.2)}{161.2} \times 100\% = 9.31\%$$

Consumer prices in Atlanta increased 9.31 percent between 1999 and 2001.

Source: U.S. Bureau of Labor Statistics. (2002). *CPI Detailed Report*. Washington, DC: U.S. Government Printing Office.

to experience retention problems because 90 percent of accountants earn more than $33,000.

Updating the Survey Data

Companies establish pay structures for future periods. Let's assume that a compensation professional wants to develop a pay structure for the period January 1, 2003, through December 31, 2003. For this illustration, it is now July 2002. The salary survey data were collected in early January 2002 to represent 2001 annual pay averages. These data will be 1 year old at the pay plan's implementation. Compensation professionals typically use historical salary data to build market-competitive pay systems because it is impossible to obtain actual 2003 salary data in 2002. So, companies update survey data with simple techniques to correct for such lags.

Several factors play an important role in updating. The most influential factors are economic forecasts and changes in the costs of consumer goods and services. Employers generally award small permanent pay increases (for example, 3 to 4 percent) when the economic forecast is pessimistic. Pessimistic forecasts suggest the possibility of recession or higher unemployment levels. Thus, employers are less willing to commit substantial amounts to fund pay increases because they may not be able to afford them. Employers typically award higher permanent pay increases when the economic forecast is optimistic. Optimistic forecasts imply enhanced business activity or lower unemployment levels. Management discretion dictates actual pay increase amounts.

Changes in the cost of living tend to make survey data obsolete fairly quickly. Over time, the average cost of goods and services increases. So, companies update salary survey data with the **Consumer Price Index (CPI)**, the most commonly used method for tracking cost changes throughout the United States. The BLS reports the CPI in *The CPI Detailed Report* every month. Each January issue provides annual averages for the prior year. Current and historical CPI data are also available on the BLS Web site (*www.bls.gov*). Table 8–8 describes some basic facts about the CPI and how to interpret it.

Table 8–9 details the procedure for updating salary survey data with the CPI.

TABLE 8-9 Updating Salary Survey, Using CPI-U, Atlanta

Jan. 1, 2002	*July 2002*	*Jan. 1, 2003*	*Dec. 31, 2003*
Market survey data for 2001 CPI-U, 176.2	Establishing pay plan for 2003 CPI-U, 178.6	Pay plan for 2003 begins	Pay plan for 2003 ends
	Price increase Jan. 1, 2002 June 2002 1.3%[1]	*Price increase* July, 2002 Jan. 1, 2003 2.61%[2]	*Price increase* Jan. 1, 2003 Dec. 31, 2003 3.28[3]
Jan. 1, 2002 Survey mean: $38,214.29	July, 2002 Survey mean: $38,711.07	Jan. 1, 2003 Survey mean: $39,721.43	Dec. 2003 Survey mean: $41,024.29

[1] [(Current CPI – Previous CPI)/Previous CPI] × 100%.

[2] Estimate based on the increase in prices for Atlanta for the second half of 2001.

[3] Estimate based on the 2001 annual increase for Atlanta.

INTEGRATING INTERNAL JOB STRUCTURES WITH EXTERNAL MARKET PAY RATES

In Chapter 7, we discussed that compensation professionals use job evaluation methods to establish internally consistent job structures. In other words, companies value jobs that possess higher degrees of compensable factors (for example, 10 years of relevant work experience) than jobs with fewer degrees of compensable factors (for example, one year of relevant work experience). Ultimately, these valuation differences should correspond to pay differences based on compensation survey data.

Earlier, we indicated that paying well below or well above the typical market rate for jobs can create a competitive disadvantage for companies. Thus, it is important that companies set pay rates by using market pay rates as reference points. To this end, we use **regression analysis**, which is a statistical analysis technique. Regression analyses enable compensation professionals to establish pay rates for a set of jobs that are consistent with typical pay rates for jobs in the external market.

We'll apply regression analysis to determine pay rates for the accountant I, accountant II, and accountant III jobs listed in Table 8–3. Before presenting the regression analysis technique, we need two sets of information—the job evaluation point totals for each accountant job based on job evaluation and the updated salary survey data. In this sample, the accountant jobs have the following job evaluation points: accountant I (100 points), accountant II (500 points), and accountant III (1,000) points.

Regression analysis enables decision makers to predict the values of one variable from another. Compensation professionals' goals are to predict salary levels for each job based on job evaluation points. Why not simply "eyeball" the list of salaries in the survey to identify the market rates? There are two reasons. First, companies pay different rates to employees who are performing the same (or very similar) jobs. Our salary survey indicates that accountant III pay rates vary between $43,500 and $55,000. "Eyeballing" the typical rate from the raw data is difficult when surveys contain large numbers of salaries.

Second, we wish to determine pay rates for a set of jobs in a particular company—accountant I, accountant II, and accountant III—based on their relative worth to typical market pay rates for the corresponding jobs contained in the salary survey. Our focus is on pricing a job structure, not pricing one job in isolation.

How does regression analysis work? Regression analysis finds the best-fitting line between two variables. Compensation professionals use job evaluation points assigned to benchmark jobs (based on the matching process discussed earlier) and the salary survey data for the benchmark jobs. They refer to the best fitting line as the **market pay line**. The market pay line is representative of typical market pay rates relative to a company's job structure. Pay levels that correspond with the market pay line are market-competitive pay rates. Figure 8–2 displays the regression results.

The following equation models the prediction.

$\hat{Y} = a + bX$

$\hat{Y}$ = predicted salary

X = job evaluation points

a = the Y intercept (This is the Y value at which $X = 0$.)

b = the slope

The slope represents the change in Y for every one unit change in job evaluation points. In other words, the slope represents the dollar value of each job evaluation point. For example, let's assume that the slope is 26. A job consisting of 301 job evaluation points is worth $26 more than a job consisting of 300 job evaluation points.

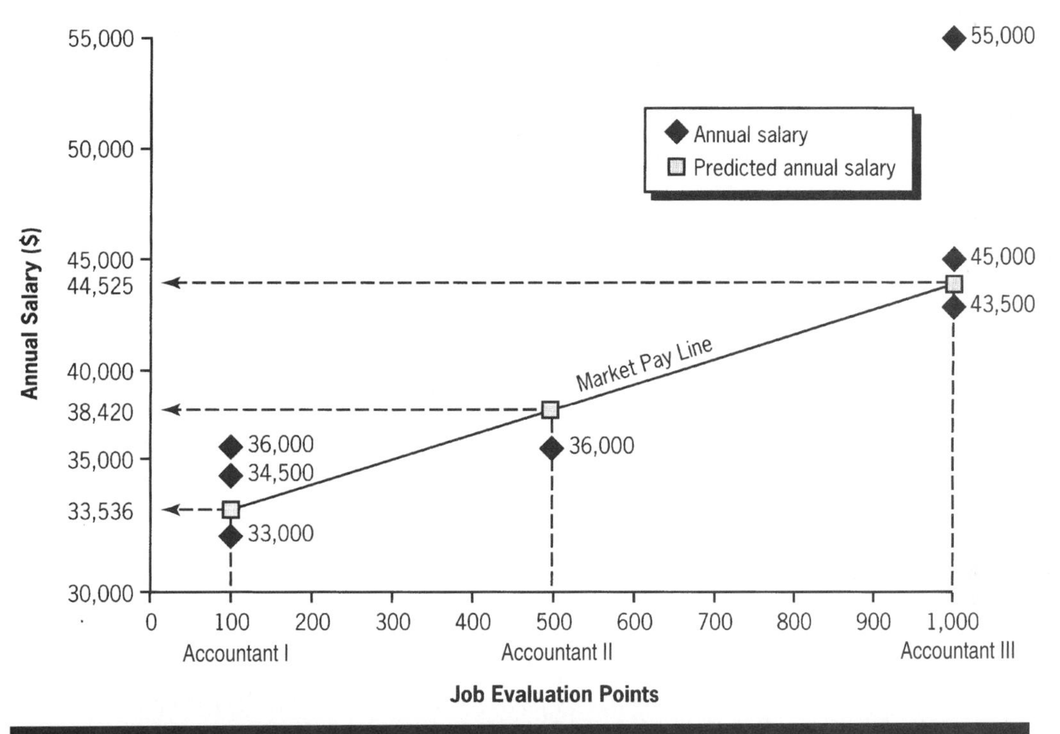

FIGURE 8-2 Regression Analysis Results for the Accountant Survey Data

For our data, the equation is:

$$\hat{Y} = \$32,315.66 + \$12.21X$$

Thus, this market policy line indicates the following market pay rates:

- Accountant I: $33,536.66

$$\hat{Y} = \$32,315.66 + \$12.21\text{ (100 job evaluation points)}$$

- Accountant II: $38,420.66

$$\hat{Y} = \$32,315.66 + \$12.21\text{ (500 job evaluation points)}$$

- Accountant III: $44,525.66

$$\hat{Y} = \$32,315.66 + \$12.21\text{ (1,000 job evaluation points)}$$

COMPENSATION POLICIES AND STRATEGIC MANDATES

Companies can choose from three pay level policies:

- Market lead
- Market lag
- Market match

The **market lead policy** distinguishes a company from the competition by compensating employees more highly than most competitors. Leading the market denotes pay levels that place in the area above the market pay line (Figure 8–2). The **market lag policy** also distinguishes a company from the competition, but by compensating employees less than most competitors. Lagging the market indicates that pay levels fall below the market pay line (Figure 8–2). The **market match policy** most closely follows the typical market pay rates because companies pay according to the market pay line. Thus, pay rates fall along the market pay line (Figure 8–2).

The market lead policy is clearly most appropriate for companies that pursue differentiation strategies. A company may choose a market lead pay policy for its accountants because the company needs the very best accountants to promote its competitive strategy of being the top manufacturer of lightest weight surgical instruments at the lowest possible cost by the year 2010.

The compensation professionals and top management officials must decide how much to lead the market—for example, 5 percent, 10 percent, 25 percent, or more. The "how much" depends on two factors. First, how much pay differential above the market is sufficient to attract and retain the most highly qualified accountants? Second, are there other funding needs for activities that promote differentiation strategies, such as research and development? Past experience and knowledge of the industry norms should provide useful information.

The market lag policy appears to fit well with lowest-cost strategies because companies realize cost savings by paying lower than the market pay line. Paying well below the market will yield short-term cost savings. However, these short-term savings will probably be offset by long-term costs. Companies that use the market lag policy may experience difficulties in recruiting and retaining highly qualified employees. Too much turnover will undercut a company's ability to operate efficiently and to market goods and services on a timely basis. Thus, companies that adopt market lag policies need to balance cost savings with productivity and quality concerns.

The market match policy represents a safe approach for companies because they generally are spending no more or less on compensation (per employee) than competitors. This pay policy does not fit with the lowest-cost strategy for obvious reasons. It does fit better with differentiation strategies. This statement appears to contradict previous ones about differentiation strategies—pay "high" salaries to attract and retain the best talent. Some companies that pursue differentiation strategies follow a market match policy to fund expensive operating or capital needs that support differentiation—for example, research equipment and research laboratories.

A "one size fits all" approach to policy selection is inappropriate. Most companies use more than one pay policy simultaneously. For example, companies generally use market match or market lead policies for professional and managerial talent because these employees contribute most directly to a company's competitive advantages. Companies typically apply market match or market lag policies to clerical, administrative, and unskilled employees (for example, janitorial). Companies' demands for these employees relative to supply in the relevant labor markets are low, and these employees' contributions to attainment of competitive advantage are less direct.

SUMMARY

This chapter discussed market-competitive pay systems and described compensation surveys. Compensation surveys provide "snapshots" of competitors' pay practices. Survey information provides the reference points for establishing pay level policies. Students should realize that conducting compensation surveys requires art, not science: These practices require compensation professionals' sound judgments for making recommendations that fit well with competitive strategies. Careful thought about the meaning underlying the facts and statistics is the key to successfully building market-competitive pay systems.

Key Terms

- market-competitive pay systems, 235
- strategic analysis, 235
- compensation surveys, 235
- National Compensation Survey (NCS), 239
- relevant labor markets, 242
- occupational classification, 242
- central tendency, 245
- mean, 245
- median, 247
- variation, 247
- real dollars, 248
- nominal dollars, 248
- standard deviation, 248
- quartiles, 250
- percentiles, 251
- Consumer Price Index (CPI), 253
- regression analysis, 254
- market pay line, 254
- market lead policy, 256
- market lag policy, 256
- market match policy, 256

Discussion Questions

1. You are a compensation analyst for Worry-Not Insurance Company, which is located in Hartford, Connecticut. Define the relevant labor market for insurance claims adjusters and for data entry clerks. Describe the rationale for your definitions.
2. Can companies easily develop compensations that are both internally consistent and market competitive? What are some of the challenges to this goal?
3. Which do you believe is most important for a company's competitive advantage: internal consistency or market competitiveness? Explain your answer.
4. Refer back to the regression equation presented earlier in this chapter. When b = 0, the market pay line is parallel to the x-axis (that is, job evaluation points). Provide your interpretation.
5. Refer to Table 8–5. Cross out salaries 26 through 35. Calculate the mean and median for this reduced data set.

Exercises

Compensation Online

For Students

Exercise 1: Find relevant journal articles

Your professor has assigned you to write a short paper outlining why market competitiveness is an important characteristic of a pay system. Use your school library's online catalog to locate articles pertaining to strategic analysis, benchmarking, and compensation surveys. Find and read several current articles in these areas.

Exercise 2: Find your appropriate salary level

Do Web searches using the term "salary survey." Find the most up-to-date salary survey. The search engines to use are:

www.yahoo.com

www.excite.com

List three positive attributes and three possible flaws for each survey. Is one survey superior to the others, or does each survey have benefits that would be helpful under different situations?

Exercise 3: Research external factors that may affect a company's compensation packages

One of the companies mentioned in this chapter was Sprint. Go to the Sprint Web site at *www.sprint.com*, scroll down to the bottom of the homepage, and click on Press Releases. Look over the titles of the releases for the last three months. Then review one from each month that you think would have a direct impact on Sprint's compensation practices. Write a brief report on why you chose the articles you did and whether you think the information will affect Sprint's compensation practices.

For Professionals

Exercise 1: Research professional resources
Conduct Web searches using the term "U.S. Industrial Outlook." Choose three search engines (try at least one that you have not used before). Pull up the most recent year of the outlook that you can find. Based upon what you have read in this chapter, what factors are prevalent in predicting industry profiles for the year in question?

Exercise 2: Keep informed on current events related to human resources
Using Yahoo, do an advanced search for "human resources." Stick to the News section of the search results. Read some of the articles and note what magazines, newspapers, or journals they can be found in so that you know where to look in the future.

Exercise 3: Find information regarding salary surveys
As VP of Human Resources, you have noticed that a lot of your company's top talent has left the firm to seek higher paychecks. To combat this, you want to make sure your pay levels are up to par with your competitors. Conduct an advanced search for "salary surveys" again. This time, find information on how to conduct such a survey, or find organizations that provide salary surveys as a service.

Endnotes

1. BridgeGate LLC. (2001). Employees again saying "show me the money," as Bridgegate survey reveals trend toward "free agent" thinking—and growing worker disillusionment. [online]. Available: *www.bridgegate.com*, accessed July 5, 2002.
2. U.S. Department of Labor (June 19, 2002). Employer costs for employee compensation—March 2002 (USDL: 02–346) [online]. Available: *www.bls.gov/ncs/ect/*, accessed July 8, 2002.
3. Milkovich, G. T., & Newman, J. M. (1996). *Compensation* (5th ed.). Homewood, IL: Irwin.

COMPENSATION IN ACTION

SALARIES IN SITE

Be prepared to deal with employees who know what they're worth.

Of all the revolutions sparked by the Internet, the democratization of information arguably has had the greatest effect on today's workplace. That's especially true for employees when it comes to their pay. A quick foray into free online salary surveys gives employees at least some idea of how their salary compares to others across the nation—or across the street.

"The bright side is that there's more salary data than I've ever seen available for free online," says Deborah Keary, SPHR, director of the Information Center at the Society for Human Resource Management (SHRM) in Alexandria, VA. And the information also may be useful to HR practitioners as they direct compensation strategy.

But it definitely puts HR on the spot. Consider a research manager, who asked not to be identified, who has worked for a market research firm in upstate New York for 3 years and regularly puts in 80-hour weeks at work. She surfed on Salary.com and was horrified to discover that her salary was $10,000 lower than the lowest number listed as a median range.

"What I wanted to do was take the information immediately to the president of the company and say, 'What's wrong with you?'" she recalls. "Instead, I did take the information to my boss, and I handed her the numbers and said, 'Tell me why I'm not anywhere near those numbers.'"

Although she ultimately got a raise that put her close to the bottom of the median range reported by Salary.com, she's now actively looking for a new job. "It made me distrust everything because I had gotten promotions and raises," she says. "I was working under the assumption that they were trying to be fair to me. But what that information from Salary.com suggests is this: If that information was so readily available to me, it must have been readily available to HR and management. And they must have looked at those numbers and blatantly said, 'Oh well, too bad for her. As long as she's not paying attention, let's save ourselves $15,000 this year.'"

Obviously, this employee was having other problems with her employer, but finding out that she was underpaid sent her on the prowl for a new position. That's common, says Tracy Herand, senior compensation analyst at Candle Corp., a technology firm in El Segundo, CA. "Salary sites are a catalyst that pushes employees to act," she says. "What they find is often the straw that broke the camel's back."

On the other hand, sometimes otherwise content employees will bring in their salary data just to see what they can get as a bargaining ploy, says Susan Barbee, HR director at Tangram Enterprise Solutions Inc., a 110-employee software firm in Cary, NC. Confrontations such as these occur in her company about four or five times a year, and they seem to follow a pattern.

For example, her director of product development recently told her that one of his employees had looked up salary information on the Web—and then stared at his paycheck. "The person walked in, said, 'This is what it says I should make on the Web. What are you going to do about it?' and walked out," she recalls.

Barbee, who does her benchmarking with the aid of many private surveys, including those from salary research firms, was confident that the salary level was adequate. So, Barbee and the employee's manager explained to the employee exactly what skills he would need to acquire to qualify for a raise. In this case, the employee seemed satisfied—and is still on the job. In fact, Barbee says she's never adjusted an individual's salary based on a Web-fueled complaint.

EVALUATE THE SALARY SITE

What makes these confrontations so difficult for HR practitioners is that while employees believe the information, it's difficult for HR professionals to know which sources of free online salary information, if any, they should trust.

Proper evaluation of online salary information is complicated because there are so many salaries sites. A recent *Google.com* search under "salary comparison sites" yielded more than 72,000 hits.

(Continued)

(Continued)

And because each site uses different methodology, HR professionals have to evaluate each one separately when confronted with an employee waving a printed Web page.

You're most likely to see data from Salary.com, arguably the most popular provider of salary comparisons. The site averages 13.4 million page views in a 6-month period and hosts 1.7 million unique visitors each month. In addition to its own site, Salary.com provides its data to 130 other sites, including portals such as AOL and Yahoo! and media sites such as *Business Week* and the *New York Times*.

Salary.com provides detailed geographic information and matching job descriptions for 1,200 positions. The primary tool used by Salary.com is the Salary Wizard, which allows users to enter a job title and ZIP code, and receive a median salary number, as well as a range from 25 percent of the median through 75 percent of the median.

The Salary Wizard is based on Salary.com's analysis of several different data sources, which the company's team of compensation specialists aggregates into a database and then uses to power the Wizard.

Exactly which data make it into the database? Bill Coleman, vice president of compensation, won't say. "We use whatever we are comfortable with as being a reliable source, primarily what we can purchase from reputable national or regional HR consulting firms," Coleman says. "We cannot name the specific names that we use out of professional courtesy to them. We don't have their permission." Many of the data providers used by Salary.com also sell their data. And knowledge that at least some of it is available for free through Salary.com might dampen sales.

Currently, the Salary Wizard is based on about a dozen separate surveys, which helps to eliminate any statistically anomalous volatility in any one survey, says Coleman. After data are aggregated, the team at Salary.com collects information about how each U.S. city relates to the national average in salaries and makes geographic calculations based on that information. From the city level, the team is able to extrapolate down to the ZIP code level, adjusting salaries downward with distance from a major metropolitan area because cost of living goes down the farther you are from a city. Salary.com verifies its numbers against salaries posted in help-wanted ads on web sites, and the team interviews some companies.

Coleman was willing to say which data categories are excluded from the database for calculations. Salary.com doesn't use magazine-based surveys or data gathered by recruiters. "Recruiter data is considered by some HR people to be data from the devil," he says. Nor does it use data gathered on Web sites directly from employees. Also, Salary.com only uses data from the Bureau of Labor Statistics as a validation tool because BLS statistics are too old to make it into the Wizard, which is updated monthly.

ANALYZE THE DATA

The *Wall Street Journal*'s salary offering is quite different. CareerJournal.com is for those who prefer data separate and "not lumped together in one bit pot," says Tony Lee, editor in chief and general manager of the site.

The predecessor to Career Journal.com, *National Business Employment Weekly*, had in-depth salary statistics on one employer, and one function was featured. Now that's all been moved online, with additional tables. In about fifty categories, there are 2 to 10 articles about compensation in a field and 4 to 10 salary tables, depending on the industry. You then can judge the credibility of the data provided.

The site is updated every week, although not all data are updated. Under "journalism" for example, CareerJournal.com offers 2 articles about the field and 4 surveys. One survey from 1999 was conducted by the *Columbia Journalism Review*. Another is a 2000 study by the Radio-Television News Directors Association in Washington, DC. Geographic information is available for surveys only where it was collected by the researcher, and there are no links to the data collector's Web site to investigate methodology.

The entity that collects the most definitive data about U.S. salaries also has a Web site aimed more toward employees than HR practitioners. America's Career InfoNet (*www.acinet.org*), a service of the federal government, provides access to BLS wage data. The site allows you to search by position and by state and provides median hourly and annual income, as well as mid-range hourly and annual figures.

ACINet's data are based primarily on the BLS Occupational Employment Statistics Survey and are supplemented by data gathered by individual states. The BLS's survey is an annual mail-based study that surveys a sample of approximately 400,000 organizations each year and, over 3 years, contacts approximately 1.2 million organizations. While you can make an estimate from a single year of data, the survey is designed to support estimates down to different levels of geography, occupational detail, and industry when analysis is based on the full sample.

One weakness of this site is that the information is old. The most recent data available at a detailed level are from 1998. Also, job descriptions are broad and, to get technical information on the survey, you have to surf back and forth between ACINET and the BLS survey site, which is not always easy to navigate.

Some sites charge for some of their data, such as WageWeb at *www.wageweb.com*. WageWeb provides national data free to all who surf there, but to get down to details, you will have to join. The price is $169 a year for organizations and $249 a year for consultants. The site provides benchmark information on more than 170 positions and claims a database of 1,400 organizations. Positions are sorted by eight categories: HR, administrative, finance, information management, engineering, health care, sales/marketing, and manufacturing.

The free information is detailed enough to make evaluation of the data easy. For each position, you learn the number of companies responding for a given position, the number of employees in a position, mean average minimum salary, mean average salary, mean average maximum salary, and average bonus paid, if any. The site also provides cursory job descriptions. Dated numbers are a weakness of this site as well; in February 2001, data posted were from July 1, 2000.

There also are specialty sites that zero in on an industry or field. DataMasters at *www.datamasters.com*, specializes in the computer industry and provides salary information on the median low, median high, and regional median for about thirty different job titles under the headings of "Management Level, Professional Staff." These are further broken into regions of the country: Northeast, Midwest, Southeast, and West Coast. The FAQs about the survey say Dowden & Co., a compensation research firm based in Drexel Hill, PA., conducted the survey in 2001.

The site says data are based on "900 employers of information systems professionals, including corporations of all sizes, in every industry group, from every U.S. region." It includes a paragraph of job descriptions for each position listed. The downside here is that the data are broken out only to the regional level.

ONE TOOL AMONG MANY

Of course, when salary data are free, there's usually some kind of trade-off, points out SHRM's Keary. "You get what you pay for." Still, if you evaluate a salary survey and find it acceptable, there's nothing wrong with bringing it into your planning mix as one data point among many, she adds.

In the age of information, the more data you can get about salaries, the better armed you will be when the next angry employees demand to know why they're not earning as much as the Internet says they should.

Source: Alison Stein, *HR Magazine*, volume 45, number 5, pp. 89–96.

WHAT'S NEW IN COMPENSATION?

Lower Pay Rates Do Not Always Represent True Market Value

Pay and benefits usually convey the relative market value of jobs across most companies. Most often, higher pay rates are typically set for jobs of greater worth based on compensable factors. Other forces such as supply of and demand for labor, economic conditions, union bargaining power, and the strategic value of jobs contribute to pay-level determination.

The *New York Times* article featured here gives us another perspective on market value, using paralegal jobs as an illustration. Paralegal jobs are becoming increasingly more important as law firms strive to limit costs. These jobs are skilled jobs that entail a variety of activities, including legal research, drawing up court papers, and verifying the accuracy of legal briefs filed by lawyers. Lawyers traditionally performed paralegal activities themselves. However, social movements such as the passage of the Civil Rights Act of 1964 and extending legal services to the poor increased the demand for legal services. Paralegal jobs were created to handle some of the work that did not require a law license. Although paralegal employees receive substantially less pay than lawyers, law firms significantly value paralegal jobs because these employees free up lawyers to generate more clients (thus, revenue). Also, because paralegal employees earn less than lawyers, the hourly rate charged to clients is substantially lower. Lower rates should help keep clients from seeking services from another law firm. Based on these reasons, opportunities for paralegals abound as does job security.

Log onto your *New York Times* account. Search the database for articles on "jobs in demand." Name some of the jobs in demand. Then, search further about one of these jobs. When reading these articles, look for the reasons why particular jobs are in high demand. Describe relevant compensation issues. Following your course instructor's specific directions, be prepared to describe the current situation, and relate it to the article contained in this text. ■

The New York Times

Paralegal Jobs Surge as Law Firms Seek to Cut Costs

The news that first-year associates at major New York law firms may soon be paid as much as $160,000 a year can only make Anthony Griffith feel a little more secure in his job.

Mr. Griffith, 30, is a legal assistant, commonly called a paralegal, a kind of paramedic for lawyers. He cannot try a case or counsel a client. But he can do legal research, draw up court papers and double-check the accuracy of briefs filed by the partners and associates he works for. And because he can perform these and other important tasks at a fraction of the fee a lawyer commands, he is vital to his firm. Not to mention the clients and their checkbooks.

Mr. Griffith and his paralegal colleagues at Goodkind, Labaton, Rudoff & Sucharow, a medium-size Manhattan firm, are members of one of the fastest growing job categories in the country at a time when law firms of all sizes have been forced to become more cost competitive.

Historically, law firms used law students, junior lawyers, secretaries and clerks to do tasks now assigned to paralegals. But in the 1960s, when the civil rights and voting rights movements sought to make legal services more available to the poor, non-lawyers were trained to perform tasks that did not require a law license. Soon, private firms and government agencies began seeing the benefits of training people for this new job category.

Mark S. Arisohn of Goodkind, Labaton, one of the partners to whom Mr. Griffith is assigned, said a paralegal's time was generally billed at $90 to $125 an hour at the firms he was familiar with, while "lawyers are typically $200 and north," reaching $500 an hour in some partners' billings.

"You don't want to have a $300 an hour lawyer doing work that can be done at $100 an hour," Mr. Arisohn said. Still, others in the legal business noted, some firms that make heavy use of paralegals retain the practice of having first-year associates handle all legal research, even elementary tasks.

On a typical morning recently, Mr. Griffith was hunched over his desk at the midtown Manhattan offices of Goodkind, Labaton preparing for a day of multiple tasks. One of the five lawyers he is assigned to had asked him to tap into the Internet to dig up articles written by an expert witness in a case. Another needed the American Arbitration Association rules for resolving employment disputes.

File cabinets and boxes nearby included more extensive assignments he had recently completed: summaries of long deposition testimony from which he had extracted the most germane parts, copies of summonses and subpoenas he had prepared and lawyers' court papers he had vetted to assure that the decisions they cited were still valid as precedents.

"I started out in high school liking the law," said Mr. Griffith, a Brooklyn resident who received a bachelor of science degree in legal assistance studies at New York City Technical College in Brooklyn. He has been working as a paralegal for seven years, the last six months at Goodkind, Labaton. The work, he said, has strengthened his interest in becoming a lawyer.

"Nothing I've seen has discouraged me," he said. "To see that what you're doing is really helping someone" has impressed him as a rewarding part of being a lawyer, he said, adding that when his personal life permits, probably in two or three years, he will apply to law school.

Mr. Griffith is among 136,000 people across the country who, government economists say, filled the paralegal ranks in 1998, the latest year for which the Bureau of Labor Statistics has figures. This is four times the number the agency estimated in 1980, and it projects that the ranks will swell to 220,000 by 2008. That is the swiftest growth rate the bureau foresees for any occupation outside the computer industry.

Paralegals are also expected to keep increasing in New York, where an estimated 13,000 work today—two-thirds of them in New York City—and where nearly 16,000 are projected 6 years from now, according to the State Department of Labor.

Explaining the occupation's surging growth since it emerged as a discrete employment category in the 1970s, Julie Sisti, who oversees the paralegal studies program at New York University, said, "We've become a more complex society, with the need to make legal services more accessible to the average person." Paralegals, with their lower-cost time, help attain this, she said.

There appear to be no shortages of candidates to fill the openings.

"Kids coming out of college don't necessarily want to go to law school but want to work in the profession, and being a paralegal is interesting work with pretty good pay," Mr. Arisohn said. His firm has 10 paralegals to assist its fifty-two lawyers.

The firm's paralegal manager, Angela L. Pariselli, would not say what Goodkind, Labaton pays its legal assistants. But she said that, generally, in the city the entry-level pay in the occupation was about $25,000 a year, and was $40,000 and up for those with more than 4 years' experience.

Besides those who decide on paralegal work as a career, many in the job are college graduates who, like Mr. Griffith, entered the occupation because they were considering becoming lawyers and decided to put in some time as legal assistants to test their affinity for the profession.

Ms. Sisti, of New York University, similarly spoke of the many who enrolled in N.Y.U.'s paralegal course because they saw a stint as a legal assistant as "a cheaper way than law school to find out if they really like the law or have a talent for it."

Many others taking the twelve-credit course, which is offered by the university's School of Continuing and Professional Studies, are looking to make paralegal work a career, she said, while still others are already employed as legal assistants but have had only on-the-job training and want to enhance their skills and advancement opportunities.

Opportunities for formal training continue to grow. The Bureau of Labor Statistics says that more than 800 programs across the country, from 4-year bachelor's degree programs to certificate courses running only a few months, are offered by universities, community colleges and proprietary business schools.

No state requires paralegals to be licensed, though some have adopted voluntary standards, said Marge Dover, executive director of the National Association of Legal Assistants, based in Tulsa, OK. She said that paralegals might perform any tasks the lawyers they work for assign to them, except that they could not give legal advice, set fees or present cases in court.

That's fine with Elizabeth Bellmar, 27, another Goodkind, Labaton paralegal, who has decided after testing the waters by working as a legal assistant that a lawyer's life is not for her.

"I don't want to write the papers, I like to fix them up," she said. "I don't want to stand up in court. It's not my nature. I like being in the background."

SOURCE: Joseph P. Fried, Paralegal jobs surge as law firms seek to cut costs (March 12, 2000) [online]. Available: *www.nytimes.com*, accessed October 1, 2002.

APPENDIX: U.S. 2002/2003 TOTAL SALARY INCREASE BUDGET SURVEY

Please Return Questionnaire No Later Than May 3, 2002.

1. NAICS code must be completed (to be included in the survey). Using the "NAICS Code" listing, enter your three-digit industry code. If your organization is multi-industry or if pay practices differ among different divisions, business units or subsidiaries, make a photocopy of the form and fill out completely for each. Please indicate the particular division, unit or subsidiary name as appropriate in the space provided for the organization listed on the back of the survey. **Please check the information sheet for new NAICS code changes.**

   ☐☐☐ North American Industry Classification System (NAICS Code)

2. Please enter brief description of organizational unit being reported:

   ____

   (e.g., Headquarters, Division, Subsidiary, Government Agency)

3. What region covers the majority of your employees reported below? If your organization is located in more than one region and pay practices are different by region, make a photocopy of the form and fill out completely for each region. If the pay practices are the same for all regions, mark the regions that apply.

   Sample: Mark like this: ●

   ○ Eastern United States—CT, DE, ME, MD, MA, NH, NJ, NY, PA, RI, VT, VA, DC, WV

   ○ Central United States—IL, IN, IA, KS, KY, MI, MN, MO, NE, ND, OH, SD, WI

   ○ Southern United States—AL, AR, FL, GA, LA, MS, NC, OK, SC, TN, TX

   ○ Western United States—AK, AZ, CA, CO, HI, ID, MT, NV, NM, OR, UT, WA, WY

Instructions for Completing Questions

All portions of question 4 are required for participation

- If your organization is on a fiscal-year basis, please use the fiscal year closest to the corresponding calendar year and make an adjustment, as necessary, to reflect the calendar-year data requested.
- Fill in the blocks carefully. Do not uses dashes. Fill in "0" if there is no increase planned where one is typically given; if not applicable (e.g., General increase/COLA) leave blank. Be sure to fill in the space for **"Total Salary Increase."**
- Use figures rounded to the nearest tenth (e.g., 2.1%).
- Reasonable estimates may be used if exact data are unavailable.
- Do not include promotional increases in your responses to Questions 4, 5 & 6 as they are covered separately in Question 8.

Base Salary Increase

4a. What is your total payroll budget for 2002? $______,______,000.00

4b. What is your base salary increase for program 2002? (PLEASE PRINT LEGIBLY.)

Number of Covered Employees		*Number of Months Between Increases*	*General Increase/ COLA*	*Merit Increase*	*Other Increase (Not Promotional Increases)*	*Total Salary Increase*
________	Nonexempt Hourly Nonunion	___	___.__%	___.__%	___.__%	___.__%
________	Nonexempt Salaried	___	___.__%	___.__%	___.__%	___.__%
________	Exempt Salaried	___	___.__%	___.__%	___.__%	___.__%
________	Officer/Executive	___	___.__%	___.__%	___.__%	___.__%
________	← **TOTAL**					

4c. If you have included an increase in the column titled "Other Increase," please explain the nature of this increase (e.g., equity increases): ____________________

5a. What are your base salary budget plans or estimates for 2003?

	Number of Months Between Increases	*General Increase/ COLA*	*Merit Increase*	*Other Increase (Not Promotional Increases)*	*Total Salary Increase*
Nonexempt Hourly Nonunion	___	___.__%	___.__%	___.__%	___.__%
Nonexempt Salaried	___	___.__%	___.__%	___.__%	___.__%
Exempt Salaried	___	___.__%	___.__%	___.__%	___.__%
Officer/Executive	___	___.__%	___.__%	___.__%	___.__%

5b. If you have included an increase in the column titled "Other Increase," please explain the nature of this increase.

____

6a. What percentage of your employees will be receiving a base salary increase (general, COLA, merit, or other) in 2002?

____.__%

6b. Does the percentage of employees receiving a base salary increase reflect a change from 2001?
○ Increase ○ Decrease ○ No change

Salary Structures

7a. If you use a formal salary range structure, by what percentage did you increase the salary range structure in 2002?

Nonexempt Hourly Nonunion	____.__%	Nonexempt Salaried	____.__%
Exempt Salaried	____.__%	Officer/Executive	____.__%

7b. By what percentage do you plan to increase the salary range structure for 2003?

Nonexempt Hourly Nonunion	____.__%	Nonexempt Salaried	____.__%
Exempt Salaried	____.__%	Officer/Executive	____ %

Promotions

8a. Are promotional increases identifiable as a separate budget item for your organization?
○ Yes ○ No **If no**, go to question 8c.

8b. If yes, budgeted promotional increases for 2002 will equal ____.__ % of total base salaries.

8c. In 2002, ____.__ % of the total employee population will receive promotional increases.

8d. The average promotional increase given is ____.__ % of a promoted employee's base salary.

Variable Pay

Variable pay is the amount established by management as a percentage of payroll to be granted for performance based, lump-sum cash rewards during the year.

9a. Does your organization use variable pay? ○ Yes ○ No
If yes, has your organization instituted variable pay in 2002? ○ Yes ○ No
If no, is your organization considering instituting variable pay in 2003?
○ Yes ○ No **Skip to question 10a**

If your organization currently uses variable pay, which of the following are included in your calculation **(mark all that apply):**

○ Yes ○ No **Organizationwide Awards:** Provided under a formal plan (not discretionary) based on the success of the whole organization (e.g., cash profit sharing—exclude retirement plans).

○ Yes ○ No **Special Individual Recognition Awards:** Given by discretion to key contributors; performance related, not for length of service or equity.

○ Yes ○ No **Group/Team Awards:** Provided under a formal plan (not discretionary) for a plant, division, work unit or team results (e.g., gainsharing; covers only a segment of organization).

○ Yes ○ No **Individual Incentive Awards:** Provided under a formal plan (not discretionary) for employees' performance in designated jobs.

9b. What percentage of base payroll was budgeted/awarded as variable pay during 2001?

	Budgeted	***Awarded***
Nonexempt Hourly Nonunion	____.__%	____.__%
Nonexempt Salaried	____.__%	____.__%
Exempt Salaried	____.__%	____.__%
Officer/Executive	____.__%	____.__%

9c. What percentage of base payroll was budgeted and what is your best estimate that is planned to be awarded as variable pay during 2002?

	Budgeted	*Awarded*
Nonexempt Hourly Nonunion	___ . __ %	___ . __ %
Nonexempt Salaried	___ . __ %	___ . __ %
Exempt Salaried	___ . __ %	___ . __ %
Officer/Executive	___ . __ %	___ . __ %

9d. What percentage of base payroll is estimated to be budgeted as variable pay during 2003?

	Budgeted
Nonexempt Hourly Nonunion	___ . __ %
Nonexempt Salaried	___ . __ %
Exempt Salaried	___ . __ %
Officer/Executive	___ . __ %

9e. How did the use of variable pay impact your base salary increase program for 2001?

○ No change ○ Partially offset base salary increase program
○ Fully offset base salary increase program

9f. If partially offset, by what percentage was your base salary increase program reduced? . %

Example: If your base salary budget would have been 5% but was reduced to 4% due to the existence of a variable pay plan, the correct answer would be 20%, not 1%,

9g. What percentage of employees in each category received a form of variable pay during 2001?

Nonexempt Hourly Nonunion	___ . __ %	Nonexempt Salaried	___ __ %
Exempt Salaried	___ . __ %	Officer/Executive	___ . __ %

Stock Plans

10a. Is your organization? ○ Publicly Traded ○ Privately Held ○ Neither
If your organization is a government agency or not-for-profit organization, continue on to question 11.

10b. Does your organization have a stock-based plan for compensation purposes in 2002?
○ Yes ○ No **If no,** please continue on to question 11.

If yes, please complete this matrix and the rest of question 10.

	Stock Purchase Program	*Stock Option Program*	*Stock Grant Program*	*Phantom Stock (SAR)*	*Co. Stock through 401(k)*
Nonexempt Hourly Nonunion	○ Yes ○ No	○ Yes ○ No	○ Yes ○ No	○ Yes ○ No	○ Yes ○ No
Nonexempt Salaried	○ Yes ○ No	○ Yes ○ No	○ Yes ○ No	○ Yes ○ No	○ Yes ○ No
Exempt Salaried	○ Yes ○ No	○ Yes ○ No	○ Yes ○ No	○ Yes ○ No	○ Yes ○ No
Officer/Executive	○ Yes ○ No	○ Yes ○ No	○ Yes ○ No	○ Yes ○ No	○ Yes ○ No

10c. Does your organization anticipate changes in the size of the grants or awards of stock for 2002?
○ Yes ○ No
If yes, what is that change? ○ Increase ○ Decrease

10d. Does your organization utilize stock as a spot award? ○ Yes ○ No

Attraction and Retention Incentive Practices

11a. In 2002, is your organization having difficulty attracting and retaining employees for key or critical jobs?
○ Yes ○ No **If yes**, please complete part 11b.

11b. What job groups or categories is your organization experiencing difficulty attracting and retaining? (mark all that apply)

☐ Business Development ☐ Health Care Professionals ☐ Marketing ☐ Research & Development
☐ Customer Service ☐ Human Resources ☐ Operations ☐ Sales
☐ Engineering ☐ Information Technology ☐ Purchasing
☐ Finance/Accounting ☐ Logistics ☐ Other

12. What actions has your organization taken to attract and retain employees? (mark all that apply)

☐ Employee referral bonus
☐ Exempt overtime pay or time off
☐ Larger merit increase budgets
☐ Market adjustment/increase to base salary
☐ Paying above market
☐ Project milestone/completion bonus
☐ Promotional/career development opportunities
☐ Retention/stay bonus
☐ Sabbaticals
☐ Separate salary structures
☐ Sign-on/hiring bonus
☐ Special cash bonus/group incentive (not organizationwide)
☐ Special training/educational opportunities
☐ Spot bonus (individual)
☐ Stock grant programs/stock options
☐ Work environment (flexible work schedule, reduced workweek, relaxed dress code, telecommuting, etc.)
☐ Have not taken any actions to address attraction and retention issues
☐ Other (please specify)

In what format would you prefer to receive your copy of the survey results?

○ Please e-mail an electronic (pdf) file of the report.

○ Please mail a hard copy of the report.

Important

Authorization for use of data in custom reports

I understand that unless I have marked the box below, WorldatWork may use our organization's data in custom designed salary budget reports. I further understand that the confidentiality of our organization's data will be maintained by WorldatWork and that our data will never be included in custom reports with fewer than 10 organizations.

X ______________________________ ______________

Signature required Date

☐ I do NOT authorize WorldatWork to use our organization's data in custom designed salary budget reports.

By submitting this survey form or electronic survey, I understand that if mandatory sections of the survey are not completed, I will not be eligible for participation in the 2002–03 Total Salary Increase Budget Survey and not eligible for the participant copy of the survey.

Please return questionnaire no later than May 3, 2002.
NO FACSIMILES PLEASE

Return to: WorldatWork, 14040 N. Northsight Blvd., Scottsdale, AZ 85260
Note any corrections to membership information below.

Name ______________________________

Title ______________________________

Organization (Required) ______________________________

Address ______________________________

City __________ State __________ Zip __________

E-mail ______________________________

CHAPTER

9 BUILDING PAY STRUCTURES THAT RECOGNIZE INDIVIDUAL CONTRIBUTIONS

Chapter Outline

- Constructing a Pay Structure
  - Step 1: Deciding on the Number of Pay Structures
  - Step 2: Determining a Market Pay Line
  - Step 3: Defining Pay Grades
  - Step 4: Calculating Pay Ranges for Each Pay Grade
  - Step 5: Evaluating the Results
- Designing Merit Pay Systems
  - Merit Increase Amounts
  - Timing
  - Recurring Versus Nonrecurring Merit Pay Increases
  - Present Level of Base Pay
  - Rewarding Performance: The Merit Pay Grid
  - Merit Pay Increase Budgets
- Designing Sales Incentive Compensation Plans
  - Alternative Sales Compensation Plans
  - Sales Compensation Plans and Competitive Strategy
  - Determining Fixed Pay and the Compensation Mix
- Designing Pay-for-Knowledge Programs
  - Establishing Skill Blocks
  - Transition Matters
  - Training and Certification
- Pay Structure Variations
  - Broadbanding
  - Two-Tier Pay Structures
- Summary
- Key Terms
- Discussion Questions
- Exercises
- Endnotes

Learning Objectives

In this chapter, you will learn about

1. Fundamental principles of pay structure design
2. Merit pay system structures

3. Sales incentive pay structures
4. Pay-for-knowledge structures
5. Pay structure variations—broadbanding and two-tier wage plans

Pay structures assign different pay rates for jobs of unequal worth and provide the framework for recognizing differences in individual employee contributions. No two employees possess identical credentials, nor do they perform the same jobs equally well. Companies recognize these differences by paying individuals according to their credentials, knowledge, or job performance. When completed, pay structures should define the boundaries for recognizing employee contributions. Employee contributions in this context correspond to the pay bases that we addressed in previous chapters—seniority, merit, incentive pay, and person-based pay.

Pay structures have strategic value. Well-designed structures should promote the retention of valued employees. Most companies support pay-for-performance systems; however, many of these companies ultimately question whether these systems add any value. The "Compensation in Action" feature at the end of this chapter calls on the expert opinion of consultants and experiences of company practitioners to emphasize the importance of design.

In this chapter, we address how companies structure these pay bases, with the exception of seniority, which is typically not the main basis for pay in companies. We start out by considering the fundamental process of constructing pay structures. Next, we examine the design elements of merit pay structures. Then, we move on to specific pay structures, including merit pay, sales incentive pay, and pay-for-knowledge.

CONSTRUCTING A PAY STRUCTURE

Compensation specialists develop pay structures based on five steps:

- Deciding on how many pay structures to construct
- Determining a market pay line
- Defining pay grades
- Calculating pay ranges for each pay grade
- Evaluating the results

Step 1: Deciding on the Number of Pay Structures

Companies often establish more than one pay structure, depending on market rates and the company's job structure. Common pay structures include exempt and nonexempt structures, pay structures based on job families, and pay structures based on geography.

Exempt and Nonexempt Pay Structures

As you will recall, these categories reflect a distinction in the Fair Labor Standards Act. Exempt jobs are not subject to the overtime pay provisions of the act. Core compensation terms for these jobs are usually expressed as an annual salary. Nonexempt jobs are subject to the overtime pay provision of the act. Accordingly, the core compensation for these jobs is expressed as an hourly pay rate. Companies establish these pay structures for administrative ease. Some broadly consistent features distinguish exempt from nonexempt jobs: Exempt jobs, by the definition of the Fair Labor Standards Act, are generally supervisory, professional, managerial, or executive jobs that contain a wide variety of duties. Nonexempt jobs are generally nonsupervisory in nature, and the duties tend to be narrowly defined.

Pay Structures Based on Job Family

Executive, managerial, professional, technical, clerical, and craft represent distinct job families. Pay structures are also defined on the basis of job family, each of which shows a distinct salary pattern in the market. For example, the Davis-Bacon Act requires contractors and subcontractors to pay wages at least equal to those prevailing in the area where work is performed. This act applies only to employers with federal or federally financed contracts worth more than $2,000 for the construction, alteration, or repair of public works or buildings. Moreover, the Davis-Bacon Act also applies only to laborers and mechanics, excluding clerical, professional, and managerial employees. Thus, companies holding federal contracts meeting these criteria have limited latitude for setting pay for certain jobs; however, the latitude for setting pay rates for other jobs is greater.

Pay Structures Based on Geography

Companies with multiple, geographically dispersed locations such as sales offices, manufacturing plants, service centers, and corporate offices may establish pay structures based on going rates in different geographic regions because local conditions may influence pay levels. The cost of living is substantially higher in the northeast region than in the south and southeast regions of the United States. For example, in 2002, a person earning $100,000 annually in Auburn, Alabama would have to earn $197,911 in Boston, Massachusetts to maintain a comparable standard of living.

Step 2: Determining a Market Pay Line

We discussed how to determine the market pay line in Chapter 8. Again, the market pay line is representative of typical market pay rates relative to a company's job structure. Pay levels that correspond with the market pay line are market-competitive pay rates. Figure 9-1 illustrates a market pay line for a series of clerical jobs. Pay rates that fall along the market pay line represent competitive pay rates based on the company's selection of a relevant labor market, and these rates promote internal consistency because they increase with the value of jobs. The clerk I job has the least complex and demanding duties and has fewer worker requirements than the remaining clerk jobs (clerk II, clerk III, and chief clerk).

Step 3: Defining Pay Grades

Pay grades group jobs for pay policy application. Human resource professionals typically group jobs into pay grades based on similar compensable factors and value. These criteria are not precise. In fact, no one formula determines what is sufficiently similar in terms of content and value to warrant grouping jobs into a pay grade.

Ultimately, job groupings are influenced by other factors, such as management's philosophy, as discussed earlier. Wider pay grades—that is, grades that include a relatively large number of jobs—minimize hierarchy and social distance between employees. Narrower pay grades tend to promote hierarchy and social distance. Figure 9-2 illustrates pay grade definitions, based on the jobs used in Figure 9-1.

Human resource professionals can develop pay grade widths as either "absolute" job evaluation point spreads or as percentage-based job evaluation point spreads. When absolute point spreads are used, grades are based on a set number of job evaluation points for each grade. For example, a compensation professional establishes pay grades equal to 200 points each. Grade 1 includes jobs that range from 1 to 200 job evaluation points, Grade 2 contains jobs that range from 201 to 400 points, and so on.

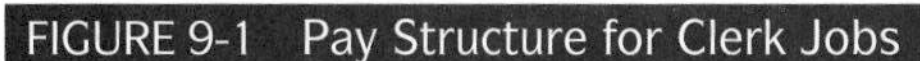
FIGURE 9-1 Pay Structure for Clerk Jobs

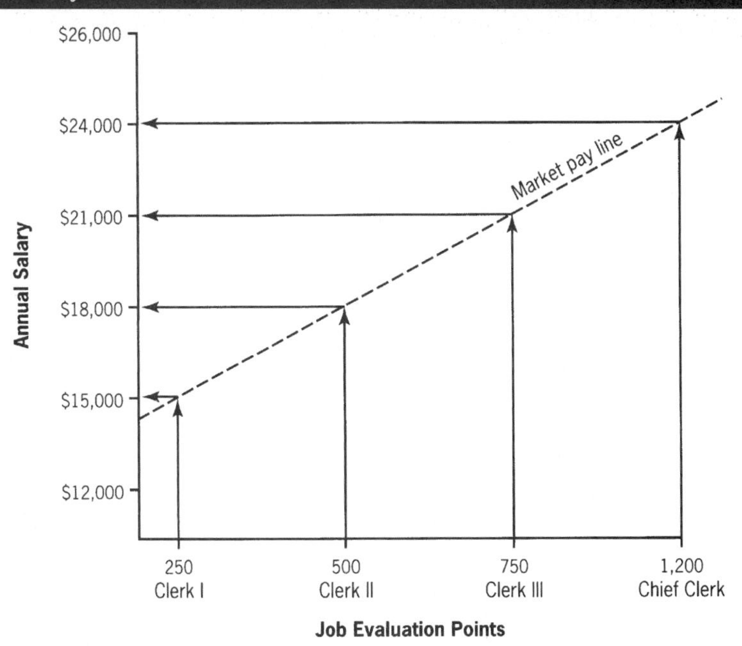

Clerk I
Employees receive training in basic office support procedures, the operation of office equipment, and the specific activities of the unit. Tasks assigned are simple and repetitive in nature and are performed in accordance with explicit instructions and clearly established guidelines. Sample duties include: files materials in established alphabetical order and prepares new file folders and affixes labels. Clerk Is must possess a high school diploma or equivalent.
Clerk II
Employees work under general supervision in support of an office. They perform routine office support tasks that require a knowledge of standard office procedures and the ability to operate a variety of office equipment. Sample duties include: prepares simple factual statements or reports involving computations such as totals or subtotals and composes memos requesting or transmitting factual information. Clerk IIs must possess a high school diploma or equivalent and 1 year work experience performing simple clerical tasks.
Clerk III
Employees work under general supervision in support of an office. They perform office support tasks requiring knowledge of general office and departmental procedures and methods and ability to operate a variety of office equipment. Sample duties include: reconciles discrepancies between unit records and those of other departments and assigns and reviews work performed by Clerks I and II. Clerk IIIs must possess a high school diploma or equivalent, 2 years work experience performing moderately complex clerical tasks, and completed coursework (five in all) in such related topics as word processing and basic accounting principles.
Chief Clerk
Employees work under direction in support of an office. They perform a wide variety of office support tasks that require the use of judgment and initiative. A knowledge of the organization, programs, practices, and procedures of the unit is central to the performance of the duties. Chief clerks must possess a high school diploma or equivalent, 4 years work experience performing moderately difficult clerical tasks, and an associate's degree in office management.

FIGURE 9-2 Pay Grade Definitions

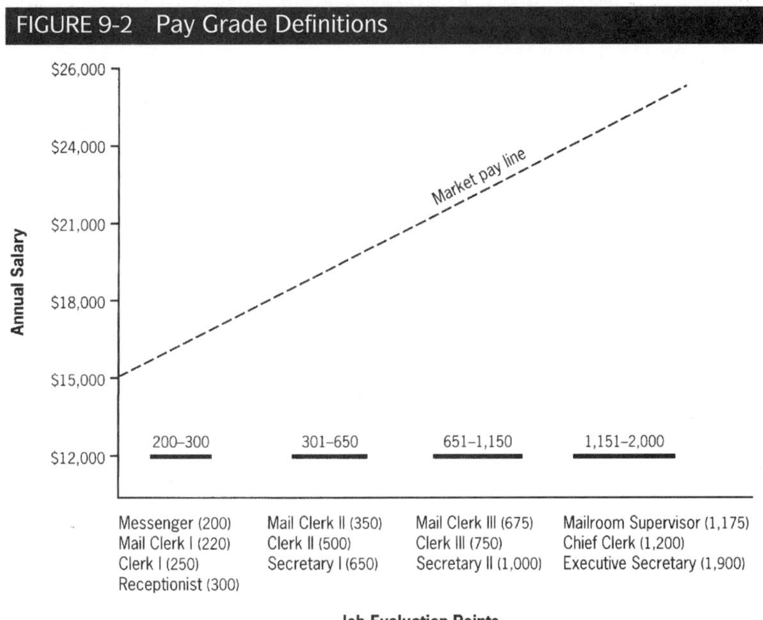

Companies may choose to vary the "absolute" point spread by increasing the point spread as they move up the pay structure, in recognition of the broader range of skills that higher pay grades represent. For example, certified public accounting jobs require a broader range of skills—knowledge of financial accounting principles and both state and federal tax codes—than do mailroom clerk jobs. Often, companies assign trainee positions to the lower, narrower pay grades because trainees generally have limited job-relevant skills. For instance, Grade 1 may contain trainee positions with job evaluation scores that range from 1 to 150, Grade 2 may contain basic jobs beyond traineeships with scores of 151 to 400, and Grade 3 may include advanced jobs with scores of 401 to 1,000.

Step 4: Calculating Pay Ranges for Each Pay Grade

Pay ranges build upon pay grades. Pay grades represent the horizontal dimension of pay structures (job evaluation points). **Pay ranges** represent the vertical dimension (pay rates). Pay ranges include midpoint, minimum, and maximum pay rates. The minimum and maximum values denote the acceptable lower and upper bounds of pay for the jobs within particular pay grades. Figure 9-3 illustrates pay ranges.

Human resource professionals establish midpoints first, followed by minimum and maximum values. The **midpoint pay value** is the halfway mark between the range minimum and maximum rates. Midpoints generally match values along the market pay line, representing the competitive market rate determined by the analysis of compensation survey data. Thus, the midpoint may reflect the market average or median (Chapter 8).

A company sets the midpoints for its pay ranges according to its competitive pay policy, as discussed in Chapter 8. If the company wants to lead the market with respect to pay offerings (market lead policy), it sets the midpoint of the ranges higher than the average for similar jobs at other companies. If the company wants to pay according to the market norm (market match policy), midpoints should equal average market midpoints. If the company is interested in lagging the market (market lag policy), it would set the midpoints below the market average. A company's base-pay policy line graphically connects the midpoints of each pay grade.

FIGURE 9-3 Pay Range Definitions

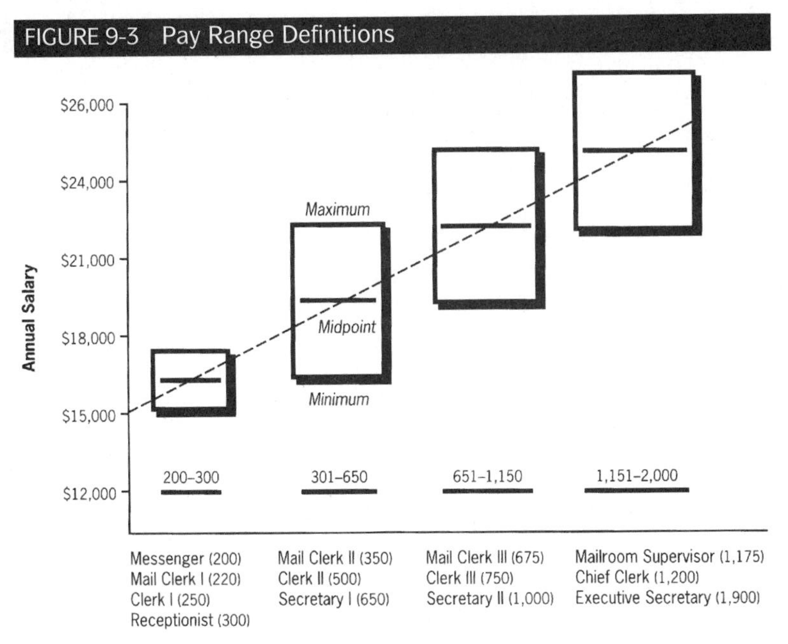

How do compensation professionals calculate pay grade minimums and maximums? They may fashion pay grade minimums and maximums after the minimums and maximums for pay grades that their competitors have established. An alternate approach is to set the pay grade minimums and maximums on the basis of range spread. A **range spread** is the difference between the maximum and minimum pay rates of a given pay grade. It is expressed as a percentage of the difference between the minimum and maximum divided by the minimum.

Companies generally apply different range spreads across pay grades. Most commonly, they use progressively higher range spreads for pay grades that contain more valuable jobs in terms of the companies' criteria. Smaller range spreads characterize pay grades that contain relatively narrowly defined jobs that require simple skills with generally low responsibility. Entry-level clerical employees perform limited duties ranging from filing folders alphabetically to preparing file folders and affixing labels. Presumably, these jobs represent bottom-floor opportunities for employees who will probably advance to higher-level jobs as they acquire the skills needed to perform these jobs proficiently. Advanced clerical employees review and analyze forms and documents to determine the adequacy and acceptability of information.

Higher-level jobs afford employees greater promotion opportunities than entry-level jobs. Employees also tend to remain in higher pay grades longer, and the specialized skills associated with higher pay grade jobs are considered valuable. Therefore, it makes sense to apply larger range spreads to these pay grades. The following are typical range spreads for different kinds of positions [1]:

- 20 to 25 percent: lower-level service, production, and maintenance
- 30 to 40 percent: clerical, technical, and paraprofessional
- 40 to 50 percent: high-level professional, administrative, and middle management
- 50 percent and above: high-level managerial and executive

After deciding on range spread, compensation professionals calculate minimum and maximum rates. Figure 9-4 illustrates the calculation of minimum and maximum

FIGURE 9-4 Calculation of Range Spread

Steps

1. Identify the midpoint: $20,000
2. Determine the range spread: 40%
3. Calculate the minimum:

$$\frac{\text{midpoint}}{100\% + (\text{range spread}/2)} = \frac{\$20{,}000}{100\% + (40\%/2)}$$

$$= \$16{,}666.67$$

4. Calculate the maximum:
   minimum + (range spread × minimum)

$$= \$16{,}666.67 + (40\% \times \$16{,}666.67)$$
$$= \$23{,}333.33$$

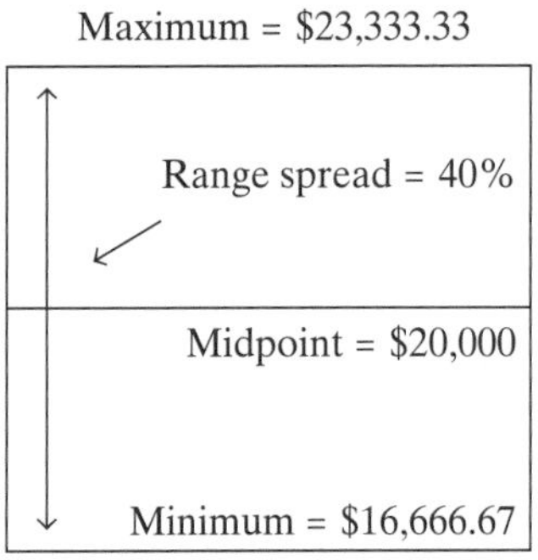

rates based on knowledge of the pay grade midpoint (as discussed earlier in Step 1) and the chosen range spread. Table 9-1 illustrates the impact of alternative range spread values on minimum and maximum values. This approach is typically applied when a company chooses to base the minimum and maximum rates budgetary constraints. We discuss budgeting issues later in this chapter.

Adjacent pay ranges usually overlap with other pay ranges so that the highest rate paid in one range is above the lowest rate of the successive pay grade. Figure 9-5 illustrates how to calculate pay range overlap. Overlapping pay ranges allow companies to promote employees to the next level without adding to their pay. Nonoverlapping pay ranges require pay increases for job promotions. Compensation professionals express overlap as a percentage. For example, the degree of overlap between pay range A and pay range B is about 33 percent.

Pay Compression

The minimum pay rate for a range usually is the lowest pay rate that the company will pay for jobs that fall within that particular pay grade. In theory, newly hired employees receive pay that is at or near the minimum. In practice, new employees often receive well above minimum pay rates, sometimes only slightly below or even higher than the pay moderately tenured employees receive. **Pay compression** occurs whenever a company's pay spread between newly hired or less qualified employees and more qualified job incumbents is small [2].

Two situations result in pay compression. The first is a company's failure to raise pay range minimums and maximums. Companies that retain set range maximums over

TABLE 9-1 The Impact of Alternative Range Spreads on Pay Range Minimum and Maximum Values, with Midpoint of $25,000

	Range Spread			
	20%	***50%***	***80%***	***120%***
Minimum: $\frac{\text{midpoint}}{100\% + (\text{range spread}/2)}$	$22,727	$20,000	$17,857	$15,625
Maximum: minimum + (range spread × minimum)	$27,272	$30,000	$32,143	$34,375
Difference between maximum and minimum values	$4,545	$10,000	$14,286	$18,750

FIGURE 9-5 Calculating Pay Range Overlap

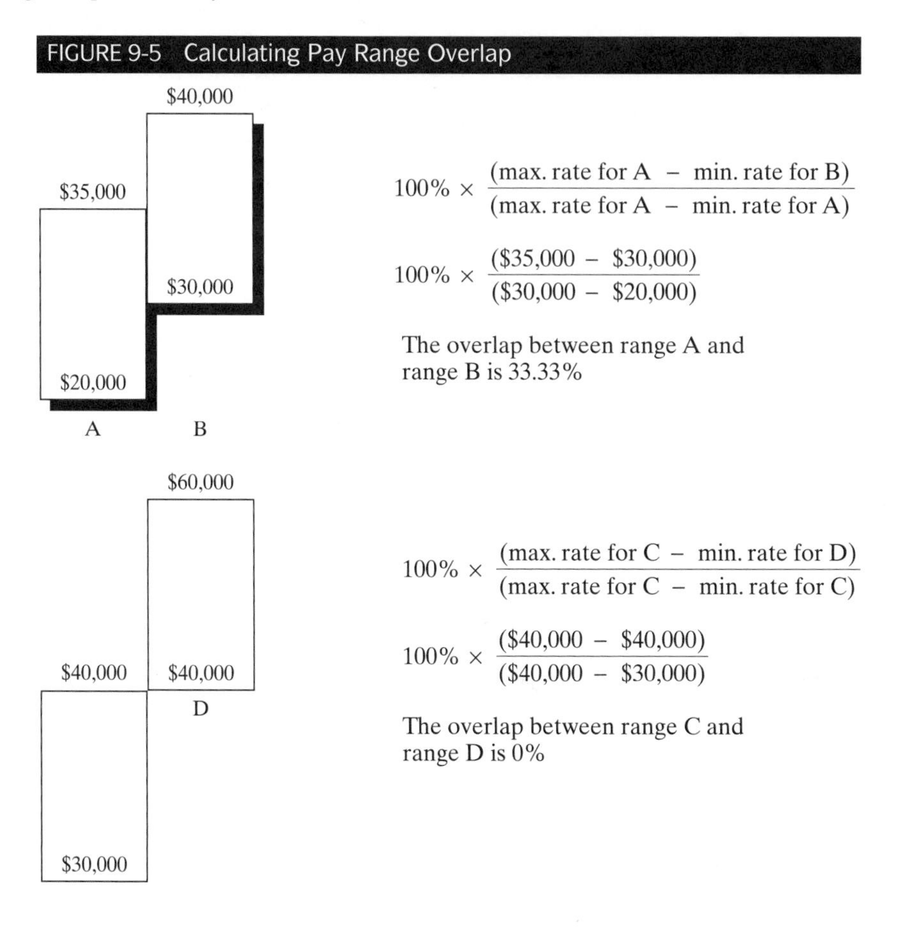

time limit increase amounts. For example, let's assume that the entry-level starting salaries for newly minted certified public accountants have increased 7 percent annually for the last 5 years. Tax-It, a small accounting firm, did not increase its pay range minimums and maximums for entry-level accountants during the same period because of lackluster profits. Nevertheless, Tax-It hired several new accountants at the prevailing market rate. Failure to pay competitive pay rates would hinder Tax-It's ability to recruit talented accountants. As a result, many of the Tax-It accountants with 5 or fewer years' experience have lower salaries (or slightly higher salaries at best) than newly hired accountants without work experience. The second situation that results in pay compression is a scarcity of qualified candidates for particular jobs. When the supply of such candidates falls behind a company's demand, wages for newly hired employees rise, reflecting a bidding process among companies for qualified candidates.

Pay compression can threaten companies' competitive advantage. Dysfunctional employee turnover is a likely consequence of pay compression. Dysfunctional turnover represents high-performing employees' voluntary termination of their employment. High-performing employees will probably perceive their pay as inequitable because they are receiving lower pay relative to their positive contributions (that is, experience and demonstrated performance) than newly hired employees who are receiving similar pay.

How can companies minimize pay compression? Maximum pay rates represent the most that a company is willing to pay an individual for jobs that fall in that particular range. Maximum pay rates should be set close to the maximum paid by other companies in the labor market for similar jobs. Setting competitive maximum rates enables a company to raise pay rates for high-quality employees who may consider employment opportunities with a competitor. However, maximum rates should not exceed maximum rates offered by competitors for comparable jobs because high maximums represent costs to the company over and above what are needed to be competitive.

Green Circle Pay Rates

Employees sometimes receive below-minimum pay rates for their pay ranges, especially when they assume jobs for which they do not meet every minimum requirement in the worker specification section of the job description. Below-minimum pay range rates are known as **green circle rates**. The pay rates of employees who are paid at green circle rates should be brought within the normal pay range as quickly as possible, which requires that both employer and employee take the necessary steps to eliminate whatever deficiencies in skill or experience that warranted paying below the pay range minimum.

Red Circle Pay Rates

On occasion, companies must pay certain employees greater than maximum rates for their pay ranges. Known as **red circle rates**, these higher pay rates help retain valued employees who have lucrative job offers from competitors. Alternatively, exemplary employees may receive red circle rates for exceptional job performance, particularly when a promotion to a higher pay grade is not granted. Red circle rates also apply to employees who receive job demotions to pay grades with lower maximum rates than the employees' current pay. Companies usually reduce demoted employees' pay over time until they receive pay that is consistent with their new jobs. In this case, red circle rates allow employees a chance to adjust to pay decreases.

Step 5: Evaluating the Results

After compensation professionals establish pay structures according to the previous steps, they must evaluate the results. Specifically, they must analyze significant differences between the company's internal values for jobs and the market's values for the same jobs. If discrepancies are evident, the company must reconsider the internal values they have placed on jobs. If their valuation of particular jobs exceeds the market's valuation of the same jobs, they must decide whether higher-than-market pay rates will undermine attainment of competitive advantage. If a company undervalues jobs relative to the market, managers must consider whether these discrepancies will limit the company's ability to recruit and retain highly qualified individuals.

Compensation professionals must also consider each employee's pay level relative to the midpoint of the pay grade. Again, the midpoint represents a company's competitive stance relative to the market. **Compa-ratios** index the relative competitiveness of internal pay rates based on pay range midpoints. Compa-ratios are calculated as follows:

$$\frac{\text{Employee's pay rate}}{\text{Pay range midpoint}}$$

Compa-ratios are interpreted as follows: A compa-ratio of 1 means that the employee's pay rate equals the pay range midpoint. Companies with market match policies strive for compa-ratios that equal 1. A compa-ratio less than 1 means that the employee's pay rate falls below the competitive pay rate for the job. Companies with market lag policies strive for compa-ratios of less than 1. A compa-ratio that is greater than 1 means that an employee's pay rate exceeds the competitive pay rate for the job. Companies with market lead policies strive for compa-ratios of greater than 1.

Human resource professionals also can use compa-ratios to index job groups that fall within a particular pay grade. Specifically, compa-ratios may be calculated to index the competitive position of a job—by averaging the pay rates for each job incumbent. Moreover, compa-ratios may be calculated for all jobs that comprise a pay grade, departments, or such functional areas as accounting.

Compa-ratios provide invaluable information about the competitiveness of companies' pay rates. Compensation professionals can use compa-ratios as diagnostic tools to judge the competitiveness of their companies' pay rates. Compa-ratios that exceed 1 tell compensation professionals that pay is highly competitive with the market. Compa-ratios that fall below 1 tell them that pay is not competitive with the market and that they should consider another course of action to increase pay over a reasonable period.

We've reviewed the elements of pay structures and the steps compensation professionals follow to construct them. Next, we consider three popular pay structures that should be familiar to compensation professionals:

- Merit pay structure
- Sales incentive compensation structure
- Pay-for-knowledge structure

DESIGNING MERIT PAY SYSTEMS

As we noted in Chapter 4, companies that use merit pay systems must ensure that employees see definite links between pay and performance. We also reviewed the rationale for using merit pay systems, as well as the possible limitations of this kind of pay system. Establishing an effective merit pay program that recognizes employee contributions requires avoiding such pitfalls as ineffective performance appraisal methods and poor communication regarding the link between pay and performance. Besides these considerations, managers interested in establishing a merit pay system must determine merit increase amounts, timing, and the type of merit pay increase—permanent or recurring increases versus one-time or nonrecurring additions to base pay. They must also settle on base pay levels relative to the base pay of functionally similar jobs [3].

Merit Increase Amounts

Merit pay increases should reflect prior job performance levels and motivate employees to perform their best. As managers establish merit increase amounts, they not only must consider past performance levels but also must establish rates that will motivate employees even after the impact of inflation and payroll deductions. Updating compensation survey data should account for increases in consumer prices (Chapter 8). As we noted in Chapter 4, "just-meaningful pay increases" refer to the minimum amounts employees will see as making a meaningful change in their compensation [4]. Trivial pay increases for average or better employees will not reinforce their performance or motivate them.

No precise mathematical formula determines the minimum merit increase that will positively affect performance; managers must consider three research findings [5]. First, boosting the merit increase amount will not necessarily improve productivity because research has shown diminishing marginal returns on each additional dollar allocated to merit increases [6]. In other words, each additional merit increase dollar was associated with smaller increases in production.

Second, employees' perceptions of just-meaningful differences in merit increases depend on their cost of living, their attitudes toward the job, and their expectations of rewards from the job. For employees who value pay for meeting economic necessity, a just-meaningful difference in pay increase tends to depend upon changes in the cost of living. On the other hand, for employees who value pay as a form of recognition, the size of the expected pay raise (versus cost of living) affects a just-meaningful difference [7].

Third, for the pay increase to be considered meaningful, the employee must see the size of the increase as substantive in a relative sense as well as in an absolute sense [8]. **Equity theory** suggests that an employee must regard his or her own ratio of merit increase pay to performance as similar to the ratio for other comparably performing people in the company. In practical terms, managers should award the largest merit pay increases to employees with the best performance, and they should award the smallest increases to employees with the lowest acceptable performance. The difference between these merit increases should be approximately equal to the differences in performance.

It is also essential that compensation professionals design plans that reinforce employees' motivation to perform well, with just-meaningful pay increases and merit increase percentages that clearly distinguish among employees based on their performance. However, the best-laid plans don't always lead to the desired results. Well-designed merit pay structures (and others that we discuss shortly) will fail without adequate funding.

Compensation budgets are blueprints that describe the allocation of monetary resources to fund pay structures. Compensation professionals index budget increases that fund merit pay programs in percentage terms. For example, a 10 percent increase for next year's budget means that it will be 10 percent greater than the size of the current year's budget. Often, this value is an indicator of the average pay increase employees will receive. Obviously, the greater the increase in the compensation budget, the more flexibility compensation professionals will have in developing innovative systems with substantial motivating potential.

Unfortunately, the magnitude of the increases in compensation budgets in recent years has been just slightly more than the average increases in cost of living. For example, the average earnings for all production or nonsupervisory employees in the United States increased only 4.3 percent in 2001 [9]. Although this value varies by occupation, industry, and region of the country, it does reflect a trend in the United States of stagnant growth in compensation budgets. The picture becomes less positive because the increase in cost of living for the same period was 2.8 percent [10]. This means that, on average, annual merit pay raises exceeded the increase in cost of living by only 1.5 percent, taking the motivational value out of pay increases.

Timing

The vast majority of companies allocate merit increases, as well as cost-of-living and other increases, annually. At present, companies typically take one of two approaches in timing these pay raises. Companies may establish a **common review date** or **common review period** so that all employees' performances are evaluated on the same date or during the same period—for example, the month of June, which immediately follows a company's peak activity period. Best suited for smaller companies, common review dates reduce the administrative burden of the plan by concentrating staff members' efforts to limited periods.

Alternatively, companies may review employee performance and award merit increases on the **employee's anniversary date—**the day on which the employee began to work for the company. Most employees will thus have different evaluation dates. Although these staggered review dates may not monopolize supervisors' time, this approach can be administratively burdensome because reviews must be conducted regularly throughout the year.

Recurring Versus Nonrecurring Merit Pay Increases

Companies have traditionally awarded merit pay increases permanently, and permanent increases are sometimes associated with some undesirable side effects, such as placing excessive cost burdens on the employer. In terms of costs, U.S. companies are increasingly concerned with containing costs as just one initiative in their quest to establish and sustain competitive advantage in the marketplace. Companies may advocate **nonrecurring merit increases**—lump sum bonuses—which lend themselves well to cost containment and have recently begun to gain some favor among unions, including the International Brotherhood of Electrical Workers [11]. Lump sum bonuses strengthen the pay-for-performance link and minimize costs because these increases are not permanent, and subsequent percentage increases are not based on higher base pay levels.

Present Level of Base Pay

Pay structures specify acceptable pay ranges for jobs within each pay grade. Thus, each job's base pay level should fall within the minimum and maximum rates for its respective pay grade. In addition, compensation professionals should encourage managers to offer similar base pay to new employees performing similar jobs unless employees' qualifications—education and relevant work experience—justify pay differences. This practice is consistent with the mandates of several laws (Chapter 3)—Title VII of the Civil Rights Act of 1964, the Equal Pay Act of 1963, and the Age Discrimination in Employment Act of 1967. Of course, employees' merit pay increases should vary with their performance.

Rewarding Performance: The Merit Pay Grid

Table 9-2 illustrates a typical merit pay grid that managers use to assign merit increases to employees. Managers determine pay raise amounts by two factors jointly: employees' performance ratings and the position of employees' present base pay rates within pay ranges. Pay raise amounts are expressed as percentages of base pay. For instance, let's say that two employees will each receive a 5 percent merit pay increase. One employee is paid on an hourly basis, earning $8.50 per hour, and the other is paid on an annual basis, earning $32,000. The employee whose pay is based on

TABLE 9-2 Merit Pay Grid

	Performance Rating				
	Excellent	*Above Average*	*Average*	*Below Average*	*Poor*
Q4 →$70,000 $65,000 $60,000	5%	3%	1%	0%	0%
Q3 →$55,000 $50,000 $45,000	7%	5%	3%	0%	0%
Q2 →$40,000 $35,000 $30,000	9%	7%	6%	2%	0%
Q1 →$25,000 $20,000 $15,000	12%	10%	8%	4%	0%

an hourly rate (usually nonexempt in accord with the Fair Labor Standards Act—that is, one who must be paid overtime for time worked in excess of 40 hours per week) receives a pay raise of $0.44 per hour, increasing her hourly pay to $8.94. The employee whose pay is based on an annual rate, typically exempt from the Fair Labor Standards Act provisions, receives a pay increase of $1,600, boosting her annual pay to $33,600.

In Table 9-2, employees whose current annual salary falls in the second quartile of the pay range and whose performance rates an average score receive a 6 percent merit pay increase. Employees whose current annual salary falls in the first quartile of the pay range and whose job performance is excellent receive a 12 percent merit pay increase. The term *cell* (as in spreadsheet software programs such as Microsoft Excel) is used to reference the intersection of quartile ranking and performance rating. Table 9-2 contains 20 cells.

Employees' Performance Ratings

Merit pay systems use performance appraisals to determine employees' performance. Where merit pay systems are in place, an overall performance rating guides the pay raise decision. In Table 9-2, an employee receives any one of five performance ratings ranging from "Poor" to "Excellent." As you can see, when we hold position in pay range constant, pay raise amounts increase with level of performance. This pattern fits well with the logic underlying pay-for-performance principles—recognize higher performance with greater rewards.

Employees' Positions Within the Pay Range

Employees' positions within the pay range are indexed by quartile ranking, which, in Chapter 8, we described as a measure of dispersion. Again, quartiles allow compensation professionals to describe the distribution of data—in this case, hourly or annual base pay amount—based on four groupings known as quartiles. In Table 9-2, the first quartile is the point below which 25 percent of the salary data lie (and above which 75 percent of the salary data are found), which is $25,000. In this example, 25 percent of the salary figures are less than or equal to $25,000, and 75 percent of these figures are greater than $25,000. The second quartile is the point below which 50 percent of the salary data lie (and above which 50 percent of the salary figures are found), which is $40,000 for this example. The third quartile is the point below which 75 percent of the salary figures lie (and above which 25 percent of the salary figures are found), which is $55,000 for this example. The fourth quartile is the point below which all of the salary data lie, which is $70,000. The lower a person's pay falls within its designated pay grade—for example, the first quartile versus the third quartile—the higher the percentage pay raise, all else being equal. Similarly, the higher a person's pay within its grade, the lower the percentage pay raise, all else being equal.

Holding performance ratings constant, compensation professionals reduce merit pay increase percentages as quartile ranks increase to control employees' progression through their pay ranges. Pay grade minimums and maximums not only reflect corporate criteria about the value of various groups of unlike jobs but also may be dictated by budgeting. We'll look at the issue of budgeting shortly. Let's take the case of two employees whose performance ratings are identical but whose base pay places them in different quartiles of the pay grade—one in the third quartile and the other in the first quartile. If these employees were to receive the same pay raise percentage, the base pay rate for the employee in the third quartile likely would exceed the maximum pay rate for the range more quickly than would the base pay rate for the employee in the first quartile.

Merit Pay Increase Budgets

Now that we've considered the design principles for merit pay grids, we'll take a closer look at budgetary considerations. Budgets limit the merit pay increase percentages in each cell. A **merit pay increase budget** is expressed as a percentage of the sum of employees' current base pay. For instance, let's assume that a company's top financial officers and compensation professionals agree to a 5 percent merit pay increase budget. Let's also assume that the sum of all employees' current base pay is $10 million. A 5 percent merit pay increase budget for this example equals $500,000 (5% × $10,000,000). In this example, employees, on average, receive a 5 percent merit pay increase. As described earlier, merit pay increases awarded to individual employees will vary according to performance level and position in the pay range. However, the average of the individual pay increases must not exceed the allotted merit pay increase budget, again 5 percent.

In practice, the typical merit pay increase budget is 4.5 percent, with some variation based on employee status [12]. For example, in 2001, nonexempt hourly employees earned an average 4.3 percent increase, exempt employees earned an average 4.6 percent increase, and executives earned an average 4.7 percent increase.

Compensation professionals generally ensure that merit pay increases do not exceed the budgeted value with the following four steps:

1. Compensation professionals ask managers and supervisors to indicate the percentage of employees who fall in each of the performance categories in the performance appraisal instrument. The sample merit pay grid illustrated in Table 9-2 lists five performance categories. For illustrative purposes, let's assume the following performance distribution for employees:

- Excellent: 10 percent
- Above average: 20 percent
- Average: 40 percent
- Below average: 25 percent
- Poor: 5 percent

2. Compensation professionals rely on position in the pay range to determine the percentage of employees whose pay falls into each quartile. For example, let's assume the following distribution of employees in each quartile:

- Q4: 20 percent
- Q3: 25 percent
- Q2: 40 percent
- Q1: 15 percent

In other words, 20 percent of employees earn pay that falls in the range from $55,000 to $70,000 (fourth quartile) in Table 9-2. Similarly, 25 percent of the employees earn pay that falls in the range from $40,000 to $55,000 (third quartile). The same rationale applies to the first and second quartiles.

3. Compensation professionals combine both sets of information to determine the percentage of employees who fall into each cell. The percentage of employees whose performance rating is excellent and whose base pay falls in the fourth quartile equals 2.0 percent (10 percent × 20 percent). The sum of the cell percentages totals 100 percent.

	Excellent	Above Average	Below Average	Average	Poor
Q4	10% × 20% = 2%	20% × 20% = 4%	40% × 20% = 8%	25% × 20% = 5%	5% × 20% = 1%
Q3	10% × 25% = 2.5%	20% × 25% = 5%	40% × 25% = 10%	25% × 25% = 6.25%	5% × 25% = 1.25%
Q2	10% × 40% = 4%	20% × 40% = 8%	40% × 40% = 16%	25% × 40% = 10%	5% × 40% = 2%
Q1	10% × 15% = 1.5%	20% × 15% = 3%	40% × 15% = 6%	25% × 15% = 3.75%	5% × 15% = 0.75%

4. Compensation professionals make recommendations for the merit pay increase amount in each cell. They combine this information with the percentage of employees who fall in each cell from the previous step to determine how much the assigned merit increase amount recommended for each cell contributes to the total merit pay increase budget. In Table 9-2, a 10 percent merit pay increase amount is recommended for employees whose performance rates above average and whose pay falls in the first quartile. Multiplying the recommended merit increase amount (10 percent) by the percentage of employees who fall in the corresponding cell from the previous step (3 percent) equals 0.30 percent. In other words, 0.30 percent of the total 5 percent merit pay increase budget will be awarded to employees whose performance rates as above average and whose pay falls in the first quartile. In this example, with a merit pay increase budget equaling $500,000, $1,500 would be available (0.30 percent × $500,000). The sum of these values should not exceed the total merit pay increase budget—5 percent in this example. Before finalizing the merit pay grid, compensation professionals may allocate different percentages to cells to determine the impact of their choices on the merit increase pay budget.

Pay structures based on merit differ from sales compensation in at least two key ways. First, whereas sales compensation programs center on incentives that specify rewards an employee will receive for meeting a preestablished—often objective—level of performance, merit pay programs generally base an employee's reward on someone else's (most often the employee's supervisor's) subjective evaluation of the employee's past performance. Second, in most instances, a sales employee's compensation is variable to the extent that it is composed of incentives. Under a merit pay system, an employee earns a base pay appropriate for the job (as discussed earlier in this chapter) that is augmented periodically with permanent pay raises or one-time bonuses.

DESIGNING SALES INCENTIVE COMPENSATION PLANS

Compensation programs for salespeople rely on incentives [13]. Sales compensation programs can help businesses meet their objectives by aligning the financial self-interest of sales professionals with the company's marketing objectives [14]. By extension, sales compensation programs can help companies achieve strategic objectives by linking sales professionals' compensation to fulfilling customer needs or other marketing objectives, such as increasing market share. Thus, sales compensation plans derive their objectives more or less directly from strategic marketing objectives, which, in turn, are derived from company competitive strategy. Particular sales objectives include [15]:

- Sales volume indicates the amount of sales that should be achieved for a specified period.
- New business refers to making sales to customers who have not purchased from the company before.
- Retaining sales simply targets a level of sales from existing customers.

STRETCHING THE DOLLAR

ETHICS OF INCENTIVE PAY

"Most short-term incentive awards are tied to the achievement of goals established . . . at the beginning of the plan year."* Although goal setting in most businesses is more an art than a science, an appropriate ethical stance would be that, once approved and announced, a goal is a goal unless extraordinary circumstances during the course of the year negatively affected goal achievement. The ethical challenge is often related to the definition of "extraordinary." So that otherwise unearned management bonuses could be paid, some CEOs have gone to great lengths to convince their directors that events that would otherwise be considered routine were in fact "extraordinary" and not subject to management control.

The human resources executive usually is responsible for the design and administration of top management incentive plans and often has input into the annual goal-setting process. In addition, the HR executive is enlisted in drafting (and sometimes presenting) the recommendations for the forthcoming year's goals and for justifying bonus targets that sometimes are not reflective of business conditions.

A common rationalization presented to the HR executive who is asked to bend the rules and draft a supportive argument to the compensation committees is management's fear that outstanding executives will leave if adequate bonuses are not paid. In some cases, this occurs. In most cases, this doesn't happen until several years of payouts have been skipped by the firm in question, while competitors have continued to award bonuses to their executives.

*Passage quoted from Rosen, S. D., & Juris, H. A. (1995). Ethical issues in human resource management. In G. R. Ferris, S. D. Rosen, & D. T. Barnum (Eds.), *Handbook of Human Resource Management*. Cambridge, MA: Blackwell Publishers, p. 205.

- Product mix rewards sales professionals for selling a preestablished mix of the company's goods or services. The rationale for the product mix objective is to help the company increase its competitiveness by promoting new products and services. Said another way, successfully meeting this sales objective rewards sales professionals for helping the company stay viable by not putting "all its eggs into one basket."
- Win-back sales is an objective that is designed to motivate sales professionals to regain business from former clients who are now buying from a competing company.

Alternative Sales Compensation Plans

Companies usually use one of five kinds of sales incentive plans. The type of plan appropriate for any given company will depend on the company's competitive strategy. The order of presentation roughly represents the degree of risk (from lowest to highest) to employees.

- Salary-only plans
- Salary-plus-bonus plans
- Salary-plus-commission plans
- Commission-plus-draw plans
- Commission-only plans

Salary-Only Plans

Under **salary-only plans**, sales professionals receive fixed base compensation, which does not vary with the level of units sold, increase in market share, or any other indicator of sales performance. From the employees' perspective, salary-only plans are relatively risk-free because they can expect a certain amount of income. From a company's perspective, salary-only plans are burdensome because the company must compensate its sales employees regardless of their achievement levels. Thus, salary-only plans do not fit well with the directive to link pay with performance through at-risk pay. Nevertheless, salary-only plans may be appropriate for particular kinds of selling situations such as:

- Sales of high-priced products and services or technical products with long lead times for sales
- Situations in which sales representatives are primarily responsible for generating demand, but other employees actually close the sales
- Situations in which it is impossible to follow sales results for each salesperson; that is, where sales are accomplished through team efforts
- Training and other periods when sales representatives are unlikely to make sales on their own

Salary-Plus-Bonus Plans

Salary-plus-bonus plans offer a set salary coupled with a bonus. Bonuses usually are single payments that reward employees for achievement of specific, exceptional goals. For a real estate agent, generating in excess of $2 million dollars in residential sales for a 1-year period may mean earning a bonus totaling several thousand dollars.

Salary-Plus-Commission Plans

Commission is a form of incentive compensation based on a percentage of the selling price of a product or service. **Salary-plus-commission plans** spread the risk of selling between the company and the sales professional. The salary component presumably enhances a company's ability to attract good employees and allows a company to direct its employees' efforts to nonselling tasks that do not lead directly to commissions, such as participating in further training or servicing accounts. The commission component serves as the employees' share in the gains they generated for the company.

Commission-Plus-Draw Plans

Commission-plus-draw plans award sales professionals with subsistence pay or draws—money to cover basic living expenses—yet provide them with a strong incentive to excel. This subsistence pay component is known as a **draw**. However, unlike salaries, companies award draws as advances, which are charged against commissions that sales professionals are expected to earn. Companies use two types of draws. **Recoverable draws** act as company loans to employees that are carried forward indefinitely until employees sell enough to repay their draws. **Nonrecoverable draws** act as salary because employees are not obligated to repay the loans if they do not sell enough. Clearly, nonrecoverable draws represent risks to companies because these expenses are not repaid if employees' sales performances are lackluster. Companies that adopt nonrecoverable draws may stipulate that employees cannot continue in the employment of the company if they fail to cover their draw for a specified number of months or sales periods during the year. This arrangement is quite common among car salespeople.

Commission-Only Plans

Under **commission-only plans**, salespeople derive their entire income from commissions. Three particular types of commissions warrant mention. **Straight commission** is based on a fixed percentage of the sales price of the product or service. For instance, a 10 percent commission would generate a $10 incentive for a product or service sold that is priced at $100, and $55 for a product or service sold that is priced at $550.

Graduated commissions increase percentage pay rates for progressively higher sales volume. For example, a sales professional may earn a 5 percent commission per unit for sales volume up to 100 units, 8 percent for each unit from 101 to 500 units, and 12 percent for each unit in excess of 500 sold during each sales period.

FLIP SIDE OF THE COIN

THE DARK SIDE OF SALES COMPENSATION PLANS

Salesmen at Chrysler's Withnell Dodge dealership in Salem, Oregon, noticed business was slow in early April of this year. Their response may have seemed odd to outsiders: They encouraged buyers to take even longer than usual to choose a car.

Why? Because of Chrysler's incentive program, which awarded bonuses to dealers who met a monthly sales goal but offered no rewards to those who did not. Once salesmen realized that they had little chance of hitting the April target, they delayed sales in the hope of achieving May's numbers instead.

Had Withnell Dodge been the only Chrysler dealership to react that way, the company might not have suffered. But other U.S. and Canadian dealerships also sought to delay sales. The carmaker's April sales dropped 18 percent that month, far more than the industry's average fall of 10 percent. Chrysler's management reassessed the incentive plan. Goals now cover a 90-day period, under the theory that sales over a longer period are more difficult to manipulate.

The trouble starts, according to Mike Jensen, managing director at the consulting firm Monitor Group, when companies pre-set sales and profits targets. "These processes are a joke," he says. In the ballet of budget negotiations, the most successful managers are seen as those who can convince bosses of poor market conditions in their particular area. Low expectations mean lower sales and profits targets, making it easier for executives to meet or beat numbers. Programs are usually structured so that hitting the target triggers a substantial bonus, while failing to reach it means no extra pay. The system leads not only to distortions in reporting but also to behavior that can permanently damage the company.

Source: Excerpt from Griffith, V., Targets that distort a company's aim. *Financial Times*, November 21, 2001 [online]. Available: *www.ft.com*, accessed July 7, 2002.

Finally, **multiple-tiered commissions** are similar to graduated commissions but with one exception. Employees earn a higher rate of commission for all sales made in a given period if the sales level exceeds a predetermined level. For instance, employees might earn only 8 percent for each item if total sales volume falls short of 1,000 units. However, if total sales volume exceeds 1,000 units, then employees might earn a per item commission equal to 12 percent for every item sold. Commission-only plans are well suited for situations in which:

- The salesperson has substantial influence over the sales.
- Low to moderate training or expertise is required.
- The sales cycle—the time between identifying the prospect and closing the sale—is short.

In contrast to salespeople on salary-only plans, commission-only salespeople shoulder all the risk: Employees earn nothing until they sell. Despite this risk, potential rewards are substantial, particularly with graduated and multiple-tiered commission plans.

Although commissions may fit well with cost-cutting measures, these incentives are not always the best tactic for compensating sales professionals. In fact, commission structures probably suffer from many of the same limitations of individual incentive plans that we discussed in Chapter 5, such as competitive behaviors among employees. Moreover, some sales experts argue that commissions undermine employees' intrinsic motivation to sell—that is, their genuine interest for the challenge and enjoyment that selling brings. These experts argue that once salespeople have lost that intrinsic motivation, commissions act essentially as controls to maintain sales professionals' performance levels. Said another way, such professionals may simply go through the motions in order to earn money without regard to quality and customer satisfaction [16].

For any sales compensation plan, it is critical that companies establish realistic total sales targets and individual performance standards. Beyond reasonable limits, it is possible that sales compensation plans will backfire. Consequences of such backfire include lower employee motivation, unprofessional behavior, and compromised profits. The "Flip Side of the Coin" feature illustrates the consequences of a poorly designed sales compensation plan.

Sales Compensation Plans and Competitive Strategy

Sales plans with salary components are most appropriate for differentiation strategies. Under salary-based sales plans, employees can count on receiving income. By design, salary plans do not require employees to focus on attaining sales volume goals or other volume indicators (for example, market share). Sales professionals who receive salaries can turn their attention to addressing clients' needs during the presale and servicing phases of the relationship. Salary-based sales compensation applies to the sale and servicing of such technical equipment as computer networks, including the hardware (for example, the individual computers and network server) and the software (applications programs such as Microsoft Excel or the Windows operating system).

Commission-oriented sales compensation plans are best suited for lowest-cost strategies because compensation expenditures vary with sales revenue. As a result, only the most productive employees earn the best salaries. Essentially, commissions represent rewards for "making the sale." For example, real estate sales agents' earnings depend upon two factors—number of houses sold and their selling price. Similarly, new-car salespersons' earnings depend on the number of cars sold and their selling price. In either situation, customers are likely to have questions and concerns following sales transactions. Many real estate sales companies employ real estate assistants at low salaries—not much more than the minimum wage—who mediate such buyers' queries of the sellers as "What grade of rock salt is most appropriate for the water softener apparatus?" Oftentimes, real estate assistants are training to be full-fledged real estate agents, and they view low pay as a necessary trade-off for learning the ropes.

In any event, the design, implementation, and effectiveness of sales compensation programs is essential for competitive advantage. For example, the Penn Mutual Life Insurance Company engaged the services of Oracle Corporation, an e-business solutions company, to develop a sales compensation system for its sales professionals:

> In the highly competitive insurance industry, the ability to motivate and compensate producers is a key factor in increasing revenue and market share. As part of its Producer Value Commitment, Penn Mutual has decided to implement this strategic compensation solution to enhance its producers' ability to track compensation and strengthen its ability to stay competitive in the compensation options that it offers. After evaluating several competing solutions, Penn Mutual determined that Oracle Sales Compensation provided the superior reporting, flexibility and ease of use necessary to support a large network of producers. Additionally, Penn Mutual cited Oracle Sales Compensation's Internet architecture as an important factor because it will help position the company for the future.
>
> "What differentiates Penn Mutual from other life insurance carriers is our strong commitment to deliver our products and services in ways that

make it easy for producers to do business with us," said Susan Kozik, Penn Mutual's senior vice president and chief technology officer. "Oracle Sales Compensation will enable producers to clearly track their compensation against sales goals and other key motivational rewards."

"Our Sales and Marketing team is very excited about this new system," added Larry Mast, executive vice president and chief marketing officer. All of the information they need will be at their fingertips, which will help them to work more productively."

"Penn Mutual is ahead of their competition in recognizing the importance of providing their producers with the tools they need to be effective," said Mark Barrenechea, senior vice president, CRM Product Division, Oracle Corp. "The strategic use of Oracle Sales Compensation will enable them to effectively grow their business by providing critical information that will help producers sell more products." [17]

Determining Fixed Pay and the Compensation Mix

Managers must balance fixed and incentive pay elements to directly affect employee motivation. The mix depends mainly on three factors:

- Influence of the salesperson on the buying decision
- Competitive pay standards within the industry
- Amount of nonsales activities required

Influence of the Salesperson on the Buying Decision

For the most part, the more influence sales professionals have on "buying" decisions, the more the compensation mix will emphasize incentive pay. Salespeople's influence varies greatly with the specific product or service marketed and the way these are sold. Many sales professionals assume an order-taker role, with little influence over purchase decisions. For example, salespeople in such large department stores as Sears have little influence over the merchandise for sale, because these stores send their buyers to manufacturers to purchase lines of products that will be sold in its stores throughout the United States and beyond. Product display and promotional efforts—television or newspaper ad campaigns—are determined by store management. Although a salesclerk with a bad attitude may prevent sales from happening, these workers control very little of the marketing effort.

On the other end of the spectrum, some employees serve as consultants to the client. For instance, when a company decides to invest in computerizing its entire worldwide operations, it may approach a computer manufacturer such as IBM to purchase the necessary equipment. Given the technical complexity of computerizing a company's worldwide operations, the client would depend on IBM to translate its networking needs into the appropriate configuration of hardware and software. Ultimately, these IBM sales professionals influence the purchaser's decision to buy.

Competitive Pay Standards Within the Industry

A company's compensation mix must be as enticing as that offered by competitors if the company wants to recruit high-quality sales professionals. Industry norms and the selling situation are among the key determinants of compensation mix. For instance, competitive standards may dictate that the company must give greater weight to either incentive or fixed pay, which we addressed earlier. Incentive (commission) pay weighs heavily in highly competitive retail industries, including furniture, home electronics, and auto sales. Salary represents a significant pay component in such high entry-barrier industries as pharmaceuticals. In the case of pharmaceuticals, barriers to entry include the U.S. Food and Drug Administration regulations on testing new products that significantly extend the time from product conception through testing to marketing for general use. Salary is an appropriate compensation choice because pharmaceutical companies face little risk of new competition.

Amount of Nonsales Activities Required

In general, the more nonsales duties salespeople have, the more their compensation package should tend toward fixed pay. Some companies and products, for instance, require extensive technical training or customer servicing activities. An excellent example is again the pharmaceuticals industry. Sales professionals employed by such companies as Bristol-Myers Squibb, Lilly, and Merck must maintain a comprehensive understanding of their products' chemical compositions, clinical uses, and contraindications.

DESIGNING PAY-FOR-KNOWLEDGE PROGRAMS

As indicated in Chapters 4 and 5, merit pay and incentive pay represent job-based approaches to compensating employees. In Chapter 6, we discussed the importance of paying for knowledge that many companies recognize. For this discussion, we use the terms *knowledge* and *skills* interchangeably, as the design features for both structures are virtually the same. In its purest form, pay-for-knowledge programs reward employees for the acquisition of job-related knowledge (or skills, in the case of skill-based pay plans). In practice, companies are concerned with how much employees' performance improve as a result of their newly acquired knowledge. Our focus in this section is on the latter.

A fundamental issue in pay-for-knowledge programs is whether investments in training provide measurable payoffs to companies. Recently, the American Society for Training and Development, a premier professional organization of training and development professionals, offered some insight. Based on a research study involving approximately 2,500 companies, training investments are positively related to future total stockholder return, gross profit margin, and income per employee [18].

Establishing Skill Blocks

Skill (knowledge) blocks are sets of skills (knowledge) necessary to perform a specific job (for example, typing skills versus analytical reasoning) or group of similar jobs (for example, junior accounting clerk, intermediate accounting clerk, and senior accounting clerk). Table 9-3 contains an example of a knowledge block familiar to us—building market competitive compensation systems (Chapters 2 and 8).

The number of skill blocks included in a pay-for-knowledge structure can range from two to several. Current plans average about 10 skill blocks [19]. The appropriate number of blocks depends on the variety of jobs within a company. The development of skill blocks should occur with three considerations in mind.

First, the company must develop job descriptions, which we discussed in Chapter 7. Job descriptions should be treated as blueprints for the creation of a pay-for-knowledge system. Well-crafted job descriptions should facilitate the identification of major skills, the training programs employees need to acquire horizontal and vertical skills, and accurate measures of performance.

Second, individual jobs should be organized into job families, or groups of similar jobs such as clerical, technical, and accounting. The information conveyed within a job description should enable the plan developers to identify skills that are common to all jobs in the family and skills that are unique for individual jobs in the family. Based on these groupings, all tasks necessary to perform the jobs in a job family should be listed to facilitate the identification of the skills necessary to perform the tasks.

TABLE 9-3 Knowledge Block: Building Market-Competitive Compensation Systems

I. Strategic analyses
  A. External market environment
    1. Industry profile
    2. Foreign demand
    3. Competition
    4. Long-term prospects
    5. Labor-market assessment
  B. Internal capabilities
    1. Financial condition
    2. Functional capabilities
    3. Human resource capabilities
II. Compensation surveys
  A. Using published compensation survey data
    1. Survey focus: Core or fringe compensation
    2. Sources of published compensation surveys
  B. Compensation surveys: Strategic considerations
    1. Defining relevant labor market
    2. Choosing benchmark jobs
  C. Compensation survey data: Summary, analysis, and interpretation
    1. Using the appropriate statistics to summarize survey data
      a. Central tendency
      b. Variation
    2. Updating the survey data
    3. Statistical analysis

Third, skills should be grouped into blocks. There are no hard-and-fast rules compensation professionals can follow to determine skill blocks. A general guideline is that the blocked knowledge should relate to specific job tasks and duties. Referring again to Table 9-3, knowledge about the external environment and a company's internal capabilities—two distinct sets of knowledge—together form the foundation of strategic analyses.

Transition Matters

A number of initial considerations arise in the transition from using job-based pay exclusively to using pay-for-knowledge programs as well. These issues include assessment of skills, alignment of pay with the knowledge structure, and access to training [20].

Skills Assessment

The skills assessment issue centers on who should assess whether employees possess skills at levels that justify a pay raise, on what basis assessments should be made, and when assessments should be conducted. Gaining employee trust is critical during the transition period, because employees may view new systems as threats to job security. Therefore, some combination of peer and self-assessments, as well as input from known "experts" such as supervisors, may be essential. The important ingredients here are employee input and the expertise of supervisors and managers. In the case of knowledge assessment, paper-and-pencil tests are useful tools.

Having established who should conduct assessments, on what basis should assessments be made? During the transition, companies use conventional performance measures that reflect employees' proficiency in skills use, complemented by employees' self-assessments. The use of both types of data is likely to increase an employee's understanding of the new system as well as build faith in it, particularly when testimony and the more conventional performance measures converge.

A final assessment matter concerns timing. During transition phases, managers should assess employees' performances more frequently to keep employees informed of how well they are doing under the new system. In addition, more frequent assessments should reinforce the key aim of pay for knowledge—to encourage employees to learn more. Performance feedback is essential for this process [21].

Aligning Pay with the Knowledge Structure

One of the most difficult tasks that managers face as they guide employees toward a pay-for-knowledge system is aligning pay with the knowledge structure. Upon implementation of pay for knowledge, employees' core compensation must reflect the knowledge or skills they have that the company incorporates into its pay-for-knowledge structure. If employees' actual earnings are more than the pay-for-knowledge system indicates, managers must develop a reasonable course of action so that employees can acquire skills that are commensurate with their current pay. If employees are underpaid, the company must provide pay adjustments as quickly as possible. The length of time required to make these necessary adjustments will depend on two factors—the number of such employees and the extent to which they are underpaid. Obviously, with limited budgets, companies will require more extended periods as either the number of underpaid employees or the pay deficit increases.

Access to Training

A final transition matter is access to training. Pay-for-knowledge systems make training necessary, rather than optional, for those employees who are motivated for self-improvement. Accordingly, companies that adopt pay for knowledge must ensure that all employees have equal access to the needed training for acquiring higher-level skills. They must do so not only to meet the intended aim of pay-for-knowledge programs—to reward employees for enhancing their skills—but also to address legal imperatives. Restricting access to training can lead to a violation of key laws (Chapter 3)—Title VII of the Civil Rights Act of 1964 and the Age Discrimination in Employment Act of 1967. Companies must also educate employees about what their training options are and how successful training will lead to increased pay and advancement opportunities within the company. In other words, employers should not assume that employees will necessarily recognize the opportunities that are available to them unless they are clearly communicated. Written memos and informational meetings conducted by HR representatives are effective communication media.

Training and Certification

Successful pay-for-knowledge programs depend on a company's ability to develop and implement systematic training programs. For many of the reasons cited in Chapter 1—intense domestic and global competition, rapid technological advancement, and educational deficits of new workforce entrants—progressive companies in the United States have adopted a continuous learning philosophy, which, like pay for knowledge, encourages employees to take responsibility for enhancing their skills and knowledge [22]. Clearly, training represents a key venue for continuous learning.

Because employees are required to constantly learn new skills, training becomes an ongoing process. Companies implementing pay for knowledge typically increase the amount of classroom and on-the-job training [23]. When training is well designed, employees should be able to learn the skills needed to increase their pay as well as the skills necessary to teach and coach other employees at lower skill levels. Accurate job descriptions are useful in determining training needs and focusing training efforts.

Employers must make necessary training available to employees so they can progress through the pay-for-knowledge system. A systematic method for ensuring adequate training coverage involves matching training programs with each skill block. Accessibility does not require that employers develop and deliver training themselves. Training that is developed and delivered by an agency not directly affiliated with the company—community college, vocational training institute, university, or private consultant—can be just as accessible when the employer integrates the offering of these other sources with its pay-for-knowledge program.

In-House or Outsourcing Training

The following criteria should be used to determine whether to develop and deliver training within the workplace or to outsource [24].

Expertise

Specialized training topics require greater expertise, and more generic topics require less expertise. Employers generally turn to in-house resources if they can draw on existing expertise. If in-house expertise is lacking, employers often seek an outside provider either to fill the need directly or to train individuals who become instructors. Employers usually rely on in-house expertise for employer- and product-specific training. Such training is governed by employer philosophies and procedures and is, therefore, not readily available in the external market.

Timeliness

Employers often seek outside services if the in-house staff does not have adequate time to develop and deliver the program within the time frame requested. For example, PeopleSoft, a business applications software development company, trains its clients (for example, Exxon-Mobil, Wal-Mart, General Motors, Ford, Citigroup, IBM, AT&T, and Verizon) on how to use the systems they install. Over time, client companies experience turnover, which often includes the departure of employees who are well trained to use installed PeopleSoft systems. To maintain effective business operations, client companies require training on demand. PeopleSoft offers training on demand to its clients through different forms of media, including the Internet and CD-ROMs.

Size of the Employee Population to Be Trained

Employers typically rely on in-house resources for larger groups of employees. The major impetus behind this decision is economics. If there is a large demand for training, the program is more likely to be delivered more than once, resulting in economies of scale.

Sensitivity or Proprietary Nature of the Subject Matter

Sensitive or proprietary training is defined as training used to gain a competitive advantage or training that gives access to proprietary, product, or strategic knowledge. Employers rarely issue security clearances to outside resources to provide training of this nature. If the area of the training is sensitive or proprietary, the training is likely to be done in-house regardless of the other factors just discussed.

Certification and Recertification

Certification ensures that employees possess at least a minimally acceptable level of skill proficiency upon completion of a training unit. Quite simply, if employees do not have an acceptable degree of skill, then the company wastes any skill-based compensation expenditure. Usually, supervisors and coworkers, who are presumably most familiar with the intricacies of their work, certify workers. Certification methods can include work samples, oral questioning, and written tests. Table 9-4 illustrates an example of WorldatWork's curriculum outline for their Certified Compensation Professional (CCP) certification.

Recertification, under which employees periodically must demonstrate mastery of all the jobs they have learned or risk losing their pay rates, is necessary to maintain the workforce flexibility offered by a pay-for-knowledge plan [25]. The recertification process typically is handled by retesting employees, retraining employees, or requiring employees to occasionally perform jobs that use their previously acquired skills.

For example, the Society for Human Resource Management offers two types of professional certification—the Professional in Human Resources and the Senior Professional in Human Resources. Individuals with at least 2 years of work experience in exempt jobs (Chapter 3) earn certification when they pass a comprehensive examination of knowledge in the HR domain. Because the field of HR knowledge changes over time, individuals with certification must periodically earn continuing education credits to maintain certification. Credits are earned through a wide variety of activities, including course and/or conference attendance, membership in professional organizations, leadership with the association, teaching, speaking, writing, and projects completed on the job. This updating process is known as recertification.

TABLE 9-4 WorldatWork Training Certification: Certified Compensation Professional (CCP)

Recognized as the world's standard since 1976, the Certified Compensation Professional (CCP) designation is known throughout the global rewards community as a mark of expertise and excellence in all areas of compensation. The CCP designation requires a passing score on nine examinations, including six required exams plus three chosen from the remaining elective exams. There is no limit for completion of these requirements.

Suggested order of required examinations

T1: Total Rewards Management
C1: Regulatory Environments for Compensation Programs
C2: Job Analysis, Documentation, and Evaluation
T3: Quantitative Methods
C4: Base Pay Management

Can be integrated at any time:

T2: Accounting and Finance for the Human Resources Professional

Electives (choose any three)

C5: Elements of Sales Compensation
C6: Elements of Executive Compensation
C6A: Advanced Concept in Executive Compensation
C9: Elements of Expatriate Compensation
C11: Performance Management: Strategy, Design, and Implementation
C12: Variable Pay: Incentives, Recognition, Rewards
T4: Strategic Communication in Total Rewards
T6: Mergers and Acquisitions: Benefits, Compensation, and Other HR Issues
T9: International Total Remuneration
T11: Fundamentals of Equity-Based Rewards

Source: WorldatWork Training Certification: Certified Compensation Professional (CCP). [online]. Available: *www.worldatwork.org*, accessed July 25, 2002.

PAY STRUCTURE VARIATIONS

The principles of pay structure development reviewed previously apply to the majority of established pay structures in companies throughout the United States. Broadbanding and two-tier pay structures represent variations to those pay structure principles.

Broadbanding

The Broadbanding Concept and Its Advantages

Companies may choose **broadbanding** to consolidate existing pay grades and ranges into fewer wider pay grades and broader pay ranges. Figure 9-6 illustrates a broadbanding structure and its relationship to traditional pay grades and ranges. Broadbanding represents the organizational trend toward flatter, less hierarchical corporate structures that emphasize teamwork over individual contributions alone [26]. Some federal government agencies including the Navy, the General Accounting Office, and the Central Intelligence Agency began experimenting with the broadbanding concept in the 1980s to introduce greater flexibility to their pay structures. Some private sector companies began using broadbanding in the late 1980s for the same reason. General Electric's plastics business is a noteworthy adopter of broadbanding. Because broadbanding is relatively new, little research describes these structures or documents their effectiveness in establishing flatter organizational structures.

Broadbanding uses only a few large salary ranges to span levels within the organization previously covered by several pay grades. Thus, HR professionals place jobs that were separated by one or more pay grades in old pay structures into the same band under broadbanding systems. For example, condensing three consecutive grades into a single broadband eliminates the hierarchical differences among the jobs evident in the original, narrower pay grade configuration. Now, employees holding jobs in a single broadband have equal pay potential, unlike employees in a multiple pay grade configuration. In addition, elimination of narrow bands broadens employees' job duties and responsibilities.

Some companies establish broadbands for distinct employee groups within the organizational hierarchy—upper management, middle management, professionals, and staff. This approach reduces management layers dramatically, and it should promote quicker decision-making cycles. Other companies create broadbands on the basis of

FIGURE 9-6 Broadbanding Structure and Its Relationship to Traditional Pay Grades and Ranges

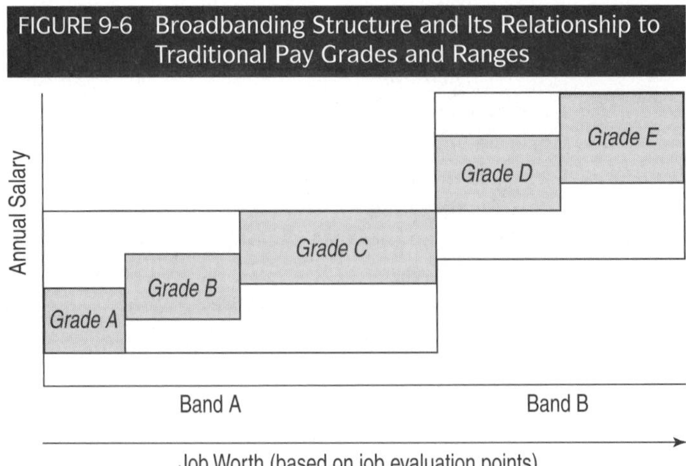

job families—clerical, technical, and administrative. Job family-based bands should give employees broader duties within their job classes. Still others may set broadbands according to functional areas, collapsing across job families. For example, a broadband may be established for all HR specialists—training, compensation, recruitment, and performance appraisal. These bands should encourage employees to expand their knowledge and skills in several HR functions.

Broadbanding shifts greater responsibility to supervisors and managers for administering each employee's compensation within the confines of the broadbands. Because broadbands include a wider range of jobs than narrowly defined pay grades, supervisors have greater latitude in setting employees' pay according to the tasks and duties they perform. Under traditional pay grades, employees receive pay and pay increases based on a limited set of duties stated in their job descriptions.

Limitations of Broadbanding

Notwithstanding the benefits of broadbanding, it does possess some limitations. Broadbanding is not a cure-all for all compensation-related dysfunction within companies. For instance, broadbanding changes how compensation dollars are allocated but not how much is allocated. Managers often think that flatter organizational structures reduce costs. To the contrary, broadbanding may lead to higher compensation expenses because managers have greater latitude in assigning pay to their employees. In fact, the federal government's limited experience showed that broadbanding structures were associated with more rapid increases in compensation costs than traditional pay structures [27].

Broadbanding also necessitates a trade-off between the flexibility to reward employees for their unique contributions and a perception among employees that fewer promotional opportunities are available. This transition from multiple narrowly defined pay grades to fewer broadbands reduces organizational hierarchies that support job promotions. Employers and employees alike need to rethink the idea of promotions as a positive step through the job hierarchy.

Two-Tier Pay Structures

The Two-Tier Pay System Concept and Its Advantages

Two-tier pay structures reward newly hired employees less than established employees. Under the temporary basis, employees have the opportunity to progress from lower entry-level pay rates to the higher rates enjoyed by more senior employees. Permanent two-tier systems reinforce the pay-rate distinction by retaining separate pay scales: Lower-paying scales apply to newly hired employees, and current employees enjoy higher-paying scales. Although pay progresses within each scale, the maximum rates to which newly hired employees can progress are always lower than more senior employees' pay scales. Table 9-5 illustrates a typical two-tier wage structure.

Two-tier wage systems are more prevalent in unionized companies. Labor representatives have reluctantly agreed to two-tier wage plans as a cost-control measure. In exchange for reduced compensation costs, companies have promised to limit layoffs. These plans represent a departure from unions' traditional stance of single base pay rates for all employees within job classifications. Approximately a third of collective bargaining agreements contained a two-tier wage provision in 1999 [28].

Two-tier pay structures enable companies to reward long-service employees while keeping costs down by paying lower rates to newly hired employees who do not have

TABLE 9-5 Two-Tier Wage Structure

The following pay rates apply to the 2003 calendar year. Employees hired on or after January 1, 2003, will be paid according to Schedule A below. Employees hired before January 1, 2003, will be paid according to Schedule B below.

Schedule A			
Job Classification	***Hourly Pay Rate***	***Cost-of-Living Adjustment***	***Total Hourly Pay Rate***
Shop floor laborers	$12.10	$1.36	$13.46
Assemblers	$14.05	$1.36	$15.41
Carpenters	$16.50	$1.36	$17.86
Plumbers	$16.90	$1.36	$18.26
Schedule B			
Job Classification	***Hourly Pay Rate***	***Cost-of-Living Adjustment***	***Total Hourly Pay Rate***
Shop floor laborers	$14.10	$1.36	$15.46
Assemblers	$16.05	$1.36	$17.41
Carpenters	$18.50	$1.36	$19.86
Plumbers	$18.90	$1.36	$20.26

an established performance record within the company. Usually, as senior employees terminate their employment—taking jobs elsewhere or retiring—they are replaced by workers who are compensated according to the lower-paying scale.

Limitations of Two-Tier Pay Structures

A potentially serious limitation of two-tier plans is that the lower pay scale applied to newly hired workers may restrict a company's ability to recruit and retain the most highly qualified individuals. Resentment can build among employees on the lower tier toward their counterparts on the upper tier, which may lead to lower tier employees' refusal to perform work that extends in any way beyond their job descriptions. Such resentment may lead employees on the upper tier to scale back their willingness to take on additional work to the extent that they perceive pay premiums are not sufficiently large to compensate for extra duties. In addition, opponents of two-tier wage systems contend that pay differentials cause lower employee morale. Finally, conflict between the tiers may lead to excessive turnover. When high performers leave, then the turnover is dysfunctional to the company and can have long-term implications for productivity and quality.

SUMMARY

In this chapter, we reviewed the pay structure concept as well as the building blocks needed to establish pay structures. Compensation professionals develop pay structures for the various pay bases. Pay structure development generally entails linking the internal job structure with the external market's pricing structure for jobs, knowledge, or skills. Once developed, pay structures recognize individual differences in employee contributions, and these structures represent operational plans for implementing and administering pay programs.

Key Terms

- pay structures, 272
- pay grades, 273
- pay ranges, 275
- midpoint pay value, 275
- range spread, 276
- pay compression, 277
- green circle rates, 279
- red circle rates, 279
- compa-ratios, 279
- equity theory, 281
- compensation budgets, 281
- common review date, 281
- common review period, 281
- employee's anniversary date, 281
- nonrecurring merit increases, 282
- merit pay increase budget, 284
- salary-only plans, 286
- salary-plus-bonus plans, 287
- commission, 287
- salary-plus-commission plans, 287
- commission-plus-draw plans, 287
- draw, 287
- recoverable draws, 287
- nonrecoverable draws, 287
- commission-only plans, 287
- straight commission, 287
- graduated commissions, 287
- multiple-tiered commissions, 288
- skill (knowledge) blocks, 291
- certification, 294
- recertification, 295
- broadbanding, 296
- two-tier pay structures, 297

Discussion Questions

1. Respond to the following statement: "Pay grades limit a company's ability to achieve competitive advantage." Do you agree? Provide a rationale for your position.
2. Two employees perform the same job, and each received exemplary performance ratings. Is it fair to give one employee a smaller percentage merit increase because his pay falls within the third quartile but give a larger percentage merit increase to the other because his pay falls within the first quartile? Please explain your answer.
3. Describe some ethical dilemmas sales professionals may encounter. How can sales compensation programs be modified to minimize ethical dilemmas?
4. React to the statement: "Merit pay grids have the potential to undermine employee motivation." Please discuss your views.
5. Compression represents a serious dysfunction of pay structures. Discuss some of the major ramifications of compression. Also, discuss how companies can minimize or avoid these ramifications.

Exercises

Compensation Online

For Students

Exercise 1: Find relevant journal articles

Use your school library's online catalog to locate articles pertaining to job families and pay structure. Find and read several current articles in these areas. Write your best explanation of these topics, as if you had to explain it to someone else who was trying to learn.

Exercise 2: Write a short paper on pay structure design

Visit *www.hr-guide.com*. Also, conduct an advanced Yahoo search for "pay structures" or "pay grades." What do you find out about creating pay grades? Describe five considerations HR professionals should take into account when designing pay structures.

Exercise 3: Research compa-ratios

One of the important topics in this chapter had to do with compa-ratios. Use Yahoo and two other search engines to find information on this topic. Which search engine did you find to be most helpful? Why?

Select one of the sites to review. Write a brief summary of the site. Did it help you understand the topic any better? Why or why not?

For Professionals

Exercise 1: Research compensation design consultants

You are working for a firm that is growing rapidly. Your current compensation administration practices were sufficient for one office and 30 employees. However, you now have offices in several cities and more than 200 employees. As the firm continues to grow, you (the human resources department) need help keeping up. From Yahoo's Business and Economy section, search the Business to Business listing for compensation system design firms. Which ones specifically mention merit pay, incentive pay, or person-focused pay? Give examples of what they say about each topic.

Exercise 2: Research and review pay scales

Audit the pay scales of the University of Pennsylvania using their Web page, *www.hr.upenn.edu/*. Click on "Compensation Salary Structure." Review the salary structure for the appropriate grade, schedule, and job type for various positions that are links at the bottom of the page. Think about the skills and responsibilities that you have had in past jobs. Based on the general level of skills and responsibilities you have had, where would your past jobs have fallen in this pay structure?

Exercise 3: Research an organization

Use Yahoo to search for the American Society for Payroll Management (ASPM). Read about this organization and read its newsletter. How would being a part of this organization be useful to the HR professional?

Endnotes

1. Bureau of National Affairs. (2002). *Skill-Based Pay.* BNA's Library on Compensation & Benefits on CD [CD-ROM]. Washington, DC: Author.
2. Myers, D. W. (1989). *Compensation Management.* Chicago: Commerce Clearing House.
3. Heneman, R. L. (1992). *Merit Pay: Linking Pay Increases to Performance.* Reading, MA: Addison-Wesley.
4. Krefting, L. A., & Mahoney, T. A. (1977). Determining the size of a meaningful pay increase. *Industrial Relations, 16*, pp. 83–93.
5. Heneman, R. L. (1992). *Merit pay: Linking Pay Increases to Performance.* Reading, MA: Addison-Wesley.
6. Rambo, W. W., & Pinto, J. N. (1989). Employees' perceptions of pay increases. *Journal of Occupational Psychology, 62*, pp. 135–145.
7. Krefting, L. A., Newman, J. M., & Krzystofiak, F. (1987). What is a meaningful pay increase? In D. B. Balkin, & L. R. Gòmez-Mejía (Eds.), *New Perspectives on Compensation.* Upper Saddle River, NJ: Prentice Hall.
8. Heneman, R. L. (1992). *Merit Pay: Linking Pay Increases to Performance.* Reading, MA: Addison-Wesley.
9. WorldatWork. (2002). Survey: Inflation continues to close in on salary increases [online]. Available: *www.worldatwork.org*, accessed: June 17, 2002.
10. U.S. Bureau of Labor Statistics. (2002). Consumer Price Index summary [online]. Available: *www.bls.gov/cpi/*, accessed July 7, 2002.
11. Erickson, C. L. & Ichino, A. C. (1994). Lump-sum bonuses in union contracts. *Advances in Industrial and Labor Relations, 6*, pp. 183–218.
12. WorldatWork. (2002). Survey: Inflation continues to close in on salary increases [online]. Available: *www.worldatwork.org*, accessed June 17, 2002.
13. Carey, J. F. (1992). *Complete Guide to Sales Force Compensation.* Homewood, IL: Irwin.
14. Kuhlman, D. C. (1994). Implementing business strategy through sales compensation. In W. Keenan Jr. (Ed.), *Commissions, Bonuses, & Beyond.* Chicago: Probus Publishing.
15. Myers, D. W. (1989). *Compensation Management.* Chicago: Commerce Clearing House.
16. Keenan, W., Jr. (1994). The case against commissions. In W. Keenan Jr. (Ed.), *Commissions, Bonuses, & Beyond.* Chicago: Probus Publishing.
17. PR Newswire. (August 9, 1999). Penn Mutual chooses Oracle customer relationship management (CRM) software [online]. Available: *findarticles.com/cf_0/m4PRN/1999_August_9/55379514/print.jhtml*, accessed June 19, 2002.
18. American Society for Training and Development. (2000). Profiting from learning: Do firms' investments in education and training pay off? [online]. Available: *www.astd.org/virtual—community/research/PFLWhitePaper.pdf*, accessed July 7, 2002.
19. Bureau of National Affairs. (2002). *Skill-Based Pay.* BNA's Library on Compensation & Benefits on CD [CD-ROM]. Washington, DC: Author.

20. Dewey, B. J. (1994). Changing to skill-based pay: Disarming the transition landmines. *Compensation & Benefits Review, 26*, pp. 38–43.
21. Karl, K., O'Leary-Kelly, A. M., & Martocchio, J. J. (1993). The impact of feedback and self-efficacy on performance in training. *Journal of Organizational Behavior, 14*, pp. 379–394.
22. Rosow, J., & Zager, R. (1988). *Training: The Competitive Edge*. San Francisco: Jossey-Bass.
23. Jenkins, G. D., Jr., & Gupta, N. (1985). The payoffs of paying for knowledge. *National Productivity Review, 4*, pp. 121–130.
24. Noe, R. A. (2001). *Employee Training and Development* (2nd ed.). Boston: Irwin/McGraw-Hill.
25. Jenkins, G. D., Jr., Ledford, G. E., Jr., Gupta, N., & Doty, D. H. (1992). *Skill-Based Pay*. Scottsdale, AZ: American Compensation Association.
26. Risher, H. H., & Butler, R. J. (1993–94). Salary banding: An alternative salary-management concept. *ACA Journal, 2*, pp. 48–57.
27. Schay, B. W., Simons, K. C., Guerra, E., & Caldwell, J. (1992). Broad-banding in the federal government—technical report. Washington, DC: U.S. Office of Personnel Management.
28. The Bureau of National Affairs. (2002). *Two-Tier Wage Structures*. BNA's Library on Compensation & Benefits on CD [CD-ROM]. Washington, DC: Author.

COMPENSATION IN ACTION

CAN PAY FOR PERFORMANCE REALLY WORK?

While pay for performance can be a solution for some organizations in search of new compensation concepts, it's not the answer for every company. Design is important, and the downside can be steep.

At a time of economic slowdowns and uncertainty, a compensation concept such as pay for performance is particularly tempting and increasingly popular. A recent survey by Hewitt Associates LLC found that nearly 8 in 10 companies have some kind of variable pay system, up from fewer than 5 in 10 in 1990. It's an understandable trend at a time when revenues slump, stock options shrivel, and across-the-board raises just aren't feasible for many organizations.

The question for HR people who wonder if they should follow suit is this: Does pay for performance really work? The answer is that while pay for performance can work, it's not the solution for every organization.

The range of opinion about pay for performance is broad and deep. Its proponents say that rigorous, long-term pay-for-performance systems offer effective methods of helping companies continually improve the workforce while getting and keeping the best people. Opponents argue that incentive pay plans tend to pit employees against one another, erode trust and teamwork, and create what critics call dressed-up sweatshops.

Sometimes, it's bad even while it's good. Lisa Weber, executive vice president of human resources for MetLife, calls the shift to a pay-for-performance model "absolutely gut-wrenching. Some people hate it."

But after MetLife placed all employees on a rating scale that is subject to change based on the performance of specific goals and core behaviors, the company's return on equity jumped from 7 percent in 1998 to 10.5 percent in 2000. "It's been tough, but it's been fabulous," she says.

The concept of pay for performance isn't new. Ever since ancient Mesopotamians were paid by the basket for picking olives, there's been some form of performance-based pay. In the modern era, the term is used fairly loosely: Commissions and bonuses are often thrown into the definition.

For the purposes of this story, pay for performance means a variable pay approach that is anchored to a measurement of performance, whether that's how many hours an attorney bills every month or a more subjective standard—how well a manager fosters teamwork, for instance. Often, evaluations are based on best-to-worst forced ranking systems—known to many employees as rank and yank—which are thought to provide a way of identifying and rewarding strong performers and encouraging everyone to work harder and smarter. True pay for performance is more formalized than an occasional attaboy bonus. It is variable compensation that must be re-earned each year and doesn't permanently increase base salary.

WHAT MAKES IT WORK?

When it is measurable and objective, pay for performance is not limited to such environments as assembly lines or the piecework arena. It can translate to any business, including banks, accountants, and legal firms, says Niki Somerset, a management consultant in Virginia Beach, Virginia, who has helped many businesses move from a straight salary plan to a performance-based program. "Incentive pay has always been quietly done in boardrooms," she says. "If you've got 250 attorneys in 30 cities, you've got to set projections, people have to be productive. Billable hours are the ticket."

MetLife measures employees and managers by comparing each person to others who are on the same level. Employees are measured on a 1-to-5 scale. The company then calculates which employees are at the top, in the middle, and at the bottom. Employees who rate a 3 receive about 65 percent more in bonuses than those who earn a 2. A person rated 3 might receive a bonus of $6,900, whereas one who rated 2 would get $4,200.

The company is concentrating a great deal of attention on the most senior 250 of the organization's 46,393 employees, says Weber. They are evaluated on their individual performance results and on questions such as: Do they show partnership? Do they demonstrate teamwork? Do they create heroes? How dedicated are they to learning and development?

Synygy, Inc., the largest provider of incentive management software and services, implemented its own plan a couple of years after the company was founded in 1991. Company spokesman Oliver Picher describes it as a bonus program that ranges in amount from 5 to 100 percent of an employee's base salary and is paid quarterly. Evaluation ratings are set by a "mentor" (supervisor) and also by coworkers who use an appraisal system called OPTIC: Ownership, Professionalism, Teamwork, (Continuous) Improvement, and Client Focus.

Employees are rated on a 1-to-5 scale. Objectives are set at the beginning of the quarter and at the end, and everyone in the company participates—whether clerical worker or top executive. As director of public relations, Picher says, he is evaluated on responsibilities that apply to his specific job, such as the number and quality of press releases and their impact, and the contacts he's made with specific people and organizations.

When it is designed for whole-company success: Pay for performance is often criticized for tilting a company toward one measure and away from another. Individual goals can pit workers against each other. A plan that focuses only on output will invariably suffer in the area of quality.

At MetLife, the focus is on individual performance, but "it's not OK to step on people's toes," Weber says. "You must rate high on partnership and teamwork. If you're a great performer but a terrible team player, you won't do well."

Financial results shouldn't be the only measure for pay-for-performance success, says Margaret Bentson, principal compensation manager at Hewitt Associates, San Francisco. Customer service should also be considered, with a scoring system that might include such factors as on-time delivery, reduction in the number of returned products, and client satisfaction surveys. "The idea is to marry the fortunes of the employee to the performance of the company."

When employees have a sizable stake in the action: At Nucor Corporation, the largest steel producer in the United States, the secret to success is to give huge bonuses of 100 or even 150 to 160 percent, says James M. Coblin, vice president of human resources. "That's when employees catch fire."

The Charlotte, North Carolina, company—which employs 8,000 people at 22 plants in nine states—has the highest productivity, the highest wages, and the lowest labor costs per ton in the American steel industry. The average pay in the year 2000 was $63,000 for a steel mill employee. Coblin says the program succeeds because every employee can see how the incentive arrangement affects his wages each week.

During the down times, of course, there's also sharing. The company doesn't lay people off, Coblin says. Rather, the plant shuts down its production lines for a day or two a week. Salaried executives still work; hourly employees aren't required to. About 80 percent of Nucor's employees are on this production incentive plan. Other employees also have performance-based compensation.

When the whole organization is involved: "To make it work, the most important thing is the involvement of the whole company," Somerset says. "Even if there's only a 1 percent profit, it should be divided among everyone, including the administration. Everyone is part of the team-building." Nucor, for instance, gives non-production employees other awards—from free dinners for outstanding work to one share of stock for every year of employment.

Involvement of another kind has been a key to success in Colorado's Douglas County School District, which has one of the oldest and most extensive pay-for-performance programs in the country. The program works, in part, because of the enormous effort that was invested in developing the system over a two-year period, says Douglas Hartman, the district's HR director. That built confidence among teachers long before the plan was implemented, he says.

Another reason for the success of the plan, now in its eighth year, is that the school district funds the program internally. "We are not dependent on outside grants or legislative programs," Hartman says. "That's one of the big reasons it's been a success in attracting, retaining, and

(Continued)

(Continued)

rewarding the best teachers. Our plan is consistent and reliable."

When there are clear expectations: At MetLife, "there is a lot more honesty in this process," Weber says. "It forces a level of openness. People meet expectations and know where they stand. The message is this: It pays to be a high performer." Weber credits the company's new pay-for-performance program as "the driving force behind our cultural transformation. We have created an environment where the top performers can thrive. No one here is 'entitled' to anything." Since the new pay system was instituted, turnover has dropped and is now 12 percent, Weber says. It is only 6 percent among the top performers.

At Synygy, "everyone knows there's an evaluation and who gives it," Picher says. "There are no surprises. What's important is that you have to evaluate people on a regular basis. People have to know why you're doing it so they can make adjustments and their job is under their control."

When there is commitment to training and support: "Pay for performance requires more of a commitment to training or it will not work." Somerset says. "And it may require more administrative support."

WHEN DOES PAY FOR PERFORMANCE FALL SHORT?

When it pits employees against each other: This is the biggest problem with pay for performance, says Stanford University professor Jeffrey Pfeffer, who has researched the subject extensively and declares pay for performance "a myth."

"A company's success is not a consequence of what an individual does. It's a consequence of what the system does," says Pfeffer, the Thomas D. Dee professor of organizational behavior at the Stanford Business School.

"These programs do more damage than good," agrees Marc Holzer, a Rutgers University business professor and president of the American Society for Public Administration. He's watched agencies and schools trot out various compensation schemes, try them out, keep them, change them, and abandon them.

"They set up competition between people. They emphasize the individual rather than the team. Virtually all innovations are group efforts. Yes, the exceptional person should be rewarded. But that exceptional person is dependent on others, on support services, which is often ignored."

"Incentive pay is toxic. . . . By the early nineties, I was spending 95 percent of my time on conflict resolution instead of on how to serve our customers," says Pat Lancaster, the chairman of Lantech, a manufacturer of packaging machinery with 325 employees, who is quoted by Pfeffer in his book *The Human Equation: Building Profits by Putting People First* (Harvard Business School Press, 1998). What the system bred wasn't profits, Lancaster told Pfeffer, but greedy rival gangs of workers.

The competitive aspects of pay for performance have made it a hotly contested issue in public agencies, including some school systems. New York Mayor Rudolph Giuliani proposed an individual merit pay program last year, drawing the ire of United Federation of Teachers/New York president Randi Weingarten. She says Giuliani's plan would worsen potential teacher shortages. "Classrooms aren't factories, and teachers don't do piecework," she says. "To do their work well, educators need to collaborate—not compete—with their colleagues."

Pfeffer says evidence indicates that incentive compensation may be more effective at a divisional or organizational rather than an individual level. "Profit sharing, stock ownership, gain sharing, and group bonuses seem more consistently to produce positive results than do individually based incentive schemes."

When it pushes one outcome to the detriment of others: Highly competitive pay systems tend to promote far less beneficial qualities, Pfeffer says. "Sears tried it and got in trouble." As he explains in his book, "Sears abandoned a commission system at its automobile repair stores when California officials found widespread evidence of consumer fraud, with employees recommending unneeded repairs to unsuspecting customers, for example."

Pfeffer says organizations that have tried and subsequently abandoned performance-for-pay plans cite problems that include overly aggressive salespeople who alienate consumers and high turnover rates.

Despite past problems with its commission system in the company's auto repair stores, Sears spokeswoman Peggy Palter says, "That was just a small part of our business." The company is still very much in favor of pay for performance, she notes, "and has been very pleased with the results." Over the years, Palter says, Sears has continued to update and improve its compensation system, and has developed different approaches for different parts of the company—the credit and retail divisions, for example. "We now incent on customer service scores," she says, adding that customer service improvements have been rapid because of bonus pay for performance.

When it is too subjective: Weber says that subjectivity in ratings is the most controversial part of MetLife's process. "If one manager rates an employee 3, but his boss rates the same person 2, there's a lot of blaming. The manager goes back to the employee and says, 'I rated you 3, but so-and-so only gave you 2.'"

When it is so subjective that it opens the company to allegations of bias: Former and current employees at Microsoft, Ford, and Conoco have filed lawsuits, alleging that the forced-ranking systems used by those companies to award bonuses and weed out underperformers were biased against some groups of workers: white males over blacks or women, for example, or younger managers over older ones.

CAN YOU MAKE IT WORK?

If you are going to embark on a pay-for-performance plan, look at these generally accepted principles:

- Success depends on the willingness of individual managers to make objective assessments of their employees.
- Managers must be willing to differentiate between performances that meet expectations and those that exceed—or fall short of—expectations.
- Competency-based systems should measure an employee's performance against a set of core behaviors that have a proven impact on business.
- Payouts should be made quarterly or at least more often than annually.
- There must be follow-up evaluations.
- The plan must be communicated clearly, frequently, and simply.
- Success depends on training, reinforcement, and companywide commitment.

A Hewitt Associates study released last year gives pay for performance mixed reviews. More companies are using the incentive plan now than in 1990, but only 22 percent said they believe that pay incentives work. Twenty-one percent of the companies surveyed said they did not think it helped; 57 percent said it "somewhat helped." An earlier Hewitt survey, conducted in 1995, found that among the 61 percent of organizations in the sample that had adopted variable compensation plans with budgets of $5 million or more, 48 percent of the plans failed to achieve their goals.

In his book, Pfeffer relates that, despite their popularity, most plans share two attributes: They absorb vast amounts of management time and resources, and they make everyone unhappy.

And yet MetLife is thrilled with its program, Weber says. "It's tough stuff," she adds. "But I go out on tour and I ask people all over the country to raise their hand if they're satisfied with the plan. Everyone raises his or her hand. It's not all about money. It's how you feel inside. We still have work to do on the program. To make something an institution, you have to change hearts as well as minds."

Whatever HR professionals decide to do about pay for performance, Pfeffer urges them to keep this in mind: "Many studies strongly suggest that this form of reward [individual incentive pay] undermines teamwork, encourages a short-term focus, and leads people to believe that pay is not related to performance at all but to having the 'right' relationships and an ingratiating personality."

That suggests that the only way pay for performance can work is if it rewards teamwork and long-term focus, and is designed to be as objective and fair as possible. Some proponents obviously think that's possible. Critics like Pfeffer think the idea is inherently flawed, and that it ignores another reason people work: "for meaning in their lives."

"In fact," he adds, "people work to have fun." Companies that ignore this fact are "essentially

(Continued)

(Continued)

bribing their employees and will pay the price in a lack of loyalty and commitment."

Jay Schuster, a partner in Schuster-Zingheim and Associates, Inc., in Los Angeles and co-author of *Pay People Right*! (Jossey-Bass, 2000), has argued with Pfeffer about pay for years. "Pfeffer is right. People do work for more than pay," he says. "But what they are concerned with is this: a compelling future, a positive workplace, individual growth, and total pay.

"The organizations that do indeed truly reward people consistently for performance out-perform those that don't," Schuster adds. "My sense is, if you're not going to pay for performance, what are you going to pay for?"

It is a question that has no easy answer. But most of those close to the issue would agree with Pfeffer when he warns that the one thing above all others that can potentially inflict the most damage on an organization is to tamper with its pay system. When considering such a major decision, the first principle for the HR professional to address should be this: First, do no harm.

HOW METLIFE MEASURES CORE BEHAVIORS FOR LEADERS, MANAGERS, AND EMPLOYEES

Lisa Weber, the executive vice president of human resources at MetLife, credits the company's upswing to a pay-for-performance program that was implemented three years ago. One of the most essential aspects of developing a good plan is to be clear about expectations, she says.

At MetLife, employees are rated on a 1-to-5 scale based on the following competency models of core behaviors—one for leaders and managers, another for individual employees:

For leaders/managers:

- Champions change. Proactively leads and embraces change with innovation, courage, and resiliency. Questions the existing ways of getting things done and endeavors to improve quality and efficiency.
- Inspires a shared vision. Creates a compelling mission and purpose for the organization and energizes people to work toward shared goals.
- Promotes key values. Consistently demonstrates. MetLife values. Emphasizes that people count, and that the company promotes winning from within.
- Communicates effectively. Shares information and encourages candid and open dialogue. Ensures that people share information and have access to the information they need to meet their business objectives.
- Develops talent for the future. Identifies critical skills needed to get results. Creates a work environment that attracts and retains top talent.
- Focuses on customers. Works to exceed expectations of customers externally and internally. Takes immediate action to resolve customers' problems.
- Produces results. Directs action toward achieving goals that are critical to MetLife's success. Sets clear performance expectations that are aligned to business priorities. Ensures that rewards—financial and nonfinancial—are linked to performance.
- Uses sound business judgment. Applies knowledge of the business and the industry, and common sense, to make the best decisions.
- Builds relationships. Excels at building partnerships and fostering teamwork. Works collaboratively within and across organizational boundaries to achieve common goals.

For individual employees:

- Adapts to and implements change. Embraces change with innovation, courage, and resiliency.
- Promotes key values. Consistently demonstrates company values. Conducts business endeavors with truth, sincerity, and fairness.
- Communicates effectively. Shares information and engages in candid and open dialogue.
- Focuses on customers. Works to exceed customers' expectations.
- Produces results. Directs action toward achieving goals that are critical to the company's success.
- Completes work without close supervision.
- Manages own performance effectively. Organizes time and priorities to achieve business results.
- Uses sound business judgment. Applies knowledge of the business and the industry, and common sense, to make the best decisions.
- Builds relationships and works collaboratively. Excels at building partnerships and working as part of a team.
- Demonstrates technical and functional expertise.

Source: Janet Wiscombe, Workforce (August 2001) pp. 28-34. ISSN: 1092–8332, Number: 76851907, Copyright: ACC Communications, Inc.

WHAT'S NEW IN COMPENSATION?

Though Pay Raises Are the Norm, Companies Sometimes Cut Pay

Pay structures assign different pay rates for jobs of unequal worth and provide the framework for recognizing differences in individual employee contributions. No two employees possess identical credentials or perform the same job equally well. Companies recognize these differences by paying individuals according to their credentials, knowledge, or job performance. When completed, pay structures should define the boundaries for recognizing employee contributions Employee contributions in this context correspond to the pay bases that we addressed in previous chapters—seniority, merit, incentive pay, and knowledge-based pay.

Generally, most companies raise employees' base pay every year according to their level of individual contributions. Most employees will tell you that they believe they deserve to receive pay raises because their job performance has contributed positively to the daily operations or competitive advantage of employers. Well-designed HR systems should facilitate these outcomes. However, with the exception of virtually all collective bargaining agreements (see Chapter 3 for a review), employers are typically not obligated to provide pay raises to employees. Employers often decide to award pay raises when management officials believe that this cost expenditure will promote the interests (profits) of the company shareholders (for example, company owners of privately owned companies or stockholders of companies that trade stock on public stock exchanges). Indeed, company management may decide to reduce base pay levels if the immediate cost savings is in the best interest of employees. Reducing compensation costs by cutting pay or benefits or through layoffs can have an immediate positive impact on a company's bottom line.

Pay-cut decisions most often occur during recessionary periods in the domestic or world economy, when actual or anticipated future demand for products and services slackens. Quite simply, less output will cut into profits. The U.S. economy experienced a deep recessionary period in the year 2001 and in most of 2002. The featured *New York Times* article describes a noteworthy example of pay cut. Computer Sciences Corporation instituted a 6-month leave program that entailed employees receiving a 6-month leave while receiving only 20 percent pay!

Log onto your *New York Times* account. Search the database for articles on "pay cuts," "pay raises," and "economic conditions." Also, search for articles on "Computer Sciences Corporation." Following your course instructor's specific directions, be prepared to describe the current situation and relate it to the article. ■

The New York Times

Computer Sciences Seeks Leaves

EL SEGUNDO, Calif., Aug. 15—The Computer Sciences Corporation, the computer-services company, said today that it would ask its 66,000 workers to volunteer to take at least 6 months' leave with 20 percent pay.

A spokesman for Computer Sciences, Frank Pollare, said the program would allow workers to receive some income and the company to "reduce costs for that time." Mr. Pollare said he could not forecast possible savings or say how many workers would take the extended leave.

Computer Sciences and two larger rivals, IBM and Electronic Data Systems, have had falling or slowing sales as customers have cut information-technology budgets in response to a lagging global economy. Computer Sciences shares have fallen 25 percent this year.

According to an e-mail message to workers in Australia, full-time employees will get approval from their managers to take 6 to 9 months of leave with an 80 percent pay cut to help the company "control costs and improve operating efficiencies."

Computer Sciences said that it had bolstered profit as workers became more productive and that the company cut 2,000 jobs last year.

On July 31, the company said first-quarter profit rose 66 percent, to $79 million, through cost cuts and an accounting change. Sales rose 1.9 percent, which was lower than expected.

The company has about 37,000 workers in the United States, 21,000 in Europe, and 8,000 in Asia. All of them will be offered extended leave if laws in the workers' nations of employment allow it, Mr. Pollare said.

It is "too early to speculate" whether the company will force workers to take the leave if too few workers volunteer, he said.

SOURCE: Computer Sciences Seeks Leaves (August 15, 2002) [online]. Available: *www.nytimes.com*, accessed October 1, 2002.

CHAPTER 10 LEGALLY REQUIRED BENEFITS

Chapter Outline

- An Overview of Legally Required Benefits
- Components of Legally Required Benefits
  Social Security Act of 1935
  State Compulsory Disability Laws (Workers' Compensation)
  Family and Medical Leave Act of 1993
- The Implications of Legally Required Benefits for Strategic Compensation
- Summary
- Key Terms
- Discussion Questions
- Exercises
- Endnotes

Learning Objectives

In this chapter, you will learn about

1. Which employee benefits are legally required
2. The Social Security Act of 1935 and its mandated protection programs—unemployment insurance, old age, survivor, and disability insurance (OASDI), and Medicare
3. Compulsory state disability laws (workers' compensation)
4. The Family and Medical Leave Act of 1993
5. Some of the implications for strategic compensation and possible employer approaches to managing legally required benefits

The Social Security programs (for example, retirement and disability) are perhaps the most widely publicized legally required benefits in the United States. For years, there have been valid concerns that there will be insufficient funding to meet promised benefits. As time passes, these concerns are growing stronger. Also, there are new and ongoing political debates about how to ensure the viability of Social Security programs. President George W. Bush signed an executive order (see

Chapter 3 for a definition of executive orders) to create the new Presidential Commission to Strengthen Social Security. "The Compensation in Action" feature at the end of this chapter discusses concerns such as the possible impact of reform on employer-sponsored retirement plans.

AN OVERVIEW OF LEGALLY REQUIRED BENEFITS

The U.S. government established programs to protect individuals from catastrophic events such as disability and unemployment. Legally required benefits are protection programs that attempt to promote worker safety and health, maintain family income streams, and assist families in crisis. The cost of legally required benefits to employers is quite high. As of March 2002, U.S. companies spent an average $3,744 per employee annually to provide legally required benefits [1]. Human resource staffs and compensation professionals in particular must follow a variety of laws as they develop and implement programs.

Historically, legally required benefits provided a form of social insurance [2]. Prompted largely by the rapid growth of industrialization in the United States in the early 19th century and the Great Depression of the 1930s, initial social insurance programs were designed to minimize the possibility that individuals who became unemployed or severely injured while working would become destitute. In addition, social insurance programs aimed to stabilize the well-being of dependent family members of injured or unemployed individuals. Further, early social insurance programs were designed to enable retirees to maintain subsistence income levels. These intents of legally required benefits remain intact today.

Nowadays, legally required benefits apply to virtually all U.S. companies, and they "level the playing field," so to speak. These programs are unlikely to directly lead to a competitive advantage for one company over another. However, legally required benefits may indirectly promote competitive advantage for all companies by enabling unemployed individuals, disabled employees, and their dependent family members to participate in the economy as consumers of products and services. As we discussed in Chapter 3, the government has a vested interest in promoting a vigorous economy that exhibits regular buying and selling, such that the demand for goods and services does not substantially outpace or fall below the supply of those goods and services. Clearly, key to maintaining a vigorous economy is the participation of individuals as consumers of the products and services sold in the marketplace. In this and the next chapter, it will become evident how many elements of fringe compensation serve this end.

COMPONENTS OF LEGALLY REQUIRED BENEFITS

The key legally required benefits are mandated by the following laws: the Social Security Act of 1935, various state workers' compensation laws, and the Family and Medical Leave Act of 1993. All provide protection programs to employees and their dependents.

Social Security Act of 1935

Historical Background

Income discontinuity caused by the Great Depression led to the Social Security Act as a means to protect families from financial devastation in the event of unemployment. The Great Depression of the 1930s was a time when many businesses failed and masses of people became chronically unemployed. During this period, employers shifted their

STRETCHING THE DOLLAR

SOCIAL SECURITY: THE EMPLOYEE BENEFIT YOU DON'T THINK ABOUT

Whether you have thousands of employees or just one or two, you're furnishing some kind of benefit package. The size of the package probably depends on the size of your business. Your employees may enjoy a range of benefits, including paid health insurance, a company pension, a profit-sharing plan or membership in a fitness club. If, however, you have a small business, you may be able to offer only a two-week vacation with pay.

There's more to your benefit package. You, like other employers, provide another very important benefit that both you and your employees probably take for granted. And it's one that's never mentioned in the recruiting ad.

The other benefit is the Social Security package of protection—retirement, survivors, disability insurance and Medicare hospital insurance. You may regard the 7.65 percent of employees' salaries that you pay to Social Security as just a business expense that's required by law. In addition, you have to withhold 7.65 percent from your employees' salaries and send that to the government.

WHY DO YOU CALL A MANDATORY TAX A BENEFIT?

The taxes you and your workers pay provide a comprehensive package of insurance for the workers and their families. The Social Security taxes you and your workers pay provide:

- Retirement insurance that will pay the employee monthly benefits as early as age 62, and the employee's spouse and dependent children as well.
- Survivors insurance that pays monthly benefits to the widow or widower and children and dependent parents of a deceased worker.
- Disability insurance that pays monthly benefits to workers of all ages who have a severe disability. (In some cases, a young worker may qualify for a disability benefit after having worked as little as one and one-half years.) The worker's spouse and dependent children may also receive monthly benefits when the worker is disabled.
- Medicare hospital insurance at age 65 or earlier if the worker has been receiving Social Security disability benefits for two years.

It's important that your employees know what Social Security means to them and their families. To help them become better informed about the value of Social Security, we hope you will encourage them to read the Social Security Statement they'll receive each year if they are 25 years or older and not already receiving Social Security benefits. Your employees can expect to receive their statement about three months before their birthday.

The *Social Security Statement* can help your workers plan their financial future by providing estimates of the retirement, disability and survivors benefits they and their families may be eligible to receive now and in the future. The statement also includes a year-by-year display of your workers' earnings. If their earnings record is not correct, ask them to let us know right away. That's important because their benefits will be based on Social Security's posted record of their lifetime earnings. Your workers should also let us know whether their date of birth is listed incorrectly on the statement.

Your employees can also get help planning their financial future when they visit *www.ssa.gov/planners* or by calling 1-800-772-1213.

Source: Social Security Administration (2002) [online]. Available: *www.ssa.gov/planners*.

focus from maximizing profits to simply staying in business. Overall, ensuring the financial solvency of employees during periods of temporary unemployment and following work-related injuries promoted the well-being of the economy and contributed to some companies' ability to remain in business. Specifically, these subsistence payments contributed to the viability of the economy by providing temporarily unemployed or injured individuals with the means to contribute to economic activity by making purchases that result in demand for products and services.

The Social Security Act of 1935 also addresses retirement income and the health and welfare of employees and their families. Many employees could not meet their financial obligations (for example, housing expenses and food) on a daily basis, and most employees could not retire because they were unable to save enough money to support themselves in retirement. Further, employees' poor financial situations left them unable to afford medical treatment for themselves and their families.

As a result of these social maladies, three programs within the act aim to relieve some of the consequences of these social problems:

- Unemployment insurance
- Old Age, Survivor, and Disability Insurance (OASDI)
- Medicare

Each of those programs will be reviewed in turn.

Unemployment Insurance

The Social Security Act founded a national federal-state unemployment insurance program for individuals who become unemployed through no fault of their own. Each state administers its own program and develops guidelines within parameters set by the federal government. States pay into a central unemployment tax fund administered by the federal government. The federal government invests these payments, and it disburses funds to states as needed. The unemployment insurance program applies to virtually all employees in the United States, with the exception of most agricultural and domestic workers (for example, housekeepers).

Individuals must meet several criteria to qualify for unemployment benefits. Unemployment itself does not necessarily qualify a person, although these criteria vary somewhat by state. Those applying for unemployment insurance benefits must have been employed for a minimum period of time. This **base period** tends to be the first four of the last five completed calendar quarters immediately preceding the individual's benefits year. In addition, all states require sufficient previous earnings, typically $1,000 during the last four quarters combined. Other criteria are listed in Table 10-1.

Individuals who meet the eligibility criteria receive weekly benefits. Because the federal government places no limits on a maximum allowable amount, the benefits amount varies widely from state to state. Most states calculate the weekly benefits as a specified fraction of an employee's average wages during the highest calendar quarter of the base period.

The majority of states pay regular unemployment benefits for a maximum of 26 weeks. A 1970 amendment to this act established a permanent program of extended

TABLE 10-1 Eligibility Criteria for Unemployment Insurance Benefits

To be eligible for unemployment insurance benefits, an individual must:

1. Not have left a job voluntarily
2. Be able and available for work
3. Be actively seeking work
4. Not have refused an offer of suitable employment
5. Not be unemployed because of a labor dispute (exception in few states)
6. Not have had employment terminated because of gross violations of conduct within the workplace

unemployment benefits, usually for an additional 13 weeks (totaling 39 weeks). The extended program in any state is triggered when the state's unemployment exceeds a predetermined level. Another type of program that offers extended unemployment insurance benefits is the **supplemental unemployment benefit (SUB)**, which is most common in industries where employment conditions are cyclical, such as in steel industry. Virtually all SUB benefits are part of collective bargaining agreements. Since the September 11th attacks and the ensuing weakened U.S. economy, President George W. Bush approved a third extension of an additional 13 weeks, permitting qualified unemployed individuals to receive benefits for up to 65 weeks. Table 10-2 illustrates the unemployment insurance benefits for selected states in 2002.

Unemployment insurance benefits are financed by federal and state taxes levied on employers under the **Federal Unemployment Tax Act (FUTA)**. Generally, state and

TABLE 10-2 Unemployment Benefit Amounts for Selected States

State	*Qualifying Wage or Employment (number × WBA or as indicated)*	*Waiting Week*	*Computation of WBA (fraction of HQW or as indicated)*	*WBA for Total Unemployment*	
				Min.	*Max.*
AL	1-½ × hqw	0	1/24 of average of 2 highest quarters	$45	$190
CO	40 or $2500 in BP, whichever is greater	1	60% of 1/26 of claimant's 2 highest quarters up to 50% of 1/52 of aww	$25	$390
DE	36	0		$20	$330
FL	1½ × hqw; $3,400 in BP	1	1/26	$32	$275
IA	1-¼ × hqw; 3.5% of the statewide aaw in HQ; 1/2 of hqw in a 2nd quarter	0		$42–$51	$283–$347
KY	1-½ × hqw; 8 × WBA in last 2 quarters; $750 in 1 quarter; $750 in other quarters	0	1.3078% of BP wages up to 62% of state aww	$39	$329
ME	2 × annual aww in each of 2 quarters and 6 × annual aww in BP	1	1/22 ave. wages paid in 2 highest quarters of BP up to 52% of state aww + $10 per dep up to ½ WBA	$47–$70	$272–$408
OH	20 weeks employment with wages averaging 27.5% of state aww	1	½ claimant's aww + da of $1–$83 based on claimant's aww and number of dep	$86	$308–$414
RI		1	4.62% of hqw up to 67% of of state aww + greater of $10 or 5% of the benefit rate per dep up to 5 deps	$56–$106	$415–$518
SD	$728 in HQ; 20 × WBA outside HQ	1	1/26 up to 50% of state aww	$28	$234
TN	40; $780.01 in highest 2 quarters		1/26 of average 2 highest quarters	$30	$275

Abbreviations: average weekly wage, **aww**; base period, **BP**; calendar quarter, **CQ**; calendar year, **CY**; dependent, **dep**; dependents allowances, **da**; high quarter, **HQ**; high-quarter wages, **hqw**; maximum, **max**; minimum, **min**; weekly benefit amount, **WBA**.

Source: U.S. Department of Labor. (2002). Significant provisions of state unemployment laws [online]. Available: *workforce security.doleta.gov/unemploy/sigpro12002.asp*, accessed June 19, 2002.

local governments, as well as not-for-profit companies (for example, the United Way), are exempt from FUTA. Employer contributions on average amount to 6.2 percent of the first $7,000 earned by each employee. Of this $434, 5.4 percent is disbursed to state unemployment commissions, and the remaining 0.8 percent covers administrative costs at the federal level. Only one state—Alaska—taxes employees to help fund its unemployment insurance program.

Although this 6.2 percent figure represents the typical tax burden, each company's actual rate depends on its prior experience with unemployment. Accordingly, a company that lays off a large percentage of its employees will have a higher tax rate than a company that lays off none or relatively few of its employees. This **experience rating system** implies that a company can manage its unemployment tax burden. In practice, the tax rate on companies varies from less than 1 percent to as high as 10 percent.

Old Age, Survivor, and Disability Insurance (OASDI)

OASDI contains a number of benefits that were amended to the act following its enactment in 1935. Besides providing retirement income, the amendments include survivors' insurance (1939) and disability insurance (1965). The phrase "old age" in the title refers to retirement benefits.

Virtually all U.S. workers are eligible for protections under the Social Security Act, except for three exempt classes. First, civilian employees of the federal government and railroad employees who were employed prior to 1984 are exempt from the retirement program; however, these individuals are not exempt from the Medicare program, which we discuss later in this chapter. Second, employees of state and local governments who are already covered under other retirement plans are exempt from Social Security retirement contributions. Third, American citizens working overseas for foreign affiliates of U.S. employers who own less than 10 percent of the foreign affiliate are exempt from the retirement program.

Old Age Benefits

Individuals may receive various benefit levels upon retirement, or under survivors' and disability programs, based on how much credit they have earned through eligible payroll contributions. They earn credit based on **quarters of coverage**. For example, in 2003, a worker earns credit for one quarter of coverage for each $890 in annual earnings on which Social Security taxes are paid. This figure is based on the average total wages of all workers as determined by the Social Security Administration (SSA). Of course, workers may earn up to four quarters of coverage credit each year. Individuals become **fully insured** when they earn credit for 40 quarters of coverage, or 10 years of employment, and remain fully insured during their lifetime. Other eligibility criteria concerning quarters of coverage are based on more complex formulas [3].

An individual who has become fully insured must meet additional requirements before receiving benefits under the particular programs. Under the retirement program, fully insured individuals may choose to receive benefits as early as age 62, although their benefit amounts will be permanently reduced if elected prior to age 65. Congress recently instituted changes in the minimum age for receiving full benefits. In 2000, the minimum age for full benefits began rising slowly from 65 to 67 in the year 2022. Table 10–3 displays examples of the number of retirees and average monthly retirement benefits for selected years between 1980 and 2002. The number of retiree beneficiaries has risen steadily since 1970. The average monthly benefits have also increased, and these benefit increases are usually tied to annual increases in the cost of

TABLE 10-3 Social Security Retirement Benefits in Current-Payment Status 1980 to 2002

Type of Beneficiary	*1980*	*1985*	*1990*	*1995*	*1999*	*2002*
Retired workers (thousands)	19,582	22,432	24,838	26,673	27,774	28,837
Average monthly benefit, current dollars						
Retired worker	$341	$479	$603	$720	$730	$874
Retired worker and spouse	$567	$814	$1,027	$1,221	$1,086	$1,455

Source: U.S. Social Security Administration (2000). *Social Security Bulletin, Annual Statistical Supplement.* Washington, DC: U.S. Government Printing Office, and *The Fact Sheet on the Old-Age Program* [online]. Available: *www.ssa.gov.*, accessed July 15, 2002.

living [4]. For example, the average monthly benefit for all retired workers rose 1.4 percent from $882 in 2002 to $895 in 2003.

Survivor Benefits

The SSA calculates survivors' benefits based on the insureds' employment status and the survivors' relationship to the deceased. Dependent, unmarried children of the deceased and a spouse of the deceased who is caring for a child or children may receive survivors' benefits if the deceased worker was fully insured. A widow or widower at least age 60, or a parent at least age 62 who was dependent on the deceased employee, is entitled to survivors' benefits if the deceased worker was fully insured. In December 2001, the average monthly benefit was $238 for children of disabled workers and $814 for widows and widowers [5].

Disability Benefits

An individual must meet the requirements of disability insured status to obtain disability benefits. **Disability insured** status requires that a worker be fully insured and have a minimum amount of work under Social Security within a recent time period. This latter element varies according to a person's age and the type of disability [6].

Disabled employees of any age are entitled to disability benefits only if they meet disability insured status. Moreover, the disability must be of a serious nature: It must be expected to endure for at least 1 year or to result in death. Finally, disability benefits are subject to a waiting period of up to 6 months. In January 2003, the average monthly disability benefit was $833.

Medicare

The Medicare program serves nearly all U.S. citizens aged 65 or older by providing insurance coverage for hospitalization, convalescent care, and major doctor bills. The Medicare program includes four separate plans:

- **Medicare Part A:** Compulsory hospitalization insurance
- **Medicare Part B:** Voluntary supplementary medical insurance
- **Medigap:** Voluntary supplemental insurance to fill in the gaps for Parts A and B
- **Medicare+Choice** or **Medicare Part C:** New choices in health care providers

Medicare Part A Coverage

This compulsory hospitalization insurance covers both inpatient and outpatient hospital care and services. Social Security beneficiaries, retirees, voluntary enrollees, and disabled individuals are all entitled. Both employers and employees finance Medicare Part A benefits through payroll taxes of 1.45 percent on all earnings. Compensation subject to Medicare tax has no limit.

Examples of Part A coverage include:

- Inpatient hospital care for up to 90 days for a single spell of illness. Covered individuals also have a lifetime reserve of 60 additional days of hospital care. A single spell of illness begins upon entering the hospital and ends upon remaining out of the hospital for 60 consecutive days.
- Medicare Part A also provides for unlimited in-home care visits. These services must be provided by a home health agency participating in Medicare. Services include intermittent nursing care, therapy treatment, and services of a home health aide.

Medicare Part B Coverage

This voluntary supplementary medical insurance covers 80 percent of medical services and supplies after the enrolled individual pays a $100 annual deductible for services furnished under this plan. Part B helps pay for physicians' services and for some medical services and supplies not covered under Part A. Participation in Part B is voluntary and financed by monthly premiums paid jointly by the federal government and by those who enroll. The monthly contribution for Part B was $54.00 in 2003.

Companies with at least 100 Medicare enrollees can establish a formal group payer arrangement with the Department of Health and Human Services. Medicare enrollees participating in the arrangement must furnish signed statements with their Social Security number to authorize the SSA to bill the employer for the premiums and to release information so that the Department of Health and Human Services can administer the group payer arrangement. Some of the terms employers must abide with include:

- All premiums currently due for enrollees included in the formal payment program will be paid.
- Premium liability will be assumed by the organization through the month in which it notifies the SSA that it is dropping an individual from its rolls, or through the month of death, whichever occurs first.

Anyone eligible for the Medicare hospital insurance plan Part A is automatically enrolled for supplementary Part B medical insurance. An individual who already is receiving monthly Social Security or railroad retirement benefits is considered to have enrolled for Part B insurance the month before the month he or she became entitled to hospital insurance. Those over age 65 who are not eligible for Social Security benefits are considered to have enrolled for Part B insurance in the month they file an application for Part A. A Social Security beneficiary can decline medical insurance coverage.

In general, the Medicare voluntary medical insurance plan pays for the following physicians' bills:

- Diagnosis, therapy, and surgery
- Consultation during home, office, and institutional calls
- Medical services and supplies ordinarily furnished in a doctor's office, such as services of an office nurse
- Medications that cannot be self-administered

Part B also covers outpatient hospital services, including diagnosis and treatment in an emergency room or outpatient clinic; other outpatient services such as surgery, physical therapy, and speech pathology; and those furnished in a comprehensive outside rehabilitation facility. Moreover, Part B provides coverage for home health services for an unlimited number of medically necessary visits as stipulated by a doctor.

Medigap Insurance

Medigap insurance supplements Part A and Part B coverage and is available to Medicare recipients in most states from private insurance companies for an extra fee. Federal and state laws limit the sale of these plans to 10 standardized choices that vary in terms of the level of protection. Some insurers offer Medicare Select plans. **Medicare Select** plans are Medigap policies that offer lower premiums in exchange for limiting the choice of health care providers. Three states—Massachusetts, Minnesota, and Wisconsin—do not subscribe to this system for offering Medigap insurance. Separate rules apply in these states.

Medicare Part C Coverage

The Balanced Budget Act of 1997 established Medicare+Choice, a third Medicare program (Medicare Part C), as an alternative to the original program (Parts A and B). The Medicare+Choice program provides beneficiaries the opportunity to receive health care from a variety of options, including private fee-for-service plans, managed care plans, or medical savings accounts. **Fee-for-service plans** provide protection against health care expenses in the form of cash benefits paid to the insured or directly to the health care provider after receiving health care services. These plans pay benefits on a reimbursement basis. Medicare Parts A and B are based on fee-for-service arrangements. **Managed care** plans often pay a higher level of benefits if health care is received from approved providers. The Medicare+Choice program also allows beneficiaries to switch health plans during an annual open enrollment period each November.

State Compulsory Disability Laws (Workers' Compensation)

Historical Background

Workers' compensation insurance came into existence during the early decades of the 20th century, when industrial accidents were very common and workers suffered from occupational illnesses at alarming rates [7]. The first constitutionally acceptable workers' compensation law was enacted in 1911. By 1920, all but six states had instituted workers' compensation laws [8]. State workers' compensation laws are based on the principle of liability without fault [9]. That is, an employer is absolutely liable for providing benefits to employees that result from occupational disabilities or injuries, regardless of fault. Another key principle of workers' compensation laws is that employers should assume costs of occupational injuries and accidents. Presumably, these expenses represent costs of production that employers are able to recoup through setting higher prices.

Workers' compensation insurance programs, run by states individually, are designed to cover expenses incurred in employees' work-related accidents. Maritime workers within U.S. borders and federal civilian employees are covered by their own workers' compensation programs. The maritime workers' compensation program is mandated by the **Longshore and Harborworkers' Compensation Act**, and federal civilian employees receive workers' compensation protection under the **Federal Employees' Compensation Act**. Thus, workers' compensation laws cover virtually all employees in the United States, except for domestic workers, some agricultural workers, and small businesses with fewer than a dozen regular employees [10].

Workers' Compensation Objectives and Obligations to the Public

Six basic objectives underlie workers' compensation laws [11]:

- Provide sure, prompt, and reasonable income and medical benefits to work-accident victims, or income benefits to their dependents, regardless of fault

- Provide a single remedy and reduce court delays, costs, and workloads arising out of personal injury litigation
- Relieve public and private charities of financial drains
- Eliminate payment of fees to lawyers and witnesses as well as time-consuming trials and appeals
- Encourage maximum employer interest in safety and rehabilitation through appropriate experience-rating mechanisms
- Promote frank study of causes of accidents (rather than concealment of fault), reducing preventable accidents and human suffering

Employers must fund workers' compensation programs according to state guidelines. Participation in workers' compensation programs is compulsory in 48 states and elective in New Jersey and Texas. Generally, these states require that employers subscribe to workers' compensation insurance through private carriers or, in some instances, through state funds. Self-insurance, another funding option allowed in the majority of states, requires companies to deposit a surety bond, enabling them to pay their own workers' claims directly [12]. Many companies select self-insurance because it gives employers more discretion in administering their own risks. Nevertheless, self-insured companies must pay their workers the same benefits as those paid by state funds or private insurance carriers.

The National Commission on State Workmen's Compensation Laws specified six primary obligations of state workers' compensation programs. This commission established these obligations to ensure prompt and just remedy for workers injured on the job [13]. Table 10-4 lists these obligations.

Claims Under Workers' Compensation Programs

Employees can incur three kinds of workers' compensation claims. The first, **injury claims**, are usually defined as claims for disabilities that have resulted from accidents such as falls, injuries from equipment use, or physical strains from heavy lifting. Employees who work long hours at computer keyboards or assembly lines, performing the same task over and over again, frequently complain of numbness in the fingers and neck as well as severe wrist pain. This type of injury is known as repetitive strain injury. A 2002 Bureau of Labor Statistics press release indicates that repetitive strain injuries typically led an employee to miss 17 days of work [14].

The second kind of claim, **occupational disease claims**, results from disabilities caused by ailments associated with particular industrial trades or processes. For example, black lung, a chronic respiratory disease, is a common ailment among coal miners.

TABLE 10-4 Primary Obligations of State Workers' Compensation Programs

1. Take initiative in administering the law.
2. Continually review performance of the program and be willing to change procedures and to request the state legislature to make needed amendments.
3. Advise workers of their rights and obligations and assure that they receive the benefits to which they are entitled.
4. Apprise employers and insurance carriers of their rights and obligations; inform other parties in the delivery system, such as health care providers, of their obligations and privileges.
5. Assist in voluntary and informal resolution of disputes that are consistent with law.
6. Adjudicate claims that cannot be resolved voluntarily.

Source: Nackley, J. V. (1989). *Primer on workers' compensation, 2nd ed.* Washington, DC: Bureau of National Affairs.

In older office buildings, lung disease from prolonged exposure to asbestos is another kind of ailment. Generally, the following occupational diseases are covered under workers' compensation programs:

- Pneumoconioses, which are associated with exposure to dusts
- Silicosis from exposure to silica
- Asbestos poisoning
- Radiation illness

The third kind of claim, **death claims**, asks for compensation for deaths that occur in the course of employment or that are caused by compensable injuries or occupational diseases. The particular injuries and illnesses covered by workers' compensation programs vary by state.

Workers file claims to the state commission charged with administering the workers' compensation program. The names of these agencies vary by state. Examples include bureaus of workers' compensation and industrial accident boards. Typically, one state agency oversees the administration of the program and disburses benefits to the individuals whose claims have been deemed meritorious. Another agency within the state, such as the board of workers' compensation appeal, resolves conflicts that may arise, such as claim denials with which claimants are dissatisfied.

Depending upon the claim, workers' compensation laws specify four kinds of benefits. The first, medical benefits, are provided without regard to the amount or time over which the benefits will be paid.

The second, disability income, compensates individuals whose work-related accident or illness has at least partially limited their ability to perform the regular duties of their jobs. The amount of disability income varies by state; the norm is two-thirds of the employee's average weekly wage for a predetermined period prior to the incident leading to disability. Two exceptions are Iowa and Michigan, where the weekly disability payment is calculated as 80 percent of spendable earnings.

Third, death benefits are awarded in two forms—burial allowances and survivors' benefits. Burial allowances reflect a fixed amount, varying by state. In 2002, the maximum burial allowance ranged from $2,000 in Mississippi to $15,000 in Minnesota [15]. Survivors' benefits are paid to deceased employees' spouses and to any dependent children. The amounts vary widely by state, based on different criteria. For example, assuming no dependent children, the minimum allowable weekly payment to a spouse varied from $20 (Arkansas, Connecticut, Florida, and Wisconsin) to $430.02 (Oregon).

The fourth benefit, rehabilitative services, covers physical and vocational rehabilitation. Claims for this benefit must usually be made within 6 months to 2 years of the accident. For instance, in Alaska, the rehabilitative benefits require the employer to pay reasonable board, lodging, and travel up to $10,000 for a 2-year period [16].

Recent Trends in Workers' Compensation

In recent years, workers' compensation claims have risen dramatically in terms of both numbers of claims and claims amounts. The increased prevalence of repetitive strain injuries resulting from the use of keyboards has contributed to this trend. In 1990, $38.2 billion was paid in workers' compensation claims, rising by 219 percent to $43.4 billion in 1999 [17]. In 2002, workers' compensation cost nearly 20 percent of all legally required benefits for all civilian employees [18]. Table 10–5 illustrates total premiums paid into workers' compensation programs and the total annual benefits paid for selected years between 1990 and 1999 by type of claim (the most recent available data at the time of publication of this book). Disability benefits represented the greatest

TABLE 10-5 Workers' Compensation Payments: 1980 to 1999

Item	*1980*	*1985*	*1990*	*1995*	*1996*	*1997*	*1998*	*1999*
Workers covered (mil.)	79	84	106	113	115	118	121	124
Premium amounts paid	**22.3**	**29.2**	**53.1**	**57.1**	**55.3**	**52.5**	**52.8**	**53.3**
Private carriers	15.7	19.5	35.1	31.6	30.5	29.5	30.1	30.2
State funds	3.0	3.5	8.0	10.5	10.2	9.5	9.8	10.1
Federal programs	1.1	1.7	2.2	2.6	2.6	2.6	2.7	2.7
Self-insurers	2.4	4.5	7.9	12.5	12.0	11.0	10.2	10.4
Annual benefits paid	**13.6**	**22.2**	**38.2**	**43.4**	**41.8**	**41.1**	**42.3**	**43.4**
By private carriers	7.0	12.3	22.2	21.1	20.4	21.0	22.8	23.9
From state funds	4.3	5.7	8.8	11.0	10.6	10.3	10.3	10.2
Employers' self-insurance	2.3	4.1	7.2	11.2	10.8	9.8	9.2	9.3
Type of Benefit:								
Medical/hospitalization	3.9	7.5	15.2	16.7	16.6	15.7	16.4	18.1
Compensation payments	9.7	14.7	23.1	26.7	25.3	25.4	25.9	25.4
Percent of covered payroll:								
Workers' compensation costs	1.96	1.82	2.18	1.83	1.67	1.47	1.37	1.29
Benefits	1.07	1.30	1.57	1.39	1.26	1.15	1.09	1.05

Source: 1980–2001, U.S. Social Security Administration, Annual statistical supplement to the Social Security Bulletin. Beginning 1994, National Academy of Social Insurance, Washington, DC, *Workers' Compensation: Benefits, Coverage, and Costs,* annual.

amount of paid workers' compensation claims for each year listed in Table 10-5. Survivor benefits represented the least amount.

Family and Medical Leave Act of 1993

The Family and Medical Leave Act (FMLA) aims to provide employees with job protection in cases of family or medical emergency. The basic thrust of the act is guaranteed leave, and a key element of that guarantee is the right of the employee to return either to the position he or she left when the leave began or to an equivalent position with the same benefits, pay, and other terms and conditions of employment. The passage of the FMLA reflects a growing recognition that many employees' parents are becoming elderly, rendering them susceptible to a serious illness or medical condition. These elderly parents are likely to require frequent (if not constant) attention for an extended period while ill, which places a burden on their adult children.

The passage of the FMLA also recognizes the increasing prevalence of two-income families and the changing roles of men regarding child care. Both partners in a marriage are now more likely to work full-time and share family responsibilities, including child rearing. The number of families with two earners increased from 29,659,000 in 1995 to 31,601,000 in 2000 [19]. Much like elderly parents, children can also become seriously ill, requiring parents' attention. Also, the FMLA enables fathers to take paternity leave to care for their newborn babies. Until the passage of the FMLA, men did not have protection comparable to what women receive under the Pregnancy Discrimination Act (Chapter 3).

Title I of the FMLA states:

> An eligible employee is entitled to 12 unpaid work weeks of leave during any 12-month period for three reasons: because of the birth or placement for adoption or foster care of a child; because of the serious health condition of a

FLIP SIDE OF THE COIN

IS THE FMLA COSTLY TO EMPLOYERS?

The FMLA was passed to enable employees to take time off from work to meet family and medical needs. Perhaps the hottest issue of debate preceding the passage of the act centered on its possible negative effects on companies' ability to compete. Opponents argued that granting 12 weeks of unpaid leave while maintaining an employee's health and medical insurance coverage would create a cost disadvantage for U.S. companies relative to foreign competition. Continuing to pay for fringe compensation is costly, especially when there is no productivity return from the beneficiary; that is, the employee who is taking leave. Ideally, filling the vacancy with temporary workers should compensate for the productivity loss associated with employees on leave. In some cases, temporary replacements do not possess as much experience as permanent employees. By the time temporary employees become proficient, the permanent employees are likely to be returning from leave.

The U.S. Department of Labor conducted two national studies to examine the impact of the FMLA on employer costs and savings.* Following are the major findings: For the great majority of work sites, compliance with the FMLA entails no costs or only small costs. Between 89.2 and 98.5 percent of covered work sites report no costs or small costs in each of four broad areas: (1) general administrative costs, (2) the cost of continuing health benefits, (3) costs associated with hiring and training replacements for leave-taking employees, and (4) other costs. Larger employers are most likely to experience an increase in costs, in part because they are more apt to have larger numbers of leave-takers. One large employer cited increased costs as the "unintended adverse consequences" resulting from implementation of the act. However, only 1.3 percent of employers report that they reduced benefits to offset costs associated with the FMLA, giving further evidence that costs overall are minimal. Very few employers (2.5 percent) report cost savings resulting from the FMLA. Interestingly, though, the larger work sites (250 employees or more) that are more likely to incur costs from the act also report slightly more cost savings (7.5 percent) than covered work sites as a whole. Some employers reported cost savings, particularly from reduced employee turnover. They also paint an overall picture of enhanced employee productivity, goodwill, and willingness to "go the extra mile" resulting from employees' ability to take leave.

*U.S. Department of Labor. (2000). Excerpts of the results of a survey conducted by the Commission on Family and Medical Leave [online]. Available: *www.dol.gov/dol/esa/fmla.htm*.

> spouse, child, or parent; or because of the employee's own serious health condition. Leave may be taken for birth or placement of a child only within 12 months of that birth or placement.
>
> . . . family leave provisions apply equally to male and female employees: "A father, as well as a mother, can take family leave because of the birth or serious health condition of his child; a son as well as a daughter is eligible for leave to care for a parent."

The minimum criteria for eligibility under this act include the following: Eligible workers must be employed by a private employer or by a civilian unit of the federal government. Also, eligible workers must have been employed for at least 12 months by a given employer. Finally, eligible workers have provided at least 1,250 hours of service during the 12 months prior to making a request for a leave. Employees who do not meet these criteria are excluded, as are those who work for an employer with fewer than 50 employees within a 75-mile radius of the employee's home.

Employers may require employees to use paid personal, sick, or vacation leave first as part of the 12-week period. If an employee's paid leave falls short of the 12-week mandated period, then the employer must provide further leave—unpaid—to total 12 weeks. While on leave, employees retain all previously earned seniority or employment benefits, though employees do not have the right to add such benefits while on leave. Further, while on leave, employees are entitled to receive health insurance benefits. Finally, employees may be entitled to receive health benefits if they do not return from leave because of a serious health condition or some other factor beyond their control.

Human resource professionals along with department managers should develop proactive plans that will enable companies to effectively manage workloads of employees who take leave. One approach is to cross-train workers, who will then have the knowledge and skills to cover vacant jobs while their coworkers are on leave. Pay-for-knowledge programs (Chapter 6) lend themselves well toward enabling employers to meet this objective, particularly when vacant jobs require company-specific knowledge, as in the case of customer service representatives, or highly specialized skills, as in the case of quality assurance inspectors. Alternatively, companies can staff temporarily vacant job openings with temporary workers. This approach is reasonable for jobs that do not require company-specific knowledge, as in the case of many clerical jobs such as filing clerks and word processor operators.

THE IMPLICATIONS OF LEGALLY REQUIRED BENEFITS FOR STRATEGIC COMPENSATION

Fringe compensation is unlike most bases for core compensation—merit, pay-for-knowledge, and incentives. Under these core programs, the amount of compensation employees receive varies with their level of contributions to the company. Instead, fringe benefits tend to emphasize social adequacy. Under the principle of social adequacy, benefits are designed to provide subsistence income to all beneficiaries regardless of their performance in the workplace [20]. Thus, although humanitarian, legally required benefits do not directly meet the imperatives of competitive strategy. However, legally required benefits may contribute indirectly to competitive advantage by enabling individuals to remain participants in the economy.

Nevertheless, legally required benefits may be a hindrance to companies in the short term because these offerings require substantial employee expenditures, such as contributions mandated by the Social Security Act and various state workers' compensation laws. Without these mandated expenditures on compensation, companies could choose to invest these funds in direct compensation programs designed to boost productivity and product or service quality. Alternatively, companies could choose investments in research and development activities essential for product differentiation. Finally, for companies pursuing lowest-cost strategies, management could simply choose to place these funds in reserve, representing a reduction in the overall cost to conceive, develop, and deliver a product or service.

How can HR managers and other business professionals minimize the cost burden associated with legally required benefits? Let's consider this issue for both workers' compensation and unemployment insurance benefits. In the case of workers' compensation, employers can respond in two ways. The first response is to reduce the likelihood of workers' compensation claims. The implementation of workplace safety programs is one strategy for reducing workers' compensation claims. Effective safety programs include teaching safe work procedures and safety awareness to employees and supervisors. Another strategy for reducing workers' compensation claims is health promotion programs that include inspections of the workplace to identify health risks, such as high levels of exposure to toxic substances, and then elimination of those risks.

The second employer response is to integrate workers' compensation benefits into the rest of the benefits program. Because of the rampant cost increases associated with workers' compensation, several state legislatures have considered integrating employer-sponsored medical insurance and workers' compensation programs. Specifically, this "24-hour" coverage would roll the medical component of workers' compensation into traditional employer-provided health insurance. Some companies have already experimented with 24-hour coverage. For instance, Polaroid Corporation has found cost advantages associated with integrating medical insurance and workers' compensation: reduced administrative expense through integration of the coverages, better access to all employee medical records, and a decrease in litigation [21].

Use of 24-hour coverage is not widespread for a number of reasons [22]. Many insurance companies view this approach as complicated. In addition, some companies are concerned that this coverage would cost them in unanticipated ways.

Employers also can contain their costs for unemployment insurance. As discussed earlier, the amount of tax employers contribute to providing unemployment insurance depends partly on their experience rating. Thus, employers can contain costs by systematically monitoring the reasons they terminate workers' employment and avoiding terminations that lead to unemployment insurance claims whenever possible. For example, it is not uncommon for companies to employ workers on a full-time basis when they experience increased demand for their products or services. Adding full-time workers is reasonable when companies expect that the higher demand will last for an extended period, such as more than 2 years. However, when demand is lower in the short term, companies usually reduce their workforce through layoffs. Unless the laid-off employees immediately find employment, they will file claims with their local employment security office for unemployment insurance. Their claims contribute to the companies' unemployment experience rating and, thus, their cost expenditures.

SUMMARY

This chapter provided a discussion of the legally required benefits concept, the rationale for legally required benefits, varieties of legally required benefits, and the implications of benefits for strategic compensation. Although companies have little choice with regard to the implementation of these benefits, the management of these companies can proactively manage the costs of these legally required benefits to some extent. In the coming years, employees, employers, unions, and the government will pay greater attention to the adequacy of Social Security benefits for the succeeding generations. Likewise, these groups will closely monitor the effectiveness of the FMLA.

Key Terms

- base period, 312
- supplemental unemployment benefit (SUB), 313
- Federal Unemployment Tax Act (FUTA), 313
- experience rating system, 314
- quarters of coverage, 314
- fully insured, 314
- disability insured, 315
- Medicare Part A, 315
- Medicare Part B, 315
- Medigap, 315
- Medicare+Choice, 315
- Medicare Part C, 315
- Medicare Select, 317
- fee-for-service plans, 317
- managed care, 317
- Longshore and Harborworkers' Compensation Act, 317
- Federal Employees' Compensation Act, 317
- injury claims, 318
- occupational disease claims, 318
- death claims, 319

Discussion Questions

1. Except for the Family and Medical Leave Act, the remaining legally required benefits were conceived decades ago. What changes in the business environment and society might affect the relevance or perhaps the viability of any of these benefits? Discuss your ideas.
2. Provide your reaction to the statement "Fringe compensation is seen by employees as an entitlement for their membership in companies." Explain the rationale for your reaction.
3. Conduct some research on the future of the Social Security programs (see the Internet site *www.ssa.gov*). Based on your research, prepare a statement not to exceed 250 words that describes your view of the Social Security programs (for example, whether they are necessary, their viability, or whether there should be changes in how the programs are funded). Refer to the information obtained from your research efforts, indicating how it influenced your views.

Exercises

Compensation Online

For Students

Exercise 1: Find relevant journal articles

You are preparing to debate a legally required benefits topic. Use your school library's online catalog to locate articles pertaining to one of the topics, such as Medicare, Social Security benefits, and workers' compensation. Find and read several current articles in these areas. Based on your review, discuss three reasons why the government should provide greater funding to support the selected program.

Exercise 2: Search for federal government information

This chapter deals, in part, with the federal government's efforts to help the disabled gain employment. Go to the U.S. Department of Labor's Web site at *www.doleta.gov/*. Click on the Research link at the top of the homepage. Look for a site that corresponds to information in this chapter and read it. How does what you read add to or change what you read in the chapter?

Exercise 3: Research current information on Social Security matters

Go to the Social Security Administration Web site at *www.ssa.gov/pressoffice/*. Review current information from the SSA Press Office. Select one of the links, read it, and write a brief summary of how the information in this site relates to the textbook chapter.

For Professionals

Exercise 1: Review a professional resource

Though the expense is minimal, your board of directors questions the worth of having membership in the International Foundation of Employee Benefits Plans. Go to the Web page of the International Foundation of Employee Benefit Plans at *www.ifebp.org*. Write a summary of what this group has to offer and how it can be a helpful resource for every HR professional in your corporation.

Exercise 2: Review company Web sites

Visit the Web pages for Kodak and Southwest Airlines at *www.kodak.com* and *www.southwest.com.* View the information on benefits at these companies. What is the purpose of this section of a company's Web site? Explain how descriptions of employee benefits may promote recruitment of talented employees.

Exercise 3: Keep informed of current events related to human resources

Employees turn to the HR department for answers on several issues, even some that do not pertain directly to company policy. Therefore, it is important to keep abreast of current issues. From Yahoo, perform an advanced search for "Medicare." Focus on the News section of Yahoo and review some of the resulting articles. Which two issues do you feel are most pressing? Why?

Endnotes

1. U.S. Bureau of Labor Statistics. (2002). Employer costs for employee compensation—March 2002 [online]. Available: *www.bls.gov/ncs/ect/home.htm*, accessed July 24, 2002.
2. The Bureau of National Affairs. (1991). *Employee Benefits Law*. Washington, DC: Bureau of National Affairs.
3. Beam, B. T., Jr., & McFadden, J. J. (1996). *Employee Benefits* (5th ed.). Chicago: Dearborn Financial Publishing.
4. U.S. Social Security Administration. (2000). *Social Security Bulletin* 63 (2), Table 1.B2. Washington, DC: U.S. Government Printing Office.
5. U.S. Social Security Administration. (2003). Social security fact sheet [online]. Available: *www.ssa.gov/cola/colafacts2003.htm*, accessed January 15, 2003
6. Beam, B. T., Jr., & McFadden, J. J. (1996). *Employee Benefits* (5th ed.). Chicago: Dearborn Financial Publishing.
7. Dulles, F. R., & Dubofsky, M. (1993). *Labor in America: A History*. Arlington Heights, IL: Harlan Davidson.
8. Rejda, G. E. (1994). *Social Insurance and Economic Security*. Upper Saddle River, NJ: Prentice Hall.
9. U.S. Chamber of Commerce. (2002). *2002 Analysis of Workers' Compensation Laws*. Washington, DC: Author.
10. Ibid.
11. Nackley, J. V. (1987). *Primer on Workers' Compensation*. Washington, DC: Bureau of National Affairs.
12. Ibid.
13. Ibid.
14. U.S. Bureau of Labor Statistics (2002). Lost-worktime injuries and illnesses: Characteristics and resulting time away from work, 2000 (USDL 02–196) [online]. Available: *www.bls.gov/bls/newsrels.htm*, accessed June 27, 2002.
15. U.S. Chamber of Commerce. (2002). *2002 Analysis of Workers' Compensation Laws*. Washington, DC: Author.
16. Ibid.
17. U.S. Department of Commerce. (2001). *Statistical Abstracts of the United States* (121st ed.). Washington, DC: Author.
18. Bureau of Labor Statistics. (2002). *Employer Cost Index, March 2002* (USDL: 02–346). Washington, DC: U.S. Government Printing Office.
19. U.S. Department of Commerce. (2001). *Statistical Abstracts of the United States* (121st ed.). Washington, DC: Author.
20. Beam, B. T., Jr., & McFadden, J. J. (1996). *Employee Benefits* (5th ed.). Chicago: Dearborn Financial Publishing.
21. Tompkins, N. C. (1992). Around-the-clock medical coverage. *HR Magazine* (June), pp. 66–72.
22. Baker, L. C., & Krueger, A. B. (1993). Twenty-four-hour coverage and workers' compensation insurance. Working paper, Princeton University Industrial Relations Section.

COMPENSATION IN ACTION

IMPACT OF NEW SOCIAL SECURITY COMMISSION

When President Bush signed an Executive Order on May 2 to create the new Presidential Commission to Strengthen Social Security, he was both fulfilling a campaign promise and attempting to reignite a national dialogue that has smoldered in recent years because of the lack of a crisis.

Indeed, most politicians and Social Security recipients (older Americans) have been content to let the debate smolder because they are keenly aware of the decisions often discussed as necessary to keep the Social Security system solvent over the long term. For both of these groups, "reform" and "modernization" have become fixed terms in the context of Social Security as lightning rods for political mobilization and action.

So why would the president purposefully want to wake this highly volatile sleeping giant called Social Security reform? And, more important, what are the potential employer implications of the recommended reforms being brought to the table by the president's new Commission to Strengthen Social Security.

A POTENTIALLY HUGE BURDEN ON PRIVATE PLANS

Employer-sponsored retirement and pension plans traditionally are thought of as being one of the three "legs" of the "three-legged stool" of American retirement. For most Americans, the three legs supporting their retirement (Social Security, private individual savings and employer-sponsored pensions) are wobbly, at best.

Ever since the first leg of the stool, Social Security, issued its first payments to recipients in 1940, the U.S. government's retirement safety net has been not only a very popular program but also highly effective in reducing poverty among the nation's retirees and elderly. It is not difficult to ascertain why the program is so popular and vigorously defended by politicians: The older Americans who receive Social Security benefits are dedicated and consistent voters, and are very well represented in the nation's capital.

But defending the status quo in the Social Security system is defending a system with fundamental, structural problems. The most prominent challenge—which both sides of the debate openly acknowledge—is the premise upon which the system is funded. When initiated in 1940, the Social Security payroll tax worked well as a funding mechanism because there were many more people paying into the system than there were retired persons receiving benefits from the system. As the U.S. population started to shift, however, this structural funding mechanism slowly began to be undermined, as the ratio of workers to retirees shrank.

Congressional changes to Social Security in 1977 and 1983 acknowledged these trends by providing some relief and extending the system's solvency. But they did not permanently "fix" the system's funding problem. Today, with the huge baby boomer generation passing 50 years of age, the mid- to long-term outlook regarding the ratio of workers paying into the system to retirees taking money out is bleak.

According to the Social Security trustees, when many baby boomers are easing into their golden years in 2016, Social Security will be facing the unpleasant prospect of having to tap its trust fund to pay benefits for the first time. The amount of revenue leaving the system in benefits payments will exceed income to the system through tax collections. Without any changes to this situation, Social Security and its trust fund will be insolvent in 2038. Thus, without substantial Social Security reform, virtually all individuals will be relying upon the two-legged stool of personal savings and employer-sponsored pension plans by 2038.

The personal savings leg, however, is clearly not America's strong suit—it never has been—and it may never be without new incentives for Americans to save. In 1974, the U.S. personal savings rate was roughly 9 percent of disposable income; by the mid-1990s, it had dropped to just 3.4 percent. The 2001 tax relief legislation signed into law in June established some new incentives to save, but historical data strongly suggest that most Americans lack the discipline necessary to make personal savings a viable "leg" for their own retirement.

Thus, without meaningful Social Security reform and significant action regarding the incentives offered to individuals for private savings, there is only one leg left to stand on for most Americans: private, employer-sponsored pension and retirement plans. The implications for employers of maintaining the status quo in Social Security will be substantial, indeed, come 2016.

IMPACT ON EMPLOYERS

Social Security often is an unavoidable presidential campaign issue. During campaign 2000, then–Texas Governor Bush spoke frequently about his belief that individuals should have more control over their Social Security benefits and how the funds they contribute to the system are invested during their lifetime.

To fulfill the broad campaign pledge of strengthening the Social Security system, newly inaugurated President Bush appointed a 16-member, bipartisan commission in May 2001, cochaired by former Sen. Patrick Moynihan (D-N.Y.) and Dick Warner, Co-COO of AOL/Time Warner.

The Commission to Strengthen Social Security did not start its task, however, with a clean slate from which to operate. Consistent with the president's campaign rhetoric, the commission started its work with a set of principles regarding reform that took many of the traditional political "hot buttons" off the table. The commission's first guiding principle (of six) states that any recommendation must not change any Social Security benefits for current or near-retirees. The third principle states that Social Security payroll tax increases will not be a component of the commission's recommendations.

With reductions in benefits to current and near-term recipients and increases in payroll taxes officially off the table—two items frequently mentioned as being required medicine for shoring up the financial structure of the system—what else might the Commission recommend to "modernize" Social Security? This is perhaps where employers need to pay the closest attention.

The sixth operational principle for the commission reflects what the president spoke about most often on the campaign trail. It states that modernization of the Social Security system must include "individually controlled, voluntary personal retirement accounts which will augment the Social Security safety net."

Currently, assets in the Social Security trust fund are invested in Treasury securities, backed by the full faith and credit of the U.S. government. The sixth principle, however, indicates that the president is interested in expanding Social Security investments, on an individual basis, to other investment vehicles.

Although it remains to be seen how the commission will recommend how this individual account concept should be implemented, it very likely could be modeled on the employer-based 401(k) system. If this is the case, experience from employers implementing 401(k) suggests that employees might take a greater interest in retirement planning and saving. As indicated above, Social Security funds currently are invested in Treasury certificates, and contributors to the system (employees) have little incentive to track their portfolio because they don't really have one.

In addition to simply having employees pay more attention to their own retirement—a circumstance that President Bush is clearly hoping to create with his proposals—the implications are broader for employers. First, there is the issue of administering the change from the employer side. The creation of individualized Social Security accounts could, presumably, result in changes to how the Social Security funds are collected through the payroll tax and deposited by employers.

In addition, because of the success of the private, employer-based 401(k) concept, it is possible that the commission's recommendations would seek to leverage this success in the public realm as much as possible. The recommendations could go as far as attempting to somehow link individual Social Security accounts to an individual's private pension accounts, causing potentially new administrative burdens and responsibilities for reporting and record keeping by employers. Further, changes to Social Security in the

(Continued)

(Continued)

individual account concept could result in competitive pressures on existing private retirement savings plans, especially if employees are allowed to make supplemental contributions to their individual Social Security accounts.

A RIPPLE EFFECT

In addition to the above possibilities, perhaps the most fundamental reason for private pension administrators to follow the work of the President's Commission to Strengthen Social Security is the fact that any changes to one or more sides of the three-legged stool will unavoidably affect the other sides. Social Security and employer-based pension plans are inextricably linked because many plans are integrated; that is, they assume the existence of the other for the beneficiary's planning purposes.

Although new payroll taxes and changes that would affect benefits to current recipients are off the table, according to the president's principles, raising the retirement age for Social Security benefits is not, and indeed has been discussed at the commission. According to a 2000 General Accounting Office (GAO) report, changes such as this will have a ripple effect on private plans. "Traditional reforms in the Social Security program, such as changing benefits or taxes, or raising the normal retirement age, may alter the incentives of workers and employers, which could prompt adjustments in private pension plans," the report said.

The President's Commission to Strengthen Social Security is scheduled to conclude its work in the fall, with a report containing recommendations that will then need to be written into legislative proposals and debated in Congress before potentially being made into law. As of press time for this article, the commission had met only once, at which time it discussed the broad concepts and principles from which it would operate. However, based on these principles and the 2000 campaign pledges of President Bush, it would seem likely that individual Social Security accounts will be a feature, if not the highlighted feature, of the recommendations. Depending upon the structure of this concept—for example, whether it is voluntary or universal, whether supplemental contributions could be made, etc.—the implications of all three legs of the traditional American retirement system could be significant.

Source: Ryan M. Johnson. *Workspan* (2001). Scottsdale, AZ: WorldatWork [online]. Available: *resourcepro.worldatwork.org/livelink/livelink/fetch/2000/2657/46405/147717/248261/3*, accessed July 12, 2002. © 2001 WorldatWork, 14040 N. Northsight Blvd., Scottsdale, AZ 85260 U.S.A.; 480/951-9191; Fax 480/483-8352; *www.worldatwork, org*; E-mail worldatwork@worldatwork.org

WHAT'S NEW IN COMPENSATION?

Politics Plays an Inescapable Role in Legally Required Employee Benefits

Just say the phrase "legally-required employee benefits" and you will find debates involving politicians and employers. Political debates are inevitable whenever two or more groups with opposing views clash. For the most part, politicians represent the interests of the people who elected them into office. Employers focus on controlling costs to promote higher profits for business owners and shareholders.

In the case of legally required benefits such as Medicare, the Social Security Act's Old-Age, Survivor, and Disability Insurance (OASDI) programs, and family and medical leave, many politicians strive to serve the interests of their individual constituents by proposing legislation or changes to existing legislation. Employees represent the greatest number of votes that elect public officials. Not surprisingly, then, it is the employees who expect politicians to promote their interests by suggesting or supporting proposed legislation that will enhance workers' welfare. Employers enter into these political debates to protect economic interests. For most businesses that means fighting against proposed legislation that, if enacted, would create cost burdens and threaten profit targets. As a side note, the political dynamics are more complex than described here. For example, although politicians ideally represent the interests of individual voters, lucrative financial support of politicians' campaigns for election or reelection may create a conflict of interest by diluting a politician's loyalties to the voters.

The featured *New York Times* article describes the passage of a law in California that allows most employees to take up to six weeks of *paid* leave to cope with family emergencies. As discussed in this chapter, the Family and Medical Leave Act of 1993 provides most employees up to 12 weeks of *unpaid* leave to cope with weighty family issues such as illness and the birth or adoption of a child. Oftentimes, state (for example, California) or municipal (for example, Chicago, Illinois) variations of federal laws offer modified benefits with at least as much protection as corresponding federal legislation.

Of course, employees and labor unions hail California's paid family leave law as a great victory that promotes the welfare and well-being of employees and their families. However, businesses are far less supportive and argue that paid leave will amount to an excessive cost burden of paying employees while they are not at work. Besides the fundamental payroll cost issue, companies stand to bear additional costs; for instance, hiring less-experienced temporary replacements.

Log into your *New York Times* account. Search the database for articles on "social security," "workers' compensation," and "family leave." When reviewing these articles, pay attention to the political tensions. Be prepared to discuss these issues in class. What are the possible gains and losses for workers? Employers? Following your course instructor's specific directions, be prepared to describe the current situation, and relate it to the article contained in this text. ■

The New York Times

Family Leave in California Now Includes Pay Benefit

LOS ANGELES, Sept. 23—Gov. Gray Davis signed a bill today to establish paid family leave to care for a new child or an ailing relative, giving California workers the most expansive family benefit in the nation.

The law, which business interests say will drive away jobs, will allow virtually any worker to take up to 6 weeks paid leave to cope with a family emergency. The benefit will be paid solely out of employee contributions.

The bill was one of several on Mr. Davis's desk pushed hard by California's powerful liberal-labor coalition. On Sunday, Mr. Davis signed a measure that would permit some stem cell research currently limited by federal law, as well as a package of bills giving patients enhanced rights in disputes with health maintenance organizations.

Political analysts read the governor's actions as an effort to strengthen support among core Democratic groups, who have been lukewarm about Mr. Davis's reelection campaign. Despite spending nearly $20 million this summer attacking his Republican opponent, Bill Simon Jr., Mr. Davis maintains only a slim lead in public opinion polls.

"This is all about shoring up and motivating his base," said Sherry Bebitch Jeffe, a senior scholar in public policy at the University of Southern California. "He has to turn out Democrats, labor, Latinos, women, none of whom are really excited about him. I don't think he can risk angering his base at this point."

The family leave bill was closely watched as a gauge of Mr. Davis's political strategy this fall. Labor activists, who have long been suspicious of the governor because of his history of courting business to attract campaign contributions, said they were pleased with his decision but still unsure where his heart lies.

Mr. Davis signed the bill this afternoon at a children's hospital in Los Angeles, calling it landmark legislation that will aid workers and businesses.

"Californians should never have to make the choice between being good workers and being good parents," the governor said. "This bill will help millions of California workers meet their responsibilities to both their family and their employers."

Organized labor and family rights groups nationwide who have been pushing states to extend the benefit to all workers lustily cheered the governor's action. It is one of the highest priorities of the A.F.L.-C.I.O., which calls on other states to enact similar legislation. Lawmakers in twenty-seven other states are considering such measures.

The measure's sponsor, State Senator Sheila Kuehl, said she was uncertain until the weekend whether Mr. Davis would sign it. The bill was heavily amended late in the legislative session to address business concerns and win passage in the Assembly. The bill's original provision for twelve weeks' paid leave was reduced to 6 weeks, and the employer contribution to the state fund that will pay the benefits was eliminated.

The bill also requires workers to use up to 2 weeks vacation time for family emergencies and caps the benefit at $728 a week.

Ms. Kuehl, who represents the Democratic strongholds of West Los Angeles, Santa Monica and Malibu, said that business opponents were "crying wolf" about the bill's impact on jobs and labor costs in California.

"Their real objection was that they simply did not want workers to take time off, no matter how needy they might be in terms of family care," she said.

But business organizations said the bill was a job killer at a time when the state's economy was slumping and California lawmakers were imposing costly new environmental and labor rules.

The leader of the state chamber of commerce warned that the bill added to a business climate that discouraged job creation.

"We're opposed to a lot of bills, but this is one of the worst," said Allan Zaremberg, president of the chamber of commerce. "When you're the only state in the country with paid family leave and they've tried it in 27 other states and it's failed in each and every one, we see it as a competitive disadvantage in attracting or keeping businesses here."

The California bill broadens a federal measure, the Family and Medical Leave Act, which former President Bill Clinton signed in 1993. That law guarantees the jobs of workers who take time off to care for a child or sick relative, but the benefit is unpaid.

The federal law also exempts businesses with fewer than fifty employees. California's new law sets no size limit.

SOURCE: John M. Broder. Family Leave in California Now Includes Pay Benefit (September 23, 2002) [online]. Available: *www.nytimes.com*, accessed October 1, 2002.

CHAPTER

11 DISCRETIONARY BENEFITS

Chapter Outline

- An Overview of Discretionary Benefits
- Components of Discretionary Benefits
  - Protection Programs
  - Paid Time-Off
  - Services
- Laws That Guide Discretionary Fringe Compensation
  - Employee Retirement Income Security Act of 1974 (ERISA)
  - Consolidated Omnibus Budget Reconciliation Act of 1985 (COBRA)
  - Additional Pertinent Legislation
- Unions and Fringe Compensation
- Designing and Planning the Benefits Program
  - Determining Who Receives Coverage
  - Financing
  - Employee Choice
  - Cost Containment
  - Communication
- The Implications of Discretionary Benefits for Strategic Compensation
- Summary
- Key Terms
- Discussion Questions
- Exercises
- Endnotes

Learning Objectives

In this chapter, you will learn about

1. The role of discretionary benefits in strategic compensation
2. The various kinds of protection programs
3. The different types of paid time-off
4. A variety of employee services
5. The considerations that go along with designing and planning discretionary benefits programs
6. How discretionary benefits fit with differentiation and lowest-cost competitive strategies

Today, discretionary benefits represent a significant fiscal cost to companies. As of March 2002, U.S. companies spent an average $9,547 per employee annually to provide discretionary benefits [1]. Discretionary benefits account for as much as 40 percent of employers' total payroll costs (that is, the sum of core compensation and all fringe compensation costs).

As the term implies, "discretionary benefits" are offered at the will of company management. Unlike well-designed pay-for-performance systems, employees view discretionary benefits such as paid vacation and holidays as an entitlement much like any of the legally required benefits. Employers reinforce an entitlement mentality toward benefits because they award discretionary benefits regardless of employee performance. The "Compensation in Action" feature at the end of this chapter discusses awarding discretionary benefits according to employee performance.

AN OVERVIEW OF DISCRETIONARY BENEFITS

Discretionary benefits fall into three broad categories: protection programs, paid time-off, and services. Protection programs provide family benefits, promote health, and guard against income loss caused by catastrophic factors such as unemployment, disability, or serious illnesses. Not surprisingly, paid time-off provides employees time off with pay for such events as vacation. Services provide enhancements such as tuition reimbursement and day care assistance to employees and their families.

In the past several decades, firms have offered a tremendous number of both legally required and discretionary benefits. In Chapter 10, we discussed how the growth in legally required benefits from a select body of federal and state legislation developed out of social welfare philosophies. Quite different from these reasons are several factors that have contributed to the rise in discretionary benefits.

Discretionary benefits originated in the 1940s and 1950s. During both World War II and the Korean War, the federal government mandated that companies not increase employees' core compensation, but it did not place restrictions on companies' fringe compensation expenditures. Companies invested in expanding their offerings of discretionary benefits as an alternate to pay hikes as a motivational tool. As a result, many companies began to offer welfare practices. **Welfare practices** were "anything for the comfort and improvement, intellectual or social, of the employees, over and above wages paid, which is not a necessity of the industry nor required by law" [2]. Moreover, companies offered employees welfare benefits to promote good management and to enhance worker productivity.

The opportunities to employees through welfare practices varied. For example, some employers offered libraries and recreational areas, and others provided financial assistance for education, home purchases, and home improvements. In addition, employers' sponsorships of medical insurance coverage became common.

Quite apart from the benevolence of employers, employee unions also directly contributed to the increase in employee welfare practices through the National Labor Relations Act of 1935 (NLRA), which legitimized bargaining for employee benefits. Union workers tend to participate more in benefits plans than do nonunion employees [3]. Table 11-1 illustrates some of the differences in benefits between nonunion and union employees. For example, in 2001, union workers were more likely than nonunion workers to receive health care benefits and retirement income benefits.

Unions also indirectly contributed to the rise in benefits offerings. As we discussed in Chapter 3, nonunion companies often fashion their employment practices after union companies as a tactic to minimize the chance that their employees will seek

TABLE 11-1 Median Weekly Earnings of Full-Time Wage and Salary Workers by Union Affiliation and Selected Characteristics, 2001

Characteristic	*2001*			
	Total	*Members of Unions*[1]	*Represented by Unions*[2]	*Nonunion*
Sex and Age				
Total, 16 years and over	$597	$718	$712	$575
16 to 24 years	376	473	475	370
25 years and over	632	733	728	612
25 to 34 years	579	654	646	563
35 to 44 years	658	743	738	637
45 to 54 years	693	776	774	663
55 to 64 years	640	744	744	613
65 years and over	472	607	605	440
Men, 16 years and over	672	765	761	647
16 to 24 years	392	482	488	387
25 years and over	722	781	779	705
25 to 34 years	621	699	691	610
35 to 44 years	755	799	794	744
45 to 54 years	799	814	813	790
55 to 64 years	766	801	807	748
65 years and over	548	686	705	520
Women, 16 years and over	511	643	639	494
16 to 24 years	354	458	456	348
25 years and over	542	656	652	519
25 to 34 years	514	600	597	503
35 to 44 years	545	643	641	523
45 to 54 years	588	721	715	554
55 to 64 years	539	656	659	512
65 years and over	372	497	487	358
Race, Hispanic Origin, and Sex				
White, 16 years and over	612	741	736	591
Men	694	784	781	669
Women	521	667	661	503
Black, 16 years and over	487	603	599	463
Men	518	649	637	498
Women	451	563	564	424
Hispanic origin, 16 years and over	414	578	578	398
Men	438	611	612	414
Women	385	503	501	372

[1]Data refer to members of a labor union or an employee association similar to a union.

[2]Data refer to members of a labor union or an employee association similar to a union as well as workers who report no union affiliation but whose jobs are covered by a union or an employee association contract.

Note: Data refer to the sole or principal job of full-time workers. Excluded are all self-employed workers regardless of whether or not their businesses are incorporated. Detail for the above race and Hispanic-origin groups will not sum to totals because data for the "other races" group are not presented and Hispanics are included in both the white and black population groups.

Source: U.S. Bureau of Labor Statistics (2002). Union members in 2001 (USDL: 02-28). Washington, DC: Author.

union representation [4] and may offer their employees benefits that are comparable to the benefits received by employees in union shops.

Employees came to view both legally required benefits and discretionary benefits as entitlements. Anecdotal evidence suggests that most employees still feel this way: From their perspective, company membership entitles them to fringe compensation. Until recently, companies have also treated virtually all elements of fringe compensation as entitlements. They have not questioned their role as social welfare mediators. However, both rising benefit costs and increased foreign competition have led companies to question this entitlement ethic. For instance, in 2002, U.S. companies typically spent nearly $15,000 per employee to provide both legally required and discretionary benefits [5].

A more recent phenomenon that gives rise to discretionary benefits is the federal government's institution of tax laws that allow companies to lower their tax liability based on the amount of money they allocate to providing employees with particular discretionary benefits. These tax laws permit companies to deduct from their pretaxable income the cost of certain benefits, thereby lowering companies' tax liabilities.

COMPONENTS OF DISCRETIONARY BENEFITS

Protection Programs

Income Protection Programs

Disability Insurance Disability insurance replaces income for employees who become unable to work because of sicknesses or accidents. Unfortunately, employees need this kind of protection. At all working ages, the probability of being disabled for at least 90 consecutive days is much greater than the chance of dying while working; one of every three employees will have a disability that lasts at least 90 days [6].

Employer-sponsored or group disability insurance typically takes two forms. The first, **short-term disability insurance**, provides benefits for a limited time, usually less than 6 months. The second, **long-term disability insurance**, provides benefits for extended periods between 6 months and life. Disability criteria differ between short- and long-term plans. Short-term plans usually consider disability as an inability to perform any and every duty of the disabled person's occupation. Long-term plans use a more stringent definition, specifying disability as an inability to engage in any occupation for which the individual is qualified by reason of training, education, or experience.

Most short-term disability plans pay employees 50 to 100 percent of their pretax salary, but long-term disability plans pay 50 to 70 percent of pretax salary [7]. Generally, long-term benefits are subject to a waiting period of 6 months to 1 year and usually become active only after an employee's sick leave and short-term disability benefits have been exhausted.

Long-term disability insurance provides a monthly benefit to employees who, due to illness or injury, are unable to work for an extended period of time. Payments of long-term disability benefits usually begin after 3 to 6 months of disability and continue until retirement or for a specified number of months. Payments generally equal a fixed percentage of predisability earnings.

Both short- and long-term disability plans may duplicate disability benefits mandated by the Social Security Act and state workers' compensation laws (discussed in Chapter 10). These employer-sponsored plans generally supplement legally required benefits established by the **Employee Retirement Income Security**

Act of 1974. Employer-sponsored plans do not replace disability benefits mandated by law.

Life Insurance Employer-provided **life insurance** protects employees' families by paying a specified amount to an employee's beneficiaries upon the employee's death. Most policies pay some multiple of the employee's salary—for instance, twice the employee's annual salary. Frequently, employer-sponsored life insurance plans also include accidental death and dismemberment claims, which pay additional benefits if death was the result of an accident or if the insured incurs accidental loss of a limb.

Most companies offer full-time employees life insurance. On average, companies spent $83 per employee in 2002 to provide life insurance and $145 per unionized worker [8].

There are two kinds of life insurance: term coverage and whole life coverage. **Term coverage**, the most common type of life insurance offered by companies, provides protection to employees' beneficiaries only during employees' work years. **Whole life coverage**, on the other hand, extends protection to beneficiaries into the insureds' retirement years.

Individuals can subscribe to life insurance on an individual basis by purchasing policies from independent insurance agents or representatives of insurance companies. Alternatively, they can subscribe to group life insurance through their employers, which has clear benefits. First, group plans allow all participants covered by the policy to benefit from coverage, and employers assume the burden of financing the plan either partly or entirely. Second, group policies permit a larger set of individuals to participate in a plan at a lower cost per person than if each person had to purchase life insurance on an individual basis.

Pension Programs **Pension programs** provide income to employees and their beneficiaries throughout their retirement. Individuals may participate in more than one pension program simultaneously. It is not uncommon for employees to participate in pension plans sponsored by their companies—for example, 401(k) plans—as well as in pension plans that they establish themselves, such as the individual retirement account (IRA). In 2002, employers' contributions to pension plans on behalf of their employees were substantial—averaging $1,664 per employee [9].

Pension program design and implementation are quite complex, largely because of the many laws that govern their operations, particularly the Employee Retirement Income Security Act of 1974 (ERISA), which we will address later in this chapter.

Three sets of terms broadly characterize pension plans:

- Financing method: Contributory versus noncontributory plans
- Tax treatment: Qualified versus nonqualified plans
- Benefit determination: Defined contribution plans versus defined benefit plans

Employers choose from four approaches to finance benefits—noncontributory, contributory, and employee-financed programs, or some combination thereof. **Noncontributory financing** means that the company pays the total costs for each discretionary benefit. Under **contributory financing**, the company and its employees share the costs. Under employee-financed benefits, employers do not contribute to the financing of discretionary benefits, and employees bear the entire cost. The majority of benefit plans today are contributory, largely because the costs of benefits have risen so dramatically.

STRETCHING THE DOLLAR

TARGETING CORPORATE RETIREMENT BENEFITS

Is your retirement plan "right" for your organization? How does your retirement income compare with your competitors'? Are your plans delivering the appropriate benefits to all employees? To address these questions, the following concepts should be examined:

- Measurement of benefit adequacy through the use of replacement ratios
- Benefit comparison between flat dollar pension plans and salary-based pension plans
- Ways of targeting higher paid participants with additional pension benefits

BENEFIT ADEQUACY

It is often assumed that, upon retirement, an individual usually will have income available from several basic sources including:

- Social Security retirement benefits
- Employer-sponsored retirement plans
- Personal savings
- Income from work after retirement

Studies show that for an individual to maintain the standard of living established prior to retirement, income during actual retirement years will need to be at levels between 79 percent to 86 percent of the preretirement income—an amount called the replacement level. Actual replacement levels required to maintain preretirement standards of living will depend on the amount of preretirement income received.

The "replacement ratio" that provides this desired benefit level is derived by dividing the retirement income expected in the first year of retirement into the compensation received in the last year of employment. Figure 1 summarizes the results of a recent study on retirement income replacement ratios that may be required for a married couple.

These results do not include the effects of employee savings, prior accumulation of assets or income from work after retirement. For purposes of this discussion, the replacement ratio results will serve as the minimum or baseline for required income needed in an individual's post-retirement years.

DEFINED BENEFIT PENSION PLANS

Defined benefit pension plans fall into two broad categories: those that provide salary-based benefits determined as some percentage of compensation or non-pay related benefits earned in some fixed amount per year of service (e.g., $25 per month, per year of service). Non-pay-related plans are often referred to as flat dollar pension plans. What follows is how participants in the flat-dollar and salary-based pension plans would fare

FIGURE 1 Required Standard of Living Replacement Ratios

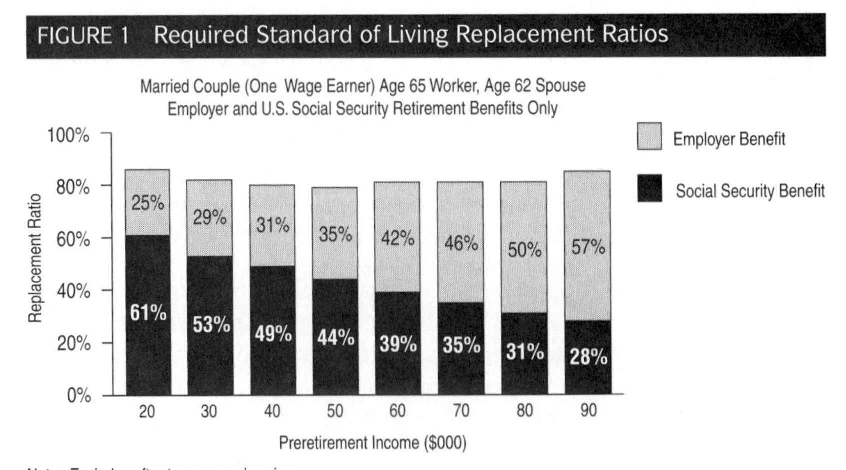

Note: Excludes after-tax personal savings

Source: Georgia State University.

FIGURE 2 Benefits Adequacy Analysis—Flat Dollar Pension Plan

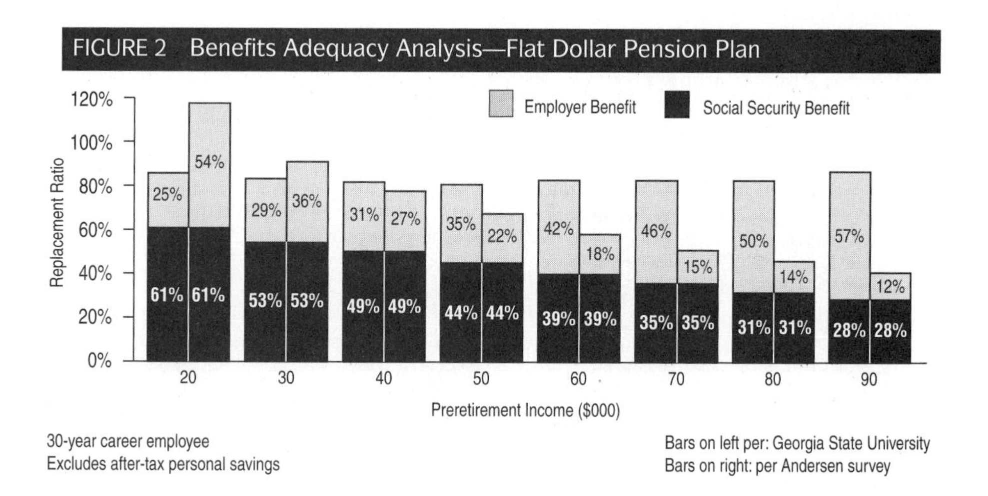

when comparing benefit adequacy on a replacement ratio upon retirement.

FLAT DOLLAR PENSION PLANS

A recent survey of retirement plans[1] found that 65 percent of collectively bargained defined benefit plans offered retirement benefits in the form of a flat dollar amount per year of service. The survey's median benefit multiplier was about $30 per month per year of service. What does this mean for the typical participant in a collectively bargained pension plan?

Figure 2 illustrates the income replaced at retirement for a typical survey participant in a collectively bargained pension plan retiring at age 65 with 30 years of service. The retirement benefits are separated by source (Social Security retirement benefit and pension benefit) and do not include the effect of any personal savings. For comparison purposes, the replacement ratios from the Georgia State University survey will represent a baseline benefit adequacy and are shown side by side at each income level.

As Figure 2 results indicate, flat dollar pension plans do an inadequate job of targeting retirement benefits. The average benefit of $30 per month per year of service appears to meet our baseline minimum level of benefit adequacy (e.g., provide benefits at the 100 percent replacement ratio level) at annual income levels between $30,000 and $40,000. At all other income levels, the retirement benefits have missed their target. At preretirement income levels above $50,000, the need to supplement retirement income from other sources such as personal savings or income from part-time work will be required.

SALARY-BASED PENSION PLANS

In a survey of noncollectively bargained pension plans,[2] nearly 81 percent of the plans surveyed provided benefits based on a participant's compensation. For a career employee retiring at age 65, with 30 years of service, most pension plans were expected to provide a median benefit equal to 36 percent of the most recent preretirement income level.

Of these retirement plans, more than three-quarters provided additional pension benefits for pay above the Social Security covered compensation amounts. Currently, the covered compensation level is $37.214 for those individuals reaching age 65 in 2001.

Figure 3 illustrates the income replaced in retirement for a career employee participating in a salary-based pension plan. Retirement benefits are split by source and do not include amounts from personal savings or income from post-retirement employment.

These results again show that as far as meeting the goal of targeting an adequate income replacement level at retirement for its participants, many pension plans may be missing their mark. Frequently, career employees at the lowest income levels will actually see their total take-home pay increase in their post-retirement years. While this may not be a major concern for most plan sponsors, and may invoke feelings of corporate parternalism, what is happening at higher

(Continued)

(Continued)

FIGURE 3 Benefit Adequacy Analysis—Salary Based Pension Plan

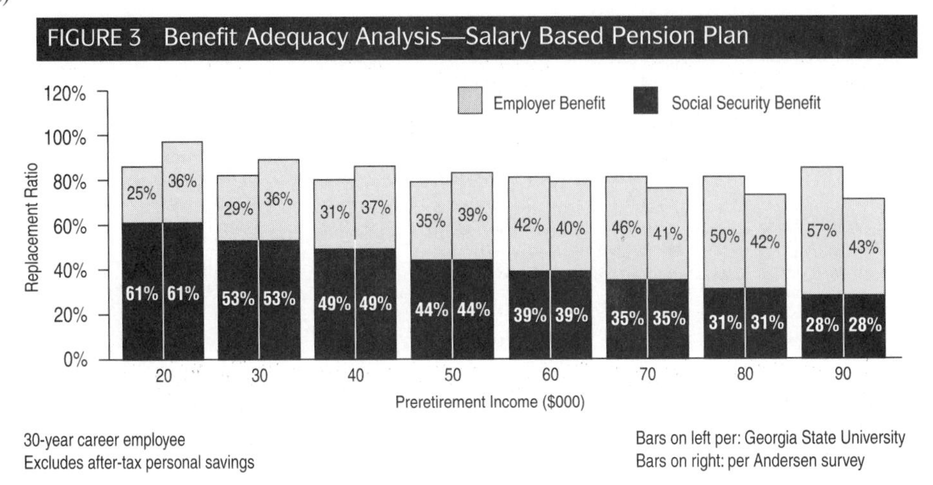

income levels gives these same plan sponsors cause for concern.

EXECUTIVE LEVEL BENEFITS

While Figure 3 shows that participants in salary-based pension plans are more closely aligned with the overall baseline of benefit adequacy, there is still a need at these higher income levels for plan sponsors to do more.

As discussed in [another] article,[3] many organizations are turning to supplemental executive retirement plans (SERPs) to help increase the retirement benefits available to their highest paid employees. Since they are not tax-qualified plans, SERPs are not subject to the design restrictions imposed by the Internal Revenue Service (IRS) qualification and nondiscrimination requirements that apply to general retirement plans.

SERPs can be either stand-alone plans or wrap-around plans. The benefits in a stand-alone SERP are determined without regard to the benefits provided in the company's general retirement plan. A wrap-around SERP establishes a gross benefit and then offsets this benefit for actual benefits paid under the general plan. A typical SERP formula may provide a benefit equal to 60 percent of final average pay at retirement for a career executive, with an offset for general plan benefits if a wrap-around plan is employed.

Interestingly, for purposes of uniformity, many excess benefit SERPs currently in use are wrap-around plans that provide benefits similar to the company's general retirement plan, without regard to the IRS limitations on compensation or on annual benefit amounts (currently $170,000 and $140,000, respectively, for 2001).

Other industry surveys indicate that the same replacement ratio levels seen in the Georgia State University study are required for higher paid individuals, as well. By extrapolating results to higher income levels,[4] Figure 4 shows clearly that without some form of supplemental retirement benefit, targeted levels of benefit adequacy are not being met for many higher paid employees.

TARGETING ADDITIONAL RETIREMENT BENEFITS

In collectively bargained plans, many middle-income participants will see their post-retirement income levels fall below the established norms of basic retirement benefit adequacy. Many responsible plan sponsors have already performed their own benefit adequacy analysis and have responded by setting up new 401(k) plans or other account balance programs to address this potential retirement benefits shortfall.

For those organizations with 401(k) plans already in place, the addition of matching employer contributions on employee deferrals will help provide the needed post-retirement income. In many cases, employers also are increasing the amount of their matching contributions. For example, instead of matching the typical 50 percent of the first 6 percent of pay deferred by 401(k) participants, employers could increase their matching contributions to 100 percent of the first 3 percent of employee pay

FIGURE 4 Benefit Adequacy Analysis—Executive Level Retirement Benefits

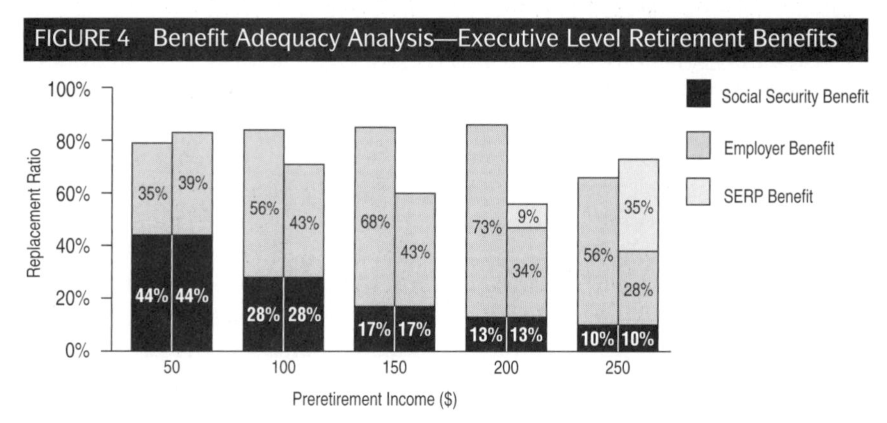

deferred and an additional 50 percent match on the next 3 percent of employee deferrals.

In many instances, without these additional benefits, the retiree will need to supplement post-retirement income with personal savings and continued full-time or part-time employment.

Many plan sponsors are attempting to address the current benefit inadequacy issue for their higher paid employees by adding another layer of benefits to their existing retirement plans—a benefit available only to a targeted select group of employees. Many defined benefit pension plans now include an account balance feature in addition to the traditional percentage of compensation accrual. While such a two-tiered benefit structure increases the administrative duties of the plan sponsor—it requires a demonstration of compliance with IRS nondiscrimination regulations—the potential benefits to participants and plan sponsors far outweigh the costs.

LOOKING AHEAD

The pension reform provisions contained in the Economic Growth and Tax Reconciliation Act of 2001 passed by Congress give plan sponsors the ability to do more for their higher paid employees. Starting in 2002, the IRS limitation on eligible compensation and annual benefits will increase to $200,000 and $160,000, respectively. The higher compensation limits in a company's general plan will result in the shifting of some retirement benefits from the SERP into the tax-qualified general plan.

These examples cover the traditional 30-year career employee. In these nontraditional times—think, New Economy—and with today's mobile workforce, the need for plan sponsors to provide additional retirement benefits is increasingly more pronounced for mid-career and late-career hires.

With the higher annual benefits limits now available, many plan sponsors will add a layer of benefits, many in an account balance format that will target participants most in need. The use of multi-tiered benefits structures within a single pension plan is likely to become more prevalent. This ability to target specific participant groups with increased pension benefits will give plan sponsors the opportunity to ensure a basic level of benefit adequacy for all employees.

ENDNOTES

1. Arthur Andersen 1999 Survey of Non-Collectively Bargained Defined Benefit Plans.
2. Arthur Andersen 1999 Survey of Collectively Bargained Defined Benefit Plans.
3. Catching On Overseas—Retirement Benefits Chart the Same Waters. (2001). WorldatWork Journal, first quarter.
4. The U.S. Bureau of Labor Statistics does not provide consumer expenditure data at income levels above $100,000. Therefore, care must be taken when extrapolating replacement ratio results to incomes above this amount.

Qualified pension plans entitle employers to tax benefits from their contributions to pension plans. This means that employers may take current tax deductions for contributions. Employees may also receive some favorable tax treatment (that is, a lower tax rate). A qualified plan generally entitles employees to favorable tax treatment of the benefits they receive upon their retirement. Any investment income that is generated in the pension program is not taxed until the employee retires. **Nonqualified pension plans** provide less favorable tax treatments for employers and employees. Table 11-2 lists the defining characteristics of qualified pension plans.

Finally, companies determine benefits based on a defined contribution approach or defined benefit approach. Under **defined contribution plans**, employers and employees make annual contributions to separate accounts established for each participating employee, based on a formula contained in the plan document. The amount each participant receives depends on the performance of the selected investment vehicle (for example, company stock, government bonds). Typically, formulas call for employers to contribute a given percentage of each participant's annual pay each year. Employers invest these funds on behalf of the employee in any of a number of ways, such as company stocks, diversified stock market funds, or federal government bond funds. In 2002, companies contributed an average $790 per employee to defined contribution pension plans [10].

The most common types of defined contribution plans are profit sharing plans, 401(k) plans, employee stock ownership plans (ESOPs), and savings and thrift plans. Regarding profit sharing plans, employers might use allocation formulas that divide contributions among participants in proportion to their relative compensation paid during the plan year, or the employer might disburse the share of profits equally among employees regardless of their earnings. Most employers allocate shares of profit proportional to employee earnings. Once employers make contributions, they are invested, as discussed previously, and held until distribution.

The 401(k) plans, named after the section of the Internal Revenue Code that established them, permit participating employees to set aside a portion of their pay-

TABLE 11-2 The General Characteristics of Qualified Pension Plans

Eligibility
Employers may impose any initial eligibility requirement but for those that pertain to age or service. No minimum age over 21 can be required, nor can more than 1 year of service be required for eligibility.
Nondiscrimination
Employers cannot provide highly compensated employees (for example, vice president, chief executive officers with preferential treatment with regard to employer contributions to the plans or the level of benefits received *unless* the employer contributions or benefit levels are based solely on employee's compensation level or years of service.
Vesting Requirements
Employers must provide employees with a nonforfeitable right to the funds they contribute to the plans on behalf of their employees after a specified period, commonly 3 to 5 years. For example, employees who terminate their employment after the 3-/to 5-year period maintain the right to the funds contributed on their behalf by the employer. However, employees who terminate their employment before the 3-/to 5-year period forfeit the right to the funds contributed on their behalf by the employer.
Payout Restrictions
Employees generally pay a penalty (usually 10 percent) on withdrawal of funds from any qualified plan before early retirement age (59-1/2 years).

checks for retirement purposes. The portion of pay that is deducted reduces an employee's taxable income, thus lowering income tax liability. The 401(k) plans differ from deferred profit sharing plans in two important ways. First, employees can decide how much of their compensation is deferred in a 401(k) plan. The Internal Revenue Service sets dollar limits on the maximum allowable pretax contribution to a 401(k) plan, adjusted for increases in the cost of living. Section 401(k) plans had contribution limits of $11,000 in 2002, and these limits will rise by increments of $1,000 annually until reaching $15,000 in 2006. The limit will be indexed for inflation in $500 increments beginning after 2006.

Employee stock ownership plans (ESOPs) may be the basis for a company's 401(k) plan, and these plans invest in company securities, making them similar to profit sharing plans and stock bonus plans. ESOPs and profit sharing plans differ because ESOPs usually make distributions in company stock rather than cash. ESOPs are essentially stock bonus plans that use borrowed funds to purchase stock.

Savings and thrift plans are savings plans that employers set up on behalf of employees. They feature employee contributions matched by the employer. Employees make contributions to savings and thrift plans on a pretax basis. Also, employees cannot withdraw their contributions from their accounts prior to their retirement without a substantial monetary penalty. The contributions by employers vary widely, usually between 1 and 50 percent of employees' annual contributions.

Stock bonus plans are governed by rules similar to those that apply to profit sharing plans, except that benefits generally are distributed in the form of stock of the employer corporation. Both employees and employers make regular contributions to these plans. The employer then invests both contributions in an investment vehicle selected by the employee—stocks, bonds, and money market funds.

Defined benefit plans guarantee the retirement benefits specified in the plan document. This benefit usually is expressed in terms of a monthly sum equal to a percentage of a participant's preretirement pay multiplied by the number of years he or she has worked for the employer. Although the benefit in such a plan is fixed by a formula, the level of required employer contributions fluctuates from year to year. The contribution depends on the amount necessary to make certain that the benefits promised will be available when participants and their beneficiaries are eligible to receive them. As a result, companies find defined benefit plans more burdensome to administer than defined contribution plans. Not surprisingly, fewer companies participate in defined benefit plans.

Health Protection Programs

Health protection has captured both employees' and employers' attention for several years. From the employees' perspective, health coverage is valuable, particularly as the costs of health care have increased dramatically. Total health care expenditures rose by more than 5,000 percent from $26.9 billion in 1960. The expenditure amounts from private sources were substantially higher than the expenditure amounts from public sources.

Companies can choose from varieties of health protection including indemnity plans, self-funded insurance, health maintenance organizations (HMOs), and preferred provider organizations (PPOs). Most companies offer more than one kind of medical and health protection coverage.

Indemnity Plans (Also Known as Fee-for-Service-Plans) **Indemnity plans** provide protection for three types of medical expenses: hospital expenses, surgical expenses, and physicians' charges. Hospital expense coverage pays for room and board charges and other in-hospital services agreed upon in the contract, such as laboratory fees and x-ray charges.

Surgical expense benefits pay for medically necessary surgical procedures but usually not for elective surgeries such as cosmetic surgical procedures. Generally, indemnity plans pay expenses according to a schedule of usual, customary, and reasonable charges. The **usual, customary, and reasonable charge** is defined as being not more than the physician's usual charge; within the customary range of fees charged in the locality; and reasonable, based on the medical circumstances. Whenever actual surgical expenses exceed the usual, customary, and reasonable level, the patient must pay the difference.

Under indemnity plans, policyholders (employees) may generally select any licensed physician, surgeon, or medical facility for treatment, and the insurance plan reimburses the policyholders after medical services are rendered. The insurance policy, or contract between the insurance company and the employees, specifies the expenses that are covered and at what rate. A common feature of indemnity plans is the **deductible**. Each year, employees must pay a deductible before insurance benefits become active. The deductible amount is modest, ranging between $100 and $600, depending on the plan.

Indemnity plans also feature coinsurance, which becomes relevant after the insureds pay their annual deductible. **Coinsurance** refers to the percentage of covered expenses paid by the insured. Most indemnity plans stipulate 20 percent coinsurance. This means that the insured will pay 20 percent of covered expenses and the insurance plan is responsible for the difference, in this case, 80 percent. Just as deductibles vary, so do coinsurance provisions. Although 20 percent is a much smaller amount than 80 percent, the rapidly rising costs of health care may make paying 20 percent cost-prohibitive to most people. Thus, most indemnity plans specify the maximum amount a policyholder must pay per year, known as the **out-of-pocket maximum** provision.

The purpose of the out-of-pocket maximum provision is to protect individuals from catastrophic medical expenses. Single individuals often have an annual out-of-pocket maximum of $800, and family out-of-pocket maximums may be as high as $3,000. Both the annual deductible and coinsurance amounts count toward meeting the out-of-pocket maximum. For example, once the total deductible and coinsurance amounts total $800 for a single individual, the insurance plan then pays 100 percent of the covered expenses in excess of the out-of-pocket maximum. Table 11-3 lists the coverage of a standard indemnity medical insurance program.

Upon deciding to offer health protection benefits to employees, companies must decide between offering these benefits through an individual policy or a group policy. Individual policies typically require evaluation of each employee's health. Group health insurance plans are negotiated by an employer to cover all employees for specific benefits. Under group plans, premiums are determined by an actuarial analysis of plan participants rather than on an actual evaluation of each employee's health. Employers may choose to pay the entire policy premium or share the cost with employees. Group plans offer advantages to both employees and employers. For employers, group plans are generally less expensive because underwriting these plans involves less risk to the insurer. For employees, insurance companies impose fewer restrictions on the terms of coverage, such as waiving physical examinations as a condition for enrollment.

Self-Funded Insurance Self-funded insurance and indemnity plans appear superficially to be the same. **Self-funded insurance plans** specify areas of coverage, deductibles, coinsurance rates, and out-of-pocket maximums, just as indemnity plans do. Differences between indemnity plans and self-funded insurance plans center on

TABLE 11-3 A Sample Fee-for-Service Plan With and Without PPO Hospital Usage

Benefit Summary

The benefits described in this summary represent the major areas of coverage. For detailed information, see the specific covered benefits section. The annual plan deductible and other updated information for each plan year will appear annually in your Benefit Choice Options booklet.

Effective Date	July 1, 2002
Plan Year	July 1–June 30 of each year
Plan Year Maximum	Unlimited
Lifetime Maximum	Unlimited
Annual Plan Deductible	(July 1, 2002)

Member Annual Plan Deductible

Annual Salary	**Deductible**
$49,800 or less	$150
$49,801–$62,300	$250
$62,301 and over	$300
Retiree/Annuitant/Survivor	$100

Dependent Annual Plan Deductible $100

Family Deductible Cap

Annual Salary	**Family Cap**
$49,800 or less	$300
$49,801–$62,300	$400
$62,301 and over	$450
Retiree/Annuitant/Survivor	$300

Coverage After Annual Plan Deductibles

Physician & Surgeon Services	In-patient or office visits	• 80% of R&C [reasonable and customary] after deductible
Out-Patient Services	Diagnostic lab/x-ray	• 100% of R&C after deductible
	Durable medical equipment & prosthetics	• 80% of R&C after deductible
	Surgical facility charges	• 90% after deductible
	PPO Hospitals	**Non-PPO Hospital**
In-Patient Hospital	90% after annual plan deductible	65% after annual plan deductible and $100 admission deductible, if member resides within 25 miles of PPO hospital. Annual non-PPO out-of-pocket maximum applies. 80% after annual plan deductible and $100 admission deductible, if member does not reside within 25 miles of PPO hospital. General out-of-pocket maximum applies.
	General	**Non-PPO Hospital**
Out-of-Pocket Maximum	Plan pays 100% of R&C after you pay $800 per individual or $2000 per family in deductibles and coinsurance.	Plans pays 100% of R&C after you pay $3000 per individual or $7000 per family in non-PPO deductibles and coinsurance.

All charges are subject to the benefit administrator's determinations of medical necessity and reasonable and customary (R&C) fees.

how benefits provided to policyholders are financed. When companies elect indemnity plans, they establish a contract with an independent insurance company such as Blue Cross and Blue Shield. Indemnity plans pay benefits from their financial reserves, which are based on the premiums companies and employees pay to receive insurance. Companies may choose to self-fund employee insurance, an alternative to indemnity plans. Such companies pay benefits directly from their own assets, either current cash flow or funds set aside in advance for potential future claims.

The decision to self-fund is based on financial considerations. Self-funding makes sense when a company's financial burden associated with covering medical expenses for its employees is less than the cost to subscribe to an indemnity insurance company for coverage. By not paying premiums in advance to an indemnity plan, a company retains these funds for current cash flow.

Health Maintenance Organizations (HMOs) and Preferred Provider Organizations (PPOs) HMOs and PPOs are popular systems that organize, deliver, and finance health care. **Health maintenance organizations (HMOs)** are sometimes described as providing "prepaid medical services," because fixed periodic enrollment fees cover HMO members for all medically necessary services, as long as the services are delivered or approved by the HMO. HMOs generally provide inpatient and outpatient care as well as services from physicians, surgeons, and other health care professionals. Most medical services may be fully covered, or participants may be required to make nominal (HMO) **copayments**. Common copayments are $10 or $15 per doctor's office visit and $5 to $10 per prescription drug.

The HMOs are regulated at both federal and state levels. At the federal level, HMOs are governed by the **Health Maintenance Organization Act of 1973** [11], amended in 1988, to encourage their use: The federal government believes that HMOs are a viable alternative method for financing and delivering health care. Companies must offer HMOs if they are subject to the minimum wage provisions of the Fair Labor Standards Act (Chapter 3). The act spurred the growth of HMOs by making development funds available to qualifying HMOs and by imposing a "dual choice" requirement on employers that sponsored health benefits programs. Under the dual choice requirement, employers with at least 25 employees had to offer at least one HMO as an alternative to a traditional indemnity plan.

In 1995, the dual choice requirement was eliminated to allow HMOs and other types of health care programs to compete on a more equal footing in two ways. First, employers now can negotiate rates based on the extent to which employees are likely to use HMO services. Employers whose employees tend to use HMO services more extensively pay higher premiums than employers whose employees tend to use HMO services less extensively.

Second, employers now can compete more equally because they must not financially discriminate against employees choosing an HMO option. In other words, companies must contribute an equal percentage regardless of employees' choices (that is, an HMO versus an indemnity or self-insured plan).

HMOs differ based on where service is rendered, how medical care is delivered, and how contractual relationships between medical providers and the HMOs are structured. **Prepaid group practices** provide medical care for a set premium, rather than on a fee-for-service basis. Physicians who have contracted to share facilities, equipment, and support staff provide services to HMO members. A group HMO usually operates on a 24-hour basis, covering emergency phones and sometimes emergency rooms.

Individual practice associations are partnerships or other legal entities that arrange health care services by entering into service agreements with independent physicians, health professionals, and group practices. Physicians who participate in this type of HMO practice may continue to see non-HMO patients. Participating physicians base fees on a capped fee schedule. This means that the HMO establishes the amount it will reimburse physicians for each procedure. If physicians charge more than the fee set by the HMO, then they must bill the difference to the patients. For example, an HMO sets a cap of $40 for a physical examination. If the physician charges $55 for the examination, then the physician bills the HMO for $40 and the patient for $15.

Under a **preferred provider organization (PPO)**, a select group of health care providers agree to provide health care services to a given population at a higher level of reimbursement than under fee-for-service plans. Physicians qualify as PPO providers by meeting quality standards, agreeing to follow cost-containment procedures implemented by the PPO, and accepting the PPOs reimbursement structure. In return, the employer, insurance company, or third-party administrator helps guarantee provider physicians with certain patient loads by furnishing employees with financial incentives to use the preferred providers.

What are the key differences between HMOs and PPOs? There are two major differences. First, PPOs do not provide benefits on a prepaid basis. Health care providers receive payment after they render services to patients. Second, employees who subscribe to PPOs are generally free to select from comprehensive lists of physicians and health care facilities.

Dental Insurance **Dental insurance** is now a relatively common component of fringe compensation packages. The likelihood of employers offering dental insurance plans increases with company size. Union employees are more likely than other employees to have dental insurance coverage.

Indemnity dental insurance plans provide cash benefits by reimbursing patients for out-of-pocket costs or by paying dentists directly for patient costs. Deductibles and coinsurance are common, and plans typically pay 50 to 80 percent of fees after deductibles are paid. With **self-insured dental plans**, employers directly finance dental benefits by using their general assets or pay into a trust from which benefits are paid. Self-insured plans often involve the services of third-party administrators. **Dental service corporations**, owned and administered by state dental associations, are nonprofit corporations of dentists. Participating dentists register their fees, and patients usually pay the difference between the fixed fee established by the corporations and the dentist's often higher actual fee. **Dental maintenance organizations** deliver dental services through the comprehensive health care plans of many HMOs and PPOs. Some independent networks of dentists, known as dental maintenance organizations, give employers access to providers that will offer discounted services, similar to dental PPOs.

Vision Insurance Fewer companies offer their employees **vision insurance** than dental insurance. Plans usually cover eye examinations, lenses, frames, and fitting of glasses. Similar to dental protection, vision insurance benefits may be delivered through indemnity plans or managed care arrangements. All forms of delivery limit the frequency and types of services. Typically, benefits are limited to eye examinations, basic prescription lenses, and frames once every 1 to 2 years. Vision plan benefits are relatively limited because they exclude coverage of specialty prescription eyeglass lenses (for example, sunglasses, lightweight plastic lenses, and photo-sensitive lenses) and they restrict the coverage amount for frames. These plans generally do not cover any of the costs of contact lenses, unless a vision care provider deems their usage a medical necessity.

Paid Time-Off

The second type of discretionary benefit is paid time-off. This category is relatively straightforward. As the name implies, paid time-off policies compensate employees when they are not performing their primary work duties. The major types of paid time-off are:

- Holidays
- Vacation
- Sick leave
- Personal leave
- Jury duty
- Funeral leave
- Military leave
- Clean-up, preparation, or travel time
- Rest period "break"
- Lunch period

Companies offer most paid time-off as a matter of custom, particularly paid holidays, vacations, and sick leave. In unionized settings, the particulars about paid time-off are in the collective bargaining agreement. The paid time-off practices that are most typically found in unionized settings are jury duty, funeral leave, military leave, clean-up, preparation, travel time, rest period, and lunch period.

Services

Employee Assistance Programs

Employee assistance programs (EAPs) help employees cope with personal problems that may impair their job performance, such as alcohol or drug abuse, domestic violence, the emotional impact of AIDS and other diseases, clinical depression, and eating disorders [12]. EAPs are widely used.

Companies offer EAPs because at any given time an estimated 10 to 15 percent of a company's employees experience difficulties that interfere with job performance [13]. Although EAP costs are substantial, the benefits seem to outweigh the costs. For example, the annual cost per employee of an EAP is approximately $40 to $50. However, anecdotal evidence indicates that employers' gains outweigh their out-of-pocket expenses for EAPs: savings from reduced employee turnover, absenteeism, medical costs, unemployment insurance rates, workers' compensation rates, accident costs, and disability insurance costs. In fact, one analysis of EAP effectiveness demonstrated that 78 percent of EAP users found resolutions to their problems [14].

Depending on the employer, EAPs provide a range of services and are organized in various ways. In some companies, EAPs are informal programs developed and run on-site by in-house staff. Other employers contract with outside firms to administer their EAPs, or they rely on a combination of their own resources and help from an outside firm.

Family Assistance Programs

Family assistance programs help employees provide elder care and child care. Elder care provides physical, emotional, or financial assistance for aging parents, spouses, or other relatives who are not fully self-sufficient because they are too frail or disabled. Child care programs focus on supervising preschool-age dependent children whose parents work outside the home. Many employees now rely on elder care programs because of their parents' increasing longevity [15] and the growing numbers of dual-income families [16]. Child care needs arise from the growing number of single parents and dual-career households with children.

A variety of employer programs and benefits can help employees cope with their family responsibilities. The programs range from making referrals to on-site child or elder care centers to company-sponsored day care programs, and they vary in the amount of financial and human resources needed to administer them. Generally, the least expensive and least labor-intensive programs are referral services. Referral services are designed to help workers identify and take advantage of available community resources, conveyed through media such as educational workshops, videos, employee newsletters and magazines, and EAPs.

Flexible scheduling and leave allows employees the leeway to take time off during work hours to care for relatives or react to emergencies. Flexible scheduling, which includes compressed work weeks (such as 10-hour days or 12-hour days), flextime, and job sharing, helps employees balance the demands of work and family [17]. Besides flexible work scheduling, some companies allow employees to extend their legally mandated leave sanctioned by the Family and Medical Leave Act (see Chapter 10). Under extended leave, employers typically continue to provide fringe compensation such as insurance and promise to secure individuals comparable jobs upon their return [18].

Day care is another possible benefit. Some companies subsidize child or elder day care in community-based centers. Elder care programs usually provide self-help, meals, and entertainment activities for the participants. Child care programs typically offer supervision, preschool preparation, and meals. Facilities must usually maintain state or local licenses. Other companies such as Stride Rite Corporation and Fel-Pro choose to sponsor on-site day care centers, offering services that are similar to community-based centers.

Tuition Reimbursement

Companies offer **tuition reimbursement programs** to promote their employees' education. Under a tuition reimbursement program, an employer fully or partially reimburses an employee for expenses incurred for education or training. A survey of tuition reimbursement programs showed that 43 percent of these plans reimbursed less than 100 percent of tuition; however, some companies vary the percentage of tuition reimbursed according to the relevance of the course to the companies' goals or the grades employees earn [19].

Tuition reimbursement programs are not synonymous with pay-for-knowledge programs (Chapter 6). Instead, they fall under the category of fringe compensation. Under these programs, employees choose the courses they wish to take when they want to take them. In addition, employees may enroll in courses that are not directly related to their work. As we discussed in Chapter 6, pay-for-knowledge is one kind of core compensation. Companies establish set curricula that employees take, and they generally award pay increases to employees who successfully complete courses within the curricula. Pay increases are not directly associated with tuition reimbursement programs.

Transportation Services

Some employers sponsor **transportation services** programs that help bring employees to the workplace and back home again by using more energy-efficient forms of transportation. They may sponsor public transportation or vanpools: employer-sponsored vans or buses that transport employees between their homes and the workplace.

Employers provide transit subsidies to employees working in metropolitan and suburban areas served by mass transportation, such as buses, subways, and trains. Companies may offer transit passes, tokens, or vouchers. Practices vary from partial subsidy to full subsidy.

Many employers must offer transportation services to comply with the law. Increasingly, local and state governments request that companies reduce the number of single-passenger automobiles commuting to their workplace each day because of government mandates for cleaner air. The Clean Air Act Amendments of 1990 require employers in large metropolitan areas such as Los Angeles to comply with state and local commuter-trip reduction laws. Employers may also offer transportation services to recruit individuals who do not care to drive in rush-hour traffic. Further, transportation services enable companies to offset deficits in parking space availability, particularly in congested metropolitan areas.

Employees obviously stand to benefit from these transportation services. For example, using public transportation or joining a vanpool often saves money by eliminating commuting costs such as gas, insurance, car maintenance and repairs, and parking fees. Moreover, commuting time can be quite lengthy for some employees. By leaving the driving to others, employees can use the time more productively by reading, completing paperwork, or "unwinding."

Outplacement Assistance

Some companies provide technical and emotional support through **outplacement assistance** to employees who are being laid off or terminated. They do so with a variety of career and personal programs designed to develop employees' job-hunting skills and strategies and to boost employees' self-confidence. A variety of factors leads to employee termination. Those best suited to outplacement assistance programs include:

- Layoffs due to economic hardship
- Mergers and acquisitions
- Company reorganizations
- Changes in management
- Plant closings or relocation
- Elimination of specific positions, often the result of changes in technology

Outplacement assistance provides such services as personal counseling, career assessments and evaluations, training in job search techniques, resume and cover letter preparation, interviewing techniques, and training in the use of basic workplace technology such as computers [20]. While beneficial to employees, outplacement assistance programs hold possible benefits for companies as well. They can promote a positive image of the company among those being terminated, as well as their families and friends, by helping these employees prepare for employment opportunities.

Wellness Programs

In the 1980s, employers began sponsoring **wellness programs** to promote and maintain employees' physical and psychological health. Wellness programs vary in scope. They may emphasize weight loss only, or they may emphasize a range of activities such as weight loss, smoking cessation, and cardiovascular fitness. Programs may be offered on- or off-site. Although some companies invest in staffing professionals for wellness programs, others contract with external vendors such as community health agencies or private health clubs.

Although wellness programs are relatively new, some evidence already indicates that these innovations can save companies money and reduce employees' needs for health care. For every $1 invested in preventive health care programs, companies can expect to save as much as $6 in medical insurance costs [21].

Smoking cessation, stress reduction, nutrition and weight loss, exercise and fitness activities, and health screening programs are the most common workplace wellness programs. **Smoking cessation** plans range from simple campaigns that stress the negative aspects of smoking to intensive programs directed at helping individuals to stop smoking. Many employers offer courses and treatment to help and encourage smokers to quit. Other options include offering nicotine replacement therapy, such as nicotine gum and patches, and self-help services. Many companies sponsor antismoking events, such as the Great American Smoke-Out, during which companies distribute T-shirts, buttons, and literature that discredit smoking.

Stress management programs can help employees cope with many factors inside and outside work that contribute to stress. For instance, job conditions, health and personal problems, and personal and professional relationships can make employees anxious and thus less productive. Symptoms of stressful workplaces include low morale, chronic absenteeism, low productivity, and high turnover rates. Employers offer stress management programs to teach workers to cope with conditions and situations that cause stress. Seminars focus on recognizing signs of stress and burnout, as well as on how to handle family- and business-related stress. Stress reduction techniques can improve quality of life inside and outside the workplace. Employers benefit from increased employee productivity, reduced absenteeism, and lower health care costs.

Weight control and nutrition programs are designed to educate employees about proper nutrition and weight loss, both of which are critical to good health. Information from the medical community has clearly indicated that excess weight and poor nutrition are significant risk factors in cardiovascular disease, diabetes, high blood pressure, and cholesterol levels. Over time, these programs should give employees better health, increased morale, and improved appearance. For employers, these programs should result in improved productivity and lower health care costs.

Companies can contribute to employees' weight control and proper nutrition by sponsoring memberships in weight-loss programs such as Weight Watchers. Sponsoring companies may also reinforce weight loss programs' positive results through support groups, intensive counseling, competitions, and other incentives. Companies sometimes actively attempt to influence employee food choices by stocking vending machines with nutritional food.

LAWS THAT GUIDE DISCRETIONARY FRINGE COMPENSATION

Many laws guide discretionary fringe compensation practices. Here we review only the major laws on this topic: the Employee Retirement Income Security Act of 1974 (ERISA), the Consolidated Omnibus Budget Reconciliation Act of 1985 (COBRA), key antidiscrimination laws, and the Fair Labor Standards Act.

Employee Retirement Income Security Act of 1974 (ERISA)

ERISA was established to regulate the implementation of various fringe compensation programs, including medical, life, and disability programs, as well as pension programs. The essence of ERISA is protection of employee benefits rights.

ERISA addresses matters of employers' reporting and disclosure duties, funding of benefits, the fiduciary responsibilities for these plans, and vesting rights. Companies must provide their employees with straightforward descriptions of their employee benefits plans, updates when substantive changes to the plan are implemented, annual synopses on the financing and operation of the plans, and advance notification if the company intends to terminate the benefits plan. The funding requirement mandates that companies meet strict guidelines to ensure having sufficient funds when employees reach retirement. Similarly, the fiduciary responsibilities require that companies not engage in transactions with parties having interests adverse to those of the recipients of the plan and not deal with the income or assets of the employee benefits plan in the company's own interests.

Vesting refers to an employee's acquisition of nonforfeitable rights to an employer's contributions to fund pension benefits. Oftentimes, employees must be 100 percent vested between 3 and 5 years of service depending on the vesting schedule. One hundred percent vested means that an employee cannot lose the pension benefits even if the employee leaves the job before retirement; employees are entitled to every dollar contributed on their behalf by the employer.

There are two minimum criteria for eligibility under ERISA. First, employees must be allowed to participate in a pension plan after they reach age 21. Second, employees must have completed 1 year of service based on at least 1,000 hours of work. There is no maximum age limit for eligibility.

Since the passage of ERISA, there have been a number of amendments to this act. The impetus for these amendments has been the ever-changing laws relating to the tax treatment of employees' contributions to pension plans. For example, the tax laws offer employees the opportunity to deduct a limited amount of their gross income (income before any federal, state, or local taxes are assessed) for investment in a pension plan. Such deductions reduce the taxable gross pay amount on which taxes are assessed, clearly lowering employees' tax burdens. The amendments are quite complex and technical, requiring familiarity with the Internal Revenue Code, the tax code administered by the Internal Revenue Service. The key amendments include the Tax Equity and Fiscal Responsibility Act of 1982, Deficit Reduction Act of 1984, the Tax Reform Act of 1986, and the **Economic Growth and Tax Relief Reconciliation Act of 2001**.

Consolidated Omnibus Budget Reconciliation Act of 1985 (COBRA)

The **Consolidated Omnibus Budget Reconciliation Act of 1985 (COBRA)** was enacted to provide employees with the opportunity to temporarily continue receiving their employer-sponsored medical care insurance under their employer's plan if their coverage otherwise would cease because of termination, layoff, or other change in employment status. COBRA applies to a wide variety of employers, with exemptions available only for companies that normally employ fewer than 20 workers, church plans, and plans maintained by the U.S. government.

Under COBRA, individuals may continue their coverage, as well as coverage for their spouses and dependents, for up to 18 months. Coverage may extend for up to 36 months for spouses and dependents facing a loss of employer-provided coverage because of an employee's death, a divorce or legal separation, or certain other qualifying events. Employee termination, retirement, layoff, and death are examples of qualifying events. Table 11-4 displays the maximum continuation period for particular qualifying events.

Companies are permitted to charge COBRA beneficiaries a premium for continuation coverage of up to 102 percent of the cost of the coverage to the plan. The 2 percent markup reflects a charge for administering COBRA. Employers that violate the COBRA requirements are subject to an excise tax per affected employee for each day that the violation continues. In addition, plan administrators who fail to provide required COBRA notices to employees may be personally liable for a civil penalty for each day the notice is not provided.

TABLE 11-4 Continuation of Coverage under COBRA

The following information applies to health, vision, and dental coverage only. If you are interested in continuing life insurance when your employment terminates, please refer to the materials provided which describe your life coverage.

COBRA (Consolidated Omnibus Budge Reconciliation Act) was signed into law on April 7, 1986, as P.L. 99-272. Under COBRA, the employer must provide covered members and their dependents who would lose coverage under the plan the option to continue coverage. The mandate is restricted to certain conditions under which coverage is lost, and the election to continue must be made within a specified election period. COBRA went into effect for members and their dependents on July 1, 1986.

A. COBRA Requirements

Qualifying Events	Maximum Continuation Period
Member	
a) Termination of employment for any reason, including termination of disability benefits and layoff, except for gross misconduct.	18 months
b) Loss of eligibility due to reduction in work hours.	18 months
c) Determination by the Social Security Administration (SSA) of disability that existed at time of qualifying event.	29 months
Dependent	
a) Member's termination of employment as stated above.	18 months
b) Member's loss of eligibility due to reduction in work hours.	18 months
c) Member's death, divorce, or legal separation.	
1) spouse or ex-spouse, under age 55	36 months
2) spouse or ex-spouse age 55 or older	The date spouse or ex-spouse becomes entitled to Medicare.
d) Member's Medicare entitlement. (Under certain conditions, this could be 36 months.)	18 months
e) Ceases to satisfy plan's eligibility requirements for dependent status.	36 months
f) Determination by the Social Security Administration (SSA) of disability that existed at time of qualifying event. Must have been covered under member's insurance at time of qualifying event.	29 months

If you are covered under COBRA and have been determined to be disabled by the federal Social Security Administration (SSA), you may be eligible to extend your coverage time from 18 months to 29. You must submit a copy of the SSA determination to the State's COBRA Administrator within 60 days of the date of the SSA determination letter and before the end of the original 18-month COBRA coverage period. Failure to notify the administrator and submit the required documentation within the 60-day period will disqualify you for the extension.

To be eligible for the extension of time, members must have been determined by the SSA to be disabled at the time of the event which qualified them for COBRA. Dependents must have been determined by the SSA to be disabled at the time of the event which qualified the member for COBRA and must have been covered by the member for insurance at that time.

Additional Pertinent Legislation

As we discussed in Chapter 3, the Civil Rights Acts of 1964 and 1991, the Age Discrimination in Employment Act, and the Pregnancy Discrimination Act prohibit discrimination in both core and fringe compensation. This means that employers must provide members of protected classes (for example, women or all individuals at least age 40) with an equal opportunity to receive the same benefits as members of the majority. In addition, we discussed the Fair Labor Standards Act, which applies to fringe compensation as well as to core compensation. Employees who are covered by this law are entitled to a pay rate of one-and-one-half times their normal hourly rate for hours worked in excess of 40 during a workweek. Fringe benefits that are linked to pay, such as unemployment insurance (Chapter 10), increase correspondingly during those overtime hours.

UNIONS AND FRINGE COMPENSATION

In Chapter 3, we reviewed the NLRA, which gives rights to employees to self-organize, form, join, or assist labor unions; bargain collectively through representatives of their own choosing; and engage in other concerted activities for the purpose of collective bargaining.

Under the NLRA, the possible subjects for bargaining fall under three categories: mandatory, permissive, or illegal. Only the lists of mandatory and permissive subjects include compensation issues. To date, the National Labor Relations Board (NLRB) has declared no compensation subjects as illegal. **Mandatory bargaining subjects** are those that employers and unions must bargain if either party makes proposals about them. In the domain of fringe compensation, the following items are mandatory subjects of bargaining:

- Disability pay (supplemental to what is mandated by Social Security and the various state workers' compensation laws)
- Employer-provided health insurance
- Paid time-off
- Pension and retirement plans

The NLRA strictly limits management discretion in unionized firms to establish major elements of the fringe compensation program. For example, the NLRB held that an employer committed an unfair labor practice when it unilaterally switched insurance carriers and changed the health protection benefits provided under its collective bargaining agreement. The NLRB held that the collective bargaining agreement contemplated that the same insurance carrier would be retained while the contract was in effect and that benefits would remain as agreed upon during negotiations [22].

Although employee health care benefits plans are mandatory subjects for bargaining, under certain circumstances the change in the identity of the plan's insurance carrier or third-party administrator is not a compulsory bargaining subject. For example, a federal appeals court ruled lawful an employer's unilateral change to a new insurance carrier that was substantively the same as the old carrier [23]. The employer had proposed that it unilaterally be able to change insurance carriers. The union countered by saying that change would come only after both parties agreed on the terms and conditions of the health care coverage. When neither could agree on the terms, an interim contract provision was inserted, which stated that the employer could not unilaterally adopt an alternate delivery system. Subsequently, the employer changed carriers without first consulting the union. The union sued to prevent the company from switching carriers, but the court held the change of carriers was lawful for two reasons: First, the coverage under the new carrier remained substantially the same. Second, the provision restricting the unilateral adoption of an alternative delivery system, although ambiguous enough to be capable of more than one meaning, did not prevent the employer from switching insurance carriers.

Permissive bargaining subjects are those subjects on which neither the employer nor union is obligated to bargain. The following are fringe compensation items in the permissive subjects category:

- Administration of funds for fringe compensation programs
- Retiree benefits (such as medical insurance)
- Workers' compensation, within the scope of state workers' compensation laws

DESIGNING AND PLANNING THE BENEFITS PROGRAM

As noted earlier, discretionary benefits can work strategically by offering protection programs, paid time-off, and services. As they plan and manage fringe compensation programs, HR professionals should keep these functions in mind. Probably no single company expects its fringe compensation program to meet all these objectives. Therefore, company management, along with union representatives as appropriate, must determine which objectives are the most important for a particular workforce.

Many experts argue that employee input is key to developing a "successful" program [24]. Such input helps companies target the limited resources they have available for fringe compensation to those areas that best meet employees' needs. For example, if a company's workforce includes mostly married couples who are raising young children, family assistance programs would probably be a priority. By involving employees in program development, they are most likely to accept and appreciate the benefits they receive. Companies can involve employees in the benefits determination process in ways such as surveys, interviews, and focus groups.

As they design fringe programs, human resource professionals must address fundamental issues, including:

- Who receives coverage
- Whether to include retirees in the plan
- Whether to deny benefits to employees during their probationary periods
- Financing of benefits
- Degree of employee choice in determining benefits
- Cost containment
- Communication

Employers can ascertain key information from employees that can be useful in designing these programs. Table 11-5 lists examples of the kinds of information employers may want from their employees. The areas of input emphasize employees'

TABLE 11-5 Types of Employee Input for Designing Benefits Programs

Ask employees:

- What they know about existing benefits
- What they perceive to be the value of possible benefit changes
- What they think about the quality and timeliness of benefits communications and administration
- What they perceive to be the value of existing benefits, compared with those provided by other employers

Source: Adapted from Haslinger, J. A. & Sheering, D. Employee input: The key to successful benefits programs. *Compensation & Benefits Review* (May–June 1994), pp. 61–70.

FLIP SIDE OF THE COIN

24/7 BENEFITS

A major computer manufacturer faced today's Internet realities by using its own IT department to develop an online benefits program with 'round the clock access.

Gateway, one of the nation's leading personal computer manufacturers, is tapping some of its own technology for an online open enrollment project involving employees who own PCs, as well as those who do not.

The move was driven in part by market realities. The number 1 reason people now purchase a PC is for Internet access, according to Jacquelyn Trask, the company's director of compensation, benefits and occupational health and safety.

"We developed a Web site in house and tried to destroy everything in print during the past three months," Trask recently told attendees of a symposium, sponsored by the Conference Board, on benefits policy and strategy for the 21st century. "Our journey was all home grown."

Gateway, which employs 19,000 employees worldwide, had enrolled roughly 3,000 of the 4,000 U.S. employees who had viewed online enrollment pages at the time of her presentation. Eventually, the company hopes to allow employees to adjust their W-4 withholding information online.

To help employees learn how to use search engines, recognize URLs and perform other online tasks, Gateway developed a Web certification program. Since the company's average employee is 28 years old, Trask quipped that this approach was partially designed to combat written benefits communications getting lost in the U.S. mail en route to the addresses of younger employees who may have moved several times.

HOME ACCESS DILEMMA

More to the point, however, was the hope that employees would enjoy the freedom of easy access to their benefits information at all times.

"Employees have got to be able to connect from home," Trask recalled telling Gateway's IT department, which she said rose to the challenge of developing secure firewalls so that benefits access could be granted outside of work. Personal identification numbers and Social Security numbers helped protect the confidentiality of employee data.

"We have this tagline in HR: Keeping it personal, making it simple," she said, adding that employees now can enjoy the freedom of enrolling in their benefits plans at 2 A.M. if they so choose.

However, 24/7 access poses a dilemma for Gateway. Although the company offers employees a discount on its computers, PC ownership is still out of reach for roughly 12,000 of 17,000 U.S. employees—mostly those in manufacturing plants. The company decided to allow these employees time off to enroll in their benefits plans via onsite kiosks.

The issue recently was dramatized when Ford Motor Co., Delta Airlines and Intel announced that they would make computers, Internet access and printers available to their employees at a substantial discount, in some cases costing as little as $5 a month. "It's something we need to look at," Trask said in response to a question about these deep discount programs.

"We find that home access is a pivotal issue," reported Mark Schumann, a principal at Towers Perrin, which has worked with Gateway. He said the issue has taken on added importance since companies have been cracking down on employees surfing the Internet for nonwork use on company time.

RELEVANT BENEFITS CONTENT

In recent years, Schumann noted that the search for health care and retirement savings information has moved to the Internet with the same intensity as shopping for products and searching for new employment.

Whereas organizational knowledge always has been imparted on a hierarchical basis (e.g., employee training conducted at a specific time and place), Schumann said the Web offers 24/7 access to all benefits information. It also places control over the flow of information firmly in the hands of employees, with both potentially good and bad results for employers. He noted that a group of highly vocal IBM employees used the Internet to pressure their employer to redesign its new and controversial cash balance savings plan to be more responsive to older workers.

"This is the most personal tool we can offer employees," Schumann said, "but it's useless unless they can relate to the content."

Since one mission of the Employee Retirement Income Security Act of 1974 (ERISA) is to put benefits plan information into plain English, Schumann suggested that employers have a good internal search engine in place. For example, if a plan participant types in "crooked teeth," then orthodontia benefits information should appear on the screen.

Another way to pass the relevance test, he said, is to enable people to compare an array of medical plan options and build their own tables and charts with just the click of a mouse. Other promising functions include resume writing and career counseling.

What makes employee benefits information sizzle, Schumann explained, is if graphics are easy to absorb, screens appear quickly and a world of information is made available at just one glance. Of course, none of this means anything unless the information is accurate, the content is frequently updated, the server is dependable and the transactions are foolproof, he added. Figure 1 lists factors that make a Web site relevant.

BENEFITING ALL AGES

While Internet access shows tremendous promise for child development and school-related research, Gateway's Trask noted that people over the age of 60 spend three times as many hours online than any other age group. About half the people who are online are between the ages of 30 and 49, she said, while 30 percent are under 30, 15 percent are 50 to 64 and 4 percent are 65 and older.

The potential is extraordinary when you consider that the Internet reached as many Americans in its first six years as the telephone did in its first four decades, according to Towers Perrin's Schumann. (Figure 2 lists other key statistics about online usage.)

Still, there are caveats to keep in mind. "We don't want organizations connected only to computers," Schumann warned. "We also want people to have social experiences. It's the debate of high-tech versus high-touch."

FIGURE 1 What Makes a Web Site Relevant?

- Information is meaningful.
- The site is easy to navigate.
- The search engine makes information easy to locate.
- Technology creates multiple routings through the information.
- The experience is unique and personal.

FIGURE 2 What's Happening Online

- There are seven new people on the Internet every second.
- 50 percent of online users believe intranet news is more accurate than traditional news sources.
- 85 percent of college freshmen use the Internet for research.
- 36 percent of current college students have developed their own Web sites.

Source: Bruce Shutan. *Workspan*. (2000). Scottsdale, AZ: WorldatWork [online]. Available: *resourcepro.worldatwork.org/livelink/livelink/fetch/2000/2657/46405/147717/204096/164*, accessed August 2, 2002. © 2000 WorldatWork, 14040 N. Northsight Blvd., Scottsdale, AZ 85260 U.S.A.; 480/951-9191; Fax 480/483-8352; *www.worldatwork.org*; E-mail WorldlatWork @worldatwork.org

beliefs about other employers' benefits offerings and employees' thoughts about the value of the benefits they receive.

Determining Who Receives Coverage

Companies decide whether to extend benefits coverage to full-time and part-time employees or to full-time employees only. The trend is toward offering part-time employees no benefits.

Deciding Whether to Include Retirees in the Plan

This decision centers on whether to extend medical insurance coverage to employees beyond the COBRA-mandated coverage period, as discussed earlier. Offering medical coverage to retirees benefits them in obvious ways because employers usually finance these benefits either wholly or partly, enabling many retirees on limited earnings to receive adequate medical protection. Until recently, extending medical insurance coverage to retirees also benefited employers: The money they spent to extend coverage to retirees was tax deductible. However, starting in 1997, employers' contributions to extend medical coverage to retirees are no longer tax deductible, which means that such expenses will reduce company earnings in the short-term. Consequently, fewer employers are expected to finance medical insurance coverage for retirees in the future.

Probationary Period

Another scope issue companies must address is employees' status. In many companies, employees' initial term of employment (usually shorter than 6 months) is deemed a **probationary period**, and companies view such periods as an opportunity to ensure that they have made sound hiring decisions. Many companies choose to withhold discretionary fringe compensation for all probationary employees. Companies benefit directly through lower administration-of-benefits costs for these employees during the probationary period. However, probationary employees may experience financial hardships if they require medical attention.

Financing

Human resource managers must consider how to finance benefits. In fact, the available resources and financial goals may influence, to some extent, who will receive coverage. Managers may decide on noncontributory, contributory, and employee-financed programs, or some combination thereof. **Noncontributory financing** implies that the company assumes total costs for each discretionary benefit. Under **contributory financing**, the company and its employees share the costs. Under **employee-financed benefits**, employers do not contribute to the financing of discretionary benefits. The majority of benefit plans today are contributory, largely because the costs of benefits have risen so dramatically.

Employee Choice

Human resource professionals must decide on the degree of choice employees should have in determining the set of benefits they will receive. If employees within a company can choose from among a set of benefits, as opposed to all employees receiving the same set of benefits, the company is using a **flexible benefits plan** or **cafeteria plan**. Companies implement cafeteria plans to meet the challenges of diversity, as discussed earlier. Although there is limited evidence regarding employees' reactions to flexible benefits, the existing information indicates benefit satisfaction, overall job satisfaction, pay satisfaction, and understanding of benefits increased after the implementation of a flexible benefits plan [25]. Many of these outcomes are desirable, as they are known to lead to reduced absenteeism and turnover.

Cafeteria plans vary [26], and the two most common are discussed here. **Flexible spending accounts** permit employees to pay for certain benefits expenses (such as child care) with pretax dollars. Prior to each plan year, employees elect the amount of salary-reduction dollars they wish to allocate to this kind of plan. Employers then use this money to reimburse employees for expenses incurred during the plan year that qualify for repayment. Table 11-6 illustrates the features of a flexible spending account for Illinois state employees. These features are typical of flexible spending accounts used in private- and public-sector employers.

Core plus option plans extend a preestablished set of benefits such as medical insurance as a program core, usually mandatory for all employees. Beyond the core, employees may choose from an array of benefits options that suit their personal needs. Companies establish upper limits of benefits values available to each employee. If employees do not choose the maximum amount of benefits, employers may offer an option of trading extra benefits credits for cash. Table 11-7 illustrates the choices of a typical core plus plan.

Cost Containment

Overall, human resource managers today try to contain costs. As indicated earlier, the rise in health care costs is phenomenal, so fringe compensation now accounts for a substantial percentage of total compensation costs incurred by companies. In 2002, fringe compensation accounted for nearly 28 percent [27]. The current amount has risen dramatically over the past few decades. This increase would not necessarily raise concerns if total compensation budgets were increasing commensurably. As we discussed in Chapter 9, the growth in funds available to support all compensation programs has stagnated. As a consequence, employers face difficult trade-offs between fringe compensation offerings and increases to core compensation.

Communication

Earlier, we noted that employees often regard fringe compensation as an entitlement. Thus, it is reasonable to infer that employees are not aware of its value. In fact, research suggests that employees either are not aware of or undervalue the fringe compensation they receive [28]. Given the significant costs associated with offering fringe compensation, companies should try to convey to employees the value they are likely to derive from having such benefits. Accordingly, a benefits communication plan is essential. An effective communication program should have three primary objectives [29]:

- To create an awareness of and appreciation for the way current benefits improve the financial security and the physical and mental well-being of employees
- To provide a high level of understanding about available benefits
- To encourage the wise use of benefits

Traditionally, companies have used printed brochures to summarize the key features of the benefits program and to help potential employees compare benefits offerings with those of other companies they may be considering. When new employees join the company, initial group meetings with benefits administrators or audiovisual presentations can detail the elements of the company's benefits

TABLE 11-6 Flexible Spending Accounts

How the FSA Program Works

The Flexible Spending Accounts (FSAs) program lets you use tax-free dollars to pay for medical expenses and/or dependent care expenses, increasing your take-home pay and giving you more spendable income. Through convenient payroll deductions, you may contribute up to $5,000 tax-free to a spending account for either one or both plans.

Spending accounts are like getting a tax rebate every time you pay for eligible health and child (dependent) care expenses. The FSA program is simple to use:

- You sign up during one of the enrollment periods and determine how much pretax earnings you wish to put into your FSA account.
- You put pretax money into your spending accounts. (The amount you choose is taken out of your paycheck through payroll deduction and deposited into your FSA account before taxes are calculated.)
- When you have an eligible expense, you send in a claim form with the required documentation.
- Then you get a check back from your account.

When you are reimbursed from your spending accounts, you receive that money tax-free. This amount doesn't appear on your W-2 Form as taxable income—and a lower taxable income means you pay less taxes.

Employees have to type of FSAs available: the Medical Care Assistance Plan (MCAP) for eligible health-related expenses and Dependent Care Assistance Plan (DCAP) for eligible child or other dependent care expenses.

Important Notes

- **Federal Tax Deductions:** Expenses reimbursed through an FSA may not also be used as itemized deductions on your federal tax return.
- **Forfeitures:** Money contributed to your FSA in any plan year can only be used to reimburse eligible expenses incurred during that same plan year. Per IRS regulations, any amounts not claimed by the end of the filing deadlines are forfeited.
- **FSA Accounts Are Separate:** The IRS requires that amounts contributed for reimbursement of health care expenses be accounted for separately from those for day care. In other words, you cannot use amounts deposited in your MCAP account to cover DCAP expenses, or vice versa.
- **Tax Savings:** The employer does not guarantee any specific tax consequence from participation in the FSA program. You are responsible for understanding the effects on your individual situation as a result of directing earnings into tax-free spending accounts. You are also responsible for the validity and eligibility of your claims. You may wish to consult with your personal tax adviser regarding your participation.
- **Changing Your FSA Midyear:** Unless you are newly hired or experience a qualifying change of family status, you may not enroll in, withdraw from, or change your contribution to an FSA account outside of the annual benefit choice period.

Dependent Care Assistance Plan (DCAP)

Who Is Eligible to Participate in DCAP?

Eligible Employees Include:

- Employees who are actively at work and are receiving a paycheck from which deductions can be made.
- If you are married, your spouse must be either gainfully employed or looking for work (but must have earned income for the year); a full-time student for at least five months during the year; or disabled and unable to provide for his or her care.

Eligible Dependents for DCAP Are Defined by the IRS and Include:

- Your spouse;
- Children or other individuals you are eligible to claim as dependents on your federal income tax return; and,
- Individuals who could have been claimed as dependents on your income tax except that the person had income which exceeded the amount allowable to be claimed as a dependent.

TABLE 11-6 (*cont.*)

What Expenses Are Eligible for Reimbursement under DCAP?

- Nursery schools and preschools;
- Schooling prior to the first grade if the amount you pay for schooling is incident to and cannot be separated from the cost of care;
- Day care centers that comply with all applicable state and local laws and regulations;
- Work-related baby-sitters—whether in or out of your home;
- Before- and after-school care;
- Housekeepers in your home if part of their work provides for the well-being and protection of your eligible dependents;
- Adult day care facilities (but not expenses for overnight nursing home facilities);
- Employment taxes you pay on wages for qualifying child and dependent care services; and,
- Other expenses which meet program and IRS criteria

Medical Care Assistance Plan (MCAP)

Who Is Eligible to Participate in MCAP?

- Employees who are working full-time or not less than half-time, are receiving a paycheck from which deductions can be taken, and are participating in one of the state's health plans are eligible.

What Expenses Are Eligible for Reimbursement under MCAP?

- Health and dental care costs not fully covered by the insurance plans in which you or your family members participate, for example:
  - deductibles
  - copayments
  - amounts in excess of the maximum benefit, or
  - amounts in excess of the reasonable and customary charge limits of the health or dental plans;
- Health and dental care not considered as covered services by the insurance plans in which you or your family members participate; and,
- Other expenses which meet program and IRS criteria.

TABLE 11-7 A Sample Core Plus Option Plan

The core plus option plan contains two sets of benefits: *core benefits* and *optional benefits*.

All employees receive a minimum level of *core benefits*:

- Term life insurance equal to 1 times annual salary
- Health protection coverage (indemnity plan, self-funded, HMO, PPO) for the employee and dependents
- Disability insurance

All employees receive credits equal to 4 to 7 percent of salary, which can be used to purchase *optional benefits:*

- Dental insurance for employee and dependents
- Vision insurance for employee and dependents
- Additional life insurance coverage
- Paid vacation time up to 10 days per year

If an employee has insufficient credits to purchase the desired optional benefits, he or she can purchase these credits through payroll deduction.

program. Shortly after group meetings or audiovisual presentations (usually within a month), new employees should meet individually with benefits administrators, sometimes known as "counselors," to select benefits options. After employees select benefits, the company should provide them with personal benefits statements that detail the scope of coverage and value of each component. Table 11-8 illustrates a personal statement of benefits. Beyond these particulars, companies may update employees on changes in benefits—reductions in or additions to benefits choices or coverage—with periodic newsletters.

TABLE 11-8 Example of a Personal Statement of Benefits

A PERSONAL BENEFITS STATEMENT FOR:
John Doe

SSN: *xxx-xx-xxxx* Date of Birth: ***04/10/61***
Marital status: ***Single***

REVIEW OF YOUR CURRENT BENEFIT CHOICES

As of March 2003, our records indicate you have chosen the following benefits (rates may change July 1, 2004):

MEDICAL

For you:
PERSONAL CARE HMO
For your dependent(s):
NONE

State's monthly contribution:	
For you:	***$185.00***
For your dependent(s):	***None***
Your monthly contribution:	***$27.50***

DENTAL

QUALITY CARE DENTAL PLAN

Your monthly contribution:	***$7.50***
State's annual contribution:	
For you:	***$90.00***
For your dependent(s):	***None***

LIFE INSURANCE

As a full-time employee you receive state-paid life insurance equal to your annual salary. If you work part-time, your state-paid amount is less. When you retire at age 60 or older, you still receive $5,000 worth of state-paid life insurance.

State's monthly contribution for your state-paid life insurance:

Basic life ($90,000): $32.50

Your monthly contribution for the following optional coverage:

For you	*(None):*	*None*
Spouse life	*(None):*	*None*
Child life	*(None):*	*None*
Accidental Death and Dismemberment:	*(None):*	*None*

FLEXIBLE SPENDING ACCOUNTS

You are enrolled in the following plan(s):

Dependent Care Assistance Plan	
Annual deduction:	***Not Enrolled***
Medical Care Assistance Plan	
Annual deduction:	***Not Enrolled***

DEPENDENTS

You have chosen to cover the following dependent(s) under your Health Plan:
No Dependents

Note: Any corrections for either premium paid or insurance coverage may only be applied retroactively for up to six months from the month in which the change was reported to the group insurance representative. Be sure to review your paycheck for proper deductions and report any concerns to your group insurance representative immediately.

DOLLAR VALUE OF YOUR BENEFITS

Your total annual compensation is your salary or retirement payment plus the value of state-paid medical, dental, and life insurance coverage.

State-paid medical insurance coverage for you:	***$2,220.00***
State contribution for medical insurance coverage for your dependent(s):	***None***
State-paid dental insurance coverage for you and your dependent(s):	***$90.00***
State-paid life insurance coverage for you:	***$390.00***
Total Value of Your State Paid Benefits:	***$2,700.00***

TABLE 11-9 Employee Benefits Overview

This section is designed to provide detailed information regarding your benefits as a University of Illinois employee. It will give you a comprehensive explanation of each benefit and the resources you will need to initiate enrollment, make changes or find answers to questions regarding your benefits.

Please select from the following categories:

- Announcements—Provides announcements of upcoming sign-up periods or events and updated information relating to your benefits
- Benefits Directory—Provides a listing of staff members, including addresses, phone numbers and E-mail addresses for the Benefits Service Center and each campus.
- Benefit Choice—Benefit Choice is an annual open enrollment period that allows employees to make changes to their state of Illinois health, dental and life insurance coverages and enroll or re-enroll in flexible spending accounts.
- Benefit Forms—Provides links to printable and online benefit forms.
- *Benefits on Call*—Provides an explanation and step-by-step instructions on how to access your benefits information by calling the Benefits On Call voice response system.
- Benefits Statement—Provides a statement outlining your current benefit enrollments and instructions for accessing that information.
- Benefits Summary—Provides a detailed, comprehensive description of each benefit plan and its provisions.
- Change in Illinois State Plan (CMS) Coverages—Provides guidelines and required documentation on when and how you can make changes to your state insurance plans.
- Frequently Asked Questions—Provides a list of commonly asked questions relating to your benefits.
- Leave Information—Provides time-off related information for benefits such as family medical leave, sick leave and vacation leave.
- Retirement Planning Seminars—Provides dates and sign-up information.
- Shared Benefit—Provides information on the sharing of sick leave between eligible employees and the process to apply for time or donate time to the shared sick leave pool.
- SURS Information—Provides links to information on the State University Retirement System.
- University Plans—Provides plan information and enrollment procedures for University administered benefit plans.

Contemporary communications methods include a company's intranet and an interactive phone system. An intranet is a useful way to communicate benefits information to employees on an ongoing basis beyond the legally required written documents. In an era of the paperless office, employees are less likely to have written materials readily available. Employees can review general information about the benefits program whenever they want. Table 11-9 lists general information about the kinds of available information. Each paragraph contains a hyperlink (for example, announcements, benefits directory) that leads to more detailed information.

Interactive phone systems communicate descriptive information about benefits, representing an alternative way to stay abreast of basic benefits information. Employees use the telephone to contact a user-friendly voice response system. These phone systems go a step further by allowing employees to make common transactions virtually 24 hours a day, 7 days a week, eliminating the need to visit the company's benefits office. For example, employees may request insurance claim forms for delivery by mail or fax. Interactive phone systems are particularly helpful to employees who work in the field or in remote facilities too small to warrant a separate benefits office. Table 11-10 shows a summary of an interactive phone system to enroll in or change benefits.

TABLE 11-10 Benefits On Call: (217)555-8422 1-800-555-1451

Benefits On Call is an interactive voice response system developed to provide employees with benefit information virtually 24 hours a day, 7 days a week. By calling the Benefits On Call system, benefit-eligible employees are able to obtain their specific benefit information and eliminate the need to visit or call the Benefit Center.

Benefits On Call is available 24 hours a day, except for the following times:

- Between 4:00 a.m. and 6:00 a.m., Monday through Saturday
- Between 10:00 p.m. Saturday and 8:00 a.m. Sunday

Benefits On Call can be used to:

- Request items to be mailed or faxed to you, such as:
  - Personal Benefits Statement
  - Claim Forms
  - Enrollment Forms
- Receive confirmation of health and dental plan enrollments, including dependent coverage.
- Confirm insurance coverage amounts for the State Term-Life plan and the Accidental Death and Dismemberment plan.
- Verify enrollment and payroll deduction amounts for the Tax-Deferred Retirement plans and Flexible Spending Accounts.
- Hear responses to frequently asked questions, such as:
  - When can I change plans?
  - When can I add a dependent?
  - How long are dependents eligible for coverage?

To Use Benefits On Call, you will need:

- Touch-tone telephone
- Social security number
- Four-digit personal identification number (PIN). You will choose your PIN the first time you call Benefits On Call. This will be your PIN that you use every time you call.

To access your information through Benefits On Call:

- Dial (217) 555-8422 or 1-800-555-1451
- After the welcome message, enter your social security number, followed by the # sign.
- Enter your PIN, followed by the # sign.
- Select from the menu of topics by pressing the appropriate numbers on your telephone keypad.

After becoming familiar with the system, you will be able to take "shortcuts" from the main menu by pressing a series of numbers as outlined in the following table.

Shortcuts from Main Menu

Benefits Statement or Forms		***Health Insurance***		***Life Insurance***	
Benefits Statement Faxed	21	Health Plan Enrollment	111	Employee Life Insurance	1211
Benefits Statement Mailed	22	Changing Plans	411	Spouse Life Insurance	1212
Forms Faxes	31	Adding Dependents	412	Child Life Insurance	1213
Forms Mailed	31	Children Covered Until . . .	413	Accidental Death and Dismemberment Insurance	122
		Filing Claims	4151		

TABLE 11-10 (*cont.*)

Tax Deferred Plans		***Dental Insurance***		***Medical and/or Dependent Care Assistance Plans***	
403(b) Enrollment	131	Enrollment	112	Enrollment, Contribution Amount	14
457 Enrollment	132	Changing Plans	411		
		Filing Claims	4152	Disability Coverage	123

THE IMPLICATIONS OF DISCRETIONARY BENEFITS FOR STRATEGIC COMPENSATION

Not unlike core compensation, discretionary benefits can contribute to a company's competitive advantage for the reasons discussed earlier, such as tax advantages and recruiting the best-qualified candidates. Discretionary benefits can also undermine the imperatives of strategic compensation. Ultimately, companies that provide discretionary benefits to employees as entitlements are less likely to promote competitive advantage than companies that design discretionary fringe compensation programs to fit the situation.

Management can use discretionary benefit offerings to promote particular employee behaviors that have strategic value. For instance, when employees take advantage of tuition reimbursement programs, they are more likely to contribute to the strategic imperatives of product or service differentiation or cost reduction. Knowledge acquired from job-relevant education may enhance the creative potential of employees, as well as their ability to suggest more cost-effective modes of work. Alternatively, ESOPs may contribute to companies' strategic imperatives by instilling a sense of ownership in employees. Having a financial stake in the company should lead employees to behave more strategically.

A company can use discretionary benefits to distinguish itself from the competition. In effect, competitive benefits programs potentially convey the message that the company is a good place to work because it invests in the well-being of its employees. Presumably, lucrative benefits programs will attract a large pool of applicants that include high-quality candidates, positioning a company to hire the best possible employees.

Discretionary benefits also serve a strategic purpose by accommodating the needs of a diverse workforce. As we discussed previously, companies choose between offering one standard set of benefits to all employees or a flexible benefits program that permits each employee to choose discretionary benefits coverage. For example, with the increased number of dual-career couples with children, the need for some form of child care for preschool-age children has grown. However, not all employees require child care because they do not have children or because their children are too old to require this kind of supervision. If a company offered a standard fixed plan of discretionary fringe compensation, then only one segment of the workforce would benefit—obviously those with very young children. Employees not needing child care assistance would be receiving a benefit of no value to them, which, in effect, reduces the entire value of the benefits program for these employees. On the other hand, a company that did not offer child care could expect absenteeism and turnover as employees with young children struggle to cope with child care. In either case, a standard benefits plan would not be helpful. However, a cafeteria plan would enable employees to receive benefits that are useful to their situation, minimizing these sorts of problems. In the long-run, accommodating the diverse needs of the workforce has strategic value by minimizing dysfunctional behaviors—absenteeism and turnover—that are disruptive to a company's operations.

Finally, the tax advantage afforded companies from offering particular discretionary benefits has strategic value. In effect, the tax advantage translates into cost savings to companies. These savings can be applied to promote competitive advantage. For example, companies pursuing differentiation strategies may invest these savings into research and development programs. Companies pursuing lowest-cost strategies may be in a better position to compete because these savings may enable companies to lower the prices of their products and services without cutting into profits.

SUMMARY

This chapter reviewed the role of discretionary benefits in strategic compensation and described the major kinds of discretionary benefits. At present, companies offer widely varied kinds of fringe compensation practices. Increasingly, companies are investing in protection programs and services that are designed to enhance the well-being of employees in a cost-efficient manner. As competition increases, placing greater pressures on cost-containment strategies, companies have already faced hard choices about the benefits they offer their employees. It is likely that this trend will continue in the foreseeable future.

Key Terms

- welfare practices, 332
- short-term disability insurance, 334
- long-term disability insurance, 334
- Employee Retirement Income Security Act of 1974, 334
- life insurance, 335
- term coverage, 335
- whole life insurance, 335
- pension programs, 335
- noncontributory financing, 335
- contributory financing, 335
- qualified pension plans, 340
- nonqualified pension plans, 340
- defined contribution plans, 340
- employee stock ownership plans (ESOPs), 341
- defined benefit plans, 341
- indemnity plan, 341
- usual, customary, and reasonable charge, 342
- deductible, 342
- coinsurance, 342
- out-of-pocket maximum, 342
- self-funded insurance plans, 342
- health maintenance organizations (HMOs), 344
- copayments, 344
- Health Maintenance Organization Act of 1973, 344
- prepaid group practices, 344
- individual practice associations, 344
- preferred provider organization (PPO), 345
- dental insurance, 345
- indemnity dental insurance, 345
- self-insured dental plans, 345
- dental service corporations, 345
- dental maintenance organizations, 345
- vision insurance, 345
- employee assistance programs (EAPs), 346
- family assistance programs, 346
- flexible scheduling and leave, 347
- day care, 347
- tuition reimbursement programs, 347
- transportation services, 347
- outplacement assistance, 348
- wellness programs, 348
- smoking cessation, 349
- stress management, 349
- weight control and nutrition programs, 349
- vesting, 350
- Economic Growth and Tax Relief Reconciliation Act of 2001, 350
- Consolidated Omnibus Budget Reconciliation Act of 1985 (COBRA), 350
- mandatory bargaining subjects, 352
- permissive bargaining subjects, 353
- probationary period, 356
- noncontributory financing, 356
- contributory financing, 356
- employee-financed benefits, 356
- flexible benefits plan, 356
- cafeteria plan, 356
- flexible spending accounts, 357
- core plus option plans, 357

Discussion Questions

1. Many compensation professionals are faced with making choices about which discretionary benefits to drop because funds are limited, and the costs of these benefits continually increase. Assume you must make such choices. Rank order discretionary benefits, starting with the ones you would *most likely drop* to the ones you would *least likely drop*. Explain your rationale. Do factors such as the demographic composition of the workforce of the company matter? Explain.

2. Discuss your views about whether discretionary fringe compensation should be an entitlement or something earned based on job performance.
3. What role can flexible benefits programs play in alleviating the potential dissatisfaction that goes along with cutting benefits? Should companies move to a flexible benefits approach to "get the most bang for the buck"? Explain.
4. Assume that you are an HRM professional whose responsibility is to develop a brochure for the purpose of conveying the value of your company's benefits program to potential employees. Your company has asked you to showcase the benefits program in a manner that will encourage recruits to join the company. Develop a brochure (of no more than two pages) that meets this objective. Conduct research on companies' benefits practices (in journals such as *Benefits Quarterly*) as a basis for developing your brochure.
5. Your instructor will assign you an industry. Conduct some research in order to identify the prevalent fringe compensation practices for that industry. Also, what factors (for example, technology, competition, government regulation) might influence the present practices? How will these practices change?

Exercises

Compensation Online

For Students

Exercise 1: Find relevant journal articles

When class discussion on discretionary benefits issues began, you immediately became intrigued and wanted to learn more. Use your school library's online catalog to locate articles pertaining to the most intriguing topic. Find and read several current articles in these areas. Be ready to explain what you learned to the other members of your class.

Exercise 2: Search for information on discretionary benefits

Using the Yahoo search engine, click on advanced search, type in "discretionary benefits," select an exact phrase match search method, and click on the search link. How many sites were found? Select one of the sites that you think will provide current information about discretionary benefits. Read the information and write a brief summary on what you learned from the site, including how the information relates to what you read in the textbook.

Exercise 3: Search for information related to ERISA of 1974

The Employee Retirement Income Security Act of 1974 was briefly reviewed in this chapter. To learn more about it, conduct an advanced search for "Employee Retirement Income Security Act." Read about the act or read the act itself. What does Part 1 of Title 1 of ERISA require?

For Professionals

Exercise 1: Review professional resources

An issue regarding employee rights according to the Consolidated Omnibus Budget Reconciliation Act of 1985 has come across your desk. Go to *www.benefitslink.com* and click the search link. Once there, type in "COBRA." Look over the results. How can this Web site be of service in your day-to-day work as an HR professional?

Exercise 2: Review a government resource

The VP of HR has approached you to head up a new employee assistance initiative. She wants you to prepare a small proposal, just enough to take to the board to show them what you have in mind. Go to the U.S. Office of Personnel Management's Web site at *www.opm.gov*. Click the site index link, scroll down, and click the employee health services link. From here, look at highlighted topics such as "employee assistance" or "employee health," and review the information given to you. Describe two issues or facts from these sources that you wish to communicate to the VP as potential benefits to the company.

Exercise 3: Review a union Web page

Unions are one of the most important parties in the work environment in regard to human resources. Visit the American Federation of State, County, and Municipal Employees Web page at *afscme.org*. Conduct a search of this site for "benefits" or some more specific topic from this chapter, such as "cafeteria plans." How can this Web site help an HR professional serve both employees and shareholders?

Endnotes

1. U.S. Bureau of Labor Statistics. (2002). Employer costs for employee compensation—March 2002 [online]. Available: *www.bls.gov/ncs/ect/home.htm*, accessed July 24, 2002.
2. U.S. Bureau of Labor Statistics. (1919). Welfare work for employees in industrial establishments in the United States. *Bulletin* # 250, pp. 119–123
3. U.S. Department of Commerce. (2001). *Statistical Abstracts of the United States* (121st ed.)
4. Solnick, L. (1985). The effect of the blue collar unions on white collar wages and benefits. *Industrial and Labor Relations Review*, *38*, pp. 23–35.
5. U.S. Bureau of Labor Statistics. (2002). Employer costs for employee compensation—March 2002 [online]. Available: *www.bls.gov/ncs/ect/home.htm*, accessed July 24, 2002.
6. Beam, B. T., Jr., & McFadden, J. J. (1996). *Employee Benefits* (5th ed.). Chicago: Dearborn Financial Publishiing.
7. Ibid.
8. U.S. Bureau of Labor Statistics. (2002). Employer costs for employee compensation—March 2002 [online]. Available: *www.bls.gov/ncs/ect/home.htm*, accessed July 24, 2002.
9. U.S. Bureau of Labor Statistics. (2002). Employer costs for employee compensation—March 2002 [online]. Available: *www.bls.gov/ncs/ect/home.htm*, accessed July 24, 2002.
10. Ibid.
11. Health Maintenance Organizations, 42, USC 300e to 330e-17.
12. Kirrane, D. (1990). EAPs: Dawning of a new age. *HR* Magazine, *35*, pp. 30–34.
13. Bureau of National Affairs. (2000). Employee Assistance Programs. *Compensation and Benefits* (CD-ROM). Washington DC: Author.
14. U.S. Bureau of Labor Statistics. (2002). Employer costs for employee compensation—March 2002 [online]. Available: *www.bls.gov/ncs/ect/home.htm*, accessed July 24, 2002.
15. Spencer, G. (November, 1992). Projection of the population of the United States, by age, sex, race, and Hispanic origin: 1992 to 2050). *Current Population Reports* (P-25, no. 1092). Washington DC: United States Government Printing Office.
16. U.S. Bureau of Labor Statistics. (2002). Employer costs for employee compensation—March 2002 [online]. Available: *www.bls.gov/ncs/ect/home.htm*, accessed July 24, 2002.
17. The Conference Board. (1999). *Work-Life Initiatives in a Global Context*. New York: The Conference Board.
18. Goodstein, J. D. (1994). Institutional pressures and strategic responsiveness: Employer involvement in work-family issues. *Academy of Management Journal*, *37*, pp. 350–382.
19. Gòmez-Mejía, L. R., Balkin, D. R. & Cardy, R. L. (1995). *Managing Human Resources*. Upper Saddle River, NJ: Prentice Hall.
20. Gibson, V. M. (1991). The ins and outs of outplacement. *Management Review*, *80*, pp. 59–61.
21. Tully, S. (1995). America's healthiest companies. *Fortune*, *131* (June 15), pp. 98–100.
22. *Wisconsin Southern Gas Co.*, 69, L.R.R.M. 1375, 173 NLRB No. 79 (1968).
23. *UAW v. Mack Trucks, Inc.*, 135, L.R.R.M. 2833 (3rd Cir. 1990).
24. Haslinger, J. A., & Sheering, D. (1994). Employee input: The key to successful benefits programs. *Compensation & Benefits Review* (May–June), pp. 61–70.
25. Barber, A. E., Dunham, R. B., & Formisano, R. (1990). The impact of flexible benefit plans on employee satisfaction. Paper presented at the 50th annual meeting of the Academy of Management, San Francisco, CA.
26. Beam, B. T., Jr., & McFadden, J. J. (1996). *Employee Benefits* (5th ed.). Chicago: Dearborn Financial Publishing.
27. U.S. Bureau of Labor Statistics. (2002). Employer costs for employee compensation—March 2002 [online]. Available: *www.bls.gov/ncs/ect/home.htm*, accessed July 24, 2002.
28. Huseman, R., Hatfield, J., & Robinson, R. (1978). The MBA and fringe benefits. *Personnel Administration*, *23*, pp. 57–60.
29. Beam, B. T., Jr., & McFadden, J. J. (1996). *Employee Benefits* (5th ed.). Chicago: Dearborn Financial Publishing.

COMPENSATION IN ACTION

DEMAND PERFORMANCE FOR BENEFITS

If your workforce still thinks benefits are entitlements, they have the wrong idea. What can HR do to make employees understand the true value of benefits?

At the threshold of a new millennium, employees should be viewing benefits as part of their total compensation package, but they rarely do.

And it's easy to see why. Though they can find salary information, tax withholding and more down to the penny on their paycheck stubs, few employees know the dollar value of the benefits they earn.

Without knowing the cost of their benefits, they also don't know that many of those costs are rising. While employees directly feel the pinch of higher gasoline prices or more expensive movie tickets, they're largely protected from price hikes in the benefits they increasingly take for granted.

But those realities are merely symptoms of a much larger phenomenon. Large organizations have eliminated hundreds of thousands of jobs over the last decade, and still are cutting jobs in record numbers. However, the job cuts aren't dominating headlines because these people are finding new jobs. The new jobs, increasingly, are at smaller organizations.

Employees who have become more accustomed to generous benefit packages, however, go to their new employers with the expectation that the benefits will still be there. Few stop to consider the difference between one organization's ability to provide those benefits and another's.

At the same time, the job market has become more competitive than at any time in a generation. In an effort to attract and retain top talent, employers of all sizes have increasingly relied on benefits; it's almost impossible for a company without benefits to hire the people it needs. The result of these circumstances is that employees now feel entitled to the benefits they receive.

It's because of this attitude that there are a lot of forces working to preserve the status quo. It isn't surprising that benefit plans have proven stubbornly resistant to the dramatic changes that have been made in compensation plans over the past few years.

Yet leading organizations have worked hard to move past the entitlement mentality. Instead, they offer pay plans linked to results and, as much as possible, rewarding top performers.

Wouldn't employees begin to see benefits as part of their total compensation package if benefits were treated like the rest of the package—that is, tied to performance? That may sound like a radical concept, but ultimately companies may find they have to make that change if they're to remain competitive.

COMPANIES MUST FIRST STANDARDIZE AND CONSOLIDATE

Although tying benefits to performance may be where we're headed, few organizations are in a position to make such a change today. Instead, most companies must do two things first: standardize and consolidate.

Consider the example of Stamford, Connecticut–based GTE Corp. Through a series of acquisitions, the telecommunications company at one time offered nearly 400 separate benefits plans. Ultimately, the number proved untenable and the company implemented a flexible benefit plan called "GTE Choices" in 1992.

The change consolidated many active employees benefits plans, eliminated benefits plan confusion and offered economies of scale. GTE now has only one summary plan description, one marketing brochure and one overall approach. The new plan is more efficient to administer and more consistent.

Employee satisfaction at GTE skyrocketed. The GTE Choices plan has allowed the company to offer more flexibility and higher quality benefits to employees, while at the same time giving its business units the ability to decide how much to subsidize the program for employees.

But not all organizations have done the hard work that GTE has accomplished. Many companies have plans that simply were cobbled

(Continued)

(Continued)

together over time—one benefit after another added to the menu as employee needs were identified or perceived. And other organizations offer patchwork plans that are the outgrowth of mergers or acquisitions.

The result is that employees who are working for the same organization—but in different locations or different business units—aren't eligible for the same benefits. And still other organizations have allowed operating units to develop unique benefit plans to meet the needs of their individual constituencies. None of these situations allows an organization to tie its benefit plan to overall business goals, which is a critical element if benefits are to be tied to performance.

"The benefits philosophy must reflect both how the firm creates competitive advantage from employee skills, knowledge and behaviors, as well as how employees value the various components of the employment product," explains Doug Merchant, a former HR manager for AT&T. "The benefits philosophy must rest on the firm's business and HR strategies."

In other words, organizations can only begin to link benefits to performance when they know the performance they want. At the simplest level, organizations that want short-term productivity increases might offer work/life benefits to those employees who demonstrate those increases. Organizations that are seeking long-term profitability are probably better off focusing on retirement plans. Such correlations already are being made.

SOME EMPLOYERS ALREADY LINK BENEFITS TO PERFORMANCE

In March 1999, the American Compensation Association (ACA) and The Segal Co. (a New York City–based employee benefits, compensation and HR consulting firm) jointly conducted a survey of ACA members to examine the extent to which their work/life programs are being used to reward employee performance. The survey, called the "1999 Survey of Performance-Based Work/Life Programs," confirms that employers are beginning to use nonmonetary compensation—particularly work/life programs—as part of their total rewards management strategy.

According to the survey findings, 18 percent of survey respondents currently use some work/life programs to reward employee performance. Although 43 percent of the surveyed organizations don't use work/life programs to reward employee performance, they believe that some of these programs should be used as rewards for performance in the future. Twenty-four percent of respondents quantitatively link work/life programs to improved employee satisfaction; 65 percent said they either are or should be linking some work/life programs to employee performance.

The work/life programs that currently are most commonly used to reward employee performance—particularly flexible work schedules and paid time-off programs—are programs that are geared toward rewarding high performers with additional time to conduct personal business. As employers seek continuously improved employee performance and strive for employer-of-choice status within their industries, while always watching expenses, low-cost work/life "add-ons" like convenience services are ideal avenues for rewarding high-level performers.

Beyond paid time-off benefits, there's great potential for employers to expand the use of convenience services, financial planning, legal assistance and other voluntary benefits—which have broad-based appeal and are relatively inexpensive.

For example, convenience services currently are offered by 30 percent of the ACA survey respondents, yet less than 1 percent of those respondents use them as rewards for employee performance. Since convenience services are typically offered as time-savers for time-starved high performers, there's an excellent opportunity to offer these services as reward incentives.

Perhaps the best-known example of a company that's linking work performance to its total rewards strategy, including benefits, is Toledo, Ohio–based manufacturer Owens-Corning. In 1996, the company overhauled its comp and benefits strategy to create a variable plan that's tied to performance. Workers clearly see how their work is rewarded with extra pay in the form of more benefit choices. Workers also get to pick from an array of options, making them responsible for their own choices.

The organization's "Rewards and Resources" program has virtually eliminated the entitlement mentality, given employees greater choice and slashed the company's fixed benefits costs.

ALIGN YOUR PLAN WITH OTHER HR BEST PRACTICES

If benefits truly are linked directly to performance, then don't they cease to exist as benefits? Aren't they then one form of compensation?

It's a question of more than just semantics. The question challenges us to think about the entire nature of the employment relationship.

To stay competitive, we've given employees more responsibility for managing their own careers. For instance, employees are taking increasingly more responsibility for their own training and education. They have grater control than ever over how their retirement funds are invested. So does it really make sense for benefits to still largely be provided, in a paternalistic sense? Don't we want employees to have more control, and doesn't tying benefits to performance ultimately give them control?

Some human resources professionals argue that it does.

"HR should get out of the benefits business. Pay employees well enough, and make independent benefit contractors available to them to handle this," says John Way, HR manager for Elf Atochem N.A. in Carrollton, Kentucky. "They're the experts. As mobile as the American worker is becoming, this would be a step in the right direction. Let individual employees be responsible for their own benefits."

It's a radical idea, but one that would bring benefit plans more closely into alignment with other human resources best practices.

One thing is certain, if employees don't understand the tie-in between their total compensation—including benefits—and how well they do on the job, employers will forever be offering something for nothing. It's not an idea employers can afford to perpetuate, nor HR will want to market.

Source: Jennifer Laabs, *Workforce* volume 79, number 1 (January 2000): pp. 42-46, ISSN: 1092-8332, Number: 47831683, Copyright ACC Communications, Inc. January 2000.

WHAT'S NEW IN COMPENSATION?

Outsourcing the Employee Benefits Function

Until now, we presumed that employers manage and administer the entire benefits function internally with a staff of benefits professionals, including managers, and support staff. Some employers have chosen to outsource some or all of the benefits function. *Outsourcing* refers to a contractual agreement by which an employer transfers responsibility to a third-party provider. In the case of benefits, third-party providers are companies with expertise in benefits design and administration. Outsourcing agreements can remain in effect from a few months to a few years.

Two factors that drive the decision to outsource are reductions in workforce size and the complexity of benefit plan administration. Increasingly, labor shortages make it difficult for companies to devote staff time to only one function. Employers expect staff members to help out in multiple areas, thereby abandoning a specialist role in favor of a generalist role.

Outsourcing some or all benefits administration can be very expensive in the short-run because most or all contract fees are due up front. Over time, efficient arrangements can be less costly than devoting several employees to benefits administration, especially when staff member flexibility allows companies to bolster critical functions by adding more employees to customer service during peak demand.

The featured *New York Times* article illustrates a joint business venture between Fidelity Investments and I.B.M. to serve as a third-party administrator for other companies' benefits programs. As discussed previously, labor market realities and tougher economic conditions are leading companies to lower costs, and outsourcing benefits administration is just one of many ways to achieve cost control objectives. In addition, sluggish economic conditions were slowing Fidelity and I.B.M. revenue growth, and both companies recognized third-party benefits administration as a new source for generating revenue.

Companies and employees face a wide variety of employee benefits issues. Log into your *New York Times* account. Search the database for articles on "employee benefits." Did you find any articles on outsourcing the benefits function? Summarize some of these. Also, describe some of the other benefits issues identified in your search. Following your course instructor's specific directions, be prepared to describe the current situation, and relate it to the article contained in this text. ■

The New York Times

Fidelity and I.B.M. in Venture to Handle Worker Benefit Plans

Fidelity Investments and I.B.M. formed a venture yesterday to manage the employee benefit plans of other companies.

Executives of both companies said they saw a promising business in selling payroll and benefits services to large employers, including government agencies and major nonprofit organizations. Fidelity would provide the benefits expertise and I.B.M. the computers and database.

Both companies are struggling to generate new revenues in the face of major downturns in their core markets. Fidelity, which is owned by the Edward C. Johnson family of Boston, depends primarily on managing retirement and other investments, charging fees based on the value of assets, a tough business in a declining stock market. I.B.M. has suffered because corporations and governments are delaying purchases of hardware and technology.

As part of the agreement, Fidelity will administer I.B.M.'s benefits. It will lease a call center in Raleigh, NC, that I.B.M. opened in 1994 to handle questions from its 140,000 workers in the United States and 120,000 retirees about retirement, health, charitable giving and other benefits.

The 450 I.B.M. workers in Raleigh will become Fidelity employees next month. Another 2,500 or so I.B.M. personnel workers will remain with the computer maker to handle hiring, firing, discipline, pay, promotions and other issues, said Towney Kennard, an I.B.M. vice president.

Terms of the deal were not disclosed.

The joint venture, which is not exclusive, comes less than a week after Hewitt Associates, a suburban Chicago company that is one of the nation's largest benefits consulting companies, completed an initial public offering. The Hewitt stock sale was premised in part on the expected growth of what it calls "human resources business process outsourcing."

"Many large employers are evaluating outsourcing their benefits administration functions so they can concentrate on their core competencies," said Peter J. Smail, president of Fidelity Employer Services.

Outsourcing is now concentrated in retirement savings and in payroll, which is dominated by companies like Automatic Data Processing and Paychex.

Fidelity, a unit of FMR, and I.B.M. said that by 2005 they expected benefits outsourcing to grow into an industry with $43 billion to $45 billion of annual revenue. The industry takes in about $12 billion today, Mr. Kennard of I.B.M. said.

Companies have been moving quickly to hire others to field questions from workers and retirees about their health, retirement and other benefits, said Wayne Cooper, chief executive of Kennedy Information, a company in Peterborough, VT, that tracks consulting and outsourcing.

He said this area of outsourcing had doubled since 1996 and was expected to grow more quickly in the next few years.

Fidelity administers benefits for more than 11,000 companies, but that function overwhelmingly involves only retirement savings, usually through a 401(k) plan.

About 200 companies pay Fidelity for its broader business administering benefits plans. Mr. Smail said customers include Hughes Electronics, Ford Motor, Monsanto, Philip Morris and Shell Oil.

Fidelity and I.B.M. said that outsourcing could save companies 15 percent to 20 percent on the cost of administering benefit plans.

The expected savings suggest that the business itself may involve thin margins. But if administering benefits brings Fidelity new clients for its asset management business then it could be an effective marketing tool that not only pays for itself, but generates some profit and increases Fidelity's technological prowess.

SOURCE: David Cay Johnston, Fidelity and I.B.M. in venture to handle worker benefit plans (July 3, 2002) [online]. Available: *nytimes.com*, accessed October 1, 2002.

PART V: CONTEMPORARY STRATEGIC COMPENSATION CHALLENGES

CHAPTER 12 INTERNATIONAL COMPENSATION

Chapter Outline

- Competitive Strategies and How International Activities Fit In
  - Lowest-Cost Producers' Relocations to Chapter Production Areas
  - Differentiation and the Search for New Global Markets
  - How Globalization Is Affecting HR Departments
  - Complexity of International Compensation Programs
- Preliminary Considerations
  - Host Country Nationals, Third Country Nationals, and Expatriates: Definitions and Relevance for Compensation Issues
  - Term of International Assignment
  - Staff Mobility
  - Equity: Pay Referent Groups
- Components of International Compensation Programs
- Setting Base Pay for U.S. Expatriates
  - Methods for Setting Base Pay
  - Purchasing Power
- Incentive Compensation for U.S. Expatriates
  - Foreign Source Premiums
  - Hardship Allowances
  - Mobility Premiums
- Establishing Fringe Compensation for U.S. Expatriates
  - Standard Benefits for U.S. Expatriates
  - Enhanced Benefits for U.S. Expatriates
- Balance Sheet Approach for U.S. Expatriates' Compensation Packages
  - Housing and Utilities
  - Goods and Services
  - Discretionary Income
  - Tax Considerations
- Repatriation Pay Issues
- Compensation Issues for HCNs and TCNs
- Summary
- Key Terms
- Discussion Questions
- Exercises
- Endnotes

Learning Objectives

In this chapter, you will learn about

1. Competitive strategies and how international activities fit in
2. How globalization affects HR departments
3. Methods for setting expatriates' base pay
4. Incentive compensation for expatriates
5. Fringe compensation for expatriates
6. The balance sheet approach
7. Repatriation issues
8. Compensation issues for HCNs and TCNs

International compensation programs have strategic value as U.S. businesses continue to establish operations in foreign countries such as Pacific Rim countries, Eastern Europe, and Mexico. The general trend for expanding operations overseas serves as just one indicator of the "globalization" of the economy. U.S. companies place professional and managerial (U.S. citizen) employees overseas to establish and operate satellite plants and offices. Although there are many glamorous aspects about working overseas, the glamor comes at the price of personal and, sometimes, professional sacrifices. Compensation takes on strategic value by providing these employees minimal financial risk associated with working overseas, as well as lifestyles for them and their families comparable to their lifestyles in the United States. Multinational companies—that is, companies with operations in more than one country—develop special compensation packages to help compensate for the personal sacrifices international assignees and their immediate families make. These sacrifices are associated with cultural variations that affect their lifestyle—dealing with an unfamiliar culture, enhanced responsibilities, and potentially higher living expenses.

The "Compensation in Action" feature at the end of this chapter describes the results of a study on the challenges associated with implementing international compensation and reward systems worldwide. In particular, the study provides insights into how managers worldwide respond when faced with this challenge.

COMPETITIVE STRATEGIES AND HOW INTERNATIONAL ACTIVITIES FIT IN

The presence of U.S. companies in foreign countries is on the rise. You might forget that you are in China while taking a taxi ride through the streets of Beijing: Billboards and establishments for such U.S. companies as McDonald's, Pizza Hut, Pepsi, Coca Cola, and Motorola are common sights.

Several factors have contributed to the expansion of global markets. These include such free trade agreements as the **North American Free Trade Agreement**, the unification of the European market, and the gradual weakening of Communist influence in Eastern Europe and Asia. Likewise, foreign companies have greater opportunities to invest in the United States.

Lowest-Cost Producers' Relocations to Cheaper Production Areas

Many U.S. businesses have established manufacturing and production facilities in Asian countries and in Mexico because labor is significantly cheaper than in the United States. There are two key reasons for the cost difference. First, labor unions generally do not have much bargaining power in developing Asian countries or in Mexico, where the government possesses extensive control over workplace affairs. Second, Asian governments do not value individual employee rights as much as the U.S. government does. As we discussed in Chapter 3, the Fair Labor Standards Act of 1938 provides employees a minimum hourly wage rate, limits exploitation of child labor, and mandates overtime pay.

Differentiation and the Search for New Global Markets

Coca Cola and Pepsi products are well known worldwide because these companies aggressively introduced their soft drink products throughout numerous countries. Establishing Coke and Pepsi products worldwide does not represent a differentiation strategy. However, Coke and Pepsi could distinguish themselves from competing companies by taking on new business initiatives that depart from "business as usual" and meet specific market needs.

For Coke and Pepsi, "business as usual" means marketing soft drink products—carbonated water with artificial colors and flavors. Marketing bottled spring water would clearly be a departure from business as usual for them. The People's Republic of China (PRC) possesses a definite need for bottled spring water: The Chinese government is unable to provide its citizens and visitors drinkable water because the country does not maintain adequate water purification plants. Coke and Pepsi could distinguish themselves from other soft drink companies by marketing spring water along with their regular soft drink products. Coke and Pepsi would be known as companies that serve necessary (bottled water) and recreational (soft drinks) beverage needs.

How Globalization Is Affecting HR Departments

The globalization of business requires that companies send employees overseas to establish and operate satellite plants and offices. Naturally, companies must invest in the development of appropriate HR practices. International business operations are destined to fail without the "right" people. Human resource professionals must be certain to identify the selection criteria that are most related to successful international work assignments. For example, do candidates possess adequate cultural sensitivity? Do they believe that U.S. customs are the only appropriate way to approach problems? Are candidates' families willing to adjust to foreign lifestyles?

Training is another key HR function. Expatriates must understand the cultural values that predominate in foreign countries; otherwise, they risk hindering business. For example, one of Procter & Gamble's Camay soap commercials was successful in the United States, but the Japanese perceived the very same commercial that aired in Japan to be rude. The commercial depicted a man barging into the bathroom on his wife while she was using Camay soap. Japanese cultural values led Japanese viewers to judge this commercial as offensive. The Japanese deemed the commercial as acceptable after Procter & Gamble modified the commercial to show a woman using Camay soap in privacy.

Companies' investments in cross-cultural training vary. Some companies provide release time from work to take foreign language courses at local colleges or universities. Highly progressive companies such as Motorola run corporate universities that offer cross-cultural training courses.

Complexity of International Compensation Programs

The development and implementation of international compensation programs typically pose four challenges to companies that U.S. compensation programs do not have to consider. First, successful international compensation programs further corporate interests abroad and encourage employees to take foreign assignments. Second, well-designed compensation programs minimize financial risk to employees and make their and their families' experiences as pleasant as possible. Third, international compensation programs promote a smooth transition back to life in the United States upon completion of the international assignment. **Repatriation** is the process of making the transition from an international assignment and living abroad to a domestic assignment and living in the home country. Fourth, sound international compensation programs promote U.S. businesses' lowest-cost and differentiation strategies in foreign markets.

PRELIMINARY CONSIDERATIONS

We must take some basic issues under advisement before examining the elements of international compensation programs. Compensation professionals must distinguish among HCNs, TCNs (discussed next), and expatriates as compensation recipients with their own unique issues. In addition, compensation professionals should consider such matters as term of the international assignment, staff mobility, and equity because these factors pertain directly to the design elements of international compensation programs.

Host Country Nationals, Third Country Nationals, and Expatriates: Definitions and Relevance for Compensation Issues

There are three kinds of recipients of international compensation:

- Host country nationals (HCNs)
- Third country nationals (TCNs)
- Expatriates

We will define these recipients as employees of U.S. companies doing business in foreign countries. However, these definitions also apply to employees of non-U.S. companies doing business in foreign countries.

Host country nationals are foreign national citizens who work in U.S. companies' branch offices or manufacturing plants in their home countries. Japanese citizens working for General Electric in Japan are HCNs.

Third country nationals are foreign national citizens who work in U.S. companies' branch offices or manufacturing plants in foreign countries—excluding the United States and their own home countries. Australian citizens working for General Motors in the People's Republic of China are TCNs.

Expatriates are U.S. citizens employed in U.S. companies with work assignments outside the United States. U.S. citizens employed in CitiBank's London, England, office are expatriates.

Our primary focus is on compensation for expatriates. Following the extensive discussion of expatriate compensation, we consider some of the challenges compensation professionals face when compensating HCNs and TCNs.

As a reminder, our focus is on U.S. companies, and these definitions reflect this focus. Other countries can be the focus as well. For example, let's define HCN, TCN, and expatriate from the Australian perspective. BHP, an Australian company, conducts business worldwide in such countries as the People's Republic of China and the United States. A Chinese citizen who works for BHP in Shanghai is an HCN. A U.S. citizen who works for BHP in Shanghai is a TCN. An Australian citizen who works for BHP in Shanghai is an expatriate.

Human resource professionals construct international compensation packages on the basis of three main factors:

- Term of international assignment
- Staff mobility
- Equity: pay referent groups

Term of International Assignment

The term of the international assignment is central in determining compensation policy. Short-term assignments—usually less than 1 year in duration—generally do not require substantial modifications to domestic compensation packages. However, extended assignments necessitate features that promote a sense of stability and comfort overseas. These features include housing allowances, educational expenses for children, and adjustments to protect expatriates from paying "double" income taxes—U.S. federal and state taxes as well as applicable foreign taxes.

Staff Mobility

Companies must also consider whether foreign assignments necessitate employees' moving from one foreign location to another—from Beijing, China, to the Special Economic Zone in China, or from England to Brazil. Such moves within and across foreign cultures can disrupt expatriates' and their families' lives. Staff mobility comes at a price to companies in the form of monetary incentives and measures to make employees' moves as comfortable as possible.

Equity: Pay Referent Groups

Well-designed U.S. compensation programs promote equity among employees: Employees' pay is commensurate with performance or knowledge attainment. Expatriates are likely to evaluate compensation, in part, according to equity considerations. Many U.S. companies use domestic employees as the pay referent groups when developing international compensation packages because virtually all expatriate employees eventually return to the United States.

Some companies use local employees as the pay referent groups for long-term assignments because they wish to facilitate expatriates' integration into foreign cultures. As we discuss later, Mexican managerial employees' compensation packages include base pay and such cash allowances as Christmas bonuses. On the other hand, the main components of U.S. managerial employees' compensation packages include base pay and long-term incentives. U.S. expatriates working in Mexico on long-term assignments are likely to have compensation packages that are similar to Mexican managerial employees' compensation packages.

COMPONENTS OF INTERNATIONAL COMPENSATION PROGRAMS

The basic structure of international compensation programs is similar to the structure of domestic compensation programs. The main components include base pay and fringe compensation. The inclusion of nonperformance-based incentives and allowances distinguishes international compensation packages from domestic compensation packages. Table 12-1 lists the main components of international compensation programs.

SETTING BASE PAY FOR U.S. EXPATRIATES

U.S. companies must determine the method for setting expatriates' base pay. Final determination should come only after companies carefully weigh the strengths and limitations of alternative methods. In addition, the purchasing power of base pay is an important

TABLE 12-1 U.S. Expatriates' Compensation Package

Core Compensation
  Base pay
  Incentive compensation
    Foreign service premium
    Hardship allowance
    Mobility premium
Fringe Compensation
  Standard Benefits
    Protection programs
    Paid time-off
  Enhanced Benefits
    Relocation assistance
    Educational reimbursement for expatriates' children
    Home leave and travel reimbursement
Rest and relaxation leave allowance

consideration. Purchasing power affects standard of living. The following quote from a U.S. expatriate stationed in Italy captures the essence of purchasing power for expatriates: "Does an Italian lira purchase as much macaroni today as it did yesterday?" Two key factors influence purchasing power—the stability of local currency and inflation.

Methods for Setting Base Pay

U.S. companies use one of three methods to calculate expatriates' base pay:

- Home country-based method
- Host country-based method
- Headquarters-based method

Home Country-Based Method

The **home country-based pay method** compensates expatriates the amount they would receive if they were performing similar work in the United States. Job evaluation procedures enable employers to determine whether jobs at home are equivalent to comparable jobs in foreign locations based on compensable factors. How does location create differences in jobs that are otherwise considered equal? One example may be that foreign language skills are probably essential outside English-speaking countries. Adjustments to expatriates' pay should reflect additional skills.

The home country-based pay method is often most appropriate for expatriates. Equity problems are not very likely to arise because expatriates' assignments are too short to establish local national employees as pay referents. Instead, expatriates will base pay comparisons on their home country standards. In general, the home country-based pay method is most suitable when expatriate assignments are short in duration and local nationals performing comparable jobs receive substantially higher pay. As we discussed earlier, expatriates may rely on local cultural norms over extended periods as the standard for judging the equitableness of their compensation.

Host Country-Based Method

The **host country-based method** compensates expatriates based on the host countries' pay scales. Companies use various standards for determining base pay, including market pricing, job evaluation techniques, and jobholders' past relevant work experience. Other countries use different standards. As we discuss later in this chapter, the Japanese emphasize seniority. Expatriates' base pay will be competitive with other employees' base pay in the host countries. The host country-based method is most suitable when assignments are of long duration. As we noted previously, expatriates are then more likely to judge the adequacy of their pay relative to their local coworkers rather than to their counterparts at home.

Headquarters-Based Method

The **headquarters-based method** compensates all employees according to the pay scales used at the headquarters. Neither the location of the international work assignment nor home country influences base pay. This method makes the most sense for expatriates who move from one foreign assignment to another and rarely, if ever, work in their home countries. Administratively, this system is simple because it applies the pay standard of one country to all employees regardless of the location of their foreign assignment or their country of citizenship.

Purchasing Power

Decreases in purchasing power lead to lower standards of living. Quite simply, expatriates cannot afford to purchase as many goods and services as before, or they must settle for lower quality. Diminished purchasing power undermines the strategic value of expatriates' compensation because top-notch employees are probably not willing to settle for lower standards of living while stationed at foreign posts. In addition, changes in the factors that immediately influence standard of living—the stability of currency and inflation—are somewhat unpredictable. This unpredictability creates a sense of uncertainty and risk. As we discuss later in this section, most U.S. companies use the balance sheet approach to minimize this risk.

Currency Stabilization

Most U.S. companies award expatriates' base pay in U.S. currency, not in the local foreign currency. However, foreign countries as a rule do not recognize U.S. currency as legal tender. Therefore, expatriates must exchange U.S. currency for local foreign currency based on daily exchange rates. An **exchange rate** is the price at which one country's currency can be swapped for another [1]. Exchange rates are expressed in terms of foreign currency per U.S. dollar or in terms of U.S. dollars per unit of foreign currency. For example, on July 29, 2002, the exchange rate for the Swedish krona was 9.46 KR for each U.S. $1.

Government policies and complex market forces cause exchange rates to fluctuate daily. Exchange rate fluctuations have direct implications for expatriates' purchasing power. For example, let's start with the previous exchange rate of 9.46 KR per U.S. $1. Also, the exchange rate was 8.50 KR per U.S. $1 on December 31, 1999. This example illustrates a rise in the exchange rate for Swedish money. U.S. expatriates experience higher purchasing power because they receive more Swedish KR for every U.S. $1 they exchange.

Inflation

Inflation is the increase in prices for consumer goods and services. Inflation erodes the purchasing power of currency. Let's assume that ABC Corporation does not award pay increases to its expatriates stationed in Australia during 2001. Expatriates' purchasing power remains unaffected as long as there isn't any inflation (and reduced exchange rate) during the same period. However, these expatriates had lower purchasing power in 2001 because inflation averaged 4.4 percent in Australia. In other words, the average costs of consumer goods and services increased 4.4 percent between 2000 and 2001. Table 12-2 shows the annual inflation rates for various countries between 1996 and 2001.

TABLE 12-2 Annual Inflation Rates (%) for Selected Countries, 1990–2001

Years	*United States*	*Canada*	*Japan*	*Australia*	*Austria*	*Belgium*	*Denmark*
1990–1991	4.2	5.6	3.3	3.2	3.3	3.2	2.4
1991–1992	3.0	1.5	1.6	1.0	4.1	2.4	2.1
1992–1993	3.0	1.8	1.3	1.8	3.6	2.8	1.2
1993–1994	2.6	0.2	0.7	1.9	3.0	2.4	2.0
1994–1995	2.8	2.1	–0.1	4.6	2.2	1.5	2.1
1995–1996	3.0	1.6	0.1	2.6	1.9	2.1	2.1
1996–1997	2.3	1.6	1.8	0.3	1.3	1.6	2.2
1997–1998	1.6	0.9	0.6	0.9	0.9	1.0	1.9
1998–1999	2.2	1.7	–0.3	1.5	0.6	1.1	2.5
1999–2000	3.4	2.7	–0.7	4.5	2.3	2.5	3.0
2000–2001	2.8	2.6	–0.7	4.4	2.7	2.5	2.4

Source: U.S. Bureau of Labor Statistics. (2002). *Consumer prices in sixteen countries.* Washington, DC: Government Printing Office.

INCENTIVE COMPENSATION FOR U.S. EXPATRIATES

In the United States, companies offer incentives to promote higher job performance and to minimize dysfunctional turnover, which results when high performers quit their jobs. International compensation plans include a variety of unique incentives to encourage expatriates to accept and remain on international assignments. These incentives also compensate expatriates for their willingness to tolerate less desirable living and working conditions. The main incentives are foreign services premiums, hardship premiums, and mobility premiums.

Foreign Service Premiums

Foreign service premiums are monetary payments above and beyond regular base pay. Companies offer foreign service premiums to encourage employees to accept expatriate assignments. These premiums generally apply to assignments that extend beyond 1 year. The use of foreign service premiums is widespread.

Companies calculate foreign service premiums as a percentage of base pay, and these premiums range between 10 and 30 percent of base pay. The percentage amount increases with the length of the assignment. Sometimes, larger amounts are necessary when there is a shortage of available candidates. Companies disburse payment of the foreign service premium over several installments to manage costs and to "remind" expatriates about the incentive throughout their assignments.

Employers that use foreign service premiums should consider the possible drawbacks. First, employees may misconstrue this premium as a regular permanent increase to base pay, and resentment toward the employer may develop following the last installment. Second, foreign service premiums may not have incentive value when employers make several small installments rather than fewer large installments. Third, employees may feel as if their standard of living has declined when they return to the United States because they no longer receive this extra money.

Hardship Allowances

The **hardship allowance** compensates expatriates for their sacrifices while on assignment. Specifically, these allowances are designed to recognize exceptionally hard living and working conditions at foreign locations. Employers disburse hardship allowances in small amounts throughout the duration of expatriates' assignments. It is easy for expatriates to lose sight of the foreign service premiums and hardship allowances because they appear as relatively small increments to their paychecks. Companies should take care to communicate the role of these payments.

Companies offer hardship allowances at exceptionally severe locations only. The U.S. Department of State has established a list of hardship posts where the living conditions are considered unusually harsh. Most multinational companies award hardship allowances to executive, managerial, and supervisory employees. Hardship allowances range from 10 percent to 25 percent of base pay—the greater the hardship, the higher the premium. The U.S. Department of State uses three criteria to identify hardship locations:

- Extraordinarily difficult living conditions, such as inadequate housing, lack of recreational facilities, isolation, inadequate transportation facilities, and lack of food or consumer services
- Excessive physical hardship, including severe climates or high altitudes and the presence of dangerous conditions affecting physical and mental well-being
- Notably unhealthy conditions, such as diseases and epidemics, lack of public sanitation, and inadequate health facilities

The U.S. Department of State has deemed more than 150 places as hardship locations. Table 12-3 lists examples of hardship locations and recommended hardship differentials.

TABLE 12-3 Hardship Locations, Differentials, and Danger Pay

Country and City	*Differential Rate Percent*
Bahrain[1]: Bahrain	0
Belize: Belize City	10
Guatemala: Guatemala City	10
India: Chennai	20
Macedonia, The Former Yugoslav Republic of: Skopje	15
Mexico[1]: Monterrey	0
Thailand: Udorn	15
Yemen: Sanaa	20

Country and City	*Danger Pay Rate Percent*
Jerusalem (other than West Bank)	15 (eff. 04/21/02)
Macedonia, The Former Yugoslav Republic of:	
Skopje	0 (eff. 02/10/02)
Other	0 (eff. 02/10/02)
Pakistan[2]: Islamabad	25 (eff. 04/07/02)
Karachi	25 (eff. 04/07/02)
Lahore	25 (eff. 04/07/02)
Other	25 (eff. 04/07/02)
Quetta	25 (eff. 04/07/02)
Yemen: Sanaa	15 (eff. 03/10/02)
Other	15 (eff. 03/10/02)

[1]The differentials were eliminated for Bahrain and Monterrey effective 03/24/02 and 02/10/02, respectively.

[2]The danger pay for the listed Pakistan posts were 20% effective 03/24/2002.

Source: A complete listing of locations with hardship differential for federal civilian employees can be found in Section 920 of the Department of State *Standardized Regulations (Government Civilians, Foreign Areas)*, available from the Superintendent of Documents, U.S. Government Printing Office, Washington, DC 20402.

FLIP SIDE OF THE COIN

OUT OF SIGHT, OUT OF MIND: OPINIONS DIFFER ON ASSIGNMENTS' SUCCESS

Almost half of expatriate employees leave their employer within two years of returning from a foreign assignment, indicating the expatriation and repatriation processes need improvement.

Companies increasingly have been extending their markets across international borders over the past decade. Expansions in business markets drastically have increased the need to send employees to overseas locations. In fact, over a three-year period, employers spend an estimated $1 million or more when sending an employee overseas. Are they getting a good return on that investment? Are employees gaining career advancement and reputation in the company that may have been promised by taking such an assignment?

A recent study by CIGNA International Expatriate Benefits, the National Foreign Trade Council (NFTC) and WorldatWork suggests that employers and employees hold significantly different opinions on the success of expatriate assignments. Forty-four percent of employees who had returned from an assignment reported leaving their employer within two years of their expatriate experience, according to *Maximizing Your Expatriate Investment*.

The study questioned 143 human resources executives and more than 400 expatriate employees on their thoughts about expatriate assignments. The survey was designed to assess employer and employee opinions on various expatriate assignment topics, such as intercultural training, health care concerns, use of technology, gender-specific experiences, surprises expatriates experience abroad and the advice expatriates offer others considering an assignment.

WHY GO THERE?

While sending employees overseas is not new to businesses, it has increased significantly in the past decade, as technology advancements have made today's business world more easily global. So, what are the top reasons employers choose to send people on expatriate assignments, and what are the motivations for employees accepting the assignments?

"With the Internet and other technological developments continually expanding the reach of business, the expatriate has become a crucial employer in the international expansion of many businesses," said Anne C. Ruddy, CPCU, executive director of WorldatWork.

There are a number of specific reasons companies send expatriates to international locations, according to the survey, ranging from "performing a specific task" (95 percent) to "no local employees with the necessary skills for a particular job" (81 percent). Employees are more personally motivated in accepting an international assignment because it is:

- Exciting (96 percent)
- Enhances their resume and makes them more marketable (92 percent)
- Interesting to work in another country (91 percent)

More company-oriented reasons, such as "pursuing a long-term career with the employer" (69 percent) and "essential for career development" (67 percent), ranked much lower for employees.

Qualifications for going on an assignment and the considerations employees take into account before accepting an assignment, however, focus directly on the employee from both perspectives. Employers most often consider cultural adaptability, enthusiasm, language ability and employee health in determining who to send on an expatriate assignment. The employees' ability and enthusiasm are important to the company and show that they will be an asset in the new assignment. As for employees' considerations in accepting an assignment, the "what's in it for me" attitude leads the pack. The top concerns for employees, according to the survey, were:

- Adequacy of total benefits package (80 percent)
- Impact on financial security (78 percent)
- Concern about ability to achieve assignment goals (75 percent)

(Continued)

(Continued)

- Ability to manage in a new environment (72 percent)
- Impact on career development.

There also are external considerations for the employee. Family considerations weigh heavily on the decision to accept an assignment. Sixty-seven percent of respondents said "education for children" was a top concern, 60 percent cited "spouse/partner adjustment" and 53 percent were concerned with their "children's adjustment."

"There are a number of things companies and employees have to take into consideration before an assignment can continue," Ruddy said. "Sometimes it seems that the process of making the offer and getting an employee to accept the offer may be the most difficult part of the assignment."

HE SAID, SHE SAID

Whether in preparation for the assignment, while on the assignment or returning from the assignment, employers and employees seem to have quite disparate opinions on the success of each step along the way. For example, 53 percent of the HR executives surveyed said they felt the company does a "good to very good" job meeting expatriates' needs as they prepare to go on an assignment. However, when expatriates were asked the same question, only 32 percent reported the company does a "good to very good" job, and 40 percent said the company did a "poor to very poor" job. (See Figure 1.)

FIGURE 1 Preparing Expatriates for Assignment

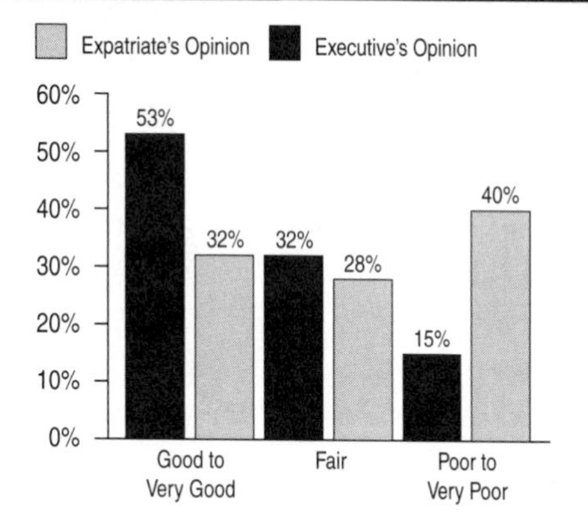

FIGURE 2 Expatriate Health Care Issues While on Assignment

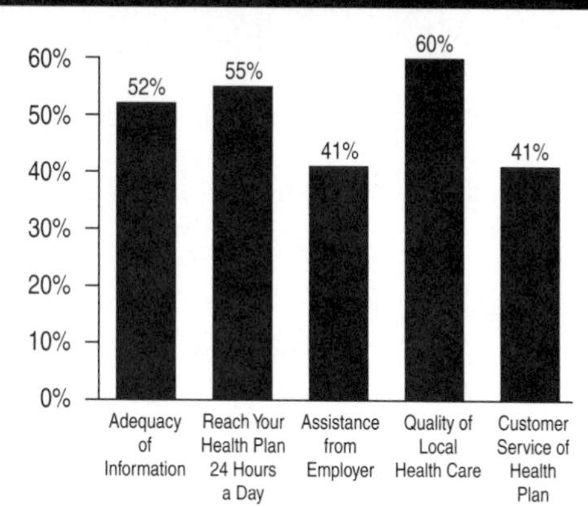

While on assignment, expatriates seem to find that the experience is what they expected (46 percent) or better (47 percent). So, it seems that once they are in place, they find that the experience is exciting and worth their while. However, there are some key tools, like the Internet and communication with headquarters, that provide the support they need to make the assignment work. (See Figure 2.) This disparity increases when asking whether the company met the needs of the employee while on assignment. Ninety-three percent of HR executives said their company does a "fair to very good" job, while one-third of expatriates said their employer does a "poor to very poor" job.

Proper communication is a top concern for employees working at headquarters, so the importance of adequate communication amplifies when that employee is perhaps halfway around the globe. Sixty-three percent of expatriates reported that communication with headquarters was about what they expected and 10 percent reported it better than expected, according to the survey.

HOME SWEET HOME

Wandering souls always come home, and repatriation of employees abroad is always around the corner. How companies handle this process and prepare employees for their return is not quite as disputed as other survey items. According to the respondents, 38 percent of executives and 26 percent of expatriates reported their company did a "good to very good" job of meeting the expatriates' needs upon return from an assignment. The disparity in this area comes in those that felt the company does a "poor to very poor" job, with 20 percent of executives and 45 percent of expatriates reporting this. Even so, employees reported rather high marks on the assignment's success, with many achieving their goals of increased marketability and professional/personal success. (See Figure 3.)

"The issue of a successful repatriation was even more dramatic for women. Whereas 29 percent of men felt that the company did a 'good to very good' job, only 7 percent of the women agreed," said Virginia Hollis, vice president of sales and marketing for CIEB. "We need to study the gender differences raised in this study further, because it became evident that women are more dissatisfied than men with the entire process, but most notably with what happens to them upon return."

A major problem of repatriation was the employees' status upon return. Twenty-one percent of employers implied a company commitment to have a job for the employee upon their return, according to the survey. More often, there was no commitment and employees found a troubling situation upon their return. Sometimes, expatriates like the overseas experience so much that they seek another assignment. Seventy-seven percent of those surveyed reported they are more likely to accept an international position with another employer than a domestic position with their current employer. Eighty-seven percent would accept another overseas assignment with their current employer.

FIGURE 3 Evaluating Success of Assignment

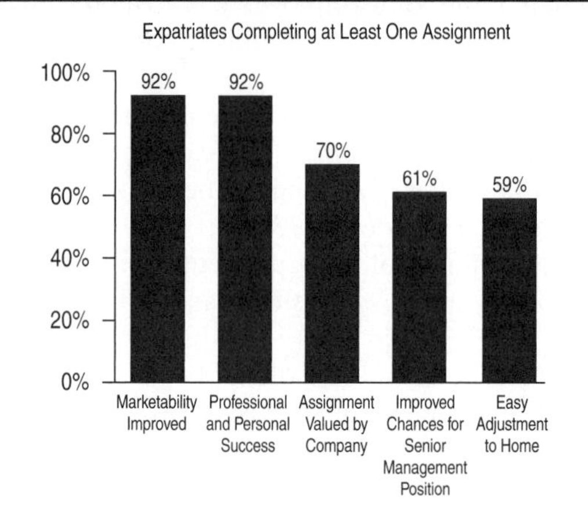

TRAINING AND SUPPORT VITAL TO ASSIGNMENT'S SUCCESS

"Obviously, as employers, we simply are not doing enough to recognize the unique needs of this important group of employees," Hollis said. "Services need to be provided which are geared specifically to their needs, and the vendors providing those services need to be managed and measured."

Expatriate assignments are critical in today's ever-expanding global market. Companies understand this and realize they need solid programs to have successful expatriate assignments. Preparing employees for an assignment, supporting them while on assignment and effectively repatriating them are essential to the success and continuation of current and future assignments.

When planning each phase of an assignment, companies should take employees' opinions into consideration. Losing expatriates upon their return, an expatriate returning home early from an assignment or another problem that ruins an assignment puts a black mark on the program for future endeavors.

Source: Jeremy Handel, *Workspan*. (2001). volume 44, © 2001 WorldatWork, 14040 N. Northsight Blvd., Scottsdale, A2 85260 U.S.A.; 480/951-9191; Fax 480/483-8352; *www.worldatwork.org*; E-mail worldatwork@worldatwork.org

Mobility Premiums

Mobility premiums reward employees for moving from one assignment to another. Companies use these premiums to encourage employees to accept, leave, or change assignments—usually between foreign posts or between a domestic position to one in a foreign country. Expatriates typically receive mobility premiums as single lump-sum payments.

ESTABLISHING FRINGE COMPENSATION FOR U.S. EXPATRIATES

Benefits represent an important component of expatriates' compensation packages. Companies design benefits programs to attract and retain the best expatriates. In addition, companies design these programs to promote a sense of security for expatriates and their families. Further, well-designed programs should help expatriates and their families maintain regular contact with other family members and friends in the United States.

Benefits fall into three broad categories—protection programs, paid time-off, and services. Protection programs provide family benefits, promote health, and guard against income loss caused by catastrophic factors such as unemployment, disability, or serious illnesses. Paid time-off provides employees such paid time-off as vacation. Service practices vary widely. Services provide enhancements such as tuition reimbursement and day care assistance to employees and their families.

Just like domestic fringe compensation packages, international fringe compensation plans include such protection programs as medical insurance and retirement programs [2]. In most cases, U.S. citizens working overseas continue to receive medical insurance and participate in their retirement programs.

International and domestic plans are also similar in that they offer paid time-off; however, international packages tend to incorporate more extensive benefits of this kind, which we discuss later. Moreover, international fringe compensation differs from domestic compensation with regard to the types of allowances and reimbursements. For international assignees, these payments are designed to compensate for higher costs of living and housing, relocation allowances, and education allowances for expatriates' children.

Employers should take several considerations into account when designing international fringe benefits programs, including [3]:

- Total remuneration: What is included in the total employee pay structure—cash wages, benefits, mandated social programs, and other perquisites? How much can the business afford?
- Benefit adequacy: To what extent must the employer enhance mandated programs to achieve desired staffing levels? Programs already in place and employees' utilization of them should be critically examined before determining what supplementary programs are needed and desirable.
- Tax effectiveness: What is the tax deductibility of these programs for the employer and employee in each country, and how does U.S. tax law treat expenditures in this area?
- Recognition of local customs and practices: Companies often provide benefits and services to employees based on those extended by other businesses in the locality, independent of their own attitude toward these same benefits and services.

International fringe compensation packages contain the same components as domestic fringe compensation packages and enhancements. U.S. expatriates receive many of the same standard benefits as their counterparts working in the United States. Expatriates also receive enhanced benefits for taking overseas assignments.

Standard Benefits for U.S. Expatriates

Protection programs and paid time-off are the most pertinent standard benefits.

Protection Programs

Previously, we discussed legally required protection programs (Chapter 10) and discretionary protection programs (Chapter 11). Let's consider the application of each kind to the international context.

The key legally required protection programs are mandated by the following laws: the Social Security Act of 1935, various state workers' compensation laws, and the Family and Medical Leave Act of 1993. All provide protection programs to employees and their dependents. Expatriates continue to participate in the main Social Security programs—retirement insurance, benefits for dependents, and Medicare. The Family and Medical Leave Act also applies to expatriates. However, state workers' compensation laws generally do not apply to expatriates. Instead, U.S. companies can elect private insurance that provides equivalent protection.

Discretionary protection programs provide family benefits, promote health, and guard against income loss caused by catastrophic factors such as unemployment, disability, or serious illnesses. U.S. companies provide these protection programs to expatriates for the same reasons they do in the United States—as a strategic response to workforce diversity and to retain the best-performing employees. Withholding these benefits from expatriates would create a disincentive for employees to take international assignments.

Paid Time-Off

Standard paid time-off benefits include annual vacation, holidays, and emergency leave.

Expatriates typically receive the same annual vacation benefits as their domestic counterparts. These benefits are particularly common among expatriates with relatively short-term assignments. Companies do not provide expatriates extended regular vacation leave because expatriates are likely to perceive the removal of these benefits on their return to domestic assignments as punitive. However, U.S. companies must comply with foreign laws that govern the amount of vacation. For example, Mexican law entitles employees to 14 days vacation per year, and Swedish law mandates 30 days!

Expatriates generally receive paid time-off for foreign national or local holidays that apply to their foreign locations. Foreign holiday schedules may provide fewer or more holidays than the United States. Also, some countries require employers to provide all employees paid time-off for recognized holidays. In the United States, companies offer paid holidays as a discretionary benefit or as set in collective bargaining agreements.

Paid leave for personal or family emergencies also is a component of most expatriate compensation packages. Such emergencies may include critically ill family members or their deaths in the United States or in the foreign posts. Most companies provide paid emergency leave, but some companies provide unpaid leaves of absence. In either case, companies cover travel expenses between the foreign post and the United States.

Enhanced Benefits for U.S. Expatriates

Enhanced benefits for U.S. expatriates include:

- Relocation assistance
- Education reimbursements for expatriates' children
- Home leave benefits and travel reimbursements
- Rest and relaxation leave and allowance

Relocation Assistance

Relocation assistance payments cover expatriates' expenses to relocate to foreign posts. Table 12-4 lists the items most commonly covered under relocation assistance programs. Relocation assistance is generally large enough to pay for major expenses.

TABLE 12-4 Relocation Assistance Payments

The relocation allowance or reimbursement provides employees with money for:

- Temporary quarters prior to departure because the expatriate's house has been sold or rented
- Transportation to the foreign post for employees and their families
- Reasonable expenses incurred by the family during travel
- Temporary quarters while waiting for delivery of household goods or while looking for suitable housing
- Moving household goods to the foreign post
- Storing household goods in the United States

Companies usually base these payment amounts on three main factors: distance, length of assignment, and rank in the company.

Education Reimbursements for Expatriates' Children

Expatriates typically place their children in private schools designed for English-speaking students. Tuition in foreign countries is oftentimes more expensive than tuition for private U.S. schools. These companies choose to reimburse expatriate children's education for two reasons. First, some foreign public schools are generally not comparable to U.S. public schools. Some are better, and others are below the U.S. standard. Companies make generous educational reimbursements where public school quality is low. Second, most U.S. children do not speak foreign languages fluently. Thus, they cannot enroll in foreign public schools.

Home Leave Benefits and Travel Reimbursements

Companies offer **home leave benefits** to help expatriates manage the adjustment to foreign cultures and to maintain direct personal contact with family and friends. As the name implies, home leave benefits enable expatriates to take paid time-off in the United States. Home leave benefits vary considerably from company to company. The length and frequency of these leaves usually depends on the expected duration of expatriates' assignments—longer assignments justify longer home leaves. Also, expatriates must serve a minimum period at the foreign post before they are eligible for home leave benefits—anywhere from 6 to 12 months. Companies offer these extended benefits along with the standard paid time-off benefits.

Companies compensate expatriates while they are away on home leave. In addition, most companies reimburse expatriates for expenses associated with travel between the foreign post and the United States. These reimbursements apply to expatriates and to family members who live with expatriates at foreign posts. Companies typically reimburse the cost of round-trip airfare, ground transportation, and accommodations while traveling to and from the foreign post.

Rest and Relaxation Leave and Allowance

Expatriates who work in designated hardship foreign locations receive **rest and relaxation leave benefits**. Rest and relaxation leave represents additional paid time-off. Progressive employers recognize that expatriates working in hardship locations may need extra time away from the unpleasant conditions to "recharge their batteries." Rest and relaxation leave benefits differ from standard vacation benefits because companies designate where expatriates may spend their time. For example, many U.S. companies with operations in China's Special Economic Zone designate Hong Kong as an acceptable retreat because it is relatively close by, and Hong Kong has many amenities not present in the Special Economic Zone, such as diverse ethnic restaurants and Western-style entertainment.

Rest and relaxation leave programs include allowances to cover travel expenses between the foreign post and the retreat location. Companies determine allowance amounts based on such factors as the cost of round-trip transportation, food, and lodging associated with the designated locations. Allowances usually cover the majority of the costs. The U.S. Department of State publishes per diem schedules for various cities. Location and family size determine per diem amounts.

BALANCE SHEET APPROACH FOR U.S. EXPATRIATES' COMPENSATION PACKAGES

Most U.S. multinational companies use the balance sheet approach to determine expatriates' compensation packages. The **balance sheet approach** provides expatriates the standard of living they normally enjoy in the United States. Thus, the United States is the standard for all payments.

The balance sheet approach has strategic value to companies for two important reasons. First, this approach protects expatriates' standards of living. Without it, companies would have a difficult time placing qualified employees in international assignments. Second, the balance sheet approach enables companies to control costs because it relies on objective indexes that measure cost differences between the U.S. and foreign countries. We discuss these indexes shortly.

The use of the balance sheet approach is most appropriate when:

- The home country is an appropriate reference point for economic comparisons.
- Expatriates are likely to maintain psychological and cultural ties with the home or base country.
- Expatriates prefer not to assimilate into the local foreign culture.
- The assignment is of limited duration.
- The assignment following the international assignment will be in the home country.
- The company promises employees that they will not lose financially while on foreign assignment [4].

Companies that use the balance sheet approach compare the costs of four major expenditures in the United States and the foreign post:

- Housing and utilities
- Goods and services
- Discretionary income
- Taxes

Employees receive allowances whenever the costs in the foreign country exceed the costs in the United States. Allowance amounts vary according to the lifestyle enjoyed in the United States. In general, individuals with higher incomes tend to live in more expensive homes, and they are in better positions to enjoy more expensive goods and services (for example, designer labels versus off-brand labels). Higher income also means higher taxes.

Where do U.S. companies obtain pertinent information about costs for foreign countries? U.S. companies may rely on three information sources. First, they can rely on expatriates who have spent considerable time on assignment or foreign government contacts. Second, private consulting companies (for example, Towers Perrin) or research companies (for example, Bureau of National Affairs) can conduct custom surveys. Third, most U.S. companies consult the *U.S. Department of State Indexes of Living Costs Abroad, Quarters Allowances, and Hardship Differentials*, which is published quarterly. It is the most cost-effective source because it is available at no charge in libraries with government-depositories as well as at *www.state.gov*.

Housing and Utilities

Employers provide expatriate employees with **housing and utilities allowances** to cover the difference between housing and utilities costs in the United States and in the foreign post. The U.S. Department of State uses the term **quarters allowances**. Table 12-5 displays pertinent information from the U.S. Department of State's quarters allowances.

The quarters allowances table contains three main sections: the survey date, exchange rate, and annual allowance by family status and salary range. The survey date is the month when the Office of Allowances received housing expenditure reports.

The exchange rate section includes three pieces of information: effective date, foreign unit, and number per U.S. dollar. We reviewed the concept of exchange rate earlier. It is expressed as the number of foreign currency units given in exchange for U.S. $1. The U.S. Department of State uses the exchange rate to compute the quarters allowances. In Yokohama, expatriates receive 130 Japanese yen for every U.S. $1 exchanged. They receive 1,263 Korean won for every U.S. $1.

TABLE 12-5 Quarters Allowances October 1999

		Exchange Rate			*Annual Allowance by Family Status and Salary Range*			
Country and City	*Survey Date*	*Effective Date*	*Foreign Unit*	*Number per US$*	*Family Status*	*Less Than $34,000*	*$34,000 to $61,999*	*$62,000 and Above*
Australia: Melbourne	October 98	December 98	Dollar	1.58	Family	$15,500	$16,800	$17,600
					Single	14,100	15,500	16,800
Azores: Lajes Field	November 98	April 99	Escudo	166	Family	9,800	10,900	12,000
					Single	8,700	9,800	11,400
Bahrain: Manama	April 99	May 99	Dinar	0.3769	Family	21,700	24,100	24,100
					Single	19,300	21,700	24,100
Barbados	November 98	December 98	Dollar	2.00	Family	23,600	26,200	28,400
					Single	21,000	23,600	26,200
Belgium: Brussels	July 99	August 99	Franc	39.4	Family	26,000	28,900	30,300
					Single	23,100	26,000	28,900
Bermuda	December 95	October 96	Dollar	1.00	Family	23,600	26,200	26,200
					Single	21,900	21,900	24,800
Canada: Calgary	March 99	April 99	Dollar	1.48	Family	16,600	18,400	20,300
					Single	14,700	16,600	19,300
Korea: Osan	June 98	December 98	Won	1359	Family	18,200	20,200	21,200
					Single	16,200	18,200	20,200
Luxembourg	February 99	March 99	Franc	35.4	Family	28,200	30,900	34,300
					Single	25,000	28,200	32,700
Mexico: Mexico, D.F.	May 95	July 95	Peso	6.36	Family	30,800	34,100	37,500
					Single	27,300	30,800	35,800

Source: U.S. Department of State. (1999). *The Department of State indexes of living costs abroad, quarters allowances, and hardship differentials—October* 1999. Washington, DC: U.S. Government Printing Office [online]. Available: *www.state.gov*.

As the name implies, the section titled "Annual Allowance by Family Status and Salary Range" contains information on family status and salary range. The table distinguishes between singles and families. The term *single* is self-explanatory. In Stuttgart, the quarters allowance is $24,000 for single expatriates with annual incomes of $70,204 and over. In Tokyo, the allowance is $36,600!

The term *family* refers to two-or-more-person families. Employees with larger families living with them at the foreign posts receive supplements. Families of three or four persons receive a 10 percent supplement, families of five or six persons receive a 20 percent supplement, and families of seven or more persons receive a 30 percent supplement. In Vicenza, Italy, the quarters allowance is $31,590 for a seven-member expatriate family earning $75,000 per year (that is, $24,300 regular family allowance × 1.30—a 30 percent supplement).

Goods and Services

Expatriates receive **goods and services allowances** when the cost of living is higher in that country than in the United States. Employers base these allowances on **indexes of living costs abroad**, which compare the costs (U.S. dollars) of representative goods and services (excluding education) expatriates purchase at the foreign location and the cost of comparable goods and services purchased in the Washington, DC, area. The indexes are place-to-place cost comparisons at specific times and currency exchange rates.

Table 12-6 displays pertinent information from the Department of State's "Indexes of Living Costs Abroad" table. The table contains three pertinent sections: the survey date, the exchange rate, and the local index. The survey date represents the month the

TABLE 12-6 Indexes of Living Costs Abroad (Washington, DC = 100)

		Exchange Rate		*Local*
Country and City	***Survey Date***	***Foreign Unit***	***Number Per US$***	***Index***
Algiers: Algeria	01/23/2001	Dinar	78.0	101
Bangladesh: Dhaka	04/15/2001	Taka	54.0	97
Bolivia: La Paz	07/09/2001	Boliviano	6.58	96
Central African Republic: Bangui	03/01/2001	CFA Franc	709	142
Egypt: Cairo	03/19/2001	Pound	3.85	103
El Salvador: San Salvador	03/19/2001	Colon	8.75	103
Finland: Helsinki	06/15/2001	Mark	6.80	130
Guinea: Conakry	11/27/2000	Franc	1,865	116
Iceland: Reykjavik	06/11/2001	Kronur	100.6	151
Jamaica: Kingston	06/27/2001	Dollar	45.5	140
Kuwait: Kuwait City	11/11/2000	Dinar	0.308	128
Latvia: Riga	05/07/2001	Lat	0.6267	112
Niger: Niamey	07/16/2001	CFA Franc	774	105
Saudi Arabia: Dhahran Area	04/14/2001	Riyal	3.75	126
Singapore: Singapore	04/11/2001	Dollar	1.79	132
Spain: Madrid	04/16/2001	Peseta	185	102
Sweden: Stockholm	06/12/2001	Kroner	10.27	135
United Kingdom: Loudwater	05/15/2001	Pound	0.6762	132
United Kingdom: Rochester	05/08/2001	Pound	0.6762	134

Source: U.S. Department of State. (2001). *The Department of State indexes of living costs abroad.* Washington, DC: U.S. Government Printing Office [online]. Available: *www.state.gov.*

Department of State received the cost data. Again, we already reviewed the exchange rate concept. The local index is a measure of the cost of living for expatriates at their foreign posts relative to the cost of living in Washington, DC.

The index for Washington, DC., is 100, representing the base comparison. The local index for Reykjavik, Iceland, is 132: On average, the costs for goods and services in Reykjavik are 32 percent higher than in Washington, DC.: $[(132 - 100)/100] \times 100$. The local index for La Paz, Bolivia, is 96. On average, the costs for goods and services in La Paz are 4 percent lower than in Washington, DC.: $[(96 - 100)/100] \times 100$. Companies should provide allowances to compensate for the higher costs in Reykjavik. Allowances are not needed for La Paz because the cost of living is lower there than in the United States.

Discretionary Income

Discretionary income covers a variety of financial obligations in the United States for which expatriates remain responsible. These expenditures are usually of a long-term nature. Companies typically do not provide allowances because expatriates remain responsible for them in spite of international assignments. Table 12-7 lists examples of discretionary income expenditures.

Tax Considerations

All U.S. citizens working overseas for U.S. corporations are subject to the Federal Unemployment Tax Act (FUTA) [5]. Expatriates continue to pay U.S. income taxes and Social Security taxes while on assignment. The Internal Revenue Service (IRS) taxes U.S. citizens' income regardless of whether they earn income in the United States or while on foreign assignment [6]. Expatriates also must pay income taxes to local foreign governments based on the applicable income tax laws. Paying taxes to both the U.S. government and foreign governments is known as "double" taxation [7]. The Internal Revenue Code (IRC) includes two rules that enable expatriates to minimize double taxation by reducing their U.S. federal income tax obligations:

- IRC Section 901
- IRC Section 911

Expatriates can minimize double taxation by claiming a tax credit under IRC Section 901. **IRC Section 901** allows expatriates to credit foreign income taxes against the U.S. income tax liability:

- If the U.S. federal income tax is greater than the foreign tax amount, then expatriates need pay only the difference to the federal government.
- If the foreign tax exceeds the U.S. federal income tax amount, expatriates can apply the foreign tax excess—the difference between the foreign income tax and the U.S. federal income tax—as a deduction from future federal taxable income for up to 5 years.

TABLE 12-7 Discretionary Income Expenditures
• Pension contributions
• Savings and investments
• Insurance payments
• Equity portion of mortgage payments
• Alimony payments
• Child support
• Student loan payments
• Car payments

IRC Section 911 permits "eligible" expatriates to exclude as much as $70,000 of foreign earned income, plus a housing allowance, from taxation. Let's look at the income exclusion and housing allowance elements separately.

Table 12-8 lists specific types of income that are eligible for exclusion under IRC Section 911, which requires that expatriates pay U.S. federal income taxes only on the income amount above $70,000. For example, an expatriate whose foreign-earned income totals $150,000 in 2002 must pay taxes on only $80,000 (that is, $150,000 – $70,000 exclusion).

Employer Considerations: Tax Protection and Tax Equalization

Although IRC Sections 901 and 911 substantially reduce expatriates' double taxation burdens, neither generally eliminates double taxation. Under the balance sheet approach, companies choose between two approaches to provide expatriates tax allowances:

- Tax protection
- Tax equalization

A key element of both tax protection and tax equalization methods is the hypothetical tax. Employers calculate the **hypothetical tax** as the U.S. income tax based on the same salary level, excluding all foreign allowances. Under **tax protection**, employers reimburse expatriates for the difference between the actual income tax amount and the hypothetical tax when the actual income tax amount—based on tax returns filed with the IRS—is greater. Expatriates simply pay the entire income tax bill when the taxes are less than or equal to the hypothetical tax. Expatriates realize a tax benefit whenever actual taxes amount to less than the hypothetical tax because they will have paid lower income taxes on their overseas assignments than on assignments in the United States.

Under **tax equalization**, employers take the responsibility for paying income taxes to the U.S. and foreign governments on behalf of the expatriates. Tax equalization starts with the calculation of the hypothetical tax. Based on this hypothetical tax amount, employers deduct income from expatriates' paychecks that totals the hypothetical tax amounts at year-end. Employers reimburse expatriates for the difference between the hypothetical tax and actual income tax whenever the actual income tax

TABLE 12-8 Cash and Noncash Income Exclusions: IRC Section 911
Cash
• Salaries and wages • Bonuses • Sales commissions • Incentives • Professional fees
Noncash
• Housing • Meals • Cars • Allowances for cost-of-living differentials, education, home leave, tax reimbursements, children's education, and moving expenses

STRETCHING THE DOLLAR

WORKSHARING PRACTICES IN EUROPE

Unemployment rates in European countries are generally much higher than in the United States. As a result, most European countries have introduced the practice of worksharing. *Worksharing* can be defined as any policy that involves a redistribution of employment through a reorganization of working time. Specifically, employed individuals reduce their work hours so that unemployed individuals have the opportunity to work. Six worksharing practices are found in European companies:

- General reductions in working time reduces work hours for employees in an attempt to create jobs for the unemployed.
- Jobsharing enables two or more employees to voluntarily share the responsibilities and duties of a full-time job with a commensurate reduction in pay and benefits.
- Part-time early retirement practices enable older workers to reduce their weekly work hours as they near retirement age, provided that unemployed individuals make up the work time and benefit from older workers' experiences.
- Voluntary part-time working practices enable workers to voluntarily cut their working hours with a commensurate reduction in pay and benefits, provided that the company actively recruits new workers to fill the remaining work hours.
- Paid-leave arrangements enable workers to take extended periods of leave from the company, with the temporary employment of previously unemployed individuals.
- Career breaks afford workers the opportunity to take unpaid leave for a variety of reasons, including travel or caring for family members.

Source: Anonymus. Worksharing in Europe—Part One. (January 1999). *European Industrial Relations Review*, 300, pp 14–19.

amount is less. Expatriates reimburse their employers whenever the actual income tax amount exceeds the hypothetical income tax amounts.

Tax equalization offers employers two important advantages over tax protection. First, expatriates receive equitable treatment regardless of their location and do not keep the unexpected tax gain from being posted in countries with income tax rates lower than in the United States. As a result, employers should have an easier time motivating expatriates to move from one foreign post to another. In addition, companies save money by not allowing expatriates to keep tax windfalls.

REPATRIATION PAY ISSUES

Special compensation considerations should not end with the completion of international assignments. Effective expatriate compensation programs promote employees' integration into their companies' domestic workforces. Returnees may initially view their domestic assignments as punishment because their total compensation decreases. Upon return, former expatriates forfeit special pay incentives and extended leave allowances. Although most former expatriates understand the purpose of these incentives and allowances, it often takes time for them to adjust to "normal" compensation practices.

Many expatriates may not adjust very well to compensation-as-usual because they feel their international experiences have made them substantially more valuable to their employers. Their heightened sense of value may intensify when former expatriates compare themselves with colleagues who have never taken international assignments. Two consequences are likely. First, former expatriates may find it difficult to work collaboratively with colleagues, which can undermine differentiation objectives.

Second, strong resentments may lead former expatriates to find employment with competitors. Adding insult to injury, competitors stand to benefit from former expatriates' international experiences.

Companies can actively prevent many of these problems by the following two measures. First, companies should invest in former expatriates' career development. Career development programs signal that companies value returnees. In addition, former expatriates may view their employers' investments in career development as a form of compensation, reducing the equity problems described earlier. Second, companies should capitalize on expatriates' experiences to gain a better understanding of foreign business environments. Also, former expatriates can contribute to the quality of international assignments by conveying what did and did not work well during their assignments.

COMPENSATION ISSUES FOR HCNs AND TCNs

Compensating HCNs and TCNs poses special challenges. In Chapter 2, we recognized that variations in national culture play a role in shaping compensation practices. Specifically, national culture creates normative expectations. Expatriates responsible for managing compensation programs may find that cultural differences reduce the effectiveness of U.S. compensation practices. Three examples illustrate this point.

Japan

A striking contrast exists between U.S. and Japanese cultures. In U.S. businesses, strategic business decisions generally originate from top management. Japanese business leaders cultivate consensus on business decisions, or *nemawashi*. U.S. culture promotes a sense of individualism, which translates into high career mobility. Japanese culture promotes a sense of collectivism, which leads to heightened loyalty.

These cultural values are apparent in compensation systems. As we discussed previously (Chapters 4, 5, and 6), the predominant bases for pay in the United States are performance and knowledge, which represent equity. In Japan, the predominant basis for pay is seniority, which represents equality. As a result, pay differences among the Japanese tend to be smaller than pay differences among U.S. employees.

China

Another noteworthy cultural contrast exists between the U.S. and the People's Republic of China (PRC). The differences between the U.S. market economy and the PRC's centralized government-controlled economy set the stage for cultural clashes. For decades, the Chinese government owned and operated virtually all business organizations. The Communist Party places substantial emphasis on equal contributions to society, group welfare, and the concern for interpersonal relationships. In addition, the Communist Party calls for greater emotional dependence of Chinese citizens on their employers. Further, the party expects employers to assume a broad responsibility for their members.

These ideals are evident in the Chinese workplace and in compensation practices. Employers provide housing and modest wages for food and clothing. The Chinese receive health care under government-sponsored protection programs. Based on the Communist ethic, the Chinese do not identify very well with pay-for-performance programs.

Mexico

The compensation packages of U.S. and Mexican managerial employees differ substantially. The most important elements of U.S. managers' compensation are base pay and long-term incentives. Base pay and cash allowances represent the lion's share of

Mexican managerial employees' compensation packages. In fact, the Mexican government mandates that employers award Christmas bonuses, profit sharing, and a minimum 20 percent vacation pay premium (that is, employers must pay employees at least an additional 20 percent of their regular pay while on vacation). U.S. employers offer these allowances at their discretion, not by government mandate.

The most noteworthy difference is Mexico's acquired right law: Employees possess the right to benefit from compensation practices that were in effect for at least 2 years. For example, let's assume that an employer institutes the practice of 40 paid vacation days per year. Employees acquire the right to 40 paid vacation days per year every year if the company instituted this practice for at least 2 consecutive years. Historically, U.S. companies do not operate under an acquired right law, although U.S. employees often view benefits as an entitlement. Nowadays, U.S. companies discourage this view because benefits represent a significant cost.

These illustrations represent only some of the challenges that U.S. companies are bound to face when compensating TCNs and HCNs. Compensation professionals need to understand the cultural contexts before they can develop effective international compensation programs. Pay-for-performance and pay-for-knowledge represent the foundation of U.S. compensation programs. Business leaders should not abandon these programs because they are inconsistent with cultural norms. Instead, it will be necessary for U.S. companies to work closely with their international partners to convey the importance of these approaches.

SUMMARY

This chapter provided a discussion of international compensation and its strategic role. The globalization of the economy necessitates U.S. companies' investments overseas. Well-designed expatriate compensation programs support strategic initiatives by attracting and maintaining the best performers. Effective expatriate compensation programs reduce risk and promote expatriate families' comfort while they are stationed at foreign posts. The balance sheet approach minimizes financial risk to expatriates, and various incentives and allowances promote comfort. We also discussed that successful expatriate compensation programs facilitate returnees' transition to domestic assignments.

Key Terms

- North American Free Trade Agreement, 373
- repatriation, 375
- host country nationals, 375
- third country nationals, 375
- expatriates, 375
- home country-based pay method, 377
- host country-based method, 377
- headquarters-based method, 378
- exchange rate, 378
- inflation, 378
- foreign service premiums, 379
- hardship allowance, 379
- mobility premiums, 383
- relocation assistance payments, 385
- home leave benefits, 386
- rest and relaxation leave benefits, 386
- balance sheet approach, 387
- housing and utilities allowances, 388
- quarters allowances, 388
- goods and services allowances, 389
- indexes of living costs abroad, 389
- discretionary income, 390
- IRC Section 901, 390
- IRC Section 911, 391
- hypothetical tax, 391
- tax protection, 391
- tax equalization, 391

Discussion Questions

1. Discuss the strengths and weaknesses of the following methods for establishing base pay in international contexts: home country-based pay, headquarters-based pay, and host country-based pay.
2. For a country of your choice, conduct research into the cultural characteristics that you believe should be important considerations in establishing a core com-

pensation program for a U.S. company that plans to locate there. Discuss these characteristics. Also, discuss whether you feel that pay-for-performance programs are compatible. If compatible in any way, what course of action would you take to promote this compatibility?
3. Discuss your reaction to the following statement: "U.S. companies should increase base pay (beyond the level that would be paid in the United States) to motivate employees to accept foreign assignments."
4. Allowances and reimbursements for international assignments are costly. Should companies avoid international business activities? Explain your answer. If you answer no, what can companies do to minimize costs?
5. Of the many reimbursements and allowances that U.S. companies make for employees who take foreign assignments, which one is the most essential? Discuss your reasons.

Exercises

Compensation Online

For Students

Exercise 1: Find relevant articles
An HR professional is coming to speak to your class about global HR issues. Your course instructor has asked a few students to do some basic research so that the discussion can be livelier and more productive. He has asked you to research compensation issues in specific. Use your school library's online catalog to locate articles pertaining to expatriates, repatriation, multinational corporations, international compensation, and global competition. Find and read several current articles in these areas.

Exercise 2: Search for latest news on international benefits
While preparing for the speaker to come to your class, you found many interesting articles and wondered what the latest developments were on certain issues. Using the Bureau of Labor Statistics Web site at *www.bls.gov/*, click on the News Releases link. Under the International Programs heading, click on one of the links. Read the article and write a brief summary of the information it contained and how it relates to the textbook information.

Exercise 3: Research employee resources
Since you are currently looking for a job, or will be soon enough, use Yahoo to search for "expat" or "expatriate." Visit resulting sites such as *www.expatforum.com* or *www.expatexchange.com.* If you had the opportunity to work as an expatriate at some foreign location, how could these sites help you?

For Professionals

Exercise 1: Devise a repatriation package
As a compensation professional, sometimes you need to look at a situation from the employee's point of view. Using the Web site at *www.insiders.com/relocation/*, devise cost-effective ways the company can ease the repatriation shock for an employee and his or her family returning from an assignment.

Exercise 2: Research income tax laws for expatriates
The federal income tax responsibilities for multinational corporations and their American employees who work overseas can be confusing. Your company is about to send some of your colleagues to France, Spain, and Germany. Go the Internal Revenue Service Web site to get a better understanding of the tax laws that pertain to working overseas: *www.irs.gov/.* Scroll down the Web page and click on the Individuals link. Click on the Overseas Taxpayers link. Review the information and write a brief summary on what you learned by accessing this site. Did you find this site helpful? What did you learn by reviewing this site that you did not know?

Exercise 3: Research global HR services

Your firm's HR staff is already spread too thin and is not growing fast enough to keep up with the global expansion of the firm as a whole. Expatriate and repatriation issues are not being handled to the satisfaction of either the employees or management. It has been decided to outsource some of these functions to make the experience more worthwhile for everyone involved. Use the Yahoo, Business and Economy and Business to Business sections to find organizations that provide services such as cross-culture training or repatriation services either to expatriates themselves or to your organization.

Endnotes

1. Munn, G. G., Garcia, F. L., & Woelfel, C. J. (1991). *Encyclopedia of Banking and Finance*. Chicago: St. James Press.
2. Bureau of National Affairs (2002). Expatriate pay. Compensation and benefits (CD-ROM). Washington, DC: Author.
3. Horn, M. E. (1992). *International Employee Benefits: An Overview*. Brookfield, WI: International Foundation of Employee Benefit Plans.
4. Sheridan, W. R., & Hansen, P. T. (1996). Linking international business and expatriate compensation strategies. *American Compensation Association Journal*, Spring, pp. 66–81.
5. Internal Revenue Code, Section 306(c), paragraph 3306(j).
6. Kates, S. M., & Spielman, C. (1995). Reducing the cost of sending employees overseas. *Practical Accountant*, *28*, pp. 50–55.
7. Ibid.

COMPENSATION IN ACTION

CROSSING A RAGING RIVER: SEEKING FAR-REACHING SOLUTIONS TO GLOBAL PAY CHALLENGES

Business executives and researchers are keenly aware of the implications of emerging globalization in the worldwide marketplace. Data supporting the ever-increasing pace of globalization only adds credence to the need for a careful treatment of the issue. In 2000, world merchandise export was valued at $6.2 trillion (World Trade Organization, 2001). During the same year, technology-related exports became the second largest among various product categories. Similarly, in the last decade technology-related investments grew at an unprecedented rate. For example, in 2000, technology represented 30 percent of the total business investment and contributed roughly 20 percent of the output growth in the United States (Lawrence, 2002). At the same time, the global mergers and acquisitions (M&A) activities hit a record level of $3.43 trillion (Hansen, 2000). The efficient movement of resources across borders, falling trade barriers, expanding markets for goods and services, and increasingly networked socio-political institutions are propelling professionals to rethink the way they manage organizations globally.

These global forces often juxtapose different national systems in ways that require novel and creative approaches to managing organizations.

Even organizations that operate only in one country have to strategically respond to these environmental changes to stay globally competitive. Multinational enterprises (MNEs), however, have little choice but to strategically respond to the new realities. In particular, MNEs must simultaneously deal with global pressures and a web of local forces including cultures, legal systems and powerful institutions. Faced with a lack of a theoretically grounded framework to explain and investigate variations across nations, scholars and managers typically sweep contextual variations under the rug of "national culture" without directly dealing with the unexplained. As a result, it is almost common to observe an MNE deploy multiple, often inconsistent, compensation and rewards systems across different nations (Milkovich and Newman, 2002). Because compensation and rewards systems are one of the most salient levers managers use to achieve organization's strategic objectives, it is imperative to gain a better understanding of how MNEs balance global and local pressures in designing and implementing international compensation and rewards system (ICRS).

An oft-cited example of how global pressures impact ICRS is the changing nature of compensation systems at DaimlerChrysler. At the time of Daimler's acquisition of Chrysler in 1997, the Chrysler CEO's compensation (more than $11 million) was more than the estimated compensation to the top ten Daimler executives (Milkovich and Newman, 2002). Faced with such an unpleasant situation, DaimlerChrysler announced its new global pay systems for its top 250 executives (Gross & Wingerup, 1999). This is most likely the first of many compensation problems DaimlerChrysler will have to address as it deals with its new identity.

Like DaimlerChrysler, many MNEs have struggled to reconcile individual country circumstances with their intent to formulate global compensation systems. Conventional models used to address ICRS issues rely heavily on one of two models: national culture or strategic alignment.

The proponents of national culture logic assert that when it comes to understanding international pay issues, national culture is destiny. Relying on the assumption that "most of a country's inhabitants share a national character . . . that . . . represents mental programming for processing ideas and information that these people have in common," this model seeks a fit between compensation and the values, norms and beliefs of a national culture (Hofstede, 1980). Depending on the model's specificity, some focus on the relationship between underlying attributes or dimensions of national culture and ICRS and others treat all idiosyncratic local host country's ICRS practices

(Continued)

(Continued)

as reflective of national culture. Based on this national culture logic, DaimlerChrysler HR executives would assess cultural differences between the United States and Germany to formulate the new global pay systems for the top 250 executives.

While the national culture model assumes that external forces solely determine compensation decisions, the strategic alignment model stresses the importance of compensation decision makers because it emphasizes aligning ICRS with MNE's internal attributes such as strategy, structure and organizational culture. Based on this model, DaimlerChrysler HR executives would focus on the firm's internal strengths to formulate the new global pay system. The strategic alignment model considers fragmentation in the external environmental attributes, including national culture, as opportunities that organizations should exploit to achieve their strategic objectives. Accordingly, DaimlerChrysler HR executives would view cultural differences between the United States and Germany as opportunities to be exploited by the global pay system.

A STUDY TO CAPTURE THE GLOBAL REALITY

The two conventional ICRS models offer starkly contrasting prescriptions and both offer only a limited perspective. To address these concerns, the following study aims to answer a simple question: When faced with identical ICRS issues (i.e., recruiting, performance, retention and human capital development), how do managers worldwide respond?

This qualitative and quantitative research not only assesses the validity of conventional wisdom about international compensation systems, but also formulates a framework that should guide scholars and managers in their thinking about global pay issues. Several unique conceptual insights resulted from on-site interviews conducted in nine countries with more than 100 managers representing 14 nationalities and five multinationals over the course of one year. Interestingly, the findings reveal that managers' thinking does not conform fully to either the strategic or national culture logic. Instead, managers seem to engage in "pragmatic experimentation" by feeling their way around the flux resulting from juxtaposing global and local pressures. Instead of treating the ICRS decisions "either as a reactive response to national cultural pressures or as a planned strategic alignment process," these managers offer a far more complex assessment that can only be captured by modeling "loose" fitting pragmatism.

Analysis of these managers' responses, along with extant field knowledge, suggests that a model of "loose" fitting pragmatism about ICRS should address five important issues:

1. Critical factors in local host contexts
2. The importance of flexibility in local host context
3. The strategic orientation
4. Types of strategic responses
5. Pragmatic experimentation about ICRS issues (Milkovich and Newman, 2002).

CRITICAL FACTORS OF LOCAL HOSTS CONTEXTS

According to managers, three categories of factors related to local host contexts are crucial to the design and implementation of ICRS issues: regulations and institutions, changing social contracts and relationships, and industry conditions and markets (Milkovich and Newman, 2002).

Regulations and Institutions

Nations use their regulatory framework and other institutions to influence MNEs' practices. In certain nations, such as Sweden, Belgium and Germany, centralized pay setting institutions have a dominant influence on pay practices of organizations. The idea of 13th month pay is widely exercised in many East Asian nations. To stave off economic slowdown and improve national competitiveness in 1998, the Singaporean government famously mandated that organizations should reduce their contributions to the Central Provident Fund (CPF) from 20 percent to 10 percent and reduce or withhold cash incentives. A national level mandate by the Singaporean government effectively reduced MNE's choices about the use of retirement funds or performance-based pay as a tool to achieve business objectives. A manager from a high-tech MNE argued that in Singapore, "The mentality is to rely on the government. The government reduced CPF from 20 percent to 10 percent and nobody complained about it."

Perhaps the most commonly cited example in this regard relates to the impact of a nation's tax on different components of ICRS. For example, favorable tax treatment of stock options in the United States, United Kingdom and Hong Kong and unfavorable treatment in Germany and Japan have significantly impacted the deployment of stock options in these countries. In India, favorable tax treatment of housing allowances have prompted MNEs to offer a large portion of total compensation in the form of housing allowance. Managers also gave us examples of how other institutions such as unions and political groups could influence their compensation design decisions.

Changing Social Contracts and Relationships

Changing social contracts and relationships among key stakeholders can shape or reinforce "habitual" or "customary" compensation practices in a variety of areas including benefits, housing, transportation, maid service, recreation, financial loans, medical coverage and pension plans. They may influence what forms of pay are salient. For example, many top executives in India's information technology (IT) sector now expect MNEs to provide golf club membership. In Europe personal wealth is usually contained in employees' pension plans while in the United States, it increasingly is in returns tied to the stock market. Much has been written about changing employment relationships in the United States with a movement away from lifetime employment at one firm and toward flexibility and variability for both employees and organizations. Preferred or undesirable ICRS practices often depend on evolutions in these social contracts and relationships. Managers must often be creative in the way they meet conditions of the prevailing social contract with the organization's budgetary and strategic constraints. One manger illustrated it this way:

> Improved housing is really important to professionals in Shanghai, but it is costly and difficult to get reasonable housing loans. At first, to attract and keep the best people, we tried building or managing apartments, town houses, and even single-family houses. But we figured out we weren't in the housing business. So now we are trying to make housing loans available at great terms based on two years of performance—and the loans get forgiven on a sliding scale over the time the individual sustains performance.

Industry and Market Conditions

The nature and dynamics of globalization create greater competitive intensity where competition increasingly comes from a greater variety of sources. As corporations extend their reach to more diverse locations, they also will have to contend with a variety of different labor, economic and financial markets. Global strategic alliances and partnerships that span several organizations and many national borders create a global marketplace. Of course some industries are more globalized than others. Industries such as IT, financial, electronic and auto already have become truly global. India now hosts customer service call centers for many Fortune 500 companies.

Managing talent on a worldwide scale is chief among the concerns that managers face; the marketplace for talent has gone global too. Managers stated that software engineers in India and Belarus know exactly how much their U.S. and UK counterparts make. These global workers from India and Belarus considered their geographic home addresses as merely places to live and argued against using them as a basis for defining labor markets. They certainly wished to have "global pay for working in a global marketplace" and their expectations and behaviors are framed by their IT industry conditions rather than the geographic locations of their homes. Several Chinese managers gave an excellent example about how they had to be pragmatic about ICRS issues after the entry of GM in Pudong, China. When GM started hiring for this new facility, they substantially raised salaries and signing bonuses. Many local companies had to quickly respond by offering performance-based incentives and bonuses to prevent mass exodus of talented employees. In a contrasting example, a U.S. manager of a Japanese company expressed that his company is unable to react to the local U.S. market conditions because Japanese companies generally do not offer stock options. Managers in Hong Kong and India have started offering housing loans in response to similar

(Continued)

(Continued)

loans offered by large global banks such as Citibank and Chase-Manhattan. One worker for a U.S. multinational summed it up this way:

> When my colleague from Singapore comes to India, is it fair to learn that my salary is one-fourth of his salary? MNEs want global quality work but do not offer global quality compensation. How can one explain the fact that if my home address changes from Bangalore to New York City, my quality of life changes dramatically? Those of who [move] globally, our expectations change significantly based on what we see. When we are in, say the U.S., we are in a dream world. When we come back to India, we continue to think about it. It is not money per se, but the comparative fairness in the global context that is important.

(Ir)relevance of National Culture to ICRS

Surprisingly, few managers in the study voluntarily suggested that national culture plays an important role in shaping global compensation systems. Specific and direct probing about the role of national culture in shaping ICRS further clarified their thinking. According to most managers, national culture itself does not directly shape their compensation choices. Their responses, however, do suggest that national culture, though a fuzzy and possibly a difficult factor to assess, may play an indirect role at some level in shaping global pay. To a great extent, these results run counter to the national culture logic suggested earlier. Equally interesting, in direct probing, many managers challenged the conventional wisdom of looking at national culture as some "averaged" value that could be used to characterize a nation. Repeatedly, managers pointed to the value of looking at subcultures and variations within a nation. Thus, rather than relying on an oversimplified notion of a single set of national cultural values (e.g., Americans are ______; Chinese are ______; Russians are ______; French are ______; etc.), managers, predictably, were more focused on variations in critical contextual factors and individual capabilities.

IMPORTANCE OF VARIATION OR FLEXIBILITY IN LOCAL HOST CONTEXT

The study found that managers knew intuitively what scholars know based on extensive research. In discussions with managers, it became clear that they are wary of averaged abstractions about local conditions, because these assumptions could blind them to the real strategic choices created by the variations in host country contexts. Managers' responses suggest that the key to gaining an understanding about global compensation design and implementation decisions lies in their ability to leverage the variations or flexibility that may be present within and across local host contexts. Variation in contextual factors allows managers to pragmatically experiment and strategically craft a global philosophy about compensation design and implementation issues. A careful analysis of managers' responses indicates that the variation that might be observed in host country contexts can be described by five factors: diversity, freedom to choose, formalization, pervasiveness, and centrality.

Diversity describes the observed differences in a host country's contextual factors. In some countries, pay-related laws vary greatly from region to region. For example, in the United States, laws about local employment taxes vary from state to state, sometimes even among cities within a state. In India, 11 different labor laws define the term *wage* differently. Laws in China permit few compensation forms. Diversity could be observed in other contextual factors, too. In many nations, like the United States and China, pay-related norms and customs vary greatly from region to region. In Japan, even though the norms are changing, they tend to be more uniform. Variation in cultural values is another good example. The U.S. society is heterogeneous; the Japanese society is homogeneous.

In addition to diversity, variation is expressed in the amount of choice the local host context offers. *Freedom to choose* is particularly critical for socio-cultural issues. In the United States, individuation and democratization processes have allowed both employers and employees to focus on multiple options. Employment-at-will and labor mobility are generally accepted norms to deal with fluctuations in the macroeconomic conditions. Institutionalization of these norms in the United States has percolated into compensation practices, evidenced from adoption of flexible and innovative benefits. In Singapore, on the other hand, limitations on individuation processes have legitimized management of pension plans at the national level.

Formalization is the degree to which contextual factors are codified into rules and enforced. Common business practices are less formalized than laws, which by definition are codified. Adherence to laws and dominant business practices may be weakly or strongly enforced by government agencies or other powerful stakeholders like unions and pressure groups. Variation also is manifested in the pervasiveness of factors in local host contexts. Pay practices that are widely adopted or adhered to by many organizations (e.g., vacation days, maid services, chauffeur-driven car, etc.) are more pervasive. Finally, employees may see certain pay practices as more central or important. For example, in some countries employees may be more interested in chauffeur-driven cars than other forms of compensation.

To summarize, factors in local host contexts may have high or low variation depending on the five attributes. Local host contexts with high variations allow MNEs to be strategic about ICRS. On the other hand, inflexible local host contexts constrain MNEs' choices and force them to conform and localize pay decisions. In other cases, MNEs may seek to resist local pressures. These three response options form the basis of pragmatic experimentation.

ORGANIZATIONAL FACTORS AND STRATEGIC ORIENTATION

Even though a local host context can constrain a specific response, according to managers, organizational context provides them with proximal and more important cues about crafting ICRS. Organizational factors (e.g., specific business needs, organizational culture, structure and strategy) play a crucial role in the design and delivery of ICRS. Analyses of managerial responses suggest that MNEs use one of the three dominant ICRS strategies to achieve their business objectives (Milkovich and Newman, 2002):

Adapter/Localizer

An adapter or localizer organization formulates global compensation systems to be consistent with most or all of the local environments in which it operates. Interestingly, this approach to compensation design often is consistent with these organizations' global business strategy to offer customized products and services consistent with needs of local host contexts. Adapter/localizer strategic orientation was evident in a Japanese MNE operating in the United States and Europe: each subsidiary had its own compensation system. In other words, this MNE believed in "when in Rome, pay as the Romans pay."

Exporter

Exporter considers headquarters compensation system as "tried and tested," and works to make the compensation systems of subsidiaries imitate the compensation system of the headquarters unit. The headquarters compensation system acts as a template and is modified only when necessary to meet local conditions. Data found this strategic orientation in the U.S. financial services MNEs that sought to utilize the U.S. system in all its global locations.

Globalizer

These MNEs are true proponents of a global pay system. They gather the best ideas worldwide and distill them into a unified set of ICRS practices that can be consistently applied across all subsidiaries. For globalizers, this strategic ICRS orientation is crucial for tapping into and deploying global marketplace talent. While both exporters and globalizers seek a common global pay system, globalizers are not tied to headquarters' dominant thinking. Instead, they develop internal structures that allow a free flow of ideas globally. Globalizers have to be more agile than exporters in order to think and act "locally and globally" simultaneously (Milkovich and Newman, 2002). This strategic orientation was found among high technology, particularly IT industry, MNEs. A prime driver for these organizations was creating a consistent performance mindset among employees throughout the world and facilitating seamless global talent mobility.

THE RANGE OF RESPONSES

An important question relates to how different MNEs respond to the global and local pressures. The study found that the dominant strategic

(Continued)

(Continued)

orientation determines the nature of an MNE's response to pressures from local host contexts. In other words, MNEs choose from one of the three possible responses—conformance, resistance, and strategic—based on their strategic orientation. A conformance response primarily reflects MNEs' attempts to adjust to local contexts. Usually this means adopting compensation practices that reflect strongly those of other organizations operating in the local host environment.

Rather than conforming to the demands of local contexts, MNEs sometimes may resist local contexts' pressure by simply refusing to comply or by trying to influence or change factors in the local host context. Among those studied, a U.S. computer company and a UK-based food product company chose the resistance response. Managers from these MNEs asserted that they resisted local pressures to institute egalitarian pay structure by implementing an individual incentive program internally consistent with their strategic orientations.

Finally, rather than conforming or resisting, a *strategic* response, in essence, reflects an MNE's desire to align ICRS with its strategic goals and mission. The overriding objective is to ensure that compensation designs support global business objectives. A British senior executive of a U.S. MNE operating in China put it this way, "we pay globally because our clients operate globally. One global pay system is, quite logically, the best for us."

PRAGMATIC EXPERIMENTATION AND ICRS

In making global pay decisions, managers overwhelmingly favored a strategic response. That is, their primary focus is the business objectives of MNEs. However, their strategic responses are constrained by a complex set of demands placed on MNEs by the interplay of local and global pressures. This complexity forces managers to take a pragmatic experimentation approach when designing global pay systems.

Adapters/localizers preferred conformance responses, irrespective of how the local host contexts were structured. While this response reduced their ability to gain competitive advantage by strategically aligning their ICRS, they considered adapting to conditions in local contexts as the main drivers of their compensation decisions.

Occasionally, globalizers also chose conformance response, mainly when the local host contexts constrained their decisions via low variation or inflexibility. Analysis suggests, however, that globalizers are more likely to resist than conform. Globalizers derive their strategic advantage from an integrated and unified global pay system; internal equity is a critical objective for globalizers. With an extensively interdependent global network of resources of globalizers, they are able to exert influence on local host contexts to allow deployment of unified global pay systems. Compensation practices such as global stock options, financial loans and salary management for virtual contracts are some of the pay-related issues suggested by globalizers as candidates for resistance responses. Greater variation in local host contexts allows globalizers to create integrated and unified international compensation systems. Managers from globalizers in this study considered strategic responses to be the most preferred responses.

Finally, since exporters seek to transport their headquarters' compensation practices to all subsidiaries, they avoid and/or resist the demands of local host contexts. Exporters conform only when absolutely necessary and often try resistance responses first in search of a way around conforming.

The design and implementation of global pay strategy necessitates a coordinated effort by headquarters managers as well as local hosts contexts' human resources managers. Data suggest that the local HR host country manager's role also differs depending on the MNE's strategic orientation. For an adapter/localizer, the local host country's HR manager acts as a strategic partner. The focus of an adapter/localizer's local country HR manager is to strategically design ICRS to conform to local pressures to meet local business objectives. Adapter/localizer MNEs provide significant autonomy to local country HR managers to act as strategic partners. For an exporter, he/she is hired to mainly implement headquarters compensation system. The local host country HR manager helps an exporter with information necessary to resist or avoid local pressure. Another important responsibility of an exporter's local country HR manager is to inform local constituents about the virtues of HQ-centric compensation practices. A globalizer expects him/her to offer advice about local ICRS practices so that the local pay-related ideas may be integrated with the global pay system.

There are also some risks associated with each of the three strategic orientations. For example, ICRS of an adapter/localizer is likely to be inconsistent and fragmented. Local host nationals may see an exporter as HQ-centric. ICRS of globalizers may become too general and cumbersome. Despite these concerns, the study's results suggest that MNEs use a different basis to glue their ICRS. A globalizer uses global processes and organizational culture as glue to craft internally consistent ICRS. For an exporter, HQ processes and culture form the basis for gluing ICRS across nations. However, and adapter/localizer does not consider internal consistency across nations as important and hence does not rely on common processes and culture.

PATTERNING THE CHAOS OF A GLOBAL COMPENSATION SYSTEM

Two contemporary approaches to international compensation system design—the national culture and strategic alignment models—offer contrasting and contradicting propositions. While the two approaches are useful for understanding and crafting global pay, neither approach captures the complexity involved in the design and implementation of international compensation. One of the primary findings is that local managers are pragmatic experimentalists: They conformed when required, resisted when needed or feasible, and strategically crafted global compensation systems to achieve organizational objectives. Clearly the pragmatic experimental framework of global compensation systems is more descriptive than prescriptive. Even though it captures the reality of the global marketplace, it certainly is messier. Yet analysis suggests that the pragmatic experimentation framework of ICRS offers several helpful tools for managers to pattern the chaos resulting from a duel between local and global pressures:

Focus on Organizational Strategy

The study's results suggest that ICRS should be carefully aligned with an organization's global business strategy. The three strategic orientations for crafting global compensation systems (i.e., localizer/adapter, exporter, and globalizer) mainly depend on organizational factors, particularly on an organization's business strategy.

Understand the Role of Local Host Factors

Factors in local host contexts such as regulations and institutions, markets, social contracts and industry conditions defined the boundary conditions that sometimes constrained their strategic choices. National culture appears to matter far less than hitherto assumed in impacting ICRS. Organizations must be willing to appreciate the chaos involved in dealing with multiple local host contexts. More importantly, organizations should nurture the value of "pragmatic experimentation" in crafting global compensation systems. A manager used an old Chinese metaphor to succinctly state this point: "We are forever crossing a raging river in our bare feet. We must take one step at a time, feeling along the bottom for sharp stones and drop-offs, while searching the way across."

The Magic of Variation: Understand the Basis for Strategic Choices

Managers in the study highlighted the importance of variation in local host contexts' factors. Flexibility in the local host context offered these managers sufficient leeway to take a strategic view of ICRS. The understanding of attributes that enhance or diminish variations in local host contexts allows mangers to strategically choose the nature of response to local pressures.

In conclusion, as the global marketplace becomes more interconnected, with effortless flow of information, the traditional mindsets of national-level social contracts, deeply rooted in employees' psyches, would be challenged. Managers in the study assert that such changes in the global marketplace will be the impetus for designing and implementing new forms of global pay systems. Questions such as "Does global pay exist?" or "Is there a set of best global pay practices?"

(Continued)

(Continued)

miss the complexity of designing a global pay system. Evidently, the new form of global pay system will avoid the "one-size-fits-all" philosophy and instead incorporate variations in local host contexts as the basis of ICRS design to meet business objectives.

References

Gross, S. E. and Wingerup, P. L. (1999). Global pay? Maybe not yet! *Compensation and Benefits Review, 31*, pp. 25–34.

Hansen, F. (2002). Global mergers & acquisitions explode. *Business Credit, 102*, pp. 22–25.

Hofstede, G. (1980). Motivation, leadership, and organizations: Do American theories apply abroad? *Organizational Dynamics, 9*, pp. 42–55.

Lawrence, S. (2002). Technology and the global economy. *Red Herring, 110* pp. 28-29.

Milkovich, G. T., and Newman, J. M. (2002). *Compensation*. New York: McGraw-Hill/Irwin.

World Trade Organization. (2001). World trade slows sharply in 2001 amid the uncertain international situation. [online]. Available: *http://www.wto.org/english/news_e/pres01_e/pr249_e.htm.*

Source: Atul Mitra, Ph.D., University of Northern Iowa; Matt Bloom, Ph.D., University of Notre Dame; and George T. Milkovich, Ph.D., Cornell University *WorldatWork Journal*. (2002). p. 11.

WHAT'S NEW IN COMPENSATION?

Japanese Compensation Systems Moving Away from Traditional Cultural Values

This chapter focused on international compensation, specifically, compensation and benefits considerations for U.S. expatriates. As discussed, U.S. expatriates are generally U.S. citizens or resident aliens working for a U.S. company outside the United States (for example, a U.S. citizen working for Bristol Myers Squibb in England). The field of international compensation is quite comprehensive, extending to other countries' compensation practices for its citizens.

In the United States, most pay decisions are related to the worth of the job and an employee's job performance. That is, an employee's compensation increases commensurately with levels of performance attainment. We reviewed pay-for-performance systems in Chapters 4 and 5, and these include merit pay and a variety of incentive pay programs (for example, behavioral encouragement plans, gain-sharing plans, and profit-sharing plans). Pay-for-performance systems fit well with the strong endorsement of individualist cultural values in the United States. Individualist values encourage an individual's achievement. For the most part, pay-for-performance systems reinforce individual achievement with pay increases.

Other countries endorse different cultural values, as discussed in Chapter 2. In that chapter, we characterized the collectivist values of Japanese culture and how those values influence the design of compensation systems. In collectivist societies, people hold dear membership in groups. Duty to group needs prevails over each individual's needs and personal feelings. Failure to meet group needs results in personal shame because society disapproves of individuals who do not hold group interests in high esteem. These principles apply to all aspects of Japanese life including employment. Traditionally, employers have highly valued employees' affiliations, and they have taken personal interest in employees' personal lives as well as work lives. The value placed on group membership leads employers to care about the well-being of their employees' families because families are important groups in Japan. Employers generally award base pay to meet families' needs and also on the basis of seniority to honor affiliation as employees.

Although collectivist values remain strong in Japan, some companies are changing their compensation systems out of economic necessity. The featured *New York Times* article describes how slowdowns in the Japanese economy are leading some major corporations to adopt performance-based plans. These changes are influencing the design of retirement pay systems that create incentives for some employees not to remain with a particular company for entire careers, and the adoption of pay-for-performance benefits.

Log onto your *New York Times* account. Search the database for articles on "international pay" and "expatriate and pay" to find articles about international compensation. When reading these articles, identify the issues about pay levels or benefits. Following your course instructor's specific directions, be prepared to describe the current situation, and relate it to the article contained in this text. ■

The New York Times

International Business: Japan's New 'Temp' Workers; Rethinking Lifetime Jobs and Their Underpinnings

OSAKA, Japan—This spring, Suguru Takamatsu, one of 814 new employees of the Matsushita Electric Industrial Company, took his destiny into his own hands.

Mr. Takamatsu, 25, declined to join the ranks of the Japanese salarymen who rarely think about financing their retirement until their employer hands them a fat check at the age of 60. Instead, he elected to have his retirement benefits, along with other perks the company would normally provide over the course of his career, paid to him directly as he advances at Matsushita.

The budding engineer plans to invest them on his own, taking advantage of the new opportunities promised by financial deregulation. "There is no guarantee that I'll keep my job at Matsushita until I retire," Mr. Takamatsu said. "There might be layoffs, or I might change my mind, find a better job or better conditions."

Listen closely. Mr. Takamatsu's choice—and Matsushita's decision to let him make it—may seem like a tiny thing, but in it you can hear the cracking of the iron links that have traditionally chained Japanese employee to employer for life.

"We want to give more opportunities to our employees to select their course," said Atsushi Murayama, managing director of personnel and general affairs at Matsushita, the electronics titan that markets products under the Panasonic and National names. "We accept that some will seek work later outside the company, but that's the reality of the changes in Japanese business and in Japanese society."

For the first time, Matsushita—long considered one of the most conventional big businesses in Japan—gave new recruits a choice of three retirement plans, knowing full well that it was striking a blow against an employment system that has been the backbone of the industrial complex that made Japan a global economic power.

"I was astonished, not just surprised," said Hiroyuki Matsui, a manager at the Nikkeiren, the Japan Federation of Employers' Associations. "The management style of Matsushita is very, very traditional, with more or less a family-style relationship to employees, so it's difficult to understand why they have introduced this kind of thing."

With a note of disapproval, he suggested that newly minted college graduates lacked the preparation to make the choices Matsushita was giving them. "It is impossible to judge the success of this program for 20 to 30 years," he said.

But Matsushita is not alone in taking what are bold steps by Japanese standards. Ever so gently, corporate Japan is trying to reduce its reliance on lifetime employment by tinkering with the rigid, seniority-based salary system. While this movement has been going on for a while, it is now picking up momentum.

Many companies have introduced management ranks to merit-based pay systems to reduce the relevance of seniority. Fujitsu has gone the furthest, announcing recently that merit would determine the pay of all 47,000 employees in Japan.

Some companies are even fiddling with the semiannual "bonus," a label that implies a link to performance but in Japan refers to a twice-yearly payment negotiated by the unions. The Toyota Motor Corporation has started calling the bonuses "lump-sum payments" in hopes that someday it can give real bonuses to employees whose work is exemplary.

Amid today's hard times and rising unemployment, early retirement is becoming more common, if not more publicly acknowledged, and companies are brazenly cutting overtime pay and other benefits. "The Japanese-type management system, such as the seniority system or lifetime employment, cannot be continued," said Isao Nakauchi, chairman, president and chief executive of Japan's largest retailer, Daiei Inc., which is grappling with a huge debt and a slowdown in consumption.

It's not that Mr. Nakauchi or any other executive here thinks lifetime employment does not have its place in Japanese industry. Everyone is well aware of the benefits of having a core group of committed employees. "Employment stability is still the biggest obligation an employer has," Mr. Matsui said.

Mr. Murayama of Matsushita agrees—to a point. "If we lose that totally, we won't have success competing with America," he said. "But those types of people who elect big businesses like Matsushita because they're looking for a stable, steady, comfortable environment, they make me a little uneasy."

Matsushita, a pillar of Japan Inc., has been cautiously chipping away at the traditional mold. The salaries of its 11,000 managers are determined by merit, not seniority, and it is negotiating with its union over a similar plan for the rest of its 83,000 employees in Japan.

This year, it introduced a performance-based stock option plan for management, and it is seeking a cost-effective way to push the mandatory retirement age to 65 from 60. With its low birth rate, Japan will eventually face a labor shortage that could be partly addressed by reversing the trend toward early retirement and extending working life—seniority-based pay makes older employees too expensive. If birth rates do not increase, the population will plummet from 125 million today to a stunning 55 million by the year 2100, according to government forecasts.

"We need team spirit, yes, but at the same time we need creative, independent thinkers who want to work outside the team," Mr. Murayama said. "To those people, the uniform pay system is something frustrating, something that gets in the way of human development."

Matsushita's retirement plan, however, seems to be somewhat of a novelty in Japan. Japan has nothing like a 401(k) program, and the notion of self-directed investment for retirement—an idea that has taken hold in the United States—is as alien as the thought of wearing shoes in the house.

Nonetheless, most Japanese are well aware that they will probably have to pay for a good portion of their retirement themselves because, all things remaining the same, the government pension fund is likely to run dry in 2025.

As for Matsushita, it is hoping the new program will attract a higher caliber of job applicant. "One of our frustrations has been that we can't recruit above-average students so easily," Mr. Murayama said. "The traditional pay system is regarded as limiting to creativity, so those creative people we want to attract look elsewhere for a job."

The new retirement program gives recruits a choice of three plans. They can, as Mr. Takamatsu did, opt to have pension benefits paid out to them as they go; they can have a portion paid out and leave a portion under the company's administration, or they can choose the traditional, lump-sum-on-retirement system.

Even in the traditional system, workers normally get a partial payment if they leave a company before retirement, but job switching has been rare, and with lifetime employment the norm, openings scarce. And while Matsushita guarantees a respectable 7.5 percent return on workers' retirement money, some employees think they can do better.

Tomohiko Hasegawa, who graduated from Meiji University this year with a law degree, chose the conventional system. It's not that Mr. Hasegawa, a 23-year-old lawyer hoping for an international posting with Matsushita in the future, isn't interested in managing his own money. But he figures he can do that by setting aside a portion of his salary.

"I have no plans to switch jobs, so why shouldn't I participate in the company plan," he said. "I'm planning to stay for a long time." Much to Matsushita's surprise, however, 39 percent of its new employees opted for the nontraditional plans.

Many of them were women like Yuka Kitadai, 22, who often do not view their careers as lifetime endeavors. Ms. Kitadai, who graduated from Keio University, chose the plan that pays her the retirement allowance portion of her total benefits package but allows her to participate in programs for housing loans and other company-sponsored investment options.

"I want to be able to use it now," she said. "I thought I could invest it myself or use it to travel and learn some other languages on my own." While she's aware that as a novice to investing, she may lose the money, Ms. Kitadai said she was prepared to take that chance. She does not expect to be laid off, but she wants to be ready just in case.

"One of the reasons I want to start learning another language is because I think I'm going to have to protect myself with my own skills," Ms. Kitadai said. "That way even if I got laid off by Matsushita, I could use my skills to find another job."

Ms. Kitadai was among the 31 percent of new employees who opted for "Plan B," which pays out retirement allowances along with the semiannual bonus but allows participants to invest in various company savings plans at attractive rates, take part in the company's stock purchase plan and qualify for special loans for their children's education and scholarships. Under that plan, a new employee who makes less than $1,478 a month would receive $597 a year in retirement pay.

"Plan A," the more radical of the company's three retirement plans, was selected by 8 percent of new employees, who had to have a specialty like law or engineering to qualify; such people would presumably have more job options in the future. They chose to forego participation in company savings, housing and stock programs in exchange for additional compensation: a new employee earning less than $1,478 a month gets $1,418 a year in advance retirement payments.

Like Ms. Kitadai, Shinichi Yamane, a graduate of Ohio State University, opted for Plan B. He liked it because it offered him the chance for some extra cash but also protected a bit of his future by allowing him to participate in various company benefits.

"I thought choosing Plan A was a little risky, but I also thought it might be better to get some of the money in my younger years rather than when I'm too old to enjoy it," he said.

Mr. Yamane, a 28-year-old electrical engineer, will join the semiconductor development division when his initial training is finished. He said he planned to use the additional money that will come with his first bonus on a new stereo, clothes, perhaps even a car.

Like Mr. Yamane, Mr. Takamatsu agreed that his choice, Plan A, raised the stakes for him considerably, but he was sanguine. "There are no guarantees anymore here," he said. "I have to take responsibility for my own future."

SOURCE: Stephanie Strom, International Business: Japan's New "Temp" Workers'; Rethinking Lifetime Jobs and Their Underpinnings (June 17, 1998) [online]. Available: *www.nytimes.com*, accessed October 3, 2002.

CHAPTER

13 COMPENSATING EXECUTIVES

Chapter Outline

Learning Objectives

In this chapter, you will learn about

1. Components of executive core compensation
2. Components of executive fringe compensation
3. Principles and processes of setting executive compensation
4. Executive compensation disclosure rules
5. The executive compensation controversy: Are U.S. executives paid too much?

Executive compensation practices in U.S. companies have received substantial attention in the press. As we will see in this chapter, executive pay practices have raised concerns that many executives receive lucrative compensation and benefits even when company performance falls below shareholder expectations. Many critics have questioned whether such practices may interfere with some executives' motivation to achieve excellent performance. The "Compensation in Action" feature at the end of this chapter describes optimal executive compensation packages that deliver the most value to a company while motivating and rewarding executives.

CONTRASTING EXECUTIVE PAY WITH PAY FOR NONEXECUTIVE EMPLOYEES

From an economic standpoint, the chief executive officer (CEO) is the seller of his or her services, and the compensation committee is the buyer of these services. Under classic economic theory, a reasonable price is obtained through negotiations that are arm's length between an informed seller and an informed buyer. An awkward situation can result when the CEO hires a professional compensation director or compensation consultant. In this case, the compensation consultant who makes the recommendation to the compensation committee works for the CEO. In theory, the CEO hires the consultant to perform an objective analysis of the company's executive pay package and to make whatever recommendations the consultant feels are appropriate. This relationship has the potential to promote a conflict of interest because of the perceived pressure for the consultant to protect the CEO's financial interests. The irony is that the consultant is often viewed as representing the shareholders' interests. In a sense, the buyers of the CEO's services are the shareholders and their representatives, the compensation committee of the board of directors. They tend to act upon the compensation consultant's recommendation [1].

This passage illustrates just one of the main differences between compensating executives and compensating other employees. There are many other contrasts. The income disparity between executives and other employees is astounding. The median annual earnings for production and other nonsupervisory employees was $31,044 in 2001 [2]. The 20 top-paid CEOs received an approximate average $5.6 million [3].

PRINCIPLES OF EXECUTIVE COMPENSATION: IMPLICATIONS FOR COMPETITIVE STRATEGY

Executives are the top leaders in their companies. Intuitively, it seems reasonable that executives should earn substantial compensation packages. After all, their skills and experience enable them to develop and direct the implementation of competitive strategies. Few dispute the key role executives play in promoting competitive advantage. However, public scrutiny of executive compensation packages intensified during the 1990s because of heightened concerns about global competitiveness and the rampant corporate downsizing initiatives that left hundreds of thousands of employees jobless. We take up the executive compensation controversy later in this chapter. Next, we review fundamental concepts—defining executive status and the components of executive compensation packages.

DEFINING EXECUTIVE STATUS

Who Are Executives?

Virtually all the components of executive compensation plans provide favorable tax treatment for both the executive and the company. Who are executives? From a tax regulation perspective, the Internal Revenue Service (IRS) recognizes two groups of employees who play a major role in a company's policy decisions: highly compensated employees and key employees. The IRS uses "key employees" to determine the necessity of top-heavy provisions in employer-sponsored qualified retirement plans that cover most nonexecutive employees; it uses "highly compensated employees" for nondiscrimination rules in employer-sponsored health insurance benefits (Chapter 11). Although these two designations were created for federal tax rule applications, employees in both groups typically participate in executive compensation and benefits plans.

FIGURE 13-1 Examples of Key Employees

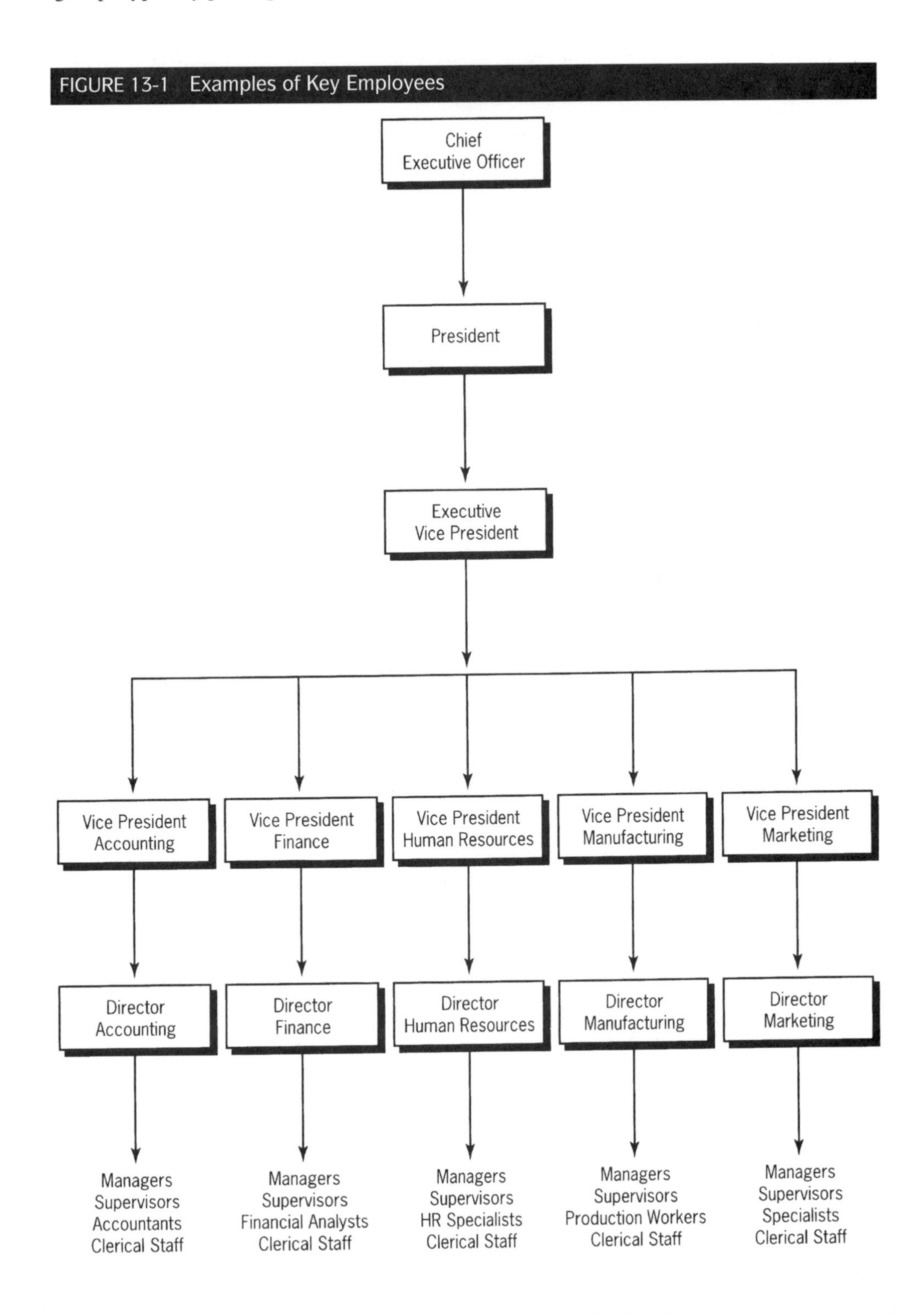

Key employees and highly compensated employees hold positions of substantial responsibility. Figure 13–1 illustrates the placement of key employees in a typical organizational structure. Although titles vary from company to company and in pay structures, CEOs, presidents, executive vice presidents, vice presidents of functional areas (for example, human resources), and directors below them usually meet the criteria for key employees.

Key Employees

The Internal Revenue Service defines a **key employee** as an employee who at any time during the current year is [4]:

- an officer of the employer having an annual compensation greater than $130,000 (indexed for inflation in increments of $5,000 beginning in 2003),
- a 5 percent owner of the employer, or
- a 1 percent owner of the employer having an annual compensation from the employer of more than $150,000.

U.S. Treasury Regulations define the term *officer* used in this definition of key employees [5]:

> Generally, the term officer means an administrative executive who is in regular and continued service. The term officer implies continuity of service and excludes those employed for a special and single transaction. An employee who merely has the title of an officer but not the authority of an officer is not considered an officer for purposes of the key employee test. Similarly, an employee who does not have the title of an officer but has the authority of an officer is an officer for purposes of the key employee test.

Highly Compensated Employees

The Internal Revenue Service (IRS) defines a **highly compensated employee** as one of the following if, during the current year or preceding year, he or she was [6]:

- a 5-percent owner at any time during the year or the preceding year, or
- for the preceding year had compensation from the employer in excess of $80,000 (indexed for inflation, $85,000 in 2001), and,
- if the employer elects the application of this clause for a plan year and was in the top-paid group of employees for the preceding year.

An employee is treated as a 5 percent owner for any year if at any time during the year the employee was a 5 percent owner of the employer. An employee is in the top-paid group of employees for any year if the employee is in the group consisting of the top 20 percent of the employees when ranked by compensation paid during the year.

EXECUTIVE COMPENSATION PACKAGES

Executive compensation has both core and fringe compensation elements, much like compensation packages for other employees. However, one noteworthy feature distinguishes executive compensation packages from nonexecutive compensation packages. Executive compensation packages emphasize long-term or deferred rewards over short-term rewards. The main components of executive compensation include:

- Current or annual core compensation
- Deferred core compensation: stock compensation
- Deferred core compensation: golden parachutes
- Fringe compensation: enhanced protection program benefits and perquisites

Components of Current Core Compensation

Executive current core compensation packages contain two components—annual base pay and bonuses. In 2001, the 20 top-paid CEOs received an approximate average $5.6 million [7]. Although quite high, current compensation dropped by more than 10 percent in just 1 year [8].

Base Pay

Base pay is the fixed element of annual cash compensation. Companies that use formal salary structures may have specific pay grades and pay ranges (Chapter 9) for nonexempt employees and exempt employees, including supervisory, management, professional, and executive jobs, with the exception of the CEO.

As discussed in Chapter 9, compensation professionals generally apply different range spreads across pay grades. Most commonly, they use progressively higher range spreads for pay grades that contain more valuable jobs in terms of a company's competitive strategies. Higher-level jobs afford employees greater promotion opportunities than entry-level jobs. Employees also tend to remain in higher pay grades longer, and the specialized skills associated with higher pay grade jobs are considered valuable. Therefore, it makes sense to apply larger range spreads to these pay grades.

Chief executive officer jobs do not fall within formal pay structures for two reasons. First, CEOs' work is highly complex and unpredictable. It is not possible to specify discrete responsibilities and duties. The choice of competitive strategy by CEOs and other executives and the influence of external and internal market factors (Chapter 2) make it impossible to describe CEOs' jobs. Second, setting CEO compensation differs dramatically from the rational processes compensation professionals use to build market-competitive pay structures (Chapter 8). We discuss agency theory, tournament theory, and social comparison theory later as explanations for setting CEO compensation.

Bonuses

Bonuses represent single pay-for-performance payments companies use to reward employees for achievement of specific, exceptional goals. As discussed in previous chapters, compensation professionals design bonuses for merit pay programs (Chapter 4), gain sharing plans and referral plans (Chapter 5), and sales incentive compensation programs (Chapter 9). Bonuses also represent a key component of executive compensation packages.

Companies' compensation committees recommend bonus awards to boards of directors for their approval (as discussed later in this chapter). Four types of bonuses are common in executive compensation:

- Discretionary bonus
- Performance-contingent bonus
- Predetermined allocation bonus
- Target plan bonus

As the term implies, boards of directors award **discretionary bonuses** to executives on an elective basis. They weigh four factors in determining the amount of discretionary bonus: company profits, the financial condition of the company, business conditions, and prospects for the future. For example, boards of directors may award discretionary bonuses to executives when a company's position in the market is strong.

Executives receive **performance-contingent bonuses** based on the attainment of specific performance criteria. The performance appraisal system for determining bonus awards is often the same appraisal system used for determining merit increases or general performance reviews for salary (Chapter 4).

Unlike the previous executive bonuses, the total bonus pool for the **predetermined allocation bonus** is based on a fixed formula. The central factor in determining the size of the total bonus pool and bonus amounts is company profits.

The **target plan bonus** ties bonuses to executives' performance. The bonus amount increases commensurately with performance. Executives do not receive bonuses when their performance falls below minimally acceptable standards. The target plan bonus differs from the predetermined allocation bonus in an important way: Predetermined allocation bonus amounts are fixed, regardless of how well executives perform.

Short-Term Incentives

Companies award short-term incentive compensation to executives to recognize their progress toward fulfilling competitive strategy goals. Executives may participate in current profit sharing plans and gain sharing plans. Table 13-1 describes these plans. We already discussed the use of current profit sharing plans and gain sharing plans for nonexecutive employees in Chapter 5. Whereas short-term objectives reward nonexempt and lower-level management employees for achieving major milestone work objectives, short-term incentives applied to executives are designed to reward them for meeting intermediate performance criteria. The performance criteria relate to the performance of a company as dictated by competitive strategy. Change in the company's earnings per share over a 1-year period, growth in profits, and annual cost savings are criteria that may be used in executives' short-term incentive plans.

Short-term incentive compensation programs usually apply to a group of select executives within a company. The plan applies to more than one executive because the synergy that results from the efforts and expertise of top executives influences corporate performance. The board of directors distributes short-term incentive awards to each executive based on rank and compensation levels. Thus, the CEO will receive a larger performance award than the executive vice president, whose position is lower than the CEO's position.

For example, let's assume that the CEO and executive vice president of a chain of general merchandise retail stores have agreed to lead the corporation as the lowest-cost chain of stores in the general merchandise retail industry. The CEO and her executive vice president establish a 5-year plan to meet this lowest-cost competitive strategy. The vice president of compensation recommends that the company adopt a gain sharing program to reward top executives for contributing to the cost reduction objective. After 1 year, the complementary decisions made by the CEO and executive vice

TABLE 13-1 Short-Term Incentive Compensation: Current Profit Sharing Plans and Gain Sharing Plans

Current Profit Sharing Plans

As we discussed in Chapter 5, profit sharing plans pay a portion of company profits to employees, separate from base pay, cost-of-living adjustments, or permanent merit pay increases. Two basic kinds of profit sharing plans are used widely today. First, current profit sharing plans award cash to employees, typically on a quarterly or annual basis. Second, deferred profit sharing plans place cash awards in trust accounts for employees. These trusts are set aside on employees' behalf as a source of retirement income. Current profit sharing plans provide cash to employees as part of their regular core compensation; thus, these payments are subject to IRS taxation when they are earned. Deferred profit sharing plans are not taxed until the employee begins to make withdrawals during retirement.

Gain Sharing Plans

As we discussed in Chapter 5, gain sharing describes group incentive systems that provide participating employees with an incentive payment based on improved company performance such as increased productivity, increased customer satisfaction, lower costs, or better safety records. Gain sharing was developed so that all employees could benefit financially from productivity improvements resulting from the suggestion system. Besides serving as a compensation tool, most gain sharing reflects a management philosophy that emphasizes employee involvement.

TABLE 13-2 Employee Stock Terminology

Stock Option. A right granted by a company to an employee to purchase a number of stocks at a designated price within a specified period of time.

Stock grant. A company's offering of stock to an employee.

Exercise of stock grant. An employees' purchase of stock, using stock options.

Disposition. Sale of stock by the stockholder.

Fair market value. The average value between the highest and lowest reported sales price of a stock on the New York Stock Exchange on any given date. The Internal Revenue Service specifies whether an option has a readily ascertainable fair market value at grant. An option has a readily ascertainable fair market value if the option is actively traded on an established stock exchange at the time the option is granted.

president have enabled the corporation to save $10,000,000. The board of directors agree that the executives' collaborative decisions led to noteworthy progress toward meeting the lowest-cost strategy and award the CEO 2 percent of the annual cost savings ($200,000) and 1 percent to the executive vice president ($100,000).

Components of Deferred Core Compensation

Stock Compensation

Deferred compensation refers to an agreement between an employee and a company to render payments to an employee at a future date. Deferred compensation is a hallmark of executive compensation packages. As an incentive, deferred compensation is supposed to create a sense of ownership, aligning the interests of the executive with those of the owners or shareholders of the company over the long term. The 20 top-paid CEOs earned an average of $101 million in long-term compensation during 2001, which represents more than a 494 percent increase from an average 1995 level of approximately $17 million [9]!

Apart from the incentive value, deferred compensation provides tax advantages to executives. In particular, deferring payment until retirement should lead to lower taxation. Why does deferment create a tax advantage? Executives do not pay tax on deferred compensation until they receive it. Presumably, executives' income tax rates will be substantially lower during retirement, when their total income is lower than while they are employed.

Company stock shares are the main form of executives' deferred compensation. As described in Chapter 5, **company stock** represents total equity of the firm. **Company stock shares** represent equity segments of equal value. Equity interest increases positively with the number of stock shares. Stocks are bought and sold every business day in a public stock exchange. The New York Stock Exchange is among the best-known stock exchanges. Table 13-2 lists basic terminology pertaining to stocks.

Companies design executive stock compensation plans to promote an executive's sense of ownership of the company. Presumably, a sense of ownership should motivate executives to strive for excellent performance. Generally, stock value increases with gains in company performance. In particular, a company's stock value rises in response to reports of profit gains. However, factors outside executives' control often influence stock prices despite executives' performance. For example, forecasts of economywide recession, increases in the national unemployment rate, and threats to national security (such as the September 11 attacks) often lead to declines in stock value.

Six particular forms of deferred (stock) compensation include:

- Incentive stock option plans
- Nonstatutory stock option plans
- Restricted stock
- Phantom stock plans

- Discount stock option
- Stock appreciation rights

Incentive Stock Options

Incentive stock options entitle executives to purchase their companies' stock in the future at a predetermined price. Usually, the predetermined price equals the stock price at the time an executive receives the stock option. In effect, executives are purchasing the stocks at a discounted price. Executives generally buy after the price has increased dramatically. An executive receives **capital gains** as the difference between the stock price at the time of purchase and the lower stock price at the time an executive receives the stock option. Executives receive income tax benefits by participating in incentive stock option plans. The federal government does not recognize capital gains until the disposition of the stock.

Nonstatutory Stock Options

Much like incentive stock options, companies award stock options to executives at discounted prices. In contrast to incentive stock options, **nonstatutory stock options** do not qualify for favorable tax treatment. Executives pay income taxes on the difference between the discounted price and the stock's fair market value at the time of the stock grant. They do not pay taxes in the future when they choose to exercise their nonstatutory stock options.

Nonstatutory stock options do provide executives an advantage. Ultimately, executives' tax liability is lower over the long term: Stock prices generally increase over time. As a result, the capital gains will probably be much greater in the future when executives exercise their options rather than when their companies grant these options.

Restricted Stock

The term **restricted stock** means that executives do not have any ownership control over the disposition of the stock for a predetermined period, often 5 to 10 years. Executives must sell the stock back to the company for exactly the same discounted price at the time of purchase if they terminate their employment before the end of the designated restriction period [10]. In addition, restricted stock grants provide executives tax incentives. They do not pay tax on any income resulting from an increase in stock price until after the restriction period ends [11]. Restricted stock is a common type of long-term executive compensation. Boards of directors award restricted stock to executives at considerable discounts.

Phantom Stock

A **phantom stock** plan is a compensation arrangement whereby boards of directors compensate executives with hypothetical company stocks rather than actual shares of company stock. Phantom stock plans are similar to restricted stock plans because executives must meet specific conditions before they can convert these phantom shares into real shares of company stock [12]. There generally are two conditions. First, executives must remain employed for a specified period, anywhere between 5 and 20 years. Second, executives must retire from the company. Upon meeting these conditions, executives receive income equal to the increase in the value of company stock from the date the company granted the phantom stock to the conversion date. Phantom stock plans provide executives with tax advantages. Executives pay taxes on the capital gains after they convert their phantom shares to real shares of company stock during retirement. Executives' retirement incomes will probably be significantly less than their incomes prior to retirement. Thus, the retirees' income tax rates will be lower.

Discount Stock Option Plans

Discount stock option plans [13] are similar to nonstatutory stock option plans with one exception. Companies grant stock options at rates far below the stock's fair market value on the date the option is granted. This means that the participating executive immediately receives a benefit equal to the difference between the exercise price and the fair market value of the employer's stock.

Stock Appreciation Rights

Stock appreciation rights provide executives income at the end of a designated period, much like restricted stock options. However, executives never have to exercise their stock rights to receive income. The company simply awards payment to executives based on the difference in stock price between the time the company granted the stock rights at fair market value to the end of the designated period, permitting the executives to keep the stock. Executives pay tax on any income from gains in stock value when they exercise their stock rights, presumably after retirement when their tax rates are lower [14].

Golden Parachutes

Most executives' employment agreements contain a golden parachute clause. **Golden parachutes** provide pay and benefits to executives after a termination resulting from a change in ownership or corporate takeover. Golden parachutes extend pay and benefits from 1 to 5 years, depending on the agreement. Planned retirement, resignation, or disability does not trigger golden parachute benefits. Boards of directors include golden parachute clauses for two reasons. First, golden parachutes limit executives' risks in the event of these unforeseen events. Second, golden parachutes promote recruitment and retention of talented executives.

Companies benefit from golden parachute payments because they can treat these payments as business expenses. This means that companies can reduce their tax liability by increasing the parachute amount. The total value of golden parachutes came to far exceed executives' annual income levels. Public outcry led to government-imposed intervention that limited tax benefits to companies. Generally, companies may receive tax deductions on golden parachutes that amount to less than three times an executive's average annual compensation for the preceding 5 years.

Fringe Compensation: Enhanced Protection Program Benefits and Perquisites

Executives receive discretionary benefits like other employees—protection program benefits, provide paid time-off, and employee services. However, executives' discretionary benefits differ in two ways. First, protection programs include supplemental coverage that provides enhanced benefit levels. Second, the services component contains benefits exclusively for executives. These exclusive executive benefits are known as **perquisites** or **perks.** Legally required benefits apply to executives, with the exception of one provision of the Family and Medical Leave Act of 1993.

Enhanced Protection Program Benefits

Supplemental life insurance and supplemental executive retirement plans distinguish protection programs for executive employees from protection programs for other employees. As discussed in Chapter 11, employer-provided life insurance protects employees' families by paying a specified amount to an employee's beneficiaries upon an employee's death. Most policies pay some multiple of the employee's salary—for instance, benefits paid at twice the employee's annual salary. Besides regular life insur-

TABLE 13-3 Alternative Life Insurance Plans for Executives

Split-Dollar Plans

The death benefit is divided or split between the employer and the employee's designated beneficiary. The premium can be paid entirely by the employer, or premium costs can be shared between the employer and employee. The employer does not receive a tax deduction for its share of the premium payments. However, employers are reimbursed for their premium payments by their share of the death benefit, which they receive tax free.

Death Benefit Only Plans

Death benefit only plans pay benefits only to a designated beneficiary upon the death of the employee. This arrangement avoids federal estate taxes on the death benefit. According to federal estate tax laws, death benefits are included in an employee's estate if he or she held the right to receive payment from the life insurance plan while alive (some life insurance plans do allow employees to receive payments under limited conditions while alive). Because the employee was never eligible to receive payment on the plan while alive, the death benefit only plan payments are not considered part of the estate and thus are not subject to estate taxes.

Group Term Life Insurance Plans

As we discussed in Chapter 11, term life insurance coverage is the most common type of life insurance offered by companies. These plans provide protection to employees' beneficiaries only during employees' employment. Group term life insurance plans provide greater amounts of insurance coverage to executives than to other employees.

Source: Adapted from Beam, B. T., Jr., & McFadden, J. J., 1996. *Employee benefits* (5th ed.). Chicago: Dearborn Financial Publishing.

ance, executives receive **supplemental life insurance** protection that pays an additional monetary benefit. Companies design executives' supplemental life insurance protection to meet two objectives [15]. First, supplemental life insurance increases the value of executives' estates bequeathed to designated beneficiaries (usually family members) upon their deaths. Life insurance programs may be designed to provide greater benefits than standard plans usually allow. Second, these programs provide executives with favorable tax treatments. Table 13-3 summarizes the main features of alternative life insurance plans for executives.

Supplemental retirement plans are designed to restore benefits restricted under qualified plans. As discussed in Chapter 11, qualified plans entitle employers to tax benefits from their contributions to pension plans. In general, this means that employers may take current tax deductions for contributions to fund future retirement income. Employees may also receive some favorable tax treatment (that is, a lower tax rate). In Chapter 11, we discussed the characteristics of qualified plans (Table 11-2). A qualified plan generally entitles employees to favorable tax treatment of the benefits they receive upon their retirement. Any investment income that is generated in the pension program is not taxed until the employee retires.

The Internal Revenue Service limited the annual earnings amount for determining qualified plan benefits to $200,000 in 2002 (beginning in 2003, indexed for inflation, in increments of $5,000). In general, all annual earnings above this level cannot be included in defined benefit plan formulas or the calculation of annual additions to defined contribution plans. Also, the Internal Revenue Service limits the annual benefit amounts for defined benefit plans to the lesser of $160,000 in 2002, indexed for inflation, or 100 percent of the highest average compensation for 3 consecutive years

TABLE 13-4 Common Executive Perks

- Company cars
- Financial services
- Legal services (for example, income tax preparation)
- Recreational facilities (for example, country club and athletic club memberships)
- Travel perks (for example, first-class airfare)
- Residential security
- Tickets to sporting events

[16]. Limits on annual additions to defined contribution plans were the lesser of $40,000 in 2002, indexed for inflation, or 100 percent of the participant's compensation [17]. For example, an executive's three highest annual salaries are $690,000, $775,000, and $1,100,000. The average of these three highest salaries is $855,000. Of course, $160,000 is less than $855,000. Thus, an executive's retirement income based on the company's qualified pension plan cannot exceed $160,000 adjusted for inflation.

A supplemental retirement plan can make up this difference. For illustrative purposes, let's assume that the annual benefit under a qualified pension plan is 60 percent of the final average salary for the past 15 years of service, which is $400,000. Based on this formula, the executive should receive an annual retirement benefit of $240,000 ($400,000 × 60%). This annual benefit exceeds $160,000—the statutory limit for qualified retirement plans. Because of the statutory limit, companies may offer a supplemental executive retirement plan that provides the difference between the value derived from the pension formula ($240,000) and the statutory limit ($160,000). In this example, the executive would receive a supplemental annual retirement benefit of $80,000.

Perquisites

Executive perquisites are an integral part of executive compensation. Perquisites cover a broad range of benefits, from free lunches to free use of corporate jets. Table 13-4 lists common executive perks. Perquisites serve two purposes. First, these benefits recognize executives' attained status. Membership in an exclusive country club reinforces executives' attained social status. Second, executives use perks for personal comfort or as a business tool. For example, a company may own a well-appointed cabin in Vail, Colorado. Executives may use the cabin for rest and relaxation or as a place to court new clients or close a lucrative business deal. Arranging relaxing weekends in Vail not only benefits executives and their families but also provides executives opportunities to develop rapport with prospective clients. Apple Computer awarded a $90 million Gulfstream V jet to Steven P. Jobs [18].

PRINCIPLES AND PROCESSES FOR SETTING EXECUTIVE COMPENSATION

We discussed the processes compensation professionals use to reward performance (merit pay and alternative incentive pay methods) and acquisition of job-related knowledge and skills (pay-for-knowledge and skilled-based pay) in previous chapters. Although pay-for-performance is the public rationale for setting executive compensation, reality often is quite different. Three alternative theories explain the principles and processes for setting executive compensation: agency theory, tournament theory, and social comparison theory. We begin by discussing the key players in setting executive compensation.

The Key Players in Setting Executive Compensation

Different individuals and groups participate in setting executive compensation. They include compensation consultants, compensation committees, and boards of directors. Each plays a different role in setting executive compensation.

Executive Compensation Consultants

Executive compensation consultants usually propose several recommendations for alternate pay packages. Oftentimes, executive compensation consultants are employed, by large consulting firms that specialize in executive compensation or advise company management on a wide variety of business issues. For example, Hay Associates, Hewitt Associates, Towers Perrin, and William M. Mercer are four widely known consulting firms that specialize in executive compensation.

Consultants make recommendations about what and how much to include in executive compensation packages based on strategic analyses, much like the analyses we discussed in Chapter 2. Recall that a **strategic analysis** entails an examination of a company's external market context and internal factors. Examples of external market factors include industry profile, information about competitors, and long-term growth prospects. Financial condition is the most pertinent internal factor regarding executive compensation. Strategic analyses permit compensation consultants to see where their client company stands in the market based on external and internal factors. Strong companies should be able to devote more financial resources to fund lucrative executive compensation programs than weaker companies. More often than not, executive compensation consultants find themselves in conflict of interest situations:

> Ostensibly, compensation consultants were hired by the CEO to perform an objective analysis of the company's executive pay package and to make whatever recommendations the consultant felt were appropriate. In reality, if those recommendations did not cause the CEO to earn more money than he was earning before the compensation consultant appeared on the scene, the latter was rapidly shown the door [19].

Executive compensation consultants' professional survival may depend on recommending lucrative compensation packages. Recommending the most lucrative compensation packages will quickly promote a favorable impression of the consultant among CEOs, leading to future consulting engagements.

Board of Directors

A **board of directors** represents shareholders' interests by weighing the pros and cons of top executives' decisions. Boards of directors have approximately 15 members. These members include CEOs and top executives of other successful companies, distinguished community leaders, well-regarded professionals (for example, physicians and attorneys), and possibly a few top-level executives of the company.

Boards of directors give final approval of the compensation committee's recommendation. Some critics of executive compensation have argued that CEOs use compensation to co-opt board independence [20]. CEOs often nominate candidates for board membership, and their nominations usually lead to candidates' placement on the board. Board members receive compensation for their service to the boards. Here are some examples based on year 2002 data available to the public per Security and Exchange Commission regulations (discussed under "Executive Compensation Disclosure Rules"): At General Electric (GE), board members receive annual monetary compensation of about $75,000 plus an additional $2,000 for each board committee meeting attended. Besides monetary and stock compensation, companies are using benefits such as medical insurance, life insurance, and retirement programs to attract top-notch individuals to join boards of directors. In general, board members' failure to cooperate with CEOs may lead to either fewer benefits or their removal.

> The board determines the pay of the CEO. But who determines the pay of the outside directors? Here, a sort of formal Japanese Kabuki has developed. The board of directors determines the pay of the CEO, and for all practical purposes, the CEO determines the pay of the board of directors. Is it any accident, then, that there is a statistical relationship between how highly the CEO is paid and how highly his outside directors are paid [21]?

As we discuss shortly, recent changes in Securities and Exchange Commission rulings have increased board members' accountability for approving sound executive compensation packages—supportive of shareholders' best interests.

Compensation Committee

Board of directors members within and outside the company make up a company's **compensation committee**. Outside board members serve on compensation committees to minimize conflict of interest. Thus, outside directors usually are the committee's membership majority.

Compensation committees perform three duties. First, compensation committees review consultants' alternate recommendations for compensation packages. Second, compensation committee members discuss the assets and liabilities of the recommendations. The complex tax laws require compensation committees to consult compensation experts, legal counsel, and tax advisors. Third, based on these deliberations, the committee recommends the consultant's best proposal to the board of directors for their consideration.

Theoretical Explanations for Setting Executive Compensation

Three prominent theories describe the processes related to setting executive compensation: agency theory, tournament theory, and social comparison theory. The following discussion provides concrete interpretations of these theories. In addition to the works cited throughout this chapter, several excellent scholarly journal articles provide full explanations of these theoretical frames as applied to executive compensation [22].

Agency Theory

Ownership is distributed among many thousands of shareholders in such large companies as Ford Motor Company, General Electric, General Motors, and IBM. For example, owning at least one share of stock in Ford Motor Company bestows ownership rights in Ford Motor Company. Each shareholder's ownership is quite small, amounting to less than 1 percent. Inability to communicate frequently or face-to-face to address business concerns is a major disadvantage of thousands of shareholders.

Under **agency theory**, shareholders delegate control to top executives to represent their ownership interests. However, top executives usually do not own majority shares of their companies' stocks. Consequently, executives usually do not share the same interests as the collective shareholders. These features make it possible for executives

STRETCHING THE DOLLAR

WORKERS' PERSPECTIVES ON U.S. EXECUTIVE COMPENSATION PRACTICES

Despite the rationale for CEO compensation levels in the United States, many workers are disgruntled. In particular, CEOs and company shareholders may be getting more bang for the buck. However, workers who rank relatively low in companies' job hierarchies believe they are getting less bang for the CEO buck. Here are some workers' perspectives:

DIALING FOR DECENCY

The CEO of our large telecommunications company will be receiving $4.27 million compensation this year, while 250 operators will be losing their jobs over the next 18 months. I have 34 years with the company, and the majority of my office (approximately 125 people) have an average of 18 to 20 years. We are being given the option of joining forces with operators in "right-to-work" states making $7 an hour less than we do, with drastically reduced vacation. If we join these other operators, our jobs will still not be secure, and we will lose severance pay ($1,100 per year worked) that we have accumulated. It does not seem fair that someone who claims our budget has been used up can still receive this kind of compensation while 250 operators stand to lose so much. I have given many years of my life to this company, and I am so ashamed of the way they treat not only their employees but also our customers, who are not getting the good service that they deserve. The company has reengineered so much that some offices have a majority of employees with less than two years' experience. Thank you for letting me vent.

SICK OF THE SITUATION

I have been a registered nurse for over 15 years. I now make about $1.60 to $2 an hour more than I did 15 years ago. During this time, my duties have greatly expanded. Sometimes, when the ward is less than full, I'm sent home with no pay. I worked years ago at a state hospital in Maryland and was active in AFSCME. In those days, we were at least listened to. Today the people that I work with are afraid to even mention unions openly. There is a general feeling that we have to take what we can get. No one in our health care system is willing to give anything but lip service to caring for people. The health care industry is increasing the workload of health care workers to cut costs, but I don't see any CEOs being sent home without pay, only those of us that have regular bills to pay. We are subjects of a repressive regime that is willing to do anything to the old and the poor to keep what they have, making sure we do not share the benefits of a booming economy. I feel too old to quit, too unempowered to complain, and too angry to care for people at the level they need. The hospitals don't care. Our company has just about found the bottom line they can get people to work for. They love it.

YOU'RE NOT ALONE IN A CROWD

I know I'm not alone when I say that the average worker is worse off now than before. Now, in addition to this being the age of the disposable employee (job security is a thing of the past), the CEOs are lining their pockets and packing their golden parachutes with not even the pretense of shame. If putting 500 long-time employees out of work will raise the stock price and increase the CEO's "performance" bonus, there isn't even so much as a thought or concern for the employees' welfare. The very employees who made the company a success do not count one iota. If they have to, the company will toss workers a bone . . . a big $1 an hour raise, while the CEO's feeling squeezed on a paltry $13 million a year . . . struggling families be damned. . . . "Don't let the door hit . . . on the way out" is the prevailing attitude of upper management. They do it because they can. No need to let annoying moral or ethical questions interfere with profits, right?

THIS LAND IS OUR LAND

Feel free to use my story as an incentive to get people to resist the destruction of the American middle class and working poor. Big profits and big salaries of CEOs are being fed by layoffs, downsizing, firings, and eliminating people who have invested years of loyalty in companies with the idea that eventually their loyalty would be repaid by a decent wage. This is true across the board in America—from professionals to factories—and we all need to stand together. Please do not use my name as I have no desire to be further cannibalized.

The CEO of my major media company is one of the richest men in the world. Yet, to "cut costs," fully half the company is now staffed by "temporaries." Employees are no longer employees but "associates," and are forbidden to discuss their salary or even listen to anyone else discuss his or her salary under threat of instant termination. The workforce has not offered the slightest resistance. Contrary to the current rhetoric, transnational corporations do not want people with knowledge, training, and experience. They want a completely conformist, sheeplike, and fearful workforce who will "buy into" all corporate dogma—referred to as "Corporate Culture."

Source: AFL-CIO (2000). Executive pay watch [online]. Available: *www.aflcio.org*.

to pursue activities that benefit themselves rather than the shareholders. The actions of executives on behalf of their own self-interest are known as the **agency problem** [23]. Specifically, executives may emphasize the attainment of short-term gains (increasing market share through lower costs) at the expense of long-term objectives (for example, product differentiation). Boards of directors may be willing to provide executives generous annual bonuses for attaining short-term gains.

Shareholders negotiate executive employment contracts with executives to minimize loss of control. Executive employment contracts define terms of employment pertaining to performance standards and compensation, specifically current and deferred compensation and benefits. The main shareholder objective is to protect the company's competitive interests. Shareholders use compensation to align executives' interests with shareholders' interests. As discussed earlier, boards of directors award company stock to align executives' interests with shareholders' interests.

Tournament Theory

Tournament theory casts lucrative executive compensation as the prize in a series of tournaments or contests among middle- and top-level managers who aspire to become CEO [24]. Winners of the tournament at one level enter the next tournament level. In other words, an employee's promotion to a higher rank signifies a win, and more lucrative compensation (higher base pay, incentives, enhanced benefits, and perks) represents the prize. The ultimate prize is promotion to CEO and a lucrative executive compensation package. The chance of winning competitions decreases dramatically as employees rise through the ranks: There are fewer positions at higher levels in corporate hierarchical structures. Figure 13-2 depicts a visual representation of CEO compensation as a tournament.

Social Comparison Theory

According to **social comparison theory**, individuals need to evaluate their accomplishments, and they do so by comparing themselves to similar individuals [25]. Demographic characteristics (for example, age or race) and occupation are common comparative bases. Individuals tend to select social comparisons who are slightly better than themselves [26]. Recently, researchers have applied social comparison theory to explain the processes for setting executive compensation [27].

As we discussed earlier, compensation committees play an important role in setting executive compensation, and compensation committees often include CEOs from other companies of equal or greater stature. Based on social comparison theory, compensation committee members probably rely on their own compensation packages and the compensation packages of CEOs in companies of equal or greater stature to determine executive compensation.

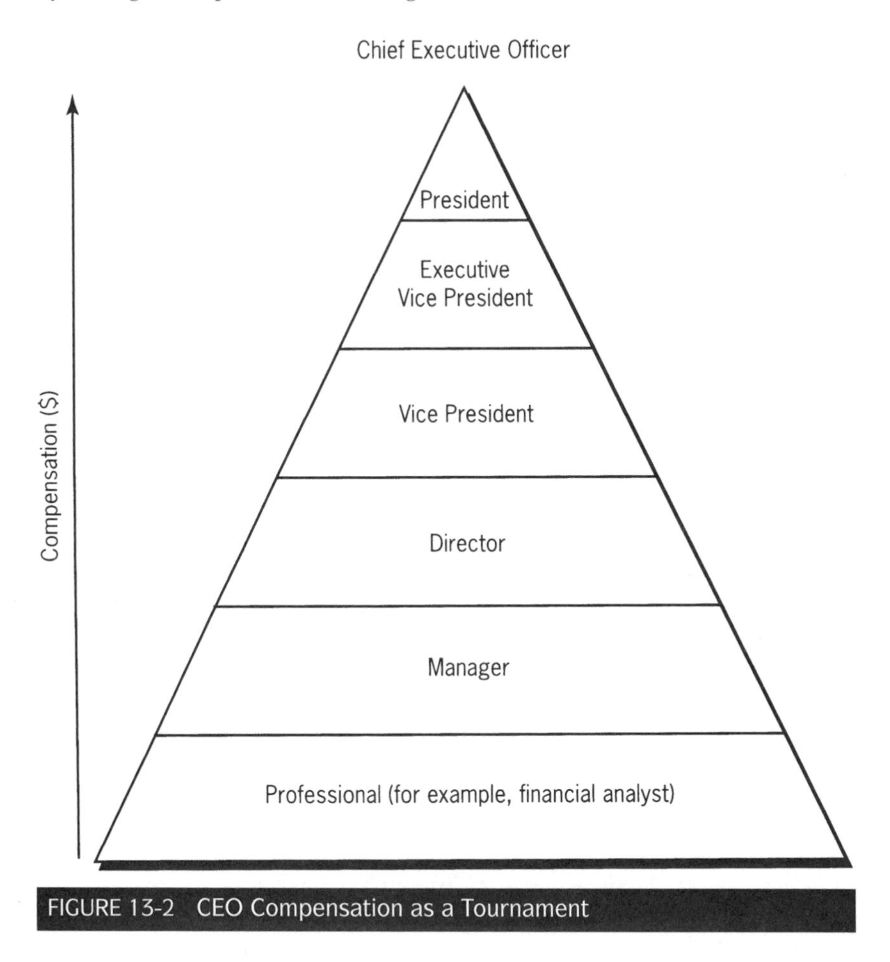

FIGURE 13-2 CEO Compensation as a Tournament

EXECUTIVE COMPENSATION DISCLOSURE RULES

Companies that sell and exchange securities (for example, company stocks and bonds) on public stock exchanges are required to file a wide variety of information with the **Securities and Exchange Commission** (SEC) including executive compensation practices. The Securities and Exchange Commission is a nonpartisan, quasijudicial federal government agency with responsibility for administering federal securities laws. The **Securities Exchange Act of 1934** applies to the disclosure of executive compensation.

In 1992 and 1993, the SEC modified its rules pertaining to the disclosure of executive pay [28]. Table 13-5 lists types of information about executive compensation that companies should disclose. The SEC rulings have two objectives. The first objective is to clarify the presentation of the compensation paid to the CEO and the four most highly paid executives. The second objective is to increase the accountability of company boards of directors for executive compensation policies and decisions. Companies' board members may be subject to personal liability for paying excessive compensation. Under securities law, publicly held corporations are required to disclose detailed information on executive compensation to shareholders and the public. Shareholders can bring derivative lawsuits on behalf of a corporation, claiming that executive compensation is excessive. Thus far, the courts are generally unwilling to substitute their judgment for the business judgment of a board of directors or compensa-

TABLE 13-5 Securities and Exchange Commission Disclosure Requirements for Executive Compensation

- Stock option and stock appreciation right tables
- Long-term incentive plan table
- Pension plan table
- Performance graph comparing the company's stock price performance against a market index and a peer group
- Report from the compensation committee of the board of directors explaining compensation levels and policies
- Description of the directors' compensation, disclosing all amounts paid or payable
- Disclosure of certain employment contracts and golden parachutes

tion committee. Nevertheless, these SEC rulings suggest that directors should exercise more independent judgment in approving executive compensation plans.

The SEC rules are presented in tabular and graphic forms, making information more accessible to the public at large than prior to the 1992 and 1993 modifications. These rules indirectly regulate compensation levels through enhanced public access to

TABLE 13-6 Summary Compensation Table

	Annual Compensation				
Name and Principal Position	*Year*	*Salary*	*Bonus*	*Other Annual Compensation*[1]	*Total Annual Compensation*
John F. Welch, Jr.	2001	$3,375,000	$12,700,000	$ 171,772	$16,246,772
Retired Chairman of the Board	2000	4,000,000	12,700,000	54,019	16,754,019
and Chief Executive Officer	1999	3,325,000	10,000,000	—	13,325,000
Jeffrey R. Immelt	2001	$2,750,000	$ 3,500,000	$ 137,954	$ 6,387,954
Chairman of the Board and Chief	2000	1,000,000	2,500,000	103,340	3,603,340
Executive Officer	1999	616,667	1,200,000	121,124	1,937,791
Dennis D. Dammerman	2001	$1,900,000	$ 4,200,000	$ 72,590	$ 6,172,590
Vice Chairman of the Board	2000	1,733,333	3,500,000	—	5,233,333
and Executive Officer	1999	1,400,000	2,800,000	—	4,200,000
Robert C. Wright	2001	$2,000,000	$ 3,725,000	$ 58,849	$ 5,783,849
Vice Chairman of the Board	2000	1,766,667	3,100,000	153,991	5,020,658
and Executive Officer	1999	1,495,833	2,500,000	105,463	4,101,296
Benjamin W. Heineman, Jr.	2001	$1,250,000	$ 2,225,000	$ 51,163	$ 3,526,163
Senior Vice President, General	2000	1,175,000	1,900,000	69,937	3,144,937
Counsel and Secretary	1999	1,050,000	1,560,000	97,036	2,707,036
Gary L. Rogers	2001	$1,391,304	$ 1,800,000	$ 130,330	$ 3,321,634
Vice Chairman of the Board	2000	1,116,667	1,500,000	165,792	2,782,459
and Executive Officer	1999	927,083	1,185,000	169,478	2,281,561

[1]This column includes the aggregate incremental cost to the company of providing various reportable perquisites and personal benefits in 2001, including financial counseling in 2001 for Mr. Welch ($143,479), Mr. Immelt ($44,908), Mr. Dammerman ($57,619), Mr. Wright ($15,300) and Mr. Heineman ($21,240), and the use of a car for Mr. Heineman in 2001 ($16,150). It also includes personal use of company aircraft in 2001 for Mr. Immelt ($83,200), Mr. Wright ($16,289), Mr. Heineman ($13,567), and for Mr. Rogers in 2001 ($114,342), in 2000 ($150,985) and in 1999 ($155,245).

TABLE 13-6 Summary Compensation Table (*cont.*)

		Long-Term Compensation		
		Awards	Payouts	
Name and Principal Position	*Year*	*Restricted Stock Units*[2]	*Number of Stock Options*	*LTIP Payouts*[3]
John F. Welch, Jr.	2001	—	—	—
Retired Chairman of the Board	2000	$48,715,625	3,000,000	—
and Chief Executive Officer	1999	—	1,875,000	$31,325,000
Jeffrey R. Immelt	2001	—	1,200,000	—
Chairman of the Board	2000	$15,000,000	550,000	—
and Chief Executive Officer	1999	—	375,000	$4,233,333
Dennis D. Dammerman	2001	—	1,012,500	—
Vice Chairman of the Board	2000	$13,093,750	550,000	—
and Executive Officer	1999	—	600,000	$8,522,135
Robert C. Wright	2001	—	750,000	—
Vice Chairman of the Board	2000	$10,475,000	400,000	—
and Executive Officer	1999	—	450,000	$10,258,333
Benjamin W. Heineman, Jr.	2001	—	262,500	—
Senior Vice President,	2000	$2,095,000	150,000	—
General Counsel and Secretary	1999	—	180,000	$3,823,913
Gary L. Rogers	2001	—	525,000	—
Vice Chairman of the Board	2000	$3,928,125	225,000	—
and Executive Officer	1999	—	270,000	$3,920,340

[2]This column shows the market value of restricted stock unit (RSU) awards on date of grant. The committee periodically grants restricted stock or RSUs to executives of the company. The aggregate holdings and market value of restricted stock and RSUs held on December 31, 2001, by the individuals listed in this table, are: Mr. Welch, no shares or units; Mr. Immelt, 758,388 shares or units/$30,396,191; Mr. Dammerman, 1,286,620 shares or units/$51,567,729; Mr. Wright, 1,470,383 shares or units/$58,932,950; Mr. Heineman, 662,023 shares or units/$26,533,881; and Mr. Rogers, 782,802 shares or units/$31,374,704. The restrictions on these shares and units lapse on a scheduled basis over the executive officer's career, or upon death, with the restrictions on 25% of the units generally scheduled to lapse three and seven years after the date of grant, and the restrictions on the remaining 50% scheduled to lapse at retirement. Regular quarterly dividends or dividend equivalents are paid on restricted stock and RSUs held by these individuals.

[3]These amounts represent the dollar value of payouts pursuant to the long-term financial performance incentive awards granted in 1997. Half of the amounts were paid in RSUs which are subject to forfeiture if the named executive terminates employment within three years following payment for any reason other than disability, death or retirement.

information by discouraging corporations from granting potentially embarrassing executive pay, especially when corporate performance is weak. There are several tables, but the most important here is the Summary Compensation Table [29], which discloses compensation information for the CEO and the four most highly paid executives over a 3-year period. Table 13-6 shows an excerpt of the Summary Compensation Table.

As you can see in Table 13-6, the Summary Compensation Table for GE covers the compensation paid to the named executive officers during the last completed fiscal year and the 2 preceding fiscal years. The table contains two main subheadings: annual compensation and long-term compensation. Annual compensation includes salary (base pay), bonus, and other annual compensation. Long-term compensation includes restricted stock awards, stock appreciation rights, and long-term incentive

TABLE 13-6 *(cont.)*

		All Other Compensation ($)			
Name and Principal Position	***Year***	***Payments Relating to Employee Savings Plan***[4]	***Earnings on Deferred Compensation***[5]	***Value of Supplemental Life Insurance Premiums***[6]	***Total***
John F. Welch, Jr.	2001	$340,375	$1,249,096	$1,056,859	$2,646,330
Retired Chairman of the Board	2000	315,050	974,005	1,269,064	2,558,119
and Chief Executive Officer	1999	242,350	746,383	51,050	1,039,783
Jeffrey R. Immelt	2001	$140,000	$ 27,643	$ 37,174	$204,817
Chairman of the Board and	2000	56,000	18,168	39,340	113,508
Chief Executive Officer	1999	36,500	13,152	25,075	74,727
Dennis D. Dammerman	2001	$127,750	$161,212	$ 17,738	$306,700
Vice Chairman of the Board	2000	109,650	107,696	26,444	243,790
and Executive Officer	1999	84,000	68,696	28,007	180,703
Robert C. Wright	2001	$ 70,050	$230,966	$ 17,768	$318,784
Vice Chairman of the Board	2000	61,850	149,649	28,698	240,197
and Executive Officer	1999	52,400	103,573	48,035	204,008
Benjamin W. Heineman, Jr.	2001	$ 77,050	$123,060	$ 13,862	$213,972
Senior Vice President,	2000	68,425	90,165	22,462	181,052
General Counsel and Secretary	1999	59,550	63,766	30,917	154,233
Gary L. Rogers	2001	$ 74,950	$106,019	$ 11,792	$192,761
Vice Chairman of the Board	2000	59,850	72,214	15,269	147,333
and Executive Officer	1999	50,800	63,961	21,768	136,529

[4]These amounts represent company payments of 3.5% of eligible pay made in connection with the company's Savings and Security Program.

[5]This compensation represents the difference between market interest rates determined pursuant to SEC rules and the 10% to 14% interest contingently credited by the company on salary deferred by the executive officers under various salary deferral plans in effect between 1987 and 2001. Under all such plans, the executive officers generally must remain employed by the Company for at least four years following the deferrals, or retire after the full year of deferral, in order to obtain the stated interest rate.

[6]This column includes the estimated dollar value of the company's portion of insurance premium payments for supplemental split-dollar life insurance provided to company officers. GE will recover all split-dollar premiums paid by it from the policies. The estimated value is calculated, in accordance with SEC rules, as if the 2001 premiums were advanced to the executive officers without interest until the time the company expects to recover its premium payments.

Source: GE annual report: Proxy statement [online]. Available: *http://www.ge.com/annual01/proxy/tables/summary_compensation.html*, accessed June 5, 2002.

payouts. The last column, "All Other Compensation ($)," is a catchall column to record other forms of compensation. Information in this column must be described in a footnote.

EXECUTIVE COMPENSATION: ARE U.S. EXECUTIVES PAID TOO MUCH?

Are U.S. executives paid too much? Popular press and newspaper accounts generally suggest that executives are overpaid. Of course, you should form your own opinion based on the following pertinent information:

- Comparison between executive compensation and other worker groups
- Strategic questions: Is pay for performance?

- Ethical considerations: Is executive compensation fair?
- International competitiveness

Comparison Between Executive Compensation and Compensation for Other Worker Groups

The median annual earnings of all full-time U.S. workers was $31,044 in 2001 [30]. Child care workers earned the least (median annual earnings = $12,792), and lawyers earned the most (median annual earnings = $72,696) [31]. In 2001, the 20 top-paid CEOs received an approximate average $5.6 million [32].

Strategic Questions: Is Pay for Performance?

There are several measures of corporate performance (Table 13-7). Are CEOs compensated commensurately with their companies' performance? It is difficult to answer just yes or no because the evidence is mixed. A study of the relationship

TABLE 13-7 Corporate Performance Measures
Size
• Sales • Assets • Profits • Market value • Number of employees
Growth
• Sales • Assets • Profits • Market value • Number of employees
Profitability
• Profit margin • Return on assets (ROA) • Return on equity (ROE)
Capital Markets
• Dividend yield • Total return to shareholders • Price/earnings ratio • Payout
Liquidity
• Current ratio • Quick ratio • Working capital from operations • Cash flow from operations
Leverage
• Debt-to-equity ratio • Short-term vs. long-term debt • Cash flow vs. interest payments

between Fortune 500 companies' CEO compensations and corporate performance found [33]:

- CEO annual base pay and annual bonuses showed strong positive relationships with pretax profit margins and return on equity. As company performance (as measured by pretax profit margins and return on equity) increased, so did CEO annual base pay and bonuses.
- All long-term CEO compensation components (for example, restricted stock, incentive stock options) were not significantly related to company performance (again, as measured by pretax profit margins and return on equity).

Since the publication of this study in 1995, several additional studies have examined the relationship between CEO pay and company performance. The evidence for substantiating this relationship is mixed. Therefore, a simple statement cannot be made about the relationship between CEO pay and company performance. Most often, shareholder returns describe company performance. For example, in 2001, Irwin Jacobs, CEO of Qualcomm, earned $5.8 million based on a shareholder return of 680 percent (that is, roughly the increase in the company's stock price between December 31, 1998, and December 31, 2001). On the other hand, John Chambers, CEO of Cisco Systems, earned $279.3 million, but Cisco's stock price declined by 70 percent!

Ethical Considerations: Is Executive Compensation Fair?

Is executive compensation fair? Three considerations drive this question: companies' abilities to attract and retain top executives, income disparities between executives and other employees, and layoffs of thousands of nonexecutive employees.

Attract and Retain Top Executives

Many compensation professionals and board of directors members argue that the trends in executive compensation are absolutely necessary for attracting and retaining top executives. Presumably, executives' decisions directly promote competitive advantage by positioning companies to achieve lowest-cost and differentiation strategies effectively. In Chapter 3, we indicated that competitive advantage invigorates the economy by increasing business activity, employment levels, and individuals' abilities to participate in the economy as consumers of companies' products and services.

Income Disparities

Table 13-8 illustrates the marked income disparity between annual pay for various nonexecutive jobs and pay for CEOs. The typical annual earnings for the lowest-paid occupation (child care workers) amounted to a mere 0.25 percent (yes, one-quarter of 1 percent) of the average annual CEO salary and bonus. The ratio of highest-paid occupation (lawyers) to the average annual CEO salary and bonus was not much better—1.42 percent. Said differently, the typical CEO's annual salary plus bonus was 398 times greater than the typical child care worker's annual pay and 70 times greater than the typical lawyer's annual pay! The income disparity between executives and nonexecutive employees is increasing. A worker earning $25,000 in 1996 would have earned $94,715 in 2002 (expected $177,470 in 2005) if his or her pay rose as quickly as CEO pay for the same period [34].

Layoffs Borne by Workers but Not Executives

Millions of workers have been laid off since 1990. In 1995 alone, more than 750,000 employees lost their jobs; the number of layoffs increased to 7,678,000 in 2001, representing a 934 percent increase [35]. Top management typically advances several reasons that necessitate these layoffs—global competition, reductions in product demand,

TABLE 13-8 Selected Median Annual Nonexecutive Earnings 2001

Occupation	*Annual Earnings ($)*
Lawyers	72,696
Physicians	65,416
Aerospace engineers	64,792
Airplane pilots and navigators	59,800
College and university teachers	52,468
Personnel and labor relations managers	48,048
Firefighters	41,340
Accountants and auditors	40,196
Elementary school teachers	38,480
Electricians	37,128
General office supervisors	30,784
Correctional institution officers	29,796
Automobile mechanics	28,132
Secretaries	24,700
Bus drivers	23,764
File clerks	20,904
Janitors and cleaners	18,980
Nursing aides, orderlies, and attendants	18,720
Waiters and waitresses	17,212
Farm workers	16,276
Teachers' aides	15,912
Child care workers	12,792

Source: U.S. Bureau of Labor Statistics (2002). *Employment and earnings*. Washington, DC: U.S. Government Printing Office.

technological advances that perform many jobs more efficiently than employees, mergers and acquisitions, establishing production operations in foreign countries with lower labor costs, and the steep economic downturn following the September 11 terrorist attacks. A scant few executives lost their jobs, as millions of workers lost their jobs between 1990 and 2001.

International Competitiveness

Increased global competition has forced companies in the United States to become more productive. Excessive expenditures on compensation can threaten competitive advantage. Compensation expenditures are excessive when they outpace the quality and quantity of employees' contributions. In addition, compensation expenditures may be excessive when they are substantially higher than competitors' compensation outlays. Concerns about U.S. companies' competitiveness in global markets are common because of the vast differences in compensation levels between the CEOs of U.S. and foreign companies.

International Compensation Comparisons

Comparisons between U.S. executive compensation and foreign executives' compensation can be made on two dimensions: total compensation amount and components.

Securities and Exchange Commission (SEC) rules require the disclosure of executive compensation in U.S. companies. However, comparable rules do not exist in for-

FLIP SIDE OF THE COIN

IN DEFENSE OF U.S. EXECUTIVE COMPENSATION PRACTICES

Popular press accounts of U.S. executive compensation practices generally advance two criticisms. First, executive compensation levels are unwarranted when the relationship between executive compensation and company performance is tenuous. Second, executives do not deserve to earn as much as they do, particularly when they authorize mass layoffs to promote competitiveness. Consider these responses in defense of U.S. executive compensation practices.

Criticism 1: Executive compensation levels are unwarranted when the relationship between executive compensation and company performance is tenuous. This criticism is consistent with basic pay-for-performance principles: Reward employees commensurately with their performance. Critics should adopt a multiyear view of corporate performance when judging the appropriateness of executive pay levels. Consistent with competitive strategies, it may be several years before the fruits of sound strategic planning are realized. In addition, factors beyond executives' control (for example, an increase in interest rates that leads consumers to spend less money on products and services) may result in lackluster short-term corporate performance.

Criticism 2: Executives do not deserve to earn as much as they do, particularly when they authorize mass layoffs to promote competitiveness. Some basic facts and assumptions are necessary before providing a response to this criticism:

- In 2001, the median annual earnings was $31,044 for production and nonsupervisory employees[1] Chief executive officers (CEOs) earned an average of $5,600,000 in annual salary and bonuses during 2001.[2]
- Let's assume that U.S. CEO compensation should be similar to a typical Japanese CEO's total compensation. Japanese CEOs typically earned a total $508,106 (annual salary, bonus, and deferred compensation) in 2001. About 65 percent of this total was awarded as salary and annual bonuses. Thus, $508,106 × 65% = $330,269.
- Based on this assumption, U.S. CEOs earned an average excess totaling $4,969,731 (that is $5,600,000 – $330,269).

Therefore, approximately 160 employees, on average, would retain their jobs ($4,969,731/ $31,044) for 1 year if the company's CEO reduced his compensation by $4,969,731. Although the livelihood of 160 employees is important, a broader perspective may be necessary. Saving 160 jobs in one year may lead to dire future consequences if the company is unable to retain a highly qualified CEO. Losing such a CEO may result in poorer corporate performance that, in turn, may lead to permanent job loss for thousands.

[1]U.S. Bureau of Labor Statistics (January 2002). *Employment and earnings*. Washington, DC: Government Printing Office.
[2]Lavalle, L., with Jesperson, F. F., & Arndt, M. (2002). Special report: Executive pay. *Business Week* (April 15), pp. 81–84, 86.

eign countries. Consequently, it is difficult to make detailed comparisons between U.S. and foreign executive compensation.

Research indicates that U.S. CEOs earn significantly more than their foreign counterparts. The following states the typical foreign CEO pay (including annual salary and bonus, deferred compensation, benefits, and perks) in 2001 [36].

- Hong Kong: $736,599
- United Kingdom: $668,526
- Singapore: $645,740
- Venezuela: $635,055
- Italy: $600,319
- Australia: $546,914

- France: $519,060
- Japan: $508,106
- Brazil: $492,465
- Germany: $454,974
- Spain: $429,725
- South Korea: $214,836
- Thailand: $137,581

Undermining U.S. Companies' Ability to Compete

At present, there is no evidence showing that U.S. executive compensation pay practices have undermined U.S. companies' ability to compete with other companies in the global marketplace. Might executive compensation practices undermine U.S. companies' competitiveness in the future?

On one hand, it is reasonable to predict that CEO pay will not undermine U.S. companies' ability to compete because CEO pay increased as company profits increased. On the other hand, the current wave of widespread layoffs may hinder U.S. companies' competitiveness. As you recall from Chapter 2, U.S. companies use layoffs to maintain profits and cut costs, heightening workers' job insecurities. The remaining workers may lose their faith in pay-for-performance systems and their trust in their employers as colleagues lose their jobs; yet, CEOs continue to receive higher compensation. Workers may not feel that working hard will lead to higher pay or job security. Thus, they may choose not to work proficiently. Consequently, reduced individual performance and destabilized workforces may make it difficult for U.S. companies to compete against foreign companies.

SUMMARY

We reviewed the components and principles of executive compensation. The components include base pay, bonuses, short-term incentives, stock and stock option plans, enhanced benefits, and perquisites. Next, we examined the principles and processes underlying executive compensation. Finally, we addressed whether U.S. executive compensation is excessive. Although popular press accounts suggest that it is, you will have to form your own opinion, particularly as you assume compensation management responsibilities for your employer. As a compensation professional, you are likely to face many difficult questions from employees regarding the rationale for and the fairness of lucrative executive compensation packages.

Key Terms

- key employee, 412
- highly compensated employee, 412
- discretionary bonuses, 413
- performance-contingent bonuses, 413
- predetermined allocation bonus, 414
- target plan bonus, 414
- deferred compensation, 415
- company stock, 415
- company stock shares, 415
- incentive stock options, 416
- capital gains, 416
- nonstatutory stock options, 416
- restricted stock, 416
- phantom stock, 416
- discount stock option plans, 417
- stock appreciation rights, 417
- golden parachutes, 417
- perquisites, 417
- perks, 417
- supplemental life insurance, 418
- supplemental retirement plans, 418
- executive compensation consultants, 420
- strategic analysis, 420
- board of directors, 420
- compensation committee, 421
- agency theory, 421
- agency problem, 423
- tournament theory, 423
- social comparison theory, 423
- Securities and Exchange Commission, 424
- Securities Exchange Act of 1934, 424

Discussion Questions

1. What can be done to make the function of compensation committees consistent with shareholders' interests? Explain your answer.
2. Which component of compensation is most essential to motivate executives to lead companies toward competitive advantage? Discuss your rationale.
3. Discuss your position on executive compensation. Is executive compensation excessive or appropriate?
4. Discuss the differences between enhanced benefits and perquisites.
5. Consult the three most recent *Business Week* special reports on executive compensation. These reports appear in the issues published during the third week of April. Pick a company that appears in the survey each year, and note the information about annual and long-term compensation. Next, review some recent materials that describe the industry and future prospects (for example, consult newspapers, business periodicals, trade magazines, or company information on the Internet, which we discussed in Chapter 2). Finally, write a one-page report summarizing your selected company's current condition and future prospects. Then, comment on whether you believe that the 3-year trend in executive compensation is appropriate. Explain your rationale.

Exercises

Compensation Online

For Students

Exercise 1: Find relevant articles

It's debate time again! This time you will be arguing over the fairness of current executive compensation practices. Use your school library's online catalog to locate articles pertaining to the agency theory, deferred compensation, the golden parachute, capital gains, and stock options. Find and read several current articles in these areas.

Exercise 2: Research executive compensation information

Using the Yahoo search engine, click on advanced search, type in "executive compensation," choose the exact phrase match search method, and click on the search button. Select Business and Economy > Employment and Work > Employee Benefits, and click on Executive Compensation and Employee Benefits—articles and news summaries concerning compensation, pensions, benefits, stock ownership, and other issues. Choose one of the articles, read it, and write a brief summary of what you learned by reading the article.

Select another search engine and conduct an "executive compensation" search. Compare and contrast the results of both searches.

Exercise 3: Review an organization's Web site

On the AFL-CIO Web site, click the "Pay Watch" link. Look up the compensation packages of several executives, and read about organized labor's views regarding executive compensation. Write a short paper outlining points you agree with, what you disagree with, and why.

For Professionals

Exercise 1: Understand stock options

Stock options are a large part of executive compensation packages. To get a better understanding of stock options go to the Chicago Board of Trade Web site at *cbot.com/*. Read over this Web site and write a brief summary describing what stock options are and their advantages and disadvantages as compensation benefits.

Exercise 2: Keep up with current events in HR

An executive in your firm has taken issue with his current compensation package. He believes he is worth much more and can find it somewhere else. You have been assigned the task of researching how much of his opinion is actually true. Using Yahoo, conduct an advanced search for "executive compensation." Click the "News" tab at the top of the resulting page and read some of the articles. Pick out an issue or trend that you notice in the articles and summarize what it is and why you believe it is happening.

Exercise 3: Learn important terms

You will be working with some senior-level analysts from the finance department to develop a stronger stock option plan to aid in recruiting top executive talent. To prepare yourself and make sure you have your proverbial ducks in a row before the first meeting, search for "financial glossary" or "financial terms." Look over some terms that may have been mentioned in this chapter and others, and make sure you understand their meaning.

Endnotes

1. Walters, B., Hardin, T., & Schick, J. (1995). Top executive compensation: Equity or excess? Implications for regaining American competitiveness. *Journal of Business Ethics*, *14*, pp. 227–234.
2. Bureau of Labor Statistics. (January 2002). *Employment and Earnings*. Washington, DC: Government Printing Office.
3. Lavelle, L., with Jespersen, F. F., & Arndt, M. (2002). Special report: Executive pay. *Business Week*, April 15, pp. 81–84, 86.
4. Internal Revenue Code, § 416 (i).
5. Treas. Reg. § 1.416-1, Q13.
6. Internal Revenue Code, § 414 (q).
7. Lavelle, L., with Jespersen, F. F., & Arndt, M. (2002). Special report: Executive pay. *Business Week*, April 15, pp. 81–84, 86.
8. Lavelle, L., with Jespersen, F. F., & Arndt, M. (2002). Special report: Executive pay. *Business Week*, April *15*, pp. 81–84; 86.
9. Byrne, J. A., with Bongiorno, L. (1995). CEO pay: Ready for takeoff. *Business Week*, April 25, pp. 88–94.
10. Internal Revenue Code 83; Treasury Regulations 1.83-1(b)(2), 1.83-1(e), 1.83-2(a).
11. Internal Revenue Code 83; Treasury Regulations 1.83-1(b)(1), 1.83-1(c).
12. Internal Revenue Code 61, 83, 162; Treasury Regulations 1.83.
13. Ibid.
14. Internal Revenue Code 61, 83, 162, 451; Treasury Regulations 1.83.
15. Beam, B. T., Jr., & McFadden, J. J. (1996). *Employee Benefits* (4th ed.). Chicago: Dearborn Financial Publishing.
16. I.R.C. § 415 (b).
17. I.R.C. § 415 (c).
18. Lavelle, L. with Jespersen, F. F., and bureau reports (2001). Executive pay. *Business Week*, no. 3728, April 16, pp. 176–80.
19. Crystal, G. S. (1991). Why CEO compensation is so high. *California Management Review*, *34*, pp. 9–29.
20. Ibid.
21. Ibid.
22. Agency Theory: Eisenhardt, K. M. (1989). Agency theory: An assessment and review. *Academy of Management Review*, *14*, pp. 57–74; Jensen, M., & Meckling, W. H. (1976). Theory of the firm: Managerial behavior, agency costs, and ownership structure. *Journal of Financial Economics*, *3*, pp. 305–360; Tosi, H. L., Jr., & Gòmez-Mejía, L. R. (1989). The decoupling of CEO pay and performance: An agency theory perspective. *Administrative Science Quarterly*, *34*, pp. 169–189; Goodman, P. S. (1974). An examination of referents used in the evaluation of pay. *Organizational Behavior and Human Performance*, *12*, pp. 170–195; Lazear, E., & Rosen, S. (1981). Rank-order tournaments as optimum labor contracts. *Journal of Political Economy*, *89*, pp. 841–864; O'Reilly, C. A., III, Main, B. G., & Crystal, G. S. (1988). CEO compensation as tournament and social comparison: A tale of two theories. *Administrative Science Quarterly*, *33*, pp. 257–274.
23. Jensen, M. C., & Meckling, W. H. (1976). Theory of the firm: Managerial behavior, agency costs, and ownership structure. *Journal of Financial Economics*, *3*, pp. 305–360.
24. Lazear, E., & Rosen, S. (1981). Rank-order tournaments as optimum labor contracts. *Journal of Political Economy*, *89*, pp. 841–864.
25. Festinger, L. (1954). A theory of social comparison processes. *Human Relations*, *7*, pp. 117–140.
26. Tversky, A., & Kahneman, D. (1974). Judgment and uncertainty: Heuristics and biases. *Science*, *185*, pp. 1124–1131.
27. O'Reilly, C. A., III, Main, B. G., & Crystal, G. S. (1988). CEO compensation as tournament and social comparison: A tale of two theories. *Administrative Science Quarterly*, *33*, pp. 257–274.
28. SEC Release No. 33–6962 (Oct. 16, 1992); SEC Release No. 33–6940 (July 10, 1992); SEC Release No. 34–33229 (Nov. 29, 1993).
29. Summary Compensation Table: 17 C.F.R 229.402(b),

as amended Nov. 29, 1993, effective Jan. 1, 1994.

30. Bureau of Labor Statistics. (January 2002). *Employment and Earnings*. Washington, DC: Government Printing Office.
31. Ibid.
32. Lavelle, L., with Jespersen, F. F., & Arndt, M. (2002). Special report: Executive pay. *Business Week*, April 15, pp. 81–84, 86.
33. Klein, Marc-Andreas (1995). *Top Executive Pay for Performance*. New York: The Conference Board.
34. AFL-CIO. (2002). Executive paywatch [online]. Available: *www.aflcio.org/home.htm*, accessed July 18, 2002.
35. Bureau of Labor Statistics. (January 2002). *Employment and Earnings*. Washington, DC: Government Printing Office.
36. Towers Perrin. (2002). 2001 Worldwide Total Remuneration [online]. Available: *www.towers.com*.

COMPENSATION IN ACTION

FINDING THE SWEET SPOTS: OPTIMAL EXECUTIVE COMPENSATION

HOW TO DETERMINE THE BEST COMPENSATION PLAN FOR YOUR BUSINESS AND YOUR LEADERS

How much should executives be paid? How competitive should executive compensation be? Why should executive compensation be competitive? Compensation plan designers in search of answers to these questions can use a new way of obtaining optimal executive compensation (OEC).

OEC represents the "sweet spot," or a compensation package that delivers the most value to a company while motivating and rewarding executives. For the company and shareholders, it achieves the most return from the investment in executive compensation. For the executive, it represents a fair and equitable compensation package. These, in turn, provide an optimal scenario for the employee, business partners and customers.

Optimal executive compensation focuses on:

- **External competitiveness**. Executive compensation is market competitive so that the organization can attract, retain and motivate the right individuals.
- **Internal strategic fit**. Executive compensation is aligned to the organization's business strategies, supporting the creation of value for shareholders and employees.

Traditionally, executive compensation plan designers have done well in analyzing external competitiveness because it is simple to do and compensation data are abundantly available. However, the same cannot be said of analyzing internal strategic fit because it is less straightforward, requires an understanding of the business strategy and there is no formal methodology. Consequently, relying mostly on external competitiveness, required analysis causes certain inefficiencies to form in executive compensation by addressing current inefficiencies:

- **Insufficient link between company strategy and executive compensation.** Executive compensation often is set or justified using industry data independent of the company's business strategy. The desired process is to set the business strategy, then structure executive compensation that can drive and support the business strategy.
- **Companies paying executives with insufficient regard for the company and individual performance.** For example, executives are paid the median salary because the company's compensation strategy is to "pay the market median," regardless of the company's performance within the market or the type of executives needed in the organization. Stock options, a popular means of executive compensation, rise and fall in value primarily based on stock market movement and not necessarily the executives' performance.
- **The market inefficiencies in executive compensation spiral further inefficiencies.** Simply focusing on external competitiveness (and not enough internal strategic fit) in executive compensation design has forced companies to match changing market compensation levels regardless of whether changes are warranted.

This is a win-win proposition for the company and executives because few executives have to cope with compensation practices inefficiencies, allowing them to focus on the business at hand. Appropriately applied, it will help attain market efficiency in executive compensation for the benefit of the company, employees and, ultimately, the public. (See Figure 1.)

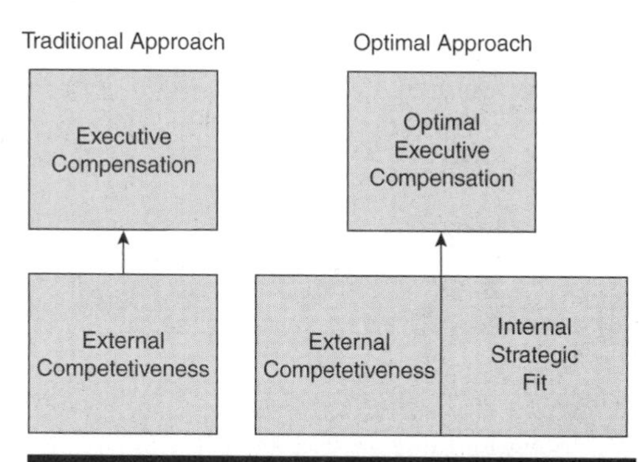

FIGURE 1 The Way to OEC

HOW DOES OEC WORK?

OEC is a concept rather than a predetermined formula because the internal strategic fit aspect of the analysis cannot be captured with a single formula for all companies. What goes into the formula and how it is analyzed should be customized and tailored to each circumstance.

The following is an example of designing optimal executive compensation for the CEO position in a specific segment of the financial industry. Although the data are actual and public information, company names are not disclosed to focus on the application of methodology rather than the specific companies. All information in this analysis was obtained from documents filed with the Securities and Exchange Commission, including the most recently available proxy statement for each company.

COMPARISON COMPANY PROFILES

Figure 2 shows the profiles of the select seven companies in the specific financial industry. Comparative and financial analysis show the following:

- There is a range of company size in terms of number of employees (from 331 to 1,114) and revenue (from $332 million to $1 billion).
- Company C shows a significantly higher revenue growth, primarily from its international operations, at the expense of profitability (net income and return on equity) and shareholder returns (earnings per share [EPS] changes). Company B, in spite of the median number of employees, had, by far, the lowest revenue and market capitalization, dismal net income and poor shareholder return.
- Companies D and E, with the highest market capitalization, had the highest net income. Company A, with the least number of employees, had the best shareholder return in the past five years. Companies F and G, overall, were close to the median levels.

FIGURE 2 Company Profitability

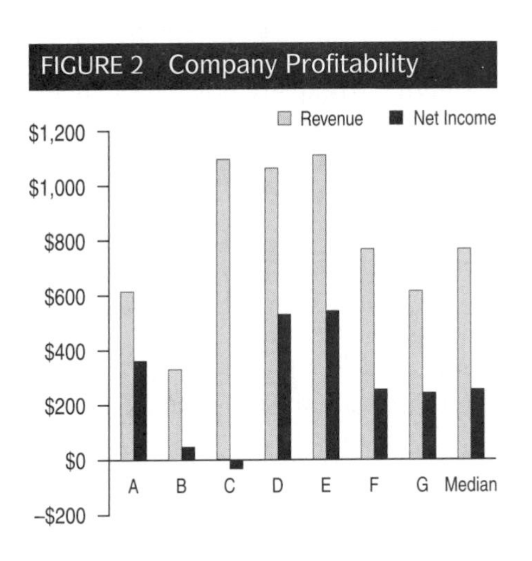

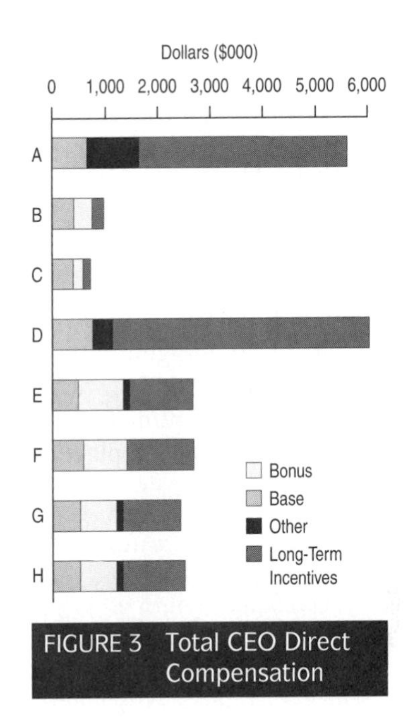

FIGURE 3 Total CEO Direct Compensation

MARKET COMPENSATION ANALYSIS

Figure 3 shows some drastically different pay structures. In the past three years, Company D has awarded its CEO long-term incentives worth $27 million ($9.2 million per year), while Company C awarded none to its CEO. As noted earlier, Company C, at negative $28 million, was the only company in the group to post a negative net income for 2000 and declining EPS in the past three years, primarily from its unsuccessful international operations. This may explain the significantly lower CEO total compensation.

BUSINESS STRATEGY LINK

To link and align business strategy to executive compensation, identifying and analyzing key strategic factors for both the company and the industry are required. For the finance industry

(Continued)

(Continued)

	Leading Indicators	Progressive Measures	Desired Results
Internal Factors	Ownership Intensity	Risk Tolerance	Business Intensity
Ext. Benchmarks	Tenure/Talent	Financial Performance	Stock Performance

FIGURE 4 OEC Strategic Factors Model

example, the six strategic factors in Figure 4 are identified. In analyzing the factors two sets of data are compiled: one set with the actual past performance to see the alignment with current compensation, and another set with the future strategy to determine an optimal future compensation. For the calculation example, the following three companies are selected:

- **Company B, the "losing" performer.** Currently, with the least revenue by far and with the negative total shareholder return in the past three years, Company B needs a "turnaround specialist" to jump-start the business. It needs a CEO who can manage higher-risk tolerance and business intensity. The CEO tenure in this specific industry is not as important as the ability to bring fresh perspective and new ideas. An A-quality CEO will need to make tough, drastic changes, even at the cost of short-term financial performance.
- **Company E, the industry "top" performer.** Company E is performing at the top of the industry in terms of revenue generation, return on equity and total shareholder return. It needs a "visionary leader" to maintain its leadership position. The company also needs a CEO with high ownership intensity who can inspire employees to attain even higher financial performance.
- **Company F, the "mediocre" performer.** Currently, a median performer, Company F needs a "seasoned superstar" CEO who can grow its market share. It needs to increase its CEO's ownership intensity. Also, against the current conservative company strategy, it needs a CEO who can implement a business strategy that is higher in risk tolerance and business intensity.

FINDING SWEET SPOTS

Now link the strategic factors to the design of CEO compensation. For simplicity here, summary analysis of three compensation components (base salary, bonus pay, stock options) are presented separately. In practice, one would analyze in greater depths all components separately, as well as together.

CEO BASE SALARY

(See Figure 5.)

Purpose

- Attract and retain key talents.
- Form a basis for other pay components.

Sample Methodology

- Pay base salary competitively (within one standard deviation of the market average) based on similar revenue size and industry.
- Adjust pay level based on the current financial condition/performance of the company and the individual executives' talent and potential.
- May consider other determinants, such as company size (market capitalization, number of employees), company developmental stage, private versus public, etc.

Analysis

Company B requires slightly higher base salary; Company E's current level is close to the OEC level; Company F requires a lower base salary.

Recall that Company B is the smallest, worst performing and it may be surprising—and counterintuitive at first—to say that the company needs to increase its CEO's base salary. However, this illustrates the importance of being strategic and forward-looking. Company B requires an A-quality CEO going forward who can turn around the ailing company.

The business strategy is set first, followed by definition of required CEO competencies, then a market competitive pay level is set. (Of course, the next nontrivial challenge for the organization is to find that A-quality CEO.)

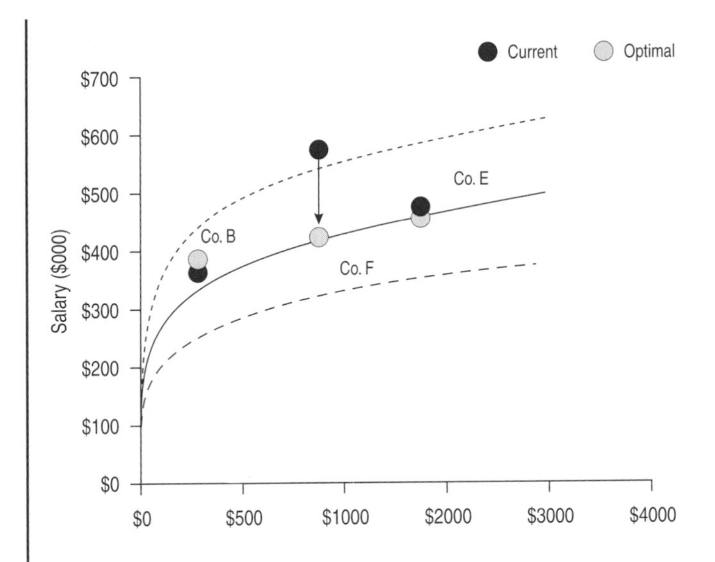

Co.	($ Millions) Revenue	Adjust Factors Fin. Perf.	Talent	OEC Salary	Curr. Salary	Diff.
A	$619				$620	
B	$332	Mid	"A"	$398	$375	–6%
C	$1,094				$395	
D	$1,057				$750	
E	$1,110	Above	"B"	$475	$463	–2%
F	$763	Above	"B"	$439	$575	31%
G	$615				$530	

FIGURE 5 OEC Base Salary Analysis

Note that the Company B business strategy of a "turnaround" is the hypothesis but, if the company does not have such a business strategy going forward, then the required CEO and the pay level may be different. The company strategy and needs determine the CEO requirement/pay—not the other way around.

CEO BONUS PAY

Purpose

- Motivate executives
- Improve short-term performance.

Sample Methodology

- Pay bonus competitively, based on similar revenue size.
- Adjust "target" level based on risk tolerance, in which higher tolerance for risks would warrant higher target bonus level.
- Adjust bonus range based on business intensity, where more CEO influence on results would warrant wider bonus range.
- May consider other determinants, such as type of industry and volatility, company goals stretch, leverage, etc.

Analysis

Based on the OEC methodology and hypotheses:

- Company B's target level should be increased with a wide range.
- Company E's target level should be decreased with a narrow range.
- Company F, whose current bonus plan information is not available, should offer a mid-range bonus plan.
- This means that Company B (in need of turnaround) needs a more aggressive incentive plan, while Company E (the top-performing company in need of leadership maintenance) needs a less aggressive/risky plan.

(Continued)

(Continued)

CEO STOCK OPTIONS

Purpose

- Align executives' and shareholders' interests.
- Improve long-term performance.

Sample Methodology

- Grant options based on market competitiveness, company strategy and stock performance.
- Adjust grant size and frequency based on the current ownership level and industry volatility.
- Adjust grant size and vesting schedule further based on the company developmental stage (e.g., new products, focus on core products, etc.)
- May consider other determinants, such as the CEO's current options holding, management intensity, etc.

Analysis

All three companies are providing a less-than-optimal amount of stock options to their CEOs. While Company B should consider a shorter vesting duration on the stock options so that its business urgencies can be better met, Company E should consider a longer vesting to encourage longer performance horizon.

ON THE MARK

Finding sweet spots in executive compensation involves analyzing many complex factors, both external (market prevalence) and internal (strategic factors). OEC methodology is meant to provide a logical, justifiable way of determining the compensation levels, but it is not meant to be applied without a sufficient thought process and consideration of individual situations. It provides flexibility to choose appropriate factors and adjustment degrees.

Optimal executive compensation can be attained when executive compensation is treated as more than just a data crunching exercise. The word *compensation* is a misnomer because compensation implies paying for services received. But the idea behind OEC is more than looking at the past or even present. It is about being more forward anticipating, goal oriented and strategically fit. Perhaps a better terminology would be "optimal executive investment." One should expect a payback from executive compensation as in any investment. There should be a justification for paying a certain salary, bonus and stock options to the executives' expectations in return.

Source: Jonathan Lee, JL Strategy. *Workspan*. (2002). volume 45. © 2002 WorldatWork, 14040 N. Northsight Blvd., Scottsdale, AZ 85260 U.S.A.; 480/951-9191; Fax 480/483-8352; *www.worldatwork.org*; E-mail worldatwork@worldatwork.org

WHAT'S NEW IN COMPENSATION?

More Controversy About Executive Compensation . . . This Time, Perquisites

Executive compensation is one of the most widely reported compensation issues in the news media. Reports about executive compensation generally focus on the lucrative levels of annual pay and bonuses as well as the value of stock options. Oftentimes, these reports are tied to issues of mismatches between executive pay amounts and company performance (high pay when the company has failed to meet its earnings targets), corporate accounting scandals, or social justice.

Executive perquisites, while a major component of executive compensation systems, receive much less attention. The featured *New York Times* article describes questions about the tax treatment of several perquisite benefits awarded to Jack Welch when he was the CEO of General Electric (GE). Some of the perquisites include GE giving Welch multiple homes, domestic workers, and the use of GE jets for all of his travel. A major question focuses on whether these benefits were essential aspects of performing CEO duties at GE. Another question focuses on whether the value of these perquisites exceeded the minimum amount set by the Internal Revenue Service for income tax exemption.

Log onto your *New York Times* account. Search the database for articles on "executive compensation" and "executive pay" to find a wide variety of articles related to pay and benefits for executives. When reading these articles, think about whether executives receive too much pay or preferential treatment. Following your course instructor's specific directions, be prepared to describe the current situation, and relate it to the article contained in this text. ■

The New York Times

GE Perks Raise Issues About Taxes

In the wake of documents that detail the long list of living expenses General Electric paid for John F. Welch Jr., its former chief, some corporate governance experts are asking why GE did not more fully disclose the information and who should pay the taxes on all these benefits.

The benefits were detailed in divorce papers that Mr. Welch's estranged wife, Jane Beasley Welch, filed in Superior Court in Bridgeport, CT, on Thursday. They include a list of corporate perks including lifetime use of a palatial Manhattan apartment complete with wine, flowers, cook, housekeeper and other amenities, as well as access to General Electric's Boeing 737 jets, helicopters and a car and driver for Mr. Welch and his wife. Also included were tickets for the couple at a number of top sporting events and the opera.

What has bothered some experts is how little GE has said about the breadth of the benefits.

"I don't think the amount of disclosure really explained to the investment community the magnitude of what was being given to the retired CEO," said Jay W. Lorsch, a professor at the Harvard Business School and an expert in corporate governance.

"The other question here is how many of these retirement expenses, such as the apartment in New York, are legitimate expenses that GE should even be willing to pay," Professor Lorsch said. "Jack Welch got paid for doing a great job. Why should he get paid twice?"

Nell Minow, editor of The Corporate Library, a corporate watchdog group, believes investors might have been more alert to how indulgent the corporate culture was at GE if they had looked more carefully at the company's compensation committee, which, she feels, did not have the independence it needed to say "no" to Mr. Welch.

Public filings state that two members of the committee, Sam Nunn and Roger Penske, "had business dealings with GE," Ms. Minow noted. "And another member, Andrew Sigler, when he was chief executive of Champion International, was widely criticized by shareholders for not relating his pay to the company's performance."

In a statement on Friday, the compensation committee said that a publicly filed 1996 employment agreement to keep Mr. Welch until 2000 agreed to give him lifetime access to "planes, cars, offices, apartments and financial planning services." And the committee said that GE had received great value from the arrangement.

In a statement also on Friday, Mr. Welch said the plan had "worked to the benefit of all constituencies."

But Graef Crystal, a compensation expert, asked whether the committee should be revisiting existing arrangements from time to time to see if they make sense in light of the current business environment. "Even if they made sense in 1996, the question is whether they do now."

According to GE's 2001 proxy statement, Mr. Welch put few benefits to personal use. He had only $171,772 in compensation beyond his salary and bonus. The single item that is detailed is $143,479 for financial counseling. That leaves only $28,293 to cover all other spending for personal reasons.

Securities and Exchange Commission rulings require that companies report any personal benefits if they are over $50,000 in total or over 10 percent of any top executive's salary and bonus, whichever figure is lower. In Mr. Welch's case, his 2001 salary and bonus were $16.2 million, so he had to declare any benefits over $50,000.

Thus General Electric is taking the position that any use of the corporate apartment and other perks beyond the $171,772 he spent during the eight months before he retired from General Electric in September 2001, was for corporate purposes. While Mr. Welch must pay taxes on that amount, General Electric can write off that money, if it can show that they are ordinary and necessary expenses of doing business.

Mr. Crystal, the compensation expert, said he found it hard to believe that all those benefits were purely for corporate use. Mr. Welch has four homes—in Connecticut, Massachusetts, New York and Florida. "How did he get to those far-flung places?" Mr. Crystal wondered. "By Amtrak?"

Mr. Sheffer said that people do not understand how GE operated. "Mr. Welch, for example, was required to use GE transportation at all times for security reasons," he said.

Mr. Crystal said there was no reason for that protection. "If he needs it, why not take a prop plane?" he said. "And now that he is retired, who is going to go after him anyway?"

The planes are also financially advantageous to Mr. Welch.

Mr. Sheffer said that under federal tax rules, personal trips by Mr. Welch using corporate transportation are not required to be disclosed to shareholders. For income tax purposes, when he uses the corporate jet for personal reasons he must pay income taxes not on the cost of the flight, but on the rough equivalent of coach fare, Mr. Sheffer said.

He said that the rules for proxy disclosure and the rules for what Mr. Welch must report as income were not identical, so all of the income Mr. Welch received in the form of personal services might not be reported in the proxy but would be on his W-2 wage statement.

Tax lawyers interviewed yesterday said that many of the items that Mrs. Welch says the company paid for are clearly personal in nature and are compensation to Mr. Welch on which he should pay taxes.

When Mr. Welch files his divorce papers, they are likely to show his income last year. And they will likely include documentation on how much of the benefits he received from G.E. were for his personal use, and therefore how much he must be taxed.

Even if he takes the position that his personal use of those benefits was minimal, some experts yesterday wondered just whether such a rich deal would stand up in court.

Nevertheless, tax defense lawyers yesterday said there was almost no prospect of a criminal tax charge against GE or Mr. Welch unless evidence appeared that there had been a deliberate attempt to conceal the spending from IRS auditors.

However, these same tax lawyers said that an audit would likely result in the company or the Welches owing taxes and interest, and that if the couple were held to be responsible, they could owe substantial penalties for under-reporting their income and filing inaccurate tax returns.

Kathryn Keneally, a tax defense lawyer in New York, said that even if GE improperly reported the payments to Mr. Welch, "there are a thousand ways they can handle this" that would allow GE to escape penalties, but not taxes and interest.

SOURCE: Geraldine Fabrikast and David Cay Johnson, G.E. perks raise issues about taxes (September 9, 2002). [online]. Available: *www.nytimes.com*, accessed October 5, 2002.

CHAPTER

14 COMPENSATING THE FLEXIBLE WORKFORCE CONTINGENT EMPLOYEES AND FLEXIBLE WORK SCHEDULES

Chapter Outline

- The Contingent Workforce
  - Groups of Contingent Workers
  - Reasons for U.S. Employers' Increased Reliance on Contingent Workers
- Core and Fringe Compensation for Contingent Workers
  - Part-Time Employees
  - Temporary Employees
  - Leased Workers
  - Independent Contractors, Freelancers and Consultants
- Flexible Work Schedules: Flextime, Compressed Workweeks, and Telecommuting
  - Flexible Schedules
  - Compressed Workweek Schedules
  - Telecommuting
  - Flexible Work Schedules: Balancing the Demands of Work Life and Home Life
- Core and Fringe Compensation for Flexible Employees
  - Core Compensation
  - Fringe Compensation
- Unions' Reactions to Contingent Workers and Flexible Work Schedules
- Strategic Issues and Choices in Using Contingent and Flexible Workers
  - Lowest-Cost Competitive Strategy
  - Differentiation Competitive Strategy
- Summary
- Key Terms
- Discussion Questions
- Exercises
- Endnotes

Learning Objectives

In this chapter, you will learn about

1. Various groups of contingent workers and the reasons for U.S. employers' increased reliance on them
2. Core and fringe compensation issues for contingent workers

3. Key features of flexible work schedules, compressed workweeks, and telecommuting
4. Core and fringe compensation issues for flexible work schedules, compressed workweeks, and telecommuting
5. Unions' reactions to contingent workers and flexible work schedules
6. Strategic issues and choices in using contingent workers

Changing business conditions and personal preferences have led to an increase in contingent workers and the use of flexible work schedules in the United States. Companies employed as many as 12.5 million contingent workers in February 2001 [1]. Likewise, the complexities of employees' personal lives—dependent children and elderly relatives, dual career couples, disabilities—make working standard 8-hour days for 5 consecutive days every week difficult. About 29 million employees worked flexible work schedules during May 2001 [2]. Altogether, contingent and flexible-schedule employees represent about 26.1 percent of the U.S. civilian labor force.

This chapter looks at compensation issues for contingent workers and demonstrates that compensating contingent workers is a complex proposition. The "Compensation in Action" feature at the end of this chapter relates some of the challenges faced by HR professionals employed in a variety of companies, including Microsoft.

The previous chapters addressed compensation issues for core employees. **Core employees** have full-time jobs (that is, they work at least 35 hours per week), and they generally plan long-term or indefinite relationships with their employers. In addition, all core employees were assumed to work standard schedules—fixed 8-hour work shifts, 5 days per week. Compensation practices differ somewhat for the flexible workforce.

THE CONTINGENT WORKFORCE

Contingent workers [3] engage in explicitly tentative employment relationships with companies. The duration of their employment varies according to their convenience and employers' business needs. Both men and women each account for 50 percent of total contingent employment in the United States. Contingent workers most commonly hold professional (for example, accountant), clerical (for example, secretary), or laborer (for example, construction worker) positions; they perform jobs in the service and retail trade industries.

Groups of Contingent Workers

There are four distinct groups of contingent workers:

- Part-time employees
- Temporary and on-call employees
- Leased employees
- Independent contractors, freelancers, and consultants

Table 14-1 shows the number of contingent workers in each category.

Part-Time Employees

The Bureau of Labor Statistics distinguishes between two kinds of part-time employees: voluntary and involuntary. A **voluntary part-time employee** chooses to work fewer than 35 hours per regularly scheduled workweek. In some cases, individuals supplement full-time employment with part-time employment to meet financial obligations.

TABLE 14-1 Number of Contingent Employees, February 2001

Type of Contingent Workers	*Number*
Part-time employees	2,245,000
Temporary employees	1,169,000
On-call employees	2,089,000
Leased employees	663,000
Independent contractors	8,585,000

Source: U.S. Bureau of Labor Statistics. (2001). *Contingent and alternative employment arrangements, February 2001* [online]. Available: *www.stats.bls.gov/newsrels.htm*, accessed July 22, 2002.

Some workers, including a small but growing number of professionals, elect to work part-time as a lifestyle choice. These part-timers sacrifice pay, and possibly career advancement, in exchange for more free time to devote to family, hobbies, and personal interests. They often have working spouses whose benefits, generally including medical and dental insurance, extend coverage to family members.

Involuntary part-time employees work fewer than 35 hours per week because they are unable to find full-time employment. Involuntary part-time work represents the lion's share of all part-time employment. There is a commonly held but inaccurate stereotype of involuntary part-time workers as being low-skilled and uninterested in career advancement. To the contrary, many involuntary part-time workers hold entry-level career-track jobs [4]. Although we have discussed voluntary and involuntary part-time work as part of the contingent workforce, it is important to emphasize that many core workers negotiate part-time schedules with employers.

Table 14-2 lists the specific reasons for part-time work and the percentage of individuals who work part-time for each reason. As previously noted, some individuals who usually work full-time also hold part-time jobs. Others typically work part-time jobs only.

Companies may experience advantages and disadvantages from employing part-time workers. Flexibility is the key advantage. Most companies realize a substantial cost savings because they offer few or no discretionary benefits. Table 14-3 shows employers' costs for providing various discretionary benefits and legally required benefits to full-time and part-time employees. Employers save considerable money in the areas of paid leave, insurance, and legally required benefits.

Companies also save on overtime pay expenses. Hiring part-time workers during peak business periods minimizes overtime pay costs. As we discussed in Chapter 3, the Fair Labor Standards Act of 1938 (FLSA) requires that companies pay nonexempt employees at a rate equaling one and one-half times their regular hourly pay rates. Retail businesses save by employing part-time sales associates during the peak holiday shopping season.

Job sharing is a special kind of part-time employment agreement. Two or more part-time employees perform a single full-time job. These employees may perform all job duties or share the responsibility for particular tasks. Some job sharers meet regularly to coordinate their efforts. Job sharing represents a compromise between employees' needs or desires not to work full-time and employers' needs to staff jobs on a full-time basis. Both employers and employees benefit from the use of job sharing. Table 14-4 lists some of the benefits of job sharing to employers and employees.

TABLE 14-2 Reasons for Part-Time Employment, by Percentage of Full-Time and Part-Time Workers, 2001

	Usually Work	
	Full-Time (%)	***Part-Time(%)***
Economic Reasons		
Slack work or business conditions	5.5	8.5
Could find only part-time work	N/A	3.6
Seasonal work	<1	<1
Job started or ended during the week	22.4	N/A
Noneconomic Reasons		
Child care problems	63.6	2.2
Other family or personal obligations	2.0	16.2
Health or medical limitations	N/A	2.6
In school or training	<1	22.2
Retired, Social Security limit on earnings	N/A	6.3
Vacation or personal day	8.9	N/A
Holiday, legal, or religious	<1	N/A
Weather-related curtailment	1.1	N/A
Other	9.3	14.0

Note: Percentages total to more than 100% because some individuals work part-time for more than one reason.

Source: U.S. Department of Commerce. (2002). *Statistical abstracts of the United States*(121st ed.). Washington, DC: U.S. Government Printing Office; U.S. Department of Labor Statistics. (January 2002). *Employment and earnings*. Washington, DC: U.S. Government Printing Office.

Temporary and On-Call Employees

Companies traditionally hire temporary employees for two reasons. First, temporary workers fill in for core employees who are on approved leaves of absence, including sick leave, vacation, bereavement leave, jury duty, and military leave. Second, temporary workers offer extra sets of hands when companies' business activities peak, during such times as the holiday season for retail businesses or summer for amusement parks.

TABLE 14-3 Employers' Hourly Costs for Full- and Part-Time Employee Benefits, March 2002

Benefit	*Full-Time*	*Part-Time*
Paid leave	$1.75	$0.40
Supplemental pay	$0.75	$0.18
Insurance	$1.69	$0.40
Retirement and savings	$0.77	$0.15
Other benefits	$0.03	<$.01
Legally required benefits	$1.96	$1.24
Total hourly benefits costs	$6.96	$2.38

Source: U.S. Bureau of Labor Statistics. (2002). *Employer costs for employee compensation* (USDL: 02-346). Washington, DC: U.S. Government Printing Office.

TABLE 14-4 Benefits of Job Sharing

Benefits to Employers

- Maintenance of productivity because of higher morale and maintenance of employee skills
- Retention of skilled workers
- Reduction or elimination of the training costs that result from retraining laid-off employees
- Greater flexibility in deploying workers to keep operations going
- Minimization of postrecession costs of hiring and training new workers to replace those who found other jobs during layoff
- Strengthening employees' loyalty to the company

Benefits to Employees

- Continued fringe benefits protection
- Continued employment when the likelihood of unemployment is high
- Maintenance of family income
- Continued participation in qualified retirement programs

Temporary employees perform jobs on a short-term basis usually measured in days, weeks, or months [5].

More recently, companies have been hiring temporary workers for three additional reasons. First, temporary employment arrangements provide employers the opportunity to evaluate whether legitimate needs exist for creating new positions. Second, temporary employment arrangements give employers the opportunity to decide whether to retain particular workers on an indefinite basis. "The temp job is often what one university placement director calls the '3-month interview'—and a gateway to a full-time job and perhaps a new career" [6]. In effect, the temporary arrangement represents a probationary period, when employers observe whether workers are meeting job performance standards. As a corollary, such temporary arrangements provide workers the chance to decide whether to accept employment on a full-time basis after they have had time to "check things out." Third, employing temporary workers is often less costly than employing core workers because temporary workers are less likely to receive costly discretionary benefits (for example, medical insurance coverage).

Companies hire temporary employees from a variety of sources. The most common source is a **temporary employment agency**. In 2001, companies employed approximately 1.2 million temporary workers [7]. Traditionally, most temporary employment agencies placed clerical and administrative workers. Nowadays, some temporary agencies also place workers with specialized skills, such as auditors, computer systems analysts, and lawyers. These agencies are becoming more common.

Companies generally establish relationships with temporary employment agencies based on several factors. First, companies consider agencies' reputations as an important factor, judging reputations by how well agencies' placements work out. Some agencies place a wide range of employees, yet others specialize in one type of placement (for example, financial services professionals). When companies plan to hire a variety of temporary workers, it is often more convenient to work with agencies that do not specialize. Ultimately, companies should judge these agencies' placement records for each type of employee.

Second, companies also should consider agencies' fees. Cost is a paramount consideration for companies that are pursuing lowest-cost competitive strategies. Temporary agencies base fees as a percentage of their placements' pay rates. The

STRETCHING THE DOLLAR

IS CONTINGENT EMPLOYMENT WORTH IT TO COMPANIES?

Employers easily can justify increased contingent employment with business necessity—cost containment, flexibility, and so forth. However, companies may be trading employee loyalty for reduced costs and greater flexibility. Employees previously expected to maintain employment within their choice companies for as long as they wished. Indeed, many employees remained with a single company for decades at a time, culminating in a retirement bash and receipt of a "gold watch" for long-time service. Such companies as Ford Motor Company, General Motors, IBM, and Lincoln Electric exemplified extended employment.

Workers now in the labor force are not likely to forget past practices that once led to job security and sound retirement nest eggs. It is probably not reasonable to expect that workers will take personal interest in companies' performance as the employment relationship becomes more tentative. Instead, more workers will probably be alert to better and possibly more secure employment alternatives and therefore less loyal to employers. As more employees assume contingent worker status, companies may become victim to reduced employee loyalty, resulting in heightened job insecurity among core employees, lower control over product or service quality, higher turnover, compliance burdens and costs, and greater training costs.

First, both core and contingent workers may develop less loyalty for their employers. Hiring contingent workers may lead core employees to feel less secure about their status because staffing companies with contingent workers generally represents a lower cost alternative to core employees. Consequently, core employees' loyalties may become diminished, which can translate into lower worker dependability and work quality.

Second, employers can lose control over product or service quality when they employ contingent workers. This problem is most likely to occur when companies engage contingent workers on short-term bases: It takes contingent workers time to learn company-specific procedures and work processes. Thus, companies that do not employ contingent workers long enough will not maintain sufficient control over quality.

Third, turnover rates among core workers will probably increase when companies employ contingent workers. As noted earlier, core employees may feel uncertain about their job status, and this uncertainty will probably lead to lower loyalty. The absence of job security and diminished loyalty will increase core employees' job search activities. Over time, the most qualified core employees will receive competitive job offers that lead to dysfunctional turnover.

Finally, companies must bear the costs of training contingent workers. In many cases, employing contingent workers can be as costly as employing core workers. That is, the savings from not offering contingent workers discretionary benefits is offset by training costs. These costs become less significant for companies that employ contingent workers long enough to realize returns on the training investment through higher productivity and work quality.

percentage varies from agency to agency. Fortunately, the competition among temporary agencies keeps these rates in check.

Although temporary employees work in a variety of companies, their legal employers are the temporary employment agencies. Temporary employment agencies take full responsibility for selecting temporary employee candidates and determine candidates' qualifications through interviews and testing. Particularly for clerical and administrative jobs, many temporary agencies train candidates to use such office equipment as fax machines, electronic mail, and spreadsheet and word processing software programs. Temporary employees receive compensation directly from the agency.

Companies may hire temporary employees through other means. For example, some companies hire individuals directly as temporary workers. Under **direct hire**

arrangements, temporary employees typically do not work for more than 1 year. In addition, the hiring companies are the temporary workers' legal employers. Thus, companies take full responsibility for all HR functions that affect temporary employees, including performance evaluation, compensation, and training.

On-call arrangements are another method for employing temporary workers. On-call employees work sporadically throughout the year when companies require their services. Some unionized skilled trade workers are available as on-call employees when they are unable to secure permanent, full-time employment. These employees' unions maintain rosters of unemployed members who are available for work. When employed, on-call workers are employees of the hiring companies. Thus, the hiring companies are responsible for managing and implementing HR policies, including compensation.

Leased Employee Arrangements

Lease companies employ qualified individuals and place them in client companies on a long-term basis. Most leasing companies bill the client for the direct costs of employing the workers—such as payroll, benefits, and payroll taxes—and then charge a fixed fee. Lease companies base these fees on either a fixed percentage of the client's payroll or a fixed fee per employee.

Leasing arrangements are common in the food service industry. ARAMARK Food Services is an example of a leasing company that provides cafeteria services to client companies. ARAMARK staffs these companies' in-house cafeterias with cooks, food preparers, and checkout clerks. These cafeteria workers are employees of the leasing company, not the client company. Leasing companies also operate in other industries, including security services, building maintenance, and administrative services.

Lease companies and temporary employment agencies are similar because both manage all HR activities. Thus, lease companies provide both wages and benefits to their employees. Lease companies and temporary employment agencies differ in an important respect, however. Lease company placements generally remain in effect for the duration of the lease company's contract with the host company.

Independent Contractors, Freelancers, and Consultants

Independent contractors, freelancers, and **consultants** (the term *independent contractor* will be used in this discussion) establish working relationships with companies on their own rather than through temporary employment agencies or lease companies. Independent contractors typically possess specialized skills that are in short supply in the labor market. Companies select independent contractors to complete particular projects of short-term duration—usually a year or less. Adjunct faculty members represent a specific example of independent contractors. Colleges and universities hire them to cover for permanent faculty members who are on sabbatical leave or until they hire tenure-track replacements. In addition, some companies staff segments of their workforces with independent contractors to contain discretionary benefits costs.

Reasons for U.S. Employers' Increased Reliance on Contingent Workers

Structural changes in the U.S. economy have contributed to the rise of contingent employment:

- Economic recessions
- International competition
- Shift from manufacturing to a service economy
- Rise in female labor force participation

Economic Recessions

Many companies lay off segments of their workforces during economic recessions as a cost control measure. Following economic recessions, some companies restore staffing levels with permanent employees. Increasingly, many companies restore staffing levels with contingent workers. Since the early 1970s, the U.S. economy experienced several economic recessions. These repeated recessions have shaken employers' confidence about future economic prosperity. Staffing segments of workforces with contingent workers represents a form of risk control because employers save on most discretionary benefits costs. In addition, companies can terminate contingent workers' services more easily: These employment relationships are explicitly tentative. Both the host employer and the workers understand that these engagements are of limited duration.

International Competition

International competition is another pertinent structural change. American companies no longer compete just against each other. Many foreign businesses have demonstrated the ability to manufacture goods at lower costs than their American competitors. As a result, successful American companies have streamlined operations to control costs. These companies are saving costs by reducing the numbers of core employees and using contingent workers as an alternative [8].

The Shift from Manufacturing to a Service Economy

The service sector refers to six broad divisions of industries: transportation, communication, and public utilities; wholesale trade; retail trade; finance, insurance, and real estate; services; and government. Manufacturing companies' (for example, automobile makers and textiles) employment declined substantially between 1980 and 2002 [9], and economic forecasts predict a loss of jobs in the manufacturing sector through 2008 [10]. During this period, a steady decrease in employment in manufacturing industries was offset by a substantial rise in employment in both the retail trade and service sectors [11]. Service sector employment is expected to add nearly 12 million new jobs to the economy by the year 2008 [12]. In addition, contingent workers typically find employment in service businesses, which are more labor intensive than capital intensive (for example, heavy manufacturing equipment).

> A number of trends depict a society that is in some ways increasingly dedicated to future investment by means of both capital and increased effort. Business-oriented services—such as upgrading of software and intelligent machinery, services related to construction, and improvement of business processes with the aid of consultants—may all be interpreted as present investments for a wealthier future. The extension of business operating hours may be interpreted in the same way. Even two rapidly increasing social services, daycare and residential care, enable some people to work outside the home instead of caring for relatives, and to contribute to economic expansion [13].

Rise in Female Labor Force Participation

The increase in female participation in the labor force has promoted growth in the use of contingent workers. One-income families were commonplace until the early 1970s, and males headed these households. Since then, several economic recessions in the United States left large numbers of individuals unemployed.

Many wives entered the labor force temporarily to supplement family income during their husbands' unemployment spells [14]. The majority took low-paying jobs as clerical or service workers because they did not have sufficient education to attain

FLIP SIDE OF THE COIN

TEMPORARY WORKERS LOSE JOBS DURING RECENT RECESSIONS DESPITE LOWER EMPLOYMENT COSTS

Oftentimes, companies employ temporary workers to more easily change staffing levels in response to business conditions. On one hand, employers commonly hire temporary workers in anticipation of a surge in demand for product or services. For example, retail stores and express mail shipping companies hire temporary workers for the holiday shopping season. Demand usually spikes a month or two prior to the December holidays and falls off dramatically in January, shortly after the flurry of gift exchange settles down.

Other companies often reduced the level of full-time, noncontingent workers during periods of recessions. Particularly during recessionary periods when business demand is sluggish, reducing these staffing levels enables companies to cut costs by not paying both wages or salaries and a full complement of employee benefits to core employees. Recently, in upbeat economies companies have maintained workforces that include a larger proportion of temporary workers to maintain staffing flexibility during future economic downturns. However, during these economic downturns, companies have included many more temporary workers than noncontingent employees. Laying off more temporary workers seems to run counter to the cost control objective. With careful consideration, this trend is not surprising. Given companies' tendency to maintain greater numbers of temporary workers, companies are hesitant to reduce core staffing levels too drastically. Presumably, core employees are likely to be more committed to employers than are temporary workers whose employment terms are explicitly tentative.

high-paying jobs. Even educated women could not find high-paying jobs because the recessions limited such opportunities. As a result, many well-educated women also assumed low-paying clerical or service positions.

A large segment of these women remained in the contingent labor force following the end of these economic recessions because their husbands' salaries did not keep up with inflation. Contingent employment enabled women to balance the demands of home and work. Although men have been taking greater responsibility for child rearing in recent years, women still bear the brunt of these duties [15]. Thus, contingent employment, compared with core employment, affords women opportunities to balance the demands of home and work. Consequently, contingent workers are disproportionately female [16].

The rise in single-parent households also contributed to the rise in contingent employment. Many single female parents possess low levels of education, which limits job opportunities. As a result, single mothers accept such low-paying contingent jobs as domestic work, retail sales, and low-level clerical positions. Apart from low educational attainment, single mothers accept contingent work because it enables them to spend more time with their children. As an aside, these women generally cannot afford to pay for regular day care services.

Nowadays, a large segment of well-educated females enter the contingent workforce because of dual-career pressures. In many areas of the country, employers have the luxury of large pools of educated, skilled workers who have followed as their spouses pursue job opportunities. These areas typically have few large employers such as in Fort Collins, Colorado, and Champaign-Urbana, Illinois, where universities are the main employers. Many spouses with professional credentials take low-paying, part-time jobs because there are few good job opportunities.

CORE AND FRINGE COMPENSATION FOR CONTINGENT WORKERS

Compensation practices for contingent workers vary. We will discuss these practices shortly. Nevertheless, all parties involved in employing contingent workers possess liability under federal and state laws, including:

- Overtime and minimum wages required under the FLSA
- Paying insurance premiums required under state workers' compensation laws
- Nondiscriminatory compensation and employment practices under the Employee Retirement Income Security Act of 1974 (ERISA), National Labor Relations Act (NLRA), Title VII of the Civil Rights Act of 1964, Americans with Disabilities Act of 1990 (ADA), and the Age Discrimination in Employment Act (ADEA).

Temporary employment agencies and leasing companies that place workers in clients' firms are liable under these laws. In addition, the client company may also be liable. "The fact that a worker is somebody else's employee while he or she is on your premises, or performing services for the business, is not necessarily a defense to alleged violations of federal and state labor laws including Title VII of the Civil Rights Act, the Fair Labor Standards Act, and the Americans with Disabilities Act" [17]. As we discussed in Chapter 3, each of these laws applies to compensation practice.

Part-Time Employees

Companies that employ part-time workers are the legal employers, as is the case for core employees. Compensating part-time employees poses the following challenges for employers:

- Should companies pay part-time workers on an hourly basis or a salary basis?
- Do equity problems arise between core employees and part-time employees?
- Do companies offer benefits to part-time workers?

Core Compensation

Part-time employees earn less, on average, than core employees. In March 2002, part-time workers earned an average $9.76 per hour while full-time employees earned $17.61 per hour [18]. Full-time white-collar employees earned $21.47 per hour while part-time white-collar employees earned $12.09 per hour. Full-time blue-collar workers earned substantially more than their part-time counterparts ($14.68 per hour versus $8.99 per hour). Similarly, full-time service employees earned more than part-timers ($9.69 per hour versus $7.08 per hour).

Companies often expect salaried part-time employees to do much more than their fair share of the work because the effective hourly pay rate decreases as the number of hours worked increases. An explicit agreement pertaining to work-hour limits can minimize this problem. Similarly, an agreement may specify explicit work goals. Alternatively, companies may avoid this problem by paying part-time employees on an hourly basis.

Part-time and full-time employees may perceive the situation as inequitable under certain circumstances. For example, equity problems may arise when salaried full-time employees and hourly part-time employees work together. It is possible that highly skilled full-time employees might effectively be underpaid relative to less skilled part-time employees performing the same work. That is, full-time employees' "hourly" pay rate will be lower when they perform more and better work in a shorter period than less-skilled part-time workers.

Fringe Compensation

Companies generally do not provide discretionary benefits to part-time employees. However, benefits practices for part-time workers vary widely according to company size as well as between the private and public sectors. In 1997, approximately half of part-time employees working in medium-size and large private companies earned paid time-off benefits [19]. Fewer received medical insurance coverage (21 percent) or retirement benefits (34 percent). Smaller private companies were less likely to offer fringe compensation to part-time employees. In 1996, approximately one-third earned pay for time not worked benefits, and even fewer received medical insurance (6 percent) or retirement benefits (13 percent) [20].

Employers are not required to offer protective insurance (that is, medical, dental, vision, or life insurance) to part-time employees. However, part-time employees who do receive health insurance coverage under employer-sponsored plans are entitled to protection under the Consolidated Omnibus Budget Reconciliation Act (COBRA). As discussed in Chapter 11, COBRA provides employees the opportunity to continue receiving employer-sponsored health care insurance coverage temporarily following termination or layoff. Employees who qualify for COBRA protection receive insurance coverage that matches the coverage level during employment.

Employers may be required to provide qualified retirement programs to part-time employees [21]. Part-time employees who meet the following two criteria are eligible to participate in qualified retirement programs:

- Minimum age of 21 years
- Completion of at least 1,000 hours of work in a 12-month period (that is, "year of service")

Special considerations apply to seasonal employees' eligibilities for qualified retirement benefits because most seasonal employees do not meet the annual service pension eligibility criterion. Maritime industries such as fishing represent seasonal employment, and fishermen are seasonal employees. The Department of Labor defines 125 service days as the "year of service" for maritime workers [22]. Part-time and seasonal employees cannot be excluded from pension plans if they meet the Department of Labor's "year of service" criterion.

Temporary Employees

Temporary employment agencies are the legal employers for temporary employees. Thus, temporary employment agencies are responsible for complying with federal employment legislation with one exception that we will address shortly—workers' compensation. Compensating temporary employees poses challenges for companies.

- Do equity problems arise between core employees and temporary employees?
- How do the FLSA overtime provisions affect temporary employees?
- Do companies offer temporary workers benefits?
- Who is responsible for providing workers' compensation protection: the temporary agency or the client company?

Core Compensation

Temporary workers in the United States earned an average $9.90 per hour in February 2001 [23]. Hourly pay rates varied widely by occupation and workers' particular qualifications. Equity problems may (or may not) arise where core and temporary employees work together. On one hand, temporary employees may work diligently because they know that their assignments in client companies are explicitly of limited duration. In addition, frequent moves from one company to the next may limit workers' opportunities or desires to build careers with any of these companies. Further, temporary workers may neither take the time nor have the time to scope out pay differences because their engagements are brief—anywhere from 1 day to a few weeks. Thus, these temporary employees are not likely to perceive inequitable pay situations.

On the other hand, some temporary employees may not work diligently because they did not choose temporary employment arrangements. Individuals who lose their jobs because of a sudden layoff and who have few core job alternatives are most susceptible. Pay differences between these temporary employees and core employees are likely to intensify perceptions of inequity.

It is important to distinguish between temporary employees and seasonal employees for determining eligibility under the FLSA minimum wage and overtime pay provisions. Companies hire temporary employees to fill in as needed. This means that companies may hire temporary employees at any time throughout a calendar year. However, seasonal employees work during set regular periods every year. Lifeguards on New England beaches are seasonal employees because they work only during the summer months, when people visit beaches to swim. Summer camp counselors are also seasonal employees.

The FLSA extends coverage to temporary employees. Thus, temporary employment agencies must pay temporary workers at least the federal minimum wage rate. Also, the FLSA requires employers to provide overtime pay at one and one-half times the normal hourly rate for each hour worked beyond 40 hours per week. Host companies are responsible for FLSA compliance if temporary employment agencies are not involved, as in the case of direct hire or on-call arrangements.

Some seasonal employees are exempt from the FLSA's minimum wage and overtime pay provisions [24]. The FLSA itself as drafted does not explicitly address minimum wage and overtime pay practices for seasonal employees. However, professional legal opinions were added as needed to resolve ambiguities and guide practice. The opinions pertain to specific employers' questions about the act's scope of coverage—for example, the applicability of FLSA overtime and minimum wage provisions to seasonal amusement park workers. Professional opinions do not automatically generalize to all seasonal employees. For example, all amusement or recreational establishment employees are covered by the FLSA's minimum wage and overtime pay provisions when the establishments operate at least 7 months per year. However, youth counselors employed at summer camps are generally exempt from the FLSA minimum wage and overtime pay provisions.

Fringe Compensation

Anecdotal evidence indicates that companies typically do not provide discretionary benefits to temporary employees. This information should not be surprising. As we discussed earlier, many companies employ temporary workers to minimize discretionary benefits costs. However, temporary employees (and seasonal workers) are eligible for qualified pension benefits if they meet ERISA's minimum service requirements for seasonal and part-time employees, as discussed earlier.

The **dual employer common law doctrine** establishes temporary workers' rights to receive workers' compensation [25]. According to this doctrine, temporary workers are employees of both temporary employment agencies and the client companies. The written contract between the employment agency and client company specifies which organization's workers' compensation policy applies in the event of injuries.

TABLE 14-5 Safe Harbor Rule Requirements

- The leased employee must be covered by the leasing company's pension plan, which must (1) be a money purchase plan with a nonintegrated employer contribution rate for each participant of at least 10 percent of compensation, (2) provide for full and immediate vesting, and (3) allow each employee of the leasing organization to immediately participate in such a plan; and
- Leased employees cannot constitute more than 20 percent of the recipient's "nonhighly compensated workforce." Nonhighly compensated workforce means the total number of (1) nonhighly compensated individuals who are employees of the recipient and who have performed services for the recipient for at least a year or (2) individuals who are leased employees of the recipient (determined without regard to the leasing rules).

Source: I.R.C. §414(n)(5).

Leased Workers

Designating leased employees' legal employers is less clear than for part-time and temporary employees. Leasing companies are the legal employers regarding wage issues and legally required benefits. However, leasing companies and client companies are the legal employers regarding particular discretionary benefits. Thus, compensating leased employees is complex.

- Do leased employees receive discretionary benefits?
- Who is responsible for providing discretionary benefits: the leasing company or the client company?

Core Compensation

In February 2001, leased employees earned an average hourly wage of $19.75 [26]. Currently, systematic compensation data for leased employees are very limited. Thus, it is not possible to compare leased employees' and core employees' wages and salaries.

Fringe Compensation

Both pension eligibility and discretionary benefits are key issues. Leased employees are generally entitled to participation in the client companies' qualified retirement programs. However, the leasing company becomes responsible for leased employees' retirement benefits when the **safe harbor rule** [27] requirements are met. Table 14-5 lists the safe harbor rule requirements.

Another section of the Internal Revenue Code influences companies' discretionary benefits policies (excluding retirement benefits) for leased employees [28]. Under this rule, client companies are responsible for providing leased employees with group medical insurance, group life insurance, educational assistance programs, and continuation coverage requirements for group health plans under COBRA.

Independent Contractors, Freelancers, and Consultants

The Bureau of Labor Statistics does not monitor pay levels for independent contractors. Companies are not obligated to pay the following on behalf of independent contractors, freelancers, and consultants:

- Federal income tax withholding.
- Overtime and minimum wages required under the FLSA. However, employers are obligated to pay financially dependent workers overtime and minimum wages.

- Insurance premiums required under state workers' compensation laws, except where states explicitly require that companies maintain workers' compensation coverage for all workers regardless of whether they are independent contractors.
- Protection under the Employee Retirement Income Security Act of 1974 (ERISA), the Family and Medical Leave Act, the National Labor Relations Act (NLRA), Title VII of the Civil Rights Act of 1964, and the Americans with Disabilities Act (ADA).

To determine whether employees are financially dependent, employers must first apply the **economic reality test**. Table 14-6 lists the criteria. For example, are topless nightclub dancers entitled to minimum wage under FLSA? A nightclub's owners claimed that the dancers were not eligible because they were independent contractors:

- The dancers could perform whenever and wherever they wanted.
- The club had no control over the manner of performance.
- The dancers must furnish their own costumes.

A federal district court ruled that the nightclub's topless dancers were entitled to minimum wage because they were economically dependent on the nightclub [29]. The dancers were economically dependent on the nightclub for the following reasons:

- The club owners set hours in which the dancers could perform.
- The club owners issued guidelines on dancers' behavior at the club.
- The club owners deducted 20 percent from the credit card tips of each dancer to cover administrative costs.

Again, employers' obligations under many federal and state employment laws depend on whether workers are employees or independent contractors. Companies must use the Internal Revenue Code's right to control test to determine whether such individuals are employees or independent contractors. Possessing the right to control work activities classifies individuals as employees rather than independent contractors. Table 14-7 lists 20 criteria of the **right to control test**.

TABLE 14-6 Economic Reality Test: Six Criteria to Determine Whether Workers Are Financially Dependent on the Employer

1. The extent to which the worker has the right to control the result of the work and the manner in which the work is performed
2. The degree to which the individual is "economically dependent" on the employer's business or, in other words, the amount of control the employer has over the individual's opportunity to realize a profit or sustain a loss
3. The extent to which the services are an integral part of the employer's business operations
4. The amount of initiative or level of skill required for the worker to perform the job
5. The permanency, exclusivity, or duration of the relationship between the employer and the worker
6. The extent of the worker's investment in equipment or materials required for the job

TABLE 14-7 Right to Control Test: 20 Factors to Determine Whether an Employer Has the Right to Control a Worker

1. *Instructions.* Requiring a worker to comply with another person's instructions about when, where, and how he or she is to work ordinarily indicates an employer-employee relationship.
2. *Training.* Training a worker indicates that the employer wants the services performed in a particular manner and demonstrates the employer's control over the means by which the result is reached.
3. *Integration.* Integration of the worker's services into the business operations and the dependence of success or continuation of the business on the worker's services generally indicate that the worker is subject to a certain amount of direction and control by the employer.
4. *Services rendered personally.* If the services must be rendered personally, presumably the employer is interested in the methods used to accomplish the work as well as the result, and control is indicated.
5. *Hiring, supervising, and paying assistants.* The employer's hiring, supervising, and paying the worker's assistants generally indicates control over the worker. However, if it is the worker who hires, supervises, and pays his or her assistants and is ultimately responsible for their work, then the worker has an independent contractor status.
6. *Continuing relationship.* A continuing relationship between the worker and the employer indicates that an employer-employee relationship exists.
7. *Set hours of work.* The establishment of set hours of work by the employer indicates control.
8. *Full-time required.* If the worker must devote full-time to the employer's business, the employer has control over the worker's time. An independent contractor, on the other hand, is free to work when and for whom he or she chooses.
9. *Doing work on employer's premises.* If the work is performed on the employer's premises, control is suggested, especially if the work could be performed elsewhere.
10. *Order or sequence set.* If a worker must perform services in the order or sequence set by the employer, control is indicated because the worker is unable to follow his or her own pattern of work.
11. *Oral or written reports.* Requiring the worker to submit regular or written reports to the employer suggests control.
12. *Payment by hour, week, month.* Payment by the hour, week, or month suggests an employer-employee relationship unless it is just a convenient way of paying a lump sum agreed upon as the cost of a job. Payment by the job or on commission generally indicates an independent contractor status.
13. *Payment of business and/or traveling expenses.* If the employer ordinarily pays the worker's business or traveling expenses, the worker is an employee.
14. *Furnishing of tools and materials.* If the employer furnishes significant tools, materials, and other equipment, an employer-employee relationship usually exists.
15. *Significant investment by worker.* If a worker invests in facilities that he or she uses to perform services and that are not typically maintained by an employee (such as rental of office space), an independent contractor status usually is indicated. Lack of investment in facilities tends to indicate that the worker depends on the employer for such facilities.
16. *Realization of profit or loss.* A worker who cannot realize a profit or suffer a loss as a result of his or her services generally is an employee.
17. *Working for more than one firm at a time.* If a worker performs more than *de minimis* services for a multiple of unrelated persons or firms at the same time, independent contractor status is generally indicated.
18. *Making services available to general public.* If a worker makes his or her services available to the general public on a regular and consistent basis, independent contractor status is indicated.
19. *Right to discharge.* The employer's right to discharge a worker indicates employee status.
20. *Right to terminate.* If a worker can terminate his or her relationship with the employer at any time without incurring liability, employee status is indicated.

Source: Rev. Rul. 87-41, 1987-1 C.B. 296.

FLEXIBLE WORK SCHEDULES: FLEXTIME, COMPRESSED WORKWEEKS, AND TELECOMMUTING

Many companies now offer employees flexible work schedules to help them balance work and family demands. Flextime and compressed workweek schedules are the most prominent flexible work schedules used in companies. Flexible work schedule practices apply to both core employees and contingent employees.

Flextime Schedules

Flextime schedules allow employees to modify their work schedules within specified limits set by the employer. Employees adjust when they will start work and when they will leave. However, flextime generally does not lead to reduced work hours. For instance, an employee may choose to work between 10 A.M. and 6 P.M., 9 A.M. and 5 P.M., or 8 A.M. and 4 P.M..

All workers must be present during certain workday hours when business activity is regularly high. This period is known as **core hours**. The number of core hours may vary from company to company, by departments within companies, or by season. Although employees are relatively free to choose start and completion times that fall outside core hours, management must carefully coordinate these times to avoid understaffing. Some flextime programs incorporate a **banking hours** feature that enables employees to vary the number of work hours daily as long as they maintain the regular number of work hours on a weekly basis.

Employers can expect three possible benefits from using flextime schedules. First, flextime schedules lead to less tardiness and absenteeism. Flexibly defining the workweek better enables employees to schedule medical and other appointments outside work hours. As a result, workers are less likely to be late or miss work altogether.

Second, flexible work schedules should lead to higher work productivity. Employees have more choice about when to work during the day. Individuals who work best during the morning hours may schedule morning hours, and individuals who work best during the afternoons or evenings can choose these times. In addition, possessing the flexibility to attend to personal matters outside work should help employees focus on doing better jobs.

Third, flexible work schedules benefit employers by creating longer business hours and better service. Staggering employees' schedules should enable businesses to stay open longer hours without incurring overtime pay expenses. Also, customers should perceive better service because of expanded business hours. Companies that conduct business by telephone on national and international bases are more likely to be open during customers' normal operating hours in other time zones.

Two possible limitations of flexible work schedules are increased overhead costs and coordination problems. Maintaining extended operations leads to higher overhead costs, including support staff and utilities. In addition, flexible work schedules may lead to work coordination problems when some employees are not present at the same time.

Compressed Workweek Schedules

Compressed workweek schedules enable employees to perform their work in fewer days than a regular 5-day workweek. As a result, employees may work four 10-hour days or three 12-hour days. These schedules can promote companies' recruitment and retention successes by:

- Reducing the number of times employees must commute between home and work
- Providing more time together for dual-career couples who live apart

Telecommuting

Telecommuting represents an alternative work arrangement in which employees work at home or at some other location besides the office. Telecommuters generally spend part of their time working in the office and the other part working at home. This alternative work arrangement is appropriate for work that does not require regular direct interpersonal interactions with other workers. Examples include accounting, systems analysis, and telephone sales. Telecommuters stay in touch with coworkers and superiors through electronic mail, telephone, and faxes. Table 14-8 summarizes the variety of possible telecommuting arrangements.

Potential benefits for employers include increased productivity and lower overhead costs for office space and supplies. Telecommuting also serves as an effective recruiting and retention practice for employees who strongly desire to perform their jobs away from the office. Employers may also increase the retention of valued employees who choose not to move when their companies relocate.

Employees find telecommuting beneficial. Telecommuting enables parents to be near their infants or preschool-age children and to be home when older children finish their school days. In addition, telecommuting arrangements minimize commuting time and expense, which are exceptional in such congested metropolitan areas as Boston, Los Angeles, and New York City. Travel time may increase threefold during peak "rush hour" traffic periods. Parking and toll costs can be hefty. Monthly parking rates alone often exceed hundreds of dollars per car. Finally, employees' involvement in office politics will be reduced, which should promote higher job performance.

Telecommuting programs may also lead to disadvantages for employers and employees. Some employers are concerned about not having direct contact with employees, which makes conducting performance appraisals more difficult. Employees sometimes feel that work-at-home arrangements are disruptive to their personal lives. In addition, some employees feel isolated because they do not personally interact as often with coworkers and superiors.

Flexible Work Schedules: Balancing the Demands of Work Life and Home Life

Some U.S. companies use flexible work schedules to help employees balance the demands of work life and home life. Flextime, compressed workweeks, and telecommuting should provide single parents or dual-career parents the opportunity to spend

TABLE 14-8 Alternative Telecommuting Arrangements

- *Satellite work center.* Employees work from a remote extension of the employer's office that includes a clerical staff and a full-time manager.
- *Neighborhood work center.* Employees work from a satellite office shared by several employers.
- *Nomadic executive office.* Executives who travel extensively maintain control over projects through use of telephone, fax, and electronic mail.
- Employees sometimes work entirely outside the office. Others might work off-site only once a month or 2 to 3 days a week.
- Telecommuters can be full- or part-time employees.
- Telecommuting arrangements can be temporary or permanent. A temporarily disabled employee may work at home until fully recovered. A permanently disabled employee may work at home exclusively.

Source: Adapted from Bureau of National Affairs, Telecommuting, 1996. *Compensation & Benefits* [CD-ROM] Washington, DC: Bureau of National Affairs.

more time with their children. Flextime gives parents the opportunity to schedule work around special events at their children's schools. Compressed workweeks enable parents on limited incomes to save on day care costs by reducing the number of days at the office. Parents can benefit from telecommuting in a similar fashion. Likewise, dual-career couples living apart also benefit from flexible work schedules. Compressed workweeks and telecommuting reduce the time spouses have to spend away from each other.

CORE AND FRINGE COMPENSATION FOR FLEXIBLE EMPLOYEES

The key core compensation issue for flexible work schedules is overtime pay. The main fringe compensation issues are pay for time not worked benefits and working condition fringe benefits.

Core Compensation

In many cases, "flexible" employees work more than 40 hours during some weeks and fewer hours during other weeks. The FLSA requires that companies compensate nonexempt employees at an overtime rate equal to one and one-half times the normal hourly rate for each hour worked in excess of 40 hours per week. The overtime provisions are based on employees' working set hours during fixed work periods. How do FLSA overtime provisions apply to flexible work schedules?

Let's assume the following flexible work schedule: An employee works 40 hours during the first week, 30 hours during a second week, and 50 hours during a third week. Although this employee worked 40 hours per week, on average, for the 3-week period ([40 + 30 + 50 hours]/3 weeks), is she entitled to overtime pay for the additional 10 hours worked during the third week?

Some employees' weekly flexible schedules may fluctuate frequently and unpredictably according to such nonwork demands as chronically ill family members. Unpredictable flexible schedules make overtime pay calculations difficult. It is possible that companies may make inadequate or excessive overtime payments. A Supreme Court ruling (***Walling v. A. H. Belo Corp.***) [30] requires employers to guarantee fixed weekly pay for employees whose work hours vary from week to week:

- The employer typically cannot determine the number of hours employees will work each week.
- The workweek period fluctuates both above and below 40 hours per week.

This pay provision guarantees employees fixed weekly pay regardless of how many hours they work, and it enables employers to control weekly labor cost expenditures.

The use of compressed workweek schedules may lead to differences in overtime practices in some states. Whereas the federal government bases overtime pay on a weekly basis, some states use other time bases to determine overtime pay eligibility. Table 14-9 lists maximum hour provisions for select states. As you can see, there is wide variation in daily overtime practices.

Fringe Compensation

Flexible workweek schedules have the greatest impact on paid time-off benefits. Many companies determine employees' sick leave benefits and vacation days based on the number of hours they work each month. The determination of paid vacation and sick leave for employees on standard work schedules is relatively straightforward. However, flexible employees work fewer hours some months and more hours during

TABLE 14-9 Maximum Hours Before Overtime for Selected States

Arkansas

- 10-hour day, 40-hour week for workers with flexible work hour plan if part of collective bargaining agreement or signed employer-employee agreement filed with state Department of Labor.

Connecticut

- 9-hour day, 48-hour week in manufacturing/mechanical establishments for workers under 18 or over 65, handicapped persons, and disabled veterans.
- 10-hour day, 55-hour week during emergencies or peak demand, with commissioner's permission.
- 6-day, 48-hour week for employees under 18 or over 66, handicapped persons, and disabled veterans in public restaurant, café, dining room, barber shop, hairdressing, or manicuring establishment; amusement or recreational establishment; bowling alley, shoe shining establishment; billiard or pool room, or photographic gallery.

Michigan

- 10 hours a day in factories, workshops, salt blocks, sawmills, logging or lumber camps, booms or drivers, mines or other places used for mechanical or manufacturing purposes.

Nevada

- 8-hour day, 40-hour week, unless mutually agreed 10-hour day, 4-day week.

other months. This variability complicates companies' calculations of paid time-off benefits.

Another issue is the treatment of paid time-off for holidays. Under standard work schedules, the vast majority of employees work five 8-hour days from Monday through Friday. For example, all employees take Thanksgiving Day off (a Thursday) with pay. Under flexible schedules, some employees may not be scheduled to work on Thursdays. Consequently, standard-schedule employees receive one day off with pay during Thanksgiving week, and some flexible employees work their regular schedules, missing a paid day off from work. Companies must establish policies that provide flexible workers with comparable paid time-off benefits or alternative holidays. Such policies are necessary to maintain equity among employees. However, scheduling alternative holidays may lead to coordination problems for small companies: Companies with small staffs may not have enough employees to cover for flexible workers during their alternative holiday time off work.

A fringe compensation issue known as **working condition fringe benefits** applies to telecommuters. Employers are likely to provide telecommuters with the necessary equipment to perform their jobs effectively while off-site: computers, modems, printers, photocopy machines, sundry office supplies, and telex machines. In addition, some employers provide similar equipment to employees who wish to work additional hours outside their regular work schedules during the evenings or weekends. This arrangement does not qualify as telecommuting.

The Internal Revenue Service treats the home use of office equipment and supplies as employees' taxable income when the use falls outside established telecommuting relationships. However, employees are not taxed when the home use of employer-provided equipment falls within established telecommuting relationships. Under this condition, the Internal Revenue Service treats the home use of employer-provided equipment as a working condition fringe benefit.

UNIONS' REACTIONS TO CONTINGENT WORKERS AND FLEXIBLE WORK SCHEDULES

Unions generally do not support companies' use of contingent workers and flexible work schedules. Most union leaders believe that alternative work arrangements threaten members' job security and are prone to unfair and inequitable treatment. The most common concerns include:

- Employers exploit contingent workers by paying them lower wages and benefits than core employees.
- Employers' efforts to get cheap labor will lead to a poorly trained and less skilled workforce that will hamper competitiveness.
- Part-time employees are difficult to organize because their interests are centered on activities outside the workplace. Thus, part-time workers probably are not good union members.
- Part-time employment erodes labor standards: Part-time workers are often denied fringe benefits, job security, and promotion opportunities. Increasing part-time employment would promote inequitable treatment.
- Temporary employees generally have little concern about improving the productivity of a company for which they will work for only a brief period.
- Unions' bargaining power becomes weak when companies demonstrate their ability to perform effectively with temporaries.
- The long days of compressed workweeks or flextime could endanger workers' safety and health, even if the workers choose these long days themselves.
- Concerns about employee isolation, uncompensated overtime, and company monitoring in the home are among the reasons unions have been reluctant to permit telecommuting by their members.

Unions' positions against contingent employment are unlikely to change because this practice undermines efforts to secure high wages and job security for members. However, some unions, particularly in the public sector, have begun to accept the use of flexible work schedules. The benefits of these arrangements—increased productivity, lower absence rates, and tardiness—strengthen unions' bargaining power.

STRATEGIC ISSUES AND CHOICES IN USING CONTINGENT AND FLEXIBLE WORKERS

As you will recall, in Chapter 2 we reviewed a framework for selecting particular compensation tactics to match a company's competitive strategy. How do contingent workers and flexible work schedules fit with the two fundamental competitive strategies: lowest-cost and differentiation? Ultimately, these innovations, when properly applied, can contribute to meeting the goals of lowest-cost and differentiation strategies. However, the rationale for the appropriateness of contingent employment and flexible work schedules differs according to the imperatives of the lowest-cost and differentiation competitive strategies.

Lowest-Cost Competitive Strategy

Lowest-cost strategies require firms to reduce output costs per employee. Contingent employment saves companies considerable amounts of money because they do not give these workers most discretionary benefits. Discretionary benefits represent a significant fiscal cost to companies.

Employers' use of well-trained contingent workers also contributes through reduced training costs. However, not all contingent workers know company-specific work practices and procedures. Company-specific training represents a significant cost to companies. Companies that do not employ contingent workers long enough to realize the productivity benefits from training undermine lowest-cost objectives. Company-sponsored training may seem to contradict the lowest-cost imperative in the short term. The following factors can increase short-term costs:

- Costs of training materials and instructors' professional fees
- Downtime while employees are participating in training
- Inefficiencies that may result until employees master new skills

However, a longer-term perspective may lead to the conclusion that contingent work arrangements support the lowest-cost imperatives. Over time, productivity enhancements and increased flexibility should far outweigh the short-run costs if companies establish track records of high productivity, quality, and exemplary customer service.

Flexible schedules should also contribute to lowest-cost imperatives. Limited evidence suggests that flexible employees demonstrate lower absenteeism than employees with fixed work schedules.

Differentiation Competitive Strategy

A differentiation strategy requires creative, open-minded, risk-taking employees. Compared with lowest-cost strategies, companies that pursue differentiation strategies must take a longer-term focus to attain their preestablished objectives. Both arrangements should contribute to innovation; however, systematic studies demonstrating these relationships are lacking. Contingent employment probably is appropriate because companies will benefit from the influx of "new" employees from time to time who bring fresh ideas with them. Over the long run, contingent employment should minimize problems of **groupthink**, which occurs when all group members agree on mistaken solutions because they share the same mindset and view issues through the lens of conformity [31].

Flexible work schedules should also promote differentiation strategies for two reasons. First, flexible work schedules enable employees to work when they are at their physical or mental best. Some individuals are most alert during morning hours while others are most alert during afternoon or evening hours because of differences in biorhythms. Second, flexible work schedules allow employees to work with fewer distractions and worries about personal matters. The inherent flexibility of these schedules allows employees to attend to personal matters as needed.

SUMMARY

This chapter discussed contingent workers and flexible work arrangements, reasons companies rely on contingent employment arrangements and flexible work schedules, special compensation issues, unions' reactions to contingent employment and flexible work schedules, and their fit with competitive strategies. Companies that choose to employ contingent workers must give serious consideration to the possible long-term benefits and consequences. Flexible work schedules seem to accommodate the changing workers' needs well. Given the possible limitations of contingent employment and flexible work schedules, companies should strike a balance between the use of core employment and contingent employment, as well as a balance between standard work schedules and flexible work schedules.

Key Terms

- core employees, 444
- contingent workers, 444
- voluntary part-time employee, 444
- involuntary part-time employees, 445
- job sharing, 445
- temporary employment agency, 447
- direct hire arrangements, 448
- on-call arrangements, 449
- lease companies, 449
- independent contractors, 449
- freelancers, 449
- consultants, 449
- dual employer common law doctrine, 454
- safe harbor rule, 455
- economic reality test, 456
- right to control test, 456
- flextime schedules, 458
- core hours, 458
- banking hours, 458
- compressed workweek schedules, 458
- telecommuting, 459
- *Walling v. A. H. Belo Corp.*, 460
- working condition fringe benefits, 461
- groupthink, 463

Discussion Questions

1. Discuss some of the problems that companies are likely to face when both contingent workers and core employees work in the same location. Does it matter whether contingent workers and core employees are performing the same jobs? Explain your answer.
2. Companies generally pay temporary employees lower wages and offer fewer benefits than they extend to their core counterparts. Nevertheless, what are some of the possible drawbacks for companies that employ temporary workers? Do you believe that these drawbacks outweigh the cost savings? Explain your reasoning.
3. What arguments can be made in favor of using compressed workweek schedules for companies that pursue lowest-cost strategies? What are the arguments against using compressed workweek schedules in such situations?
4. What impact will flexible work schedules have on employees' commitment to their employers? On employee productivity? On company effectiveness?
5. Provide your reactions to the following statement: Contingent workers should be compensated on a pay-for-knowledge system.

Exercises

Compensation Online

For Students

Exercise 1: Find relevant journal articles

You have been given a case study regarding a company that attempted to use flexible work arrangements and failed for lack of planning. Use your school library's online catalog to locate articles pertaining to part-time employees, contingent workers, telecommuting, and contingent worker compensation. Find and read several current articles in these areas. Write a paper on what aspects of a flexible system are necessary for success.

Exercise 2: Search for information on flexible work options

The case study you analyzed in class has left you wanting a more in-depth look at alternative work arrangements. To learn more about flexible work options, go to *www.context.org/* and click on "Search all the IC Issues." Select one of the articles and write a brief summary about its contents.

Next, use the search engine of your choice and look for sites about "flexible work options." Which search engine was easier to use? Which search engine gave you the most options?

Exercise 3: Research flextime schedules

Your professor has given the class an opportunity for extra credit. You must bring information about or examples of flextime to class and be able to describe and explain the system to the rest of class. Using the Yahoo search engine, click on the advanced search link, type in "flextime schedules," select "an exact phrase match," and search. Scan over a couple of the sites. What did you learn about flextime schedules from these sites? Be prepared to discuss your findings in class.

Next, use the search engine of your choice and search for "flextime schedules." Which search engine was easier to use? Which search engine gave you the most options?

For Professionals

Exercise 1: Research a temporary help company

Your manufacturing firm is cutting back on production, but, rather than lay off workers, you would like to institute an employee leasing program. This way, your employees can continue to earn wages and benefits, and the firm can generate some revenue. To get off on the right foot, you are assigned the task of researching how temporary help companies operate. To gain an understanding of how a temporary help company markets and operates its business, go to Manpower's Web site at *www.manpower.com/*. What did you learn about Manpower? What audiences do you think the Web site is geared toward? How effective do you think it will be in reaching each audience?

Exercise 2: Review worker classification policy and compliance

For tax and benefits purposes, it may suit a company to classify as a temporary worker what is, in essence, a full-time worker. Recently, firms have come under government scrutiny for how they classify their workers. To be sure your firm is on the up and up, conduct an advanced search on Yahoo for the exact phrase match of "worker classification." Review several of the sites and pay specific attention to what implications classifying workers has on their compensation, as well as the financial impact on the employer.

Exercise 3: Keep up with current events in human resources

Visit the Public Policy Association of Senior Human Resource Executives Web site at *www.lpa.org*. Search this site for "contingent workers," "flexible workers," "telecommuting," and any other topics of interest from this chapter. Read news releases and articles published by human resource executives, and try to identify trends and significant issues. How would these issues have an impact on your role as an HR professional?

Endnotes

1. U.S. Bureau of Labor Statistics. (2002). Employer costs for employee compensation—March 2002 [online]. Available: *www.bls.gov/ncs/ect/home.htm*, accessed July 24, 2002.
2. U.S. Bureau of Labor Statistics. (2002). Employer costs for employee compensation—March 2002 [online]. Available: *www.bls.gov/ncs/ect/home.htm*, accessed July 24, 2002.
3. U.S. Bureau of Labor Statistics. (2001). Contingent and alternative employment arrangements, February 2001 (USDL 01-153) [online]. Available: *www.bls.gov/bls/newsrels.htm*, accessed July 22, 2002.
4. Fallick, B. B. (1999). Part-time work and industry growth. *Monthly Labor Review, 122*, pp. 22–29.
5. Callaghan, P., & Hartmann, H. (1991). *Contingent Work: A Chartbook on Part-Time and Temporary Employment*. Washington DC: Economic Policy Institute.
6. Burgess, P. M. (1994). *Making it in America's new economy*. Commencement Address, University of Toledo, June 11.
7. U.S. Bureau of Labor Statistics. (2002). Employer costs for employee compensation—March 2002 [online]. Available: *www.bls.gov/ncs/ect/home.htm*, accessed July 24, 2002.
8. Caudron, S. (1994). Contingent workforce spurs HR planning. *Personnel Journal*, July, pp. 52–60.
9. U.S. Bureau of Labor Statistics. (2002). Employer costs for employee compensation—March 2002 [online]. Available: *www.bls.gov/ncs/ect/home.htm*, accessed July 24, 2002.
10. U.S. Bureau of Labor Statistics. (2002). Employer costs for employee compensation—March 2002

[online]. Available: *www.bls.gov/ncs/ect/home.htm*, accessed July 24, 2002.

11. U.S. Bureau of Labor Statistics. (2002). Employer costs for employee compensation—March 2002 [online]. Available: *www.bls.gov/ncs/ect/home.htm*, accessed July 24, 2002.
12. U.S. Bureau of Labor Statistics. (2002). Employer costs for employee compensation—March 2002 [online]. Available: *www.bls.gov/ncs/ect/home.htm*, accessed July 24, 2002.
13. U.S. Bureau of Labor Statistics. (2002). Employer costs for employee compensation—March 2002 [online]. Available: *www.bls.gov/ncs/ect/home.htm*, accessed July 24, 2002.
14. England, P. (1992). *Comparable Worth: Theories and Evidence*. New York: Aldine DeGruyler.
15. Hayghe, H. V. (1990). Family members in the workforce. *Monthly Labor Review*, *113*, pp. 14–19.
16. U.S. Bureau of Labor Statistics. (2002). Employer costs for employee compensation—March 2002 [online]. Available: *www.bls.gov/ncs/ect/home.htm*, accessed July 24, 2002.
17. Cooper, S. F. (1995). The expanding use of contingent workers in the American economy: New opportunities and dangers for employers. *Employee Relations Law Review*, *20*, pp. 525–539.
18. U.S. Bureau of Labor Statistics (2002). Employer costs for employee compensation—March 2002 [online]. Available: *www.bls.gov/ncs/ect/home.htm*, accessed July 24, 2002.
19. U.S. Bureau of Labor Statistics. (1999). *Employee Benefits in Medium and Large Private Establishments, 1997*. Washington, DC: U.S. Government Printing Office.
20. U.S. Bureau of Labor Statistics. (1998). *Employee Benefits in Small Private Establishments, 1996*. Washington, DC: U.S. Government Printing Office.
21. Internal Revenue Code 410(a)(1).
22. Coleman, B. J. (1993). *Primer on ERISA* (4th ed.). Washington DC: Bureau of National Affairs.
23. U.S. Bureau of Labor Statistics. (2002). Employer costs for employee compensation—March 2002 [online]. Available: *www.bls.gov/ncs/ect/home.htm*, accessed July 24, 2002.
24. Internal Revenue Code 411(b)(4)(c).
25. Bureau of National Affairs. *Employee relations weekly, October 24, 1994*. Washington, DC: Author.
26. U.S. Bureau of Labor Statistics. (2002). Employer costs for employee compensation—March 2002 [online]. Available: *www.bls.gov/ncs/ect/home.htm*, accessed July 24, 2002.
27. Internal Revenue Code 414(n)(5).
28. Internal Revenue Code 414(n)(1)(2)(3).
29. *Martin v. Priba Corp.*, USDC N. Texas, No. 3:91-CV-278-G (11/6/92).
30. *Walling v. A. H. Belo Corp.*, 316, U.S. 624, 2WH Cases 39 (1942).
31. Sheppard, C. R. (1964). *Small Groups.* San Francisco: Chandler.

COMPENSATION IN ACTION

HR TAKES CHARGE OF CONTINGENT STAFFING

It's not always seen as HR's job, but unless HR manages its organization's use of temporary workers, it runs the risk of serious legal, financial, and security problems.

With all the workplace issues that HR has to juggle, the hiring and management of contingent workers might be low on the list. Why worry about temps, who are here today, gone tomorrow, and as expendable as paper clips? They're hardly as important as the hiring, training, and compensation of a cadre of regular employees.

That's one school of thought. But some HR professionals realize that temps aren't quite so trivial. In their view, it's critical to have a clear concept of how temps are hired, managed, and released. A company that uses contingent workers but doesn't track them can find itself on shaky legal, financial, and security ground:

Microsoft Corporation agreed to a $97 million settlement in 2000 to end a long court battle with its "permatemps" contingent workers who were hired for years at a time by the software company, allegedly in an attempt to avoid paying them for health benefits, pensions, and employee stock-purchase plans.

A Minneapolis company that makes medical devices estimated that its outlay for contingent workers was Number 9 on a list of its 10 largest expenditures. Once the company began to track its actual spending with itiliti, a company that provides Web-based workforce procurement and management software, it found that the cost of contingent workers actually ranked No. 2.

Another company's records showed that 1,200 security badges had been issued to IT contractors, but the company had only 400 temps in its workforce. That meant that 800 active security badges were in the hands of people who could "come in and do what they wanted," although they no longer worked at the site, says Chad Wells, vice president of marketing and business development for itiliti, which is based in Edina, Minnesota.

HR'S ROLE IN CONTINGENT STAFFING

How does HR fit into all this? That depends on the organization involved. In many large companies, procurement hires contingent workers. IT groups also do much of their own contingent hiring, given the specialized nature of the work.

But there are organizations in which procurement isn't responsible, and neither is HR, says Bill Rothenbach, vice president and service director in Syndicated Research Group's human capital strategies service. "Sometimes there's a distrust of HR that makes line managers unwilling to bring it into the process," he says.

And in some companies, HR has no interest in being involved, even though the interviewing and "hiring" process of temps is more akin to HR than procurement.

That's been the experience of Gene Zaino, CEO of Contractors Resources. His company provides administrative and business management services for independent contractors and acts as the third-party employer of record for the companies that engage them. "HR says, 'We don't do [contingent or consulting hiring]—that's procurement,'" he says. "We'd love to pull HR in. We think it would be of tremendous value to the organization."

HR absolutely should be in the business of managing contingent workers if those workers make up a regular, significant part of an organization's staffing, says Linda Merritt, human resources strategic planning director for AT&T.

"It's a workforce capability management issue," she says. Contingent staffing "becomes a place where capabilities are housed. If you can't see into it, you don't know if it's being managed well.

"You might want to see some people re-employed in your organization [after an assignment ends]," she says. "But if the only person who knows about them is a local line manager, or procurement, who just got them paid but doesn't

(Continued)

(Continued)

know about their skill sets," HR can't begin to make that decision.

Part of the problem lies in business systems that don't talk to each other, or don't collect the same sets of information. Procurement cares only about making sure that contingent workers get paid. It doesn't have to collect information about their performance or skills. But there are ways around that, Merritt says. "It's HR's responsibility to reach out to procurement, to find ways to get the data you need, and they don't. You can access it through some IT solutions."

And what if hiring managers are hiring as they see fit, and no one is keeping tabs on them? That's where the problems begin.

THE CONTINGENT MESS

Without oversight, contingent staffing becomes "a hidden cost to an organization," Rothenbach says. "It's extremely difficult for anyone except finance to know what's being spent on contractual workers."

It's possible for companies to lose track of how many temps they actually have, says Ed Remus, vice president of procurement for NextSource, a human-capital management software company based in New York City. Remus previously worked as senior procurement manager for Lucent Technologies.

While Remus was at Lucent, the company had more than 7,000 temporary IT employees, but because of the way they were hired, the day-to-day head count was nearly impossible to gauge.

"There was no one place we could go and find that out," he says. "The way we had to get information on contingent workforces was to send letters and e-mails to all the VPs, who farmed the letters down to the project managers, saying, 'OK, how many do we have today?' It was a difficult thing." And, Remus adds, Lucent's problem isn't unique. "I see it now with a lot of our customers."

Without some set of controls, line managers use certain staffing companies because they've developed a good relationship with them, or believe they're getting a good price (whether they really are or not). Companies have no opportunity to save money through price comparison and competition, volume discounts, or other negotiating strategies.

That was the situation when Gary Anderson joined Carlson Companies, Inc. The privately held marketing, travel, and hospitality giant owns more than 745 hotels, among them the Radisson chain, and has a restaurant empire that includes TGI Friday's. It employs more than 188,000 people worldwide, but its temporary workforce generally runs "in the hundreds," he says.

Anderson, who is now the manager of contract labor in Carlson corporate procurement, initially was hired to deal with contingent staffing in IT.

"There were the normal things you'd find: maverick buying, paying too much, contracts not in place." Also, staffing companies did not consistently run criminal and educational background checks. To top things off, Carlson was using 144 different staffing companies. So despite its size, the company had no leverage with its vendors. Quality, both of the staffing companies and the temps they supplied, also was an issue. Anderson points out that Carlson's problems were not unique. He hears plenty of similar stories from his procurement colleagues.

Other firms wind up with a temp-management mess because of mergers and acquisitions, says Chris Mortonson, chief sales officer for Fieldglass, another software technology company that has a Web-based application to help companies procure and manage their contingent workforces. In one company that Fieldglass worked with, "There were multiple business units with different purchasing processes, different HR management rules, and no consistent job descriptions across the company or the business units," he says. "There was no common definition of recruiters or procurement, and disparity on what staffing companies were used to hire, even in the same organization. The rates varied, and the quality of the workers varied."

Contingent chaos, in short.

SETTING UP CONTROLS

The first thing a company has to do is assess how much it uses contingent workers. Remus recommends a look at accounts-payable records first. Sometimes that's the only central repository of information about contingent hiring.

Some accounting systems have coding that makes the information easy to find. If the payables list isn't long, "You can eyeball lists of providers. Staffing jumps right out at HR. And if you see lots of payments to individuals [who might be independent contractors], that's a red flag," he says.

Once HR knows the extent of the organization's use of contingent workers, it can work with procurement, finance, and hiring managers to develop a process. Anderson said he began by going to staff meetings of various work groups and collecting information there. How many workers were being hired? How long did they stay? Who did the hiring?

Once the patterns are apparent, the organization (perhaps led by a strategic HR professional, as Merritt suggests) can start to create some parameters for contingent hiring. It can decide which vendors to use, on the basis of cost, expertise, and track record, for example. It can determine how long assignments will be, in order to avoid any co-employment problems such as those encountered by Microsoft. It can establish payment limits that can be exceeded only with approval from someone above the hiring manager's level.

As it has in other areas of HR, technology has made contingent workforce management a lot easier. In addition itiliti, Fieldglass, and NextSource, Chimes, eLabor, Cascade Works, and other companies all have software suites that manage contingent staffing from the employer end. More and more staffing companies are introducing systems of their own, and many of them are forming partnerships with the software companies mentioned above.

Most of the systems include instantaneous e-requisitions that greatly speed up the hiring process. These systems can be set up so that only requisitions that fit the guidelines established by HR or procurement can be sent out to staffing companies.

Once the organization has chosen a process for contingent hiring, it's crucial to get the hiring managers to go along with it. No one is going to fire hiring managers for doing an end-run around the new process, but it's a waste of time and money if they don't use it.

"It's an education process, and it takes excellent communication," Anderson says. "You tell the [hiring managers] over and over what you're doing, and you get their buy-in to the process."

What works best, he says, is to create and present a process that shows them why it's in their best interest to use it. "Does it remove work? Lower costs? Remove hassles? What are the deliverables? When you show them that, people get on board." he says.

Remus agrees. "You've got to have something that the users see as a value-add. If they see it as a nuisance, or as work, you're not going to get them to use it."

He recommends selling the new process not only by emphasizing its ease of use, but also by telling the managers, frankly, what risks the company runs by not standardizing and managing the process: higher costs, possible lawsuits, and more. "We've found it's not something you jam down people's throats. You say, 'Here are the risks, and it won't upset your apple cart to do it this way.'"

With technology, the process really can be faster, easier, and cheaper, Anderson says. And when a technology solution is in place, HR or procurement is out of the day-to-day decision-making, and won't become a bottleneck for the hiring manager who needs a temp right now.

In the case of Carlson, implementing itiliti's system meant that the company reduced its list of IT vendors from 144 to 9. Every contract is reviewed at 90 days or at termination so that the company can determine if the vendor and the worker it supplied were up to snuff. Anderson stresses that technology is just a tool, however. "The processes have to be in place first."

HELP FROM THE STAFFING COMPANIES

HR and procurement also have allies on the other end of the process, says Joanie Moran, director of operations for the southern division of Adecco. For starters, companies such as Adecco can help firms analyze their contingent-staffing history. "Sometimes they don't even know how many people they're using. They might think it's

(Continued)

(Continued)

10, and it's 40," says Joyce Russell, senior vice president of Adecco's southern division.

"They might think they have a formal process, but it's not as formal as HR thinks, or the supervisors have gotten a little lax when it comes to requisitions," Moran says. "On their own, they'll requisition 10 people HR doesn't know about."

Once a staffing agency knows an organization's processes, it can serve as a friendly enforcer. "When we come back and say, 'You're not on the approved [hiring manager] list; do you want us to call HR?' they say, 'No, no,'" Moran relates. They go back to the process, she says. The order gets approved in a timely way, but there's been a reminder that there are guidelines, and someone other than HR is keeping an eye on it. "We play the gatekeeper in that process."

LET HR DO IT

Here's a radical concept: Let the HR department do the organization's contingent hiring directly. It knows how to hire. It understands how to use job boards. It probably has an applicant-tracking system for permanent hires. It can save money.

So says Gene Zaino, CEO of Contractors Resources, a company that provides administrative and business-management services for independent contractors and acts as the third-party employer of record for the companies that engage them.

"The HR department has the talent to recruit these people, or even just source them and send them to the chief information officer [who often does IT hiring] or the line managers," Zaino says. "We're saying, Wake up! Give HR a shot at filling the job in three days or so. Let them present three or four people on a contract basis, rather than going to a staffing company."

Granted, Zaino is not a disinterested party. Companies that hire Contractors Resources as the third-party employer of record pay it 1.2 percent of the contractor's gross hourly wage. The idea, Zaino says, is that companies can save 20 percent or more by using his service, which focuses on consultant employment services, and not on recruiting contractor talent.

Zaino says that one client, a major financial brokerage firm that has had as many as 2,200 IT independent consultants and now has 1,400, saved $40 million in 2000 by sourcing its own contractors, while Contractors Resources handled the employer-of-record duties.

A small consultant management group in the company is the central point for the requisitions, Zaino says. Instead of managing vendors, the group started finding contractors on its own. "They're seeing there's a tremendous amount of dollars they can save."

Would that approach work in any company? Zaino thinks so. "It might take an HR executive with a little bit of leadership to bring this forward," he says. "The mind-set with HR that needs to be adjusted is this: The contingent workforce is a valuable part of the workforce. They need to start learning about it, embracing it, and adding value to it."

Source: Carroll Lachnit. *Workforce, 8(3)*, pp. 50–56 (March 2002). ISSN: 1092-8332, Number: 110436491, Copyright ACC Communications, Inc., March 2002.

WHAT'S NEW IN COMPENSATION?

The Cost of Health Insurance Is Out of Reach for Most Independent Contractors

This case addresses health insurance coverage for independent contractors. As we know, health insurance covers the costs of a variety of services that promote sound physical and mental health. Independent contractors must purchase health insurance on their own, oftentimes at much higher rates than rates charged to employers that extend health insurance coverage as a discretionary benefit.

Independent contractors purchase individual coverage. Individual coverage extends insurance protection to one person and possibly to his or her dependents, including children and spouse. The insurance provider (for example, Blue Cross) typically requires that prospective participants furnish evidence of health status based on a medical examination. Insurance providers use mortality tables and morbidity tables to decide whether to offer insurance and, if so, the terms and premium amount. This decision-making process is known as *underwriting*. Mortality tables indicate yearly probabilities of death based on factors such as age and sex. Morbidity tables express annual probabilities of the occurrence of health problems. Actuaries create these tables. In general, insurance companies set insurance rates higher as the probability of death or the occurrence of health problems increases.

In the case of employer-sponsored health insurance, group coverage extends protection to a group of employees and their dependents under a single master contract. Insurance providers issue master contracts to employers, professional associations, labor unions, and trust funds established to provide health insurance to designated people. The underwriting process is somewhat different for group policies. Group policies generally do not exclude any group member based on health status. Instead, they focus mainly on establishing the premium for the master contract, usually expressed on an annual basis. Insurance providers use experience ratings issued by actuaries to set premiums. Actuaries establish experience ratings to specify the incidence, type, and financial cost of insurance claims for groups (that is, everyone as a whole covered under a group plan). Experience ratings hold employers (and other group entities described earlier) financially accountable for past claims thereby establishing the basis for charging different premiums.

Insurance companies typically charge independent contractors substantially higher premiums than the per-employee premium found in employer-sponsored health insurance plans offering comparable health insurance coverage. It is more likely that many of the employees covered under employer plans will not make claims. As a result, health insurance companies will experience a reduced financial burden when considering the large amount of revenue generated through premiums. On the other hand, insurance companies generally charge much more for individual coverage because the cost of claims paid for individual generally far outweighs the amount of revenue generated in premiums by an individual policy holder.

The *New York Times* article featured here highlights a model for extending affordable health insurance coverage to independent contractors. Specifically, the article describes the experience of Working Today, a not-for-profit company that provides health insurance to independent contractors in New York. The article focuses on Working Today's challenge of extending affordable health insurance coverage to approximately 15,000 people who lost their income or experienced significant income declines as a direct result of the September 11, 2001, attacks. The article also describes how Working Today serves as a model for how to provide health insurance to people who do not receive health insurance from an employer or state government. In large part, this model may enable independent contractors to afford health insurance coverage because it would purchase a group policy to cover multiple independent contractors, much like companies purchase group coverage for employees.

Log onto your *New York Times* account. Search the database for articles on "contingent workers" to find a variety of articles about the employment situation of various contingent worker groups (for example, temporary workers, independent contractors, freelancers, consultants). What are some of the compensation issues? Following your course instructor's specific directions, be prepared to describe the current situation, and relate it to the article contained in this text. ■

The New York Times

Health Insurance for Freelancers; A New Group Focuses on an Overlooked Group of Workers

Finding a silver lining in the events of September 11, 2001, isn't easy, and capitalizing on it is even harder.

"I almost don't like to talk about it," said Sara Horowitz, whose nonprofit insurance organization, Working Today, may have hit pay dirt as a result of the attack. "It's, well, sort of unseemly."

Working Today provides portable, affordable health insurance for freelance workers in New York. The concept would seem to be an easy sell, given the swelling ranks of part-time, contract and temporary workers across the country.

But the organization has struggled since its inception to find financing to stay afloat long enough to stand on its own two feet. "It has been a lot harder than I thought it would be," Ms. Horowitz said.

Then, the September 11 Fund, the second-largest pool of philanthropic money raised to help victims of the disaster (after the Red Cross), faced a vexing problem that only Working Today could solve: how to provide a year's worth of health insurance to 15,000 people who are linked only by the effects of the attack.

Suddenly, Working Today looks poised to be a model for delivering health insurance and other benefits in a new way, one better suited to today's mobile, more fluid workforce, which is exactly what Ms. Horowitz, winner of a MacArthur "genius" award in 1999, had hoped when she cooked it up.

"It's sort of sadly ironic that it took something like September 11 to get this concept noticed," said Mara Manus, a former program officer at the Ford Foundation who granted Working Today a $1 million working-capital loan to start it. "She's on to something, she really is."

Health insurance is provided to groups largely by employers and, to a lesser extent, governments and unions. Employees working for the same company are one kind of group. Veterans are another. Poor people are another.

The fund wanted to insure as many as 15,000 people working below Canal Street and in parts of Chinatown north of it who lost jobs or suffered a significant reduction in income as a result of the attacks. They work for an array of employers or none at all. They are rich and poor. They are healthy and sick. They are United States citizens, permanent residents and illegal aliens.

Victims of the trade center attack are in the same boat as part-time and freelance workers: the health insurance system simply is not set up to deal with them.

Ms. Horowitz, whose grandfather was the president of the International Ladies Garment Workers Union and whose father represented labor unions, saw the trends when she was working as a lawyer for the health care union 1199/S.E.I.U., and immediately understood the implications.

"Look, we didn't set ourselves up and create this organization because we knew this would happen," she said. "We were seeing large national trends that showed a growing number of people working independently, not connected to any one long-term employer, and thus unable to get affordable health insurance. It's not like we were brilliant visionaries."

The number of workers who are free agents of one type or another now make up almost a third of the workforce, or 41.8 million people, according to the Economic Policy Institute. Between one-quarter and one-third of them probably do not get insurance from their employers, according to health insurance experts.

But Ms. Horowitz found that the concept of providing health insurance to a group representing a segment of the workforce, rather than a group linked by an employer or income, was too radical for many foundations and other organizations.

"Why is there no competition?" Ms. Horowitz asked. "Because there's no funding in it."

She recalled a meeting in spring 2001 with a foundation that is one of the largest health care underwriters in the country.

"It lasted 10 minutes," she said. "Usually, these presentations turn into discussions, but they had absolutely no interest. I got on the train afterward and was just numb. I couldn't believe that they couldn't see my point."

Ms. Manus, who backed Working Today when she was at Ford, said foundations that back health care focus almost single-mindedly on overhauling existing systems rather than exploring new ones. "In the workforce development field, there's a burgeoning awareness that the structure of work is changing," she said. "So funding is going to come from the people paying attention to those changes, not from the health field, which may not even be aware of this issue."

James R. Tallon Jr., president of the United Hospital Fund, which is the only traditional health care financier among Working Today's backers, said skepticism of Ms. Horowitz's concept by traditional health care backers was understandable if unfortunate. "Public policy has been very skeptical about simply allowing groups to go out and form themselves out of thin air, and for good reason," he said. "To do so would provide an incentive for healthy people to group together and get a great insurance rate, making it almost impossible for less healthy people to get health insurance."

But in 2000, Ms. Horowitz convinced Neil D. Levin, then the state insurance commissioner, that the freelancers, contract workers and temporary employees working in Silicon Alley were a group no different from the employees of, say, Lehman Brothers or Pfizer.

Mr. Levin, who later headed the Port Authority of New York and New Jersey and who was killed in the attack on the World Trade Center, pushed his officials to be creative, and Working Today was classified as an association, a designation that enabled it to provide insurance.

Working Today is not an insurer. Rather, it forms a group and then buys insurance for it from HIP and other providers. On September 4, 2001, Working Today opened for business; 24,000 people tapped into its Web site (*www.workingtoday.org*) in the first week. "Then no one signed up after September 11," Ms. Horowitz recalled. "For the first three months, we thought, oh my God, maybe this won't work."

But in January, eligible uninsured workers started signing up, and now Working Today has almost 1,000 subscribers. They had to show proof that they earned $9,000 in a six-month period or that they were employed in technology jobs for at least 120 hours. Technology is defined as everything from software development to online journalism. The insurance costs an average of $255 a month, which is automatically deducted from their checking accounts.

"The monthly cost is very affordable," said Chris Lombardi, a writer with multiple sclerosis who pays $235 a month.

Before she signed up with Working Today in July, Ms. Lombardi and her partner had been getting by on her partner's COBRA, a federal program that lets workers get insurance at a reduced cost from their former employer for up to 18 months after they leave a job, which cost them $763 a month. She had looked into an insurance program through the National Writers Union, which would have cost about $600.

Ann Quinn, a marketing consultant, started her own business two years ago and began searching for insurance for her family when her COBRA began running out. "It was really expensive," she said.

She read about Working Today and then attended a seminar for free agents at which Ms. Horowitz spoke. "She was like an evangelist," Ms. Quinn said. For coverage for herself, her husband and her daughter, Ms. Quinn pays $740 a month, almost $300 less than she was paying through COBRA, and the insurance she has through Working Today includes preventive dental care.

"There are other options for free agents, but they're pricier and not as flexible," she said.

Working Today will one day be about more than just health insurance, too, if Ms. Horowitz has her way. She intends the organization to evolve into a sort of human resources department for the nation's floating workforce, offering a smorgasbord of benefits. Already, it offers life and disability insurance as well as free checking.

"Through a fluke, September 11 exposed this huge national problem of how to provide health insurance to people who don't get benefits from an employer or the state," Ms. Horowitz said. "It's not like the problem didn't exist before September 11, but it took that disaster to highlight this huge, other disaster we have."

SOURCE: Stephanie Strom, Health insurance for freelancers (October 2, 2002) [online]. Available *www.nytimes.com*, accessed October 10, 2002.

GLOSSARY

Aaron v. City of Wichita, Kansas, a court ruling, offered several criteria to determine whether City of Wichita fire chiefs are exempt employees, including the relative importance of management as opposed to other duties, frequency with which they exercise discretionary powers, relative freedom from supervision, and the relationship between their salaries and wages paid to other employees for similar nonexempt work.

Ability, based on Equal Employment Opportunity Commission guidelines, refers to a present competence to perform an observable behavior or a behavior that results in an observable product.

Age Discrimination in Employment Act of 1967 (ADEA) protects older workers age 40 and over from illegal discrimination.

Agency problem describes an executive's behavior that promotes his or her self-interests rather than the interests of the company owners or shareholders.

Agency theory provides an explanation of executive compensation determination based on the relationship between company owners (shareholders) and agents (executives).

Alternation ranking, a variation of simple ranking job evaluation plans, orders all jobs from lowest to highest, based on alternately identifying the jobs of lowest and highest worth.

Americans with Disabilities Act of 1990 (ADA) prohibits discrimination against individuals with mental or physical disabilities within and outside employment settings, including public services and transportation, public accommodations, and employment.

Andrews v. DuBois, a district court ruling, determined that the following activities at employees' home associated with the care of dogs used for law enforcement are compensable under the Fair Labor Standards Act of 1938 (FLSA): feeding, grooming, and walking the dogs. The court reasoned that these activities were indispensable to maintaining dogs as a critical law enforcement tool, they are part of officers' principal activities, and they benefit the employer.

Aptitudes represent individuals' capacities to learn how to perform specific jobs.

Atonio v. Wards Cove Packing Company, a Supreme Court case, ruled that plaintiffs (that is, employees) in employment discrimination suits must indicate which employment practice created disparate impact and demonstrate how the employment practice created disparate impact (intentional discrimination).

Baby boom generation refers to the generation of people born between 1946 and 1964.

Balance sheet approach provides expatriates the standard of living they normally enjoy in the United States.

Banking hours refers to a feature of flextime schedules that allows employees to vary the number of hours they work each day as long as they work a set number of hours each week.

Base pay represents the monetary compensation employees earn on a regular basis for performing their jobs. Hourly pay and salary are the main forms of base pay.

Base period is the minimum period of time an individual must be employed before becoming eligible to receive unemployment insurance under the Social Security Act of 1935.

Behavioral encouragement plans are individual incentive pay plans that reward employees for specific behavioral accomplishments, such as good attendance or safety records.

Behavioral observation scale (BOS), a specific kind of behavioral system, displays illustrations of positive incidents (or behaviors) of job performance for various job dimensions. The evaluator rates the employee on each behavior according to the extent to which the employee performs in a manner consistent with each behavioral description.

Behavioral systems, a type of performance appraisal method, requires that raters (for example, supervisors) judge the extent to which employees display successful job performance behaviors.

Behaviorally anchored rating scale (BARS), a specific kind of behavioral system, is based on the critical incident technique (CIT), and these scales are developed in the same fashion with one exception. For the CIT, a critical incident would be written as "the incumbent completed the task in a timely fashion." For the BARS format, this incident would be written as "the incumbent is expected to complete the task in a timely fashion."

Benchmark jobs, found outside the company, provide reference points against which the values of jobs within the company are judged.

Bennett Amendment allows employees to charge employers with Title VII violations regarding pay only when the employer has violated the Equal Pay Act of 1963.

Bias errors happen in the performance evaluation process when the rater evaluates the employee based on the rater's negative or positive opinion of the employee rather than on the employee's actual performance.

Board of directors represents shareholders' interests by weighing the pros and cons of top executives' decisions. Members include chief executive officers and top executives of other successful companies, distinguished community leaders, well-regarded professionals (for example, physicians and attorneys), and a few of the company's top-level executives.

Boureslan v. Aramco, a Supreme Court case in which the Supreme Court ruled that federal job discrimination laws do not apply to U.S. citizens working for U.S. companies in foreign countries.

Brito v. Zia Company, a Supreme Court ruling, deemed that the Zia Company violated Title VII of the Civil Rights Act of 1964 when a disproportionate number of protected-class individuals were laid off on the basis of low performance appraisal scores. Zia Company's action was a violation of Title VII because the use of the performance appraisal system in determining layoffs was indeed an employment test. In addition, the court ruled that the Zia Company had not demonstrated that its performance appraisal instrument was valid.

Broadbanding is a pay structure form that leads to the consolidation of existing pay grades and pay ranges into fewer wider pay grades.

Cafeteria plan (see flexible benefits plan).

Capital gains is the difference between the company stock price at the time of purchase and the lower stock price at the time an executive receives the stock options.

Capital requirements include automated manufacturing technology and office and plant facilities.

Capital-intensity refers to the extent to which companies' operations are based on the use of large-scale equipment. On average, capital-intensive industries (for example, manufacturing) pay more than less capital-intensive industries (such as service industries).

Career development is a cooperative effort between employees and their employers to promote rewarding work experiences throughout employees' work lives.

Cash balance plans represent a cross between traditional defined benefits and defined contributions retirement plans. The rate of monetary accumulation slows as the employee's years of service increase.

Central tendency represents the fact that a set of data clusters or centers around a central point. Central tendency is a number that represents the typical numerical value in a data set.

Certification ensures that employees possess at least a minimally acceptable level of skill proficiency upon completion of a training unit. Certification methods can include work samples, oral questioning, and written tests.

Civil Rights Act of 1964 is a major piece of federal legislation designed to protect the rights of underrepresented minorities.

Civil Rights Act of 1991 shifted the burden of proof of disparate impact from employees to employers, overturning several 1989 Supreme Court rulings.

Classification plans, particular methods of job evaluation, place jobs into categories based on compensable factors.

Coinsurance refers to the percentage of covered expenses paid by the insured. Most commercial plans stipulate 20 percent coinsurance. This means that the insured will pay 20 percent of covered expenses while the insurance company pays the remaining 80 percent.

Collective bargaining agreements are written documents that describe the terms of employment reached between management and unions.

Commercial dental insurance provides cash benefits by reimbursing patients for out-of-pocket costs for particular dental care procedures or by paying dentists directly for patient costs.

Commission is a form of incentive compensation, based on a percentage of the product or service selling price and the number of units sold.

Commission-only plans are specific kinds of sales compensation plans. Salespeople derive their entire income through commissions.

Commission-plus-draw plans award sales professionals commissions and draws.

Common review date is the designated date when all employees receive performance appraisals.

Common review period is the designated period (for example, the month of June) when all employees receive performance appraisals.

Company stock represents the total equity or worth of the company.

Company stock shares represent equity segments of equal value. Equity interest increases with the number of stock shares held.

Comparable worth represents an ongoing debate in society regarding pay differentials between men and women who perform similar but not identical work.

Compa-ratios index the relative competitiveness of internal pay rates based on pay range midpoints.

Comparison systems, a type of performance appraisal method, require that raters (for example, supervisors) evaluate a given employee's performance against other employees' performance attainments. Employees are ranked from the best performer to the poorest performer.

Compensable factors are job attributes (for example, skill, effort, responsibility, and working conditions) that compensation professionals use to determine the value of jobs.

Compensation budgets are blueprints that describe the allocation of monetary resources to fund pay structures.

Compensation committees contain board of directors members within and outside a company. Compensation committees review executive compensation consultants' alternate recommendations for compensation packages, discuss the assets and liabilities of the recommendations, and recommend the consultant's best proposal to the board of directors for their consideration.

Compensation strategies describe the use of compensation practices that support human resource and competitive strategies.

Compensation surveys involve the collection and subsequent analysis of competitors' compensation data.

Competency-based pay refers to two specific types of pay programs: pay-for-knowledge and skill-based pay.

Competitive advantage describes a company's success based on employees' efforts to maintain market share and profitability over several years.

Competitive strategy refers to the planned use of company resources—technology, capital, and human resources—to promote and sustain competitive advantage.

Compressed workweek schedules enable employees to perform their full-time weekly work obligations in fewer days than a regular 5-day workweek.

Concessionary bargaining focuses on unions promoting job security over large wage increases in negotiations with management.

Consolidated Omnibus Budget Reconciliation Act of 1985 (COBRA) was enacted to provide employees the opportunity to temporarily continue receiving their employer-sponsored medical care insurance under their employer's plan if their coverage otherwise would cease due to termination, layoff, or other change in employment status.

Consultants (see independent contractors).

Consumer Price Index (CPI) indexes monthly price changes of goods and services that people buy for day-to-day living.

Contingent workers engage in explicitly tentative employment relationships with companies.

Continuous learning is a philosophy that underlies most training efforts in companies. Progressive companies encourage employees to continuously develop their skills, knowledge, and abilities through formal training programs.

Contractors, for the purposes of compensation-related laws, are businesses that provide services to the government (for example, repair of public buildings).

Contrast errors occur when a rater (for example, a supervisor) compares an employee to other employees rather than to specific, explicit performance standards.

Contributory financing implies that the company and its employees share the costs for discretionary benefits.

Contributory pension plans require monetary contributions by the employee who will benefit from the income upon retirement.

Copayments represent nominal payments individuals make for office visits to their doctors or for prescription drugs.

Core compensation describes the monetary rewards employees receive. There are six types of core compensation: base pay, seniority pay, merit pay, incentive pay, cost-of-living adjustments (COLAs), and pay-for-knowledge and skill-based pay.

Core employees possess full-time jobs, and they generally plan long-term or indefinite relationships with their employers.

Core hours, as applied to flextime schedule, are the hours when all workers must be present.

Core plus option plans establish a set of benefits, such as medical insurance, as mandatory for all employees who participate in flexible benefits plans.

Cost leadership strategy focuses on gaining competitive advantage by being the lowest-cost producer of a good or service within the marketplace, while selling the good or service at a price advantage relative to the industry average.

Cost shifting refers to the practice used by physicians and hospitals to offset health care expenses for individuals who are unable to pay by charging higher fees to individuals with health insurance.

Cost-of-living adjustments (COLAs) represent periodic base pay increases that are based on changes in prices, as indexed by the Consumer Price Index (CPI). COLAs enable workers to maintain their purchasing power and standard of living by adjusting base pay for inflation.

Critical incident technique (CIT), a specific kind of behavioral system, requires job incumbents and their supervisors to identify performance incidents—on-the-job behaviors and behavioral outcomes—that distinguish successful performance from unsuccessful performance. The supervisor then observes the employees and records their performance on these critical job aspects.

Cross-departmental models, a kind of pay-for-knowledge program, promote staffing flexibility by training employees in one department with some of the critical skills they would need to perform effectively in other departments.

Current profit sharing plans award cash to employees, typically on a quarterly or annual basis.

Davis-Bacon Act of 1931 established employment standards for construction contractors holding federal government contracts valued at more than $2,000. Such contractors must pay laborers and mechanics at least the prevailing wage in their local area.

Day care refers to programs that supervise and care for young children and elderly relatives when their regular caretakers are at work.

Death claims under workers' compensation are claims for deaths that occur in the course of employment or that are caused by compensable injuries or occupational diseases.

Deductible is the out-of-pocket expense that employees must pay before dental, medical, or vision insurance benefits become active.

Deferred compensation refers to an agreement between an employee and a company to render payments to an employee at a future date. Deferred compensation is a hallmark of executive compensation packages.

Deferred profit sharing plans place cash awards in trust accounts for employees. These trusts are set aside on employees' behalf as a source of retirement income.

Defined benefit plans guarantee retirement benefits specified in the plan document. This benefit usually is expressed in terms of a monthly sum equal to a percentage of a participant's preretirement pay multiplied by the number of years he or she has worked for the employer.

Defined contribution plans require that employers and employees make annual contributions to separate retirement fund accounts established for each participating employee, based on a formula contained in the plan document.

Dental insurance provides reimbursement for routine dental checkups and particular corrective procedures.

Dental maintenance organizations deliver dental services through the comprehensive health care plans of many health maintenance organizations (HMOs) and preferred provider organizations (PPOs).

Dental service corporations, owned and administered by state dental associations, are nonprofit corporations of dentists.

Depth of knowledge refers to the level of specialization, based on job-related knowledge, an employee brings to a particular job.

Depth of skills refers to the level of specialization, based on skills, an employee brings to a particular job.

Derivative lawsuits represent legal action that is initiated by company shareholders claiming that executive compensation is excessive.

Dictionary of Occupational Titles (DOT) includes over 20,000 private and public sector job descriptions. It has been replaced by the Standard Occupational Classification system.

Differentiation strategies focus on product or service development that is unique from those of its competitors. Differentiation can take many forms, including design or brand image, technology, features, customer service, or price.

Direct hire arrangements refer to companies' recruitment and selection of temporary workers without assistance from employment agencies.

Disability insured refers to an employee's eligibility to receive disability benefits under the Social Security Act of 1935. Eligibility depends on the worker's age and the type of disability.

Discharge represents involuntary termination, specifically for poor job performance, insubordination, or gross violation of work rules.

Discount stock options, a kind of executive deferred compensation, entitle executives to purchase their companies' stock in the future at a predetermined price. Discount stock options are similar to nonstatutory stock options with one exception. Companies grant stock options at rates far below the stock's fair market value on the date the option is granted.

Discretionary benefits are benefits that employers offer at their own choice. These benefits fall into three broad categories: protection programs, pay for time not worked, and services.

Discretionary bonuses are awarded to executives on an elective basis by boards of directors. Boards of directors weigh four factors in determining discretionary bonus amounts: company profits, the financial condition of the company, business conditions, and prospects for the future.

Discretionary income covers a variety of financial obligations in the United States for which expatriates remain responsible.

Disparate impact represents unintentional employment discrimination. It occurs whenever an employer applies an employment practice to all employees, but the practice leads to unequal treatment of protected employee groups.

Disparate treatment represents intentional employment discrimination, occurring whenever employers intentionally treat some workers less favorably than others because of their race, color, sex, national origin, or religion.

Draw is a subsistence pay component (that is, to cover basic living expenses) in sales compensation plans. Companies usually charge draws against commissions that sales professionals are expected to earn.

Early retirement programs contain incentives designed to encourage highly paid employees with substantial seniority to retire earlier than they planned. These incentives expedite senior employees' retirement eligibility and increase retirement income. In addition, many companies include continuation of medical benefits.

Economic reality test helps companies determine whether employees are financially dependent on them.

Education, based on Equal Employment Opportunity Commission guidelines, refers to formal training.

Education reimbursements apply to expatriates' children. Companies generally reimburse expatriates for the cost of children's private-school tuition in foreign posts.

EEOC v. Chrysler, a district court ruling, deemed that early retirement programs are permissible when companies offer them to employees on a voluntary basis. Forcing early retirement upon older workers represents age discrimination.

EEOC v. Madison Community Unit School District No. 12, a circuit court ruling, shed light on judging whether jobs are equal based on four compensable factors: skill, effort, responsibility, and working conditions.

Employee assistance programs (EAPs) help employees cope with personal problems that may impair their job performance, such as alcohol or drug abuse, domestic violence, the emotional impact of AIDS and other diseases, clinical depression, and eating disorders.

Employee benefits include any variety of programs that provide paid time-off (for example, vacation), employee services (for example, transportation services), and protection programs (for example, life insurance).

Employee Retirement Income Security Act of 1974 (ERISA) was established to regulate the establishment and implementation of various fringe compensation programs. These include medical, life, and disability insurance programs, as well as pension programs. The essence of ERISA is the protection of employee benefits rights.

Employee stock ownership plans (ESOPs) may be the basis for a company's Section 401(k) plan, and these plans invest in company securities, making them similar to profit sharing plans and stock bonus plans, presumably when the value of stock has increased.

Employee-financed benefits mean that employers do not contribute to the financing of discretionary benefits.

Employee's anniversary date represents the date an employee began working for his or her present employer. Often, employees receive performance appraisals on their anniversary dates.

Employment termination takes place when employees' agreement to perform work is ended. Employment terminations are voluntary or involuntary.

Equal benefit or equal cost principle contained within the Older Workers Benefit Protection Act (OWBPA) requires employers to offer benefits to older workers of equal or greater value than the benefits offered to younger workers.

Equal Employment Opportunity Commission, a federal government agency, oversees and enforces various employment laws that guard against illegal discrimination including Title VII of the Civil Rights Act of 1964.

Equal Pay Act of 1963 requires that men and women should receive equal pay for performing equal work.

Equity theory suggests an employee must regard his or her own ratio of merit increase pay to performance as similar to the ratio for other comparably performing people in the company.

Errors of central tendency occur when raters (for example, supervisors) judge all employees as average or close to average.

Exchange rate is the price at which one country's currency can be swapped for another.

Executive branch enforces the laws of various quasi-legislative and judicial agencies and executive orders.

Executive compensation consultants propose recommendations to chief executive officers and board of director members for alternate executive compensation packages.

Executive Order 11141 prohibits companies holding contracts with the federal government from discriminating against employees on the basis of age.

Executive Order 11246 requires companies holding contracts (worth more than $50,000 per year and employing 50 or more employees) with the federal government to develop written affirmative action plans each year.

Executive orders influence the operation of the federal government and companies that are engaged in business relationships with the federal government.

Exempt refers to an employee's status regarding the overtime pay provision of the Fair Labor Standards Act of 1938 (FLSA). Generally, administrative, professional, and executive employees are exempt from the FLSA overtime and minimum wage provisions.

Expatriates are U.S. citizens employed in U.S. companies with work assignments outside the United States.

Experience rating system establishes higher contributions (to fund unemployment insurance programs) for employers with higher incidences of unemployment.

Extrinsic compensation includes both monetary and nonmonetary rewards.

Fair Labor Standards Act of 1938 (FLSA) addresses major abuses that intensified during the Great Depression and the transition from agricultural to industrial enterprises. These include substandard pay, excessive work hours, and the employment of children in oppressive working conditions.

Family and Medical Leave Act of 1993 (FMLA) requires employers to provide employees 12 weeks of unpaid leave per year in cases of family or medical emergency.

Family assistance programs help employees provide elder care and child care. Elder care provides physical, emotional, or financial assistance for aging parents, spouses, or other relatives who are not fully self-sufficient because they are too frail or disabled. Child care programs focus on supervising preschool-age dependent children whose parents work outside the home.

Federal Employees' Compensation Act mandates workers' compensation insurance protection for federal civilian employees.

Federal government oversees the entire United States and its territories. The vast majority of laws that influence compensation were established at the federal level.

Federal Unemployment Tax Act (FUTA) specifies employees' and employers' tax or contribution to unemployment insurance programs required by the Social Security Act of 1935.

Fee-for-service plans provide protection for three types of medical expenses: hospital expenses, surgical expenses, and physician's charges.

First-impression effect occurs when a rater (for example, a supervisor) makes an initial favorable or unfavorable judgment about an employee and then ignores or distorts the employee's actual performance based on this impression.

Flexible benefits plan allows employees to choose a portion of their discretionary benefits based on a company's discretionary benefits options.

Flexible scheduling and leave allows employees to take time-off during work hours to care for relatives or react to emergencies.

Flexible spending accounts permit employees to pay for certain benefits expenses (such as childcare) with pretax dollars.

Flextime schedules allow employees to modify work schedules within specified limits set by the employer.

Forced distribution is a specific kind of comparison performance appraisal system in which raters (for example, supervisors) assign employees to groups that represent the entire range of performance.

Foreign service premium is a monetary payment awarded to expatriates above their regular base pay.

Freelancers (see independent contractors).

Fringe compensation (see employee benefits).

Fully insured refers to an employee's status in the retirement income program under the Social Security Act of 1935. Forty quarters of coverage lead to fully insured status.

Gain sharing describes group incentive systems that provide participating employees an incentive payment based on improved company performance, whether for increased productivity, increased customer satisfaction, lower costs, or better safety records.

General educational development (GED) refers to education of a general nature that contributes to reasoning development and to the acquisition of mathematical and language skills. The GED has three components: reasoning development, mathematical development, and language development.

General Schedule (GS) classifies federal government jobs into 15 classifications (GS-1 through GS-15), based on such factors as skill, education, and experience levels. In addition, jobs that require high levels of specialized education (for example, a physicist), significantly influence public policy (for example, law judges), or require executive decision making are classified in three additional categories: Senior level (SL), Scientific & Professional (SP) positions, and the Senior Executive Service (SES).

Glass Ceiling Act established the Glass Ceiling Commission—a 21-member bipartisan body appointed by President Bush (U.S. president between 1989 and 1993) and Congressional leaders and chaired by the Secretary of Labor. The committee conducted a study of opportunities for, and artificial barriers to, the advancement of minority men and all women into management and decision making positions in U.S. businesses, and it prepared and submitted to the president and Congress written reports containing the study's findings, conclusions, and recommendations.

Golden parachutes, a kind of executive deferred compensation, provide pay and benefits to executives following their termination resulting from a change in ownership or corporate takeover.

Goods and services allowances compensate expatriates for the difference between goods and services costs in the United States and in the foreign post.

Graduated commissions increase percentage pay rates for progressively higher sales volume in a given period.

Great Depression refers to the period during the 1930s when many businesses failed and many workers became chronically unemployed.

Green circle rates represent pay rates for jobs that fall below the designated pay minimums.

Group incentive programs reward employees for their collective performance, rather than for each employee's individual performance.

Groupthink occurs when all group members agree on mistaken solutions because they share the same mindset and view issues through the lens of conformity.

Hardship allowance compensates expatriates for their sacrifices while on assignment.

Headquarters-based method compensates all employees according to the pay scales used at the headquarters.

Health Maintenance Organization Act of 1973 encouraged the use of HMOs as an alternative approach to delivering health care services.

Health maintenance organizations (HMOs) are sometimes described as providing "prepaid medical services," because fixed periodic enrollment fees cover HMO members for all medically necessary services, provided that the services are delivered or approved by the HMO. HMOs represent an alternative to commercial and self-funded insurance plans.

Home country-based pay method compensates expatriates the amount they would receive if they were performing similar work in the United States.

Home leave benefits enable expatriates to take paid time-off in the United States.

Horizontal knowledge refers to similar knowledge (for example, record keeping applied to payroll applications and record keeping applied to employee benefits).

Horizontal skills refer to similar skills (for example, assembly skills applied to lawn mowers and assembly skills applied to snow blowers).

Host country nationals (HCNs) are foreign national citizens who work in U.S. companies' branch offices or manufacturing plants in their home countries.

Host country-based methods compensate expatriates based on the host countries' pay scales.

Hourly pay is one type of base pay. Employees earn hourly pay for each hour worked.

Housing and utilities allowances compensate expatriates for the difference between housing and utilities costs in the United States and in the foreign post.

Human capital refers to employees' knowledge and skills, enabling them to be productive (see also human capital theory).

Human capital theory states that employees' knowledge and skills generate productive capital known as human capital. Employees can develop knowledge and skills from formal education or on-the-job experiences.

Human resource strategies specify the particular use of HR practices to be consistent with competitive strategy.

Hypothetical tax is the U.S. income tax based on the same salary level, excluding all foreign allowances.

Illegal discriminatory bias occurs when a supervisor rates members of his or her race, gender, nationality, or religion more favorably than members of other classes.

Improshare is a specific kind of gain sharing program that rewards employees based on a labor hour ratio formula. A standard is determined by analyzing historical accounting data to find the number of labor hours needed to complete a product. Productivity is then measured as a ratio of standard labor hours and actual labor hours.

Incentive pay or variable pay is defined as compensation, other than base wages or salaries, that fluctuates according to employees' attainment of some standard, such as a preestablished formula, individual or group goals, or company earnings.

Incentive stock options entitle executives to purchase their companies' stock in the future at a predetermined price. Usually, the predetermined price equals the stock price at the time an executive receives the stock options. Incentive stock options entitle executives to favorable tax treatment.

Independent contractors are contingent workers who typically possess specialized skills that are in short supply in the labor market. Companies select independent contractors to complete particular projects of short-term duration—usually a year or less.

Indexes of living costs abroad compare the costs (U.S. dollars) of representative goods and services (excluding education) expatriates purchase at the foreign location and the cost of comparable goods and services purchased in the Washington, D.C., area. Companies use these indexes to determine appropriate goods and service allowances.

Individual incentive plans reward employees for meeting work-related performance standards, such as quality, productivity, customer satisfaction, safety, and attendance. Any one or a combination of these standards may be used.

Individual practice associations, a particular kind of HMO, are partnerships or other legal entities that arrange health care services by entering into service agreements with independent physicians, health professionals, and group practices.

Individualism-collectivism, a dimension of national culture, is the extent to which individuals value personal independence versus group membership.

Industry represents the narrowest (that is, the most specific) classification of an industry within the North American Industry Classification System.

Industry group is the fourth broadest classification of industries within the North American Industry Classification System.

Industry profiles describe such basic industry characteristics as sales volume, the impact of relevant government regulation on competitive strategies, and the impact of recent technological advances on business activity.

Inflation is the increase in prices for consumer goods and services. Inflation erodes the purchasing power of currency.

Injury claims, under workers' compensation, are claims for disabilities that have resulted from accidents such as falls, injuries from equipment use, or physical strains from heavy lifting.

Interests represent individuals' liking or preference for performing specific jobs.

Internally consistent compensation systems clearly define the relative value of each job among all jobs within a company. This ordered set of jobs represents the job structure or hierarchy. Companies rely on a simple, yet fundamental principle for building internally consistent compensation systems: Jobs that require greater qualifications, more responsibilities, and more complex job duties should be paid more highly than jobs that require lesser qualifications, fewer responsibilities, and more complex job duties.

Intrinsic compensation reflects employees' psychological mindsets that result from performing their jobs.

Involuntary part-time employees work fewer than 35 hours per week because they are unable to find full-time employment.

Involuntary terminations are initiated by companies for a variety of reasons, including poor job performance, insubordination, violation of work rules, reduced business activity due to sluggish economic conditions, or plant closings.

IRC Section 901 allows expatriates to credit foreign income taxes against their U.S. income liability.

IRC Section 911 permits eligible expatriates to exclude as much as $70,000 of foreign earned income from taxation, plus a housing allowance.

Job analysis is a systematic process for gathering, documenting, and analyzing information in order to describe jobs.

Job characteristics theory describes the critical psychological states that employees experience when they perform their jobs (that is, intrinsic compensation). According to job characteristics theory, employees experience enhanced psychological states when their jobs rate high on five core job dimensions—skill variety, task identity, task significance, autonomy, and feedback.

Job content refers to the actual activities that employees must perform in the job. Job content descriptions may be broad, general statements of job activities or detailed descriptions of duties and tasks performed in the job.

Job control unionism refers to a union's success in negotiating formal contracts with employees and establishing quasi-judicial grievance procedures to adjudicate disputes between union members and employers.

Job descriptions summarize a job's purpose and list its tasks, duties, and responsibilities, as well as the skills, knowledge, and abilities necessary to perform the job at a minimum level.

Job duties, a section in job descriptions, describe the major work activities and, if pertinent, supervisory responsibilities.

Job evaluation systematically recognizes differences in the relative worth among a set of jobs and establishes pay differentials accordingly.

Job sharing is a special kind of part-time employment agreement. Two or more part-time employees perform a single full-time job.

Job summary, a statement contained in job descriptions, summarizes the job based on two to four descriptive statements.

Job titles, listed in job descriptions, indicate job designations.

Job-content evaluation, an approach to evaluating job worth, takes skill, effort, responsibility, and working conditions into account.

Job-lock phenomenon occurs whenever an employed individual experiences a medical problem, and this individual is "locked" into the current job because most health insurance plans contain preexisting conditions clauses.

Job-point accrual model, a type of pay-for-knowledge program, provides employees opportunities to develop skills and learn to perform jobs from different job families.

Just-meaningful pay increase refers to the minimum pay increase that employees will see as making a substantial change in compensation.

Key employee, as defined by the Internal Revenue Service, is an employee who, at any time during the current year or any of the 4 preceding years, is one of 10 employees owning the largest percentages of the company, an employee who each owns more than 5 percent of the company, or an employee who earns more than $150,000 per year and owns more than 1 percent of the company.

Knowledge, based on Equal Employment Opportunity Commission guidelines, refers to a body of information applied directly to the performance of a function.

Labor market assessments enable companies to determine the availability of qualified employees.

Labor-management relations involve a continuous relationship between a company's HR professionals and a group of employees-members of a labor union and its bargaining unit.

Layoff represents involuntary termination that results from sluggish economic conditions or from plant closings.

Lease companies employ qualified individuals and place them in client companies on a long-term, presumably "permanent" basis. Lease companies place employees within client companies in exchange for fees.

Legally required benefits are protection programs that attempt to promote worker safety and health, maintain family income streams, and assist families in crisis. The key legally required benefits are mandated by the following laws: the Social Security Act of 1935, various state workers' compensation laws, and the Family and Medical Leave Act of 1993.

Leniency errors occur when raters (for example, supervisors) appraise an employee's performance more highly than it really rates, compared with objective criteria.

Life insurance protects employees' families by paying a specified amount to employees' beneficiaries upon employees' deaths. Most policies pay some multiple of the employees' salaries.

Line employees are directly involved in producing companies' goods or service delivery. Assembler, production worker, and sales employee are examples of line jobs.

Local governments enact and enforce laws that are most pertinent to smaller geographic regions—for example, Champaign County in Illinois or Los Angeles.

Longevity pay systems reward with permanent additions to base pay those employees who have reached pay grade maximums and who are not likely to move into higher pay grades.

Longshore and Harborworkers' Compensation Act mandates workers' compensation insurance protection for maritime workers.

Long-term disability insurance provides income benefits for extended periods of time, between 6 months and life.

Lorance v. AT&T Technologies, a Supreme Court case, limited employees' rights to challenge the use of seniority systems to only 180 days from the system's implementation date.

Lowest-cost strategy (see cost leadership strategy).

Management by objectives (MBO), a goal-oriented performance appraisal method, requires that supervisors and employees determine objectives for employees to meet during the rating period, and then employees appraise how well they have achieved their objectives.

Management incentive plans award bonuses to managers who meet or exceed objectives based on sales, profit, production, or other measures for their division, department, or unit.

Mandatory bargaining subjects are issues that employers and unions must bargain on if either constituent makes proposals about them.

Market lag policy distinguishes companies from the competition by compensating employees less than most competitors. Lagging the market indicates that pay levels fall below the market pay line.

Market lead policy distinguishes companies from the competition by compensating employees more highly than most competitors. Leading the market denotes pay levels above the market pay line.

Market match policy most closely follows the typical market pay rates because companies pay according to the market pay line. Thus, pay rates fall along the market pay line.

Market pay line is representative of typical market pay rates relative to a company's job structure.

Market-based evaluation, an approach to job evaluation, uses market data to determine differences in job worth.

Market-competitive pay systems represent companies' compensation policies that fit the imperatives of competitive advantage.

Masculinity-femininity, a dimension of national culture, refers to whether masculine or feminine values are dominant in society. Masculinity favors material possessions. Femininity encourages caring and nurturing behavior.

McNamara-O'Hara Service Contract Act of 1965 requires that all federal contractors employing service workers must pay at least the minimum wage as specified in the FLSA. In addition, contractors holding contracts with the federal government that exceed $2,500 in value must pay the local prevailing wages and offer fringe compensation equal to the local prevailing benefits.

Medicare serves nearly all U.S. citizens aged 65 or older by providing insurance coverage for hospitalization, convalescent care, and major doctor bills. The Medicare program includes four separate plans: compulsory hospitalization insurance, Part A, voluntary supplementary medical insurance, Part B, Medigap insurance to cover gaps in Parts A and B coverage, and new choices in health care, Part C. The Social Security Act of 1935 established Medicare.

Merit bonuses or nonrecurring merit increases are lump sum monetary awards based on employees' past performances. Employees do not continue to receive nonrecurring merit increases every year. Instead, employees must earn them each time.

Merit pay increase budget limits the amount of pay raises that can be awarded to employees for a specified time period. A merit pay increase budget is expressed as a percentage of the sum of employees' current base pay.

Merit pay programs reward employees with permanent increases to base pay according to differences in job performance.

Midpoint pay value is the halfway mark between the range minimum and maximum rates. Midpoints generally match values along the market pay line, representing the competitive market rate determined by the analysis of compensation survey data.

Mobility premiums reward employees for moving from one assignment to another.

Multiple-tiered commissions increase percentage pay rates for progressively higher sales volume in a given period only if sales exceed a predetermined level.

National culture refers to the set of shared norms and beliefs among individuals within national boundaries who are indigenous to that area.

National Labor Relations Act of 1935 (NLRA) establishes employees' rights to bargain collectively with employers on such issues as wages, work hours, and working conditions.

Negative halo effect occurs when a rater (for example, a supervisor) generalizes an employee's negative behavior on one aspect of the job to all aspects of the job.

Noncash incentives complement monetary sales compensation components. Such noncash incentives as contests, recognition programs, expense reimbursements, and benefits policies can encourage sales performance and attract sales talent.

Noncontributory financing implies that the company assumes total costs for discretionary benefits.

Noncontributory pension plans do not require employee contributions to fund retirement income.

Nonexempt refers to an employee's status regarding the overtime pay provision of the Fair Labor Standards Act of 1938 (FLSA). Generally, employees whose jobs do not fall into particular categories (that is, administrative, professional, and executive employees) are covered by overtime and minimum wage provisions.

Nonqualified pension plans provide less favorable tax treatments for employers than qualified pension plans.

Nonrecoverable draws act as salary because employees are not obligated to repay the loans if they do not sell enough.

Nonrecurring merit increases or merit bonuses are lump sum monetary awards based on employees' past job performances. Employees do not continue to receive nonrecurring merit increases every year. Instead, employees must earn them each time.

Nonstatutory stock options, a kind of executive deferred compensation, entitle executives to purchase their companies' stock in the future at a predetermined price. Usually, the predetermined price equals the stock price at the time an executive receives the stock options. Nonstatutory stock options do not entitle executives to favorable tax treatment.

North American Free Trade Agreement (NAFTA) became effective on January 1, 1994. NAFTA has two main goals. First, NAFTA was designed to reduce trade barriers among Mexico, Canada, and the United States. Second, NAFTA also set out to remove barriers to investment among these three countries.

North American Industry Classification System (NAICS). NAICS codes represent keys to pertinent information for strategic analyses. The NAICS codes contain five digits, representing the sector (first two digits), subsector (the first three digits), industry group (first four digits), and the industry (all five digits).

North American Industry Classification System Manual classifies industries based on the NAICS.

Occupational disease claims are workers' compensation claims for disabilities caused by ailments associated with particular industrial trades or processes.

Occupational Information Network (O*NET) is a database designed to describe jobs in the relatively new service sector of the economy and to more accurately describe jobs that evolved as the result of technological advances. O*NET replaces the *Revised Handbook for Analyzing Jobs.*

Older Workers Benefit Protection Act (OWBPA), the 1990 amendment to the ADEA, indicates that employers can require older employees to pay more than younger employees for health care insurance coverage. This practice is permissible when older workers collectively do not make proportionately larger contributions than the younger workers.

On-call arrangements are a method for employing temporary workers.

O*NET database [see Occupational Information Network (O*NET)]

Operating requirements encompass all HR programs.

Organizational and product life cycles describe the evolution of company and product change using human life cycle stages. Much like people are born, grow, mature, decline, and die, so do companies, products, and services. Business priorities, including human resources, vary with life cycles.

Organizational culture is a system of shared values and beliefs that produce norms of behavior.

Out-of-pocket maximum provisions in medical insurance plans limit the total dollar expenditure a beneficiary must pay during any plan year. This provision is most common in commercial medical insurance plans.

Outplacement assistance refers to company-sponsored technical and emotional support to employees who are being laid off or terminated.

Paid time-off represents discretionary employee benefits (for example, vacation time) that provide employees time-off with pay.

Paired comparison, a variation of simple ranking job evaluation plans, orders all jobs from lowest to highest based on comparing the worth of each job in all possible job pairs. Paired comparison also refers to a specific kind of comparison method for appraising job performance. Supervisors compare each employee to every other employee, identifying the better performer in each pair.

Part A refers to compulsory hospitalization insurance under Medicare.

Part B refers to voluntary supplementary medical insurance under Medicare.

Part C refers to a broad variety of healthcare choices under Medicare.

Pay compression occurs whenever a company's pay spread between newly hired or less qualified employees and more qualified job incumbents is small.

Pay grades group jobs for pay policy application. Human resource professionals typically group jobs into pay grades based on similar compensable factors and value.

Pay ranges represent the span of possible pay rates for each pay grade. Pay ranges include midpoint, minimum, and maximum pay rates. The minimum and maximum values denote the acceptable lower and upper bounds of pay for the jobs within particular pay grades.

Pay structures represent pay rate differences for jobs of unequal worth and the framework for recognizing differences in employee contributions.

Pay-for-knowledge plans reward managerial, service, or professional workers for successfully learning specific curricula.

Pension programs provide income to individuals throughout their retirement. Sometimes, companies use early retirement programs to reduce workforce size and trim compensation expenditures.

Percentiles describe dispersion by indicating the percentage of figures that fall below certain points. There are 100 percentiles ranging from the first percentile to the 100th percentile.

Performance appraisal describes an employee's past performance and serves as a basis to recommend how to improve future performance.

Performance-contingent bonuses, awarded to executives, are based on the attainment of such specific performance criteria as market share.

Perks (see perquisites).

Permissive bargaining subjects are those subjects on which neither the employer nor the union is obligated to bargain.

Perquisites are benefits offered exclusively to executives—for example, country club memberships.

Person-focused pay plans generally reward employees for acquiring job-related competencies, knowledge, or skills rather than for demonstrating successful job performances.

Phantom stock, a type of executive deferred compensation, is an arrangement whereby boards of directors compensate executives with hypothetical company stock rather than actual shares of company stock. Phantom stock plans are similar to restricted stock plans because executives must meet specific conditions before they can convert these phantom shares into real shares of company stock.

Physical demands represent the physical requirements made on the worker by the specific situation.

Piecework plan, an individual incentive pay program, rewards employees based on their individual hourly production against an objective output standard, determined by the pace at which manufacturing equipment operates. For each hour, workers receive piecework incentives for every item produced over the designated production standard. Workers also receive a guaranteed hourly pay rate regardless of whether they meet the designated production standard.

Point method represents a job-content evaluation technique that uses quantitative methodology. Quantitative methods assign numerical values to compensable factors that describe jobs, and these values are summed as an indicator of the overall value for the job.

Portal-to-Portal Act of 1947 defines the term *hours worked* that appears in the FLSA.

Positive halo effect occurs when a rater (for example, a supervisor) generalizes employees' positive behavior on one aspect of the job to all aspects of the job.

Poverty threshold represents the minimum annual earnings needed to afford housing and other basic necessities. The federal government determines these levels each year for families of different sizes.

Power distance, a dimension of national culture, is the extent to which people accept a hierarchical system or power structure in companies.

Predetermined allocation bonuses, awarded to executives, are based on a fixed formula. Often, company profits is the main determinant of the bonus amounts.

Preexisting conditions apply to all health insurance plans. These are conditions for which medical advice, diagnosis, care, or treatment was received or recommended during the 6-month period preceding the beginning of coverage.

Preferred provider organizations (PPOs) are select groups of health care providers that provide health care services to a given population at a higher level of reimbursement than under commercial insurance plans.

Pregnancy Discrimination Act of 1978 (PDA) is an amendment to Title VII of the Civil Rights Act of 1964. The PDA prohibits disparate impact discrimination against pregnant women for all employment practices.

Prepaid group practices, a specific type of HMO, provide medical care for a set premium, rather than a fee-for-service basis.

Probationary period is the initial term of employment (usually less than 6 months) during which companies attempt to ensure that they have made sound hiring decisions. Often, employees are not entitled to participate in discretionary benefits programs during their probationary periods.

Production plan (see piecework plan).

Profit sharing plans pay a portion of company profits to employees, separate from base pay, cost-of-living adjustments, or permanent merit pay increases. Two basic kinds of profit sharing plans are used widely today: current profit sharing and deferred profit sharing.

Protection programs are either legally required or discretionary employee benefits that provide family benefits, promote health, and guard against income loss caused by catastrophic factors such as unemployment, disability, or serious illnesses.

Qualified pension plans entitle employers to tax benefits from their contributions to pension plans. In general, this means that employers may take current tax deductions for contributions to fund future retirement income.

Quarters allowance is the U.S. Department of State term for housing and utilities allowances.

Quarters of coverage refers to each 3-month period of employment during which an employee contributes to the retirement income program under the Social Security Act of 1935.

Quartiles allow compensation professionals to describe the distribution of data, usually annual base pay amount, based on four groupings.

Range spread is the difference between the maximum and the minimum pay rates of a given pay grade.

Rating errors in performance appraisals reflect differences between human judgment processes versus objective, accurate assessments uncolored by bias, prejudice, or other subjective, extraneous influences.

Recertification ensures that employees periodically demonstrate mastery of all the jobs they have learned.

Recoverable draws act as company loans to employees that are carried forward indefinitely until employees sell enough (that is, earn a sufficient amount in commissions) to repay their draws.

Recruitment entails identifying qualified job candidates and promoting their interest in working for a company.

Red circle rates represent pay rates that are higher than the designated pay range maximums.

Referral plans are individual incentive pay plans that reward employees for referring new customers or recruiting successful job applicants.

Relevant labor markets represent the fields of potentially qualified candidates for particular jobs.

Reliable job analysis yields consistent results under similar conditions.

Relocation assistance payments cover expatriates' expenses to relocate to foreign posts.

Repatriation is the process of making the transition from an international assignment and living abroad to a domestic assignment and living in the home country.

Rest and relaxation benefits provide expatriates assigned to hardship locations with paid time-off. Rest and relaxation leave benefits differ from standard vacation benefits because companies designate where expatriates may spend their time.

Restricted stock, a type of executive deferred compensation, requires that executives do not have any ownership control over the disposition of the stock for a predetermined period, often 5 to 10 years.

Revised Handbook for Analyzing Jobs (RHAJ) documents the Department of Labor method of job analysis, which is used to develop the job descriptions contained in the *Dictionary of Occupational Titles*. It has been replaced by the Occupational Information Network (O*NET).

Right to control test helps companies determine whether their workers are employees or independent contractors.

Rucker Plan is a particular type of gain sharing program that emphasizes employee involvement. Gain sharing awards are based on the ratio between value added (less the costs of materials, supplies, and services rendered) and the total cost of employment.

Salary is one type of base pay. Employees earn salaries for performing their jobs, regardless of the actual number of hours worked. Companies generally measure salary on an annual basis.

Salary-only plans are specific types of sales compensation plans. Sales professionals receive fixed base compensation, which does not vary with the level of units sold, increase in market share, or any other indicator of sales performance.

Salary-plus-bonus plans are specific types of sales compensation plans. Sales professionals receive fixed base compensation, coupled with a bonus. Bonuses usually are single payments that reward employees for achievement of specific, exceptional goals.

Salary-plus-commission plans are particular types of sales compensation plans. Sales professionals receive fixed base compensation and commission.

Scanlon Plan is a specific type of gain sharing program that emphasizes employee involvement. Gain sharing awards are based on the ratio between labor costs and sales value of production.

Scientific management practices promote labor cost control by replacing inefficient production methods with efficient production methods.

Sector is the broadest classification of industries within the North American Industry Classification System (NAICS).

Securities and Exchange Commission (SEC) is a nonpartisan, quasi-judicial federal government agency with responsibility for administering federal securities laws.

Securities Exchange Act of 1934 applies to the disclosure of executive compensation.

Selection is the process HR professionals employ to hire qualified candidates for job openings.

Self-funded insurance plans are similar to commercial insurance plans with one key difference. Companies typically draw from their own assets to fund claims when self-funded.

Self-insured dental plans are similar to fee-for-service dental plans, except companies fund payment for dental procedures themselves.

Seniority pay systems reward employees with permanent additions to base pay periodically, according to employees' length of service performing their jobs.

Services represent discretionary employee benefits that provide enhancements to employees and their families, such as tuition reimbursement and day care assistance.

Severance pay usually includes several months of pay following involuntary termination and, in some cases, continued coverage under the employer's medical insurance plan. Oftentimes, employees rely on severance pay to meet financial obligations while searching for employment.

Short-term disability insurance provides income benefits for limited periods of time, usually less than 6 months.

Similar-to-me effect refers to the tendency on the part of raters (for example, supervisors) to favorably judge employees they perceive as similar to themselves.

Simple ranking plans, specific methods of job evaluation, order all jobs from lowest to highest according to a single criterion, such as job complexity or the centrality of the job to the company's competitive strategy.

Skill, based on Equal Employment Opportunity Commission guidelines, refers to an observable competence to perform a learned psychomotor act.

Skill level-performance matrix, a type of pay-for-knowledge program, rewards employees according to how well they have applied skills and knowledge to their jobs.

Skill-based pay, used mostly for employees who do physical work, increases these workers' pay as they master new skills.

Skills blocks model, a kind of pay-for-knowledge program, applies to jobs from within the same job family. Just as in the stair-step model, employees progress to increasingly complex jobs. However, in a skill blocks program, skills do not necessarily build on each other.

Small group incentive plans reward groups of individuals with financial awards when a specific objective is met.

Smoking cessation plans are particular types of wellness programs that stress the negative aspects of smoking and can include intensive programs directed at helping individuals stop smoking.

Social comparison theory provides an explanation for executive compensation determination based on the tendency for the board of directors to offer executive compensation packages that are similar to those in peer companies.

Social Security Act of 1935 established four main types of legally required benefits: unemployment insurance, retirement income, benefits for dependents, and medical insurance (Medicare).

Specific vocational preparation (SVP) is defined as the amount of lapsed time required by a typical worker to learn the techniques, acquire the information, and develop the facility needed for average performance in a specific job situation.

Staff employees support the functions performed by line employees. Human resources and accounting are examples of staff functions.

Stair-step model, a type of pay-for-knowledge program, resembles a flight of stairs. The steps represent jobs from a particular job family that differ in terms of complexity. Skills at higher levels build upon previous lower-level skills.

Standard deviation refers to the mean distance of each salary figure from the mean—how larger observations fluctuate above the mean and how small observations fluctuate below the mean.

Standard Occupational Classification System (SOC) describes 23 major occupational groups. It replaces the *Dictionary of Occupational Titles.*

State governments enact and enforce laws that pertain exclusively to their respective regions—for example, Illinois and Michigan.

Stock appreciation rights, a type of executive deferred compensation, provide executives income at the end of a designated period, much like restricted stock options. However, executives never have to exercise their stock rights to receive income. The company simply awards payment to executives based on the difference in stock price between the time the company granted the stock rights at fair market value to the end of the designated period, permitting the executives to keep the stock.

Stock compensation plans are companywide incentive plans that grant employees the right to purchase shares of company stock.

Stock options describe an employee's right to purchase company stock.

Straight commission is based on a fixed percentage of the sales price of the produce or service.

Strategic analysis entails an examination of a company's external market context and internal factors. Examples of external market factors include industry profile, information about competitors, and long-term growth prospects. Internal factors encompass financial condition and functional capabilities—for example, marketing and human resources.

Strategic decisions support business objectives.

Strategic management entails a series of judgments, under uncertainty, that companies direct toward achieving specific goals.

Stress management is a specific kind of wellness program designed to help employees cope with many factors inside and outside their work that contribute to stress.

Strictness errors occur when raters (for example, supervisors) judge employee performance to be less than what it is compared against objective criteria.

Subsector is the second broadest classification of industries within the North American Industry Classification System (NAICS).

Summary Compensation Table discloses compensation information for CEOs and the four most highly paid executives over a 3-year period employed by companies whose stock is traded on public stock exchanges. The information in this table is presented in tabular and graphic forms to make information more accessible to the public.

Supplemental life insurance protection represents additional life insurance offered exclusively to executives. Companies design executives' supplemental life insurance protection to increase the value of executives' estates, bequeathed to designated beneficiaries (usually family members) upon their death and to provide greater benefits than standard plans usually allow.

Supplemental retirement plans, offered to executives, are designed to restore benefits restricted under qualified plans.

Supplemental unemployment benefit (SUB) refers to unemployment insurance that is usually awarded to individuals who were employed in cyclical industries. This benefit supplements unemployment insurance that is required by the Social Security Act of 1935.

Tactical decisions support competitive strategy.

Target plan bonuses, awarded to executives, are based on executives' performance. Executives do not receive bonuses unless their performance exceeds minimally acceptable standards.

Tax equalization is one of two approaches (the other is tax protection) to provide expatriates tax allowances. Employers take the responsibility for paying income taxes to the U.S. and foreign governments on behalf of the expatriates.

Tax protection is one of two approaches (the other is tax equalization) to provide expatriates tax allowances. Employers reimburse expatriates for the difference between the actual income tax amount and the hypothetical tax when the actual income tax amount—based on tax returns filed with the Internal Revenue Service—is greater.

Team-based incentives (see small group incentive plans).

Telecommuting represents alternative work arrangements in which employees perform work at home or some other location besides the office.

Temperaments are adaptability requirements made on the worker by the situation.

Temporary employment agencies place individuals in client companies as employees on a temporary basis.

Term coverage is a type of life insurance that provides protection to an employee's beneficiaries only during the insured person's employment.

Third country nationals (TCNs) are foreign national citizens who work in U.S. companies' branch offices or manufacturing plants in foreign countries—excluding the United States and their home countries.

Time-and-motion studies analyzed the time it took employees to complete their jobs. Factory owners used time-and-motion studies and job analysis to meet this objective.

Title I of the Americans with Disabilities Act of 1990 (ADA) requires that employers provide "reasonable accommodation" to disabled employees. Reasonable accommodation may include such efforts as making existing facilities readily accessible, job restructuring, and modifying work schedules.

Title II of the Civil Rights Act of 1991 enacted the Glass Ceiling Act.

Title VII of the Civil Rights Act of 1964 indicates that it shall be an unlawful employment practice for an employer to discriminate against any individual with respect to compensation, terms, conditions, or privileges of employment because of such individual's race, color, religion, sex, or national origin.

Tournament theory provides an explanation for executive compensation determination based on substantially greater competition for high-ranking jobs. Lucrative chief executive compensation packages represent the prize to those who win the competition by becoming chief executives.

Training is a planned effort to facilitate employees' learning of job-related knowledge, skills, or behaviors. Effective training programs lead to desired employee learning, which translates into improved future job performance.

Trait systems, a type of performance appraisal method, requires raters (for example, supervisors or customers) to evaluate each employee's traits or characteristics, such as quality of work, quantity of work, appearance, dependability, cooperation, initiative, judgment, leadership responsibility, decision-making ability, and creativity.

Transportation services represent energy-efficient ways to transport employees to and from the workplace. Employers cover part or all of the transportation costs.

Tuition reimbursement programs promote employees' education. Under a tuition reimbursement program, an employer fully or partially reimburses an employee for expenses incurred for education or training.

Two-tier pay structures reward newly hired employees less than established employees on either a temporary or permanent basis.

Uncertainty avoidance, a dimension of national culture, represents the method by which society deals with risk and instability for its members.

Universal compensable factors, based on the Equal Pay Act of 1963, include skill, effort, responsibility, and working conditions.

Usual, customary, and reasonable charges are defined as being not more than the physician's usual charge, within the customary range of fees charged in the locality, and reasonable, based on the medical circumstances. Commercial insurance plans generally do not pay more than this amount.

Valid job analysis method accurately assesses each job's duties.

Variable pay (see incentive pay).

Variation represents the amount of spread or dispersion in a set of data.

Vertical knowledge refers to knowledge traditionally associated with supervisory activities—for example, performance appraisal and grievance review procedures.

Vertical skills are those skills traditionally considered supervisory skills, such as scheduling, coordinating, training, and leading others.

Vesting refers to employees' acquisition of nonforfeitable rights to pension benefits.

Vision insurance provides reimbursement for routine optical checkups and particular corrective procedures.

Voluntary part-time employees choose to work fewer than 35 hours per regularly scheduled workweek.

Voluntary terminations are initiated by employees, who do so to work for other companies or to begin their retirements.

Wage (see hourly pay).

Wagner-Peyser Act established a federal-state employment service system.

Walling v. A. H. Belo Corp., a Supreme Court ruling, requires that employers guarantee fixed weekly pay when the following conditions prevail: the employer typically cannot determine the number of hours employees will work each week, and the workweek period fluctuates both above and below 40 hours per week.

Walsh-Healey Public Contracts Act of 1936 mandates that contractors with federal contracts meet guidelines regarding wages and hours, child labor, convict labor, and hazardous working conditions. Contractors must observe the minimum wage and overtime provisions of the FLSA. In addition, this act prohibits the employment of individuals younger than 16 and convicted criminals. Further, it prohibits contractors from exposing workers to any conditions that violate the Occupational Safety and Health Act.

Weight control and nutrition programs, a particular type of wellness program, are designed to educate employees about proper nutrition and weight loss, both of which are critical to good health.

Welfare practices were generous endeavors undertaken by some employers, motivated to minimize employees' desire to seek union representation, to promote good management, and to enhance worker productivity.

Wellness programs promote employees' physical and psychological health.

Whole life coverage is a type of life insurance that provides protection to employees' beneficiaries during employees' employment and into the retirement years.

Work Hours and Safety Standards Act of 1962 requires that all contractors pay employees one-and-one-half times their regular hourly rate for each hour worked in excess of 40 hours per week.

Worker requirements represent the minimum qualifications and skills that people must have to perform a particular job. Such requirements usually include education, experience, licenses, permits, and specific abilities, such as typing, drafting, or editing.

Worker specification, a section in job descriptions, lists the education, skills, abilities, knowledge, and other qualifications individuals must possess to perform the job adequately.

Workers' compensation laws established state-run insurance programs that are designed to cover medical, rehabilitation, and disability income expenses resulting from employees' work-related accidents.

Working condition fringe benefits refer to the work equipment (for example, computer) and services (for example, an additional telephone line) employers purchase for telecommuters' use at home.

Author Index

Note: The numbers in italic type indicate endnotes.

T

U

W

Z

Subject Index

D

F

J

N

O

Q

R

T

U

V

W

Z